Meditations
ON THE
GOSPELS

According to His Word

CONCORDIA PUBLISHING HOUSE · SAINT LOUIS

This edition © 2009 Concordia Publishing House
3558 S. Jefferson Avenue, St. Louis, MO 63118-3968
1-800-325-3040 • www.cph.org

Originally published in 1948 as *The Devotional Bible*

This publication may be available in braille, in large print, or on cassette tape for the visually impaired. Please allow 8 to 12 weeks for delivery. Write to Lutheran Blind Mission, 7550 Watson Rd., St. Louis, MO 63119-4409; call toll-free 1-888-215-2455; or visit the Web site: www.blindmission.org.

Cover photos of stained glass windows ©shutterstock.com/V. J. Matthew
Cover background image ©shutterstock.com/Sergey Vasilyev

Manufactured in the United States of America

Library of Congress Cataloging-in-Publication Data

Meditations on the Gospels : according to His Word.
    p. cm.
Originally published 1948.
ISBN 978-0-7586-1506-0
    1. Bible. N.T. Gospels--Devotional literature. I. Concordia Publishing House.
    BS2555.54.L58 2009
    242'.5--dc22
                                                                2009004778

1 2 3 4 5 6 7 8 9 10   18 17 16 15 14 13 12 11 10 09

FOREWORD FROM THE 1948 EDITION

WHEN 90 years ago the Altenburg Bible was reprinted in St. Louis, Dr. Walther wrote in *Der Lutheraner,* "Now these Jews were more noble than those in Thessalonica; they received the word with all eagerness, examining the Scriptures daily to see if these things were so" (Acts 17:11). By these words the Holy Spirit also testifies that nothing else is as necessary and salutary for a Christian as that he himself diligently and daily reads the Holy Scriptures and searches them. All the great men of God who have issued manifold writings for the edifying of Christians did not mean to invite them to seek their edification in human books instead of in the Holy Bible; the purpose of all upright theologians has always been to lead Christians into the Book of Books, the Bible, by their writing. But many Christians, though eagerly desiring to draw the counsel of God to their salvation directly from the fountain, yet are kept from doing so because in so many instances, if they were asked: "Do you understand what you are reading?" And he said, 'How can I, unless someone guides me?' " (Acts 8:30–31). No doubt many a father would gladly gather his family around the table to read them the precious Word of God again and again from beginning to end; but he sadly misses a Bible book which at the same time offers him guidance to understand what he reads and to apply it with wholesome effect. A Bible exactly adapted for that purpose was the Altenburg Bible, issued in 1676 in the city of Altenburg and now [sic] republished by the Evangelical Lutheran Central Bible Society of St. Louis.

For the same purpose the Evangelical Lutheran Synod of Missouri, Ohio, and Other States in 1944 resolved to publish, as part of its Centennial program, "a devotional work of the nature of the incomparable Altenburger Bibelwerk." The committee in charge of carrying out this resolution herewith offers the first volume of the proposed work, meditations on the Gospels of Matthew, Mark, [Luke, and John]. In concluding our labors we join in the prayer of Dr. Walther on the above-mentioned occasion:

"May God, the Father of our Lord Jesus Christ, who will have all men to be saved and to come unto the knowledge of the truth, attend this undertaking, begun solely to His honor and for the salvation of our fellow redeemed, with His blessing; may He by His Holy Spirit arouse in many of them hunger and thirst for the bread of life here offered to them; may He especially further this endeavor that soon the whole work can be given to thousands and prove to uncounted numbers a means of salvation until the Last Day dawns."

The Synodical Centennial Committee
Dr. Theodore Hoyer
Rev. H. W. Romoser
Dr. L. Fuerbringer
Dr. H. B. Hemmeter
Dr. E. T. Lams
Teacher A. H. Kramer
Mr. G. A. Fleischer

Introductory Meditation
Search the Scriptures
In the Name of Jesus

> You search the Scriptures because you think that in them
> you have eternal life; and it is they that bear witness about Me.
> John 5:39

WE begin our reading of the Gospels in the name of Jesus. Christians are moved to read and study the Word of God chiefly by two considerations: God's will and their own welfare.

It is God's will that we diligently and daily study His Word. St. Paul wrote, "Let the word of Christ dwell in you richly, teaching and admonishing one another in all wisdom, singing psalms and hymns and spiritual songs, with thankfulness in your hearts to God" (Colossians 3:16). That means more than hearing the Word on a Sunday. The Word of Christ should dwell in us, live where we live, be our constant companion wherever we go, in whatever we do. Paul addresses all Christians; all should study the Word so as to be able to teach and guide one other.

Long before St. Paul wrote this letter, when the Bible was young and consisted of only the five books of Moses, God said by him, "These words that I command you today shall be on your heart. You shall teach them diligently to your children, and shall talk of them when you sit in your house, and when you walk by the way, and when you lie down, and when you rise" (Deuteronomy 6:6–7). And to Joshua, God said, "This Book of the Law shall not depart from your mouth, but you shall meditate on it day and night, so that you may be careful to do according to all that is written in it. For then you will make your way prosperous, and then you will have good success" (Joshua 1:8).

God's will is never arbitrary. It always has a purpose. It is our blessed lot that we are the children of God and heirs of His eternal riches. Christ, our Brother and Savior, has gone ahead to prepare a place for us in the mansions of the Father's glory. And although this place is ours and nothing and no one can rob us of it, the actual possession of it lies in the future. We must live in this world until the Father calls us home, and of this life Paul says, "through many tribulations we must enter the kingdom of God" (Acts 14:22). What will strengthen and sustain us in this life?

There is a fine answer in the story of the two disciples going to Emmaus on Easter Day. They were sad because they had lost their beloved Friend and Master; they lost Him in a terrible way: He had been crucified. With Him had died all their hopes for the restoration of Israel. Surely reason enough for sadness. But a few hours later they returned to Jerusalem rejoicing! What had happened? That very Friend had joined them, walked with them, talked with them, listened to them, and said to them: " 'O foolish ones, and slow of heart to believe all that the prophets have spoken! Was it not necessary that the Christ should suffer these things and enter into His glory?' And beginning with Moses and all the Prophets, He interpreted to them in all the Scriptures the things concerning Himself" (Luke 24:25–27). That conversation changed everything for them. The real cause of their sadness, then, was that because they had neglected to study and take to heart what God long ago had told them in His Word, they had no understanding of the terrible events that had happened. Therefore, the world was indeed a dark place to them. But Jesus opened the Scriptures to them and they saw the light.

The world is still a dark place. Wars and rumors of war, bitter hatred among nations, towering ambition, utter selfishness—it all leads to conditions that are about as bad as we can imagine. And the world's wise men, trying to find a remedy, are groping in the dark, proposing this, that, and the other to arrive at peace among the nations. But even if peace could be secured, the world would still be a dark place. Even if all fear for the entire duration of our life could be removed—the fear of war, of want—there remains another fear that embitters men's lives and drives them to despair: the fear of death and of the judgment to come. This fear is rooted in the demand written in every heart: "For I am the LORD your God. . . . and be holy, for I am holy" (Leviticus 11:44), in the conviction that we have not done and cannot do what we should do, and in the terrifying question, What will become of us when we face the great Judge? Men try to drown this fear in the pursuit of riches, ambition, and pleasure, but it always rises again. There is only one cure, one way to true happiness; it is found in the testimony of divine love and forgiveness in God's Word.

All Christians find this to be true. "Through Your precepts I get understanding," says David; "Your word is a lamp to my feet and a light to my path" (Psalm 119:104–5). This does not mean we will always fully understand all the ways of God. He still "moves in a mysterious way His wonders to perform" (*LSB* 765:1). But from His Word we learn that whatever He does, His motive is love and His object is our salvation. And in that knowledge, we take the good and the evil as it comes and are content. When our sins trouble us, there is peace in the promise: "The blood of Jesus His Son cleanses us from all sin" (1 John 1:7). When night descends and we feel forsaken by God and man, here is cheer and hope: "Behold, I am with you always, to the end of the age" (Matthew 28:20). We must carry our dearest and best out to God's acre; but we can return comforted by His Word: "I am the resurrection and the life. Whoever believes in Me, though he die, yet shall he live" (John 11:25). And when, finally, we are alone to battle with the last foe, there is even then courage and strength in the divine Word: "Even though I walk through the valley of the shadow of death, I will fear no evil, for You are with me; Your rod and Your staff, they comfort me" (Psalm 23:4).

"A lamp shining in a dark place, until the day dawns and the morning star rises in your hearts," so St. Peter calls the divine Word

(2 Peter 1:19). Let us read it devoutly, study it diligently, believe it implicitly, and so be prepared for the good and the evil day.

Prayer

Blessed Lord, who has caused all Holy Scriptures to be written for our learning, grant that we hear, read, mark, learn, and inwardly keep them that by patience and comfort of Your Holy Word we may embrace and ever hold fast the blessed hope of everlasting life, which You have given us in our Savior Jesus Christ. Amen.

Theodore Hoyer

MEDITATIONS FOR
THE GOSPEL ACCORDING TO
SAINT MATTHEW

A PUBLICAN BECOMES A DISCIPLE

Matthew 9:9–13

Jesus Calls Matthew

As Jesus passed on from there, He saw a man called Matthew sitting at the tax booth, and He said to him, "Follow Me." And he rose and followed Him. And as Jesus reclined at table in the house, behold, many tax collectors and sinners came and were reclining with Jesus and His disciples. And when the Pharisees saw this, they said to His disciples, "Why does your teacher eat with tax collectors and sinners?" But when He heard it, He said, "Those who are well have no need of a physician, but those who are sick. Go and learn what this means, 'I desire mercy, and not sacrifice.' For I came not to call the righteous, but sinners."

HOW wonderful is the grace of God! When Jesus selected disciples to follow Him, to be instructed by Him and to become His apostles and witnesses to the world, He did not always choose them from the mighty, prominent, and learned, but from the poor and lowly and despised. He chose fishermen, like Peter and his brother Andrew, James and his brother John, and publicans like Matthew, the writer of the first Gospel in our Bible.

We do not know much about Matthew. He does not state in specific words that he is the writer of this book. Neither does he provide details about his life before or after his calling. He mentions only his call into the discipleship of the Lord (9:9–10). But if we compare this account of his call with the words of St. Mark and St. Luke, who clearly record the same incident, we learn that Matthew's original name was Levi and that by profession he was a publican, a tax collector. Mark 2:14–15 says: "And as He passed by, He saw Levi the son of Alphaeus sitting at the tax booth, and He said to him, 'Follow Me.' And he rose and followed Him. And as he reclined at table in his house, many tax collectors and sinners were reclining with Jesus and His disciples, for there were many who followed Him." And

Luke 5:27–29 states: "After this He went out and saw a tax collector named Levi, sitting at the tax booth. And He said to him, 'Follow Me.' And leaving everything, he rose and followed Him. And Levi made Him a great feast in his house, and there was a large company of tax collectors and others reclining at table with them."

It was customary for Jews to change their name at an important event in their life, as conversion or being called into the apostolate would have been. And Levi chose a name with a beautiful meaning. Matthew, according to the original Hebrew name, means "gift of the Lord." By choosing this name, the disciple confesses that his conversion was an act of divine grace, a gift of God. But Matthew did not forget his former sinful life. We know that publicans were usually classified with "sinners" because they frequently used their authority as customs collectors of the Roman emperor to enrich themselves by fraud and deceit to the detriment of their fellow countrymen. Note the confession of Zacchaeus, a chief among the publicans, in Luke 19:8: "And Zacchaeus stood and said to the Lord, 'Behold, Lord, the half of my goods I give to the poor. And if I have defrauded anyone of anything, I restore it fourfold.'" That is why, when Matthew records the names of the twelve apostles of Jesus, he says, "Matthew the tax collector" (Matthew 10:3). But this is the last time he mentions himself, and in the other books of the New Testament, his name is merely recorded in the list of apostles (Mark 3:18; Luke 6:15; Acts 1:13).

Neither do we know much of Matthew's life after the ascension of the Lord. Church Fathers and ancient historians tell us that at first he preached among Jews and Jewish Christians in Palestine and later to other groups, and this is undoubtedly a true report because it agrees with his Gospel. Other reports about his life, ministry, and death are mere traditions that cannot be substantiated. In the church calendar, the day of St. Matthew is observed on September 21, and the lessons appointed to be read and considered on that day are 1 Corinthians 12:4–11, or Ephesians 4:7–14 and Matthew 9:9–13.

Prayer

Lord Jesus, in the days of Your sojourn on earth, You said to Levi the tax collector, "Follow Me." And he arose and followed You and became Your apostle Matthew. Through Word and Sacrament, You also call me to follow You. Give me grace to heed Your call and follow You in true faith. Amen.

L. Fuerbringer

THE FIRST GOSPEL
Luke 1:1–2

Dedication to Theophilus

In as much as many have undertaken to compile a narrative of the things that have been accomplished among us, just as those who from the beginning were eyewitnesses and ministers of the word have delivered them to us.

IN the preceding devotion, we considered the person and the life of Matthew, the writer of the first Gospel in our Bible. Now we look at his book in a general way to better understand some of the details contained in it.

It is nowhere stated expressly in the Bible that Matthew wrote this first Gospel, but it is the unanimous opinion of Church Fathers since the first and second centuries, who were close to the New Testament events, so their opinion may be accepted without hesitation. They also tell us that Matthew wrote his Gospel for Jewish Christians to prove that Jesus of Nazareth is the Messiah promised by the prophets of the Old Testament and that His appearing on this earth is to establish the kingdom of God. Therefore, if we wish to give to each of the Gospels a distinctive label expressing its purpose and its characteristics, we can call this book the Gospel of the Promised Savior. The symbol of the evangelist, taken from the symbols of the Early Church, is a winged man because Matthew stresses the incarnation. This theme is very evident throughout the Gospel. We note that throughout his book, Matthew presents the life and work of the Savior in the context of Old Testament prophecy and shows the exact fulfillment of such prophecy by using the phrase "All this took place to fulfill what the Lord had spoken by the prophet" (1:22) or "This was to fulfill what the Lord had spoken by the prophet" or "Then was fulfilled what was spoken by the prophet Jeremiah." (See 2:15, 17, 23; 4:14; 8:17; 12:17; 13:35; 21:4; 26:54,56; 27:9.) Matthew traces the genealogy of Christ to Abraham, the father of the Jews (1:1–17), while Luke, who presents Christ as the Savior of all mankind, traces it to Adam, father of the human race (Luke 3:23–38).

Matthew records many of Jesus' words against the Pharisees and the Sadducees, indicating a polemical and at the same time an apologetic purpose. This enables his readers to oppose the false teachings and practices of the Jews. Thus we read in his book the long Sermon on the Mount (chs. 5–7), with its central theme, "For I tell you, unless your righteousness exceeds that of the scribes and Pharisees, you will never enter the kingdom of heaven" (5:20), and the dreadful woe against the scribes and the Pharisees (ch. 23). (See also chs. 12, 15, 16, 22.) Matthew generally does not translate Jewish names, explain Jewish customs, or describe Jewish localities because he assumes these are known and familiar to his readers. See, for instance, 26:25, where he does not translate the Hebrew word *rabbi* (teacher, master) because he assumes his readers will understand. But John, writing for different readers, says, " 'Rabbi' (which means Teacher)" (John 1:38). See also Matthew 15:1–3, where the evangelist does not explain the Jewish custom of washing the hands. But Mark, writing for non-Jewish readers, fully explains this custom, saying, "Now when the Pharisees gathered to Him, with some of the scribes who had come from Jerusalem, they saw that some of His disciples ate with hands that were defiled, that is, unwashed. (For the Pharisees and all the Jews do not eat unless they wash their hands, holding to the tradition of the elders, and when they come from the marketplace, they do not eat unless they wash. And there are many other traditions that they observe, such as the washing of cups and pots and copper vessels and dining couches" (Mark 7:1–4). (See also Matthew 23:5, 24.)

It is not known definitely where this book was written, but the assumption is that it was composed in Palestine, probably Jerusalem. Also, we do not know exactly when Matthew wrote his Gospel, but twice he uses a peculiar phrase. He says that the potter's field, bought with the money Judas Iscariot obtained for betraying Christ, was called "the Field of Blood to this day" (27:8). Also, when recording the fact that after the resurrection of Jesus, the watchmen at His grave were bribed by the Jewish elders and told to say to the governor that "His disciples came by night and stole Him away while we were asleep," Matthew adds, "this story has been spread among the Jews to this day" (28:13, 15). These statements indicate that the Book of Matthew was probably written a considerable time after the events recorded in it, but before the year 70, since we find no reference to the destruction of Jerusalem by the Romans (which Jesus had clearly and definitely prophesied in Matthew 23:38 and 24:1–2). Therefore, the approximate date of the writing of this Gospel is placed in the sixties but before the year 70. This dating is accepted by many Bible students. In addition, a number of well-informed Church Fathers maintained that it was the first of the four Gospels.

Regarding the contents and the arrangement of his Gospel, Matthew follows the so-called synoptic plan, as do Mark and Luke. We call these three books the Synoptic Gospels because they "see" the life, the discourses, and the work of Jesus "together;" they generally present them from the same viewpoint; and they are in much agreement with one another. They differ in this respect from John, who follows a different plan of presentation, has different content, and records other discourses of the Master. In this way, God has given us, through the four writers, a full record of the life and work of Jesus, the so-called "fourfold Gospel," one Gospel but in a fourfold form. Accordingly, Matthew has at the beginning of his book the "infancy Gospel": the birth and infancy of Jesus (chs. 1–2; see also Luke 1–2). Then, in 3:1–4:11, Matthew introduces the forerunner of Christ, John the Baptist, and tells of the Baptism and temptation of Jesus (Mark 1:1–13; Luke 3:1–4:13). Matthew adds the story of the journey of Jesus to Galilee; then presents the large first part of his book, the Galilean ministry of the Savior preaching the Gospel of the kingdom of God and performing miracles as confirmation (4:12–18:35). (See Mark 1:14–9:50; Luke 4:14–9:50.)

Then follows the second major part of the book, the continuation and conclusion of the life and work of Jesus on earth: His last journey to Jerusalem, His suffering, His death, and His resurrection (19:1–28:20). (See Mark 10:1–16:20; Luke 9:51–24:53.) Although each of the evangelists has his own style of recording the life and work of Jesus, Matthew includes discourses and deeds of the Master that are either not provided in the two other Synoptic Gospels or are given in a briefer or longer form. Matthew uses the term "kingdom of heaven" at least 32 times, the term "kingdom of God" 5 times, and the short term "kingdom" 18 times. Matthew closes his wonderful book with the great commission that Jesus addressed to His disciples and apostles and to the Church after them: "Go therefore and make disciples of all nations, baptizing them in the name of the Father and of the Son and of the Holy Spirit, teaching them to observe all that I have commanded you" (28:19). He adds the blessed promise that has been the comfort of millions and millions of men: "Behold, I am with you always, to the end of the age" (28:20).

Prayer

Lord Jesus, we thank You that You have given us Your saving Gospel through Your faithful apostle Matthew. Bless our reading of it from day to day. Grant that by Your grace we may accept it in true faith for the salvation of our souls and be guided by it in our daily life. And fulfill Your blessed promise to be with us always in life and death, even unto the end of the world. Amen.

L. Fuerbringer

JUST NAMES?
Matthew 1:1–17

NAMES, nothing but names, and many hard to pronounce. Why all these names?

God put them into this chapter, and God does nothing without purpose. These names prove that Jesus of Nazareth is the Messiah, the promised and chosen Savior of the world. The Messiah must be of the house of David, the tribe of Judah, and the seed of Abraham. These names prove it. Who else could trace his lineage to David, to Judah, to Abraham? We have in Jesus, born in Bethlehem, of the house of David, the one and only man born of woman who can redeem the world and save sinful mankind.

Again, these names prove that Jesus is Savior of all. Look at them! You see saints and sinners, Gentiles and Jews, men and women, kings and farmers, free men and captives, rich and poor, men known and men unknown. But all were ancestors of Jesus. Their bloodline flows in this Babe of Bethlehem. He took the transgressions of all these men and women to the cross and was crucified for them that they might be forgiven.

These names are given in three groups of fourteen. These men and women did not find their way onto this roster by chance. According to the eternal plans of God, all this was done that in the fullness of the time Jesus would be born of Mary in Bethlehem of Judea.

The Genealogy of Jesus Christ

The book of the genealogy of Jesus Christ, the son of David, the son of Abraham.

Abraham was the father of Isaac, and Isaac the father of Jacob, and Jacob the father of Judah and his brothers, and Judah the father of Perez and Zerah by Tamar, and Perez the father of Hezron, and Hezron the father of Ram, and Ram the father of Amminadab, and Amminadab the father of Nahshon, and Nahshon the father of Salmon, and Salmon the father of Boaz by Rahab, and Boaz the father of Obed by Ruth, and Obed the father of Jesse, and Jesse the father of David the king.

And David was the father of Solomon by the wife of Uriah, and Solomon the father of Rehoboam, and Rehoboam the father of Abijah, and Abijah the father of Asaph, and Asaph the father of Jehoshaphat, and Jehoshaphat the father of Joram, and Joram the father of Uzziah, and Uzziah the father of Jotham, and Jotham the father of Ahaz, and Ahaz the father of Hezekiah, and Hezekiah the father of Manasseh, and Manasseh the father of Amos, and Amos the father of Josiah, and Josiah the father of Jechoniah and his brothers, at the time of the deportation to Babylon.

And after the deportation to Babylon: Jechoniah was the father of Shealtiel, and Shealtiel the father of Zerubbabel, and Zerubbabel the father of Abiud, and Abiud the father of Eliakim, and Eliakim the father of Azor, and Azor the father of Zadok, and Zadok the father of Achim, and Achim the father of Eliud, and Eliud the father of Eleazar, and Eleazar the father of Matthan, and Matthan the father of Jacob, and Jacob the father of Joseph the husband of Mary, of whom Jesus was born, who is called Christ.

So all the generations from Abraham to David were fourteen generations, and from David to the deportation to Babylon fourteen generations, and from the deportation to Babylon to the Christ fourteen generations.

Names identify us. Our family name links us to a certain group of people. Our given name sets us apart from all others of our own family group. We are individuals, with obligations, duties, and responsibilities all our own. We are born into the world with a family name. But our given name is ours. When we are baptized and made part of the family of God and joint heirs with Christ Jesus, we are given an additional name: Christian.

Our names are written in God's book, the Book of Life. This makes us citizens of His kingdom and certain of our salvation. "I will never blot his name out of the book of life. I will confess his name before My Father and before His angels" (Revelation 3:5).

My name gives me individuality. I am a person and I am precious in God's sight. "The Lord takes thought for me" (Psalm 40:17). He knows me by name and orders my footsteps. Because He loves me in Christ Jesus, I cannot perish but will live and reign with Him forever.

Reading the strange and unknown names in Matthew 1 assures me that whoever comes to Jesus, the Savior, will not be cast out. No one who reads the Gospel needs to question whether God loves him. God does love us and He includes us in His gracious plan of salvation.

Prayer

Heavenly Father, grant me the grace to abide in the sacred wounds of my Savior and find forgiveness, peace, hope, and eternal life in Him who was made flesh to seek and to save the lost, the straying, and the erring. Draw me day after day with Your secure love, and keep me steadfast in the faith. Let sinner and saint, young and old, rich and poor, find in Jesus Christ their all in all. Amen.

THE NAME ABOVE ALL NAMES
Matthew 1:18–25

THERE is none other like Jesus. There never can be, for only Jesus, according to divine prophecy, was to be born of a virgin (Isaiah 7:14). His origin is in God; therefore His unique name—Immanuel—which means "God with us."

Jesus must be virgin-born if He is to be the Savior of the world. If He had been conceived in the natural manner, He would have been born in sin. But the Holy Spirit overshadowed Mary, and therefore that child born of her is God of very God (Luke 1:35).

Because Jesus was conceived by the Holy Spirit, He was without sin and fulfilled the Law of God in every detail. This He did for us, who are born in sin, who have sin transmitted to us from our fathers from generation to generation.

Only if Jesus is born without sin of the Virgin Mary can He be our Savior. A sinful man cannot even redeem himself, much less his brother. David was willing and ready to die for his son Absalom, but this would not redeem him because David himself was conceived and born in sin.

Here we have a miracle of miracles. Finite mind exclaims that this cannot be. Modern thought rejects this truth. But the believers of the ages realize that there is no salvation unless we have a sinless Savior who is perfect in His holiness. Such a perfect Savior is possible only if Jesus of Bethlehem is born of the Virgin Mary.

The Birth of Jesus Christ

Now the birth of Jesus Christ took place in this way. When His mother Mary had been betrothed to Joseph, before they came together she was found to be with child from the Holy Spirit. And her husband Joseph, being a just man and unwilling to put her to shame, resolved to divorce her quietly. But as he considered these things, behold, an angel of the Lord appeared to him in a dream, saying, "Joseph, son of David, do not fear to take Mary as your wife, for that which is conceived in her is from the Holy Spirit. She will bear a son, and you shall call His name Jesus, for He will save His people from their sins." All this took place to fulfill what the Lord had spoken by the prophet:

"Behold, the virgin shall conceive and bear a son, and they shall call His name Immanuel"(which means, God with us).

When Joseph woke from sleep, he did as the angel of the Lord commanded him: he took his wife, but knew her not until she had given birth to a son. And he called His name Jesus.

God gave to the Babe of Bethlehem the name Jesus. Jesus is Greek for Joshua, "the Lord saves." Joshua of old led Israel out of the wilderness into the promised land of Canaan. The Joshua-Jesus of Bethlehem, the Christ, delivers us from the slavery of sin and leads us into the heavenly Canaan, where we have peace and eternal salvation. He is called Jesus because He saves us from our sin. This He did on Calvary, where He shed His blood for the whole human race. Jesus is the Savior, my Savior, who has taken upon Himself my sins, no matter what they may be, and paid for them with His own blood.

Jesus could be wounded for my transgressions and heal me from my iniquities only because He is the Christ, the chosen of God, His only Son. He was set aside in the eternal counsel of God to come to the rescue of man. Because He is Christ, He is God made flesh.

Although He is God from all eternity, nevertheless He is my Friend, who loves with an undying love. Daily He walks with me, guides me, protects me. Because of His great love, no one will pluck me out of my Father's hand. In Christ's friendship, I find joy and a richer and fuller life. I can go in and out through prayer and know He will not turn away from me. When every other helper fails, even when I pass through death's valley, He is with me to lead me to glory, where He is King forever and ever.

Prayer

Lord Jesus, Keeper of my body, Lover of my soul, and Friend of sinful man, wrap me with Your love, and forgive me all my sins. Keep me, through Word and Sacrament, faithful, loyal, and true. Draw all mankind with Your secure love, and hasten the day of Your coming that all Your saints may live and reign with You in the glory of eternal life. Then Yours shall be the honor and praise forevermore. Amen.

WISE MEN STILL GO TO BETHLEHEM

Matthew 2:1–15

SURELY the star did not shout that the King was born! How, then, did the Wise Men of the East know that this unusual star announced the coming of the King of kings? They learned this truth the same way you and I did: through the Word of God.

Centuries before the coming of the Christ Child, King Nebuchadnezzar invaded Judah and led many of God's people into captivity. In this Babylonian exile, the people of God spoke of their hope that God would send to Israel the greater Son of David, who would establish an everlasting kingdom. And although this promise of God was misunderstood—for many thought it would be an earthly kingdom—nevertheless, this hope was expressed again and again by the captives of the East. The Wise Men surely knew the story. When they saw this unusual star, they concluded that the King had been born.

So they traveled to Jerusalem to pay the King homage. There, again through God's Word, they were directed to Bethlehem, where they found the Christ Child and worshiped Him as their Lord God and presented Him with gold, frankincense, and myrrh.

The Visit of the Wise Men

Now after Jesus was born in Bethlehem of Judea in the days of Herod the king, behold, wise men from the east came to Jerusalem, saying, "Where is He who has been born king of the Jews? For we saw His star when it rose and have come to worship Him." When Herod the king heard this, he was troubled, and all Jerusalem with him; and assembling all the chief priests and scribes of the people, he inquired of them where the

Christ was to be born. They told him, "In Bethlehem of Judea, for so it is written by the prophet:

"*'And you, O Bethlehem, in the land of Judah,*
  are by no means least among the rulers of Judah;
for from you shall come a ruler
  who will shepherd My people Israel.'"

Then Herod summoned the wise men secretly and ascertained from them what time the star had appeared. And he sent them to Bethlehem, saying, "Go and search diligently for the child, and when you have found Him, bring me word, that I too may come and worship Him." After listening to the king, they went on their way. And behold, the star that they had seen when it rose went before them until it came to rest over the place where the child was. When they saw the star, they rejoiced exceedingly with great joy. And going into the house they saw the child with Mary His mother, and they fell down and worshiped Him. Then, opening their treasures, they offered Him gifts, gold and frankincense and myrrh. And being warned in a dream not to return to Herod, they departed to their own country by another way.

The Flight to Egypt

Now when they had departed, behold, an angel of the Lord appeared to Joseph in a dream and said, "Rise, take the child and His mother, and flee to Egypt, and remain there until I tell you, for Herod is about to search for the child, to destroy Him." And he rose and took the child and His mother by night and departed to Egypt and remained there until the death of Herod. This was to fulfill what the Lord had spoken by the prophet, "Out of Egypt I called My Son."

Jesus is the Star of Bethlehem. We, too, go to Bethlehem in spirit and worship the Christ Child as our Lord and Savior. We know from the Scriptures that this babe of Bethlehem is the Messiah of prophecy.

He is the Star of love. The greatest gift came to us when God so loved the world that He gave His only Son. This gift reveals to us that amazing love that moved this Son to die for us while we were yet sinners.

He is the star of peace. He came to reconcile us to His Father through His death on the cross. Now we can come to the eternal God and know that He loves us. We are at peace with God and, therefore, at peace with our own conscience.

He is the Star of hope. All the weary and heavy-laden can turn to Him and find rest for their souls. We can look to the future and see heaven with all its glory. This hope takes the sting of disappointment out of our hearts, our lives, and our homes.

He is the Star of comfort. Earthly life is filled with sorrow and tears and death. But Jesus is the resurrection and the life. He heals broken hearts and promises that we will live because He lives.

He is the Star of joy. Bethlehem's angels announced good tidings of great joy. Sin is forgiven, salvation is certain, and heaven is our home.

Wise men still go to Bethlehem. We, too, are wise if we go. Only if the Christ Child finds room in our hearts will we daily rejoice that unto us is born a Savior, who is Christ the Lord.

Prayer

Christ Child of Bethlehem, enter our hearts and cleanse them from all sin, that we may worship and adore and serve You, who are the King of kings and the Savior of us all. Amen.

GOD CANNOT BE DEFEATED

Matthew 2:16–23

THOSE who sought the child's life are dead." And Christ Jesus still is King of kings. He lives in the hearts of millions. The gates of hell do not prevail against Him and His Church. Those who oppose the Christ Child finally go down in defeat.

Through the Wise Men of the East and Scripture, King Herod learned that the newborn King would be found in Bethlehem. Thinking it over, Herod decided to get rid of the Child. So he ordered all the innocent babies to be murdered to make sure that the newborn King would be destroyed. But before Herod could carry out his plot and kill all the baby boys, Joseph, Mary, and Jesus are on their way to Egypt. And although Herod succeeded in slaughtering many innocent boys, he failed in his unholy scheme to defeat the new King. After a time, the holy family returned to Israel. "Those who sought the child's life are dead."

Evil, wicked, brutal men had their little day. Seemingly triumphant, no one seems to be able to put a halt to their vicious plans. Righteousness, truth, and justice are trampled underfoot. However, when the last chapter is written, they are dead.

Even when Jesus was nailed to the accursed tree, even when He breathed His last human breath, sin did not win the ultimate victory. For that one day the disciples were stunned. They could not understand. Total darkness also entered their hearts and minds. But before the sun set that Friday, Jesus exclaimed: "It is finished!" Satan, sin, and death were defeated, and man was redeemed.

Through the ages, the nonbeliever has sought to wipe out the Gospel by edicts, by sword, by ridicule, and by criticism. But to this day, the Gospel message reaches the ends of the earth to bring salvation, peace, hope, and guidance to sin-troubled and weary souls.

They are dead who seek to destroy Jesus and His Gospel. Christ lives forever!

Herod Kills the Children

Then Herod, when he saw that he had been tricked by the wise men, became furious, and he sent and killed all the male children in Bethlehem and in all that region who were two years old or under, according to the time that he had ascertained from the wise men. Then was fulfilled what was spoken by the prophet Jeremiah:

"A voice was heard in Ramah,
  weeping and loud lamentation,
Rachel weeping for her children;
  she refused to be comforted, because they are no more."

The Return to Nazareth

But when Herod died, behold, an angel of the Lord appeared in a dream to Joseph in Egypt, saying, "Rise, take the child and His mother and go to the land of Israel, for those who sought the child's life are dead." And he rose and took the child and His mother and went to the land of Israel. But when he heard that Archelaus was reigning over Judea in place of his father Herod, he was afraid to go there, and being warned in a dream he withdrew to the district of Galilee. And he went and lived in a city called Nazareth, that what was spoken by the prophets might be fulfilled: "He shall be called a Nazarene."

Sometimes we feel as though God has forgotten us. We ask with anxious hearts: Does God really care? Why doesn't He do something about all this wickedness? We pray, and the heavens are silent. The world taunts: Where is your God? But not even a sparrow falls without the knowledge of our heavenly Father. "God moves in a mysterious way His wonders to perform" (*LSB* 765:1). His ways are not our ways, and His time clock of eternity does not tick with the same staccato as that of our hectic lives. As the years unfold, we will see that all came to pass that the Scriptures might be fulfilled, that God's will be done. "Be still, and know that I am God" (Psalm 46:10).

In the times when all goes wrong according to our planning and thinking and we feel that God has turned from us, let us look toward Calvary. There we see what God has done that we might have life in its fullness. Although floods destroy our fields, windstorms shatter our homes, misfortune consumes our filled barns, and death takes those we love, God cares. Did He not send His only Son to the cross that we might have those treasures that even death cannot take out of our hands?

All opposition in the end fails. We cannot perish because no one can pluck us out of our Father's hand.

That is enough to know.

Prayer

Heavenly Father, I seek refuge in You. You are my present helper in every trouble of life, the keeper of my body, and the lover of my soul in Christ, my Redeemer. I come to be healed of my sin, to be strengthened against temptation, and to be comforted in sorrow. For Jesus' sake, help me and save me. Amen.

OUTWARD REFORM WILL NOT DO
Matthew 3:1–12

EVERY generation has its own particular and peculiar sins. In each age, you hear older people say that the younger set is "going to the devil." That we all are born in sin and are by nature the children of wrath is undeniably true. This sinfulness of man shows itself from generation to generation.

John the Baptist denounced the sins of his age. To attract attention to himself, he lived an unusual life. He went out into the wilderness, lived on locusts and wild honey—as some in that region of the world still do—and clothed himself in camel's hair, a heavy cloth that would keep him warm as he slept out on the cool nighttime desert sands. By doing all this, he did not bury himself and hide from society. Instead, he aroused curiosity and people came out, even from Jerusalem, to hear him.

John used this opportunity to preach to them the Law in all its severity. He called sin by its real name. He warned the people of their oncoming doom if they did not turn from their evil ways. He emphasized that they were not saved merely because they were descendants of Abraham; they would need to repent, to turn to God and to Him who was sent of God, the Lamb for sinners slain. Only then could they escape the judgments to come.

The hour had struck, the fullness of the time was at hand, Scripture was being fulfilled, the Messiah was come. As John the apostle records, John the Baptist pointed to Jesus, saying, "Behold, the Lamb of God, who takes away the sin of the world" (John 1:29)!

John the Baptist Prepares the Way

In those days John the Baptist came preaching in the wilderness of Judea, "Repent, for the kingdom of heaven is at hand." For this is he who was spoken of by the prophet Isaiah when he said,

"The voice of one crying in the wilderness:
'Prepare the way of the Lord; make His paths straight.'"

Now John wore a garment of camel's hair and a leather belt around his waist, and his food was locusts and wild honey. Then Jerusalem and all Judea and all the region about the Jordan were going out to him, and they were baptized by him in the river Jordan, confessing their sins.

But when he saw many of the Pharisees and Sadducees coming to his baptism, he said to them, "You brood of vipers! Who warned you to flee from the wrath to come? Bear fruit in keeping with repentance. And do not presume to say to yourselves, 'We have Abraham as our father,' for I tell you, God is able from these stones to raise up children for Abraham. Even now the axe is laid to the root of the trees. Every tree therefore that does not bear good fruit is cut down and thrown into the fire.

"I baptize you with water for repentance, but He who is coming after me is mightier than I, whose sandals I am not worthy to carry. He will baptize you with the Holy Spirit and fire. His winnowing fork is in His hand, and He will clear His threshing floor and gather His wheat into the barn, but the chaff He will burn with unquenchable fire."

We all are sinners. We must be reminded of this fact time and again. Otherwise we may become callous and hard-hearted and unconcerned about our transgressions. But why rub it in? That is not the purpose of denouncing sin and calling attention to it. God wants us to see our shortcomings and trespasses so that we may turn from our sinful ways and be saved.

John the Baptist says, "Repent." Ezekiel says, "Turn back, turn back from your evil ways, for why will you die, O house of Israel?" (Ezekiel 33:11). However, repentance is more than reforming; a sinner can reform and still be lost. We must turn to Jesus as the Savior who redeemed us with His blood. As we turn to Him in faith, He cleanses us and sends us on our way, transformed and renewed. We are new creations in Christ. Reborn, we bear the fruits of this rebirth. We now live for Christ and in Christ. We love Him because He first loved us. Therefore we bring forth the fruit of the Spirit—love, joy, peace, patience, kindness, goodness, faithfulness, gentleness, and self-control (Galatians 5:22–23).

Baptized with the Holy Spirit, we are aglow with an enthusiasm, consecration, and zeal for Christ that shows itself in word and action as we go through life. Daily we dedicate ourselves to Christ, who has laid down His life that we might be God's own, reconciled and saved forevermore.

Prayer

Spirit of God, descend on us and take full possession of our hearts. Make us Your temples and preserve us in faith until we stand before the throne of the Lamb and adore Him as our eternal King and Lord. Amen.

MY SON AND MY CHILDREN
Matthew 3:13–17

THE Baptism of John was not the New Testament sacrament. This is clearly indicated in Acts 19:1–5: "And it happened that while Apollos was at Corinth, Paul passed through the inland country and came to Ephesus. There he found some disciples. And he said to them, 'Did you receive the Holy Spirit when you believed?' And they said, 'No, we have not even heard that there is a Holy Spirit.' And he said, 'Into what then were you baptized?' They said, 'Into John's baptism.' And Paul said, 'John baptized with the baptism of repentance, telling the people to believe in the one who was to come after him, that is, Jesus.' On hearing this, they were baptized in the name of the Lord Jesus."

John's Baptism was a ceremonial cleansing of the Old Testament dispensation, to which Jesus submitted to fulfill all Law. Luke tells us that another ceremonial law was observed when Jesus was brought to the temple forty days after His birth (Luke 2:22–23). As Jesus, made under the Law, began to fulfill it, God the Father gave His approval as the heavens opened and He declared, "This is My beloved Son, with whom I am well pleased." And the Holy Spirit descended upon Jesus in the form of a dove to let the whole world know that the entire Godhead is deeply involved in the work and mission of the Son. This Son had become flesh, that He might suffer and die and shed His blood as the eternal Lamb of God, foreshadowed in prophecy and the sacrifices at the temple.

Through this act of being baptized, Jesus officially begins His public ministry as Prophet and Priest, that He might also be the King of kings. Now He goes forth from Bethany across the Jordan to proclaim to the world that He is the Messiah, whom the Father sent into the world to reconcile the lost and again draw to Himself mankind as His forgiven children.

The Baptism of Jesus

Then Jesus came from Galilee to the Jordan to John, to be baptized by him. John would have prevented Him, saying, "I need to be baptized by You, and do You come to me?" But Jesus answered him, "Let it be so now, for thus it is fitting for us to fulfill all righteousness." Then he consented. And when Jesus was baptized, immediately He went up from the water, and behold, the heavens were opened to Him, and He saw the Spirit of God descending like a dove and coming to rest on Him; and behold, a voice from heaven said, "This is My beloved Son, with whom I am well pleased."

Jesus instituted the New Testament Sacrament of Baptism as a Means of Grace by which we are made His disciples. Through Baptism, we of the New Testament age are brought into God's kingdom, adopted into His family, and made new creatures who walk in the newness of life. In Baptism, God claims us as His own. God made a covenant with us that we are to be His children and He our heavenly Father.

God never breaks this agreement of grace. A child may run away and not enjoy the blessings of home. So we may stray from God and live without hope. But as the erring child comes home penitently, his parents will not turn from him. So we know because of this baptismal covenant that God will not close the door on us as we come confessing our sins. It may happen that a father will refuse to be reconciled to his son, that a mother may forget her baby, but day after day, year in and year out, God in Christ stretches out His hands to erring and sinful mankind and pleads: "Come!" And he who comes will not be cast out.

Prayer

Lord, You have received me as Your own in my Baptism and through the years You have been faithful to me. Give me the grace to hold fast to You as my God and Father and to confess Jesus Christ as my Savior, who has washed and cleansed me from all sin. Amen.

WHEN TO SAY NO
Matthew 4:1–11

WHEN Jesus refused to turn stones into bread, He clearly declared that bread is not the biggest issue of life. Man may have a big supply of food on hand, his barns and coffers filled, and still starve to death. Man does not live by bread alone. Friendship, love, contentment, and national and familial peace are essential to a well-rounded life. More than that, to enjoy daily bread we must have a good conscience, forgiveness, hope, and faith. Jesus refuses to make bread the main issue of life.

When Jesus refused to leap from the roof of the temple, He emphasized that man is not to throw caution to the wind. God says, "He will command His angels concerning you to guard you in all your ways" (Psalm 91:11). But the promises of God do not guarantee safety if we do something foolhardy. God never promised protection if we have ourselves nailed up in a barrel and then rolled over

Niagara Falls. Satan came to Jesus with just such a temptation: "You say You are the Son of God; You build upon His Word. Now show us that You take God at His Word—ignore all obstacles, leap and trust." But Jesus says this is tempting God.

When Jesus refused to share with Satan the glories of the world and refused to avoid suffering and dying for the sin of mankind, He resisted triumphantly and He clearly affirmed that there can be no allegiance or compromise with evil and sin. He must drink the cup to its last drop. He must shed His precious blood for our transgressions. He must trample Satan under His feet. Christ and Satan have nothing in common. Satan must go. He must depart in the end into everlasting fire. The world can be saved only through suffering and the cross. And Jesus went uncomplaining to Calvary, that we might be redeemed from sin, Satan, and eternal death.

The Temptation of Jesus

Then Jesus was led up by the Spirit into the wilderness to be tempted by the devil. And after fasting forty days and forty nights, He was hungry. And the tempter came and said to Him, "If you are the Son of God, command these stones to become loaves of bread." But He answered, "It is written,

"'Man shall not live by bread alone,
but by every word that comes from the mouth of God.'"

Then the devil took Him to the holy city and set Him on the pinnacle of the temple and said to Him, "If You are the Son of God, throw Yourself down, for it is written,

"'He will command his angels concerning you.'

and

"'On their hands they will bear you up,
lest you strike your foot against a stone.'"

Jesus said to him, "Again it is written, 'You shall not put the Lord your God to the test.'" Again, the devil took Him to a very high mountain and showed Him all the kingdoms of the world and their glory. And he said to Him, "All these I will give

You, if You will fall down and worship me." Then Jesus said to him, "Be gone, Satan! For it is written,

> " 'You shall worship the Lord your God
> and Him only shall you serve.' "

Then the devil left Him, and behold, angels came and were ministering to Him.

Satan still is busily seeking to destroy our faith by cunning insinuations. But we can resist and say no when we are tempted. Christ crushed the serpent's head on Calvary. And Christ gives us weapons with which to overcome and win victories: the Gospel, the Lord's Supper, prayer. Then Jesus Himself intercedes for us: "I have prayed for you that your faith may not fail" (Luke 22:32).

Satan wants us to believe that all troubles are settled if we have the food problem solved. He blinds us to the fact that sin creates hunger and greed breeds strife, envy, war, crime, and wickedness. He wants us to see in Jesus one who turns stones into bread and then have us clamor for a gospel that makes for a utopian world. He wants us to believe that filled barns take care of every need of life. But man cannot live by bread alone.

Satan wants us to believe that we can get along just as well if we do not pay too close attention to the Word. Why worry about sin? God is love. The Bible says so. Why go to church? The thief on the cross did not go and yet was promised paradise that very day. The Bible says so. Why be a stickler? "Did God actually say ..." (Genesis 3:1)? When the devil whispers these thoughts to us, let us resist steadfastly in the faith.

Satan wants us to believe that we can have anything we desire and not be harmed. Why suffer, sacrifice, restrain, and discipline? We can have health without restraint, faith without binding ourselves too closely to the Word, character without discipline, salvation without the blood of Christ. So says the old evil foe.

It is not always easy to say when tempted: "Get behind me, Satan," and then serve and worship the Lord God. To do so, we must look to Jesus and hold fast to His Word and promises. Then, with the power of our Lord on our side, will we conquer and win one victory after another.

Prayer

In Your compassion, look on me, gracious Savior, when I am tempted by the archenemy of my soul. Give me and all Your children strength to resist the cunning devices of the devil and sinful men. Bring to naught the plots and plans that seek to overthrow Your kingdom and Your work being done among the lost children of the world. Keep us steadfast in faith, precious Savior. Amen.

8

ONE GREATER THAN MOSES IS HERE

Matthew 4:12–25

JESUS is the great Prophet in Israel, greater than Moses, greater than Elijah. He is the Light of the world. "The people dwelling in darkness have seen a great light, and for those dwelling in the region and shadow of death, on them a light has dawned" (Matthew 4:16).

Jesus came teaching. He taught us to love our neighbor as much as we love ourselves, and He demanded that we love God above all things. He taught us that we must obey more than the letter of the Law; that lustful desires of the heart make us transgressors of the divine will. He opened our eyes to see sin in all its ugliness and inhuman brutality. He taught us that sin banishes us from the presence of God until sin is completely removed.

Jesus came preaching: "Repent, for the kingdom of heaven is at hand." It was He of whom the prophets and Moses spoke—the light to take away the blindness and darkness of sinful man. Turn to

Him and live. He will draw all men to Himself. Jesus came preaching that "God so loved the world, that He gave His only Son, that whoever believes in Him should not perish but have eternal life" (John 3:16).

Jesus came calling men and women from every walk of life to follow Him and serve Him who first loved us and gave Himself as a ransom for all. Following Jesus would not always mean ease, comfort, wealth, but rather bearing a cross—then, in the end, finding everlasting life and salvation.

Jesus came healing. All manner of diseased people came to Him, even those possessed of the devil. Jesus healed them of ills of the body and the leprosy of sin. No wonder people followed Him from all parts of the country in great number. They found in Him the answer to all of life's questions and problems.

Jesus Begins His Ministry

Now when He heard that John had been arrested, He withdrew into Galilee. And leaving Nazareth He went and lived in Capernaum by the sea, in the territory of Zebulun and Naphtali, so that what was spoken by the prophet Isaiah might be fulfilled:

"The land of Zebulun and the land of Naphtali,
the way of the sea, beyond the Jordan, Galilee of the Gentiles—

the people dwelling in darkness
have seen a great light,
and for those dwelling in the region and shadow of death,
on them a light has dawned."

From that time Jesus began to preach, saying, "Repent, for the kingdom of heaven is at hand."

Jesus Calls the First Disciples

While walking by the Sea of Galilee, He saw two brothers, Simon (who is called Peter) and Andrew his brother, casting a net into the sea, for they were fishermen. And He said to them, "Follow Me, and I will make you fishers of men." Immediately they left their nets and followed Him. And going on from there

He saw two other brothers, James the son of Zebedee and John his brother, in the boat with Zebedee their father, mending their nets, and He called them. Immediately they left the boat and their father and followed Him.

Jesus Ministers to Great Crowds

And He went throughout all Galilee, teaching in their synagogues and proclaiming the gospel of the kingdom and healing every disease and every affliction among the people. So His fame spread throughout all Syria, and they brought Him all the sick, those afflicted with various diseases and pains, those oppressed by demons, epileptics, and paralytics, and He healed them. And great crowds followed Him from Galilee and the Decapolis, and from Jerusalem and Judea, and from beyond the Jordan.

The weary, the troubled, the sin-sick, and the dying still come to Jesus and find rest for their weary life, peace for their mind, healing for their body, and salvation for their soul.

Graciously, tenderly, continuously, Jesus is calling us. Whatever may be our problem, our heartache, or our disappointment, we can come to Him and find comfort, strength, and guidance. He loves us and says, "I have redeemed you; I have called you by name, you are Mine" (Isaiah 43:1).

Are we weeping and mourning? He asks why we cry: "I am the resurrection and the life. Whoever believes in Me, though he die, yet shall he live" (John 11:25).

Are we doubting and asking questions that seem unanswerable? "He said to Thomas, 'Put your finger here, and see My hands; and put out your hand, and place it in My side. Do not disbelieve, but believe' " (John 20:27).

Have we denied Him and been ashamed of Him? He calls: " 'Simon, son of John, do you love Me more than these?' He said to Him, 'Yes, Lord; You know that I love You.' He said to him, 'Feed My lambs' " (John 21:15).

Have we stubbornly resisted Him? He calls: "Saul, why are you persecuting Me?" (Acts 26:14).

And so He calls you and me today. His love and compassion are just as tender now as in the days of His earthly walk. He still stretches out His pierced hands and pleads with us to come.

What folly to resist!

Prayer

Just as I am, Thou wilt receive,
Wilt welcome, pardon, cleanse, relieve;
Because Thy promise I believe,
O Lamb of God, I come, I come. Amen.
(LSB 570:5)

WHO'S WHO IN GOD'S KINGDOM
Matthew 5:1–12

THE Sermon on the Mount is the longest recorded discourse of our Lord Jesus Christ. Its purpose is twofold. First, Jesus teaches that the Law is not fulfilled by keeping ourselves respectable in the eyes of the world. We have not fulfilled the commandment if we have refrained from killing our neighbor. Jesus tells us that if we have not loved our fellow men as much as ourselves, we have broken the Law and are condemned in the court of God as transgressors. Therefore no man is good enough in God's sight to save his own soul.

Second, Jesus teaches what we are to do to please God. Having been saved by His grace, we want to do His will. Here it is. The Law serves as a rule and regulation for Christian living.

The Sermon on the Mount

Seeing the crowds, He went up on the mountain, and when He sat down, His disciples came to Him.

The Beatitudes

And He opened His mouth and taught them, saying:

"Blessed are the poor in spirit, for theirs is the kingdom of heaven.
"Blessed are those who mourn, for they shall be comforted.
"Blessed are the meek, for they shall inherit the earth.
"Blessed are those who hunger and thirst for righteousness,
*   for they shall be satisfied.*
"Blessed are the merciful, for they shall receive mercy.
"Blessed are the pure in heart, for they shall see God.
"Blessed are the peacemakers, for they shall be called sons of God.
"Blessed are those who are persecuted for righteousness' sake,
*   for theirs is the kingdom of heaven.*
"Blessed are you when others revile you and persecute you and utter all
kinds of evil against you falsely on My account. Rejoice and be glad,
*   for your reward is great in heaven,*
*   for so they persecuted the prophets who were before you."*

In these opening sentences of the Sermon on the Mount, we have Christ's roster of who's who. Qualifications for admission into this registry are quaint and unique, judged by the standards of this world. Money does not count; neither does power or success. "How difficult it is to enter the kingdom of God!" (Mark 10:24). "Whoever seeks to preserve his life will lose it, but whoever loses his life will keep it" (Luke 17:33).

First, Jesus lists those who are poor in spirit, those who feel their own spiritual helplessness and need. These people realize that they do not merit salvation because they are sinful and unclean. They know that salvation can be theirs only by grace. To such is promised the kingdom of heaven.

Next, Jesus names those who mourn. They mourn over their sins and are comforted with the Gospel that the blood of Jesus Christ completely cleanses them from that sin.

Then come the meek, the humble, those who know that none of us, not even the most noble of society, can boast of their own salvation. God's grace has called us into the kingdom, and His Gospel preserves us in the faith. These believers shall be rich, for all that is God's is theirs to enjoy.

Following are those who hunger and thirst for righteousness. They long for and strive to do what is pleasing to God in appreciation of His love in Christ. Jesus promises that they will be satisfied; they will find their greatest joy in the service they render to God.

The register continues with those who are merciful; they are kind, patient, thoughtful. They sympathize with those who suffer and go about doing good out of the goodness of their renewed heart. They are repaid in kind; they are shown mercy.

The roll would not be complete without those who are pure in heart. No guile or deceit is found in them. These people shall see God.

The record includes the peacemakers. We need them. They lubricate life and keep down friction. God calls them His special children. They are His favorites because they keep things running smoothly in the home, in the church, and in the nation.

Last but not least, Jesus' roster of who's who names the persecuted. Because they are God's people, confessing Christ as their Savior and Lord, the world reviles and hates them. All manner of lies and accusations are thrown at them. Life is hard, bitter, and dangerous, but they can rejoice despite all because their names are written in the Book of Life.

Prayer

Merciful Lord, keep me in Your grace day after day, forgiving sin and guiding me into the paths of uprightness. Comfort me with the assurance that my name is written in Your Book of Life because I am chosen of You through Jesus Christ, my Lord and Savior. Amen.

SALTY CHRISTIANS

10

Matthew 5:13–16

SALT is more essential than gold. We can live without gold, but not without salt. Salt was used by the ancients as pay. The root word in salary is sal—salt.

Salt vitalizes. If our body is depleted of this mineral, we lag, lose our zest, and droop. Adding a few grains of salt to the daily diet gives new energy to the body.

Salt preserves. Food that is salted down can be kept for months. This method of preserving meats is as old as the hills.

Salt flavors. Food has no taste, is bland, indeed, without salt. One vegetable tastes much like the other without this mineral, and a meal cannot be fully enjoyed unless it is properly seasoned with salt. If salt loses its quality of saltiness, it is valueless. But salt cannot be eaten by itself. It must be mixed in proper proportion with other food. Only then does salt serve its purpose.

Jesus also mentions light as something we cannot live without. The very nature of light is to be seen. The tiniest light can be seen at a great distance. During wartime blackouts, not even a match can be struck because even a little light would reveal the movements of men to the enemy.

Light spreads cheer:

How far that little candle throws his beams!

So shines a good deed in a naughty world. (The Merchant of Venice, act 5, scene 1)

Salt and Light

"You are the salt of the earth, but if salt has lost its taste, how shall its saltiness be restored? It is no longer good for anything except to be thrown out and trampled under people's feet.

"You are the light of the world. A city set on a hill cannot be hidden. Nor do people light a lamp and put it under a basket, but on a stand, and it gives light to all in the house. In the same way, let your light shine before others, so that they may see your good works and give glory to your Father who is in heaven."

Christians are the salt of the earth. Because of us, and for our sake, the world stands. We preserve it. Our lives give flavor to the populace. The more believers within a city, town, or nation, the better it will be. A truly Christian community has little need of a sheriff and a jail. The Christians make the city a safer place in which to live, and peace and quiet prevail.

Salt, by itself, has no value. The Christian is not to separate himself from the world and live in seclusion. He is to be in the world, but not of the world. If Christians lose their invigorating influence, society falls into decay. If Christians lose their salty qualities, they are of no value to God or man. Their lives will be a discredit to the Christian Church and the Gospel of Jesus Christ.

Christians are also the light of the world. Just as a city on a hill cannot be hidden, so can we neither hide our Christian identity if we are all out for Christ. We need not go about saying, "I am a Christian; see I am a Christian," for the very nature of a Christian life is to live the Christian way. Our life as believers radiates peace, hope, joy, and certainty. Our outlook is upward. We do not go through the day grumpy, long-faced, or spiteful.

"Let your light shine before others," said Jesus. Our Christian hopefulness cannot be hidden. Others will know by our conduct and speech that we are God's children.

By such a Christian life, God's name is glorified. The Early Church Father Tertullian records that of the early Christians it was said, "See, how they love one another!" Yes, they were kind even to their persecutors.

A light cannot be hidden; salt cannot serve its purpose by itself. We must move in the world without being worldly, shine forth as children of God who by word and act serve God and man.

Prayer

Lord Jesus, take full possession of my heart and mind that daily I may consecrate my life to Your service. Grant that my every act give evidence to the world of the blessedness that comes from Christian living. May my life be an example to all and draw others to You, who alone can enrich the day with worthwhile living. Forgive me all my failings and ennoble my day with Your continual presence. Amen.

THE RIGHTEOUSNESS THAT SAVES

Matthew 5:17–37

THE Scriptures speak of a threefold righteousness. They tell us of the righteousness of God. "The heavens proclaim His righteousness, and all the peoples see His glory" (Psalm 97:6). "Then my tongue shall tell of Your righteousness and of Your praise all the day long" (Psalm 35:28). The Bible tells of the perfect holiness of God. Sin and evil are far removed from Him, who is from everlasting to everlasting. Therefore, all that comes from God is holy and righteous. His Law is perfect. His Word is truth. His ways are altogether right. His judgments are just. God cannot err or sin. He is completely just and righteous. Therefore, His commandments and demands upon us are in keeping with His holiness.

The Scriptures also speak of the righteousness of man. "Not because of works done by us in righteousness" (Titus 3:5). "Not having a righteousness of my own that comes from the law" (Philippians 3:9). This is that uprightness and goodness that makes us respected as men and women in the world in which we live. Nobility of character, kindness of heart, and virtuous living can be found even among pagan people. In Christians, though, this uprightness of character is the fruit of faith. We walk in the light. But this righteousness does not save because it is not perfect. "All our righteous deeds are like a polluted garment" (Isaiah 64:6). For this very reason, Jesus said that we must have a righteousness that exceeds that of the Pharisees.

And the Scriptures speak of the righteousness of Jesus that comes to us by faith. "But that which comes through faith in Christ, the righteousness from God that depends on faith" (Philippians 3:9). "The righteousness of God through faith in Jesus Christ for all who believe" (Romans 3:22). Christ Jesus, for us and in our place, fulfilled the Law of God. In Him was no blemish or flaw. None could convict Him of sin. This perfect Christ carried our sin to the cross to make complete atonement for our transgressions. This righteousness of Jesus is credited by faith to us, who are falling short of doing the will of God. "For what does the Scripture say? 'Abraham believed God, and it was counted to him as righteousness' " (Romans 4:3). As God looks at us through Christ, who is ours by faith, we are whiter than the new-fallen snow because His blood cleanses us from all sin.

This is the righteousness that saves. God, in His perfect holiness, can accept imperfect, sin-ridden man because he has in Christ Jesus a perfect Savior. The Law is perfectly upheld, not destroyed. Justice is executed, not set aside. And man is redeemed through Christ and saved by faith in Him who was crucified for us.

Christ Came to Fulfill the Law

"Do not think that I have come to abolish the Law or the Prophets; I have not come to abolish them but to fulfill them. For truly, I say to you, until heaven and earth pass away, not an iota, not a dot, will pass from the Law until all is accomplished. Therefore whoever relaxes one of the least of these commandments and teaches others to do the same will be called least in the kingdom of heaven, but whoever does them and teaches them will be called great in the kingdom of heaven. For I tell you, unless your righteousness exceeds that of the scribes and Pharisees, you will never enter the kingdom of heaven.

Anger

"You have heard that it was said to those of old, 'You shall not murder; and whoever murders will be liable to judgment.' But I say to you that everyone who is angry with his brother will be liable to judgment; whoever insults his brother will be liable to the council; and whoever says, 'You fool!' will be liable to the hell of fire. So if you are offering your gift at the altar and there remember that your brother has something against you, leave your gift there before the altar and go. First be reconciled to your brother, and then come and offer your gift. Come to terms quickly with your accuser while you are going with him to court, lest your accuser hand you over to the judge, and the judge to the guard, and you be put in prison. Truly, I say to you, you will never get out until you have paid the last penny.

Lust

"You have heard that it was said, 'You shall not commit adultery.' But I say to you that everyone who looks at a woman with lustful intent has already committed adultery with her in his heart. If your right eye causes you to sin, tear it out and throw it away. For it is better that you lose one of your members than that your whole body be thrown into hell. And if your right hand causes you to sin, cut it off and throw it away. For it is better that you lose one of your members than that your whole body go into hell.

Divorce

"It was also said, 'Whoever divorces his wife, let him give her a certificate of divorce.' But I say to you that everyone who divorces his wife, except on the ground of sexual immorality, makes her commit adultery, and whoever marries a divorced woman commits adultery.

Oaths

"Again you have heard that it was said to those of old, 'You shall not swear falsely, but shall perform to the Lord what you have sworn.' But I say to you, Do not take an oath at all, either by heaven, for it is the throne of God, or by the earth, for it is his footstool, or by Jerusalem, for it is the city of the great King. And do not take an oath by your head, for you cannot make one hair white or black. Let what you say be simply 'Yes' or 'No'; anything more than this comes from evil."

Only because of this righteousness of Jesus can God accept the sinner. This we must realize and understand. We can at no time perfectly do the will of God by observing the letter of the Law. Many think they can. "I have never killed anyone," they say, "therefore I cannot see why God should reject me." This commandment, however, demands a perfect fulfillment. God asks us to love our fellow men with a perfect love. If, then, we are angry without cause, or have called our neighbor ugly names in our spite, then we have not loved as we should. We have not kept the commandment.

Man does not become guilty of unchasteness only if he puts away his wife for another woman. He has broken God's Law if he lusts in his heart for a woman and has impure and unchaste thoughts.

Man is not using God's name in vain only when he curses God, as did Goliath. But he is also sinning against God and this commandment when he disguises his oaths, saying, "O my gosh" or "I'll be darned."

Now if that is the demand of the holy and perfect God, who can stand in the light of His righteousness? No wonder God said, "Surely there is not a righteous man on earth who does good and never sins" (Ecclesiastes 7:20). But in Christ Jesus this righteous God is merciful and gracious to all who come pleading, "God, be merciful to me, a sinner."

Finding forgiveness and reconciliation with God through Christ and His cross, we go from His presence as transformed people. The Holy Spirit has created in us new hearts. If we then remember that we have wounded someone, or estranged him from ourselves by unkind words and unfriendly acts, we seek him out and try to be reconciled. Having tasted the sweetness of forgiveness at the throne of God, we can no longer nurse any grudges in our heart against our fellow men. They have been redeemed by the same Jesus Christ who has given His lifeblood that we might be reconciled with the Father, who does abundantly pardon.

Prayer
My hope is built on nothing less
Than Jesus' blood and righteousness;
No merit of my own I claim,
But wholly lean on Jesus' name.
On Christ, the solid Rock, I stand;
All other ground is sinking sand. Amen. (LSB:575:1)

LIVING SUCCESSFULLY WITH OTHER PEOPLE
Matthew 5:38–48

MANY successful businessmen make a complete failure of their home life. In public they appear very amiable, while in family life they are irritable and domineering. At home, they reveal no nobility of character or kindness of heart. Others are kind only to their kind. They help only those who help them.

The philosophy of the natural heart, untouched by the Gospel of Jesus, demands "an eye for an eye and a tooth for a tooth." "Love your neighbor and hate your enemy." The Christian precept, however, asks that you overcome evil with good (Romans 12:21).

We cannot live successfully or peaceably with other people if we refuse to follow the Christian maxims Jesus laid down for us in the Sermon on the Mount. He gave five distinct directives to those who want to get along with other people:

"If anyone slaps you on the right cheek, turn to him the other also." Do not seek revenge, but forgive.

"If anyone would sue you and take your tunic, let him have your cloak as well." Yield rather than being stubborn and uncompromising.

"If anyone forces you to go one mile, go with him two miles." Do the extra. Give with a smile.

"Give to the one who begs from you." Do not live self-centered and selfish lives.

"Love your enemies." Show kindness to those who are unkind. But why should we go out of our way for those who are nasty and ugly to us? To show that we are the children of God.

Christians are different. If we are thoughtful only to friends and show favors only to those who show us favors, then we are no better than heathens. The gangster does favors for his ilk. Thieves protect one another and are on good terms with their kind. As Christians, on the other hand, we do the extra and show kindness to the undeserving. We are to love our enemies and be forgiving to those who show us no consideration. That is one way we show the world that we are different. This will enable us to live successfully with difficult people.

Retaliation

"You have heard that it was said, 'An eye for an eye and a tooth for a tooth.' But I say to you, Do not resist the one who is evil. But if anyone slaps you on the right cheek, turn to him the other also. And if anyone would sue you and take your tunic, let him have your cloak as well. And if anyone forces you to go one mile, go with him two miles. Give to the one who begs from you, and do not refuse the one who would borrow from you.

Love Your Enemies

"You have heard that it was said, 'You shall love your neighbor and hate your enemy.' But I say to you, Love your enemies and pray for those who persecute you, so that you may be sons of your Father who is in heaven. For He makes His sun rise on the evil and on the good, and sends rain on the just and on the unjust. For if you love those who love you, what reward do you have? Do not even the tax collectors do the same? And if you greet only your brothers, what more are you doing than others? Do not even the Gentiles do the same? You therefore must be perfect, as your heavenly Father is perfect."

Is this possible? Can we be as perfect as our Father in heaven? Can we really love our enemies?

We can love the unlovable and show kindness to the unkind only if we take to heart "that while we were still sinners, Christ died for us" (Romans 5:8). God reconciled a rebellious world to Himself through His beloved Son. Countless times, God shows mercy to us who day after day sin much. He is always ready to forgive sin and blot out our transgressions. If God does this for us, ought we not ask Him for grace to do likewise?

Then, too, we must remember that our enemy was redeemed by the same Savior who has loved us. As we look at people who repulse us, we must not forget that Christ loves them as well and gave His life for them also. If Christ loved and redeemed them, have we a right to treat them with contempt and arrogance?

At the foot of the cross, we learn to love disagreeable people. We make hard lives easier as we strive to live with difficult people, knowing they are also forgiven and forgiving children of God.

Prayer

Heavenly Father, You know how difficult it is for us to be kind, thoughtful, and forgiving to those who make life hard and bitter for us. Only Your grace can create in us a forgiving spirit and teach us to overcome evil with good. Draw us closer to You as You forgive sin and make us gracious and merciful in Christ Jesus, our Savior. Amen.

EMPTY WORSHIP
Matthew 6:1–18

GOD'S people worship Him. Love compels us because God sent His Son into the world to redeem us from the guilt of sin and the terrors of death, and then He called us by His grace into the kingdom of His only-begotten Son. This worshiping must be done in truth and sincerity of spirit. Lip service will never do. Merely saying, "Lord, Lord," does not open the door to God's heart. Out of the fullness of a reborn heart, we must come into His presence. "The sacrifices of God are a broken spirit; a broken and contrite heart, O God, You will not despise" (Psalm 51:17).

Giving alms and bringing offerings on Sundays to make a show handicaps our worship. If we give to make a name for ourselves, if we bring our gifts merely to be praised by others, then our worship loses all value. The only motive that should prompt us to come must be our love for Christ, who has given Himself as a ransom for sin.

Praying to be seen that we may be credited with piety and praised for our devotion and zeal also handicaps our worship. Such praying easily can turn into babbling and meaningless repetitions. We pray amiss if we come with lip service.

Sacrificing to obtain sympathy or denying ourselves to be counted among the most religious in the group handicaps our worship. All this pretense displeases God.

God is a spirit and He is truth, and they that worship Him must do so in spirit and truth. The first requisite is sincerity. Therefore, Paul prays in Philippians 1:10, "So that you may approve what is excellent, and so be pure and blameless for the day of Christ." In such worship and prayer the Savior delights.

Giving to the Needy

"Beware of practicing your righteousness before other people in order to be seen by them, for then you will have no reward from your Father who is in heaven.

"Thus, when you give to the needy, sound no trumpet before you, as the hypocrites do in the synagogues and in the streets, that they may be praised by others. Truly, I say to you, they have received their reward. But when you give to the needy, do not let your left hand know what your right hand is doing, so that your giving may be in secret. And your Father who sees in secret will reward you.

The Lord's Prayer

"And when you pray, you must not be like the hypocrites. For they love to stand and pray in the synagogues and at the street corners, that they may be seen by others. Truly, I say to you, they have received their reward. But when you pray, go into your room and shut the door and pray to your Father who is in secret. And your Father who sees in secret will reward you.

"And when you pray, do not heap up empty phrases as the Gentiles do, for they think that they will be heard for their many words. Do not be like them, for your Father knows what you need before you ask Him. Pray then like this:

"Our Father in heaven, hallowed be Your name.
Your kingdom come, Your will be done, on earth as it is in heaven.
Give us this day our daily bread, and forgive us our debts,
    as we also have forgiven our debtors.
And lead us not into temptation,
    but deliver us from evil.

For if you forgive others their trespasses, your heavenly Father will
    also forgive you, but if you do not forgive others their trespasses,
    neither will your Father forgive your trespasses.

Fasting

"And when you fast, do not look gloomy like the hypocrites, for they disfigure their faces that their fasting may be seen by others. Truly, I say to you, they have received their reward. But when you fast, anoint your head and wash your face, that your fasting may not be seen by others but by your Father who is in secret. And your Father who sees in secret will reward you."

"Prayer is the Christian's vital breath." However, we say many prayers and yet are not praying. The prayer Jesus taught us might be said more frequently than any other and yet often not prayed. A prayer must rise from the heart. But do these seven petitions come from the heart? Do we always realize and understand what we are saying as we repeat the Lord's Prayer?

Our Father. God is our Father and we are His adopted children through Christ Jesus, who has reconciled us to God with His precious and holy blood. As children of the one spiritual family, we are to pray for and with one another.

Who art in heaven. God is almighty and can do far more for us than our earthly father.

Hallowed be Thy name. Holy and revered is God's name among us as we teach His Word in its truth and completeness and believe it with all our heart. We then lead Christian lives in agreement with these instructions that His name be glorified before the people of the Church and of the world.

Thy kingdom come. Through the preaching of the Gospel and our faithful witnessing, we ask God to enter into many more sin-troubled souls until the last of the elect has come to faith and His kingdom has become the glorious kingdom of heaven throughout eternity.

Thy will be done on earth as it is in heaven. May the Lord God's holy will prevail. May the wickedness of the world and the cunning wiles of Satan be restrained. And may God's gracious will be accomplished and more immortal souls come to faith and be saved.

Give us—our—bread. All that we have comes as a gift from God, who opens His hand in His goodness and grace to supply us with all that we need for this life in food, clothing, protection. This we ask not only for ourselves but also for all mankind.

Give us this day—daily. God gives us sufficient means for the present moment and for each day of our life. He guards and protects us through this daily bread from the worries and anxieties of life that rob us of contentment and the enjoyment of our food we have at the present hour.

And forgive us our trespasses as we forgive those who trespass against us. God cancels all our sins with the precious blood of our Savior. And herewith we also promise to be forgiving to those who sin against us.

And lead us not into temptation. We ask God to keep from us the temptations of the devil, the world, and our own sinful passions. Through a victorious faith, we ask him to give us the grace and strength to withstand such temptations when they come.

But deliver us from evil. God will save us from all troubles and sins of body and soul, that by His grace we come to life's closing days as faithful children who can depart in peace to be with Him forever.

For Thine is the kingdom. All things belong to the Lord.

And the power. God alone is almighty and can give to us what we ask of Him.

And the glory. All praise and honor goes to God the Father.

Forever and ever. Amen. It shall be so for all eternity. Of this we are certain because of God's promises.

Prayer

*Lord, Creator of all living things, open Your hand to supply us
with the needs of the day. Remove from us all worrisome thoughts,
and let us confidently trust that Your goodness will not fail.
Guard us from selfishness and greed, and let us find our greatest
joy in our Savior, the Bread of Life, and in His glorious Gospel.
Forgive us daily our trespasses, and protect us from the deceptions
of Satan, through Jesus Christ, our Lord. Amen.*

14

CHRISTIANS, YET ACTING LIKE HEATHENS

Matthew 6:19–34

FOOD plays a tremendous role in the world and in our homes. Every day, millions ask what and when they shall eat.

God knows the importance of food. That is why He grows it in great abundance and with clocklike regularity. But He does not give food first place. There are greater things.

"Man shall not live by bread alone." Most people make bread the chief concern of their lives. They want to accumulate treasures they can see and hold in their hands. But earthly treasures bring many worries and anxieties with them. Possessions often lose their value; moth and rust corrupt them. Treasures can be lost; thieves and schemers can take them from us. And eventually, death shakes them out of our trembling hands. Therefore, earthly possessions can cause us constant worry. We are afraid that someone else has more than we have and lives better than we do and makes a bigger show than we.

So we profess to be Christians and yet act like heathen, being more concerned about bread for the body than manna for the soul. If food is our chief concern, then God is put in the background and, in the end, is forgotten.

For that reason, Jesus says,

Lay Up Treasures in Heaven

"Do not lay up for yourselves treasures on earth, where moth and rust destroy and where thieves break in and steal, but lay up for yourselves treasures in heaven, where neither moth nor rust destroys and where thieves do not break in and steal. For where your treasure is, there your heart will be also.

"The eye is the lamp of the body. So, if your eye is healthy, your whole body will be full of light, but if your eye is bad, your whole body will be full of darkness. If then the light in you is darkness, how great is the darkness!

"No one can serve two masters, for either he will hate the one and love the other, or he will be devoted to the one and despise the other. You cannot serve God and money.

Do Not Be Anxious

"Therefore I tell you, do not be anxious about your life, what you will eat or what you will drink, nor about your body, what you will put on. Is not life more than food, and the body more than clothing? Look at the birds of the air: they neither sow nor reap nor gather into barns, and yet your heavenly Father feeds them. Are you not of more value than they? And which of you by being anxious can add a single hour to his span of life? And why are you anxious about clothing? Consider the lilies of the field, how they grow: they neither toil nor spin, yet I tell you, even Solomon in all his glory was not arrayed like one of these. But if God so clothes the grass of the field, which today is alive and tomorrow is thrown into the oven, will He not much more clothe you, O you of little faith? Therefore do not be anxious, saying, 'What shall we eat?' or 'What shall we drink?' or 'What shall we wear?' For the Gentiles seek after all these things, and your heavenly Father knows that you need them all. But seek first the kingdom of God and His righteousness, and all these things will be added to you.

"Therefore do not be anxious about tomorrow, for tomorrow will be anxious for itself. Sufficient for the day is its own trouble."

God wants us to live one day at a time. "Sufficient for the day is its own trouble."

The birds do. They don't plant crops in the spring or harvest them for the winter. Least of all do they worry about tomorrow. God takes care of them. But what is a raven or a sparrow compared with people? After all, can we make a single grain grow faster or add one sixteenth of an inch to our height by worrying all through the night? Consider the lilies of the field. Beautiful, indeed, but what lasting value is there to the lily? The lily makes the roadside more beautiful—that is all. Yet God made this flower of the field and clothed it in all this beauty. Will He forget us when we are the ones His Son died for? What folly to worry!

God knows we need food, clothing, and shelter. And He gives these things to us as we need them and tells us to live trustingly from day to day, confident that His goodness will not fail us.

We have a far greater concern in life. Jesus tells us to give first place, the highest priority, to the kingdom of God and His own righteousness. If we live faithful to Christ, His Gospel, and His Sacraments, then God will give us the things we need for this present day.

God guarantees the necessary things to those who give themselves to Him and love Him with all their heart.

Prayer

Lord, with a heart full of praise we acknowledge Your goodness in remembering us day after day. Upon the palms of Your hands You have written our names, chosen us to be Your own in Christ the Lord. Remove from our hearts all worries and anxious thoughts, and forgive us all our sins. Preserve to us Your Word and Sacraments, that our souls may be nourished and our faith strengthened, through Jesus, our eternal Redeemer. Amen.

GUARDING THE DOOR OF OUR LIPS

Matthew 7:1–14

THE most quoted sentence in all Scripture is the Golden Rule, found in Christ's Sermon on the Mount: "Whatever you wish that others would do to you, do also to them." We insist that others practice this but too often we neglect to do so ourselves. We judge the actions and the conduct of others by this standard, and we are ever ready to condemn them and their sins. At the same time, we excuse our own transgressions and sinful behavior by calling them mere slips. When we do the wrong, it seems less sinful. Jesus puts it rather quaintly when He says we enlarge our neighbor's faults into logs while our own we shrink into splinters.

We must guard against the "holier than thou" attitude that sees faults in others and none in ourselves. Therefore, Jesus urges us to apply the Golden Rule. Instead of looking for faults in others at all times, we are to seek our own salvation with fear and trembling by entering the straight gate and going the narrow way. This way leads to life eternal. Heartless faultfinding is evidence of a loveless heart, in which Christ cannot abide. How important that we think on these things!

Judging Others

"Judge not, that you be not judged. For with the judgment you pronounce you will be judged, and with the measure you use it will be measured to you. Why do you see the speck that is in your brother's eye, but do not notice the log that is in your own eye? Or how can you say to your brother, 'Let me take the speck out of your eye,' when there is the log in your own eye? You hypocrite, first take the log out of your own eye, and then you will see clearly to take the speck out of your brother's eye.

"Do not give dogs what is holy, and do not throw your pearls before pigs, lest they trample them underfoot and turn to attack you.

Ask, and It Will Be Given

"Ask, and it will be given to you; seek, and you will find; knock, and it will be opened to you. For everyone who asks receives, and the one who seeks finds, and to the one who knocks it will be opened. Or which one of you, if his son asks him for bread, will give him a stone? Or if he asks for a fish, will give him a serpent? If you then, who are evil, know how to give good gifts to your children, how much more will your Father who is in heaven give good things to those who ask Him!

The Golden Rule

"So whatever you wish that others would do to you, do also to them, for this is the Law and the Prophets.

"Enter by the narrow gate. For the gate is wide and the way is easy that leads to destruction, and those who enter by it are many. For the gate is narrow and the way is hard that leads to life, and those who find it are few."

Instead of being critical, always finding fault with everyone and everything, pray.

"But what good will that do?" some may ask. "You do not have, because you do not ask. You ask and do not receive, because you ask wrongly, to spend it on your passions" (James 4:2–3).

Maybe we are not persistent enough in prayer. This is the burden of Jesus' words. Ask; and if there is no answer, seek; and if there still is no reply, knock. Do not give up after the first attempt. If sinful parents give good gifts to their children, how much more will our heavenly Father, who loves us in Christ Jesus, give His beloved children!

Our God always gives us what is best for the well-being of our body and our soul. We can be sure of that. Parents do not give stones to their boy when he asks for bread or a snake when their daughter begs for fish. Parents will not always give the child cake, because that would be harmful in the end; they will never give a stone to their boy and say, "Chew on that."

God will not always give us the sweets of life, for then we would forget that we need Him. But He does not feed us the stones of hopelessness and despair either. We can trustingly and with a believing heart pray and be certain that God always answers our cry, not always in our way but in the wiser way. Our best security for this is Christ, who was crucified for our sins that we might be God's reconciled children and thus members of God's household and family.

Prayer

Lord, take the bitterness of sin out of our lives and sweeten our souls with Your grace and love. Your will is always wiser than our own. Therefore, we say with believing hearts, "Thy will be done." Graciously forgive all our sins of this day, keep us in Your protective care, and guide us into ways that lead to life everlasting, through Jesus Christ, our Redeemer. Amen.

BUILDING FOR PERMANENCY
Matthew 7:15–29

TRUTH is eternal. Public opinion, ecclesiastical edicts, and majority votes do not make truth. That the public has spoken and the majority voted in favor of something does not make it right nor true. By a resolution of a church convention Jesus cannot be dethroned as the Son of God. Truth is eternal, and right is right through the centuries. Man may feed his soul on ashes and build his foundations on sand, but ashes will not nourish and sand will not make for solidity.

The world is full of frauds and offers us counterfeit "isms" every day. And we Christians are often beguiled by the prophets who speak to itching ears and gullible people. As Jesus brings His Sermon on the Mount to a close, He calls attention to and warns us against three paramount dangers that so easily attract us.

A Tree and Its Fruit

"Beware of false prophets, who come to you in sheep's clothing but inwardly are ravenous wolves. You will recognize them by their fruits. Are grapes gathered from thornbushes, or figs from thistles? So, every healthy tree bears good fruit, but the diseased tree bears bad fruit. A healthy tree cannot bear bad fruit, nor can a diseased tree bear good fruit. Every tree that does not bear good fruit is cut down and thrown into the fire. Thus you will recognize them by their fruits.

I Never Knew You

"Not everyone who says to Me, 'Lord, Lord,' will enter the kingdom of heaven, but the one who does the will of My Father who is in heaven. On that day many will say to Me, 'Lord, Lord, did we not prophesy in Your name, and cast out demons in Your name, and do many mighty works in Your name?' And then will I declare to them, 'I never knew you; depart from Me, you workers of lawlessness.'

Build Your House on the Rock

"Everyone then who hears these words of Mine and does them will be like a wise man who built his house on the rock. And the rain fell, and the floods came, and the winds blew and beat on that house, but it did not fall, because it had been founded on the rock. And everyone who hears these words of Mine and does not do them will be like a foolish man who built his house on the sand. And the rain fell, and the floods came, and the winds blew and beat against that house, and it fell, and great was the fall of it."

The Authority of Jesus

And when Jesus finished these sayings, the crowds were astonished at His teaching, for He was teaching them as one who had authority, and not as their scribes.

First of all, Jesus tells us to beware of false prophets who come to us with teachings and doctrines that are not the revelations of God. Counterfeits and fraudulent substitutes are offered in the name of the Lord, while these men claim that their man-made teachings are just as good. By a slow process of poisoning, the soul is made indifferent to the truth and gives a ready ear to the smooth things that have at times a greater appeal to the carnal mind than the revealed truth. Jesus says: Beware!

Then Jesus warns against insincerity. "You will recognize them by their fruits." Our creed is reflected in our deeds. Believers cannot be lukewarm or cold toward the Scripture and the worshiping of God. Their joy in the Lord constrains them to serve Him. We cannot say one thing and do another. Our conduct in daily living gives evidence of our loyalty and devotion to Christ. "Every healthy tree bears good fruit, but the diseased tree bears bad fruit." Beware of counterfeit lives!

And third, Jesus warns against lip service. Merely saying, "Lord, Lord," will not do. Isaiah says that in his day, the children of Israel walked away backward. They would not turn their backs upon God and ignore Him, yet with every step they were getting farther away from God. "Yes, I hold membership in the church." "Yes, I was confirmed." "Yes, I believe the church is a good institution," many say lightly or with arrogance. But their empty words reveal an empty heart. Beware of counterfeit worship!

We can remain loyal to Christ and His Gospel only if we stand firmly upon the Word. Building on anything else is building on sand. If we want permanency for time and eternity, Christ must be our all in all. No matter how beguiling and bewitching and appealing the "isms" and cults may be, they offer no peace of heart and mind, no hope of heaven, no joy in the Lord. No greater mistake can be made than the one made by those who deceive themselves into believing that it matters little what they believe and think as long as they are sincere. Such will find that their foundation cannot withstand the storms of an accusing conscience and the terrors of death.

But if we build on the Rock of Ages, on Christ Jesus, our Savior, we cannot perish. Our conscience may accuse, we may have sinned greatly and often, but if we come confessing to Him and pleading for mercy, this Jesus, who hates sin with a perfect hatred yet loves us sinners with an unbounded love, will receive us and wash us and cleanse us from every sin and, by His grace, give us peace of heart and eternal life.

Prayer

Lord, grant that no one take from us this blessed salvation that is ours only through Your death on the cross. Nothing in our hands we bring, simply to Your cross we cling. Amen.

THE HEALING TOUCH
Matthew 8:1–15

SUFFERING is the common state of mankind. Suffering is due to sin. Sin has made us a pain-bearing and dying race. Our very blood is tainted even as we are born. "Behold, I was brought forth in iniquity, and in sin did my mother conceive me" (Psalm 51:5).

Suffering and sickness may be due to personal transgression of God's Law. The death of David's son was the direct consequence of David's and Bathsheba's wrongdoing (2 Samuel 12:14). As Rudyard Kipling said, "For the sin ye do by two and two ye must pay for one by one."

However, not all suffering can be traced to personal sins. In John 9, we are told that the disciples thought that the man born blind was guilty of some special trespassing, and if not he, then at least his parents. Jesus declares: "It was not that this man sinned, or his parents, but that the works of God might be displayed in him" (John 9:3). When the tower in Siloam fell and killed eighteen men, some people claimed that the victims were greater sinners than the usual run of men. Jesus emphatically says no. In fact, if we do not repent, we will likewise perish (Luke 13:4–5). As humans, we are heirs to suffering, sickness, and death.

Our suffering also can be brought on by others. Sickness and pain come to us in the course of human events. But no matter what may come and whether the ills are physical, mental, or moral, Jesus can help with His healing touch.

Jesus Cleanses a Leper

When He came down from the mountain, great crowds followed Him. And behold, a leper came to Him and knelt before Him, saying, "Lord, if You will, You can make me clean." And Jesus stretched out His hand and touched him, saying, "I will; be clean." And immediately his leprosy was cleansed. And Jesus said to him, "See that you say nothing to anyone, but go, show yourself to the priest and offer the gift that Moses commanded, for a proof to them."

The Faith of a Centurion

When He entered Capernaum, a centurion came forward to Him, appealing to Him, "Lord, my servant is lying paralyzed at home, suffering terribly." And He said to him, "I will come and heal him." But the centurion replied, "Lord, I am not worthy to have You come under my roof, but only say the word, and my servant will be healed. For I too am a man under authority, with soldiers under me. And I say to one, 'Go,' and he goes, and to another, 'Come,' and he comes, and to my servant, 'Do this,' and he does it." When Jesus heard this, He marveled and said to those who followed Him, "Truly, I tell you, with no one in Israel have I found such faith. I tell you, many will come from east and west and recline at table with Abraham, Isaac, and Jacob in the kingdom of heaven, while the sons of the kingdom will be thrown into the outer darkness. In that place there will be weeping and gnashing of teeth." And to the centurion Jesus said, "Go; let it be done for you as you have believed." And the servant was healed at that very moment.

Why does suffering and death come into our Christian life? Suffering brings us to Jesus. In the day of trouble, we realize how much we are dependent upon the Lord. As we turn to the Savior, we find Him to be sympathetic and mindful of our well-being. We discover that He moves in His wise ways to bless us and to save us. Understanding the graciousness of His heart, we say, "if You will," and then believe that His will is good and gracious and better than our own. Living in His kingdom, we want His plans and purposes to be carried out.

Suffering moves others to pray for us. Sympathetic Christians plead and storm the gates of heaven in our behalf. "The prayer of a righteous person has great power" (James 5:16). Through our prayers, we can send loads of blessings to others. As we see pain and sickness all around us, we can cram our prayers with petitions for our fellow men. We are sure that God can and will help suffering humanity. Christ's healing hand still touches the lives of men and women and lifts them out of their troubles.

The Christian who has been healed serves Christ with grateful heart and hands. Christians rise from their sickbed to give appreciative service to Jesus by helping His cause and being active in His kingdom. The sympathetic help of Jesus transforms us into willing workers. We find no greater joy than traveling up and down the Jericho road of life to help the fallen, the erring, the sick, and the dying. Christ's healing touch is revealed through us as we serve Him in appreciation and love.

Prayer

*Lord, today we, too, dedicate ourselves anew to You who has, for
Christ's sake, so graciously helped us out of all our troubles. You
not only heal the soul by daily forgiving sin but You also preserve
the body and sustain our lives with Your almighty arm. Protect us
from the ills of life and the temptations of Satan. For Jesus' sake,
hear our prayers. Amen.*

MAJESTIC GLORY AND DEEP ABASEMENT
Matthew 8:16–27

IN the ages to come, Jesus will remain the most unique character
in history. No one is like Him. In His deepest humility, we behold
a glory so sublime that we fall to our knees. In the majesty of His
glory, we see Him in such lowliness that many ask, Can this be the
promised King? Nowhere to lay His head, not a cent He can call
His own. How can He be God of God, Light of Light, very God
of very God?

Neverthless there is something about Jesus that awakens the
admiration of mankind. In every generation, people are prompted
to say, "I will follow You wherever You go." These faithful souls
faced wild and hungry lions, were burned at the stake, and were
exiled all because they were convinced that there is no one except
Jesus who can save them.

How do we account for such undying devotion to this humble
Nazarene? It can be explained only if we look beyond His humiliation and, by a faith created through the Holy Spirit, see Him as the
Savior who brings peace and hope to the hearts of men, who otherwise would die in utter despair.

Jesus demands such adoration. Nothing must come ahead of Him. No one dare share the same allegiance that we give Him. This man whom the wind and the waves obey is God made flesh, who came to ransom us from the hopelessness of condemning sin and make us heirs of the glory that He had before the foundation of the world.

As long as we look to Him as Lord and Savior, we cannot perish. We may be forced to face danger, sorrow, hunger, pain, and death, but we will not perish—we will have life everlasting. That is why He calls us to follow Him no matter where He leads us.

> That evening they brought to Him many who were oppressed by demons, and He cast out the spirits with a word and healed all who were sick. This was to fulfill what was spoken by the prophet Isaiah: "He took our illnesses and bore our diseases."

The Cost of Following Jesus

> Now when Jesus saw a crowd around Him, He gave orders to go over to the other side. And a scribe came up and said to Him, "Teacher, I will follow You wherever You go." And Jesus said to him, "Foxes have holes, and birds of the air have nests, but the Son of Man has nowhere to lay His head." Another of the disciples said to Him, "Lord, let me first go and bury my father." And Jesus said to him, "Follow Me, and leave the dead to bury their own dead."

Jesus Calms a Storm

> And when He got into the boat, His disciples followed Him. And behold, there arose a great storm on the sea, so that the boat was being swamped by the waves; but He was asleep. And they went and woke Him, saying, "Save us, Lord; we are perishing." And He said to them, "Why are you afraid, O you of little faith?" Then He rose and rebuked the winds and the sea, and there was a great calm. And the men marveled, saying, "What sort of man is this, that even winds and sea obey Him?"

Jesus makes tremendous demands on those who follow Him. Some think the demands are unreasonable, so Jesus wants us to consider the cost.

"I will follow You wherever You go." Will you? asks Jesus. Even the fox has a den and the bird a nest; but if you follow Me, says Jesus, you may not even have that, for "the Son of Man has nowhere to lay His head."

"Lord, let me first go and bury my father." Jesus answers, "Follow Me, and leave the dead to bury their own dead." There comes a time when the believer will have to break all human ties for the sake of Jesus. Men and women were compelled to cut loose from their families for the sake of their faith. Jesus put the truth bluntly so this man would realize what it may cost in human relationship to follow Him.

But if we realize who Jesus is and what He means to us, we will give up everything and anything rather than lose Him, for He alone is the way by which we come to the Father and eternal life.

Prayer

Jesus, glorious Savior, no greater treasure is ours than Your love, which led You to Calvary, that we might be the forgiven children of Your heavenly Father. Take our life and make it Yours. Grant that nothing becomes more precious to us than the sacrifice of Calvary, which brings peace to our mind and salvation to our soul. Amen.

19

THE CITY THAT VOTED JESUS OUT
Matthew 8:28–34

HE came to His own, and His own people did not receive Him"
(John 1:11). Ever since Jesus was born, people have rejected Him
and have chosen to go through life serving Satan and sin. What has
Jesus done that multitudes refuse to receive Him into their hearts?
He has taken from them their swine. We cannot live in uncleanness and lawlessness, in sin and wickedness, when Jesus comes into
our lives. Selfishness and greed, dishonesty and lovelessness, vice and
hatred do not thrive in Christ's presence.

That is the reason why many choose against Jesus. His presence
disturbs. He does not let them lie and lust, or steal and stab. They are
not comfortable even in their uprightness. Nor can they feel smug
and satisfied with their charities and good works as they look into
His all-seeing eyes. And too often they do not want to be grieved
by their denials and betrayals and compromises. So Jesus is rejected.
Their lives and tactics do not agree with His divine principles. Swine
and holiness do not run side by side. So they evade Jesus. If they are
indifferent to truth and deaf to the call of conscience, if they stop
their ears to the Gospel message, then indeed Jesus must go. But in
the end they go with the swine to destruction.

That is the truth we learn at Gadara.

Jesus Heals Two Men with Demons

And when He came to the other side, to the country of the
Gadarenes, two demon-possessed men met Him, coming out
of the tombs, so fierce that no one could pass that way. And
behold, they cried out, "What have You to do with us, O Son
of God? Have You come here to torment us before the time?"
Now a herd of many pigs was feeding at some distance from
them. And the demons begged Him, saying, "If You cast us

out, send us away into the herd of pigs." And He said to them, "Go." So they came out and went into the pigs, and behold, the whole herd rushed down the steep bank into the sea and drowned in the waters. The herdsmen fled, and going into the city they told everything, especially what had happened to the demon-possessed men. And behold, all the city came out to meet Jesus, and when they saw Him, they begged him to leave their region.

Sin and Satan are always out to destroy. Sin damages the body, robbing us of our health; it damages the mind, poisoning our thoughts; sin destroys our soul, taking from us the faith that saves.

The men in today's Bible passage did not live normal lives. Sin makes us abnormal, immoral, unbelieving, and unspiritual. Jesus restores us completely. He came into the world to destroy the works of the devil and has given us His Word as the sword that conquers the forces of hell and prayer so we can resist steadfastly every temptation of Satan every day of our Christian life.

The mind is at peace only through Christ, the soul is washed clean through His blood, and the body is given freedom as we follow Jesus. No happier person is to be found in the world than the person who walks with the Savior of Calvary.

Prayer

Lord Jesus, come to our hearts and in our lives so Satan and sin have no dominion and power over our thoughts, words, and actions. Forgive us graciously wherever we have strayed and erred and ruled You out of our lives. Grant us the grace to find our greatest joy in You. Amen.

20

THAT WHICH IS GREATER THAN SIN

Matthew 9:1–8

SUFFERING is universal. By no stretch of our imagination can we deny its existence. But how do we account for all this misery in our human lives? Jesus has the answer.

Sin is the cause of all ills of life. Sin causes physical suffering. Therefore, Jesus says to the afflicted, "Your sins are forgiven." Sin must be removed should we be truly healed.

That is the teaching of the Bible. Proof is found on many pages of Scripture. Cain killed his brother and that caused sorrow and tears. Absalom rebelled, Achan stole, Ahab coveted his neighbor's vineyard. Each instance was followed by suffering.

Sin causes mental suffering. Man does a moral wrong, and his own conscience will not let him sleep. Man neglects God and finds no peace of heart and mind.

Sin brings suffering to others. The erring son breaks his mother's heart. The selfish and lazy father brings hunger and want to the family. A man or a nation lusting for power upsets the peace of the world, and hundreds of thousands suffer loss of life, possessions, and happiness.

Sin is always destructive. It destroys body, mind, soul, property, good name, faith, and love. All that is wrong in the world has been brought on by sin. That's why Jesus takes up the problem of sin first as the ill are brought to Him.

Jesus Heals a Paralytic

And getting into a boat He crossed over and came to His own city. And behold, some people brought to Him a paralytic, lying on a bed. And when Jesus saw their faith, He said to the paralytic, "Take heart, My son; your sins are forgiven."

And behold, some of the scribes said to themselves, "This man is blaspheming." But Jesus, knowing their thoughts, said, "Why do you think evil in your hearts? For which is easier, to say, 'Your sins are forgiven,' or to say, 'Rise and walk'? But that you may know that the Son of Man has authority on earth to forgive sins"—He then said to the paralytic—"Rise, pick up your bed and go home." And he rose and went home. When the crowds saw it, they were afraid, and they glorified God, who had given such authority to men.

Millions go to physicians and hospitals each year for help and healing. They are upset or distraught, their bodies are in great distress. They have a malignancy or a heart ailment. As they face death, they remember their sin and conscience drives them to despair. But more often, we need more than physical and medical care.

Jesus knows that. So He went to the cross to pay the penalty of our transgressions so we can be forgiven. This Gospel cures souls, changes hearts, puts the mind at ease by reconciling us with God through His blood. And all this because of His boundless love and grace. His love is greater than any sin.

No one who comes to this Great Physician is sent away uncured. Jesus makes the foulest clean.

What no philosophy of man can do, what no scientific discovery can accomplish, Jesus has done: He has washed and cleansed us from our sin. He puts the song of forgiveness into our hearts. Hopelessness and despair need not grip us because He pardons abundantly. That is the reason why the Gospel is good news—it is the love of Christ for poor sinners, whom He forgives and saves.

Prayer

Come to our hearts, Lord Jesus, and cleanse us and heal us. In Your grace, look upon all sin-troubled souls and all those who suffer and are in pain. Touch them with Your healing hands that their minds be at ease and their nerves relaxed and their bodies restored to health through Your loving promises. Be with us all in Your grace and goodness today and forevermore. Amen.

21
LIVING SECOND-RATE LIVES
Matthew 9:9–17

PUTTING a few patches of good deeds on our garments of uprightness will not work. We must be clothed in the robe of Christ's righteousness to be acceptable to God. This is a difficult lesson to learn. Ask men and women of today, "How do you hope to be saved?" They will likely answer immediately with a list of good deeds they have done and say, "See how good I am." "I never turn a beggar from my door." "I support my family as best I can." "I give to charities." "I never get drunk or cheat on my spouse." "What more can you want? I associate with the best people and even support the church."

All that is superficial. That's why Jesus confronted the Pharisees. They patched a few good deeds on their reputation and thought this made them fit for His kingdom. Anyone can fast and diet without being transformed into a child of God.

Jesus demands more than outward uprightness. He wants transformed hearts. Patches do not make a clean heart. Jesus wants us to know how sick and sinful we are; otherwise we will not come to Him and follow Him as Savior and Lord. This truth He stresses as He ad-dresses Himself to the Pharisees, who are living second-rate lives.

Jesus Calls Matthew

As Jesus passed on from there, He saw a man called Matthew sitting at the tax booth, and He said to him, "Follow Me." And he rose and followed Him.

And as Jesus reclined at table in the house, behold, many tax collectors and sinners came and were reclining with Jesus and His disciples. And when the Pharisees saw this, they said to His disciples, "Why does your teacher eat with tax collectors and sinners?" But when He heard it, He said, "Those who are well have no need of a physician, but those who are sick. Go and learn what this means, 'I desire mercy, and not sacrifice.' For I came not to call the righteous, but sinners."

A Question about Fasting

Then the disciples of John came to Him, saying, "Why do we and the Pharisees fast, but Your disciples do not fast?" And Jesus said to them, "Can the wedding guests mourn as long as the bridegroom is with them? The days will come when the bridegroom is taken away from them, and then they will fast. No one puts a piece of unshrunk cloth on an old garment, for the patch tears away from the garment, and a worse tear is made. Neither is new wine put into old wineskins. If it is, the skins burst and the wine is spilled and the skins are destroyed. But new wine is put into fresh wineskins, and so both are preserved."

Matthew broke with the past. He knew he could not find peace and salvation where he was. Most of all, he knew he couldn't save himself. Matthew told this to his friends as he invited Jesus to his house to meet his associates. They, too, should know that he had broken with his yesterdays and that Jesus had brought about this change. He was a new creature through Christ. He was born again. But the Pharisees could not understand that. A man like Matthew did not fit into their pattern, and so they ruled him out.

We must ever be on the alert lest we, too, depend on our own virtues and try to make them do. But no matter how good we appear to others, these patches of our own goodness do not clothe us as acceptable to God. Outward reforming does not transform the heart. Jesus must enter and take full possession of us. When that happens, joy fills our lives, peace comes to our mind, and we look forward with hope that goes beyond old age and death. Through Christ and His cross we see beyond this life heaven and God.

Prayer

*O Lord, for Jesus' sake, remake me day after day, creating in me
a clean heart. I confess my sins to You. They have bruised and
wounded my soul. You alone can blot out all these wrongs and
transgressions through Christ. Make me acceptable to You, and
grant that every word and act of mine may please You. I will
praise in Christ Jesus forevermore. Amen.*

MIGHTIER THAN DEATH
Matthew 9:18–26

FOR the first time in His public ministry, Jesus is confronted with
the problem of death. Does He have anything to say to the hopeless
heart that sees all that is precious fade from life and home?

"The girl is not dead but sleeping," Jesus said. "And they
laughed at Him." But Jesus has made death a sleep. He has removed
the terror and sting of dying. Death cannot hold us. This body will
live. As the kernel of wheat decays in the ground in order to come
forth more glorious, so the bodies of the believers are sown in corruption and come out of the grave in glory. And we believers will
rise with a body like His glorious body. Suffering and pain, decay
and handicap, will not affect our risen body. The believer's body
will be perfect, glorious, and deathless.

Death loses its terror, and dying becomes easier when we know
we are passing from this world to a fuller and richer life into the very
presence of God. For the Christian's body the grave is a resting place
from the toiling and sufferings of life.

Could this truth be taught in a more beautiful manner than Jesus
taught it to Jairus?

A Girl Restored to Life and a Woman Healed

While He was saying these things to them, behold, a ruler came in and knelt before Him, saying, "My daughter has just died, but come and lay Your hand on her, and she will live." And Jesus rose and followed him, with His disciples. And behold, a woman who had suffered from a discharge of blood for twelve years came up behind Him and touched the fringe of His garment, for she said to herself, "If I only touch His garment, I will be made well." Jesus turned, and seeing her He said, "Take heart, daughter; your faith has made you well." And instantly the woman was made well. And when Jesus came to the ruler's house and saw the flute players and the crowd making a commotion, He said, "Go away, for the girl is not dead but sleeping." And they laughed at Him. But when the crowd had been put outside, He went in and took her by the hand, and the girl arose. And the report of this went through all that district.

"He went in and took her by the hand, and the girl arose." Once more she lived. As we go on from day to day, certain that each step brings us closer to the grave, we can say with David: "I will fear no evil" (Psalm 23:4). And why? Because Jesus died, rose, and lives. He says to us, "Because I live, you also will live" (John 14:19). So our physical death is an interlude between time and eternity.

If this life is all there is, then what has Christ done for us? We suffer and die like everything else. "If in Christ we have hope in this life only, we are of all people most to be pitied" (1 Corinthians 15:19). But Jesus' resurrection is the triumphant assurance that we will live on. Therefore, we say, "I believe in the resurrection of the body, and the life everlasting."

Heaven is our home. There the multitude will praise the Lamb upon the throne, saying, "To Him who loves us and has freed us from our sins by His blood and made us a kingdom, priests to His God and Father, to Him be glory and dominion forever and ever. Amen" (Revelation 1:5–6).

And all heaven will resound with the great amen of victory and eternal peace. Knowing this, we can face all the bitterness and sin of this present life with courage and confidence. In Jesus, we have a hope, the glorious hope that after the tears and sorrows of our earthly life comes a glory that will never be dimmed or fade away.

Prayer

You are the resurrection and the life, Lord Jesus. Grant that in every sorrow of this world this glorious revelation will fill my heart with hope. Forgive me all my murmurings, and teach me to look to my redemption in the midst of this confused and dying race of men. Keep me on the narrow way that brings me into Your presence, where with all Your saints I will praise You in the eternal glory. Amen.

LIFTING THE BLACKOUTS OF LIFE
Matthew 9:27–38

WHEN Marie Antoinette rode to Notre Dame in Paris, she gave orders that all beggars be kept out of sight. She did not want her day spoiled by seeing the misery and want of the people.

Jesus came to the people with a heart full of compassion. As He walked the streets and lanes of the towns and villages, He looked upon them with sympathetic eyes and reached out His hand to help them in their distress. To the blind He gave sight, to the mute He gave speech. He delivered the demon-oppressed from the devil's tyranny and restored their sanity. No matter what the disease or sickness, Jesus was ever ready to touch them with His healing hand.

And then He went to Calvary in His intense love to lay down His life for the souls of men to redeem us all from the guilt of sin and the fear of death. Sin, our sin, made Calvary a necessity.

Such a compassionate Jesus we behold in the Gospels.

Jesus Heals Two Blind Men

And as Jesus passed on from there, two blind men followed Him, crying aloud, "Have mercy on us, Son of David." When He entered the house, the blind men came to Him, and Jesus said to them, "Do you believe that I am able to do this?" They said to Him, "Yes, Lord." Then He touched their eyes, saying, "According to your faith be it done to you." And their eyes were opened. And Jesus sternly warned them, "See that no one knows about it." But they went away and spread His fame through all that district.

Jesus Heals a Man Unable to Speak

As they were going away, behold, a demon-oppressed man who was mute was brought to Him. And when the demon had been cast out, the mute man spoke. And the crowds marveled, saying, "Never was anything like this seen in Israel." But the Pharisees said, "He casts out demons by the prince of demons."

The Harvest Is Plentiful, the Laborers Few

And Jesus went throughout all the cities and villages, teaching in their synagogues and proclaiming the gospel of the kingdom and healing every disease and every affliction. When He saw the crowds, He had compassion for them, because they were harassed and helpless, like sheep without a shepherd. Then He said to His disciples, "The harvest is plentiful, but the laborers are few; therefore pray earnestly to the Lord of the harvest to send out laborers into His harvest."

Like sheep scattered abroad, having no shepherd, Jesus saw the whole of humanity erring, straying, and losing itself in the grief of sorrows and death. They were scattered by doubt, unbelief, and indifference. They were lost in fear, self-pity, and the worries of life. And no one cared for their souls.

Then came Jesus to give His life as a ransom, to gather us into His fold. In Him, the souls of men found healing from the sores of their sins and assurance of His protection against the hellish wolf; they found certainty and sight amid the fog of human philosophy.

And none of the ransomed ever knew
How deep were the waters crossed;
Nor how dark was the night that the Lord passed through
Ere He found His sheep that was lost.
("The Ninety and the Nine"by Elizabeth C. Clephane)

Sheep still are scattered. People are without hope in this world, seeking to save themselves by their own efforts, by self-appointed acts of mercy. Blindly they stumble on in spiritual darkness, Satan taking full possession of their lives.

However—and this is Gospel—Jesus is just as compassionate today as He ever was. He still offers Himself in the Word as the light and the hope and the Savior of the world. And to us, who know how much He loves us and all, He gives the commission to go and seek and tell. Surely our hearts must be stirred with pity as we see the masses going away as straying and wandering sheep. The harvest truly is plenteous, opportunities are limitless, and time is getting shorter each day. Let us beseech God to send forth workers. No effort should seem too great or too small as we support people who go to the ends of the earth to tell that salvation message.

Prayer

In Your tender compassion, Shepherd of our souls, look upon all Your wounded and straying sheep and bring them back to the fold. Keep us faithful and feed us abundantly in the green pastures of Your Word. Let us not tire of making known the saving truths of Your merciful love. Forgive us our neglects and our lovelessness, and make us compassionate, sympathetic, understanding, and patient as we bear witness in a lost world of Your redeeming cross. Amen.

24

LIVING ADVENTUROUSLY FOR CHRIST

Matthew 10:1–15

NOTHING is more surprising to the man of the world and to many Christians than the fact that Jesus chose His disciples from such low strata of society. These hand-picked twelve were not men of influence or men of means; they were not even religious leaders of their generation. Yet they turned the world upside down as they went forth to preach Christ crucified and resurrected. This they accomplished because Jesus gave them power from on high and filled them with His Holy Spirit.

Jesus ordained twelve—eleven from Galilee and one from Judea. Some were fishermen, one a tax collector, and one was a political agitator, a zealot belonging to an underground political party of Palestine. James the son of Zebedee and his brother John were cousins of Jesus, being the sons of Mary's sister. James the son of Alphaeus, Thaddaeus, and Simon the Cananaean may also have been His cousins. Matthew, John, and Simon Peter wrote New Testament books: the Gospels of Matthew and John; First and Second Peter; First, Second, and Third John; and Revelation.

Jesus called and commissioned these men to gather, first, the lost sheep of the house of Israel. Jesus ordained them, set them aside for a special task. He sent them, "apostlelized" them. He commissioned them to preach, to spread the glad news that unto us is born a Savior, who is Christ the Lord. He gave them power to help the troubled lives of humanity by miraculously healing their bodies and—by the Word—bringing forgiveness to their souls. The results of their efforts they were to leave to God.

So the apostles went and preached everywhere, in season and out of season, the message of reconciliation. They dedicated themselves

to Christ, living adventurously for Him who died to make them—
and us—free.

The Twelve Apostles

And He called to Him His twelve disciples and gave them
authority over unclean spirits, to cast them out, and to heal
every disease and every affliction. The names of the twelve
apostles are these: first, Simon, who is called Peter, and
Andrew his brother; James the son of Zebedee, and John
his brother; Philip and Bartholomew; Thomas and Matthew
the tax collector; James the son of Alphaeus, and Thaddaeus;
Simon the Cananaean, and Judas Iscariot, who betrayed Him.

Jesus Sends Out the Twelve Apostles

These twelve Jesus sent out, instructing them, "Go nowhere
among the Gentiles and enter no town of the Samaritans, but
go rather to the lost sheep of the house of Israel. And proclaim
as you go, saying, 'The kingdom of heaven is at hand.' Heal
the sick, raise the dead, cleanse lepers, cast out demons. You
received without paying; give without pay. Acquire no gold nor
silver nor copper for your belts, no bag for your journey, nor
two tunics nor sandals nor a staff, for the laborer deserves his
food. And whatever town or village you enter, find out who is
worthy in it and stay there until you depart. As you enter the
house, greet it. And if the house is worthy, let your peace come
upon it, but if it is not worthy, let your peace return to you.
And if anyone will not receive you or listen to your words,
shake off the dust from your feet when you leave that house or
town. Truly, I say to you, it will be more bearable on the day of
judgment for the land of Sodom and Gomorrah than for that
town.

We, too, are confronted with a troubled and sin-sick world. We,
too, are called to bear witness to Christ, the great physician of souls,
and to speak of the hope that is within us. We, too, are to go out
into this troubled world and alleviate its misery. And to that end,
Christendom has built hospitals and facilities for the blind, the ill, the

aged, the challenged, and the parentless to shelter and aid these people in their affliction. We should not become weary of such work but daily give evidence of our faith by offering food to the hungry and encouragement to the famished souls of men.

Christ Jesus is the bread of life. He satisfies the need of our soul because He blots out sin, cleanses the conscience, and gives salvation to all who come in faith to Him. But how can they believe unless they have heard? Jesus tells us that it is our obligation to see to it that this Gospel reaches the ends of the earth. We are not responsible for the results, but we are duty-bound to do the sowing. As we sow and the seed takes root, we make ourselves friends for eternity. We, too, can live adventurously for Christ.

Prayer

You, O Lord, the Father of my Savior, Jesus Christ, desire to blanket the earth with Your saving Word, that the souls of sinners may be converted to You. Grant that we do our part in the spreading of Your message. Forgive us all our sluggishness and indifference. May we grow more zealous by Your grace and, through Your Holy Spirit, grow more eager from day to day to tell of Jesus and His redeeming love. Amen.

DID CHRIST BRING PEACE ON EARTH?
Matthew 10:16–36

IT certainly does not seem as though Christ has brought peace on earth. Nation rises against nation in one gigantic struggle after another. As history unfolds, the lifeblood of millions is poured out on the battlefields, and continents and cities that have stood for centuries are leveled to the ground. Homes are destroyed, hearts are broken, women are widowed, children are orphaned, and men lie in hospitals, broken in body and in spirit. This goes on century after century, each war becoming more destructive than the one before. The years of peace are but short interludes between colossal conflicts. How can we, then, say that Christ brought peace on earth?

Not only do nations go to war, but individuals and families also feud and quarrel. Brothers and sisters refuse to speak to one another, parents and children are estranged, husbands and wives are divorced. How can we say that Jesus brought peace on earth?

Not even the Christian Church is united. Persecutions, false prophets, errors, and contentions have torn Christendom asunder. Did Christ really bring peace on earth?

Ironically, this Jesus, the Prince of Peace, foretold just these things. Because of the enmity that exists between Christ and the devil, wars, dissensions, errors, falsehoods, and hatred will continue. Sin brings all this into the world, the home, and the church.

Jesus and His Gospel will never make peace with the devil. That is why Jesus tells His disciples and us, "you will be hated of all for My name's sake."

Persecution Will Come

"Behold, I am sending you out as sheep in the midst of wolves, so be wise as serpents and innocent as doves. Beware of men, for they will deliver you over to courts and flog you in their synagogues, and you will be dragged before governors and kings for My sake, to bear witness before them and the Gentiles. When they deliver you over, do not be anxious how you are to speak or what you are to say, for what you are to say will be given to you in that hour. For it is not you who speak, but the Spirit of your Father speaking through you. Brother will deliver brother over to death, and the father his child, and children will rise against parents and have them put to death, and you will be hated by all for My name's sake. But the one who endures to the end will be saved. When they persecute you in one town, flee to the next, for truly, I say to you, you will not have gone through all the towns of Israel before the Son of Man comes.

"A disciple is not above his teacher, nor a servant above his master. It is enough for the disciple to be like his teacher, and the servant like his master. If they have called the master of the house Beelzebul, how much more will they malign those of his household.

Have No Fear

"So have no fear of them, for nothing is covered that will not be revealed, or hidden that will not be known. What I tell you in the dark, say in the light, and what you hear whispered, proclaim on the housetops. And do not fear those who kill the body but cannot kill the soul. Rather fear him who can destroy both soul and body in hell. Are not two sparrows sold for a penny? And not one of them will fall to the ground apart from your Father. But even the hairs of your head are all numbered. Fear not, therefore; you are of more value than many sparrows. So everyone who acknowledges Me before men, I also will acknowledge before My Father who is in heaven, but whoever denies Me before men, I also will deny before My Father who is in heaven.

Not Peace, but a Sword

"Do not think that I have come to bring peace to the earth. I have not come to bring peace, but a sword. For I have come to set a man against his father, and a daughter against her mother, and a daughter-in-law against her mother-in-law. And a person's enemies will be those of his own household."

But Jesus did bring peace to the earth. Through His death on the cross, He reconciled us with God. Men may torture our bodies and even take our lives, but they cannot destroy our soul. This is in the safekeeping of our reconciled Father, who will not let us perish. If the sparrow does not fall to the ground without His permission, then certainly we will not slip out of our Father's hand, we, who are redeemed and saved through faith by the blood of His only Son. The world may hate us, but we can be of good cheer and full of confidence and hope because our Savior has overcome sin and death and has conquered Satan.

Although battles rage about us and many hate us and quarrel with us, nevertheless, in our own heart can be the peace that the world cannot give. We can have the blessed assurance that nothing in this world today or in the future can separate us from His love, which is ours through Christ's death on Calvary. Our sin is forgiven, our salvation is a fact, and heaven is our eternal home—and our mind is at peace.

Did Christ bring peace on earth? Yes, a glorious peace with God in heaven, and, praise the Lord, this peace, which abides in our hearts, cannot be taken from us.

Prayer

Lord Jesus, eternal Prince of Peace, You alone can speak peace to our souls. Let Your divine presence in our lives and our home keep us in Your grace as reconciled children of the household of our heavenly Father. Amen.

LOYALTY AT ITS BEST
Matthew 10:37–42

LOYALTY is always at a premium. Loyalty is at its best when we forget self and place all at the feet of Jesus. And Jesus demands just that. Nothing less will do. He will not tolerate a divided allegiance. Parent, child, and spouse must step down from the pedestal of adoration and give first place to Jesus. Does this mean we are to neglect our families? Never. In fact, if Christ takes full possession of our hearts and lives, we will be more faithful to one another. In our loyalty to Him, we will be loyal to others.

Following Jesus loyally, we are to take up our cross. But we do not want crosses, do we? We want ease. We are soft and do not like hardship, opposition, or ridicule. But time and again Jesus places a cross upon us. Such a cross disciplines us. It stabilizes us. As we bear opposition or ridicule for His sake, we will in the end be rewarded with peace in eternal life.

Life is not worth living if we close the door to Christ Jesus. "Whoever finds his life will lose it, and whoever loses his life for My sake will find it." Does that mean we should give up living? Should we move out of society and into some cave? Hardly! What we should give up is an aimless life that has no purpose or goal. We are to give up the self-centered life, which is only interested in eating, drinking, ease, and good times.

Wealth does not last. Depressions, bad investments, and death shake everything out of our hands. Honor does not stay; others come along and take it from us. Popularity fades; one misstep, and the crowd seeks other heroes.

But if we lose our lives in Christ and in service to Him, He gives us treasures that last longer than the world itself. These treasures come to us in terms of forgiveness, peace, salvation, and heaven. Loyalty is at its best only when Jesus takes full possession of us. Such is His claim.

"Whoever loves father or mother more than Me is not worthy of Me, and whoever loves son or daughter more than Me is not worthy of Me. And whoever does not take his cross and follow Me is not worthy of Me. Whoever finds his life will lose it, and whoever loses his life for My sake will find it.

Rewards
"Whoever receives you receives Me, and whoever receives Me receives Him who sent Me. The one who receives a prophet because he is a prophet will receive a prophet's reward, and the one who receives a righteous person because he is a righteous person will receive a righteous person's reward. And whoever gives one of these little ones even a cup of cold water because he is a disciple, truly, I say to you, he will by no means lose his reward."

"Behold, I stand at the door and knock," says Jesus (Revelation 3:20). Today He comes to us through His Word. And we receive this Word from Him, who comes to us as the eternal Word made man. In Him, we see very God of very God. Jesus is more than a prophet. He is more than a righteous man. He is all that, but there is a divine plus. This prophet, this righteous and sinless man, is God Himself. "Before Abraham was, I am" (John 8:58).

As we hear His Word through His messengers, we must accept it as the eternal truth and follow it. This Word alone makes us wise for salvation. This Word shows us that Jesus is the way, the truth, and the life. For this Jesus, the Savior who redeemed us with His blood, gave His life as a full payment that was accepted by God. A greater love and a more perfect sacrifice never was made. No other could make it.

Our redeemed souls, then, must worship and serve Him continually. And we can. The simplest act of service done in love for Him does not remain unrecognized. A cup of cold water, a kind word, a sacrificial cent is appreciated. Jesus does not look at the size of the gift or the greatness of the effort, but at the motive that prompts the act. If love is the all-consuming motive in our loyal services to Christ, then loyalty is at its best.

Prayer

Pour out on me, Savior of my soul, the riches of Your grace, and fill my heart with a greater loyalty to You, whose love rendered me the most precious service in redeeming my soul. Grant me grace to dedicate myself to Your service day upon day. Open my eyes to see opportunities to do something for You. Amen.

WHAT MAKES MAN GREAT?
Matthew 11:1–15

NONE greater than John the Baptist has ever been born! We have Jesus' word for this. But leading historians are not likely to mention John on their list of great people. They speak of Alexander the Great, Julius Caesar, Napoleon, Gandhi, or Abraham Lincoln. The history of man calls these men "great" and ignores John the Baptist. Jesus must have a different standard by which He measures the worth of a man. What makes man great? We certainly would like to know.

John is called great because he proved himself victorious over discouragement. He pointed the people of his day to Jesus as the Lamb of God, who takes away the sin of the world. John urged his own disciples to follow Jesus. Truly, he was a real herald. He forgot himself and announced that Jesus of Nazareth is the Messiah of prophecy. He refused to take honor for himself, although the people were ready to bestow it upon him. And what was John's reward? Prison and death by beheading.

John had told the ruler of the country that he was living in sin by entering into a marriage with his brother's divorced wife. John had done his duty, performed his God-appointed task. For that, Herod, the king, put him into a dungeon. John saw his fondest hopes shattered, his days dark, and the nights dismal and drear. In his plight, John sent his disciples to Jesus with the question, "Are You the one who is to come?" Jesus sent back an answer by quoting prophecy that was fulfilled in that very hour.

John believed, and that made him great. He believed that Jesus was the Messiah, the Lamb for sinners slain, the Savior of the world. Faith in the Word of God and in Jesus, the Savior, makes us great, so great that our names are written in the Book of Life and we are made heirs of heaven.

John is called great because he was not offended at Jesus. Jesus seemingly failed him. John had enthusiastically espoused Jesus' cause. Faithfully, John bore witness to Jesus—and he was imprisoned. Jesus did not help him out of the dungeon. Yet John is not offended. He is not shaken like a reed in the wind. No matter what happens to him, Jesus is still his adorable Savior, whom he will not doubt. Therefore, Jesus says of John that none born of woman is greater.

Into our lives comes Jesus, and He is not always complimentary as He speaks to us. He tells us of our sins and faults. He tells us how filthy our righteousness is. It will never do. It offends.

And we know we cannot save ourselves; we have not done the will of God. But we come believing that Jesus redeems and saves. He removes our guilt, heals our griefs, and cleanses our hearts. And if we come, we, too, will be great in His sight, for our faith has made us heirs of heaven and children of the kingdom.

When Jesus had finished instructing His twelve disciples, He went on from there to teach and preach in their cities.

Now when John heard in prison about the deeds of the Christ, he sent word by his disciples and said to Him, "Are You the one who is to come, or shall we look for another?" And Jesus answered them, "Go and tell John what you hear and see: the blind receive their sight and the lame walk, lepers are cleansed and the deaf hear, and the dead are raised up, and the poor have good news preached to them. And blessed is the one who is not offended by Me."

As they went away, Jesus began to speak to the crowds concerning John: "What did you go out into the wilderness to see? A reed shaken by the wind? What then did you go out to see? A man dressed in soft clothing? Behold, those who wear soft clothing are in kings' houses. What then did you go out to see? A prophet? Yes, I tell you, and more than a prophet. This is he of whom it is written,

'Behold, I send My messenger before your face,
who will prepare your way before you.'

Truly, I say to you, among those born of women there has arisen no one greater than John the Baptist. Yet the one who is least in the kingdom of heaven is greater than he. From the days of John the Baptist until now the kingdom of heaven has suffered violence, and the violent take it by force. For all the Prophets and the Law prophesied until John, and if you are willing to accept it, he is Elijah who is to come. He who has ears to hear, let him hear."

Too often we are blinded by outward pomp and display. We even mistake brute power and domineering authority for greatness. But what makes man great is faith in Jesus Christ as the Savior from sin. Such faith enables us to live hopefully amid all the trials, sufferings, and tears of life. Without this faith, this world is a terrible place in which to live. However, through faith in Christ, we have a hope even now in this present world, a hope we are not ashamed of. After the toiling of life comes glory. Such is our expectancy.

Prayer

Heavenly Father, Your redeeming grace has made us heirs of all the glory that is Yours from everlasting to everlasting. Mindful of these eternal treasures, help us to overcome through a triumphant faith every discouraging thought and all earthly disappointments. Bless us with Your continued presence, and let us find in You contentment and peace. In Jesus' name we ask it. Amen.

A DO-FOR-ME CHRISTIANITY
Matthew 11:16–19

NO matter what the Christian Church teaches and preaches, someone will object to the message and use it as an excuse for neglecting the worship of God and fellowship with Christian people. John the Baptist fasted and abstained from the use of wine. Because of this, some of the religionists of the day said he was possessed by a devil. Jesus went to the homes of His friends and also sat down to eat with notorious sinners, and these same people said He was a glutton and winebibber, or tippler. You simply cannot please everybody, especially those who are looking for something to find fault with.

What should we do, then? Nothing? That would be the easier course. However, that is not a God-pleasing way to face objection and criticism. So what should we do? Continue with patience and determination to teach and to preach and to carry out what God has directed us to do in His Word. The rest we leave to God.

We will never be able to please everybody. This Jesus experienced, and He was the sinless Son of God.

> *"But to what shall I compare this generation? It is like children sitting in the marketplaces and calling to their playmates,*
>
> *'We played the flute for you, and you did not dance;*
> *we sang a dirge, and you did not mourn.'*
>
> For John came neither eating nor drinking, and they say, 'He has a demon.' The Son of Man came eating and drinking, and they say, 'Look at Him! A glutton and a drunkard, a friend of tax collectors and sinners!' Yet wisdom is justified by her deeds."

Jesus probably shook His head when He heard the criticism of His opponents. "To what shall I compare this generation?" we hear Him say. They act like children who say you cannot play in our yard because you do not play by our rules. We have played our music, and you have not danced according to our tune.

This holds true today. Many have played—they want an easy-going Christianity, charming preachers who say "smooth things" (Isaiah 30:10). Many want sin denounced as long as it is not their sin. It's fun to sit in the pew and hear the preacher shoot darts at the absentees, but he must not say anything against our conduct. He must not strike too close to home. We want him to dance to the tune we play.

We have mourned, but you have not lamented. This is another tune many play. They want a do-for-me Christianity. They come to church to be entertained and to be catered to. They never lift a hand for anyone. But let them have some kind of problem, and they expect everyone to immediately jump and come to their rescue.

We mourn, and when we do, we want the church. We look for an emergency device that will take all the bitter pain out of our lives. In sickness, we want the helpful hand of the church to be conveniently near. When death comes to our home, we want the services of the church and a minister to say nice things. Are we merely looking for a membership that will bring immediate service in a crisis?

John came neither eating nor drinking, and he was faulted for his ascetic conduct. Jesus ate and drank with publicans and sinners, and He was accused of loose living. Some people cannot be pleased. No matter what the church does, it is wrong in the opinion of such faultfinders.

"To what shall I compare this generation?" says Jesus. The crowd is critical. No matter what is done, it is wrong. If we are joyful, then we are taking our Christianity lightly. If we are sad, then we are told about the joy of the Gospel. But these faultfinders of 2,000 years ago did not harm Jesus and His Gospel. They only closed the door of hope and salvation upon themselves. Surely, we do not want to make the same tragic mistake!

Prayer

*Lord, eternal God, You know how selfish we are by nature. We
always want our way and think we know even better than You how
to guide and direct the events of life and the world. Forgive us
and lead us to Your Word, that through it we may learn that Your
will and Your thoughts are better than our own. Grant us grace to
say with a believing heart, "Thy will be done," and be confident
and sure that it is a good and gracious will in Christ Jesus, our
eternal Savior. Amen.*

THE MOST GRACIOUS INVITATION EVER GIVEN TO MAN
Matthew 11:20–30

ALONG the northern shore of the Sea of Galilee during Jesus'
earthly life stood three mighty and flourishing cities—Capernaum,
Chorazin, and Bethsaida—with a population of a million people.
Today not a trace of them, save a very few ruins, is to be seen as you
walk along the seashore.

What happened? In their heyday, Jesus came to these cities and
did most of His mighty works in their midst. He performed miracle after miracle there. He preached many of His greatest sermons
there. But the people did not receive Him. They refused to receive
Him as the Messiah. So Jesus pronounced woe and judgment upon
them because they turned from Him. "It will be more tolerable on
the day of judgment for the land of Sodom than for you."

Following this scathing indictment, Jesus immediately utters
the most winsome words that ever fell from His lips. Although Jesus

pronounces upon these cities His greatest woe, He pleads with the most gracious invitation ever given to man. No matter how often men reject His love, Jesus still asks them to come. If we do, we will find rest, peace, hope, and life in Him. It is no wonder that we still turn to Him amid our sorrows and tears!

Woe to Unrepentant Cities

Then He began to denounce the cities where most of His mighty works had been done, because they did not repent. "Woe to you, Chorazin! Woe to you, Bethsaida! For if the mighty works done in you had been done in Tyre and Sidon, they would have repented long ago in sackcloth and ashes. But I tell you, it will be more bearable on the day of judgment for Tyre and Sidon than for you. And you, Capernaum, will you be exalted to heaven? You will be brought down to Hades. For if the mighty works done in you had been done in Sodom, it would have remained until this day. But I tell you that it will be more tolerable on the day of judgment for the land of Sodom than for you."

Come to Me, and I Will Give You Rest

At that time Jesus declared, "I thank You, Father, Lord of heaven and earth, that You have hidden these things from the wise and understanding and revealed them to little children; yes, Father, for such was Your gracious will. All things have been handed over to Me by My Father, and no one knows the Son except the Father, and no one knows the Father except the Son and anyone to whom the Son chooses to reveal Him. Come to Me, all who labor and are heavy laden, and I will give you rest. Take My yoke upon you, and learn from Me, for I am gentle and lowly in heart, and you will find rest for your souls. For My yoke is easy, and My burden is light."

Who is not restless today? Mankind has always been so. Ages ago, David exclaimed, "Oh, that I had wings like a dove! I would fly away and be at rest" (Psalm 55:6). But you cannot get away from yourself.

Jesus invites the restless millions to come to Him, and find rest for their souls. He does not take every unpleasant thing from us and lift every burden of life from our shoulders. That is not the promise. But He makes every burden lighter and every yoke easier. He shares the weight of the load and takes the abrasive edges off the cross. We arrive at the end of the day with sufficient strength to go on and find restful sleep as we place ourselves into His care. Rest implies certainty and reconciliation. In Christ, we are sure of forgiveness. Through His cross we are reconciled with God. Sin is removed and peace is restored be-cause the blood of Jesus makes full atonement for sin.

This forgiveness opens the door to the throne of prayer. We are living in grace. In this grace, our past misdeeds are canceled and our whole life is transformed. Burdens are lifted and anxieties are placed at Jesus' feet. Our lives are enriched by serving, following, and loving Him, whose compassion and patience invite us daily to come and find rest for our weary souls.

Prayer

Lord Jesus, Shepherd of our souls, we come to You and place all our burdens and anxieties at Your feet. We are so helpless, so weary, so exhausted. Draw us to Your bosom, and soothe us with Your promises. We have no other refuge—so we come. Patiently receive us once more. Amen.

BETTER THAN A SHEEP

Matthew 12:1–21

IT is possible to obey the letter of the Law but at the same time maliciously transgress the spirit of the same Law. Yes, we can hide behind outward observances of the commandments of God to excuse our negligence. This was the case with the Pharisees. With an exactness that extended to the dividing of an anise plant in the garden, they followed the instruction concerning the tithe. Then they excused themselves from all acts of mercy on the Sabbath day by hiding behind the letter of the commandment to "remember the Sabbath day to keep it holy . . . on it you shall not do any work" (Exodus 20:8–9).

But the rules of love apply in the observance of the Ten Commandments. For instance, Jesus healed a man on the Sabbath. He justified this act of mercy by saying that no man would leave his sheep to die if it fell into a pit on the Sabbath. God's Law did not demand the neglect of the animal. Man is humane to his sheep. And any person in trouble is better than a sheep. And why? Because God has endowed man with gifts never given to the sheep. God has given man a soul. This soul, lost in sin, fallen into pits that Satan has dug, was redeemed by God through His own Son, who gave His life as a ransom for sin. And then God gave to this redeemed man His Word, the Law and the Gospel, that he would be saved.

If man is better than a sheep, then we ought to treat him accordingly. We are not to behave like animals, yet we often we act worse than the beast of the field. We do things an animal would never do. As Christians, living in grace, we ought to live daily as God's redeemed people, obeying the Law and always showing mercy—as Jesus did when He healed the man with the withered hand.

Jesus Is Lord of the Sabbath

At that time Jesus went through the grainfields on the Sabbath. His disciples were hungry, and they began to pluck heads of grain and to eat. But when the Pharisees saw it, they said to Him, "Look, Your disciples are doing what is not lawful to do on the Sabbath." He said to them, "Have you not read what David did when he was hungry, and those who were with him: how he entered the house of God and ate the bread of the Presence, which it was not lawful for him to eat nor for those who were with him, but only for the priests? Or have you not read in the Law how on the Sabbath the priests in the temple profane the Sabbath and are guiltless? I tell you, something greater than the temple is here. And if you had known what this means, 'I desire mercy, and not sacrifice,' you would not have condemned the guiltless. For the Son of Man is lord of the Sabbath."

A Man with a Withered Hand

He went on from there and entered their synagogue. And a man was there with a withered hand. And they asked Him, "Is it lawful to heal on the Sabbath?"—so that they might accuse Him. He said to them, "Which one of you who has a sheep, if it falls into a pit on the Sabbath, will not take hold of it and lift it out? Of how much more value is a man than a sheep! So it is lawful to do good on the Sabbath." Then He said to the man, "Stretch out your hand." And the man stretched it out, and it was restored, healthy like the other. But the Pharisees went out and conspired against Him, how to destroy Him.

God's Chosen Servant

Jesus, aware of this, withdrew from there. And many followed Him, and He healed them all and ordered them not to make Him known. This was to fulfill what was spoken by the prophet Isaiah:

"Behold, My servant whom I have chosen,
  My beloved with whom My soul is well pleased.
I will put My Spirit upon Him,
  and He will proclaim justice to the Gentiles.

He will not quarrel or cry aloud,
  nor will anyone hear His voice in the streets;
a bruised reed He will not break,
  and a smoldering wick He will not quench,
until He brings justice to victory;
  and in His name the Gentiles will hope."

"A bruised reed He will not break, and a faintly burning wick He will not quench," said Isaiah centuries before the coming of the promised Messiah (42:3). If there is one fact that is undeniable in the Gospels, it is this: Jesus seeks us and loves us. We are lost, and Jesus searches until He finds us. We must be reclaimed; we must be forgiven.

Jesus went to the multitude in a world of sin and sought the lost, one by one. He brought each of us into the fold and remade us into children of light. He calls us by name: the bruised, the discouraged, the disillusioned, the sick, the sinner. Each of us can say with David: "The Lord takes thought for me" (Psalm 40:17). Jesus makes time for me. He loves me. "Simon, son of John, do you love Me?" (John 21:17). "Zacchaeus, hurry and come down, for I must stay at your house today" (Luke 19:5). "He said to Thomas, 'Put your finger here, and see My hands; and put out your hand, and place it in My side. Do not disbelieve, but believe' " (John 20:27). All this Jesus does in His love because we are more valuable than a sheep.

Prayer
Savior of my soul, I turn to You, the rock that is higher than I.
Draw me to Your wounded side, and let me find rest and healing
and salvation there. Then I can be at peace with You and
with myself, most gracious Redeemer. Amen.

THE BANE OF UNBELIEF

Matthew 12:22–37

THE Christian religion is the most universal in the world. It is not limited to any age group, ethnic group, or language. Its message is for all; its promises for every generation of men. It offers the one satisfying remedy for sin and places no one outside the circle of God's love in Christ Jesus.

At the same time, the Christian religion is extremely narrow. It allows for no other way to eternal life but by Jesus Christ, the Son of God made flesh. It permits no divided allegiance. Jesus allows no serving of two masters at the same time. You are either for Him or against Him. There is no other God but Yahweh; there is no other Savior but Jesus; there is no other revelation but the Scriptures; there is no other code of ethics but the Law of God; there is no other way to life but by the blood of Christ.

Christ includes all mankind in His gracious invitation, "Come to Me, all who labor and are heavy laden, and I will give you rest" (Matthew 11:28)—but each one must come to Him, to His wounded side. The countless number in heaven who praise the Lamb come from every kindred, nation, and tongue. But no matter where they come from, each was washed white in the blood of the Lamb (Revelation 7:9). "Whoever believes in the Son has eternal life" (John 3:36). No other shall have life, and therefore our allegiance must be undivided. So says Jesus.

Blasphemy Against the Holy Spirit

Then a demon-oppressed man who was blind and mute was brought to Him, and He healed him, so that the man spoke and saw. And all the people were amazed, and said, "Can this be the Son of David?" But when the Pharisees heard it, they said, "It is only by Beelzebul, the prince of demons, that this man casts out demons." Knowing their thoughts, He said to them, "Every kingdom divided against itself is laid waste, and no city or house divided against itself will stand. And if Satan casts out Satan, he is divided against himself. How then will his kingdom stand? And if I cast out demons by Beelzebul, by whom do your sons cast them out? Therefore they will be your judges. But if it is by the Spirit of God that I cast out demons, then the kingdom of God has come upon you. Or how can someone enter a strong man's house and plunder his goods, unless he first binds the strong man? Then indeed he may plunder his house. Whoever is not with Me is against Me, and whoever does not gather with Me scatters. Therefore I tell you, every sin and blasphemy will be forgiven people, but the blasphemy against the Spirit will not be forgiven. And whoever speaks a word against the Son of Man will be forgiven, but whoever speaks against the Holy Spirit will not be forgiven, either in this age or in the age to come.

A Tree Is Known by Its Fruit

"Either make the tree good and its fruit good, or make the tree bad and its fruit bad, for the tree is known by its fruit. You brood of vipers! How can you speak good, when you are evil? For out of the abundance of the heart the mouth speaks. The good person out of his good treasure brings forth good, and the evil person out of his evil treasure brings forth evil. I tell you, on the day of judgment people will give account for every careless word they speak, for by your words you will be justified, and by your words you will be condemned."

"Whoever speaks a word against the Son of Man will be forgiven, but whoever speaks against the Holy Spirit will not be forgiven, either in this age or in the age to come." Did you think that all sin is forgiven? Didn't Jesus redeem us from all transgressions? Why, then, does He say that the sin against the Holy Spirit will not be forgiven in this age or the next? What is this sin against the Holy Spirit?

The sin against the Holy Spirit is the stubborn and obstinate refusal to believe in Jesus as the one atoning Savior from sin. Unbelief persistently closes the door of heaven. You cannot refuse and believe at the same time. This faith in Christ Jesus is created in us by the Holy Spirit. "No one can say 'Jesus is Lord' except in the Holy Spirit" (1 Corinthians 12:3). But we can resist Him, and when we do, we close the only door that opens the glories of heaven to us.

So the person who persistently continues in unbelief remains outside of this world and the world to come. That is the curse of unbelief; it does not permit you to have the forgiveness Jesus purchased for you on the cross.

This sin against the Holy Spirit is committed only by those who have heard the Gospel of reconciliation and have resisted its gracious call. That they go on in this unforgiven state is their own fault. The Gospel call rings into their ears and the Savior stands at the door of their hearts and knocks, but they refuse Him admittance. "He destroys you, O Israel, for you are against Me, against your helper" (Hosea 13:9).

But someone may become alarmed and despairingly exclaim, "I am guilty of this sin! There is no hope for me; I am lost." To this person, we can give the assurance that he has not committed this sin against the Holy Spirit. Those who have committed it never become alarmed; they never despair, but they go on in cold indifference. Their hearts are closed to all appeals of the Gospel. As long as man listens to the message of reconciliation, he is not under the curse of this unforgivable sin.

Prayer

Gracious Lord, merciful in Christ Jesus, our Savior, keeps us steadfast in the Gospel, through which our faith is nourished and sustained. All around us we hear the hiss of unbelief, seeking to destroy in us the love for Christ Jesus, our Redeemer and Lord. Let not the foolishness of the worldly wise upset and disturb us. Preserve us in Your grace, and keep us in Your Kingdom until we, too, stand before the throne of the Lamb to praise Him forevermore. Amen.

THE SIGN OF THE PROPHET JONAH
Matthew 12:38–50

ARE You the Messiah?" Jesus answered this vital question by saying that He would perform one outstanding miracle that would prove once and for all that He was the promised Christ, the Savior of the world. That sign was the sign of the prophet Jonah. As Jonah was in the belly of a great fish for three days and lived, so shall Jesus, the Son of Man, be put to death, placed in a grave, and on the third day walk out of the tomb.

The priests and the leaders of Jerusalem did not forget this challenging assertion. After Jesus was placed in Joseph of Arimathea's sepulcher on that Friday of the crucifixion, these men of the Sanhedrin went to Pilate and said, "Sir, we remember how that impostor said, while He was still alive, 'After three days I will rise' " (Matthew 27:63). So they made doubly sure that no one would come near the tomb to attempt to take the body. The tomb was officially sealed and a detail of soldiers placed in front of it to guard it.

But this was of no avail. On the third day, the tomb was empty and Jesus was alive. By this miracle of miracles, Jesus proved to the ages that He is God and that He accomplished His task of redeeming the souls of men from the deadly clutches of Satan. But many do not believe, and on the Last Day, they will rise again to testify against such unbelief.

The Sign of Jonah

Then some of the scribes and Pharisees answered Him, saying, "Teacher, we wish to see a sign from You." But He answered them, "An evil and adulterous generation seeks for a sign, but no sign will be given to it except the sign of the prophet Jonah. For just as Jonah was three days and three nights in the belly of the great fish, so will the Son of Man be three days and three nights in the heart of the earth. The men of Nineveh will rise up at the judgment with this generation and condemn it, for they repented at the preaching of Jonah, and behold, something greater than Jonah is here. The queen of the South will rise up at the judgment with this generation and condemn it, for she came from the ends of the earth to hear the wisdom of Solomon, and behold, something greater than Solomon is here.

Return of an Unclean Spirit

"When the unclean spirit has gone out of a person, it passes through waterless places seeking rest, but finds none. Then it says, 'I will return to my house from which I came.' And when it comes, it finds the house empty, swept, and put in order. Then it goes and brings with it seven other spirits more evil than itself, and they enter and dwell there, and the last state of that person is worse than the first. So also will it be with this evil generation."

Jesus' Mother and Brothers

While He was still speaking to the people, behold, His mother and His brothers stood outside, asking to speak to Him. But He replied to the man who told Him, "Who is My mother, and who are My brothers?" And stretching out His hand toward His disciples, He said, "Here are My mother and My brothers! For whoever does the will of My Father in heaven is My brother and sister and mother."

Since Jesus is risen from the dead, unbelievers are without excuse. He has shown beyond a shadow of a doubt that He is God and the Savior of mankind. Those who reject Him in this present age and generation have no excuse for their unbelief. If the Ninevites believed Jonah and the queen of Sheba accepted Solomon's word, what excuse can anyone offer now since Jesus is risen from the dead?

How do we explain obstinate refusal to accept the risen Christ? Satan has taken full possession of their hearts. They refuse to give Jesus the right of way in their lives. They reform but they refuse to turn to Christ. So Satan takes full possession of their empty hearts.

He allows them to be religious and good in the eyes of the world. Satan does not care how religious you are as long as you do not come to the sacred wounds of Christ and look up to His cross for your salvation and eternal life. He does not object to respectability and self-righteousness as long as you do not lean upon Jesus but upon your own self instead.

If we seek heaven without the Christ, we close the one door that opens the way to life. Therefore, many have ears and do not hear and eyes and do not see that the labors of their hands are not sufficient to save their souls.

Blessed are they, indeed, who hear the Gospel and believe it. Peace comes to their heart as the risen Savior takes full possession of their lives and abides.

Prayer

Lord God, I am grateful that You have given the indisputable sign of Jesus' resurrection and, in this risen Christ, the assurance of forgiveness of my sin, the hope of life everlasting, and the promise of a personal resurrection of this dying body. I know that my Redeemer lives, and because He lives, I will see Him face-to-face in a life in which death and sorrow and decay cannot touch me. Praise to You, most gracious Father, for this blessed hope given to me through my risen and ever-living Savior. Amen.

NO DEPTH OF SOIL
Matthew 13:1–9, 18–23

THE parables of Jesus have always aroused the imagination of those who read or hear them. Jesus takes the ordinary events of life and hallows them into a spiritual significance. How often have we seen a farmer plant crops and thought only of the backbreaking and tedious hours in the extremes of weather?

But Jesus saw more. To the simple act of sowing seed, the Savior gives a heavenly interpretation. He sees the lilies of the field, as common as the dandelion, and says that in all his rich attire, Solomon never looked so magnificent. The sower throws out a handful of seed. Because it does not fall on fertile ground to take root, the plant dies before the grain ripens. There is no depth of soil on the hard roadside, the stony plot, or the weed-infested corner. It is amazing on what tiny bit of ground a weed will grow, but not the wheat. Without proper moisture and sunshine, the plant withers and dies. The toiling has been in vain, and the disappointment is keen.

But what does all this mean? Jesus says, "He who has ears, let him hear," and explains the parable.

The Parable of the Sower

That same day Jesus went out of the house and sat beside the sea. And great crowds gathered about Him, so that He got into a boat and sat down. And the whole crowd stood on the beach. And He told them many things in parables, saying: "A sower went out to sow. And as he sowed, some seeds fell along the path, and the birds came and devoured them. Other seeds fell on rocky ground, where they did not have much soil, and immediately they sprang up, since they had no depth of soil, but when the sun rose they were scorched. And since they had no root, they withered away. Other seeds fell among thorns, and the thorns grew up and choked them. Other seeds fell on good soil and produced grain, some a hundredfold, some sixty, some thirty. He who has ears, let him hear." . . .

The Parable of the Sower Explained

"Hear then the parable of the sower: When anyone hears the word of the kingdom and does not understand it, the evil one comes and snatches away what has been sown in his heart. This is what was sown along the path. As for what was sown on rocky ground, this is the one who hears the word and immediately receives it with joy, yet he has no root in himself, but endures for a while, and when tribulation or persecution arises on account of the word, immediately he falls away. As for what was sown among thorns, this is the one who hears the word, but the cares of the world and the deceitfulness of riches choke the word, and it proves unfruitful. As for what was sown on good soil, this is the one who hears the word and understands it. He indeed bears fruit and yields, in one case a hundredfold, in another sixty, and in another thirty."

Jesus does not always explain His parables, but in this instance He makes some pertinent points and gives some significant interpretations.

The devil goes to church, but not to hear. He goes to divert our attention from the preaching so it does not benefit us and strengthen our belief. Each time we go to church, the possibility is there that we will begin to daydream and the Word will not take root.

Or we may go to church and our feelings may be hurt. Someone was not as cordial as he ought to be. Or we thought the preacher was aiming his darts and arrows at us. We leave in a huff and the Word finds no room in our unreceptive heart.

Or we may go to church burdened with financial or family problems. The utilities bill is not paid, the mortgage is due, the car needs repair, or the family budget never balances. We worry and fret. This closes the door of our heart and the Word finds no footing. We return to our problems without having benefited by the promises of God.

So we may go to church, each of us, and not take home a benediction. Solomon was inspired to say, "Guard your steps when you go to the house of God. To draw near to listen is better" (Ecclesiastes 5:1). If we are to benefit from listening to the Word and the sermon, we must do so with concentration, earnest prayer, and watchful preparation.

Therefore Jesus says, "Take care then how you hear" (Luke 8:18).

Prayer

Humbly we come into Your presence, O Lord God, mindful of our own unworthiness. As we worship You with all Your children on earth, let no distracting thoughts nor vexing problems of life rob us of Your Word. Bless the preaching of the Gospel upon our hearts, and give us the grace to do Your will day after day as we move among our fellow men and perform our daily tasks. In Jesus' name. Amen.

CUSTODIANS OF A GREAT TASK
Matthew 13:10–17, 31–35

"TAKE care then how you hear" (Luke 8:18). Scripture speaks of "stopped ears" and "heavy ears." People have grown so fat with prosperity and are so steeped in pleasure that nothing penetrates their mind. They have no interest in anything spiritual. With their filled barns and granaries, they are satisfied to feed the soul on the husks and ashes of temporal gratifications. They have goods laid up for many years, so they may just as well eat and drink and enjoy life.

But if we do not appreciate the Gospel, it will be taken from us and given to others. If we persistently turn from Him, God's judgment will strike us, and then, when we hear, we will not understand, and when we see, we will not perceive. Paul says to the Thessalonians: "They refused to love the truth and so be saved. Therefore God sends them a strong delusion, so that they may believe what is false" (2 Thessalonians 2:10–11). For this very reason Scripture bids us to have hearing ears, paying attention to what is said, and obedient ears, practicing what we hear.

That is why sermons fail. Our mind is closed to the spiritual truths, and our interests lie in another direction. Jesus urges us to hear properly and adds, "Blessed are your eyes, for they see, and your ears, for they hear." So Jesus uses this parable to emphasize the importance of recognizing our responsibility as custodians of this great task.

The Purpose of the Parables

Then the disciples came and said to Him, "Why do You speak to them in parables?" And He answered them, "To you it has been given to know the secrets of the kingdom of heaven, but to them it has not been given. For to the one who has, more will be given, and he will have an abundance, but from the one who has not, even what he has will be taken away. This is why I speak to them in parables, because seeing they do not see, and hearing they do not hear, nor do they understand. Indeed, in their case the prophecy of Isaiah is fulfilled that says:

'You will indeed hear but never understand,
    and you will indeed see but never perceive.
For this people's heart has grown dull,
    and with their ears they can barely hear,
    and their eyes they have closed,
lest they should see with their eyes
    and hear with their ears
and understand with their heart
    and turn, and I would heal them.'

But blessed are your eyes, for they see, and your ears, for they hear. For truly, I say to you, many prophets and righteous people longed to see what you see, and did not see it, and to hear what you hear, and did not hear it." . . .

The Mustard Seed and the Leaven

He put another parable before them, saying, "The kingdom of heaven is like a grain of mustard seed that a man took and sowed in his field. It is the smallest of all seeds, but when it has grown it is larger than all the garden plants and becomes a tree, so that the birds of the air come and make nests in its branches."

He told them another parable. "The kingdom of heaven is like leaven that a woman took and hid in three measures of flour, till it was all leavened."

Prophecy and Parables

All these things Jesus said to the crowds in parables; indeed, He said nothing to them without a parable. This was to fulfill what was spoken by the prophet:

"I will open my mouth in parables;
I will utter what has been hidden since the foundation of the world."

Even if some do not listen to the Word of God, even if they foolishly close the door of their hearts to the Gospel of Jesus Christ, the Kingdom will continue to grow, the Church will add daily to those who are saved. This truth is taught by the parable of the mustard seed and the parable of the leaven. "So shall My word be that goes out from My mouth; it shall not return to Me empty" (Isaiah 55:11).

The Church may have very small beginnings; it may appear in some communities as though all efforts are in vain. But the mustard seed will grow and grow, and, in fact, has grown to such porportions that the birds find shelter under its beneficent influence.

The Kingdom grows in a twofold manner: it grows outwardly like the mustard plant, getting larger and larger, and it grows inwardly like the leaven, each individual increasing in faith and developing in Christian character. Through this twofold growth, the Church becomes a beacon of hope and the cornerstone for uprightness and justice in the community. Its light cannot be hid under a bushel.

As we join a congregation in Christian worship and fellowship, we should ask ourselves whether by our testimony and conduct we are drawing the world to the Gospel. Men and women observing us note something about us that makes us different. Being reconciled to God through Christ's blood makes us new creatures whose lives radiate an inward peace and confident hope. Those who don't have that hope see it in us and would like to have it. It is our God-given task to let our light shine before men that others may know we belong to Jesus.

Prayer

*Lord most holy, use us as Your servants and messengers who,
by word and conduct, reveal to the world the transforming
power of Your grace. Through Your Holy Spirit we have been
called out of the darkness of sin into the Kingdom of Your
Son, called to be saints, who are to let their light shine in this
benighted world by serving You and confessing Jesus Christ as
Savior and Lord. Forgive us the coldness of our hearts, and set
aglow in us a greater zeal for Your cause, through Jesus Christ,
our Lord. Amen.*

LIVING ON THE OUTSIDE OF THINGS

Matthew 13:24–30, 36–43

THE darnel is a weed that resembles wheat. That's why it is so difficult to eradicate it from the field. Its early blade looks so very much
like the sprouting wheat. Only when it begins to ripen does it reveal
its true nature. These weeds have the vexing characteristic of ripening earlier than wheat, so by the time the crop is ready for harvest,
the seed of the weed has fallen to the ground for the following year.
To get rid of this troublesome weed, one must let the field lie idle
for a year and uproot the weeds before they go to seed again.

Spitefulness is all you can call this man's behavior as he goes out
in the darkness of the night to sow weeds into his neighbor's field.
Sin always does its worst under cover and brings in its wake grief,
trouble, loss, and death. Sin is always destructive and, when it has
finished its work, it brings death.

In the parable of the weeds, Jesus emphasizes these facts.

The Parable of the Weeds

He put another parable before them, saying, "The kingdom of heaven may be compared to a man who sowed good seed in his field, but while his men were sleeping, his enemy came and sowed weeds among the wheat and went away. So when the plants came up and bore grain, then the weeds appeared also. And the servants of the master of the house came and said to him, 'Master, did you not sow good seed in your field? How then does it have weeds?' He said to them, 'An enemy has done this.' So the servants said to him, 'Then do you want us to go and gather them?' But he said, 'No, lest in gathering the weeds you root up the wheat along with them. Let both grow together until the harvest, and at harvest time I will tell the reapers, Gather the weeds first and bind them in bundles to be burned, but gather the wheat into my barn.'" . . .

The Parable of the Weeds Explained

Then He left the crowds and went into the house. And His disciples came to Him, saying, "Explain to us the parable of the weeds of the field." He answered, "The one who sows the good seed is the Son of Man. The field is the world, and the good seed is the sons of the kingdom. The weeds are the sons of the evil one, and the enemy who sowed them is the devil. The harvest is the close of the age, and the reapers are angels. Just as the weeds are gathered and burned with fire, so will it be at the close of the age. The Son of Man will send His angels, and they will gather out of His kingdom all causes of sin and all law-breakers, and throw them into the fiery furnace. In that place there will be weeping and gnashing of teeth. Then the righteous will shine like the sun in the kingdom of their Father. He who has ears, let him hear."

In this parable, the good seed are the children of God, the believers. They have come to faith by the seed of the Word of God, which was sown into their hearts. But they live in the world. In the field of the world, believers grow and bring forth the fruit of the Spirit as an evidence of their faith and spiritual life. Although they are in the world, they are not worldly. They did not turn into weeds but, by God's grace, they increase in faith and develop in Christian character. Without the Gospel, they spiritually go to weed.

These believers are not disturbed by the weeds. Unbelievers, hypocrites, atheists, scoffers, and the worldly-wise do not upset them. Christians continue to grow in God's grace. And when time ends for us believers, the Lord will recognize us as His own and gather us into His eternal granaries.

We must not be anxious and irritated by the godless and wicked world that takes on at times the appearance of Christian virtues while the selfish heart continues to serve sin and self. As children of God's family, we hold fast to Word and Sacrament that feeds and nourishes our souls.

We abide in Him and His Gospel. We do not mimic the world in its worldliness, but serve Christ and confess Him who in turn will confess us in eternity before His Father and give us a glory that is everlasting.

Prayer

Heavenly Father, gracious in Christ Jesus, keep us faithful amid the faithlessness of the world and the wickedness of sinful men. Grant that the allurements of the day and the enticements of sin do not draw us away from You and our Savior, Jesus Christ. Open our eyes to see the folly of unbelief and the emptiness of a life in which there is no hope. Abide with us "in cloud and sunshine," for Jesus' sake. Amen.

TREASURES OLD AND NEW

Matthew 13:44–52

PALESTINE has been invaded time and again. In the Esdraelon Valley, to the south of Nazareth, twenty decisive battles were fought through the centuries. On the rocky cliffs of the Dog River in Syria, there are more than twenty inscriptions, from the days of King Sargon of Babylon to the invasion of Allenby in World War I, telling of accomplishments and victories. Because the country was open to invasion from the north and the south, the people never felt secure. All their treasures must be portable. As they fled before an oncoming enemy, the people did two things with their treasures—they buried some of them and exchanged others for pearls. The pearls would pay for food and shelter while the people were in exile, and the buried treasures would take care of them upon their return.

Some refugees, however, never returned. Their treasures remained hidden until someone else stumbled upon them when digging a garden or plowing a field.

In the following parable, Jesus tells about a servant who finds treasure while working in the field. If he wants to claim it as his own, he must buy the land. Knowing the value of his find, he pools all he has and buys the farm. Everything else loses its value when compared to the treasure hidden in the ground.

In the other parable, Jesus has a merchant discover a pearl of unusual value, size, and beauty. He, too, gives up everything so he might have this one gem.

And this is the story of the Kingdom. It offers the one thing each one of us needs, the thing we ought to sacrifice everything for, if need be. We take none of our earthly possessions with us when death knocks at our door. But the Gospel gives us the glory of heaven.

As we believers go through each day, we may differ little from those around us. They may do the same kind of work, eat the same kind of food, have the same cultural environment, but in the end we all are separated into those who are Christ's and those who are not. Those who have spurned the pearl of the Gospel and turned aside to gather only earthly treasures will find themselves in outer darkness, eternally separated from God and the Lamb upon the throne. So says Jesus as He urges us to seek the goodly pearl and the priceless treasure.

The Parable of the Hidden Treasure

"The kingdom of heaven is like treasure hidden in a field, which a man found and covered up. Then in his joy he goes and sells all that he has and buys that field.

The Parable of the Pearl of Great Value

"Again, the kingdom of heaven is like a merchant in search of fine pearls, who, on finding one pearl of great value, went and sold all that he had and bought it.

The Parable of the Net

"Again, the kingdom of heaven is like a net that was thrown into the sea and gathered fish of every kind. When it was full, men drew it ashore and sat down and sorted the good into containers but threw away the bad. So it will be at the close of the age. The angels will come out and separate the evil from the righteous and throw them into the fiery furnace. In that place there will be weeping and gnashing of teeth.

New and Old Treasures

"Have you understood all these things?" They said to Him, "Yes." And He said to them, "Therefore every scribe who has been trained for the kingdom of heaven is like a master of a house, who brings out of his treasure what is new and what is old."

"Out of his treasure what is new and what is old." What can this treasure be? Nothing but the Gospel of reconciliation. It is as old as the hills, for it was first proclaimed to Adam and Eve in the garden (Genesis 3:15), and it is as new as the present day, for at this very moment our sins must be forgiven if we are to sleep in peace.

This old Gospel must be proclaimed with ever-renewing zeal, new approaches, fresh eagerness, and bold determination. No message is more essential, for no heart is more joyous than the one that has been cleansed from sin.

As long as the world stands, men and women will find in the treasure house of God's Word hope in the dark night of sorrow, comfort at the open grave, peace as the conscience accuses, and salvation as the doors of heaven open in the hour of death.

Those are wise, indeed, who amid all the uncertainties of the day hold fast to this one thing, the Gospel, that Christ died for us that we might be His own now and forevermore.

Prayer

Precious Savior, who has given us these eternal treasures of grace purchased with Your own blood, give us the necessary wisdom to choose this one thing, the Gospel of reconciliation and the strength to hold fast as Satan and the world try to take it from us. Continue Your presence in our midst, and bless our household with Your divine forgiveness and the peace that makes us heirs of Your Kingdom and children of our heavenly Father. Amen.

THE TRUTH ABOUT JESUS

Matthew 13:53–58

THE greatest person in history is Jesus of Nazareth. Yet not everyone accepts His claim that He is God. Many admit that He is a great teacher, an outstanding example of uprightness and nobility of character, the universal ideal of man. But after all, is He not a carpenter's son? Countless believers answer with us, "He is more than a carpenter's son." Would it make any difference to us if Jesus were only a man born of woman?

If only a carpenter's son, only a man, then Jesus could not have fulfilled the Law of God because He would also be a sinner, and His claim to be God would be a lie.

If only a carpenter's son, then Jesus could not have atoned for our disobedience and could not be the Lamb of God who takes away the sin of the world.

If only a carpenter's son, then you and I would not have a Savior who would make restitution for each transgression or go to eternal damnation for us. Nothing unclean will enter the Kingdom, and because we are born in sin our plight would be hopeless. There would be no forgiveness, no cleansing from sin, and no heaven if Jesus were only a carpenter's son.

Thank God and praise Him forever, Jesus is more than a carpenter. The Scriptures declare Him to be the Son of God, the only-begotten of the Father, very God of very God. Already in prophecy, we are told that a virgin will conceive and bear a Son and will name Him Immanuel, God with us. Then prophecy exclaims: "For to us a child is born, to us a son is given; and the government shall be upon His shoulder, and His name shall be called Wonderful Counselor, Mighty God, Everlasting Father, Prince of Peace" (Isaiah 9:6).

Jesus Himself claims to be this Messiah-God. "Before Abraham was, I am" (John 8:58). He is the Eternal One of the burning bush (Exodus 3). "I and the Father are one" (John 10:30). "Whoever has seen Me has seen the Father" (John 14:9).

But is this, perhaps, an empty, meaningless claim? No. "See My hands and My feet" (Luke 24:39). Here He is, risen from the dead. The grave and death could not hold Him. This Jesus, whom they crucified, has been raised up by God and acclaimed by Him to be the conqueror of Satan, deliverer of man, and eternal King of heaven. They broke the temple of His body, but Jesus raised it again on the third day.

He cannot merely be a carpenter's son. He is God and Lord and Savior. My problem of sin, then, is solved. I am justified by faith. My death is a sleep and my eternal home is in heaven—all because Jesus of Nazareth is more than a carpenter's son. This we must understand and believe, or we will be offended in Him.

Jesus Rejected at Nazareth

And when Jesus had finished these parables, He went away from there, and coming to His hometown He taught them in their synagogue, so that they were astonished, and said, "Where did this man get this wisdom and these mighty works? Is not this the carpenter's son? Is not His mother called Mary? And are not His brothers James and Joseph and Simon and Judas? And are not all His sisters with us? Where then did this man get all these things?" And they took offense at Him. But Jesus said to them, "A prophet is not without honor except in his hometown and in his own household." And He did not do many mighty works there, because of their unbelief.

This Jesus of Nazareth is undeniable. Yet unbelief will not accept His claim. Human nature does not want to grovel in dust and ashes and plead, "God, be merciful to me, a sinner." Man's pride turns away and will not accept mercy and be saved by grace.

That is the curse of unbelief. It spurns the love of Christ, the greatest love in the world. It closes the door of salvation upon itself and sends man to eternal damnation. For "whoever does not believe will be condemned" (Mark 16:16).

But can we be sure that Jesus has saved us? The risen Christ and the empty tomb proclaim aloud that Jesus has redeemed us, and whosoever accepts this Christ and His atoning blood, shed on Calvary, will not perish, but have everlasting life. Jesus is inescapable.

What is Jesus to us? If He is only a carpenter's son, then we have no Gospel and no hope of salvation. But if He is our Lord and God, our Savior and Redeemer, then we need not be afraid of anything in life and in death, for heaven is our home.

Prayer

Jesus, lover of my soul, let me come to Your sacred wounds and find healing. I have nothing to offer but my unworthiness. I come just as I am, clinging to Your atoning cross. There is no other refuge, no other Savior, and no other salvation. Preserve me in Your grace and keep me steadfast in faith until I see You in glory as the Lord of heaven and eternity and praise You as my Savior and Redeemer. Amen.

38

THE TANGLED WEB OF SIN
Matthew 14:1–14

IF it were done when 'tis done, then 'twere well It were done quickly" (Macbeth, act 1, scene 7). But there's the rub. Sin is not done only when the dastardly act of transgression is committed. Herod found that out. The "ghost" of John the Baptist, whom he had slain, rises in his dreams as well as in his waking hours. As soon as Herod hears of the mighty works and forceful preaching of Jesus, his conscience arises to strike him. "This is John the Baptist. He has been raised from the dead." He has come back to torment Herod and curse him.

That is always the way of sin. At the most unexpected moment, sin leaps back into remembrance to say, "You are guilty and vengeance will have you." Sin gets us into deep waters and finally drowns us in the slough of despondency and despair—unless Jesus comes to our rescue.

Herod had become infatuated with his brother's wife. He was determined to have her, although the Law of God said otherwise. John, therefore, told the king that he was living in sin. That irritated Herod. Such preaching did not please him or his wife. "John will not say such things to us and get away with it," Herodias likely said to herself, and before long the opportunity came and she got the head of John. She had taken revenge.

So goes the account in Matthew's Gospel:

The Death of John the Baptist

At that time Herod the tetrarch heard about the fame of Jesus, and he said to his servants, "This is John the Baptist. He has been raised from the dead; that is why these miraculous powers are at work in him." For Herod had seized John and bound him and put him in prison for the sake of Herodias, his brother Philip's wife, because John had been saying to him, "It is not lawful for you to have her." And though he wanted to put him to death, he feared the people, because they held him to be a prophet. But when Herod's birthday came, the daughter of Herodias danced before the company and pleased Herod, so that he promised with an oath to give her whatever she might ask. Prompted by her mother, she said, "Give me the head of John the Baptist here on a platter." And the king was sorry, but because of his oaths and his guests he commanded it to be given. He sent and had John beheaded in the prison, and his head was brought on a platter and given to the girl, and she brought it to her mother. And his disciples came and took the body and buried it, and they went and told Jesus.

Jesus Feeds the Five Thousand

Now when Jesus heard this, He withdrew from there in a boat to a desolate place by Himself. But when the crowds heard it, they followed Him on foot from the towns. When He went ashore He saw a great crowd, and He had compassion on them and healed their sick.

Herod had John beheaded because he feared the ridicule of his subjects more than he feared God. To have them laughingly say that he was not a man of his word would never do. So Herod commits the dastardly crime and adds more sin to his sinful record.

How easily is set the trap that drags us down into the depths of transgressions. We go out with a group of friends whose company we enjoy and whose conduct has been fairly harmless. Then one day someone suggests something we do not approve of. Our conscience says that it is sin, but we don't have the courage to stand apart and say no. The crowd will laugh, sneer, call us goody-goody, shun us in the future. Rather than have that happen, we put our conscience on hold and go the way of the transgressors. Before long, God has been put out of our life, and we go on to death and damnation.

Herod could not sleep with his troubled conscience. Neither can we. But Jesus is still the compassionate and forgiving Savior, who never casts out any who come seeking mercy and pardon.

Prayer

Morning, noon, and night we seek You, O God, for we sin daily and need help and healing that only You can give. Your loving-kindness reaches into our sinful hearts, cleanses us, and brings peace to our troubled souls. We rejoice in You, who abundantly pardons us in Christ Jesus. Let us always find refuge in You, that sin and Satan may have no power over us. In Jesus' name we plead. Amen.

THE OVERFLOW OF GOD'S GOODNESS
Matthew 14:15–21

ORDINARILY we need more than five small loaves to feed five thousand men. But Jesus touches the bread in the wilderness with His almighty hand, and it increases and piles up until all are fed. Jesus feeds the multitudes by a miracle.

God still multiplies bread. We plant a single kernel of wheat into the ground, and it produces fifty to a hundredfold. That, too, is a miracle of God.

To this day, we are fed out of the abundant goodness of God. Each day, God provides sufficient bread to satisfy the world's hunger. If anyone goes hungry, God cannot be blamed. The greed and selfishness of man withholds and destroys the bread that God so richly provides.

God gives for today. He challenges us to live trustingly from day to day. There is enough bread to spare. At times, we think otherwise because we see our refrigerators empty. But wait, God opens His hands and at His appointed time supplies all our needs. This is the lesson Jesus taught in the wilderness.

> Now when it was evening, the disciples came to Him and said, "This is a desolate place, and the day is now over; send the crowds away to go into the villages and buy food for themselves." But Jesus said, "They need not go away; you give them something to eat." They said to Him, "We have only five loaves here and two fish." And He said, "Bring them here to Me." Then He ordered the crowds to sit down on the grass, and taking the five loaves and the two fish, He looked up to heaven and said a blessing. Then He broke the loaves and gave them to the disciples, and the disciples gave them to the crowds. And they all ate and were satisfied. And they took up twelve baskets full of

the broken pieces left over. And those who ate were about five thousand men, besides women and children.

Most of the time, God gives us more than we need for today. He pours out upon us in greater abundance than we can use at the present hour. What should we then do, if we have more than we can use? Gather the fragments. We are stewards of our earthly possessions, and we dare not squander or waste them. We are to use our supplies wisely. We are not to forget to break our bread with the needy and to use our possessions to build the Kingdom.

A twofold precept is laid down in Scripture concerning our daily bread: If God gives us only enough for today, then we are to eat it with thanksgiving and trust, certain that He will again open His storehouses tomorrow. If God gives us more than we possibly can use, then we are to gather this abundance and use it to His glory and the well-being of our fellow men. If we do that, we will find great joy from our daily living.

Prayer

With grateful hearts, we come to Your throne of grace, O Lord, recognizing Your goodness and abundant mercy. You have opened Your hands to supply our needs for this day and have given us also the heavenly manna—the Gospel—to nourish our souls and preserve us in faith. Accept our praise and thanks arising from our appreciative hearts, which You have cleansed from all sin through Christ's most precious blood. Amen.

THE CHALLENGE TO LIVE TRUSTINGLY
Matthew 14:22–36

THE peaceful little Sea of Galilee can become very turbulent. Small boats are tossed helplessly across the waves and often are upset. Fishermen are always prepared for a plunge and make ready to face a sudden gust of wind that turns the sea into a boiling caldron.

That is a parable of life. Suddenly, out of the blue sky, comes a storm that threatens to wreak destruction and death. Then comes Jesus into our day with His outstretched hands of mercy, and once again we find hope in His promises and strength in His Word.

These adverse winds vary. At times, they come in the form of doubt. We question the mercies of God. Some forgotten sin comes to our remembrance and greatly distresses us. We ask, *Can God love me?*

Or sickness and death cross the threshold of our home. Or misfortune and trouble take from us our long-cherished possessions. Frustration, disappointment, and failure make the future look black and dismal.

Unless Jesus comes into the dark nights of life with His good cheer, life ebbs out into bitterness, hopelessness, and despair. Jesus removes fear, uncertainty, and anxiety, and in the end brings peace and heaven. No matter what storms arise, Jesus pilots us to safety through each of them and at last brings us to the haven of eternal security.

Jesus Walks on the Water

Immediately He made the disciples get into the boat and go before Him to the other side, while He dismissed the crowds. And after He had dismissed the crowds, He went up on the mountain by Himself to pray. When evening came, He was there alone, but the boat by this time was a long way from the land, beaten by the waves, for the wind was against them. And in the fourth watch of the night He came to them, walking on the sea. But when the disciples saw Him walking on the sea, they were terrified, and said, "It is a ghost!" and they cried out in fear. But immediately Jesus spoke to them, saying, "Take heart; it is I. Do not be afraid."

And Peter answered Him, "Lord, if it is You, command me to come to You on the water." He said, "Come." So Peter got out of the boat and walked on the water and came to Jesus. But when he saw the wind, he was afraid, and beginning to sink he cried out, "Lord, save me." Jesus immediately reached out His hand and took hold of him, saying to him, "O you of little faith, why did you doubt?" And when they got into the boat, the wind ceased. And those in the boat worshiped Him, saying, "Truly You are the Son of God."

Jesus Heals the Sick in Gennesaret

And when they had crossed over, they came to land at Gennesaret. And when the men of that place recognized Him, they sent around to all that region and brought to Him all who were sick and implored Him that they might only touch the fringe of His garment. And as many as touched it were made well.

"Take heart," says Jesus. The darkest night is less lonely and less empty with the Savior at our side. Under us, holding us up, are His everlasting arms. We need not face a single issue of life alone. With every problem, we can come to Him and know that He has salvation. That, indeed, is encouraging.

"Take heart," said Jesus to the man who was paralyzed (Matthew 9:1–8). "Your sins are forgiven." Therefore, good cheer filled his day. The feeling of guilt takes the joy out of life. Do we realize this? The forgiven soul has been released from the bondage of sin. This fills the heart with an unspeakable blessedness. Christian people are joy-filled people.

"Take heart," said Jesus to His disciples on the way to the garden where He was betrayed (John 16:33). "I have overcome the world." Wickedness, injustice, cruelty, dishonesty, hatred, and deception seem to take over things and control all the important positions of life. We Christians often feel as though we are fighting a losing battle with sin, error, and unbelief. But in the darkest hour, Jesus is here to help, to save and to cheer. By His grace and in His strength, we can face even death and smile, "for You are with me; Your rod and Your staff, they comfort me" (Psalm 23:4).

Prayer

Jesus, gracious Savior, take me by the hand today and lead me through each perplexing and troubling hour. Without You I sink, I faint, I fall. Help me. Give me a greater faith, a larger hope, and an abiding sense of security. Grant that Your promises fill my heart and mind with a blessed cheerfulness and undying courage that leans on You, the rock. Amen. Hear my cry, Lord Jesus. Amen.

SUBSTITUTES WILL NOT DO

Matthew 15:1–20

FROM the beginning of time, man has sought to substitute his own natural religion for the revelations of God. These self-appointed traditions always make man's salvation an accomplishment of his own hands and virtues. Man does not want to admit that he cannot save his own soul.

One of the characteristics of these self-appointed ways shows itself in the substituting of lesser and easier tasks that can be done with propriety and decency. The Savior gives us an interesting illustration.

Some sons neglect to respect their parents; they treat them unkindly and shabbily, and then they absolve themselves by making a gift of some kind to the church. So they do the one duty but neglect the other that has been definitely prescribed by God in the Law. You cannot excuse yourself from helping the man who lies half dead on the road by saying you must be at the temple. You must do the one and not leave the other undone.

Another characteristic of these self-appointed ways is observed in the substituting of mechanical adoration for a sincere and honest worship of God. We can say, "Lord, Lord," and yet be miles away in our thoughts. We can offer perfunctory participation in rituals and rites, and yet allow our whole life to be a glaring contradiction to all we profess. Man by nature always prefers outward observances of rituals to a genuine worship of the heart. We can do many things by rote without having any love within us.

Such self-appointed homage to God merits nothing; least of all does it make us acceptable to the Lord of heaven and earth. Cain learned this to his own sorrow. Through Samuel, God reminded King Saul of this: "To obey is better than sacrifice" (1 Samuel 15:22). Self-appointed works and man-made devices of worship cannot satisfy God or save the soul. This truth Jesus stresses as He meets the objections of the Pharisees and scribes.

Traditions and Commandments

Then Pharisees and scribes came to Jesus from Jerusalem and said, "Why do Your disciples break the tradition of the elders? For they do not wash their hands when they eat." He answered them, "And why do you break the commandment of God for the sake of your tradition? For God commanded, 'Honor your father and your mother,' and, 'Whoever reviles father or mother must surely die.' But you say, 'If anyone tells his father or his mother, "What you would have gained from me is given to God," he need not honor his father.' So for the sake of your tradition you have made void the word of God. You hypocrites! Well did Isaiah prophesy of you, when he said:

> " 'This people honors Me with their lips,
>   but their heart is far from Me;
> in vain do they worship Me,
>   teaching as doctrines the commandments of men.' "

What Defiles a Person

And He called the people to Him and said to them, "Hear and understand: it is not what goes into the mouth that defiles a person, but what comes out of the mouth; this defiles a person." Then the disciples came and said to Him, "Do you know that the Pharisees were offended when they heard this saying?" He answered, "Every plant that My heavenly Father has not planted will be rooted up. Let them alone; they are blind guides. And if the blind lead the blind, both will fall into a pit." But Peter said to Him, "Explain the parable to us." And He said, "Are you also still without understanding? Do you not see that whatever goes into the mouth passes into the stomach and is expelled? But what comes out of the mouth proceeds from the heart, and this defiles a person. For out of the heart come evil thoughts, murder, adultery, sexual immorality, theft, false witness, slander. These are what defile a person. But to eat with unwashed hands does not defile anyone."

If all that comes out of the heart is sinful, if hearts are unclean and by nature evil, how, then, will man find peace? If nothing that man does in his own strength and through his natural ability can satisfy God, how, then, will he be reconciled to his Maker?

God reveals the way. Christ became flesh and was made under the Law to fulfill the Law for us. But that is not all, nor is that enough. God laid on Christ the sins of the world. This made Jesus the greatest of sinners, and God treated Him as such and penalized Him when He forsook Him on the cross. By that death, Jesus atoned for the sin of all mankind. The guilty are redeemed and justified by faith. The sinlessness of Jesus is credited to the transgressor who comes to the cross. Only this substitutionary death of Jesus can set us free. This is the one substitution that has merit. His blood makes the foulest clean. And faith, created by the Holy Spirit, puts us under the cross. As God beholds us through this Jesus-cross, we look pure and clean and righteous because Christ's righteousness covers us.

This righteousness does not merely cover us; it transforms us. By faith we are made into new creatures who out of a purified heart bring forth the fruit of Christian living and service acceptable to our reconciled Father.

Prayer

Divine Lord, send Your Holy Spirit anew into our hearts and cleanse us from all sin so we may adore and worship You in spirit and in truth. Create in us a greater love for Your Word and a keener desire to serve You and our fellow men. Remove all malice, bitterness, and resentment from our minds, and fill us with Your abundant grace. In Christ Jesus, our Savior and Friend. Amen.

BUILDING A GREATER FAITH
Matthew 15:21–31

WHEN we talk about trouble, we are speaking a universal language. We all face suffering, go through pain, and by the goodness of God, survive most of the time. We have our troubles and disappointments, and after that life is never the same.

Some people have a greater staying power when misfortunes strike then than others. Although trials, troubles, and tribulations pile up like the winter snows, they sing. Their suffering grows them into heroes of faith. The Canaanite woman was one such as these.

The faith that wins must face the test of adversity. This woman of Canaan did. Her daughter was grievously vexed with a demon.

The mother could not get away from her misfortune. Such an ordeal she could not face alone indefinitely. She must get help. To obtain relief, she needed a faith that could give her the courage to go to Jesus. To go to the Prophet of Israel was not easy to do. She was a Gentile and a stranger. But faith won out. She went.

The faith that wins must face the test of silence. Jesus did not say a word to her; He paid no attention to her. But His silence was the silence of love. And faith that wins will not take silence for an answer. God had promised, and He has the power to fulfill the promises He makes. This the woman believed. She saw in Jesus a greater man than Elijah and John the Baptist. To her He was God.

The faith that wins must face the test of patience and delay. The woman came and found no enthusiastic reception. The disciples were irritated, and Jesus paid no attention to her. No help seemed to be in sight. However, the persistent woman won out.

The faith that wins must even face the test of rebuke. Jesus compares her to dogs. He reminds her of her past. Even that does not drive her away. Dogs get the crumbs. She, too, is entitled to that consideration.

So faith wins. Christ does not let her down. He tests her and develops a heroic faith in her that sends her on her way a perpetual example to all of us who are tempted to become impatient and discouraged because our burdens and troubles are not lifted at our first cry.

With these thoughts in mind, we can read the woman's story with greater appreciation.

The Faith of a Canaanite Woman

And Jesus went away from there and withdrew to the district of Tyre and Sidon. And behold, a Canaanite woman from that region came out and was crying, "Have mercy on me, O Lord, Son of David; my daughter is severely oppressed by a demon." But He did not answer her a word. And His disciples came and begged Him, saying, "Send her away, for she is crying out after us." He answered, "I was sent only to the lost sheep of the house of Israel." But she came and knelt before

Him, saying, "Lord, help me." And He answered, "It is not right to take the children's bread and throw it to the dogs." She said, "Yes, Lord, yet even the dogs eat the crumbs that fall from their masters' table." Then Jesus answered her, "O woman, great is your faith! Be it done for you as you desire." And her daughter was healed instantly.

Jesus Heals Many

Jesus went on from there and walked beside the Sea of Galilee. And He went up on the mountain and sat down there. And great crowds came to Him, bringing with them the lame, the blind, the crippled, the mute, and many others, and they put them at His feet, and He healed them, so that the crowd wondered, when they saw the mute speaking, the crippled healthy, the lame walking, and the blind seeing. And they glorified the God of Israel.

Suffering is universal. However, all our suffering can be lightened and made easier if we come to the Great Physician who never fails us. Our case is never hopeless. But we must not become impatient with Him! How patient He has been with us!

God sends us through the clinic of suffering, where pain is often acute. But by His grace we come through it as heroes of faith who can face every ordeal of life with greater confidence and with a greater courage. "I can do all things through Him who strengthens me" (Philippians 4:13).

Prayer

Jesus, full of compassion and tender mercies, look upon our distress and also the affliction of multitudes, and touch them with Your healing hand. Many are weary of the struggle, discouraged by the outcome, footsore and heartsick. Draw nigh to them, and bless them with Your forgiving peace. Ease their suffering, and put their minds at ease. Give and preserve in them an unconquerable faith unto the end of days. Hear us, gracious Friend and Lord. Amen.

ASHES FOR BREAD

Matthew 15:32–39; 16:1–12

JESUS loved people. He witnessed their struggles for existence and, with a sympathetic touch, healed them and helped them. He saw the spiritual plight of many who were steeped in vain traditions and cunning superstitions, and He was distressed and grieved. He not only fed the multitudes with bread and fish but also warned them against the poisoned bread that destroys immortal souls. Religious leaders were misleading them. The Pharisees were entangling them in formalism and ritual. And the Sadducees, through their laxity and indifference, led them astray in doctrine. The Sadducees even went so far as to deny the resurrection. They were giving the people ashes for bread.

A twofold danger threatened them: worrying about physical food to sustain their body and becoming indifferent to the truth and giving way to false doctrine, which would rob them of faith and destroy their soul. Jesus does not merely warn them; as the sympathetic Savior, He offers help that provides bread for the body and manna for the salvation of the soul.

That's why He fed the multitudes with bread and taught them all things about His Father.

Jesus Feeds the Four Thousand

Then Jesus called His disciples to Him and said, "I have compassion on the crowd because they have been with Me now three days and have nothing to eat. And I am unwilling to send them away hungry, lest they faint on the way." And the disciples said to Him, "Where are we to get enough bread in such a desolate place to feed so great a crowd?" And Jesus said to them, "How many loaves do you have?" They said, "Seven, and a few small fish." And directing the crowd to sit down on the ground, He took the seven loaves and the fish, and having given thanks He broke them and gave them to the disciples, and the disciples gave them to the crowds. And they all ate and were satisfied. And they took up seven baskets full of the broken pieces left over. Those who ate were four thousand men, besides women and children. And after sending away the crowds, He got into the boat and went to the region of Magadan.

The Pharisees and Sadducees Demand Signs

And the Pharisees and Sadducees came, and to test Him they asked Him to show them a sign from heaven. He answered them, "When it is evening, you say, 'It will be fair weather, for the sky is red.' And in the morning, 'It will be stormy today, for the sky is red and threatening.' You know how to interpret the appearance of the sky, but you cannot interpret the signs of the times. An evil and adulterous generation seeks for a sign, but no sign will be given to it except the sign of Jonah." So He left them and departed.

The Leaven of the Pharisees and Sadducees

When the disciples reached the other side, they had forgotten to bring any bread. Jesus said to them, "Watch and beware of the leaven of the Pharisees and Sadducees." And they began discussing it among themselves, saying, "We brought no bread." But Jesus, aware of this, said, "O you of little faith, why are you discussing among yourselves the fact that you have no bread? Do you not yet perceive? Do you not remember the five loaves for the five thousand, and how many baskets you gathered? Or the seven loaves for the four thousand, and how many baskets you gathered? How is it that you fail to understand that I did not speak about bread? Beware of the leaven of the Pharisees and Sadducees." Then they understood that He did not tell them to beware of the leaven of bread, but of the teaching of the Pharisees and Sadducees.

The Pharisees and Sadducees were sticklers for outward observances and forms. Not only that, they were tricky, cunning, and deceitful. They never ignored an opportunity to undermine and discredit the works and words of Jesus. They did not want to accept Him as the promised Savior; nor were they pleased to see the multitudes follow Him because He would not follow their way or comply with all their wishes.

On this occasion, when Jesus had fed the multitude in the wilderness, His enemies demanded a greater sign that would prove His Messiahship. And Jesus complied: the sign would be the sign of Jonah. As Jonah was in the belly of the fish and emerged alive after three days (Jonah 1–2), so Jesus would go into death and rise again on the third day. Jesus' resurrection was to be the one miracle that would prove for all time that He is God, the promised Messiah, and the Savior of the world.

Jesus died. And on the third day He did rise. The tomb was empty, and He was alive.

What further proof do we need?

Prayer

Gracious Savior and Friend, lift us to You and keep us in Your grace. Protect us from hunger and want, and shield us from the cunning of Satan, sin, and the deceitfulness of error and unbelief. Feed all Your children with the manna from heaven, and the Gospel of reconciliation, and satisfy the needs of every living thing with daily bread. Accept our hymns of praise for all You have given us to sustain this life. Hear our psalms of thanksgiving as we receive abundant pardon from all sins and transgressions. Continue to abide with us in this household, and bless us with Your gracious benediction. Amen.

THE MUCH-DISPUTED PASSAGE

Matthew 16:13–23

ON this rock I will build My church." Which rock? The Roman Catholic Church believes that the rock is Simon Peter and that the Church is built upon him and his direct successors, the popes of Rome; that the papacy has been established to represent Christ on earth, to speak for Christ, and to proclaim the truths given by God; and that the pope makes infallible utterances that must be accepted by the Christian people as revelations of God.

Protestant scholars do not agree with this interpretation. The Greek text plainly shows that Jesus did not intend to build the Church upon Peter and the papacy. Jesus said, You are *petros* [masculine form], and on this *petra* [feminine form] I will build My Church. Jesus here uses a play on words that cannot be reproduced in English with the same word, *rock*. However, it can be accurately illustrated with the word *confession* in this way: "You are a confessionalist, and on this *confession* I will build My Church."

What confession? The one Peter made: "You are the Christ, the Son of the living God."

This puts Christ Jesus in the center. On Him the Church is built. That is why Paul says to the Corinthian Christians: "For no one can lay a foundation other than that which is laid, which is Jesus Christ" (1 Corinthians 3:11). Again, "the household of God, built on the foundation of the apostles and prophets, Christ Jesus Himself being the cornerstone" (Ephesians 2:19–20). As long as the Church adheres to this truth and makes Christ its foundation, head, and founder, the gates of hell cannot prevail.

That makes sense and is in full harmony with the rest of the Scripture. Even Simon Peter understood the words of Jesus to mean that the Church was built upon Christ, for he says in his Epistle, quoting Isaiah: "Behold, I am laying in Zion a stone, a cornerstone chosen and precious, and whoever believes in Him will not be put to shame" (1 Peter 2:6).

We still confess that the Church has no other head than Jesus Christ Himself.

Peter Confesses Jesus as the Christ

Now when Jesus came into the district of Caesarea Philippi, He asked His disciples, "Who do people say that the Son of Man is?" And they said, "Some say John the Baptist, others say Elijah, and others Jeremiah or one of the prophets." He said to them, "But who do you say that I am?" Simon Peter replied, "You are the Christ, the Son of the living God." And Jesus answered him, "Blessed are you, Simon Bar-Jonah! For flesh and blood has not revealed this to you, but My Father who is in heaven. And I tell you, you are Peter, and on this rock I will build My church, and the gates of hell shall not prevail against it. I will give you the keys of the kingdom of heaven, and whatever you bind on earth shall be bound in heaven, and whatever you loose on earth shall be loosed in heaven." Then He strictly charged the disciples to tell no one that He was the Christ.

Jesus Foretells His Death and Resurrection

From that time Jesus began to show His disciples that He must go to Jerusalem and suffer many things from the elders and chief priests and scribes, and be killed, and on the third day be raised. And Peter took Him aside and began to rebuke Him, saying, "Far be it from You, Lord! This shall never happen to You." But He turned and said to Peter, "Get behind Me, Satan! You are a hindrance to Me. For you are not setting your mind on the things of God, but on the things of man."

What do *you* think of Christ? We can make no improvement on the answers given by Simon Peter or by Luther in his explanation of the Second Article of the Apostles' Creed in the Small Catechism:

"I believe that Jesus Christ, true God, begotten of the Father from eternity, and also true man, born of the Virgin Mary, is my Lord, who has redeemed me, a lost and condemned person, purchased and won me from all sins, from death, and from the power of the devil; not with gold or silver, but with His holy, precious blood and with His innocent suffering and death, that I may be His own and live under Him in His kingdom and serve Him in everlasting righteousness, innocence, and blessedness, just as He is risen from the dead, lives and reigns to all eternity. This is most certainly true."

This Jesus, the head of the Church, gave His life as a ransom for all, and our response is to teach, preach, and believe. If anyone comes with any other doctrine or claim than this—that Jesus sacrificed Himself for us and shed His blood for our redemption—we must say, "Get behind me, Satan, because such teachings do not come from God."

Prayer

Lord Jesus, founder and foundation of the New Testament Church, grant that we do not turn aside from this glorious and comforting truth that You are the head of the Church and have given us Your Gospel to lead us to Your eternal throne. Grant us the grace to abide in You and Your Word and to not turn away from that narrow way that leads to glory. Give us faithful pastors and loyal members who confess with us at all times that You are the Christ, the only-begotten Son of God, our Savior, our Friend, and our Lord. Amen.

THE WORTH OF THE SOUL
Matthew 16:24–28

NO ONE, not even Solomon, John D. Rockefeller, or Bill Gates, has gained the whole world. Very few have accumulated as much as these men have amassed, yet millions have lost their soul for far less. Thousands have sold their soul to Satan for the smile of popularity, for the glitter of gold, or for a night of revelry. They have gambled away an eternity of glory for a moment's satisfaction. It is human nature to want just a little more than we have. But when the goal is obtained, we reach out again because we did not find the pot of gold at the end of the rainbow.

As Jesus sees this covetous desire for riches, He declares that man gains nothing, no matter how much he piles up, if he loses his soul's salvation. After all, money can buy very little that makes for happiness, and finally death shakes all our earthly possessions out of our trembling hands. No amount of money can buy the way into heaven, no matter what you are willing to pay in the end. It will not be enough. If you want to save yourself by merit, you must fulfill the Law of God, that is, live in perfect holiness, a life in which there is no sin. This is not possible, for we are born of sinful flesh.

But the soul is the most precious part of us, for it is our immortal self. If this is lost, everything is lost. This soul can miss heaven's door through unbelief. It can be sold to Satan for the pleasures of life and the riches of the world. But man gains nothing, for that stuff called gold has no value in the court of God.

How much must we have to be rich? Only what we need for today plus the peace of God in our hearts. Realizing this, we have better understanding of Jesus' significant words spoken to His disciples in the reading for today and to His followers of all times.

Take Up Your Cross and Follow Jesus

Then Jesus told His disciples, "If anyone would come after Me, let him deny himself and take up his cross and follow Me. For whoever would save his life will lose it, but whoever loses his life for My sake will find it. For what will it profit a man if he gains the whole world and forfeits his soul? Or what shall a man give in return for his soul? For the Son of Man is going to come with His angels in the glory of His Father, and then He will repay each person according to what he has done. Truly, I say to you, there are some standing here who will not taste death until they see the Son of Man coming in His kingdom."

Jesus urges us to follow Him, but He does not promise immunity from trouble, sickness, or death. To follow Him, we must take up the cross, crucify our sinful desires, deny and curb our unholy passions, and do without things for which the world craves and slaves.

However, for those who hear His voice and follow Him, Jesus leads to everlasting glory. They cannot perish. When He comes in death or at the end of time, His own, the sheep, enter into His presence, where there is no want, no crying, no dying, only completeness of joy that has no end.

Prayer

You are the shepherd of our souls, Lord Jesus, and have purchased us with Your own blood, that the riches of eternity may be ours. Open our eyes to see the folly of chasing the fleeting rainbows of pleasure and the elusive enjoyment of wealth. Grant us the grace to use these earthly possessions to serve You and our fellow men. Let not the corruptible things enslave our soul and rob us of our salvation. Take us by the hand, precious Redeemer, and guide us along the narrow way to glory. Amen.

THE OVER-SHADOWING CLOUD
Matthew 17:1–21

PETER, James, and John get a glimpse of heaven on the Mount of Transfiguration. Jesus is on His way to Jerusalem to face His deepest humiliation—His death on the cross. Before that eventful hour comes, God reveals to these disciples that this Jesus is still His beloved Son. Christ was completing His prophetic work, and He performed His task to the full satisfaction of God. The Father is still pleased with His Son.

As Jesus enters the final stage of His prophetic mission and now, as High Priest, prepares to offer Himself as the Lamb of God, Moses and Elijah talk with Him of His great task—the redemption of a sinful world. All mankind has broken the Law given to Moses and has not heeded the call to repentance urged by Elijah. Moses' Law and Elijah's denunciation of sin could not save the world from its ruin.

But just as the three disciples exalt at the glory they behold, a cloud overshadows all. Significant in this sudden change that captivates our thoughts is the fact that Jesus remains. He is still with them as Peter, James, and John return to the colorless, disappointing, and frustrated life of that day.

That is true to this day. Amid all the changes of our hectic existence, Jesus remains the same yesterday, today, and forever. This comforting message comes to us from the transfiguration.

The Transfiguration

And after six days Jesus took with Him Peter and James, and John his brother, and led them up a high mountain by themselves. And He was transfigured before them, and His face shone like the sun, and His clothes became white as light. And behold, there appeared to them Moses and Elijah, talking with

Him. And Peter said to Jesus, "Lord, it is good that we are here. If You wish, I will make three tents here, one for You and one for Moses and one for Elijah." He was still speaking when, behold, a bright cloud overshadowed them, and a voice from the cloud said, "This is My beloved Son, with whom I am well pleased; listen to Him." When the disciples heard this, they fell on their faces and were terrified. But Jesus came and touched them, saying, "Rise, and have no fear." And when they lifted up their eyes, they saw no one but Jesus only.

And as they were coming down the mountain, Jesus commanded them, "Tell no one the vision, until the Son of Man is raised from the dead." And the disciples asked Him, "Then why do the scribes say that first Elijah must come?" He answered, "Elijah does come, and he will restore all things. But I tell you that Elijah has already come, and they did not recognize him, but did to him whatever they pleased. So also the Son of Man will certainly suffer at their hands." Then the disciples understood that He was speaking to them of John the Baptist.

Jesus Heals a Boy with a Demon

And when they came to the crowd, a man came up to Him and, kneeling before Him, said, "Lord, have mercy on my son, for he is an epileptic and he suffers terribly. For often he falls into the fire, and often into the water. And I brought him to Your disciples, and they could not heal him." And Jesus answered, "O faithless and twisted generation, how long am I to be with you? How long am I to bear with you? Bring him here to Me." And Jesus rebuked the demon, and it came out of him, and the boy was healed instantly. Then the disciples came to Jesus privately and said, "Why could we not cast it out?" He said to them, "Because of your little faith. For truly, I say to you, if you have faith like a grain of mustard seed, you will say to this mountain, 'Move from here to there,' and it will move, and nothing will be impossible for you."

From this heavenly majesty of the glorious transfiguration, Jesus and His disciples descend into the abject misery of life's bitterness and see a child terribly afflicted. It is always that way in this life. Joy and sorrow, laughter and tears, comprise our day. On the magnificent cathedrals of Europe are ugly gargoyles. Their hideousness emphasizes the elegant beauty of the carvings. If the sun would shine continually, all the world would be a desert. If it would rain continually, then all the world would be a swamp. God gives sunshine and rain, each in its appointed time. As a result, we have a beautiful world of trees and flowers. If we had only joy, we would forget God; but if we had only sorrow, we would despair. Life holds both, and God's mercy keeps us balanced and steadfast in faith.

Prayer

Your loving-kindness, O God, enables us to see through the sorrows and tears of life Your hand of goodness and heart of compassion. Draw us to You, and lead us to the cross of Calvary when we question Your mercies and doubt Your love. Forgive us our rebellious thoughts, and grow in us a greater faith and a surer hope by the power of Your Spirit, through Jesus Christ, our Redeemer. Amen.

UNDER TWO FLAGS
Matthew 17:22–27

JESUS was a law-abiding citizen who observed all regulations of the government and met every stipulated obligation of the state. In this He also fulfilled the Commandments. Although injustice and sin boldly lifted their heads, Jesus never lost His balance. Although the demands may not be equitable, Jesus suffered all things done to Him without protest or rebellion. He adjusted Himself to every situation without complaint. When He, the Lord of heaven and earth, was asked to pay His personal taxes, He complied. Although it was taxation without representation, Jesus had Simon Peter pay the required sum without protest.

The Christian is in the world but not of the world. However, if the laws are not in direct opposition to God's divine command, although they may be unreasonable and unfair, the Christian obeys them and does what is asked of him. Jesus urges us to do this, just like He requested Simon Peter to go down to the sea and open the mouth of a fish where there would be a coin that would pay their taxes.

Jesus Again Foretells Death, Resurrection

As they were gathering in Galilee, Jesus said to them, "The Son of Man is about to be delivered into the hands of men, and they will kill Him, and He will be raised on the third day." And they were greatly distressed.

The Temple Tax

When they came to Capernaum, the collectors of the two-drachma tax went up to Peter and said, "Does your teacher not pay the tax?" He said, "Yes." And when he came into the house, Jesus spoke to him first, saying, "What do you think, Simon? From whom do kings of the earth take toll or tax? From their sons or from others?" And when he said, "From others," Jesus said to him, "Then the sons are free. However, not to give offense to them, go to the sea and cast a hook and take the first fish that comes up, and when you open its mouth you will find a shekel. Take that and give it to them for Me and for yourself."

Jesus had more important things to think about than taxes and money. He came to seek and to save the lost. The hour had come—the hour of betrayal, of an unjust trial, of a cruel crucifixion. But in the mind of Jesus there never was, not even for a moment, any doubt as to the outcome of this conflict.

Victory day was a certainty. Death and the grave could not hold Him. The sign of Jonah would be fulfilled; the third day after His crucifixion and death, He would rise again.

With the same confidence and conviction, we can go onward and forward in life. Misfortunes may be piled high, yet as Christians we are certain of the ultimate victory over death and the grave. Although an army surround us and take all that we have, even our very life, nothing can pluck us out of our Father's hand or take from us the glories of heaven. That is enough to know in this world of sorrow and tears.

Therefore, with confident hope we say: I believe in the resurrection of the body and the life everlasting. Amen. It is so. Amen.

Prayer

Lord, You have placed us into the world to be witnesses of Your grace. But we are not to be of the world or walk in the sinfulness of wicked man. Watch over us and guard us from temptation and unbelief. Daily give us the grace to walk in Your Law and to be an example to the community. Protect Your Church, and guide and give wisdom to the authorities in our government, for Jesus' sake. Amen.

THE CHILD IN OUR MIDST
Matthew 18:1–14

JESUS was greatly concerned with children. They, too, have been redeemed with His own precious blood. What an empty world it would be if the children were not in it with their laughter and with their play! Jesus puts the little ones into our midst to teach us important object lessons.

Like the child, we should be trusting. The child believes its mother; it is enough that she has said so. We should have this same childlike faith in God, our eternal caretaker, and in Jesus Christ, our

Savior from sin. No matter how little we have for the moment, we should believe that God provides because He has said so. No matter what sins we have done, we should believe that Jesus' blood blots them out. He has said so.

Like a child, we should be joyous. The child is happy because he knows he is loved. God loves us. His love is greater and deeper than a mother's love. He says so. "Can a woman forget her nursing child, that she should have no compassion on the son of her womb? Even these may forget, yet I will not forget you" (Isaiah 49:15).

Like a child, we should be carefree. The boy at school does not fret all through the morning wondering whether he will get something to eat that night. He may not know what will be on the table, but he knows his mother will have something. We, too, are children in the school of life and have a heavenly Father who provides.

Who Is the Greatest?

At that time the disciples came to Jesus, saying, "Who is the greatest in the kingdom of heaven?" And calling to Him a child, He put him in the midst of them and said, "Truly, I say to you, unless you turn and become like children, you will never enter the kingdom of heaven. Whoever humbles himself like this child is the greatest in the kingdom of heaven.

"Whoever receives one such child in My name receives Me, but whoever causes one of these little ones who believe in Me to sin, it would be better for him to have a great millstone fastened around his neck and to be drowned in the depth of the sea.

Temptations to Sin

"Woe to the world for temptations to sin! For it is necessary that temptations come, but woe to the one by whom the temptation comes! And if your hand or your foot causes you to sin, cut it off and throw it away. It is better for you to enter life crippled or lame than with two hands or two feet to be thrown into the eternal fire. And if your eye causes you to sin, tear it out and throw it away. It is better for you to enter life with one eye than with two eyes to be thrown into the hell of fire.

The Parable of the Lost Sheep

"See that you do not despise one of these little ones. For I tell you that in heaven their angels always see the face of My Father who is in heaven. What do you think? If a man has a hundred sheep, and one of them has gone astray, does he not leave the ninety-nine on the mountains and go in search of the one that went astray? And if he finds it, truly, I say to you, he rejoices over it more than over the ninety-nine that never went astray. So it is not the will of My Father who is in heaven that one of these little ones should perish."

Children are precious in God's sight. He wants them as His own and loves them. Jesus came into the world to make them heirs of heaven. God has placed the duty and responsibility upon all parents to teach their children from infancy the Holy Scriptures, that they may grow wise for salvation. Beware of offending their faith! How easily they are influenced by us grown-ups! One thoughtless word, one unbecoming act, or one disparaging remark about the Bible, the Church, or the ministry and the child is never the same.

Therefore, Jesus said, "It would be better for him to have a great millstone fastened around his neck and to be drowned in the depth of the sea" than to have him undermine the faith of a little child. If a shepherd will go down into ravines and up mountains to reclaim a lost sheep, how much more ought we to do to preserve a child in faith and develop in him or her a Christian character! We should rather lose an eye or a foot than be the cause of a child's moral and spiritual downfall. Each child born into the world, every boy and every girl playing in the park, has been redeemed by Christ Jesus.

Let us not forsake any of them but help them grow in grace and in knowledge of our Lord Jesus Christ.

Prayer

Lord Jesus, Friend of children, bless all children born into the world with Christian homes; receive them into Your baptismal grace and keep them in Your kingdom as they grow up.

Give us the desire to teach boys and girls by word and example the truth that is revealed in Your cross and the Gospel of Your Word. Amen.

49
LIVING LIFE
ON GOD'S TERMS
Matthew 18:15–35

SOME people are difficult to live with. They are unlovable, quarrelsome, unkind, and spiteful. Some get on our nerves. They irritate us. What can we do to live successfully with such trying people? Jesus tells us two things. First, go and tell them their faults between you and them. Do not hold in your feelings of anger. Talk to them about their offending conduct—but do so in love. Be sure to pray about the efforts you are making, and ask others to pray with you. Be sympathetic. Second, forgive seventy times seven. Overcome evil with a forgiving spirit. "Seek peace and pursue it" (1 Peter 3:11). Some souls are sensitive, so why dwell on the unpleasant past and yesterday's quarrels with them? Some people like to pick a fight, but always remember that it takes two to quarrel. Be forgiving.

But they have offended us so often, you say! Consider this: how often have we offended God? Yet daily He forgives. As He forgives, so should we. Coming from the throne of God, where we have been forgiven, we must feel kindlier toward others. Because the Lord has been so gracious to us, we cannot demand an eye for an eye, can we? This is Jesus' contention in the parable of the unforgiving servant.

If Your Brother Sins Against You

"If your brother sins against you, go and tell him his fault, between you and him alone. If he listens to you, you have gained your brother. But if he does not listen, take one or two others along with you, that every charge may be established by the evidence of two or three witnesses. If he refuses to listen to them, tell it to the church. And if he refuses to listen even to the church, let him be to you as a Gentile and a tax collector. Truly, I say to you, whatever you bind on earth shall be bound in heaven, and whatever you loose on earth shall be loosed in heaven. Again I say to you, if two of you agree on earth about anything they ask, it will be done for them by My Father in heaven. For where two or three are gathered in My name, there am I among them."

The Parable of the Unforgiving Servant

Then Peter came up and said to Him, "Lord, how often will my brother sin against me, and I forgive him? As many as seven times?" Jesus said to him, "I do not say to you seven times, but seventy times seven.

"Therefore the kingdom of heaven may be compared to a king who wished to settle accounts with his servants. When he began to settle, one was brought to him who owed him ten thousand talents. And since he could not pay, his master ordered him to be sold, with his wife and children and all that he had, and payment to be made. So the servant fell on his knees, imploring him, 'Have patience with me, and I will pay you everything.' And out of pity for him, the master of that servant released him and forgave him the debt. But when that same servant went out, he found one of his fellow servants who owed him a hundred denarii, and seizing him, he began to choke him, saying, 'Pay what you owe.' So his fellow servant fell down and pleaded with him, 'Have patience with me, and I will pay you.' He refused and went and put him in prison until he should pay the debt. When his fellow servants saw what had taken place, they were greatly distressed, and they went and reported to their master all that had taken place. Then his master summoned him and said to him, 'You wicked servant! I forgave you all that debt because you pleaded with me. And should not you have had mercy on your fellow servant, as I had mercy on you?' And in anger his master delivered him to the jailers, until he should pay all his debt. So also My heavenly Father will do to every one of you, if you do not forgive your brother from your heart."

In the opening words, Jesus gives us specific instruction on the distinct Church authority known as the Office of the Keys. Jesus has given this authority to the Christian congregation, which may consist of as few as two or three. To such a congregation, Jesus says, "Whatever you bind on earth shall be bound in heaven, and whatever you loose on earth shall be loosed in heaven."

But we must not be rash in binding impenitent sinners. If a fellow Christian is overcome by a fault, go, talk to Him personally and privately, says Jesus. Most likely you will win him over. If you do, the incident should be considered closed.

If he will not listen to your kindly plea, then seek out other sympathetic Christians, take them into your confidence, and let them also talk to the erring brother. Only after he refuses to listen to them and the church should the congregation place him outside of its Christian fellowship.

But even after the erring and obstinate brother has been banned from the Christian congregation, the members of the church should continue to pray for him and still try to win him for Christ and save his soul. No matter how often he sins, if he repents, he should be forgiven by the church.

Prayer

Savior of us all, forgive us our quarrels and take from us the unforgiving spirit that refuses to be reconciled. Remind us that You have blotted out all our sin for days without number. As we come from Your throne of grace, forgiven of all our sins, kindle in us a kindlier attitude toward those who have hurt our feelings and wounded us with slanderous words. Create in us a heart filled with love, as was in You, who prayed for those who crucified You. Amen.

50

JESUS IS ALL IN ALL
Matthew 19:1–12

IN the beginning, God instituted marriage for the well-being and happiness of mankind. This union of one man and one woman should not be broken until death steps in and takes one or the other out of this world. Countless husbands and wives are happy indeed that such is the case and are content that their marriage is to be, and is, a lifelong union.

It is of greatest importance to the home, the Church, and the state, that husbands and wives make a success of their matrimonial venture. This can be done best if Jesus Christ is the unseen Friend who abides in their homes, their lives, and their thinking. God's Word guides them, prayer draws them closer to Christ and to each other, and the regular worship at the house of the Lord consecrates their whole living and being.

Where Christ abides, misunderstandings and rifts have less chance to grow. If we have ourselves sought and found forgiveness with our heavenly Father, we will come from the presence of the Savior forgiving, thoughtful, considerate, and patient.

Such Christian husbands and wives will be faithful to each other and find their joy in each other's companionship. Divorce and separation will be far removed from their thoughts. The question of leaving will not arise. Suspicion and jealousy will find no room in their hearts as daily they unite at the throne of grace in prayer. Separation and divorce arise only where there is a hardness of heart, indifference to God's instruction, and a turning away from the Scriptures and prayer.

That is why Moses allowed divorce, even as our laws of the state do today, for the state governs its people by natural laws, which in many instances do not follow the biblical precept. Christians, however, are bound by the Word of God. In these Scriptures, Jesus allows divorce only if the husband or the wife has been guilty of adultery. Then the innocent one may divorce the other, for the guilty has already broken the sacred bond. In homes where husband and wife and children live Christian lives, close to the heart of the Savior, happiness and contentment will abide, and the question of divorce and separation will be ruled out readily.

Teaching About Divorce

Now when Jesus had finished these sayings, He went away from Galilee and entered the region of Judea beyond the Jordan. And large crowds followed Him, and He healed them there.

And Pharisees came up to Him and tested Him by asking, "Is it lawful to divorce one's wife for any cause?" He answered, "Have you not read that He who created them from the beginning made them male and female, and said, 'Therefore a man shall leave his father and his mother and hold fast to his wife, and the two shall become one flesh'? So they are no longer two but one flesh. What therefore God has joined together, let not man separate." They said to Him, "Why then did Moses command one to give a certificate of divorce and to send her away?" He said to them, "Because of your hardness of heart Moses allowed you to divorce your wives, but from the beginning it was not so. And I say to you: whoever divorces his wife, except for sexual immorality, and marries another, commits adultery."

The disciples said to Him, "If such is the case of a man with his wife, it is better not to marry." But He said to them, "Not everyone can receive this saying, but only those to whom it is given. For there are eunuchs who have been so from birth, and there are eunuchs who have been made eunuchs by men, and there are eunuchs who have made themselves eunuchs for the sake of the kingdom of heaven. Let the one who is able to receive this receive it."

The family is the first unit of human relationship. No other tie binds humans so closely to one another. Parents are ready to make sacrifices so their children may enjoy advantages that they themselves never had. In the ideal family circle, all are thoughtful, considerate, and unselfish. They share the tasks, the responsibilities, and the obligations. If one suffers, all do; if one rejoices, all are glad; if one is successful, all are proud of the achievements. For the sake of the family, parents, as well as children, make sacrifices, deny themselves that the others may have.

In such an ideal family, Christ is the center of all thoughts, the example all follow, and the Savior all adore.

Prayer

We bow our heads, Savior and Friend, to receive Your benediction. Let Your presence bring to our souls peace, to our hearts joy, and to our minds contentment. Protect each of us as we go to and fro, and bring us safely back to the family circle. Bless all homes with Your peace, and establish more Christian families in all parts of the world, who with us worship and adore You as Savior, Lord, and God, now and forever. Amen.

LET THE CHILDREN COME
Matthew 19:13–15

LITTLE children were brought to Jesus, and He laid His hands on them and blessed them.

We still bring children to this Friend. We do this in Baptism, where they are reborn and become part of God's family, living in His grace and under His protection. We bring them to Jesus day after day in prayer. Job would rise early in the morning and offer burnt offerings for his sons and daughters, lest they sin and curse God in their hearts (Job 1:5). So we carry children on our praying hearts. We bring them to Jesus by nurturing them in the Word of God and leading them into the Church. In the Gospel, children meet Jesus, their Friend and their Savior.

However, the disciples thought that Jesus had more important things to do. Even today, some people believe that the time given to children is wasted and that children's minds are too immature to understand the words of Jesus, so they wait to take them to the Savior.

We also hinder children from coming to Jesus by our conduct and speech. If we are neglectful of prayer, if we do not attend church, if we are faultfinding with the church and ridicule Christians and Christian worship, we are hindering children from coming to Jesus. We cannot expect little ones to grow up as exemplary Christians, steadfast in faith, if we fail to let them know from infancy that Jesus loves them.

Therefore, Jesus says: "Let the little children come to Me and do not hinder them."

Let the Children Come to Me

Then children were brought to Him that He might lay His hands on them and pray. The disciples rebuked the people, but Jesus said, "Let the little children come to Me and do not hinder them, for to such belongs the kingdom of heaven." And He laid His hands on them and went away.

Jesus wants children in His kingdom. He has room for them. In fact, He tells us, unless we have the same childlike faith, we will not enter His kingdom.

Jesus had time for children. In pagan lands and among heathen people, the child is placed into the background. As Christian lands fall into spiritual decay, they neglect the training of children and spoil them to such a degree that it becomes impossible to live with them. But boys and girls who are trained in the saving truths of the Savior's Gospel will be a joy to their parents, a delight to the home, a blessing to the Church, and a definite asset to the state.

God bless them!

Prayer

Heavenly Savior and Friend, You have entrusted to the home
and the Church the precious souls of children, that they through
Your Word be taught the way of life eternal and trained to walk
in the paths of Your commandments. Make us keenly aware of the
greatness of this responsibility, that we may apply ourselves with
all diligence to this task of bringing up children, who are disci-
plined by Your Law and made wise unto salvation by Your Gospel.
Bless all children with Christian homes and Christian training,
for Your name's sake. Amen.

HE DARED TO GO AWAY

Matthew 19:16–30

A RICH young man came running to Jesus, all out of breath, and
asked the biggest and most important question of time: "What can
I do to have eternal life?"

The way the young man put the question was all wrong, for he
evidently thought he could take care of himself, so he said, "All these
I have kept. What do I still lack?" He was self-reliant.

Jesus made clear to that young man that he had not learned
the basics of the revealed truth. He did not know or understand
Scripture. Jesus first of all corrected the young man's interpretation
of what is good. The young man was not thinking of Jesus in terms
of Lord and God but saw Him instead as an exceptionally good man
and a great prophet—a teacher.

Jesus' argument is this: God is good—but if the man does not
see in Him God Almighty, then why come to Him to learn what
is "good"? Most likely, the young man did not catch the point.

Otherwise, he would have been ready to put Jesus in the center of his life.

Therefore, Jesus' second point: if the young man wants to be truly good, then he should go and sell all he owns, give his money to the poor, and follow Him. Jesus wanted to show the man that he did not have the full understanding of life and of things and of the Gospel. He had transgressed the very First Commandment, for he loved something more than God.

Did he?

He went away sorrowful, it is true, but neverthless he dared to leave. His possessions meant more to him than Jesus. He hoped that salvation would be possible without giving himself and his all to Christ.

What would we do if such a demand were made of us? No wonder Jesus speaks of the deceitfulness of riches as the young man goes away, never to return as far as we know.

The Rich Young Man

And behold, a man came up to Him, saying, "Teacher, what good deed must I do to have eternal life?" And He said to him, "Why do you ask Me about what is good? There is only one who is good. If you would enter life, keep the commandments." He said to Him, "Which ones?" And Jesus said, "You shall not murder, You shall not commit adultery, You shall not steal, You shall not bear false witness, Honor your father and mother, and, You shall love your neighbor as yourself." The young man said to Him, "All these I have kept. What do I still lack?" Jesus said to him, "If you would be perfect, go, sell what you possess and give to the poor, and you will have treasure in heaven; and come, follow Me." When the young man heard this he went away sorrowful, for he had great possessions.

And Jesus said to His disciples, "Truly, I say to you, only with difficulty will a rich person enter the kingdom of heaven. Again I tell you, it is easier for a camel to go through the eye of a needle than for a rich person to enter the kingdom of God." When the disciples heard this, they were greatly astonished, saying, "Who then can be saved?" But Jesus looked at them and said, "With man this is impossible, but with God all things are possible." Then Peter said in reply, "See, we have left everything and followed You. What then will we have?" Jesus said to them, "Truly, I say to you, in the new world, when the Son of Man will sit on His glorious throne, you who have followed Me will also sit on twelve thrones, judging the twelve tribes of Israel. And everyone who has left houses or brothers or sisters or father or mother or children or lands, for My name's sake, will receive a hundredfold and will inherit eternal life. But many who are first will be last, and the last first.

Scripture does not reveal the name of this rich young man because that is not what is important here. God wants us to know how fatal was this man's mistake when he dared to walk away from his Savior.

The young man was rich in possessions. No criticism is made because he has this wealth. He did not squander it in riotous living. He was respected in his community and conducted his affairs wisely.

He was rich in influence. He had been made president of the synagogue. He ranked high in social life. His money gave him prestige.

He was rich in nobility of character. Morally, he was good. Mothers told their sons to follow his example. He was upright, clean, decent.

He was rich in personality. He had a pleasing way in meeting people. His winsomeness won the heart of Jesus. "And Jesus, looking at him, loved him" (Mark 10:21).

But he was poor because he left Jesus for the sake of his wealth. The irony is that eventually he gave it all up. He could not take it with him into eternity. In the end, he lost everything, even his very soul.

Thinking on these things, Jesus exclaims: "It is easier for a camel to go through the eye of a needle than for a rich person to enter the kingdom of God."

Can a camel pass through the eye of a needle? Whether you explain these words to mean an ordinary needle or, as some do, a very narrow gate in Jerusalem called the Needle's Eye, the fact remains that wealth has kept many a person out of the kingdom of heaven. Mankind clings to riches with a tenacity that clearly reveals a heart full of greed and selfishness and sin.

Can no one be saved who has riches? Must we live in voluntary poverty to enter the Kingdom? Jesus does not say that. "With difficulty" will a rich man enter, says the Savior. And why? Because he trusts in his wealth rather than in his God.

But God can do the impossible. By the power of the Gospel, He can raise up the spiritually dead. Wealth in itself is not a barrier to salvation. But if we place our possessions ahead of Christ, if we believe we can buy salvation with our gifts, our riches become obstacles that close the door to heaven. Because the young man in this story was a slave to his possessions, he was made a beggar in eternity, even though he stood in high esteem with the people of the synagogue.

If we must make a choice—Christ or gold, Christ or parents, Christ or children—Christ must be the all in all of our life. No matter how noble we are, we still lack the wherewithal if Christ does not take full possession of our hearts. And as He enters and abides, we place our all at His feet and crown Him Lord of all.

Prayer
Take my love, my Lord, I pour
At Thy feet its treasure store;
Take myself, and I will be
Ever, only, all for Thee. Amen.
(LSB 783:6)

IF THIEVES ARE SAVED, WHY BE GOOD?

Matthew 20:1–16

IT doesn't seem fair that a person who works one hour is paid the same amount as one who has worked for twelve hours. We object. That a scoundrel who has robbed widows and orphans repents in the last hour of his life and is saved brings no joy to most of our hearts. We object and say, It is not right that someone like this also goes to heaven.

The parable of the laborers in the vineyard addresses this argument. We, who from childhood have been in the Kingdom, are the privileged people of the world although we have toiled and labored. Sin gives no pleasure. In the end, the transgressor gets far less out of life than we who have lived in the grace of God. We have fewer worries. We begin the day in the name of the Lord and find comfort in His promises. We sleep peacefully, knowing that the Lord neither slumbers nor sleeps. The fear of judgment to come and the sting of guilt does not keep us awake.

We need not envy the man who lives without God and without hope in this world, although his pastures seem to be greener, his land richer, and his income bigger. By God's grace, we Christians live sheltered lives in the Lord's household and family.

This is the truth that Jesus wants to impress upon our hearts in the following parable.

Laborers in the Vineyard

For the kingdom of heaven is like a master of a house who went out early in the morning to hire laborers for his vineyard. After agreeing with the laborers for a denarius a day, he sent them into his vineyard. And going out about the third hour he saw others standing idle in the marketplace, and to them he said, "You go into the vineyard too, and whatever is right I will give you." So they went. Going out again about the sixth hour and the ninth hour, he did the same. And about the eleventh hour he went out and found others standing. And he said to them, "Why do you stand here idle all day?" They said to him, "Because no one has hired us." He said to them, "You go into the vineyard too." And when evening came, the owner of the vineyard said to his foreman, "Call the laborers and pay them their wages, beginning with the last, up to the first." And when those hired about the eleventh hour came, each of them received a denarius. Now when those hired first came, they thought they would receive more, but each of them also received a denarius. And on receiving it they grumbled at the master of the house, saying, "These last worked only one hour, and you have made them equal to us who have borne the burden of the day and the scorching heat." But he replied to one of them, "Friend, I am doing you no wrong. Did you not agree with me for a denarius? Take what belongs to you and go. I choose to give to this last worker as I give to you. Am I not allowed to do what I choose with what belongs to me? Or do you begrudge my generosity?" So the last will be first, and the first last."

There is an old tale about two men in heaven who had lived under different environments on earth. The one had been a thief, while the other had been a saint. The robber had repented in his dying hour, and God's grace had saved him. In heaven, he praised God, saying that to none had the Lord shown such grace as to him. But the saint objected and claimed that God had shown him greater grace. "How so?" asked the first. "You fell," said the saint, "and God's boundless grace lifted you. That is wonderful. However, I was just as wicked at heart as you, but God's grace kept me from falling—that was a still greater accomplishment of God's grace."

If you and I have enjoyed the blessing of the Gospel throughout our lives, let us thank God for this limitless grace that preserves us and keeps us in the faith. When God shows mercy to some other poor sinner whose misspent life has robbed him of years of joy, let us remember that the bestowing of grace to such does not detract from the grace given to us. Let us not wonder or complain when God shows to others this same grace, which is ours so abundantly.

Prayer

Lord, today we are mindful of Your goodness and mercy You have shown to us through these many years. Accept our thanksgiving as we praise Your wondrous name. Continue to bless us and keep us in Your grace, through Jesus Christ, our redeeming Lord. Amen.

THE SUFFERING JESUS SAVES
Matthew 20:17–34

JESUS went to Jerusalem to suffer and die, and by His death on the cross He saved us. Everything He endured was for us. He was scourged so we would not be sent from the presence of God condemned. He was forsaken on the cross so we would not be forsaken throughout eternity.

Jesus was fully aware of the tremendous cost of our redemption. Yet He did not evade the issue or sidestep the hour. Dark and dreadful as it was, He faced it with confidence, sure of the ultimate victory. No matter what man would do to Him, on the third day He would rise to proclaim to all the world that each and every human soul has been redeemed through His death. None need to perish. If any go to eternal damnation, they go because they obstinately refused the salvation offered them through the risen Christ.

This winepress of agony Jesus would tread alone. Not even John and James, sons of Zebedee, could drink with Him one drop of this cup of Passion. They would be compelled to suffer for His sake and be persecuted because they followed Him, but redemption came solely and alone by Jesus Christ, the Son of God, made man. He gave His life as a ransom for all, sinner and saint, Gentile and Jew, farmer and king.

The suffering Jesus saves. On His way to Calvary, He showed Himself as the compassionate Savior. The two blind men on the roadside near Jericho did not plead in vain. Jesus opened their eyes. And they saw more than trees and flowers and faces and children. Their spiritual blindness was removed. They saw in this Jesus one who saves from sin. Immediately, they followed Him as Lord and Redeemer.

Jesus Foretells His Death a Third Time

And as Jesus was going up to Jerusalem, He took the twelve disciples aside, and on the way He said to them, "See, we are going up to Jerusalem. And the Son of Man will be delivered over to the chief priests and scribes, and they will condemn Him to death and deliver Him over to the Gentiles to be mocked and flogged and crucified, and He will be raised on the third day."

A Mother's Request

Then the mother of the sons of Zebedee came up to Him with her sons, and kneeling before Him she asked Him for something. And He said to her, "What do you want?" She said to Him, "Say that these two sons of mine are to sit, one at Your right hand and one at Your left, in Your kingdom." Jesus answered, "You do not know what you are asking. Are you able to drink the cup that I am to drink?" They said to Him, "We are able." He said to them, "You will drink My cup, but to sit at My right hand and at My left is not Mine to grant, but it is for those for whom it has been prepared by My Father." And when the ten heard it, they were indignant at the two brothers. But Jesus called them to Him and said, "You know that the rulers of the Gentiles lord it over them, and their great ones exercise authority over them. It shall not be so among you. But whoever would be great among you must be your servant, and whoever would be first among you must be your slave, even as

the Son of Man came not to be served but to serve, and to give
His life as a ransom for many."

Jesus Heals Two Blind Men

And as they went out of Jericho, a great crowd followed
Him. And behold, there were two blind men sitting by the
roadside, and when they heard that Jesus was passing by, they
cried out, "Lord, have mercy on us, Son of David!" The crowd
rebuked them, telling them to be silent, but they cried out all
the more, "Lord, have mercy on us, Son of David!" And stopping, Jesus called them and said, "What do you want Me to
do for you?" They said to Him, "Lord, let our eyes be opened."
And Jesus in pity touched their eyes, and immediately they
recovered their sight and followed Him.

Jesus died to deliver all mankind—from what?

From the terrors and fears, from the heartaches and uncertainties
of life. Because He died, we have a Good Shepherd who will not let
us perish; we have a keeper who neither slumbers nor sleeps.

Jesus came to deliver us, above all, from the power and the
clutches of sin. The sense of guilt, along with the shame and despair
caused by it, makes life a nightmare. If life is to be livable, we must
have an escape from the accusing finger of our own conscience.

The forces of sin are tremendous, as we see it in its destructive-
ness, brutality, and the selfishness of man. Only Jesus could break
the grip of the claws of sin and Satan.

Jesus came to bring to us an eternal and perpetual victory. He
rose, and with Him we rise to a newness of life (Ephesians 2:5–6).
We also share with Him the glory of heaven. "Because I live, you
also will live" (John 14:19).

Sinful and hopeless man can look up to the cross and find healing, salvation, and peace.

Prayer

Just as I am, poor, wretched, blind;
Sight, riches, healing of the mind,

Yea, all I need, in Thee to find,
O Lamb of God, I come, I come. Amen. (LSB 570:4)

THE MAXIMUM CHRISTIAN
Matthew 21:1–16

LOYALTY is always at a premium. Loyalty gives expression to the noblest qualities of which we are capable. When you say of a man he is true to the very marrow, you are paying him a handsome compliment indeed.

Jesus also looked for loyalty. Allegiance to Him must be undivided. "Whoever is not with Me is against Me" (Matthew 12:30). Repeatedly, Jesus told His disciples that one of them would betray Him. One would be disloyal, and this troubled His soul.

It must have been a great sight when Jesus came down from the Mount of Olives, surrounded by loyal followers. Thousands could view this procession from the temple courts, for the temple site bordered on the eastern wall of Jerusalem, opposite the Mount of Olives, with the Brook of Kidron between.

The disciples recognized the significance of this triumphant entrance. Knowing the Scriptures, they recalled the words of the prophet Zechariah: "Say to the daughter of Zion, 'Behold, your king is coming to you' " (Matthew 21:5).

But not all welcome Jesus. Those who are satisfied with their own accomplishments, and those who are selfish and self-centered, do not want this Jesus. He disturbs. Jesus does not approve of a life that places other interests ahead of Him who came to redeem us from the clutches of sin. He wants first place in our hearts and in our lives.

This His entry, triumphant and glorious, wants to emphasize.

The Triumphal Entry

Now when they drew near to Jerusalem and came to Bethphage, to the Mount of Olives, then Jesus sent two disciples, saying to them, "Go into the village in front of you, and immediately you will find a donkey tied, and a colt with her. Untie them and bring them to Me. If anyone says anything to you, you shall say, 'The Lord needs them,' and he will send them at once." This took place to fulfill what was spoken by the prophet, saying,

"Say to the daughter of Zion, 'Behold, your king is coming to you,
humble, and mounted on a donkey,
and on a colt, the foal of a beast of burden.' "

The disciples went and did as Jesus had directed them. They brought the donkey and the colt and put on them their cloaks, and He sat on them. Most of the crowd spread their cloaks on the road, and others cut branches from the trees and spread them on the road. And the crowds that went before Him and that followed Him were shouting, "Hosanna to the Son of David! Blessed is He who comes in the name of the Lord! Hosanna in the highest!" And when He entered Jerusalem, the whole city was stirred up, saying, "Who is this?" And the crowds said, "This is the prophet Jesus, from Nazareth of Galilee."

Jesus Cleanses the Temple

And Jesus entered the temple and drove out all who sold and bought in the temple, and He overturned the tables of the money-changers and the seats of those who sold pigeons. He said to them, "It is written, 'My house shall be called a house of prayer,' but you make it a den of robbers."

And the blind and the lame came to Him in the temple, and He healed them. But when the chief priests and the scribes saw the wonderful things that He did, and the children crying out in the temple, "Hosanna to the Son of David!" they were indignant, and they said to Him, "Do you hear what these are saying?" And Jesus said to them, "Yes; have you never read,

*" 'Out of the mouth of infants and nursing babies
You have prepared praise'?"*

"Behold, your king is coming to you." Jesus is that King.

Jesus is the universal King. There is nothing provincial about Him. He favors no nationality or special interests; He shows no partiality. He protects no big industries but is equitable and just in all His dealings with mankind. He came to seek and to save the lost. His kingdom ignores all boundaries and limitations of man.

Jesus is a sympathetic King. He is compassionate and understands our needs. He remembers that we are dust—frail, sinful, erring humans, who need guidance and help and forgiveness. Therefore, He intercedes for us.

Jesus is a redeeming King. He must redeem our souls from destruction and from the dominion of Satan. To do so, He gave His life. He came to save to the utmost. The penitent thief on the cross discovered this to be true and found in Him peace and heaven, the eternal kingdom of the King of kings.

Jesus is also our King. He purchased us with His own blood. He wants us to pledge our loyalty and service to Him. He has chosen human agencies to build His kingdom. As sinful yet transformed people, we serve Him. As faulty yet willing followers, we do His bidding. We, too, welcome Him to our hearts and homes with the hosannas of devotion and abiding faithfulness.

Prayer

Sun of my soul, King of the universe and of my heart, again I pledge allegiance to You and confess and acknowledge You as my Savior in whose kingdom I am protected against the cunning of Satan and the deceitfulness of the world. With all Your saints and angels, I kneel at Your throne and give to You my heart, my life, and my hands. Accept me with all my frailties, and cause even my feeble efforts to praise You. Grant that my hosannas may arise from a loyal heart that loves You and that I may in Your eternal kingdom glorify You with the alleluias of a devoted child who lives with You forevermore. Amen.

THE HALO OF A USEFUL LIFE

Matthew 21:17–32

BY an unusual, visual demonstration, Jesus pressed home important lessons to His disciples and the Passover multitude, lessons that otherwise would have been dismissed with a shrug. On a wayside fig tree, Jesus found no fruit as He was returning to Bethany after a day of preaching and teaching. Disappointed, He said that the tree would grow no fruit hereafter. The next day, the tree was withered. It did not serve the purpose for which it was planted—it grew no figs. A fruit tree must have more than leaves.

Like the fig tree, our lives are to be more than ornamental. We are to be rich in service toward God and useful and helpful to humanity. Our Christian faith must prove itself by Christian living and faithful service. Otherwise, we are valueless in the sight of the Savior. Opportunities to serve are limitless. There are always people who have never heard the Gospel, others who have never understood its significance, and still others who are in need of an encouraging word and a sympathetic hand.

"Night is coming, when no one can work" (John 9:4). If we abide in Christ, we bring forth much fruit. If we do what is worthwhile as we go through life, we receive the approval of Him who has sent us into the vineyard to make ourselves useful. No amount of stalling will do; Jesus wants action. Delays and excuses displease Him.

Of what good is a son who says, "I will go and work," and then plays truant? Such behavior does not plow fields and gather in the grain. Better a son who says, "I will not," and then later regrets that he has acted so unseemly and returns to serve. Such a son, after all, is of greater worth to the household.

This is the assertion of Jesus.

And leaving them, He went out of the city to Bethany and lodged there.

Jesus Curses the Fig Tree

In the morning, as He was returning to the city, He became hungry. And seeing a fig tree by the wayside, He went to it and found nothing on it but only leaves. And He said to it, "May no fruit ever come from you again!" And the fig tree withered at once.

When the disciples saw it, they marveled, saying, "How did the fig tree wither at once?" And Jesus answered them, "Truly, I say to you, if you have faith and do not doubt, you will not only do what has been done to the fig tree, but even if you say to this mountain, 'Be taken up and thrown into the sea,' it will happen. And whatever you ask in prayer, you will receive, if you have faith."

The Authority of Jesus Challenged

And when He entered the temple, the chief priests and the elders of the people came up to Him as He was teaching, and said, "By what authority are You doing these things, and who gave You this authority?" Jesus answered them, "I also will ask you one question, and if you tell me the answer, then I also will tell you by what authority I do these things. The baptism of John, from where did it come? From heaven or from man?" And they discussed it among themselves, saying, "If we say, 'From heaven,' He will say to us, 'Why then did you not believe him?' But if we say, 'From man,' we are afraid of the crowd, for they all hold that John was a prophet." So they answered Jesus, "We do not know." And He said to them, "Neither will I tell you by what authority I do these things.

The Parable of the Two Sons

"What do you think? A man had two sons. And he went to the first and said, 'Son, go and work in the vineyard today.' And he answered, 'I will not,' but afterward he changed his mind and went. And he went to the other son and said the same. And he answered, 'I go, sir,' but did not go. Which of the two did the will of his father?" They said, "The first." Jesus said to them, "Truly, I say to you, the tax collectors and the prostitutes go into the kingdom of God before you. For John came to you in the way of righteousness, and you did not believe him, but the tax collectors and the prostitutes believed him. And even when you saw it, you did not afterward change your minds and believe him."

Some people don't want to make decisions. They are always asking questions that they might delay action. They stall. They can neither make up their minds nor commit themselves. "By what authority are You doing these things?" asked the priests and elders of the people. They hemmed and hawed from morning until night, even when Jesus had given them sufficient proof of His Messiahship. They would not say yes; they would not say no. "We do not know."

Jesus is not satisfied with such following. Speak the truth, speak it in love, but speak out. The world must know that we belong to Christ. If we are disciples, our lives will be dedicated to Him and consecrated to His service. People will know by our conduct and speech that we belong to Him. Of Peter and John, it was said: "And they recognized that they had been with Jesus" (Acts 4:13).

Some will not like us for this reason. We will not be welcome in their circles. But, after all, those who confess Christ and walk the royal road of Christian service produce more than an ornamental life. Such faithful servants of Jesus are transparently sincere and a credit to the community. And Jesus will confess them before His Father in heaven as they enter as heirs of the eternal kingdom.

Prayer

As we bow in humble adoration, Lord of the Church and Savior of all mankind, we acknowledge our shortcomings and our many neglects. Graciously forgive us, and let the Holy Spirit take full possession of our hearts, that, sanctified by His grace, we render to You a greater service in faithful devotion, who gave Your life that we might live the more abundant and fuller life in Your grace. Amen.

CHRIST'S AUTOBIOGRAPHY

Matthew 21:33–46

ARTISTS paint portraits of themselves and authors write the story of their own lives. These are self-revealing, as a rule, especially if the autobiography takes the form of a confession.

As Jesus moved among men, He spoke to them significant truths by parables. A number of these parables were told during Jesus' last visit to Jerusalem. Some of these are not as appealing as others because through them, Jesus pronounces severe judgments upon the church leaders. Such is the parable of the tenants. It is not warm like the parable of the lost sheep or sentimental like the parable of the prodigal son or charming like the parable of the Good Samaritan. Nevertheless, it stresses the limitless patience of God's love. "Finally he sent his son to them." And him they killed. The parable carries with it a sting the chief priests and the Pharisees keenly felt, as we see from the closing remarks of the parable.

The Parable of the Tenants

"Hear another parable. There was a master of a house who planted a vineyard and put a fence around it and dug a winepress in it and built a tower and leased it to tenants, and went into another country. When the season for fruit drew near, he sent his servants to the tenants to get his fruit. And the tenants took his servants and beat one, killed another, and stoned another. Again he sent other servants, more than the first. And they did the same to them. Finally he sent his son to them, saying, 'They will respect my son.' But when the tenants saw the son, they said to themselves, 'This is the heir. Come, let us kill him and have his inheritance.' And they took him and threw him out of the vineyard and killed him. When therefore the owner of the vineyard comes, what will he do to those tenants?" They said to Him, "He will put those wretches to a miserable death and let out the vineyard to other tenants who will give him the fruits in their seasons."

Jesus said to them, "Have you never read in the Scriptures:

" 'The stone that the builders rejected
has become the cornerstone;
this was the Lord's doing,
and it is marvelous in our eyes'?

Therefore I tell you, the kingdom of God will be taken away from you and given to a people producing its fruits. And the one who falls on this stone will be broken to pieces; and when it falls on anyone, it will crush him."

When the chief priests and the Pharisees heard His parables, they perceived that He was speaking about them. And although they were seeking to arrest Him, they feared the crowds, because they held Him to be a prophet.

The vineyard in the parable represents the Jewish people. "Finally he sent his son to them." This implies that God had done much before He sent His Anointed. He had given Israel the Law on Mount Sinai; He had promised them the Messiah; He had blessed them with privileges; and He had divinely protected them through the centuries. They had Moses to lead them, Elijah to call them to repentance, Isaiah to plead with them, and Jeremiah to warn them patiently.

The tenants are the leaders to whom the people had been entrusted. But they made Israel sin. The tenants were unfaithful and selfish. The servants sent by the master of the house are the prophets, who plead: "Turn back, turn back from your evil ways, for why will you die?" (Ezekiel 33:11). Last is the Son—and Him they crucify.

Jesus let the priests and Pharisees know that He was fully aware of their plans and plottings. They could not deceive Him.

The parables are not given only to Israel. They are recorded in the sacred Scriptures for our learning and warning.

God has given us greater privileges even than He gave Israel. We have seen the victorious and triumphant Christ, who rose from the dead and lives. Israel knew the Christ of prophecy, who dwelled among them in humility. We know the Christ of power. Christ and His Church have withstood the assaults of the ages. Therefore, Jesus expects to find abundant fruit on the tree of the Gentile dispensation, the New Testament age. Of us, the children of the Gospel, the Lord expects greater things than He did of the children of the Law.

And what are we doing? What does He find? We prefer the bright lights of Sodom to the Sun of Righteousness. We busy ourselves with buying fields and examining oxen (see Luke 14:18–20). We tire ourselves out with Saturday night's revelry—we bypass Jesus.

How patient is God with us! He is looking for fruit and finds none. As faithful stewards of His grace, we are to come, bring others, tell all who will listen, pray daily for grace and growth, and support Christ's kingdom with our earthly possessions.

"Finally he sent his son to them." And they killed Him. They crucified Him, and His blood has been on them and their children ever since.

Today, God in His grace still is sending us His messengers of peace. If we fail to appreciate this Gospel of reconciliation, it will be taken from us and given to others, even as it was taken from Jerusalem and many other places.

But if we are faithful, bearing the fruits of service and devotion, the Lord will receive us to glory, saying: "You have been faithful over a little; I will set you over much. Enter into the joy of your master" (Matthew 25:21).

Prayer

Let me be Thine forever, My faithful God and Lord;
Let me forsake Thee never Nor wander from Thy Word.
Lord, do not let me waver, But give me steadfastness,
And for such grace forever Thy holy name I'll bless. Amen.
(LSB 689:1)

58

WHAT IS WRONG WITH MY GOODNESS?

Matthew 22:1–14

TO us who are not acquainted with the customs of Jesus' day, the parable of the wedding feast makes no sense. A man walking along the street in his everyday clothes is stopped by a stranger who begs him to come to a king's wedding feast. He is not given time even to go home and change clothes. He is urged to come just as he is.

An hour later, as he is seated in the banquet hall, he is chided for not having on the proper clothes and then thrown out because he does not have on a wedding garment. Surely, the king could not expect a man off the street to have on a suitable robe for the occasion.

But the other guests, all of them, were picked from the streets and the lanes and alleys to attend, and they, one and all, had on a wedding garment. Where did they get theirs? Custom prescribed that the king furnish his guests with suitable clothes to grace his banquet hall.

If this was the practice of the day, why then did this one man fail to put on the proper garment? Undoubtedly, as he compared himself with others as they came in, he found his clothes to be adequate, so fine in fact, that he believed them to be good enough for any king's banquet. So he did not make the change.

However, as soon as these others put on the kingly robes, his looked out of place, like a filthy rag. So he did not fit in and he was sent out. His conduct offended the king and marred the beauty of the gorgeous setting of the banquet room. Knowing this to be the background, we can better understand the parable.

The Parable of the Wedding Feast

And again Jesus spoke to them in parables, saying, "The kingdom of heaven may be compared to a king who gave a wedding feast for his son, and sent his servants to call those who were invited to the wedding feast, but they would not come. Again he sent other servants, saying, 'Tell those who are invited, See, I have prepared my dinner, my oxen and my fat calves have been slaughtered, and everything is ready. Come to the wedding feast.' But they paid no attention and went off, one to his farm, another to his business, while the rest seized his servants, treated them shamefully, and killed them. The king was angry, and he sent his troops and destroyed those murderers and burned their city. Then he said to his servants, 'The wedding feast is ready, but those invited were not worthy. Go therefore to the main roads and invite to the wedding feast as many as you find.' And those servants went out into the roads and gathered all whom they found, both bad and good. So the wedding hall was filled with guests.

But when the king came in to look at the guests, he saw there a man who had no wedding garment. And he said to him, 'Friend, how did you get in here without a wedding garment?' And he was speechless. Then the king said to the attendants, 'Bind him hand and foot and cast him into the outer darkness. In that place there will be weeping and gnashing of teeth.' For many are called, but few are chosen."

Again, Jesus teaches a spiritual lesson by means of an earthly custom. What is this wedding garment the King provides? It is the righteousness of Jesus with which we are clothed and made acceptable to God. This righteousness is a gift of God's grace and is put on by faith. As God looks at us, clothed in Jesus' righteousness, His perfect holiness, He sees us as pure and acceptable to be present in His heavenly banquet hall.

But why do not all people array themselves in this righteousness of Jesus, since it is ours by grace? Too many think that their own goodness is satisfactory and sufficient to admit them to eternal life. They compare themselves with others around them and see plenty who do not possess the goodness that they themselves have. Why bother, then, about Christ's righteousness?

But at the throne of God their uprightness looks like a filthy rag. And because they wanted to be judged by their own merits, they are and the Lord must send them away, for they fall short of doing His perfect will.

All those, however, who are aware of their unworthiness, foul as they may be, are perfect in the sight of God if by faith they put on Christ's righteousness. The blood of Jesus washes them free from all sin. They are acceptable through the merits of Jesus Christ, their Savior.

Prayer
Remove from us, dear Lord, all vanity of heart and self-glorification, and clothe us in the robe of Jesus' righteousness. In Jesus' name. Amen.

OUR DUAL CITIZENSHIP
Matthew 22:15–22

THE leaders of Jerusalem tried continually to trap Jesus. They thought they could ask Him questions that could not be answered to the satisfaction of both the people and the state officials.

This time, the Pharisees put their heads together with the Herodians, the political party in Palestine that wanted to keep the Herods in power. They came to Jesus with a very important question. Their plot, however, was masked as harmless inquiry. First, the Herodians paid Jesus compliments. They addressed Him as "Teacher." They told Him how profoundly they respected Him for His knowledge of the truth. And then came the trick question:

is it lawful to pay taxes to Caesar, the emperor of Rome? They reasoned that if Jesus said no, they could report Him to the state as a dissenter. If Jesus said yes, then they could go to the people and say, See, He cannot be the Messiah because He favors Caesar.

Jesus saw through their deceit and said, "You hypocrites . . . show Me the coin."

Shrewdly, they showed Him a denarius, a Roman coin that bore the image of Caesar, a human being. The Pharisees would not use such a coin at the temple; after all, didn't Moses say: "You shall not make for yourself a carved image?"

Jesus looked at the coin, saw the image, and asked, "Whose likeness and inscription is this?" They answered, "Caesar's." Then Jesus uttered that great pronouncement that has made us Christians citizens of two governments: "Therefore render to Caesar the things that are Caesar's, and to God the things that are God's."

Give Caesar what is due him and, at the same time, give God the greater loyalty of the heart. Think on these things as Matthew gives an account of the Herodians' plot.

Paying Taxes to Caesar

Then the Pharisees went and plotted how to entangle Him in His words. And they sent their disciples to Him, along with the Herodians, saying, "Teacher, we know that You are true and teach the way of God truthfully, and You do not care about anyone's opinion, for You are not swayed by appearances. Tell us, then, what You think. Is it lawful to pay taxes to Caesar, or not?" But Jesus, aware of their malice, said, "Why put Me to the test, you hypocrites? Show Me the coin for the tax." And they brought Him a denarius. And Jesus said to them, "Whose likeness and inscription is this?" They said, "Caesar's." Then He said to them, "Therefore render to Caesar the things that are Caesar's, and to God the things that are God's." When they heard it, they marveled. And they left Him and went away.

Christians are in a unique place in this world because we are citizens of two governments and live under two flags. Yet our loyalty to the one does not break down our allegiance to the other. Christians are loyal both to Christ and to their country.

As citizens of an earthly government, we obey its laws unless they are contrary to a direct instruction of God. We support the government with our prayers and taxes, and we assume the responsibilities and obligations that help to maintain the nation and make it possible to live normal lives in the community.

As citizens of Christ's kingdom, we worship and adore Him as Savior and Lord, are obedient to His Word, support His Church with our prayers and earthly possessions, and walk in our daily life as becomes the people of God.

Jesus does not allow us to live indifferently. We dare not ignore Him who died that we might be forgiven. He wants us to be loyal and faithful. Our loyalty to Him makes for a greater loyalty to the nation. The more faithful we are as Christians, the more loyal we will be as citizens of our country. The best way to put to silence those who question our allegiance to the state is to be faithful to God and His Word. The Christian ought always be an exemplary and valuable citizen to his country.

Prayer

Heavenly Father, bless our native land and protect the nation from war and destruction, that in this country we may live peaceable and normal lives, faithful to You and dutiful in the performances of all our national tasks. Preserve us in our saving faith through Jesus Christ, our Lord. Amen.

IS HEAVEN WISHFUL THINKING?
Matthew 22:23–33

THE Sadducees were the liberal theologians of Jesus' day. They denied all that is supernatural. They rejected, above all, the doctrine of the resurrection, saying that our bodies will not rise from the dead. They tried to make this revelation of God appear as fantasy and asked Jesus a question they thought was unanswerable: if a woman marries a second and third time because her husbands die, which of the three would be her husband in heaven?

Jesus had the answer. He told them that marriages do not exist in heaven. Marriages, as they are here on earth, exist to propagate the human race. In heaven, no new generations will be born. The resurrection and the full glory of eternity does not begin until the complete number of the elect has come to faith and been saved. After that, no new names and generations are to be added to the Book of Life.

But definitely there is a resurrection and a heaven, where joy is complete and love abides, for God is not a God of the dead, but of the living. So Jesus informs His opponents and us also.

Sadducees Ask About the Resurrection

The same day Sadducees came to Him, who say that there is no resurrection, and they asked Him a question, saying, "Teacher, Moses said, 'If a man dies having no children, his brother must marry the widow and raise up children for his brother.' Now there were seven brothers among us. The first married and died, and having no children left his wife to his brother. So too the second and third, down to the seventh. After them all, the woman died. In the resurrection, therefore, of the seven, whose wife will she be? For they all had her."

But Jesus answered them, "You are wrong, because you know neither the Scriptures nor the power of God. For in the resurrection they neither marry nor are given in marriage, but are like angels in heaven. And as for the resurrection of the dead, have you not read what was said to you by God: 'I am the God of Abraham, and the God of Isaac, and the God of Jacob'? He is not God of the dead, but of the living." And when the crowd heard it, they were astonished at His teaching.

We ask many questions about heaven that are never answered this side of the grave and need not be answered. God did not see fit to answer every question we ask. In fact, if He did describe to us heaven in all its beauty and bliss, we could not even comprehend it. Paul tells us that the glory is so magnificent it cannot be put into words. However, God has plainly revealed to us the way that leads to heaven. Jesus tells us that there is only one way—Himself. Believing in Him gives life. We must believe one great fact and truth: that Jesus atoned for our sin by shedding His blood for us. As we stand beneath the cross and cry for mercy, God must look at us through this cross and abundantly pardon.

All who stand before the throne of the Lamb in heaven have been washed white in His blood. So John tells us in Revelation 7. It is foolish, therefore, to speculate in fantastic musings about heaven. There is no value to cunning and tricky questions that intend to make heaven and eternity look absurd. Day after day, we should contemplate the marvels of God's love that through Christ's redemptive death has opened to us heaven's door and receives us by faith and by grace into eternal life.

Prayer

We praise and glorify Your name, Lord of heaven and earth, because You have called us out of the darkness of sin into the kingdom of Your victorious Son. Grant that we live forever with You in glory, where joy and peace and love abide forever by Your grace because of the redeeming blood of Your Son, Jesus Christ, our risen, ever-loving Savior. Amen.

CHRIST HAS THE ANSWER

Matthew 22:34–46

ALTHOUGH the Pharisees and Sadducees were at swords' points in their views on the resurrection—the Sadducees denying that man will rise from the dead—the two groups formed a united front in their opposition to Jesus. They were continually putting their heads together to formulate questions that would trap Him or trick Him into making a mistake. They phrased their question in such a way that no matter what the answer might be, a larger group of people would resent Christ's reply. At least that's what the Pharisees and Sadducees thought.

In the week following Jesus' entry into Jerusalem, these opposing forces again plotted against the Son of Man and came with a question that seemed to them unanswerable: "Which is the great commandment in the Law?"

But Jesus had the right answer: "You shall love the Lord your God with all your heart and with all your soul and with all your mind. . . . You shall love your neighbor as yourself."

Love God with all your heart and you will love your neighbor as much as yourself. If you say you love God and hate your fellow men, then you are not telling the truth. If you say that you love all mankind as yourself and deny and ignore God, then you are not speaking the truth.

The Law is fulfilled in one word: love. But there is not a just man on earth who loves with a perfect heart. Appeal, then, to the Law, and this Law will condemn you. By nature, we live in sin because we are born in sin, "by nature children of wrath" (Ephesians 2:3). As much as we brag about our good works, we are not by such isolated acts fulfilling the Law of God. This Jesus wants us to know.

The Great Commandment

But when the Pharisees heard that He had silenced the Sadducees, they gathered together. And one of them, a lawyer, asked Him a question to test Him. "Teacher, which is the great commandment in the Law?" And He said to him, "You shall love the Lord your God with all your heart and with all your soul and with all your mind. This is the great and first commandment. And a second is like it: You shall love your neighbor as yourself. On these two commandments depend all the Law and the Prophets."

Whose Son Is the Christ?

Now while the Pharisees were gathered together, Jesus asked them a question, saying, "What do you think about the Christ? Whose son is He?" They said to Him, "The son of David." He said to them, "How is it then that David, in the Spirit, calls Him Lord, saying,

" 'The Lord said to my Lord, Sit at my right hand,
until I put your enemies under your feet'?

If then David calls Him Lord, how is He his son?" And no one was able to answer Him a word, nor from that day did anyone dare to ask Him any more questions.

Jesus put a real counterquestion to those men who were trying to ensnare Him: "What do you think about the Christ? Whose son is He?" A more important question never confronted a human being. Our salvation is dependent upon the right answer.

The Pharisees rightly answered, "The Son of David." But if that is true, then this particular Son of David, Jesus of Nazareth, is God, for Psalm 2 says of this greater Son of David that He is God's only-begotten Son. Yet the Pharisees and many with them do not accept Jesus as the Christ, the Son of the living God.

However, if Jesus is not the Christ, then we have no Savior and no salvation. If we reject Jesus, we are headed for eternal damnation because we have not fulfilled the two great commandments.

So we must give the right answer to the question Who is this Jesus? We must fall to our knees with Thomas and worship Him with the confession, "My Lord and my God!"

Jesus must be to us very God of very God. We must see in Him our Savior, who has redeemed us with His own blood and made us His own and heirs of salvation. No greater question than this faces us as we go through life. What do you think about the Christ? Who is this Jesus of Nazareth?

Prayer

Lord Jesus, we believe and are convinced that You are the promised Christ, the eternal Son of God made flesh, our Savior and Friend. To Your wounded side we come to obtain cleansing from sin, deliverance from Satan, and salvation throughout eternity. Preserve us in faith, and keep us in Your grace until we stand before Your throne in the glories of heaven. Amen.

A DECADENT CHRISTIANITY

Matthew 23:1–28

TRADITIONS, ceremonies, customs, and trends always have had a strong influence on mankind. So much so that they may become burdensome enough to retard the growth and progress of humanity.

The Pharisees and scribes bound themselves to many self-made regulations such as washing hands before eating or wearing broad phylacteries. In and of themselves, these regulations were good and not at all objectionable. (Phylacteries are oblong lockets worn on the forehead and also on the arm. They contain small paper rolls on which are written Scripture passages such as "Hear, O Israel:

The Lord our God, the Lord is one" [Deuteronomy 6:4]. Nothing wrong about that.)

However, the Pharisees insisted that a man committed a sin if he did not wash his hands before eating or neglected to wear phylacteries. They were very punctilious about these man-made regulations and neglected or circumvented the Law of God given on Sinai.

The Pharisees declared that swearing by the temple was not a serious offense, but if you swore by the gold of the temple, you were indebted; no one swearing by the altar of sacrifice committed a sin, but anyone swearing by the sacrifice on the altar did a grievous wrong. That was making distinctions that do not exist. No man-made distinction does away with God's definite instructions. Nor do any observances of human regulation excuse us from doing the will of God. We must do more than those things that appeal to us or are easier to do or make a bigger showing. We must observe more than the letter of the Law.

Not only the outside of the cup is to be clean, but also the inside. Putting on a clean apron over a filthy dress does not make the garment clean.

But Pharisees of all generations have been exacting about externals but have broken the spirit of the Law. Observing the etiquette of the flag does not permit us to break the statutes of the state or evade them. Making a donation to the church does not allow us to neglect the Word and Sacrament. We may be doctrinally correct, yet not practice the doctrine by a Christian life. When we do the one, such as giving tithes or paying our church contributions, we cannot excuse ourselves from doing the other, such as showing mercy, loving our neighbor, hearing the Gospel, and walking the Christian way. If we keep only the outside clean, do that which is showy, but do not keep the heart with God, then all this avails us nothing.

These are the truths that Jesus emphasizes.

Seven Woes to the Scribes and Pharisees

Then Jesus said to the crowds and to His disciples, "The scribes and the Pharisees sit on Moses' seat, so practice and observe whatever they tell you—but not what they do. For they preach, but do not practice. They tie up heavy burdens, hard to bear, and lay them on people's shoulders, but they themselves are not willing to move them with their finger. They do all their deeds to be seen by others. For they make their phylacteries broad and their fringes long, and they love the place of honor at feasts and the best seats in the synagogues and greetings in the marketplaces and being called rabbi by others. But you are not to be called rabbi, for you have one teacher, and you are all brothers. And call no man your father on earth, for you have one Father, who is in heaven. Neither be called instructors, for you have one instructor, the Christ. The greatest among you shall be your servant. Whoever exalts himself will be humbled, and whoever humbles himself will be exalted.

"But woe to you, scribes and Pharisees, hypocrites! For you shut the kingdom of heaven in people's faces. For you neither enter yourselves nor allow those who would enter to go in. Woe to you, scribes and Pharisees, hypocrites! For you travel across sea and land to make a single proselyte, and when he becomes a proselyte, you make him twice as much a child of hell as yourselves.

"Woe to you, blind guides, who say, 'If anyone swears by the temple, it is nothing, but if anyone swears by the gold of the temple, he is bound by his oath.' You blind fools! For which is greater, the gold or the temple that has made the gold sacred? And you say, 'If anyone swears by the altar, it is nothing, but if anyone swears by the gift that is on the altar, he is bound by his oath.' You blind men! For which is greater, the gift or the altar that makes the gift sacred? So whoever swears by the altar swears by it and by everything on it. And whoever swears by the temple swears by it and by Him who dwells in it. And whoever swears by heaven swears by the throne of God and by Him who sits upon it.

"Woe to you, scribes and Pharisees, hypocrites! For you tithe mint and dill and cumin, and have neglected the weightier matters of the law: justice and mercy and faithfulness. These you ought to have done, without neglecting the others. You blind guides, straining out a gnat and swallowing a camel!

"Woe to you, scribes and Pharisees, hypocrites! For you clean the outside of the cup and the plate, but inside they are full of greed and self-indulgence. You blind Pharisee! First clean the inside of the cup and the plate, that the outside also may be clean.

"Woe to you, scribes and Pharisees, hypocrites! For you are like whitewashed tombs, which outwardly appear beautiful, but within are full of dead people's bones and all uncleanness. So you also outwardly appear righteous to others, but within you are full of hypocrisy and lawlessness."

Jesus looks for more than an outward goodness and ceremonial precision. Such things can be done mechanically. Jesus is looking for a contrite heart and consecrated lives. Despite our faults, He wants us to be sincere.

Jesus was always compassionate with stumbling and erring people, but He has no patience with those who yell "Lord, Lord" and hypocritically make pious faces. He who would not cast out one soul that came to Him weary and sin-troubled has no time for self-righteous, proud, and conceited snobs.

But remember, the door was open to the penitent thief, to the weeping Magdalene, to the questioning Thomas, and even to the erring Simon Peter. To us also, this door of His mercy is open wide if we confess our sin. To all such Jesus says, Your sin is forgiven— go in peace, and in My name go from strength to strength.

Prayer

Bruised, wounded, worried, and troubled, we come to You, O God. Turn Your face of love and mercy toward us and all those who are heavy of heart and perplexed. Call each one by name and draw such to Yourself with Your compelling love in Christ. Watch over all Your children, and remove all pretense and insincerity from our hearts, for Jesus' sake. Amen.

THE HEART CRY OF JESUS
Matthew 23:29–39

THE heart of Christ breaks as He weeps over Jerusalem. The history of the city of David has been a story of obstinate resistance to the most gracious call of a loving God. Prophets were stoned, and the blood of Zechariah was shed on the very temple site where God wanted man to go and make peace with his eternal Maker.

And it is not over. Even the contemporary generation of Jesus' day is no better than their fathers. They will lead the Son of God to Calvary and shed His holy, precious blood and let Him die on that accursed tree. No wonder Jesus weeps!

His heart breaks as He beholds the obstinacy of stubborn Jerusalem. To come to His own people with healing hands, to come to save them from their own doom and then to be rejected while helping them is tragic indeed. Jesus hates sin, yet how profound and all-embracing is His love for sinners! He does not want any of them to perish.

His heart breaks as He sees the perversity of mankind. Here He is, Redeemer and Friend, and yet man goes his own way, thinking that he needs no Savior. Man sneers and laughs at the cross. Who wants to be saved by one hanging between two transgressors? Who wants to grovel in the dust and plead unworthiness and helplessness? Not man. See what he has accomplished! Look at his magnificent civilization! Behold the mighty works of art, the endless chains of highways running over mountains and under rivers! Look at the towers reaching into the sky! Look at his glorious history, tomes of books, conquests of disease. Why, man is great, greater than ever! Look at the hospitals, medical procedures, financial strength, technological advances. Why, man is good, better than ever!

Such a world is too busy to give any thought to Jesus. But this vaunted civilization offers no hope, gives no peace, opens no heaven to mankind. It may provide clean shirts, but not clean hearts. It may place man on high pedestals and praise him to the sky, but man nevertheless has feet of clay, and out of his sinful heart comes hatred, destruction, atrocities, brutality, and wars. That brilliant mind plots death and crime and adultery. Woe to the soul that strikes Jesus in the face! It is on its march to damnation and hell.

No wonder Jesus weeps!

Woe to you, scribes and Pharisees, hypocrites! For you build the tombs of the prophets and decorate the monuments of the righteous, saying, "If we had lived in the days of our fathers, we would not have taken part with them in shedding the blood of the prophets." Thus you witness against yourselves that you are sons of those who murdered the prophets. Fill up, then, the measure of your fathers. You serpents, you brood of vipers, how are you to escape being sentenced to hell? Therefore I send you prophets and wise men and scribes, some of whom you will kill and crucify, and some you will flog in your synagogues and persecute from town to town, so that on you may come all the righteous blood shed on earth, from the blood of innocent Abel to the blood of Zechariah the son of Barachiah, whom you murdered between the sanctuary and the altar. Truly, I say to you, all these things will come upon this generation.

Lament over Jerusalem

O Jerusalem, Jerusalem, the city that kills the prophets and stones those who are sent to it! How often would I have gathered your children together as a hen gathers her brood under her wings, and you would not! See, your house is left to you desolate. For I tell you, you will not see Me again, until you say, "Blessed is He who comes in the name of the Lord."

Jesus weeps because Jerusalem would not come to Him and be saved. He pleads; all day long He reaches out His hands begging man to turn and live. He wants to help, to forgive, and to save.

He is calling; He is seeking the lost, the erring, the sorrowing, the confused, and the despairing. He wants to draw us to His bosom, that there we may sob out the tragic story of our misspent selves. And He heals. He takes our broken lives and makes us new. He wipes away our penitent tears and sends us on our way with the song of forgiveness. He takes us by the hand and leads us over the rocky road of sin's temptation to keep us from stumbling and falling. What an amazing love!

This is Gospel. Taking a lost son and clothing him in clean garments, loving him who had been in the company of swine, feeding his soul with food that satisfies, giving him peace and hope and a pure heart.

This is Gospel. The message is for all. All are included. All are wanted. If we were to say that all this big news is only for the elite, for those who have lived worthwhile lives, for those who have given a cup of cold water to the thirsty and spoken a kind word to the unlovable—then it would not be Gospel. This message cannot be limited. It is for all. It invites all to come.

Only our perversity of heart and our stubborn resistance keep us out of the arms of a forgiving Savior. His blood makes the foulest clean.

What blessed consolation to be found in Him who can give peace and heaven to sinful mankind!

Prayer
Just as I am; Thy love unknown Has broken ev'ry barrier down;
Now to be Thine, yea, Thine alone, O Lamb of God, I come,
I come. Amen. (LSB 570:6)

64

FORETELLING
MORE THAN
THE WEATHER
Matthew 24:1–14

THE temple Herod the Great built was not completed in all its details when Jesus lived. Every so often, some new ornamentation was added by some well-to-do Jew expressing "appreciation" to God. In the week of Christ's Passion, the disciples saw an addition in the temple court and called His attention to its beauty. On that occasion, Jesus foretold the destruction of the temple and the destruction of the city of Jerusalem. This would be the beginning of the final judgment.

The two, the destruction of the temple and of Jerusalem, run together and were to be signs preceding the end of the world. These are not the only signs of the final judgment and the end of time. Signs will be found in the decadent church: False prophets will arise, claiming to be the Christ. Indifference in the church will grow as the love of many will diminish.

Signs will be seen in the nations and the governments of the world: wars and rumors of wars, nation rising against nation and kingdom against kingdom. Signs will be observed among the races of men: famines, pestilences, betrayals, distrust, deceit, and hatred. Signs will be seen in the natural world: earthquakes, tidal waves, and falling stars.

All these things we see fulfilled again and again as Jesus foretold.

Jesus Foretells Destruction of the Temple

Jesus left the temple and was going away, when His disciples came to point out to Him the buildings of the temple. But He answered them, "You see all these, do you not? Truly, I say to you, there will not be left here one stone upon another that will not be thrown down."

Signs of the Close of the Age

As He sat on the Mount of Olives, the disciples came to Him privately, saying, "Tell us, when will these things be, and what will be the sign of Your coming and of the close of the age?" And Jesus answered them, "See that no one leads you astray. For many will come in My name, saying, 'I am the Christ,' and they will lead many astray. And you will hear of wars and rumors of wars. See that you are not alarmed, for this must take place, but the end is not yet. For nation will rise against nation, and kingdom against kingdom, and there will be famines and earthquakes in various places. All these are but the beginning of the birth pains.

"Then they will deliver you up to tribulation and put you to death, and you will be hated by all nations for My name's sake. And then many will fall away and betray one another and hate one another. And many false prophets will arise and lead many astray. And because lawlessness will be increased, the love of many will grow cold. But the one who endures to the end will be saved. And this gospel of the kingdom will be proclaimed throughout the whole world as a testimony to all nations, and then the end will come."

Should we be afraid of the coming judgment? Not if we are loyal and faithful to Christ to the end. There is no condemnation for those who believe. Why not? Are we not aware of our own sin and guilt? The believer has one plea that exempts him and sets him free: "Jesus died for me and paid for my transgression." Behind this truth and fact, we seek refuge. And God, who is just and righteous, does not condemn those who seek shelter in the sacred wounds of their atoning Savior. That is Gospel—the Gospel that covers the earth as snow covers the mountains and the dales.

Then the end will come—time will cease and eternity begin. To those who followed His voice and believed His Gospel will be given the glory of heaven, where there is no more death and where we will see Him face-to-face as heirs of His kingdom.

Prayer

As time ends and eternity begins, grant, Lord Jesus, that we are found among those who confess You as Savior and Lord, that You may acknowledge us and receive us into the eternal mansions. Abide in us, and preserve us daily in grace. Make us watchful and prayerful. Add daily to the number of those who are to be saved. Cover the earth with Your Gospel of reconciliation, that peace may reign and hope abide in many hearts. Amen.

THE HISS OF THE SCOFFER
Matthew 24:15–35

TWO reactions are quite typical when one speaks of the second coming of Christ. One is that of intense, even fanatical interest in predicting when it will happen: predicting the year, month, day, and hour when Jesus will return. All such predictions fail. This is to be expected because Scripture tells us that "concerning that day or that hour, no one knows, not even the angels in heaven, nor the Son, but only the Father" (Mark 13:32). "The day of the Lord will come like a thief" (2 Peter 3:10). Jesus will come in glory when no one is looking for Him, at a day and a time that cannot been predicted.

The other extreme reaction is disbelief at all prophecy of a coming judgment. "Where is the promise of His coming? For ever since the fathers fell asleep, all things are continuing as they were from the beginning of creation" (2 Peter 3:4). Scoffers hiss that the second coming is ridiculous and that it is a mere fantasy of some religious enthusiasts.

Jesus emphatically stated that He is coming again in glory to judge the living and the dead. However, certain events will precede His return. False christs will arise, great tribulations will vex humanity, the sun and the moon will not give their proper light, and, according to the apostle Paul, the Antichrist will make his appearance to deceive many.

As these things come to pass, we should be watchful and remind ourselves daily of Christ's appearing. Prayerfully, we should observe and ponder these signs and evidence, for Jesus Himself says, "See, I have told you beforehand."

The Abomination of Desolation

"So when you see the abomination of desolation spoken of by the prophet Daniel, standing in the holy place (let the reader understand), then let those who are in Judea flee to the mountains. Let the one who is on the housetop not go down to take what is in his house, and let the one who is in the field not turn back to take his cloak. And alas for women who are pregnant and for those who are nursing infants in those days! Pray that your flight may not be in winter or on a Sabbath. For then there will be great tribulation, such as has not been from the beginning of the world until now, no, and never will be. And if those days had not been cut short, no human being would be saved. But for the sake of the elect those days will be cut short. Then if anyone says to you, 'Look, here is the Christ!' or 'There He is!' do not believe it. For false christs and false prophets will arise and perform great signs and wonders, so as to lead astray, if possible, even the elect. See, I have told you beforehand. So, if they say to you, 'Look, He is in the wilderness,' do not go out. If they say, 'Look, He is in the inner rooms,' do not believe it. For as the lightning comes from the east and shines as far as the west, so will be the coming of the Son of Man. Wherever the corpse is, there the vultures will gather.

The Coming of the Son of Man

"Immediately after the tribulation of those days the sun will be darkened, and the moon will not give its light, and the stars will fall from heaven, and the powers of the heavens will be shaken. Then will appear in heaven the sign of the Son of Man, and then all the tribes of the earth will mourn, and they will see the Son of Man coming on the clouds of heaven with power and great glory. And He will send out His angels with a loud trumpet call, and they will gather His elect from the four winds, from one end of heaven to the other.

The Lesson of the Fig Tree

"From the fig tree learn its lesson: as soon as its branch becomes tender and puts out its leaves, you know that summer is near. So also, when you see all these things, you know that He is near, at the very gates. Truly, I say to you, this generation will not pass away until all these things take place. Heaven and earth will pass away, but My words will not pass away."

But none of Jesus' contemporaries is living today. Was He mistaken? Not at all!

The judgment began with the destruction of Jerusalem and its temple, which was never rebuilt. The generation that crucified Jesus and saw their temple destroyed witnessed the downfall of Jerusalem. All this occurred in AD 70, about forty years after Jesus rose from the dead. That generation saw the beginning of the judgment to come. Since then, other signs have been fulfilled and are being fulfilled to this very day.

These signs, described in our reading today, guarantee Christ's return. As we note these things and observe them, we should be assured of His faithfulness to us, become more loyal to our Lord, and be more dutiful in the performing of our tasks so that when He comes, we will be found faithful to Him and enter with Him into the kingdom of eternity.

Prayer

O Lord, Father of our Savior Jesus Christ, You have given us Your Word for our learning and warning. Grant us grace to heed Your revelations and believe Your Gospel and obey Your commandments. Forgive us our many neglects, and make us ever more diligent in the searching of the Scriptures and of Your will. Preserve us from the errors of the indifferent and sinful world, and forgive us all our sins for Jesus' sake. Amen.

YOU HAVE BEEN WARNED

Matthew 24:36–51

PREPAREDNESS has always been a key to victory in warfare and peacetime security. The commander who can spring a surprise attack on the enemy and catch the opponent off guard has won half of the battle. Nations and people must constantly be on the alert, lest they find themselves in a hopeless situation.

Jesus urges Christians to be ready at all times. He is coming again, and He wants us to be faithful so He finds us prepared. But the world of sin wants to make us indifferent. The world tells us there is plenty of time to make preparation to meet Christ, the heavenly judge. Enjoy life for the moment. Eat, drink, and be merry! Why be so concerned about heaven and salvation? We can worry about that in our old age. We all have heard such whisperings, have we not?

Such ideas are not new. The people of Noah's day said the same things and acted accordingly until the very day Noah went into the ark. There was no sign of a flood, said they, so why get excited if an old, pious fanatic gets crazy notions and ideas about sin and judgment? But the rain fell, the waters of the earth opened up, and all life perished except Noah, his family, and the animals on the ark.

"Stay awake," says Jesus, "for you do not know on what day your Lord is coming."

No One Knows That Day and Hour

But concerning that day and hour no one knows, not even the angels of heaven, nor the Son, but the Father only. For as were the days of Noah, so will be the coming of the Son of Man. For as in those days before the flood they were eating and drinking, marrying and giving in marriage, until the day when Noah entered the ark, and they were unaware until the flood came and swept them all away, so will be the coming of the Son of Man. Then two men will be in the field; one will be taken and one left. Two women will be grinding at the mill; one will be taken and one left. Therefore, stay awake, for you do not know on what day your Lord is coming. But know this, that if the master of the house had known in what part of the night the thief was coming, he would have stayed awake and would not have let his house be broken into. Therefore you also must be ready, for the Son of Man is coming at an hour you do not expect.

Who then is the faithful and wise servant, whom his master has set over his household, to give them their food at the proper time? Blessed is that servant whom his master will find so doing when he comes. Truly, I say to you, he will set him over all his possessions. But if that wicked servant says to himself, "My master is delayed," and begins to beat his fellow servants and eats and drinks with drunkards, the master of that servant will come on a day when he does not expect him and at an hour he does not know and will cut him in pieces and put him with the hypocrites. In that place there will be weeping and gnashing of teeth.

"Two men will be in the field." That is midday. "Two women will be grinding at the mill." That is morning. Two shall be in bed, says Luke 17:34. That is night.

How can it be morning, midday, and night at the same time? Because the earth is round. We can read these passages and know that Jesus is coming to all the world at the same hour. We will not hear by news media that Jesus has come to Australia or China for judgment, neither will the Europeans hear that Jesus has appeared to the United States and started the judgment. No, Jesus will come to all simultaneously.

But the hour has not as yet struck. The Lord still delays, giving all mankind room for repentance. And we who love Him should continue to serve Him even with greater faithfulness so that even more people hear this Gospel that saves.

Jesus looks for loyalty. He must be first in our lives. Whether we eat or drink, marry or are given in marriage, whatever we do, we are to do it in the name of the Lord Jesus Christ, giving thanks to God the Father by Him. Then the inevitability of judgment need not fill us with fear because Jesus is coming as our Savior and Friend and Brother. He will receive us into glory as His faithful and loyal followers.

Prayer

O Lord, Father of our Savior Jesus Christ, You have sent Your Word to the ends of the earth that the souls of all may be converted to You. While it is day, and Your grace and mercy still call men to repentance, grant that we speak of this hope to all and that we bear witness to the atoning sacrifice of Your Son, Jesus Christ. May we with prayerful hearts make ready at all times for His coming and be found faithful at His appearing, to enter with Him, our Savior, into the glory that is unending. Amen.

ON THE ALERT
Matthew 25:1–13

WEDDINGS are always human interest events. The outcome of a marriage is so unpredictable. No one knows whether the uniting of two hearts in the bond of matrimony will endure "till death do us part." Customs and fashions of the ceremony vary from generation to generation.

In Jesus' day, marriage ceremonies were performed at the home of the bride, and the festivities and the celebration were held at the home of the groom. The bride joined the husband's family and household. On the evening of the wedding, the invited guests would wait for the procession to pass along a given point, to join the crowd and go to the home of the bridegroom. It was customary to walk.

Because the streets of ancient cities were not illuminated, each person carried some kind of light. If one was to use the oil lamp for some hours, an extra jar of oil was taken along to replenish the lamp from time to time.

Five of the young women in this parable did not take extra oil. They hoped they would have enough for the procession. It was rather inconvenient to carry the extra vessel, so they took the chance—and were left out.

The courtyard was in the center of the building, not to the rear of the house, as our yards are. To avoid the rowdiness of the uninvited and to keep out those who might cause a disturbance, the door of the house was shut and bolted. Even when the women, who claimed they were invited, came to the bolted door, the servants refused to open it, fearing some foul play. So the door remained closed, and the maidens missed the wedding festivities.

The Parable of the Ten Virgins

Then the kingdom of heaven will be like ten virgins who took their lamps and went to meet the bridegroom. Five of them were foolish, and five were wise. For when the foolish took their lamps, they took no oil with them, but the wise took flasks of oil with their lamps. As the bridegroom was delayed, they all became drowsy and slept. But at midnight there was a cry, "Here is the bridegroom! Come out to meet him." Then all those virgins rose and trimmed their lamps. And the foolish said to the wise, "Give us some of your oil, for our lamps are going out." But the wise answered, saying, "Since there will not be enough for us and for you, go rather to the dealers and buy for yourselves." And while they were going to buy, the bridegroom came, and those who were ready went in with him to the marriage feast, and the door was shut. Afterward the other virgins came also, saying, "Lord, lord, open to us." But he answered, "Truly, I say to you, I do not know you."Watch therefore, for you know neither the day nor the hour.

The bridegroom in this parable is Jesus Christ. The bride is the Church. The young women are those who hold membership in a Christian congregation. Some are believers and others have no faith or "believe for a while" (Luke 8:13).

The oil is faith. This we cannot give to another. That is why we say "I believe" and not "we believe" in the Apostles' and the Nicene Creeds.

The shut door is death and judgment to come. After that door is shut, the time of grace has come to an end. No second chance is given after death. "Now is the favorable time; behold, now is the day of salvation" (2 Corinthians 6:2).

Therefore, "watch," says Jesus. We are to prepare and be on the alert and not let the routine of life and the monotony of this routine distract us. The dull hours deaden our enthusiasm. The eternal sameness of things makes us tired and weary. So faith and hope grow dim.

Faith must be nourished through the Word and Sacraments. Only then are we on the alert. When prolonged sickness comes to our home, when friends fail us, when business is disappointing and life is full of frustrations, we need a faith built upon the eternal Word. And that faith must be nourished and strengthened before the crisis comes or it may be too late.

Across the ages comes the exhortation of Jesus, the Bridegroom of our souls: "Be faithful unto death, and I will give you the crown of life" (Revelation 2:10).

Prayer

As the day unfolds before us, Lord, let us learn to know the real value of life and choose what is acceptable to You. Grant that we find our greatest joy in serving You and be ever watchful against that coldness of heart and that lukewarmness that rob us of heaven and its glory. Keep open the door of Your mercy to our household and friends, for Jesus' sake. Amen.

TRUSTEES OF GOD'S HOLDINGS
Matthew 25:14–30

IN the days of Jesus, a steward was the general manager of a rich man's estate. Often, he was a slave, as had been Joseph in Potiphar's household. All business of his master's domain was under his supervision, so such a steward was given many assistants.

In the following parable, we read that the owner had a number of stewards to whom he entrusted his wealth. To one he gave five talents, to another, two, and to a third, one. Their ability to handle money was not equal, so he gave more responsibility to one than the other.

A talent was equal to about twenty years' wages. Two of the men invested the money, but the third buried the treasure in the ground. He would take no chance whatsoever. He did nothing.

In due time, the men had to report to their master. The two who had been conscientious and faithful were rewarded accordingly, but the man who buried his money was severely chided and dismissed. The least he could have done, said the master, was to put the money with bankers to accrue interest. That he had done nothing was inexcusable.

The Parable of the Talents

For it will be like a man going on a journey, who called his servants and entrusted to them his property. To one he gave five talents, to another two, to another one, to each according to his ability. Then he went away. He who had received the five talents went at once and traded with them, and he made five talents more. So also he who had the two talents made two talents more. But he who had received the one talent went and dug in the ground and hid his master's money. Now after a long time the master of those servants came and

settled accounts with them. And he who had received the
five talents came forward, bringing five talents more, saying,
"Master, you delivered to me five talents; here I have made
five talents more." His master said to him, "Well done, good
and faithful servant. You have been faithful over a little; I will
set you over much. Enter into the joy of your master." And he
also who had the two talents came forward, saying, "Master,
you delivered to me two talents; here I have made two talents
more." His master said to him, "Well done, good and faithful servant. You have been faithful over a little; I will set you
over much. Enter into the joy of your master." He also who
had received the one talent came forward, saying, "Master, I
knew you to be a hard man, reaping where you did not sow,
and gathering where you scattered no seed, so I was afraid,
and I went and hid your talent in the ground. Here you have
what is yours." But his master answered him, "You wicked and
slothful servant! You knew that I reap where I have not sown
and gather where I scattered no seed? Then you ought to have
invested my money with the bankers, and at my coming I
should have received what was my own with interest. So take
the talent from him and give it to him who has the ten talents.
For to everyone who has will more be given, and he will have
an abundance. But from the one who has not, even what he
has will be taken away. And cast the worthless servant into the
outer darkness. In that place there will be weeping and gnashing of teeth."

In this parable, Jesus teaches that God is the owner and all we possess we are holding in trust and are accountable to Him. God has a
threefold claim on us. He created us; He redeemed us through His
Son; and He brought us to faith by the power of the Holy Spirit. So
we live in His grace and are of His household.

God has given to each of us as trustees of the family certain
earthly possessions. To some He has given more, to others less,
undoubtedly according to ability. With our fellow men, we can
claim certain possessions as our own, but with God we are stewards. Therefore, we cannot do with our own as we please. We

are responsible and accountable to Him. He expects His proportionate share. In the Old Testament, this share was a tenth. In the New Testament, living under grace, we are to give as the Lord has blessed us. He expects us to be conscientious and faithful in our stewardship.

God does not limit our stewardship to things. He also demands faithfulness in the use of our natural gifts, abilities, and talents. If we have ability in leadership, in counseling, in teaching, in administration, in music—whatever that gift may be—we are to use it in the service of God. We cannot use these gifts as we please. We dare not be indifferent as to the outcome. Our duty is to consecrate all that we have and all that we are to God. Otherwise, we are unfaithful, and what we have will be taken from us and given to those who are faithful in the performance of their duties and obligations.

Most of us are one-talent Christians. But we can all serve the Lord faithfully with whatever ability we have.

Prayer

Heavenly Father, in Your goodness, You have opened Your hands and given us all we need for life. With thanksgiving, we accept these gifts from Your bountiful hand. Grant, we beseech You, that we use them rightly and be worthy of this trust. As we acknowledge Your bounty, may we day after day perform our tasks and duties pleasing to You. We dedicate this day and ourselves and all that we have and are to You and Your Son, Jesus Christ, our Lord and Savior. Amen.

THE FINAL JUDGMENT
Matthew 25:31–46

JESUS said a good deal about His return to judge the living and the dead: signs would precede His coming and warnings will help us to be on the alert. His promises assure us that after the sorrows of life and the sinfulness of this world, He will return to end all wickedness. Satan and his followers will be imprisoned in the utter darkness of damnation, and God's saints will stand before the throne and live forevermore in glory.

Before Jesus concludes these prophetic statements of the last days, He gives an account of the actual judgment, how it will be, and what are to be the great issues and the far-reaching consequences. Some like to call this account a parable. But it is not a parable in the same sense as the parables of the ten virgins, the talents, or the prodigal son. The only parable form in the account of the final judgment is the comparison of the believers to sheep and the unbelievers to goats.

We keep this in mind as we read the story.

The Final Judgment

When the Son of Man comes in His glory, and all the angels with Him, then He will sit on His glorious throne. Before Him will be gathered all the nations, and He will separate people one from another as a shepherd separates the sheep from the goats. And He will place the sheep on His right, but the goats on the left. Then the King will say to those on His right, "Come, you who are blessed by My Father, inherit the kingdom prepared for you from the foundation of the world. For I was hungry and you gave Me food, I was thirsty and you gave Me drink, I was a stranger and you welcomed Me, I was naked and you clothed Me, I was sick and you visited Me, I was in prison and you came to Me." Then the righteous will answer Him, saying, "Lord, when did we see You hungry and feed You, or thirsty and give You drink? And when did we see You a stranger and welcome You, or naked and clothe You? And when did we see You sick or in prison and visit You?" And the King will answer them, "Truly, I say to you, as you did it to one of the least of these My brothers, you did it to Me."

Then He will say to those on His left, "Depart from Me, you cursed, into the eternal fire prepared for the devil and his angels. For I was hungry and you gave Me no food, I was thirsty and you gave Me no drink, I was a stranger and you did not welcome Me, naked and you did not clothe Me, sick and in prison and you did not visit Me." Then they also will answer, saying, "Lord, when did we see You hungry or thirsty or a stranger or naked or sick or in prison, and did not minister to You?" Then He will answer them, saying, "Truly, I say to you, as you did not do it to one of the least of these, you did not do it to Me." And these will go away into eternal punishment, but the righteous into eternal life.

Jesus is coming again. He is coming in glory. He came the first time in deep humility when He was born in Bethlehem and died on the accursed tree. When He returns at the end of the world, He will come in His heavenly majesty and every knee will bow and every tongue confess that He is King of kings and Lord of lords.

As the peoples of the ages and time appear before Him, they divide into two groups: one on the right and one on the left. Those on the right Jesus calls sheep.

Who are the sheep? What makes them sheep? Jesus tells us, "My sheep hear My voice, and I know them, and they follow Me. I give them eternal life" (John 10:27–28). At that occasion, Jesus also said to some of the contemporaries, "But you do not believe because you are not part of My flock" (John 10:26). The believers are called sheep. They believe that Jesus, by the shedding of His blood on the cross, has redeemed them. "They have washed their robes and made them white in the blood of the Lamb" (Revelation 7:14).

The goats are people who did not believe and do not accept Jesus as the Savior from sin.

So belief and unbelief determine the destinies of eternity. "Whoever believes and is baptized will be saved, but whoever does not believe will be condemned" (Mark 16:16).

If they are already separated as they approach the judgment seat, why, then, the judgment? Faith cannot be seen, but faith reveals itself in the conduct and lives of people. A good tree bears good fruit. That those on the right had a living faith showed itself in their daily life on earth. Their love for Christ compelled them to feed the hungry, visit the sick, and encourage those who were depressed in spirit. They were saved by grace and faith, but, as saved believers, they gave proof of their love for Christ by living the Christian way.

The unbelief of those on the left was revealed in their selfishness. They had no interest in Christ and ignored Him and His cause. So they are eternally separated from God and the everlasting glory of heaven. But the believers, made righteous through Christ's blood, enter into the marriage feast of the Lamb to live in the fullness of joy forever.

Prayer

Divine Savior, by whose blood we are redeemed and by whose grace we are cleansed from our sins, send Your Holy Spirit into our hearts day after day, that we may love You more and more and in a fuller measure serve You and our fellow men. Enrich our lives with the graces of Your Spirit so we may open our hearts and hands to the needs of the troubled and distressed. Amen.

THE GOSPEL OF GRATITUDE

Matthew 26:1–16

THE hour is approaching when Jesus is to lay down His life that sinners might be forgiven and saints have a glorious hope.

The religious leaders of Jerusalem can no longer delay. The hour has come, they realize, that if they are to retain the balance of power, Jesus must be silenced. For these Jewish officials, the situation has become intolerable. Yet Jesus is the most popular prophet in all Palestine. They cannot openly seize Him and put Him out of the way. Eventually, the opportunity comes. Judas Iscariot, the treasurer of Jesus' followers, is ready to strike a bargain.

Why would Judas want to put Jesus into the hands of His enemies? Volumes have been written analyzing the motives and the character of Judas. What could have induced Judas to take this fatal step and to betray his Master?

The decision to see the thing through was reached at the banquet table in the home of Simon the Leper.

The Plot to Kill Jesus

When Jesus had finished all these sayings, He said to His disciples, "You know that after two days the Passover is coming, and the Son of Man will be delivered up to be crucified."

Then the chief priests and the elders of the people gathered in the palace of the high priest, whose name was Caiaphas, and plotted together in order to arrest Jesus by stealth and kill Him. But they said, "Not during the feast, lest there be an uproar among the people."

Jesus Anointed at Bethany

Now when Jesus was at Bethany in the house of Simon the leper, a woman came up to Him with an alabaster flask of

very expensive ointment, and she poured it on His head as
He reclined at table. And when the disciples saw it, they were
indignant, saying, "Why this waste? For this could have been
sold for a large sum and given to the poor." But Jesus, aware
of this, said to them, "Why do you trouble the woman? For
she has done a beautiful thing to Me. For you always have the
poor with you, but you will not always have Me. In pouring
this ointment on My body, she has done it to prepare Me for
burial. Truly, I say to you, wherever this gospel is proclaimed in
the whole world, what she has done will also be told in memory of her."

Judas to Betray Jesus

Then one of the twelve, whose name was Judas Iscariot,
went to the chief priests and said, "What will you give me if
I deliver Him over to you?" And they paid him thirty pieces
of silver. And from that moment he sought an opportunity to
betray Him.

Jesus had raised Lazarus of Bethany from the dead. Simon the leper
gave a dinner to honor Jesus and Lazarus. As it was customary, people
reclined on couches at the table with body outstretched, away from
the table. At the meal, a woman entered with an alabaster jar filled
with precious ointment, which may have cost several hundred dollars. The woman poured the oil on Jesus' head as a sign of her deep,
sincere devotion, loyalty, and gratitude to the Savior.

"Why this waste?" asked the disciples indignantly. "This could
have been sold for a large sum and given to the poor."

Then and there Judas came to a wicked decision. Judas realized
at that meal that Jesus would never make His popularity a paying enterprise. So Judas concluded that he must act to take care of
himself. He left the house, met with the leaders of the temple, and
agreed to deliver Jesus to them at the bargain price of thirty pieces
of silver.

Was it wrong for the woman to pour all this ointment upon
the head of Jesus? Is it sinful to build beautiful churches and have
in them beautiful appointments? Must the Christian congregation

refrain from placing costly windows into the building and purchasing costly altar paraments or furnishings?

Jesus says no. Our gratitude and appreciation can and must express itself in building a house to the Lord compatible with our environment and ability. That does not say that the poor should be neglected. Men and women who love the Lord Jesus with all their hearts will not do the one and neglect the other. However, too many use the one as an excuse to do neither.

Our gratitude lifts our hearts and hands to Christ and reaches out to the needs of our fellow men.

Prayer

With grateful hearts, we lift our voices and hands in service to You, good Lord. You have supplied us with the needs of our bodies, and You have graciously given us the manna from heaven to feed and nourish our souls. Accept the gifts we humbly offer, and use them to build Your Church and proclaim the Gospel to the multitudes of people in all lands and places, to the honor and glory of Your Son, Jesus Christ, our Lord. Amen.

NIGHT OF PARADOXES
Matthew 26:17–35

THE Upper Room of Jerusalem is crowded with intensity. The Twelve are gathering with Jesus for His last Passover meal. Hearts are troubled and souls are anxious as Jesus makes the shocking revelations of unfaithfulness and cowardice. Yet His compassionate love is so compelling that He lays down His life for these men who are so disappointing in this critical hour. What a generous love as He washes their feet; what indescribable patience as He breaks for them the bread of His body. Amid the pettiness of sinful and envious disciples, the Lord of all makes a covenant of grace that erring man, ashamed of himself, may come to the Redeemer's bosom and sob out a confession of sin and be forgiven.

For the last time, Jesus gathers with the chosen amid ominous forebodings. What a doleful night it is to be! "One of you will betray Me." Startled, surprised, disturbed, they ask, one after another: "Is it I, Lord?" No one wants to think himself so devilish and so contemptible. Even Judas joins the questioning group: "Is it I, Rabbi?"

What inexpressible love as Jesus indicates to Judas that He knows that he, a trusted disciple, would sell his Master and his soul for a few paltry pieces of silver! "He who has dipped his hand in the dish with Me will betray Me." Although black plottings are hidden away in Judas's heart, Jesus still loves him and as Friend offers the same choice morsels of the Passover meal to him as the other disciples received. What an unconditional love!

"Before the rooster crows, you will deny Me three times." Not I, Lord, says Simon Peter. "Even if I must die with You, I will not deny You!" But within a few hours, Simon warmed himself at the fire of the courtyard and sank to the taunts of cursing men and completely hid his identity.

"You will all fall away because of Me this night." Never! they exclaim. But before the night grows into its wee hours, they all flee, leaving Jesus alone. What a sorry group of men! After three years of continuous training, the result seems overwhelmingly tragic. How could they ever forget that Upper Room where they witnessed such amazing events?

To prepare for this eventful night, Jesus sends two of His disciples into the city of Jerusalem to find the room, large and furnished, to get ready for the Feast of the Unleavened Bread.

The Passover with the Disciples

Now on the first day of Unleavened Bread the disciples came to Jesus, saying, "Where will You have us prepare for You to eat the Passover?" He said, "Go into the city to a certain man and say to him, 'The Teacher says, My time is at hand. I will keep the Passover at your house with My disciples.' " And the disciples did as Jesus had directed them, and they prepared the Passover.

When it was evening, He reclined at table with the twelve. And as they were eating, He said, "Truly, I say to you, one of you will betray Me." And they were very sorrowful and began to say to Him one after another, "Is it I, Lord?" He answered, "He who has dipped his hand in the dish with Me will betray Me. The Son of Man goes as it is written of Him, but woe to that man by whom the Son of Man is betrayed! It would have been better for that man if he had not been born." Judas, who would betray Him, answered, "Is it I, Rabbi?" He said to him, "You have said so."

Institution of the Lord's Supper

Now as they were eating, Jesus took bread, and after blessing it broke it and gave it to the disciples, and said, "Take, eat; this is My body." And He took a cup, and when He had given thanks He gave it to them, saying, "Drink of it, all of you, for this is My blood of the covenant, which is poured out for many for the forgiveness of sins. I tell you I will not drink again of this fruit of the vine until that day when I drink it new with you in My Father's kingdom."

Jesus Foretells Peter's Denial

And when they had sung a hymn, they went out to the Mount of Olives. Then Jesus said to them, "You will all fall away because of Me this night. For it is written, 'I will strike the shepherd, and the sheep of the flock will be scattered.' But after I am raised up, I will go before you to Galilee." Peter answered Him, "Though they all fall away because of You, I will never fall away." Jesus said to him, "Truly, I tell you, this very night, before the rooster crows, you will deny Me three times." Peter said to Him, "Even if I must die with You, I will not deny You!" And all the disciples said the same.

In this Upper Room, on that never-to-be-forgotten night, Jesus instituted one of two New Testament sacraments. As a testament of His grace, He offers us, the children of the new covenant, dispensation—forgiveness of all our sins and peace with God and hope of everlasting life.

Jesus took bread and said, "This is My body." It was real and genuine bread, something visible, that the disciples saw before their eyes. With the bread, Jesus gave them His body. This is invisible in the Sacrament. We do not behold the body with our natural eye. Nevertheless, the body is as real as the visible bread.

Then Jesus took the cup and said, "This is My blood of the covenant." This cup contained the fruit of the vine; also visible and real. With it, Jesus gave His blood, which was shed for many on Calvary. This also is real.

We have with the visible bread the invisible body, and with the visible cup, in which is the fruit of the vine, the invisible blood, shed for the remission of our sins. Of the bread we are to eat, and of the cup we are to drink; we receive with this eating and drinking the very body and blood of our Lord. We are to eat and to drink; nothing more, nothing less.

The purpose of this is stressed by Jesus. On the one hand, it is to seal to us forgiveness of all sins: the sins of the heart as well as the sins of the tongue; the ugly, nasty, and contemptible things we do; sins known to our fellow men and sins known only to God and us; even sins we are not aware of. Whose sins are to be forgiven? Those of all penitent sinners. No one who comes is to be cast out.

This Sacrament is for disturbed disciples. As Jesus announced, "One of you will betray Me," they crowded around Him, asking, "Is it I?" Jesus wants us to look into our hearts and become upset over our sins that He might offer His peace to us.

This Sacrament is for anxious disciples. Often we are uneasy, worried, troubled. As we come, Jesus whispers, "Take heart; I have overcome the world" (John 16:33).

This Sacrament is for sorrowing disciples. Those men in the Upper Room were sad; their Master was about to die. Today many hearts are sorrowing. They seek comfort. The Lord's Supper gives them the assurance that Christ is coming again and will raise up all those who believe unto life eternal.

This Sacrament is for sinning disciples. Those Twelve were about to deny, betray, and forsake. Jesus knew that. But later their consciences would awake and disturb them. Then they, as well as we, must know that the Lord forgives seventy times seven.

This Sacrament is for disappointing disciples. Jesus expected more. Had He not patiently taught them for three years? Yet, in the face of crisis, they fail Him. We, too, fall short in our loyalties and in our devotion to the Lord. Dare we come? Just for such Jesus instituted this sacred meal.

So all disturbed, anxious, sorrowing, disappointing Christians should come. What a pity that we so often reject this invitation!

On the other hand, this testament seals to us His return. "I tell you I will not drink again of this fruit of the vine until that day when I drink it new with you in My Father's kingdom." Jesus is going into death. Before another twenty-four hours have passed, His lifeless body will be placed into the tomb. This covenant is the surety that Jesus will not remain in death. He will rise again.

And now Jesus has ascended on high as the risen Savior. This Sacrament gives us the guarantee that He will come again. Until He does, He tells us to do this in remembrance of Him.

This Sacrament also seals to us the continuance of His Father's kingdom. When heaven and earth have passed away, the Kingdom still will stand. The gates of hell will not prevail against it. Christ is the final victor over sorrow, sin, and death. Each time we observe the Lord's Supper, we are telling the world that Jesus, His cause, and His Gospel will survive the wrecks of time, and we, who have been washed white in His blood, will be kings with Him forever and ever.

Prayer

Jesus, lover of souls, we are deeply aware of our failings and transgressions. Too often we have lived on the fringe of things

*and have forgotten You. The finger of guilt points at us; we have
sinned. O Savior, cast us not away from Your presence, but let us
find even this day in You forgiveness, peace, hope, and heaven.
Amen.*

THE AGONY
OF THE GARDEN
Matthew 26:36–46

JESUS did not stumble into His Passion blindly. He knew the very
hour, appointed from all eternity, in which He was to suffer and
to die. Already in Galilee, before He made the eventful journey to
Jerusalem with His disciples, Jesus announced that the time had come
and He would be put to death the next time they would go to the
Holy City. But He did not doubt for a moment as to the outcome:
"He will be raised on the third day" (Matthew 20:19).

Jesus gathered the Twelve in the Upper Room to wash their feet
and to institute the new covenant, giving His body and His blood
with the bread and the cup as a continual Means of Grace through
which weary and troubled souls may find forgiveness and peace for
their mind and heart.

After they sang the Passover hymn (Psalms 113–18), they went
out into the moonlit night, out of the Sheep's Gate, down into the
Kidron Valley and across the brook to the Garden of Gethsemane on
the western slope of the Mount of Olives. That garden still stands. In
it are eight venerable olive trees. No one can prove that they stood
there 2,000 years ago, but they are extremely old, and some look as
though they are growing from the stump of a hewn-down tree.

Jesus went to this garden on that eventful night when He was betrayed. There He fought with the forces of darkness, drinking the cup of His Passion to the last drop, that Satan's head be crushed and his power broken.

That is why Jesus went to Gethsemane.

Jesus Prays in Gethsemane

Then Jesus went with them to a place called Gethsemane, and He said to His disciples, "Sit here, while I go over there and pray." And taking with Him Peter and the two sons of Zebedee, He began to be sorrowful and troubled. Then He said to them, "My soul is very sorrowful, even to death; remain here, and watch with Me." And going a little farther He fell on His face and prayed, saying, "My Father, if it be possible, let this cup pass from Me; nevertheless, not as I will, but as You will." And He came to the disciples and found them sleeping. And He said to Peter, "So, could you not watch with Me one hour? Watch and pray that you may not enter into temptation. The spirit indeed is willing, but the flesh is weak." Again, for the second time, He went away and prayed, "My Father, if this cannot pass unless I drink it, Your will be done." And again He came and found them sleeping, for their eyes were heavy. So, leaving them again, He went away and prayed for the third time, saying the same words again. Then He came to the disciples and said to them, "Sleep and take your rest later on. See, the hour is at hand, and the Son of Man is betrayed into the hands of sinners. Rise, let us be going; see, My betrayer is at hand."

The battle of the ages was on. And Jesus must drink the cup of His Passion alone. No one could share it with Him.

With twelve He came to Jerusalem. Then there were eleven at Gethsemane. Eight stayed outside the garden; three went with Him into the grove. But even these three stayed behind as He went a "little farther," far enough that they could not see Him, for it was night and there were trees. But they could hear, if their ears were not too dull.

There in His loneliness, Jesus drank the cup of agony. Sin, damning sin, brutal sin, pet sins, hidden sins—all that is ugly in life, all that tortures the conscience, all that sends man to hell—your sin, mine—was in that cup.

No wonder Jesus drew back. All that was hideous and satanic to His sensitive and sinless soul was there. "Nevertheless, not as I will, but as You will." And why? He saw you and me—helpless, hopeless, condemned. Something had to be done and only He, the almighty God, could do it.

So He drank—He went into the battle of battles. Unseen forces attacked Him. And He battled alone. "And He came to the disciples and found them sleeping." They did nothing. A sleeping disciple is helpless and useless. Man contributes nothing to his own redemption. He is dead in trespasses and sin until the breath of the Holy Spirit comes upon him. But that the disciples slept—did not move a finger—did not deter Jesus from going into the conflict and agony to save sinful man.

And this He did with His lifeblood. That is what the agony of the garden means to you and to me.

Jesus saves worthless, useless, helpless, condemned, lost mankind. He suffered. He died that you and I might have a reconciled God, a good conscience, and an open heaven.

Prayer

In holy awe and deepest humility, we ponder upon Your Passion, Savior of lost humanity. What an amazing love! And we so undeserving and so unworthy! Precious Redeemer, draw us closer to Your wounded side, and cleanse us altogether from sin and the desire to sin. Amen.

"DO WHAT YOU CAME TO DO"

Matthew 26:47–57, 59–68

AS we see one event stumbling and tumbling after another in the frantic night of betrayal and arrest, we marvel that so many things could have happened in so short a time.

The night is dark with evil. All the world seems to have plotted against the Son of God. All the disciples forsake Him, and Jesus, in whose heart was no sin and whose noble character was without blemish, was treated like a common criminal—accused and condemned to death without one single charge proved against Him.

Yet, throughout it all, Jesus moves with the majesty of very God of very God, even touching with His healing hand the ear of the high priest's servant, which an erring disciple had cut off. Erring—because he thought that Jesus' cause must be defended and upheld by the power of the sword.

Yet the religious leaders of Jerusalem will not accept proof. They are blinded to truth and to facts. They had decided before the trial, even before the betrayal, that Jesus would be put to death regardless of evidence. Whether witnesses agree makes no difference. Although Jesus testifies under oath that He is God, the Sanhedrin do not rest until Jesus is condemned to the cross. Their hour has come. Sin and wickedness are doing their worst.

Such is the scene we behold as we go with Jesus to the judgment hall.

Betrayal and Arrest of Jesus

While He was still speaking, Judas came, one of the twelve, and with him a great crowd with swords and clubs, from the chief priests and the elders of the people. Now the betrayer had given them a sign, saying, "The one I will kiss is the man; seize Him." And he came up to Jesus at once and said,

"Greetings, Rabbi!" And he kissed Him. Jesus said to him, "Friend, do what you came to do." Then they came up and laid hands on Jesus and seized Him. And behold, one of those who were with Jesus stretched out his hand and drew his sword and struck the servant of the high priest and cut off his ear. Then Jesus said to him, "Put your sword back into its place. For all who take the sword will perish by the sword. Do you think that I cannot appeal to My Father, and He will at once send Me more than twelve legions of angels? But how then should the Scriptures be fulfilled, that it must be so?" At that hour Jesus said to the crowds, "Have you come out as against a robber, with swords and clubs to capture Me? Day after day I sat in the temple teaching, and you did not seize Me. But all this has taken place that the Scriptures of the prophets might be fulfilled." Then all the disciples left Him and fled.

Jesus Before Caiaphas and the Council

Then those who had seized Jesus led Him to Caiaphas the high priest, where the scribes and the elders had gathered.

Now the chief priests and the whole Council were seeking false testimony against Jesus that they might put Him to death, but they found none, though many false witnesses came forward. At last two came forward and said, "This man said, 'I am able to destroy the temple of God, and to rebuild it in three days.'" And the high priest stood up and said, "Have You no answer to make? What is it that these men testify against You?" But Jesus remained silent. And the high priest said to Him, "I adjure You by the living God, tell us if You are the Christ, the Son of God." Jesus said to him, "You have said so. But I tell you, from now on you will see the Son of Man seated at the right hand of Power and coming on the clouds of heaven." Then the high priest tore his robes and said, "He has uttered blasphemy. What further witnesses do we need? You have now heard His blasphemy. What is your judgment?" They answered, "He deserves death." Then they spit in His face and struck Him. And some slapped Him, saying, "Prophesy to us, You Christ! Who is it that struck You?"

As we look at these men, whom do we recognize? Do we see our own features in them? We, too, betray. We, too, sell the Savior for other interests: pleasure, good times, friends. We, too, forsake Him. We are afraid to show our colors and stand boldly in the world's highways to defend Him and confess Him. How often are we ready to say, "I am one of His disciples," and let all mankind know to whom we belong?

We, too, err. We try to build the kingdom with means and ways foreign to Jesus. We want to build with glamor, numbers, methods. Jesus wants no sword, no force, no pomp, and no impressive show to make the world take notice. Only through the Word, the Gospel, does He build His Church.

We, too, often fail to see the graciousness and glory of Jesus as Savior. Jesus is more than a reformer, more than an example, and more than a prophet. He is God's only Son, made flesh, sent to die for us and our transgressions.

There's no blasphemy in this assertion: Jesus is God. You and I want to confess Him as such and then acknowledge Him as our Savior from sin, although others betray, forsake, err, stray, and condemn. To you and to me He is the Lord God, eternally the Savior, who has redeemed us, that He might be the way by which we go to the throne, to stand in His eternal presence, washed white in His blood. So Jesus is condemned that we might be acquitted forevermore.

Prayer

Lord, open our hearts and ears to receive Your Word, that we may at all times follow its instruction and walk in the paths of righteousness. Protect us from error and falsehood, indifference and unbelief. Graciously forgive us whenever we have sinned and done contrary to Your will, for Jesus' sake. Amen.

THE SAVING LOOK

Matthew 26:58, 69–75

IN the Upper Room, where Jesus instituted His Sacrament of the bread and the cup, Jesus said to Simon Peter: "Before the rooster crows twice, you will deny Me three times" (Mark 14:30). Simon Peter thought that could never be: "I will lay down my life for You" (John 13:37). He was confident that he never would be guilty of such a contemptuous act. But Jesus knew of what He was speaking.

Then a little later Jesus said to Simon Peter: "Simon, Simon, behold, Satan demanded to have you, that he might sift you like wheat, but I have prayed for you that your faith may not fail. And when you have turned again, strengthen your brothers" (Luke 22:31–32). Note that Jesus did not use the name Peter. The disciple was not the confessor in this night. He was going to be ashamed of Jesus, deny Him, and sink to the low-character pattern of the courtyard. He was going to revert to Simon, son of Jonas.

And all his protestations meant nothing. As he warmed himself at the fire of the calloused servants, Simon declared up and down to the men and women of the courtyard, "I do no know the man."

But as we read the account of Peter's denial, do we not find in him a counterpart of ourselves?

And Peter was following Him at a distance, as far as the courtyard of the high priest, and going inside he sat with the guards to see the end.

Peter Denies Jesus

Now Peter was sitting outside in the courtyard. And a servant girl came up to him and said, "You also were with Jesus the Galilean." But he denied it before them all, saying, "I do not know what you mean." And when he went out to the entrance, another servant girl saw him, and she said to the bystanders, "This man was with Jesus of Nazareth." And again he denied it with an oath: "I do not know the man." After a little while the bystanders came up and said to Peter, "Certainly you too are one of them, for your accent betrays you." Then he began to invoke a curse on himself and to swear, "I do not know the man." And immediately the rooster crowed. And Peter remembered the saying of Jesus, "Before the rooster crows, you will deny Me three times." And he went out and wept bitterly.

Was Peter a hypocrite? If not, how, then, do we account for his conduct, one moment blowing hot and the other cold? Peter had been too self-confident. He was not leaning upon the Rock higher than he, but standing on his own feet, and they were of clay. Peter followed from afar. He wanted to be a secret disciple, hiding his identity. He mingled with bad company, and he had to be like them and act as they do. To do so, he had to deny Jesus.

Analyzing his conduct does not minimize his sin. It only explains it and warns us.

The sin of denial can be committed only by a follower of Jesus. We Christians are guilty of this transgression, denying our Christian faith. Often we are chameleons, with Christians boldly confessing and with the world shamefully denying Christ. We all act at times as Peter. But Jesus looked on Peter. The Savior still loved him.

And Peter went out and wept bitterly. Why? Because he still loved Jesus. He realized now how he had hurt and grieved his best Friend, his Savior.

And Jesus did not cast him out. Jesus fully restored Peter to grace. He forgave him all. That's what Jesus does with us as well. He takes us and makes us new.

Prayer

Out of the depth of the consciousness of our sin we come, heavenly Father, in Christ and beseech You to heal our bruised spirit. Let us again hear of Your pardoning grace in Christ Jesus. Only in Him can we find peace. As He looks at us in tender compassion, may we weep repentant tears. Lift us to His bosom,

and create in us clean hearts. May we confess Him at all times
before friend and foe and abide in His presence now and
forevermore. Amen.

THE BLINDING POWER OF SIN
Matthew 27:1–18

"SIN when it is fully grown brings forth death" (James 1:15). In the end it always drives us to despair. And yet we choose sin time and again. Strange that we should be more at home with Barabbas than with Jesus.

The first trial of Jesus in the court of the Council is over. He has been condemned for blasphemy. The Council (also known as the Sanhedrin) was the church court. The high priest presided, and the chief priests and leaders formed the Council. This court, however, did not have the right to pronounce a death sentence. That was reserved for the Romans, according to Roman law. But in the court of Pilate, the charge of blasphemy would not be understood, nor would a Roman judge deem that charge worthy of death. So these leaders had to find some other charge. They must accuse Jesus of sedition, an accusation that would get a hearing. Therefore, they decide to bring Jesus before Pilate and accuse Him of making Himself king. With the plot completed, they appear before the governer.

But into his record, Matthew places a strange interlude. He takes time out to tell us of the end of Judas Iscariot and the origin of the potter's field.

Jesus Delivered to Pilate

When morning came, all the chief priests and the elders of the people took counsel against Jesus to put Him to death. And they bound Him and led Him away and delivered Him over to Pilate the governor.

Judas Hangs Himself

Then when Judas, His betrayer, saw that Jesus was condemned, he changed his mind and brought back the thirty pieces of silver to the chief priests and the elders, saying, "I have sinned by betraying innocent blood." They said, "What is that to us? See to it yourself." And throwing down the pieces of silver into the temple, he departed, and he went and hanged himself. But the chief priests, taking the pieces of silver, said, "It is not lawful to put them into the treasury, since it is blood money." So they took counsel and bought with them the potter's field as a burial place for strangers. Therefore that field has been called the Field of Blood to this day. Then was fulfilled what had been spoken by the prophet Jeremiah, saying, "And they took the thirty pieces of silver, the price of Him on whom a price had been set by some of the sons of Israel, and they gave them for the potter's field, as the Lord directed me."

Jesus Before Pilate

Now Jesus stood before the governor, and the governor asked Him, "Are You the King of the Jews?" Jesus said, "You have said so." But when He was accused by the chief priests and elders, He gave no answer. Then Pilate said to Him, "Do You not hear how many things they testify against You?" But He gave him no answer, not even to a single charge, so that the governor was greatly amazed.

The Crowd Chooses Barabbas

Now at the feast the governor was accustomed to release for the crowd any one prisoner whom they wanted. And they had then a notorious prisoner called Barabbas. So when they had gathered, Pilate said to them, "Whom do you want me to release for you: Barabbas, or Jesus who is called Christ?" For he knew that it was out of envy that they had delivered Him up.

Pontius Pilate knew that the leaders of Jerusalem were delivering Jesus into his court out of envy. Although Pilate is little interested in his conscience and what it says, he hesitates at this moment to give way to the demands and to condemn Jesus without a hearing. The more Pilate hears and sees, the less he is inclined to do the bidding of these leaders. Yet he could not afford to lose their good will.

Therefore, Pilate believes he has found a way out. He will outwit them in their cunning. Custom and tradition dictated that a prisoner be released at the Passover to symbolize man's release by the gracious God and deliverance from the bondage of Egypt.

Pilate selects Barabbas, a criminal feared by everyone. He is so dangerous that mothers may have even frightened their children into obedience by saying, "Barabbas will get you."

Pilate places this criminal next to Jesus, the holy and sinless Son of God, and directs the people to choose between them. Pilate never dreamed they would choose Barabbas. How could they pick such a man?

Man is unpredictable. You and I will adamantly say that righteousness and truth and goodness must prevail, and yet we may go right on in sin and with the world. Strange that we feel more at home with Barabbas than with Jesus! Jesus disturbs, until we fall prostrate at His feet, crying for mercy, and then are lifted graciously by His pierced hands and forgiven altogether.

Prayer

Lord God, eternal and gracious, let us never despair of Your mercy but hold fast at all times to Your promises and find peace for our mind, rest for our soul, and healing for our conscience, for Jesus' sake. Amen.

76

WATERS THAT CANNOT CLEAN
Matthew 27:19–31

CENTURIES ago, the Jewish nation made a choice. Jesus came to His own people and they rejected Him. They refused to accept Him as Messiah, the Savior from sin and the deliverer from eternal death.

"Away with Him! Crucify Him! Give us Barabbas!" they cried.

Pilate granted them their request, although his wife begged him to have nothing to do with this just Man. But Pontius Pilate had to appease the leaders of Jerusalem—he had to do their bidding, for they had something on him that made him squirm and afraid to carry out justice. Pilate wanted to get rid of the case—at least, he wanted to face his wife with a valid excuse. He would wash his hands clean of this mess. So Pilate called for a basin and a pitcher of water, and then he ceremoniously washed his hands.

"That's all right with us," shouted the frenzied mob. "If any wrong is being done, we will take the blame. Let His blood be on us and on our children!" And it is!

The people chose Barabbas. The mob took the whole blame, and Jesus was crowned with thorns and garbed in an old, discarded, purple robe. He was condemned to die. And they led Him away to be crucified.

> Besides, while [Pilate] was sitting on the judgment seat, his wife sent word to him, "Have nothing to do with that righteous man, for I have suffered much because of Him today in a dream." Now the chief priests and the elders persuaded the crowd to ask for Barabbas and destroy Jesus. The governor again said to them, "Which of the two do you want me to release for you?" And they said, "Barabbas." Pilate said to them, "Then what shall I do with Jesus who is called Christ?"

They all said, "Let Him be crucified!" And he said, "Why, what evil has He done?" But they shouted all the more, "Let Him be crucified!"

Pilate Delivers Jesus to Be Crucified

So when Pilate saw that he was gaining nothing, but rather that a riot was beginning, he took water and washed his hands before the crowd, saying, "I am innocent of this man's blood; see to it yourselves." And all the people answered, "His blood be on us and on our children!" Then he released for them Barabbas, and having scourged Jesus, delivered Him to be crucified.

Jesus Is Mocked

Then the soldiers of the governor took Jesus into the governor's headquarters, and they gathered the whole battalion before Him. And they stripped Him and put a scarlet robe on Him, and twisting together a crown of thorns, they put it on His head and put a reed in His right hand. And kneeling before Him, they mocked Him, saying, "Hail, King of the Jews!" And they spit on Him and took the reed and struck Him on the head. And when they had mocked Him, they stripped Him of the robe and put His own clothes on Him and led Him away to crucify Him.

And "he took water and washed his hands." But all the water in the world could not wash those hands clean. Only the blood of Jesus Christ, God's only-begotten Son, cleanses us from all sin.

"His blood be on us and on our children!" That is the cry of a defying mob that will not have Jesus. They prefer going to destruction rather than letting Jesus enter their hearts and rather than giving up sin and self-righteousness.

This cry is also that of the condemned. They have gone on in their sins and turned away from Him who alone gives healing and peace to the sin-troubled soul.

But we have here also the cry of the redeemed. "Thou hast washed us and made us white in Thy blood" (cf Revelation 7:14).

The believers know that nothing can save them but faith in the redeeming death of Christ. Cleansed by His blood, which is upon them by grace, they have peace with God.

Every day Jesus comes through His Word, stands at the door of our hearts, and knocks. He is inescapable; He cannot be evaded. It is still Jesus or Barabbas. No neutral stand can be taken. If we reject Him, we go with Barabbas. We are following one of the two.

Is it Jesus? If so, then His cleansing blood is on us to wash us altogether from all sin, and salvation is sure.

Prayer
Not the labors of my hands Can fulfill Thy Law's demands;
Could my zeal no respite know, Could my tears forever flow,
All for sin could not atone; Thou must save, and Thou alone.
Nothing in my hand I bring; Simply to Thy Cross I cling. Amen.
(LSB 761:2–3*)*

THE CAUSE FOR WHICH CHRIST DIED
Matthew 27:32–49

"THEY . . . crucified Him."

Crucifixion was introduced into Palestine by Alexander the Great. It was a most torturous way of putting a human being to death. It meant hours of suffering, dizziness, loss of blood, cramping, fever, labored breathing, and exposure to the hot sun, shame, and humiliation. After hours of agonizing pain, the legs would be broken with a sledgehammer to hasten death.

Three forms of crosses were used. The T, the X, and the one with a projection over the top. The victim was nailed to the cross while it was lying on the ground. With the victim hanging on it, the cross was lifted and dropped into a hole that had been dug in the ground. All this caused additional pain to the man who was being executed.

Man always has been inhuman to man since sin came into the world.

Jesus was subjected to such atrocities upon Golgotha, the Place of a Skull.

Thus we behold Him, in whom was no sin and who went about doing good. He suffered the pangs of hell that we might be redeemed. All this He suffered for us and for our disobedience.

The Crucifixion

As they went out, they found a man of Cyrene, Simon by name. They compelled this man to carry His cross. And when they came to a place called Golgotha (which means Place of a Skull), they offered Him wine to drink, mixed with gall, but when He tasted it, He would not drink it. And when they had crucified Him, they divided His garments among them by casting lots. Then they sat down and kept watch over Him there. And over His head they put the charge against Him, which read, "This is Jesus, the King of the Jews." Then two robbers were crucified with Him, one on the right and one on the left. And those who passed by derided Him, wagging their heads and saying, "You who would destroy the temple and rebuild it in three days, save Yourself! If You are the Son of God, come down from the cross." So also the chief priests, with the scribes and elders, mocked Him, saying, "He saved others; He cannot save Himself. He is the King of Israel; let Him come down now from the cross, and we will believe in Him. He trusts in God; let God deliver Him now, if He desires Him. For He said, 'I am the Son of God.' " And the robbers who were crucified with Him also reviled Him in the same way.

The Death of Jesus

Now from the sixth hour there was darkness over all the land until the ninth hour. And about the ninth hour Jesus cried out with a loud voice, saying, "Eli, Eli, lema sabachthani?" that is, "My God, My God, why have You forsaken Me?" And some of the bystanders, hearing it, said, "This man is calling Elijah." And one of them at once ran and took a sponge, filled it with sour wine, and put it on a reed and gave it to Him to drink. But the others said, "Wait, let us see whether Elijah will come to save Him."

They gave Him sour-wine vinegar to drink, mingled with gall, and Jesus refused. Why? He did not want His senses dulled and His mind clouded. He was confronted with the powers of darkness, and He must have all His wits together—too much was at stake to take any chances.

They took His garments and gambled for them. While the salvation of the whole world is hanging in the balance, sinful and calloused man plays dice, greedily looking for a little earthly gain. But this very act proved that He who hung there was the Messiah. Concerning the Anointed of God, the Scriptures had foretold this very thing (see Psalm 22:16–18). This marked Jesus as the Son of God made flesh.

They placed a sign above His head that told the passing crowd why this Man was dying on that cross: "This is Jesus, the King of the Jews."

That He was, and more. He is Lord and Ruler of the universe, and the day will come when every knee will bow to acknowledge Him as the Lord God. But many in that day will exclaim with fear and trembling: "Mountains, 'Fall on us,' and to the hills, 'Cover us'" (Luke 23:30).

Men mocked and jeered Him: "If You are the Son of God, come down from the cross." Why did Jesus not do so? Love held Him to the cross, not the nails. Had He come down, as He could have done, you and I would have no Savior and no salvation.

However, God plainly showed that this is His Son, even as He hung there, despised and rejected. For three long hours, a total darkness covered the earth. God hid from the sight of man the deepest humiliation of His Son.

Out of that darkness, Jesus cried: "My God, My God, why have You forsaken Me?"

There is only one place where Jesus could be forsaken altogether—in hell. In this world, no one experiences such utter aloneness and abandonment.

But out of the darkness, Jesus cried, "My God." He still clung to God and prayed to Him out of the depths of hell. That is the only time in history that a trusting heart prayed from that place to God. This means victory. Satan could not separate Jesus from His Father. The devil's power is broken. He is defeated and crushed; Jesus is the eternal victor.

And because He was forsaken of God, we need not go to that forsaken place to be forever separated from the Lord. Heaven's door is opened so we may live in our heavenly Father's presence forever.

Prayer

In deep humility, we kneel at Your cross, O Savior, mindful that our sins brought You to the accursed tree. We look to You for cleansing and healing and peace. Embrace us daily with Your love, and preserve us in the saving faith, which brings us into Your presence and to glory. Amen.

WAS JESUS DEFEATED?

Matthew 27:50–66

"HE was crucified, died, and was buried." Seemingly, Christ Jesus lost out. His earthly enemies have triumphed, the opposition holds the fort.

However, the leaders of Jerusalem are uneasy. They want to believe that all is over, yet they do not feel secure in their new victories. They recall the words of Jesus: "After three days I will rise." We'd better make sure, lest a hoax be played on us, say the chief priests and some of the Pharisees. Those disciples may take the body out of the tomb and then claim He is risen. We better see to it that this does not happen.

So to Pilate they go to obtain a patrol of soldiers to guard the tomb. And, fortunately for them, they think, Pontius Pilate is accommodating. This act will later make doubly sure that the body was not stolen and prove positively that Jesus raised Himself from the dead. Besides all this, the leaders have the tomb officially sealed after the body has been placed there by loving hands and bleeding hearts, as Matthew relates.

> And Jesus cried out again with a loud voice and yielded up His spirit.
>
> And behold, the curtain of the temple was torn in two, from top to bottom. And the earth shook, and the rocks were split. The tombs also were opened. And many bodies of the saints who had fallen asleep were raised, and coming out of the tombs after His resurrection they went into the holy city and appeared to many. When the centurion and those who were with him, keeping watch over Jesus, saw the earthquake and what took place, they were filled with awe and said, "Truly this was the Son of God!"

There were also many women there, looking on from a distance, who had followed Jesus from Galilee, ministering to Him, among whom were Mary Magdalene and Mary the mother of James and Joseph and the mother of the sons of Zebedee.

Jesus Is Buried

When it was evening, there came a rich man from Arimathea, named Joseph, who also was a disciple of Jesus. He went to Pilate and asked for the body of Jesus. Then Pilate ordered it to be given to him. And Joseph took the body and wrapped it in a clean linen shroud and laid it in his own new tomb, which he had cut in the rock. And he rolled a great stone to the entrance of the tomb and went away. Mary Magdalene and the other Mary were there, sitting opposite the tomb.

The Guard at the Tomb

The next day, that is, after the day of Preparation, the chief priests and the Pharisees gathered before Pilate and said, "Sir, we remember how that impostor said, while He was still alive, 'After three days I will rise.' Therefore order the tomb to be made secure until the third day, lest His disciples go and steal Him away and tell the people, 'He has risen from the dead,' and the last fraud will be worse than the first." Pilate said to them, "You have a guard of soldiers. Go, make it as secure as you can." So they went and made the tomb secure by sealing the stone and setting a guard.

Jesus dies. Immediately, the curtain in the temple is torn in two. This curtain separated the Holy Place from the Most Holy Place. None but the high priest could enter beyond this curtain, and that only once a year. Now everyone can look in—everyone can enter into the very presence of God, for we are reconciled though the death of Jesus. All ceremonial laws have served their purpose, and no more offerings of lambs and bulls and turtledoves need to be made. "For by a single offering He has perfected for all time those who are being sanctified" (Hebrews 10:14).

Still more, at Jesus' death the earth quakes, and saints rise to show that death has been conquered and that the resurrection and eternal life are a reality.

Not only nature testifies, but the power of Christ's suffering and death is also demonstrated through the conversion of the centurion who confesses, "Truly this was the Son of God!" And Joseph of Arimathea, himself a Pharisee, comes forward and openly acknowledges his discipleship and asks Pontius Pilate for permission to place this crucified Jesus into his own new tomb.

We are truly grateful for these detailed accounts of the death and burial of Jesus. We know that He truly died. And this death was for our transgressions. He paid the wages of sin so that we, by His grace, can rise even now to newness of life.

With all believers of the ages, we can sing our hymns of praise to Him who has redeemed us by His blood out of every race of people, in every age, and through each generation, and has made us unto our God kings and priests, clothed in the pure white robes of Christ's righteousness.

Prayer

With all the saints and angels, we lift our hearts and voices in praise of Your eternal victory, Lord Jesus, Friend of sinners. We are Yours by grace, never to perish but to have eternal life. Accept our hallelujahs as we kneel in adoration before You, the only Savior and only Lord, world without end. Amen.

79

IF EASTER WERE
NOT TRUE
Matthew 28:1–10

IT is true, Christ rose. Two facts stand undeniable in the Easter message: on the third day the tomb was empty, and Jesus was seen alive.

This is the crowning evidence of His Messiahship and His eternal Sonship. When Jesus was challenged by the opposition to perform one master miracle and give them one indisputable sign by which they were to know that He is God, Jesus said He would give them the sign of the prophet Jonah. Again Jesus challenged them: "Destroy this temple, and in three days I will raise it up" (John 2:19).

The sign of Jonah is fulfilled. As Jonah was in the belly of the fish and came forth alive after three days, so Jesus was in the tomb until the third day, and then He was seen alive. "See My hands and My feet, that it is I myself. Touch Me, and see. For a spirit does not have flesh and bones as you see that I have" (Luke 24:39).

Friend and foe alike say that He rose. The women, unsuspecting, came to anoint Jesus early on Sunday morning for His final entombment, to hear to their utter amazement, "He is not here, for He has risen, as He said. Come, see the place where He lay."

The Resurrection

Now after the Sabbath, toward the dawn of the first day of the week, Mary Magdalene and the other Mary went to see the tomb. And behold, there was a great earthquake, for an angel of the Lord descended from heaven and came and rolled back the stone and sat on it. His appearance was like lightning, and his clothing white as snow. And for fear of him the guards trembled and became like dead men. But the angel said to the women, "Do not be afraid, for I know that you seek Jesus who was crucified. He is not here, for He has risen, as He said.

> Come, see the place where He lay. Then go quickly and tell His disciples that He has risen from the dead, and behold, He is going before you to Galilee; there you will see Him. See, I have told you." So they departed quickly from the tomb with fear and great joy, and ran to tell His disciples. And behold, Jesus met them and said, "Greetings!" And they came up and took hold of His feet and worshiped Him. Then Jesus said to them, "Do not be afraid; go and tell My brothers to go to Galilee, and there they will see Me."

What difference does it make that Jesus rose? All the difference in the world! If He has not risen, then we are still unforgiven sinners, then we must face a condemning judgment, then heaven is closed forever to us, then we have no hope as we stand at open graves, then we are the most miserable creatures on the earth. Truly, it would have been better if we had never been born.

But the Easter victory brings to us life and heaven, joy and peace, certainty and security. Sin cannot condemn us, for we are justified by a faith that holds fast to the eternal truth that the blood of Jesus cleanses us from all our transgressions.

Death has lost its grip on us, and we can pass through its dark valley with Christ at our side. Death is man's greatest foe. Death stopped Alexander, stopped Caesar, stopped thousands of others, but death did not stop Jesus. He rose, He ascended, and He lives. Because He lives, we, too, will live. We will see God. In us is indestructible life by faith in Christ, the living Savior.

A new life is given us even now. We have been made alive together with Christ. We are reborn creatures by the power of the Holy Spirit. Forgiven, we are transformed into the children of light. Sinners by nature, we are saints by grace. We can resist evil. We have a new and hopeful outlook. We have protection. No one can take us from the Savior's hand.

We have a living hope. This expectation does not center around earthly, material things. All of these will fall from our trembling, feeble hands when death knocks at our door. It is certain that we will carry nothing out. But our redeemed and saved soul will see glory that no sorrow can lessen, no death can shorten. Easter makes heaven our home, where there shall be no more separation, no more crying, no more death.

Easter is the brightest spot on the horizon of life. Each year, we celebrate the greatest victory in history when we sing our Easter hallelujahs. We need not despair. We need not perish. We believers shall behold Christ in glory.

And so shall we be forever with the Lord—all because He died and rose again.

Prayer

Lord Jesus, risen and ever-living Savior, with all Your people we adore You as our Lord and God, who has conquered sin and death and redeemed all mankind. We praise You because of the glorious hope You bring to us. We need not weep desperate tears as we stand at the open graves of Your saints; we need not be afraid of the judgment to come as long as You are our living Redeemer. Take full possession of our hearts and make us Yours forever. Hallelujah! Amen.

80

THE AMEN OF CERTAINTY AND PEACE

Matthew 28:11–20

CHRISTIANITY rises and falls with the resurrection of Jesus. The opponents always have recognized this fact. For this reason, many and varied attempts have been made to discredit the historic fact of Easter morning that Christ is risen.

The first attempts were extremely crude. The leaders of Jerusalem bribed the soldiers to go out and spread a lie that His body had been stolen. But that story was quickly hushed—people saw Jesus alive.

Since then, other theories have been advanced.

1. The vision theory, claiming that the disciples and followers saw Jesus only in visions and dreams. This theory holds that their impressions of Jesus were so profound that for some time after His death they dreamed of Him and even in their daydreaming claimed to have seen Him. But daydreams do not take physical form that can be touched, as Jesus was.

2. The removal theory, saying that His body had been removed by the gardener or some other person or group to another place and that the disciples, learning of this, spread the news that He rose from the dead. If this were so, then the enemies could have silenced them very readily by producing the lifeless body. But that was not done because Jesus actually rose from the tomb to live.

3. The swooning theory, declaring that Jesus fainted on the cross from loss of blood and suffering and then revived as He was placed into the cool tomb. But that does not hold water, for Jesus was stabbed with a huge spear, making an opening in His side large enough for Thomas to put his hand into. Then Jesus was placed into the tomb by His friends. If there had been doubt in their mind that Jesus was dead, they would never have sealed Him in that tomb.

4. The legend theory, saying that the whole account is just a story made up by devoted followers. However, it takes years for a legend to grow around a person, and this message of the resurrection was proclaimed at once, and fifty days later the disciples, still at Jerusalem, testified before great crowds that Jesus was risen.

One after the other, these theories must be discarded when the infallible proof shows that the tomb was empty and that the lifeless body could not be produced. The living Christ was seen time and again during those forty days.

Jesus lives and abides to this day. Christianity and the continuation of the Church could not be explained if Christ did not rise from the dead.

Those disciples and we have a message that only the living and abiding Jesus could perpetuate to this day.

The Report of the Guard

While they were going, behold, some of the guard went into the city and told the chief priests all that had taken place. And when they had assembled with the elders and taken counsel, they gave a sufficient sum of money to the soldiers and said, "Tell people, 'His disciples came by night and stole Him away while we were asleep.' And if this comes to the governor's ears, we will satisfy him and keep you out of trouble." So they took the money and did as they were directed. And this story has been spread among the Jews to this day.

The Great Commission

Now the eleven disciples went to Galilee, to the mountain to which Jesus had directed them. And when they saw Him they worshiped Him, but some doubted. And Jesus came and said to them, "All authority in heaven and on earth has been given to Me. Go therefore and make disciples of all nations, baptizing them in the name of the Father and of the Son and of the Holy Spirit, teaching them to observe all that I have commanded you. And behold, I am with you always, to the end of the age."

So we come to the close of the Gospel according to Saint Matthew, once a tax collector and sinner, but, by the grace of the Lord Jesus, an apostle, evangelist, and martyr.

Matthew concluded his Gospel with Christ's Great Commission, urging us, one and all, to bear witness to the hope within us. Surely we want others to share this peace that passes all understanding. We want others to live in this grace wherein we stand. We want others also to die in peace, knowing that faith in Christ means heaven and glory.

Matthew closes his Gospel with Jesus' promise: "Behold, I am with you always, to the end of the age." As living Savior, He abides with us, no matter where we are compelled to go. There is no situation in our life where Jesus does not help, no sorrow that He does not comfort, no sin He is not ready to forgive. Today we can say, tomorrow we still can believe, and to the end of days we can confess: Jesus loves me. Amen—Amen—that is true.

Prayer

And now, Lord Jesus, Friend and Savior, abide with us until the journey's end, keeping us steadfast in faith and obedient to Your Gospel. We thank and praise You for the victories You have won, for the peace You have brought into our lives, and for the hope that conquers every frustration of this present world. Until You call us home into glory, we worship and adore You with our hosannas and our hallelujahs. Amen—come and abide, Lord Jesus. Amen.

MEDITATIONS FOR
THE GOSPEL ACCORDING TO
SAINT MARK

AN APOSTLE'S DISCIPLE BECOMES AN EVANGELIST
Acts 12:11–17

When Peter came to himself, he said, "Now I am sure that the Lord has sent His angel and rescued me from the hand of Herod and from all that the Jewish people were expecting."

When he realized this, he went to the house of Mary, the mother of John whose other name was Mark, where many were gathered together and were praying. And when he knocked at the door of the gateway, a servant girl named Rhoda came to answer. Recognizing Peter's voice, in her joy she did not open the gate but ran in and reported that Peter was standing at the gate. They said to her, "You are out of your mind." But she kept insisting that it was so, and they kept saying, "It is his angel!" But Peter continued knocking, and when they opened, they saw him and were amazed. But motioning to them with his hand to be silent, he described to them how the Lord had brought him out of the prison. And he said, "Tell these things to James and to the brothers." Then he departed and went to another place.

IN the meditation introducing the Gospel of Matthew (page 10), we read, "How wonderful is the grace of God!" Jesus chose the first evangelist, Matthew, from the ranks of tax collectors and sinners. Now we direct our prayerful attention and devotion time to the second Gospel. When we consider the writer, purpose, and composition of this book, we must again admire and praise the grace of God, who chose the young son of a Jewish woman to record this Gospel of Jesus Christ for Gentile readers.

The name of this second evangelist, like that of the first, is a double name, and both names are recorded repeatedly in the New Testament. We read in the passage above that when the apostle Peter was miraculously delivered from prison by an angel of the Lord, he came to the house of Mary, the mother of John, whose surname was Mark. She seems to have been a prominent Christian woman of Jewish origin, in whose house other Christians in Jerusalem gathered. This house has been found in archeological digs conducted in the last century. Her son's Jewish name was John; in Hebrew, it was Jehochanan, which means "Jehovah is gracious"; his Latin, or Roman, name was Marcus, "the manly one." He may have been the young man who followed Jesus after His capture in Gethsemane, since he is the only evangelist who recorded this incident (Mark 14:51–52). He probably adopted the name Mark not long afterward when he entered the Greco-Latin world as the companion of an apostle, according to the Jewish custom of assuming a second name befitting the circumstances when an important change in a man's life took place. He may have been influenced by Peter, indicated when this apostle, a visitor at his mother's home, called him "son" in 1 Peter 5:13. But because he was a cousin to Barnabas (Colossians 4:10), he was brought into contact with St. Paul, and we learn from Acts 12:25 and 13:5 that he accompanied Paul and Barnabas on their first missionary journey at the beginning of the fifties in the first century of our Christian era.

However, we also read that Mark left them after some time and returned to Jerusalem, perhaps because he felt discouraged and was not willing to continue in the work of the Lord (Acts 13:13). Pastors or other church workers may lose heart for ministry and even leave such service, but their friends, colleagues, and congregation members should uphold them and encourage them in all possible ways. Therefore, when Paul prepared for his second missionary journey in AD 52–54, saying to Barnabas, "Let us return and visit the brothers in every city where we proclaimed the word of the Lord, and see how they are" (Acts 15:36), and Barnabas was determined to take Mark with them, Paul declined to do it. He did not think it wise to take with them someone who had not joined them in ministry.

The contention between Paul and Barnabas became so pronounced that they parted company. Barnabas took Mark, and Paul chose Silas (Acts 15:36–40). Paul and Barnabas were together again during Paul's first and second imprisonments in Rome in the sixties of the first century (Colossians 4:10–11; Philemon 24; 2 Timothy

4:11). But in those years, Mark also had contact with Peter, as indicated in Peter's letter to the Christians in Asia Minor: "She [the church] who is at Babylon, who is likewise chosen, sends you greetings, and so does Mark, my son" (1 Peter 5:13). This verse may refer to the old Mesopotamian city of Babylon, but some Church Fathers and historians believe it refers to Rome, which had become a New Testament Babylon in those days of persecution. Some of them also tell us that Mark later went from Rome to Alexandria in Egypt and founded the Church there.

Prayer

Lord Jesus, we thank You that You have given us not only one Gospel but four, which present the sacred story of Your life and work on earth in order to make us sure of our salvation. Help us to become earnest and diligent in assisting the preaching of Your Holy Gospel, and forgive us all our weaknesses and shortcomings. Strengthen our faith in You, and keep us steadfast in such faith to the end of our lives. Amen.

THE SECOND GOSPEL
Colossians 4:10;
2 Timothy 4:11; 1 Peter 5:13

Aristarchus my fellow prisoner greets you, and Mark the cousin of Barnabas (concerning whom you have received instructions— if he comes to you, welcome him). Luke alone is with me. Get Mark and bring him with you, for he is very useful to me for ministry. She who is at Babylon, who is likewise chosen, sends you greetings, and so does Mark, my son.

WE have looked at the life and work of St. Mark, the second evangelist. Now we consider his book. If we inquire about its origin, we meet with a remarkable but well-substantiated tradition. The apostles were the men who recorded the life of Jesus on earth, they were the foreordained witnesses (Acts 10:41). However, Mark was not an apostle. He was merely a companion and disciple of apostles, but his Gospel was accepted by the Church without contradiction. This is because Mark, according to the Church Fathers, was Peter's interpreter and wrote his book in a certain dependency on Peter. This is confirmed by certain characteristics of his book. It was not written by an eyewitness of the events recorded in it, yet it is written in a remarkably concrete and vivid way. Although the shortest Gospel, it tells us more about Peter than any other disciple (see 1:16–17, 29–31; 3:16; 8:29; 9:5; 10:28; 11:21; 14:29–31, 37, 66–72; 16:7), and it records matters concerning Peter fully and accurately, even his weaknesses and frailties. For example: Peter rebukes Jesus because he does not want Him to suffer and die; Peter is reprimanded by Jesus (8:32–33); Peter denies Jesus three times (14:66–72). Here we note the completeness and the details of the report as compared with Matthew 26:70–75 and with Luke 22:57–62. In 16:7, Mark adds that the resurrection of Jesus was told to Peter, who had denied Him, when Matthew and John speak about the disciples in general (Matthew 28:7; John 20:17). For this reason, we refer to the Petrine character of Mark's Gospel. God has indeed wonderfully formed and shaped His Word, but we are apt to read it superficially and overlook the peculiarities and characteristics of the individual books.

Regarding the purpose of the book, Mark's intention is to narrate the beginning of the Gospel of Jesus Christ (1:1) to show how this worldwide Gospel had its origin in the mighty person of Christ and how this Christ proved Himself by His deeds to be the true Son of God bringing the kingdom of God. See 3:11; 5:7; 15:39, where the centurion at the cross confesses, "Truly this man was the Son of God!" (1:15; 9:1; 10:15, 25; 12:34). In doing this, Mark, like the other evangelists, intends to kindle and strengthen faith, and in simple but vivid language he stresses the miracles of Christ more so than His discourses and doctrinal presentations. This indicates that he writes for readers who were not close to the events narrated in Gospel history—not Jewish Christians, but Gentile Christians. This is more evident if we remember that he includes far fewer quotations from the Old Testament than does Matthew. Mark frequently translates Aramaic words (see 3:17; 5:41; 7:11, 34; 14:36) and explains Jewish customs (for instance, the washing of hands, 7:2–5; the day of Unleavened Bread, 14:12; the day of Preparation for the Sabbath, 15:42). He does not record discourses and events that were primarily significant for Jewish readers and, therefore, we do not find in his Gospel the contents of Matthew 5:17–48 or Matthew 23, which were directed against the scribes and Pharisees. And if we consider that in his Greek language, he frequently used Latin words and phrases (for instance, *legion*, 5:9. 15; *centurion*, 15:39, 44–45)—we can assume that he wrote for Gentile Christians in Italy, particularly in Rome, where he lived with Peter (1 Peter 5:13) and where Rufus lived (Romans 16:13), whom Mark identifies as a son of Simon of Cyrene (Mark 15:21), a fact not found in the other Gospels (Matthew 27:32; Luke 23:26.)

There is a legend that Mark's body was transferred from Alexandria to Venice and that a lion accompanied it. Therefore, the lion became a symbol for Mark in paintings and on statuary. While this legend is without historical consequence, it can be said that Mark's Gospel presents Jesus as the Lion of Judah (Revelation 5:5), the Mighty One, and is, therefore, called the Gospel of the mighty Savior. In the symbolism of the Early Church, Mark is depicted as a winged lion because he emphasized the power and the miracles of the Savior. The lion, as king of beasts, was a symbol of strength. A modern-day interpretation is that Mark is the Gospel for youth, so vivid, so stirring, so strong; these same qualities adapt the story to the restless, active, vigorous spirit of the whole modern world. It represents our Lord as the mighty, wonder-working Son of God and therefore bears a special message to an age that needs a word of divine authority and a new vision of the limitless, redeeming power of Christ.

Nowhere is it stated definitely when and where the Gospel of St. Mark was written. But if we consider that the readers were Gentile Christians living in a Latin-speaking country and that the author was a disciple and attendant of Peter, it seems evident that the book was written toward the late sixties in the first century. Rome can be assumed to be the place where it was composed and where Peter was martyred in about AD 67. That it was written before the capture of Jerusalem by the Romans (AD 70) is substantiated by the fact that there is no mention in the book of such capture, although it is prophesied in 14:58. These statements also rest on the information handed down to us by reliable Fathers and historians of the Early Church.

Mark, the shortest of the Gospels, narrates only the public ministry of Jesus after giving a brief introduction that speaks of the activity of John the Baptist and of Christ's Baptism and temptation (1:1–13). In agreement with the synoptic plan (see the introduction to St. Matthew's Gospel), the ministry of Jesus is divided into two parts: first, His messianic activity in Galilee (1:14–9:50); second, its continuation and consummation in Judea through His suffering, death, resurrection, and ascension (10:1–16:20).

Prayer

Lord Jesus, we thank You for the strong and powerful Gospel of St. Mark, which tells us of Your mighty deeds during Your walk on this earth. As we read it, help us to take it to heart. Strengthen our faith in You as the true Son of God, who came into this world to seek and save us. You are the Lion of Judah, mighty in word and deed before God and all people. Help us to be strong and faithful witnesses to Your Gospel and to serve gladly as workers in Your kingdom. And when we fail or falter, forgive us and sustain us to the end. Amen.

1

THE MASTER AND HIS SERVANT

Mark 1:1–8

THE author of this Gospel, Mark, whose Jewish name was John, was a citizen of Jerusalem. As a young man, he may have been a disciple of Jesus. His mother, Mary, had a house in Jerusalem (Acts 12:12). By inspiration of the Holy Spirit, Mark's Gospel is compact and vivid, full of evidence of the faith and devotion of a man who truly loved his Lord and Savior. No wonder that he reveled in telling about things he saw and heard or that were told him by the apostles, particularly Peter. He was delighted to tell of the great miracles performed by his Savior. Moreover, Mark served his Lord by taking part in Paul's first missionary journey. For some reason, he turned back before the journey was finished, so Paul (who spared neither himself nor others when it came to serving the Savior) lost faith in Mark for a time. But later Mark became a valuable co-worker of both Paul and Peter.

In his opening paragraph, Mark gives us the superscription of his book and then draws a word picture of John the Baptist, the messenger who was sent to prepare the way of the Lord, and his relationship to his Master.

John the Baptist Prepares the Way

The beginning of the gospel of Jesus Christ, the Son of God.
As it is written in Isaiah the prophet,
"Behold, I send My messenger before Your face,
  who will prepare Your way,
the voice of one crying in the wilderness:
  'Prepare the way of the Lord,
  make His paths straight,'"

John appeared, baptizing in the wilderness and proclaiming a baptism of repentance for the forgiveness of sins. And all
the country of Judea and all Jerusalem were going out to him
and were being baptized by him in the river Jordan, confessing
their sins. Now John was clothed with camel's hair and wore
a leather belt around his waist and ate locusts and wild honey.
And he preached, saying, "After me comes He who is mightier than I, the strap of whose sandals I am not worthy to stoop
down and untie. I have baptized you with water, but He will
baptize you with the Holy Spirit."

St. Mark was fully aware of the nature of the Gospel of which he
has given us a record. For him and all true believers, the glad tidings
focus on our blessed Savior Jesus Christ. Mark was conscious of the
meaning of the name above every name—Jesus, the Savior from sin.
To him He is the Christ, the Anointed, consecrated by the Holy
Spirit to be our Prophet, Priest, and King. In contrast to those who
either deny the deity of Christ or do not know what to make of
Him, Mark stands in holy awe before Him and confesses Him to be
the Son of God, for he, like John, had beheld His glory, the glory as
of the only-begotten of the Father, full of grace and truth. May our
meditations on this Gospel produce the same result in us!

In this passage, Mark gives us not only a picture of the Master,
but also of the servant who was the humblest and yet the greatest,
the man Jesus called the greatest of all prophets because he went
before Him in the power and spirit of Elijah. Of John the Baptist, it
was written: "Behold, I send My messenger, and he will prepare the
way before Me" (Malachi 3:1). And again, "A voice cries: 'In the
wilderness prepare the way of the Lord; make straight in the desert
a highway for our God' " (Isaiah 40:3). John was not the Christ, as
some thought, nor one of the earlier prophets returned in the flesh.
Mark portrays him as the messenger, the forerunner, of the Lord,
whose only purpose was to prepare the way before Him that He
might find a ready room in the hearts of men.

What greater purpose can a servant of the Lord have! John
wanted only to be a voice, no attention for himself, all things for

Christ. Nothing but a voice, and by that voice was made known the coming of the Savior in all the joy of the Lamb of God who takes away the sin of the world. What a vivid picture the Gospel writer paints of the rugged prophet of the wilderness! Nothing soft about John! No elegant clothing for him, no gourmet food. What little he needed was provided by the wilderness. There was nothing affected or arrogant about John, yet great and small bowed in respect before him.

All things for Christ was also the meaning and significance of the Baptism John performed, while at the same time he lifted his voice with authority, preaching to priest and Pharisee as well as to sinner about the need for true repentance. His one purpose was that sinners would come to faith in the promised Christ and receive forgiveness of sins, life, and salvation. Note how anxious John is that his hearers turn to the Savior. He assures them that Christ will baptize them with the Holy Spirit. Christ's service to all people, if only they turn to Him in faith, is that He will pour out upon them His Holy Spirit and give new life through the Word and the Sacraments as the means of their salvation. If people would only use those means so near at hand, so freely given!

Prayer

Our heavenly Father, as You filled the heart of Your servant Mark with the perfect knowledge of the Gospel, so let that same knowledge come to us through Your Word, which works repentance and faith in Christ Jesus, Your Son, our Lord and Savior. As John the Baptist humbly adored Him whose way he was to prepare, considering it a privilege beyond all earthly honors to be His humblest servant, so let us receive our Savior. Make His knowledge glorious in the hearts and lives of people through our believing and loyal testimony in word and deed. We ask it in the name of Him who was and is and is to come. Amen.

THE BEGINNING OF CHRIST'S MINISTRY
Mark 1:9–20

HERE Mark presents in quick succession four contrasting images. Although Jesus makes His appearance in all humility, the glory of His divinity shines through. In connection with His Baptism, the voice from heaven declares Him to be the Son of God. When He is tempted by Satan, the angels minister to Him. A lowly rabbi, Jesus preaches with authority. Soon He becomes the beloved Master who gathers His disciples about Him.

The Baptism of Jesus

In those days Jesus came from Nazareth of Galilee and was baptized by John in the Jordan. And when He came up out of the water, immediately He saw the heavens being torn open and the Spirit descending on Him like a dove. And a voice came from heaven, "You are My beloved Son; with You I am well pleased."

The Temptation of Jesus

The Spirit immediately drove Him out into the wilderness. And He was in the wilderness forty days, being tempted by Satan. And He was with the wild animals, and the angels were ministering to Him.

Jesus Begins His Ministry

Now after John was arrested, Jesus came into Galilee, proclaiming the gospel of God, and saying, "The time is fulfilled, and the kingdom of God is at hand; repent and believe in the gospel."

Jesus Calls the First Disciples

Passing alongside the Sea of Galilee, He saw Simon and Andrew the brother of Simon casting a net into the sea, for they were fishermen. And Jesus said to them, "Follow Me, and I will make you become fishers of men." And immediately they left their nets and followed Him. And going on a little farther, He saw James the son of Zebedee and John his brother, who were in their boat mending the nets. And immediately He called them, and they left their father Zebedee in the boat with the hired servants and followed Him.

Here we read how John, the humble servant of the Lord, is privileged to baptize Jesus and thus assist in consecrating Him for His great and holy ministry. Everyone else was to be baptized for the remission of their sins. But here comes One who needs no remission of sin, a man John immediately recognizes and proclaims as "the Lamb of God, who takes away the sin of the world!" (John 1:29). Why should John baptize the One who needed no repentance? It was because Jesus had to fulfill all righteousness for us. Therefore, it happened that John baptized his cousin Jesus in the waters of the same ancient river that the children of Israel had crossed centuries earlier to enter the Promised Land. Now the waters of Baptism, combined with the Word, are to all spiritual children of Israel a "washing of regeneration and renewal of the Holy Spirit" (Titus 3:5), so that they, being born again of water and the Spirit, may enter into the kingdom of God by faith. The Father was there when His Son publicly began His ministry. Before the loyal Baptist and the astonished multitude, God's voice came down from heaven: "You are My beloved Son; with You I am well pleased" (v. 11). Only the very Son of God could receive such a testimony.

All others were disobedient. No one is perfect; no, not one. But in Jesus, God found no fault at all. He fulfilled all the Law for us. It is significant that here, at the beginning of His ministry, all three persons of the Godhead are revealed. The Father speaks from heaven, calling on those present to behold His beloved Son. The Spirit from heaven descends upon Him like a dove, thus anointing Him as our Prophet, Priest, and King.

The next event, one that happened "immediately," is recorded also by Matthew and Luke. But Mark gives information that the others do not. He tells us that the Holy Spirit drove Jesus into the wilderness to be tempted by Satan for forty days. It was a part of Christ's redemptive work to be subjected to the temptation of the devil. Under the compulsion of the Holy Spirit, Jesus goes out for His first great encounter with the archenemy of God and man, before whom all others had gone down in defeat. Not so with our Savior. In the end, the angels come and minister to Him. With the sword of the Spirit, Christ conquers Satan as our Champion. With Christ, we are safe when Satan tries us beyond our strength.

Soon, "the voice of one crying in the wilderness" (Mark 1:3) is no longer heard on the mountainside or riverbank. Because of his bold testimony, John is thrown into prison by cruel King Herod. But the word of the faithful forerunner is fulfilled. "He must increase, but I must decrease" (John 3:30). In Galilee, Jesus began to preach His Gospel. And His message is clear: if the kingdom of God, so near at hand, is to come into the hearts of people, they must repent and believe the Gospel. Turning from their sins to the promises of God's redeeming love, they will become the children of God.

Jesus also foresaw and prepared for the time when His mission on earth would be fulfilled and the message of the Kingdom should be carried to the ends of the world. So in the early days of His ministry, He gathered a special group of disciples whom He trained for apostleship. Our text mentions two pairs of brothers, all fishermen on the Sea of Galilee: Simon Peter and Andrew, and the two sons of Zebedee, James and John. The call "Follow Me" and the divine commission to be fishers of men kindled their faith and stirred their souls so they followed Jesus without hesitation. We know they never regretted it, as is true for all those who follow Him in faith.

Prayer

Lord Jesus, how can we ever thank You for putting Yourself under the Law for our sakes and fulfilling all righteousness for us! Through the washing of regeneration, we are now the blessed children of God. A thousand thanks to You that You conquered Satan for us. Be near us in every hour of temptation. By Your gracious call, lead us to true repentance and to saving faith in You. May we not hesitate to follow You. Be our Teacher so we may teach others to know You and find rest for their souls. Amen.

JESUS ASTONISHES THE PEOPLE OF CAPERNAUM

Mark 1:21–38

THE Galilean ministry of Jesus, of which Mark speaks in the first part of his Gospel, centered in Capernaum, where Jesus made His headquarters. Here Mark gives us a characteristic picture of how Jesus conducted His work. At this time, preaching is Jesus' chief concern, but Mark records a number of miracles by which Jesus proved that He was indeed the Savior to whom John the Baptist had pointed and before whom the devil with all his cruel power could not stand. May that Savior with His power to save and help be our hope and comfort!

Jesus Heals a Man with an Unclean Spirit

And they went into Capernaum, and immediately on the Sabbath He entered the synagogue and was teaching. And they were astonished at His teaching, for He taught them as one who had authority, and not as the scribes. And immediately there was in their synagogue a man with an unclean spirit.

And he cried out, "What have You to do with us, Jesus of Nazareth? Have You come to destroy us? I know who You are—the Holy One of God." But Jesus rebuked him, saying, "Be silent, and come out of him!" And the unclean spirit, convulsing him and crying out with a loud voice, came out of him. And they were all amazed, so that they questioned among themselves, saying, "What is this? A new teaching with authority! He commands even the unclean spirits, and they obey Him." And at once His fame spread everywhere throughout all the surrounding region of Galilee.

Jesus Heals Many

And immediately He left the synagogue and entered the house of Simon and Andrew, with James and John. Now Simon's mother-in-law lay ill with a fever, and immediately they told Him about her. And He came and took her by the hand and lifted her up, and the fever left her, and she began to serve them.

That evening at sundown they brought to Him all who were sick or oppressed by demons. And the whole city was gathered together at the door. And He healed many who were sick with various diseases, and cast out many demons. And He would not permit the demons to speak, because they knew Him.

Jesus Preaches in Galilee

And rising very early in the morning, while it was still dark, He departed and went out to a desolate place, and there He prayed. And Simon and those who were with Him searched for Him, and they found Him and said to Him, "Everyone is looking for You." And He said to them, "Let us go on to the next towns, that I may preach there also, for that is why I came out."

After calling His first disciples, Jesus lost no time getting to work. The very next day was the Sabbath, so He used the opportunity not only to worship in the synagogue at Capernaum but also to address the people. His sermon made a deep impression. While the scribes usually harangued the people about their man-made traditions without regard to their spiritual needs or their salvation, this young rabbi clearly had a profound understanding of the Scriptures and was deeply concerned about the souls of men. His teaching was not a vague philosophizing about some academic aspect of the Law, but was a scriptural and, therefore, authoritative discourse on the way of salvation by repentance and faith. No wonder the people were immediately attracted to Him! (How thankful we should be when our pastors proclaim the way to salvation from and with the Word of God and not their personal opinions about what is interesting or entertaining!)

Then something happened that left the people almost stunned with amazement. By God's providence, there was a man there who was possessed by a demon, unclean as the devil always is. He confessed that he had nothing in common with Jesus, whom he knew and acknowledged as the Holy One of God and whom he feared and hated. Nor did this demon want to give up his helpless human prey, for it was his delight to torture and destroy. But for him and others like him, the Lord had only contempt and righteous anger. The demon knew he could not resist Jesus' stern command to be silent and leave the man. With devilish cruelty, he threw down his poor victim in a final spasm as he left his human host with a fiendish shriek. We can well imagine the awestruck amazement of the people. They could hardly believe their eyes and ears. But there lay the once-possessed man so gloriously delivered. There stood the Man whom unclean spirits must obey. Soon the whole region of Galilee was filled with news about Jesus. Thank God, that you and I are set free from Satan's cruel bondage by that same Savior.

Peter and Andrew had a house at Capernaum. They went there after the service in the synagogue, taking Jesus, James, and John with them. What was theirs they shared, but it appeared as though there would be no joyful Sabbath meal. Peter's mother-in-law was ill with a fever. When told of the situation, Jesus immediately brought healing to the afflicted woman and joy to her family. What a happy scene as the one who was so quickly and completely restored to health rose to serve her beloved Lord.

As the sun was setting on that memorable day and the Sabbath was over, it became apparent that the incident in the synagogue that morning and the miracle in Simon's house that noon had become known far and wide. What a sight that must have been! The street to Simon's house was swarming with people as the afflicted from countless sickrooms were brought to Jesus. Prominent among them were those afflicted by the devil, the possessed. Jesus proves Himself to be the Master of the situation. No sickness could remain before His healing power. No devil could hold on to his victim. They were not even allowed to cry out against Him; their power was gone. Jesus had come to heal and help.

How tired the Lord must have been that night! Many more such days would come to tax His human strength. But before the sun rose over the quiet lake the next morning, Jesus sought a place of solitude where He could commune with His heavenly Father to gather new strength for His superhuman work. The anxious disciples soon found their beloved Master and interrupted Him with the message that people were up bright and early looking for Him. But it was not popularity that Jesus craved. Neither could He devote Himself to one city only. He must be on His way. Others, too, were to hear His message in the short time allotted to Him.

Prayer

O Lord Jesus, how great was Your compassion that moved You to bring the message of salvation to souls imprisoned by the power of Satan! Surely You came to destroy the works of the devil. Taking upon Yourself our weaknesses, You brought health, healing, and happiness to suffering bodies and distressed souls. Into Your hands we commit ourselves with all that we are and all that we have. Hear us, Lord, for the sake of Your divine compassion. Amen.

THE TRIUMPHANT FAITH OF A LEPER

Mark 1:39–45

TODAY'S text could be the subject of a separate meditation because it presents an outstanding example of faith, belief, and prayer. After that memorable day at Capernaum, Jesus began His second journey through Galilee with His disciples. His first short visit at Jerusalem had made it clear that the leaders of the people would not accept Him and His message. Over mounting opposition from these leaders, Jesus made His appeal to the people, neglecting no opportunity to preach in the synagogues. Since services were held there on Mondays and Thursdays as well as on the Sabbath, Jesus had many opportunities to present His message. The healing of the leper in today's reading took place during such a meeting in a synagogue in Galilee.

And He went throughout all Galilee, preaching in their synagogues and casting out demons.

Jesus Cleanses a Leper

And a leper came to Him, imploring Him, and kneeling said to Him, "If You will, You can make me clean." Moved with pity, He stretched out His hand and touched him and said to him, "I will; be clean." And immediately the leprosy left him, and he was made clean. And Jesus sternly charged him and sent him away at once, and said to him, "See that you say nothing to anyone, but go, show yourself to the priest and offer for your cleansing what Moses commanded, for a proof to them." But he went out and began to talk freely about it, and to spread the news, so that Jesus could no longer openly enter a town, but was out in desolate places, and people were coming to Him from every quarter.

Note how prominently again the casting out of devils is mentioned. Satan was well aware that the Son of God had come in the flesh, so the devil entered the bodies of men to torture them.

It was on this Galilean journey that Jesus met a leper who, in great distress, dared to come near enough to kneel before Him and ask for help. What a great faith is revealed in his words, "If You will, You can make me clean"! The man sincerely believed that Jesus could help him. He was also sure that whatever Jesus did, even if He decided it was better for the poor sufferer to go to his grave with his loathsome disease, he would worship Jesus still and submit to His will. (How this man puts us to shame whenever we complain about our trials and cannot wait patiently for Jesus or even doubt His will or power to help!) Jesus was deeply touched by this man's faith; compassion welled up within Him. Reassuringly, He touched the man, so long an outcast, and assured him that He was both able and willing to help him. Without further ceremony or delay, the man was completely healed.

But why did Jesus, when He sent the man away, insist that he keep this event to himself? Because the healed leper was not knowledgeable enough about Jesus to proclaim Him as the Savior from sin. Consequently, he placed all emphasis on His healing power, thus giving people a wrong impression of Jesus. Jesus, who did not want this kind of acclaim, insisted instead that the man go to the priests and make the sacrifices demanded by the law so His enemies, whose opposition was growing, would be compelled to acknowledge that a great Prophet had arisen and would be warned to not fight the truth.

We can understand why the leper, in great joy and with sincere gratitude, gave his healing the widest possible publicity. But the immediate result was that Jesus was definitely hindered in His ministry of the Word. People were so enthusiastic about this miracle that Jesus had to avoid the crowds and seek the privacy of the desert for a while instead of staying in the city to preach the truth.

But even in the desert, people came from all parts of Galilee to find Him. We see how well-meaning friends of Jesus and the

Church, not taking time or making the effort to get better acquainted with Christ and His Word but acting on their own initiative and shortsighted enthusiasm, actually may harm the cause of the Gospel by giving others a false conception of Christianity. It is necessary to follow every command of Christ and take His every word seriously, never setting our human judgment against Him and His Word. Even the sincerest enthusiasm cannot take the place of believing obedience.

Prayer

Dearest Lord Jesus, how we marvel at Your compassion toward suffering mankind! No one is so unclean but that the touch of Your almighty hand and the sound of Your gracious voice can bring healing and health to soul and body. We thank You for Your saving grace, which found us in the filth of our sins and brought us happiness and healing when there was no other help. We give glory to You alone. And may we learn to be obedient to Your every word that we may learn to know and do Your will. Amen.

5

SIN AND SICKNESS MUST YIELD BEFORE THE LORD
Mark 2:1–12

QUITE some time must have elapsed before Jesus returned to Capernaum. His plan and desire to bring the Gospel to others also was carried out. Mark tells us fewer of the sermons Jesus preached but relates, in his own vivid manner, a remarkable healing. (See also Matthew 9:2–8; Luke 5:18–26.)

Jesus Heals a Paralytic

And when He returned to Capernaum after some days, it was reported that He was at home. And many were gathered together, so that there was no more room, not even at the door. And He was preaching the word to them. And they came, bringing to Him a paralytic carried by four men. And when they could not get near Him because of the crowd, they removed the roof above Him, and when they had made an opening, they let down the bed on which the paralytic lay. And when Jesus saw their faith, He said to the paralytic, "Son, your sins are forgiven." Now some of the scribes were sitting there, questioning in their hearts, "Why does this man speak like that? He is blaspheming! Who can forgive sins but God alone?" And immediately Jesus, perceiving in His spirit that they thus questioned within themselves, said to them, "Why do you question these things in your hearts? Which is easier, to say to the paralytic, 'Your sins are forgiven,' or to say, 'Rise, take up your bed and walk'? But that you may know that the Son of Man has authority on earth to forgive sins"—He said to the paralytic—"I say to you, rise, pick up your bed, and go home." And he rose and immediately picked up his bed and went out before them all, so that they were all amazed and glorified God, saying, "We never saw anything like this!"

Back home, perhaps in Peter's house again, Jesus may have longed for quiet days and peaceful nights, but people who saw Him arrive were quick to tell others. And there they were, crowding into every available space to be near Him, craning their necks to see, straining their ears to hear. Many must have turned away in disappointment, reluctant to leave. And Jesus? What else could He do but raise His voice and preach to them the Word of salvation in plain language and full of life and power.

Suddenly, there was a stir in the crowded street. Four determined men carried a fifth, a helpless paralytic lying on a pallet, a

sight to move anyone's heart. We can well imagine how the piti-
ful little procession was met with the cry "Too late. Too crowded.
Nobody can get in there!" But the men would not turn back. Was
there no chance? Faith knows there is a way. Love is quick to find
it. There was a stairway leading to the flat roof of the house. Once
on the roof, the four men took up the tiles and gently lowered their
friend to the room below, just where the Lord stood.

Whatever the consternation of the people in the room, there
was no question as to the Lord's reaction. Here was a person who
needed His love. One look into that troubled face, and Jesus saw the
need that only He could meet. Here was not only a tortured body,
but also a troubled soul. Glancing up into the faces peering down
through the roof so confidently looking to Him for help, beholding the gleam of hope and faith in the eyes of the helpless sufferer,
the Lord responded with words only He could speak: "Son, your
sins are forgiven." We can be assured that hope did not turn into
disappointment when the man heard these words. He must have
known that what he needed above all was the assurance that in and
through his Lord and Savior, he was at peace with God. With that,
he could be content, even if his friends had had to carry him away
on the same bed of pain.

There were others in the crowd who were not so happy about
these words. The scribes, who more and more dogged the footsteps
of Jesus, had so far found nothing wrong in His words or conduct,
although they had come early and found a seat where they could
watch His every move. But here was something, they thought, that
could not go unchallenged. Jesus was speaking blasphemy. Who can
forgive sins but God alone?

That is true—only God can forgive sins. But they didn't believe
that Jesus' claim might be the truth and He might be God. Quickly
enough, He proved it. The fact that He knew their thoughts must
have shocked them into some recognition of His divinity. But they
were to see more. Would they like to see further proof of His divine
power? How about healing this paralytic? Impossible?

No. With God, nothing is impossible. Jesus turned to the helpless sufferer, whose soul, now free from the burden of a guilty conscience, was bound to Him in gratitude and faith. With simple but majestic words, Jesus said, "Rise, pick up your bed, and go home." He sent the happiest man in that great gathering of people on his way rejoicing. Readily the crowd made room for him and watched in wonder and awe as homeward-bound he left to share his joy with his loved ones.

Do they now believe that Jesus has power to forgive sins? Perhaps not the scribes, for no one is so blind as he that will not see. But that day and to this day, believers have found abiding comfort in the assurance that He can and does forgive sins. May we, like the people of Capernaum that day, truly appreciate the amazing power of Him who can do what no other can do—take from us the shame and guilt, the bondage and power, and the curse and punishment of sin and glorify God for His unspeakable gift!

Prayer

O Lord our God, we know the indescribable misery sin has brought into the world. Sin is with us daily, and sickness and sorrow are never far away. The world is filled with woe, and we are so helpless. But thanks be to You for Your unspeakable mercy that You sent Your Son to destroy the works of the devil and to take from us the curse and punishment of sin. May we never foolishly doubt or negligently cast aside this blessing, but ever rejoice and take comfort in our salvation, through Jesus Christ, our Lord. Amen.

THE LORD IS NOT AFRAID OF HIS CRITICS
Mark 2:13–28

THE calling of Matthew, the tax collector, into the discipleship of Jesus was the occasion for more opposition on the part of the scribes and Pharisees. At the same time, it gave Jesus an opportunity to point out the real difference between Him and the leaders of the Church. Although the truth silenced them, it did not convince them because they were not open to conviction. Thus truth—rejected willfully—will finally rise up in judgment against the unbeliever.

Jesus Calls Levi

He went out again beside the sea, and all the crowd was coming to Him, and He was teaching them. And as He passed by, He saw Levi the son of Alphaeus sitting at the tax booth, and He said to him, "Follow Me." And he rose and followed Him.

And as He reclined at table in his house, many tax collectors and sinners were reclining with Jesus and His disciples, for there were many who followed Him. And the scribes of the Pharisees, when they saw that He was eating with sinners and tax collectors, said to His disciples, "Why does He eat with tax collectors and sinners?" And when Jesus heard it, He said to them, "Those who are well have no need of a physician, but those who are sick. I came not to call the righteous, but sinners."

A Question About Fasting

Now John's disciples and the Pharisees were fasting. And people came and said to Him, "Why do John's disciples and the disciples of the Pharisees fast, but Your disciples do not fast?" And Jesus said to them, "Can the wedding guests fast while the bridegroom is with them? As long as they have the bridegroom with them, they cannot fast. The days will come when the bridegroom is taken away from them, and then they will fast in that day. No one sews a piece of unshrunk cloth on an old garment. If he does, the patch tears away from it, the new from the old, and a worse tear is made. And no one puts new wine into old wineskins. If he does, the wine will burst the skins— and the wine is destroyed, and so are the skins. But new wine is for fresh wineskins."

Jesus Is Lord of the Sabbath

One Sabbath He was going through the grainfields, and as they made their way, His disciples began to pluck heads of grain. And the Pharisees were saying to Him, "Look, why are they doing what is not lawful on the Sabbath?" And He said to them, "Have you never read what David did, when he was in need and was hungry, he and those who were with him: how he entered the house of God, in the time of Abiathar the high priest, and ate the bread of the Presence, which it is not lawful for any but the priests to eat, and also gave it to those who were with him?" And He said to them, "The Sabbath was made for man, not man for the Sabbath. So the Son of Man is lord even of the Sabbath."

After healing the paralyzed man, Jesus sought the open spaces He loved so. Was not this the creation in which He, as the eternal Word, had taken part? But above all, He sought contact with the multitudes, the souls He had come to redeem. He delighted in teaching them about life on this earth and the life to come. Passing by, He saw one of those despised tax collectors, Levi (whom we call Matthew), sitting in his place of business on or near the highway where merchants and others had to pay customs to the Roman government. The Lord's call, "Follow Me," was enough to make this man give up his profitable business for a life of hardship and self-denial. But no one who has made that choice has ever regretted it.

Soon Levi's house became the scene of a remarkable gathering. Perhaps those same rooms had seen other meetings of Levi and his fellow sinners. How astonished his friends must have been when they saw that Levi had invited another guest, not of their kind but that famous rabbi, Jesus of Nazareth. Why would Jesus associate with them, or they with Him for that matter? Even His disciples would have felt ill at ease. But there is no arrogance, no superior attitude from this great and holy man who had just healed one of their neighbors. He dined with them in a spirit of perfect friendliness. How could they not realize that life offers better things than making money and carousing and that Levi had found One who was more friend than anyone they had known until then? How they must have listened with rapt attention when He spoke to them of the one thing needful! True, the scribes and Pharisees, ever watchful of everything Jesus did, were scandalized. "How can that be right?" they asked the disciples with derision. "People are judged by the company they keep. A friend of sinners must be a sinner himself."

But Jesus has His answer ready. Self-satisfied, the Pharisees believed that they did not need a Savior. They think they are healthy and strong and holy. But the sick, the sinful, and the sorrowing will not be deprived of the blessings His healing love brought to their souls. What a blessing to you and me that Jesus is, indeed, the Friend of sinners!

All this brought out another issue. Although the Pharisees did not heed John the Baptist's cry of repentance, they zealously conformed to the same man-made rules of strict fasting and sorrow as did John's disciples, which gave them something in common with one another. But Jesus says the fact that the Messiah, the long-predicted Bridegroom, was in their midst was a cause for feasting and rejoicing. True, He tells them, the time for sorrow will come soon enough, when the Bridegroom will be taken from them. Then, they would weep and lament until they saw Him again. With two examples from everyday life, Jesus further illustrated the difference between the old doctrine of the Pharisees and the new teachings of Jesus. First, a new patch cannot be expected to stay in place when sewn to an old, worn-out garment. Second, it is foolish to put new wine, still in the process of fermentation, into old, weak wineskins and take the chance of bursting them. Neither could the old, dead formalism and legalism of the Pharisees be brought into harmony with the new, vigorous, authoritative Gospel of Jesus.

Another clash between Jesus and the Pharisees occurred when He wandered along the narrow paths of fields of ripening grain. The natural act of the disciples in plucking grain to satisfy their hunger did not violate the law (see Deuteronomy 23:25), but it did give the Pharisees something else to nitpick about. Plucking the stalks and rubbing the chaff off the grains was unnecessary labor, they said; it broke the Sabbath! Jesus easily showed how foolish they were. Did David do wrong when he ate the bread of the Presence that the priest gave him, although ceremonial law reserved this food for the priests? Is not love the fulfillment of the Law? Is not the Sabbath made for mankind, and not mankind for the Sabbath? Moreover, is He not the Lord of the Sabbath, who has authority to change the Law? Let us be careful that we do not become legalists, bound by man-made laws long abolished by God.

Prayer

We thank You, Lord and Savior, that You have called us out of sin and into Your fellowship and service. Give us courage to confess You before others so they also may know and love You. Let no one rob us of the joy that comes from knowing You as Lord and Savior. May no dead doctrine bind us with the chains of human laws, but may we freely and gladly serve and praise You here in time and hereafter in eternity. Amen.

DESPITE OPPOSITION, JESUS CONTINUES HIS WORK

Mark 3:1–19

HERE, we read on one hand of the increasing enmity and opposition of the Pharisees, who were growing more desperate and determined, and on the other hand of the increasing interest and enthusiasm of the people to hear Jesus' words, see His miracles, and benefit from His power as He calmly goes about the work God sent Him to do. One essential part of His plan was to call and prepare apostles so they could, after He had finished His work on earth, go out and proclaim the saving Gospel to all mankind.

A Man with a Withered Hand

Again He entered the synagogue, and a man was there with a withered hand. And they watched Jesus, to see whether He would heal him on the Sabbath, so that they might accuse Him. And He said to the man with the withered hand, "Come here." And He said to them, "Is it lawful on the Sabbath to do good or to do harm, to save life or to kill?" But they were silent. And He looked around at them with anger, grieved at their hardness of heart, and said to the man, "Stretch out your hand." He stretched it out, and his hand was restored. The Pharisees went out and immediately held counsel with the Herodians against Him, how to destroy Him.

A Great Crowd Follows Jesus

Jesus withdrew with His disciples to the sea, and a great crowd followed, from Galilee and Judea and Jerusalem and Idumea and from beyond the Jordan and from around Tyre and Sidon. When the great crowd heard all that He was doing, they came to Him. And He told His disciples to have a boat ready

for Him because of the crowd, lest they crush Him, for He had
healed many, so that all who had diseases pressed around Him
to touch Him. And whenever the unclean spirits saw Him,
they fell down before Him and cried out, "You are the Son of
God." And He strictly ordered them not to make Him known.

The Twelve Apostles

And He went up on the mountain and called to Him those
whom He desired, and they came to Him. And He appointed
twelve (whom He also named apostles) so that they might be
with Him and He might send them out to preach and have
authority to cast out demons. He appointed the twelve: Simon
(to whom He gave the name Peter); James the son of Zebedee
and John the brother of James (to whom He gave the name
Boanerges, that is, Sons of Thunder); Andrew, and Philip, and
Bartholomew, and Matthew, and Thomas, and James the son of
Alphaeus, and Thaddaeus, and Simon the Cananaean, and Judas
Iscariot, who betrayed Him.

The following Sabbath, Jesus entered the synagogue (probably the
same one mentioned in 1:21). The suspicious Pharisees would not
let Him out of their sight. Among the audience that day (by chance
or by the design of His enemies?) was a man whose hand was withered, either by an accident or through some disease. Jesus' enemies
saw here an occasion to cause Him trouble. They figured that if He
healed the man, they would accuse Him of breaking the Sabbath. If
Jesus did not heal the man, they would question His ability or willingness to help someone in trouble. But Jesus was not to be put on
the defensive. In His usual direct way, He took the lead. His command to the afflicted man to come forward was quickly obeyed.
Jesus presented the case in such a way that His enemies would either
have to concede that He was right or else keep silent: "Is it lawful
on the Sabbath to do good or to do harm, to save life or to kill?" To
refuse help and save a life is the same as to harm and kill. The ethics
of the question had not even occurred to the Pharisees. They were
speechless. And everyone could feel the righteousness of the anger
that shone from Jesus' eyes. At the same time, Jesus was grieved

by the blindness of their hearts. Are men not to be pitied who will not see the power of His saving love? Only one thing remained to be done. Jesus said to the man, "Stretch out your hand," and He healed him.

Now let the Pharisees do their worst. Since they would not be convinced that they stood in the presence of the Light from heaven, they would stand with the prince of darkness. So the Pharisees, along with the Herodians, adherents of King Herod, began decisively to plot the death and destruction of Jesus.

But His time had not yet come. Indeed, His popularity with the people grew as the unreasonable hatred of His enemies increased. As the Lord withdrew to the Sea of Galilee with His disciples, a great multitude followed Him, not only from Galilee, but from Judea, from Jerusalem, from Idumea farther to the south, from the hills to the east of the Jordan, and even from the great cities of Tyre and Sidon far to the north. His fame drew them into a vast multitude. Standing by the seashore, He might have been crowded into the water had He not asked His disciples to have a boat ready for Him from which to preach the Word of life. Especially prominent again were those vexed with unclean spirits, who could not help themselves but confessed that Jesus was the Son of God.

Jesus was fully aware that His time of suffering and death was drawing nearer. Having spent the night in prayer, seeking strength from His heavenly Father, He selected men from among His many followers to be His assistants in preaching and healing—the twelve apostles. Forever are their names recorded, the names of these "common" men who turned the world upside down: Simon, whom He honored with the surname Peter, the rock; the two sons of Zebedee, James and John, whom He nicknamed Sons of Thunder; Andrew, Peter's brother; Philip; Bartholomew; Matthew (Levi); Thomas; the other James, son of Alphaeus; Thaddaeus; and Simon the Cananaean. Mentioned last is Judas Iscariot, whom the evangelists describe only as Jesus' betrayer. What a sad thing to have one's name recorded as a traitor! May God keep us faithful and true to our glorious Master and Savior!

Prayer

O Lord Jesus, we know that the proud Pharisees of our day and the worldly minded Sadducees within and without the visible Church cannot crucify You again, but they scorn Your saving love and would rob You of Your greatest glory, the glory of being the Savior of sinners, such as we confess ourselves to be. Help us that we may not look upon You with passing wonder or come near only when it is the popular thing to do. Help us to turn from the sins that would destroy our souls, from sinful pride and prejudice. Help us, because it is Your greatest desire to save us from our sins through Your suffering and death, to ever be witnesses and messengers of Your redeeming love. Hear us in Your mercy. Amen.

8
BEWARE OF THE SIN AGAINST THE HOLY SPIRIT
Mark 3:19–35

AMID growing opposition from the Pharisees, note that Jesus' "friends" did not understand Him either. Even His relatives, including His mother, worried about Him in a way that showed they did not fully appreciate His divine mission. But the worst was that His enemies, so definitely confronted with the truth, were beginning to harden their hearts and to blaspheme. To disregard the evidence that God's Holy Spirit was working through Jesus and say that it was Beelzebul by whose power He worked miracles was a serious matter indeed. Therefore, we read the warning not to commit the sin against the Holy Ghost:

Then He went home, and the crowd gathered again, so that they could not even eat. And when His family heard it, they went out to seize Him, for they were saying, "He is out of His mind."

Blasphemy Against the Holy Spirit

And the scribes who came down from Jerusalem were saying, "He is possessed by Beelzebul," and "by the prince of demons He casts out the demons." And He called them to Him and said to them in parables, "How can Satan cast out Satan? If a kingdom is divided against itself, that kingdom cannot stand. And if a house is divided against itself, that house will not be able to stand. And if Satan has risen up against himself and is divided, he cannot stand, but is coming to an end. But no one can enter a strong man's house and plunder his goods, unless he first binds the strong man. Then indeed he may plunder his house.

"Truly, I say to you, all sins will be forgiven the children of man, and whatever blasphemies they utter, but whoever blasphemes against the Holy Spirit never has forgiveness, but is guilty of an eternal sin"—for they were saying, "He has an unclean spirit."

Jesus' Mother and Brothers

And His mother and His brothers came, and standing outside they sent to Him and called Him. And a crowd was sitting around Him, and they said to Him, "Your mother and Your brothers are outside, seeking You." And He answered them, "Who are My mother and My brothers?" And looking about at those who sat around Him, He said, "Here are My mother and My brothers! For whoever does the will of God, he is My brother and sister and mother."

Having called and ordained the twelve apostles, Jesus clearly intended to devote as much time as possible to their training and instruction. Because their journey had been a long one, their immediate intentions upon entering a certain house were to rest, refresh themselves with some food, and have some privacy. But the multitude was so anxious to see Jesus, primarily because of His miracles, that there was no time to eat. Here some of Jesus' relatives tried to intervene. They were concerned about His well-being, so they tried to stop Him. They even declared that He must be beside Himself, out of His mind. Many people today are unable to comprehend the zeal and devotion, the all-absorbing interest that sincere Christians show for the cause of the Lord, least of all do they understand the passion for the souls of men that burns in the heart of Jesus.

As for the people, we learn from St. Matthew's account that they were seriously considering that Jesus was the Son of David. This did not suit the pharisaical scribes at all, who felt that they must counteract the growing power and popularity of Jesus. Therefore, the Pharisees came out with the vicious statement: "He is possessed by Beelzebul, . . . by the prince of demons He casts out the demons." In their impotent rage, they could not have said anything harsher or more insulting. But note: although Jesus may humble Himself, no one can humiliate Him. He boldly takes the offensive. Knowing their thoughts, He summons them into His presence, not to defend Himself, but to point out the seriousness of their blasphemy and the danger that threatened their souls. How foolish the enmity of those who harden their hearts against the truth! "How can Satan cast out Satan?" He points out that a divided kingdom, a divided house, cannot stand. Satan cannot be against Satan and drive him out. Rather, Jesus has come as the stronger man to storm the stronghold of the mighty ruler of the darkness of this world and thus to overcome Satan, thief that he is, who must give up his prey.

It was easy enough to point out the foolishness of the blasphemy uttered by His enemies. It was a far more serious matter that they were in danger of losing their souls. In the strongest and most impressive way, Jesus points out that there is forgiveness in the heart of God for all sins of all men, even for their blasphemies. But there is one sin that because of its very nature can never be forgiven— blasphemy against the Holy Spirit, His blessed work. In the works of Christ and in the testimony of the Gospel, the Holy Spirit attests His presence. He who consciously, willfully, and persistently hardens himself against the testimony of the Holy Spirit cuts himself off from the only power that can save him. Let us be cautious that we do not harden ourselves against the truth.

Now a remarkable thing occurred. Jesus' mother and His brothers, unable to get to Him in the crowded house, sent Him an urgent message with the best of intentions. They, particularly Mary, were truly concerned about His welfare and were convinced that the strain and stress of the work was too much for Him. But the flaw in their concern was that they did not realize that Jesus must do the work of Him who sent Him, and do it now.

Never did any man love and honor his mother as Jesus did. But here was an occasion to show that we must put God and the cause of His kingdom first. When word reached Him that His mother and brothers wanted to see Him, Jesus answered, "Who are My mother and My brothers?" Looking around at the circle of His disciples and dramatically pointing to them, He claimed them to be the nearest and dearest to Him, those who do the will of God in the faith and love of their reborn hearts. What a privilege, and a comfort to be so close to our Savior and Lord!

Prayer

Our precious Lord and Savior, we shudder to think that we were Satan's easy and helpless prey until You came as a mightier One and snatched us out of his cruel claws. Since Your blood has atoned for our sins, Satan can no longer effectively accuse us or claim us as his own. Help us that we may never be offended in You when blind Pharisees and cunning enemies ridicule Your claim to be our only Savior, but that we may rejoice in the knowledge that our souls are precious in Your sight, unworthy though we are in ourselves. May we truly do Your will and abide in Your love. Amen.

9

A SOWER
WENT OUT TO
SOW HIS SEED
Mark 4:1–20

IN today's reading, we have a typical and well known parable of our Lord. We read again and again that Jesus taught the people. This parable is a lesson about His doctrine. It is foolish to believe that mere entertainment or even exhortation can take the place of indoctrination. And as He taught, and all true preachers make it their chief object to teach, to impart knowledge, so it must ever remain our obligation to listen and learn so the seed sown in our hearts may bear fruit now unto life eternal.

The Parable of the Sower

Again He began to teach beside the sea. And a very large crowd gathered about Him, so that He got into a boat and sat in it on the sea, and the whole crowd was beside the sea on the land. And He was teaching them many things in parables, and in His teaching He said to them: "Listen! A sower went out to sow. And as he sowed, some seed fell along the path, and the birds came and devoured it. Other seed fell on rocky ground, where it did not have much soil, and immediately it sprang up, since it had no depth of soil. And when the sun rose, it was scorched, and since it had no root, it withered away. Other seed fell among thorns, and the thorns grew up and choked it, and it yielded no grain. And other seeds fell into good soil and produced grain, growing up and increasing and yielding thirtyfold and sixtyfold and a hundredfold." And He said, "He who has ears to hear, let him hear."

The Purpose of the Parables

And when He was alone, those around Him with the twelve asked Him about the parables. And He said to them, "To you has been given the secret of the kingdom of God, but for those outside everything is in parables, so that

"they may indeed see but not perceive, and may indeed hear
but not understand, lest they should turn and be forgiven."

And He said to them, "Do you not understand this parable? How then will you understand all the parables? The sower sows the word. And these are the ones along the path, where the word is sown: when they hear, Satan immediately comes and takes away the word that is sown in them. And these are the ones sown on rocky ground: the ones who, when they hear the word, immediately receive it with joy. And they have no root in themselves, but endure for a while; then, when tribulation or persecution arises on account of the word, immediately they fall away. And others are the ones sown among thorns. They are those who hear the word, but the cares of the world and the deceitfulness of riches and the desires for other things enter in and choke the word, and it proves unfruitful. But those that were sown on the good soil are the ones who hear the word and accept it and bear fruit, thirtyfold and sixtyfold and a hundredfold."

Immediately after the incident with His mother and brothers, and with hardly enough time even to eat, Jesus yielded to the demands of an exceptionally large crowd to come out. Regardless of what they expected of Him, He knew what the people needed above all things. From the vantage point of a boat put out a little way from the shore, where all could see and hear Him, He began to teach them many things. His favorite method of teaching was to speak in parables. These parables, taken from the everyday life of His hearers, communicated eternal truths adapted to the understanding of anyone, even the least educated or capable. Here Jesus spoke of a farmer who went out to sow his seed. The fields around Jesus' listeners were not large fenced-in areas, but were little patches of hilly ground crisscrossed by narrow paths leading from village to village and from city to city. How easily some of the scattered seed could fall onto one of these paths, where the birds would eagerly devour it. There were also patches of shallow ground on rocky ledges, where the seed would readily sprout but would quickly wither under the noonday sun. Other seed would fall into apparently good ground, but the roots of weeds that had grown there the previous year had not been entirely removed and would smother the tender grain before it could take firm root and produce. But some, perhaps most, of the seed, fell into excellent ground, where it could grow and produce, some thirty-, sixty-, or a hundredfold. To emphasize the point of the lesson, Jesus added, "He who has ears to hear, let him hear."

St. Mark includes a conversation that took place later in the day, when Jesus was alone with the Twelve and other disciples. They had evidently been particularly impressed by this parable and wanted to make sure they understood Him and got the full import of this lesson. It is a good thing to meditate on a sermon we've heard or on a text we've read and to find occasion to get further information.

In His reply, Jesus first reminded the disciples about the privilege they enjoyed, namely, to know the things revealed to them concerning the kingdom of God. We must always keep in mind that such knowledge is not the result of human speculation, but that God has, in His Word, revealed to those who love Him the things that eyes have not seen and ears have not heard and that have not entered into the heart of man. Some people are like the unbelieving Jews. The parables do them no good. One wonders why they do not understand what is plainly before them and why they do not take to heart what is spoken in simple words; but when people continually harden their hearts against the truth and do not believe, it comes upon them as a judgment of God that they will not be saved.

As to the meaning of the parable, Jesus said it was so plain that if they did not understand this one, how would they understand others? What the sower sows, what the Lord and His servants preach, is the Word. That Word is all-powerful. But what good will it do if hard, unrepentant hearts will not receive it? Many hear the Word but without any longing, without any realization that they need it, without interest or attention. Soon even the remembrance of it is gone. Others receive it with enthusiasm and apparent emotion, but it does not take root. A little opposition or ridicule, and their fragile faith withers like a tender plant in the midday heat. In others, the Word may take deeper root at first but brings no fruit because the thorns of foolish cares or earthly joys smother the tender plant of faith. But, thank God, there are those who receive the Word with open hearts. The Word asserts its divine power in these people, although the fruit of faith vary according to their gifts and circumstances. How important it is not only that we hear the Word but how we hear it!

Prayer

Jesus, gentle, loving Savior, we who hear and read Your Word today enjoy a glorious privilege over so many who do not even know there is a life-saving Gospel. How awful it would be if the power of that Gospel would be lost, if we pay no prayerful attention to it and it takes no root in our hearts, or if it takes root and does not grow, or if it grows but does not bear fruit. Give us truly repentant hearts to receive Your Word. Strengthen our faith, and do not let foolish cares and earthly concerns smother Your Word in our hearts, but help it to bring forth in us an abundant harvest of loving, faithful service. Amen.

MORE PARABLES BY THE MASTER OF WIND AND WAVES
Mark 4:21–41

IT is evident that while His enemies hardened themselves more and more to His teaching until His simple parables only confused them, Jesus devoted Himself all the more to His disciples, who were willing to hear and to learn. For their sake, He devoted the rest of that busy day to telling many more parables, some of which are recorded here for our benefit. When evening came, His human nature asserted itself—He was tired. He slept aboard their little ship, and even the howling wind and the tossing waves did not disturb Him. But the cry of distress from those He loved caused Him to rise up in all the majesty of His divine power and bid the storm to be still. Let us read the story:

A Lamp Under a Basket

And He said to them, "Is a lamp brought in to be put under a basket, or under a bed, and not on a stand? For nothing is hidden except to be made manifest; nor is anything secret except to come to light. If anyone has ears to hear, let him hear." And He said to them, "Pay attention to what you hear: with the measure you use, it will be measured to you, and still more will be added to you. For to the one who has, more will be given, and from the one who has not, even what he has will be taken away."

The Parable of the Seed Growing

And He said, "The kingdom of God is as if a man should scatter seed on the ground. He sleeps and rises night and day, and the seed sprouts and grows; he knows not how. The earth produces by itself, first the blade, then the ear, then the full grain in the ear. But when the grain is ripe, at once he puts in the sickle, because the harvest has come."

The Parable of the Mustard Seed

And He said, "With what can we compare the kingdom of God, or what parable shall we use for it? It is like a grain of mustard seed, which, when sown on the ground, is the smallest of all the seeds on earth, yet when it is sown it grows up and becomes larger than all the garden plants and puts out large branches, so that the birds of the air can make nests in its shade."

With many such parables He spoke the word to them, as they were able to hear it. He did not speak to them without a parable, but privately to His own disciples He explained everything.

Jesus Calms a Storm

On that day, when evening had come, He said to them, "Let us go across to the other side." And leaving the crowd, they took Him with them in the boat, just as He was. And other boats were with Him. And a great windstorm arose, and the waves were breaking into the boat, so that the boat was already filling. But He was in the stern, asleep on the cushion. And they woke Him and said to Him, "Teacher, do You not care that we are perishing?" And He awoke and rebuked the wind and said to the sea, "Peace! Be still!" And the wind ceased, and there was a great calm. He said to them, "Why are you so afraid? Have you still no faith?" And they were filled with great fear and said to one another, "Who then is this, that even the wind and the sea obey Him?"

The disciples had received the explanation of the parable of the sower. To them it was a privilege and a blessing to know the mysteries of His kingdom. But the greater the knowledge, the greater the responsibility. They were to use their gifts for the benefit of others. Therefore, Jesus told them the parable of the lamp. They all had such lamps in their houses; they knew what they were for and wouldn't think of hiding one. So, Jesus told them, they must not hide the light they were receiving, but let it shine hope and life into the dark hearts of others. They were not to keep these things in their hearts like secrets, but make them known abroad. Considering how important this is, it is no wonder that He warned them to heed and understand His words. For the more they give to others, the more they will receive. To impart knowledge means to increase your own understanding. Prayerful attention and careful Bible study will never be in vain. Thus, those who have such knowledge will always receive more, while those who do not seek to learn more will lose what little they have. Are we gaining by sharing our knowledge with others? A teacher who does not learn cannot teach.

Next follows a beautiful parable about the power and reliability of the Gospel. As we let our light shine, confessing and teaching the Gospel, we certainly would be foolish to worry about its success. What does the Christian farmer do when he sows good seed into his field? Does he lie awake at night, worrying about the result of his labor? He leaves that to the Lord. He remembers God's promise that as long as the earth remains, seedtime and harvest will continue. The seed will sprout and grow. The success of the Word cannot be forced or hurried any more than we can change the growth process of the crops in the field—but it is assured, by virtue of the promise of God, that His Word will not return to Him void. The happy harvest time will surely come.

Another parable of cheer and comfort is that of the mustard seed. Like this relatively small seed, so the preaching of the Word and the beginning of the Church are small and disregarded. Nevertheless, the marvelous growth of the Church and the success of the Word are the wonder of the ages. As the birds find rest in the branches of the mustard tree, Jesus teaches, so countless souls have found peace in Christ's kingdom.

Here, then, is how Jesus customarily taught the Word of life to the people. His hearers did not always understand the parables, as Mark says, but they heard these plain illustrations from their own everyday life, thought about them, and discussed them with one another. And to this day, these parables help us to remember and understand the deep mysteries of the eternal truths of our salvation. What a blessed privilege that these lessons are preached to us, even as He preached them to His disciples. No more blessed hours can be spent than in the company of Jesus.

Now the long, busy day came to an end. True man that He was, Jesus needed to rest and get away from the crowd. So He told the disciples to row the boat to the other side of the lake, without any preparation on His part, not even stopping for supper. They could not keep other boats from following. Exhausted, He fell asleep, resting His head on a railing in the stern of the boat. Yes, truly human, but still the almighty God! His despairing disciples do not call Him in vain. The howling winds, rushing down from the surrounding mountains with tornadic intensity, must stop; the towering waves must be still immediately—because God the Son commanded it. With Him in their midst, why, indeed, were they so frightened? so lacking in faith? Are our troubles and trials beyond control? Remember, "Who then is this, that even the wind and the sea obey Him?"

Prayer

Lord, strengthen our faith, that we may boldly confess You, never doubt the power of Your Word, and have unfailing confidence in the success of Your kingdom and the assurance that in Your presence nothing can harm us. Amen.

THE LEGION OF DEVILS CAST OUT
Mark 5:1–20

JESUS had calmed the raging sea and stilled the howling storm, but upon His landing on the other side of the lake, He was confronted by a force far more fierce and dangerous to mankind than the destructive power of nature. Let us read how the Lord met the old evil foe on his own ground and put him to flight.

Jesus Heals a Man with a Demon

They came to the other side of the sea, to the country of the Gerasenes. And when Jesus had stepped out of the boat, immediately there met Him out of the tombs a man with an unclean spirit. He lived among the tombs. And no one could bind him anymore, not even with a chain, for he had often been bound with shackles and chains, but he wrenched the chains apart, and he broke the shackles in pieces. No one had the strength to subdue him. Night and day among the tombs and on the mountains he was always crying out and cutting himself with stones. And when he saw Jesus from afar, he ran and fell down before Him. And crying out with a loud voice, he said, "What have You to do with me, Jesus, Son of the Most High God? I adjure You by God, do not torment me." For He was saying to him,

"Come out of the man, you unclean spirit!" And Jesus asked him, "What is your name?" He replied, "My name is Legion, for we are many." And he begged Him earnestly not to send them out of the country. Now a great herd of pigs was feeding there on the hillside, and they begged Him, saying, "Send us to the pigs; let us enter them." So He gave them permission. And the unclean spirits came out, and entered the pigs, and the herd, numbering about two thousand, rushed down the steep bank into the sea and were drowned in the sea.

The herdsmen fled and told it in the city and in the country. And people came to see what it was that had happened. And they came to Jesus and saw the demon-possessed man, the one who had had the legion, sitting there, clothed and in his right mind, and they were afraid. And those who had seen it described to them what had happened to the demon-possessed man and to the pigs. And they began to beg Jesus to depart from their region. As He was getting into the boat, the man who had been possessed with demons begged Him that he might be with Him. And He did not permit him but said to him, "Go home to your friends and tell them how much the Lord has done for you, and how He has had mercy on you." And he went away and began to proclaim in the Decapolis how much Jesus had done for him, and everyone marveled.

On the other side of the Sea of Galilee is the country of the Gerasenes, a predominantly heathen land. Far from finding rest here, Jesus was immediately confronted with a problem far beyond the power and ingenuity of man to solve. He met a man possessed by a demon full of devilish wickedness. Matthew tells us that there were two such men, but one was evidently more grievously tortured than the other. Worse than a maniac, this man was considered beneath even wild animals. He lived among the bones of the dead in the caves among the hills overlooking the lake. The people of the neighborhood had no rest day or night, for at any time they might hear him and his companion shriek as they hurt themselves. Brave men had tried time and again to subdue them by binding them with ropes or chains, but nothing could tame their wildness. They tore all fetters.

Jesus and His disciples arrived amid all this excitement. Immediately the situation changed. Even when Jesus was far away, the possessed man recognized Him as the Lord. He ran to meet Jesus, and fell at His feet. With a loud voice, he proclaimed Jesus as the Son of the Most High God. When Jesus commanded the unclean spirit to come out of the man, the spirit begged pitifully that He not cast him out, but that he might be spared the torment he justly deserved. For the sake of His disciples and those who stood near, Jesus asked the unclean spirit his name. He replied, "My name is Legion, for we are many." Feeling sure that their request would not be granted and in their satanic desire to do as much harm as possible, the demons pleaded with Jesus that they might be permitted to enter into a nearby herd of pigs that the heathen inhabitants maintained (much to the disgust of the Jews). It was only upon the express permission of Jesus, who wanted to teach that the unclean fittingly were associated with the unclean, that the two thousand pigs, driven wild by the demons, ran violently down a steep hill and into the lake to their death.

We can well understand the distress of the keepers of the herd as they hurried to spread the story throughout the countryside. The people lost little time in finding out what had happened. What they saw must have amazed them. In fact, it must have also frightened them, as if they were in the presence of some mysterious power, to see the once-possessed man now free from the legion of devils, decently clothed, evidently in his right mind, and sitting calmly at the feet of this stranger, Jesus. There could be no question about the authenticity of the miracle. There were plenty of witnesses to tell what had happened to the poor man and to the pigs, whose carcasses may have been floating in the water. But whether it was the loss of the herd or their fear of the mysterious stranger who moved them, they begged Jesus to leave. They were not ready for the Gospel. How many are just like that to this day! They do not appreciate Him who came to destroy the power of the devil. Earthly loss means more to them than heavenly gain.

But there was one person who did appreciate, who was ready. As Jesus and His disciples were about to board their ship to return to Galilee, the healed man earnestly begged to go along. But Jesus, in His wisdom, would have it otherwise. He had an important assignment for this man, who was so full of gratitude and faith. Jesus told him to go home to his friends and tell them, as no one else could, what great things the Lord had done for him in His divine compassion. Gladly the man obeyed. So eloquently he told what his Savior had done for him throughout the region that people were filled with amazement. Oh, that all who have experienced the Redeemer's saving power and love would tell it to others!

Prayer

We thankYou, Lord Jesus, thatYou have indeed come to destroy the works of the devil and to redeem us from his cruel power. Help us that we may not drive You from us through ignorance or the love of earthly gain. May we rather be privileged to be witnesses and messengers of Your saving love, telling others what great things You have done for us that they, too, may rejoice in their redemption. Amen.

A SICK WOMAN IS RESTORED TO HEALTH; JAIRUS'S DAUGHTER IS RESTORED TO LIFE
Mark 5:21–43

THIS amazing story, the first record of Jesus raising someone from the dead, is also told by Matthew and Luke, along with the account of His healing of the sick woman. But Mark adds graphic details not recorded by the other writers. Let us, then, read the account of this faith-strengthening miracle of the almighty Son of God, who has conquered death for us.

Jesus Heals a Woman and Jairus's Daughter

And when Jesus had crossed again in the boat to the other side, a great crowd gathered about Him, and He was beside the sea. Then came one of the rulers of the synagogue, Jairus by name, and seeing Him, he fell at His feet and implored Him earnestly, saying, "My little daughter is at the point of death. Come and lay Your hands on her, so that she may be made well and live." And He went with him.

And a great crowd followed Him and thronged about Him. And there was a woman who had had a discharge of blood for twelve years, and who had suffered much under many physicians, and had spent all that she had, and was no better but rather grew worse. She had heard the reports about Jesus and came up behind Him in the crowd and touched His garment. For she said, "If I touch even His garments, I will be made well." And immediately the flow of blood dried up, and she felt in her body that she was healed of her disease. And Jesus, perceiving in Himself that power had gone out from Him, immediately turned about in the crowd and said, "Who touched My garments?" And His disciples said to Him, "You see the crowd pressing around You, and yet You say, 'Who touched Me?'" And He looked around to see who had done it. But the woman, knowing what had happened to her, came in fear and trembling and fell down before Him and told Him the whole truth. And He said to her, "Daughter, your faith has made you well; go in peace, and be healed of your disease."

While He was still speaking, there came from the ruler's house some who said, "Your daughter is dead. Why trouble the Teacher any further?" But overhearing what they said, Jesus said to the ruler of the synagogue, "Do not fear, only believe." And He allowed no one to follow Him except Peter and James and John the brother of James. They came to the house of the ruler of the synagogue, and Jesus saw a commotion, people weeping and wailing loudly. And when He had entered, He said to them, "Why are you making a commotion and weeping? The child is not dead but sleeping." And they laughed at Him. But He put them all outside and took the child's father and mother and those who were with Him and went in where the child was. Taking her by the hand He said to her, "Talitha cumi," which means, "Little girl, I say to you, arise." And immediately the girl got up and began walking (for she was twelve years of age), and they were immediately overcome with amazement. And He strictly charged them that no one should know this, and told them to give her something to eat.

Because the Gerasenes did not want Him there, Jesus returned to the western shore of the Sea of Galilee, where He had preached to great multitudes just the day before. It seems that many of these people lingered at the same place near the shore as if they were waiting for Him. But before Jesus could begin to teach the people, Jairus, one of the rulers of the synagogue, who must have heard Jesus preach often and who probably saw Him heal many people, hurried to Him in great agitation. In his anxiety, his words fairly tumble over one another. His little daughter, so dear to his heart, was that very moment lying at the point of death. But Jairus had full confidence that if Jesus would come and lay His healing hands on her, she would live. Without hesitating a moment, the Lord went with him. And, of course, the crowd followed.

But the faith of the anxious father was put to a severe test. In the crowd that was pushing and crowding Jesus was a sorely afflicted woman. Her condition not only was a physical affliction of a most distressing nature, but it also caused her to be unclean. Therefore, she was excluded from the synagogue and shunned by all who knew her. She had spent all her money on doctors, but none had been able to cure her. After twelve years of suffering and humiliation, her condition grew steadily worse. We can imagine how hope surged in her heart when she heard of the incredible cures performed by Jesus, and we admire both her humility and the greatness of her faith. Here was her opportunity. Everybody was crowding the Lord, so she would not be noticed if she merely touched the hem of His robe, believing that was all she needed to be healed.

And it was. That faith-filled touch brought instant, perfect relief, new vigor and health. But she did not go unnoticed. Such faith was not to be hidden. Jesus knew that His divine power had been drawn upon. His action in making the woman confess what she had done and calling attention to her was to point out to the crowd her remarkable faith and to strengthen it at the same time. Publicly telling her, in front of the crowd, that her faith had made her whole and she should go in peace also helped to reinstate her according to levitical law. She went on her way, a happy woman, indeed.

But what about Jairus? This delay must have made him frantic with worry about his young daughter, And, to be sure, what he dreaded most did happen. Messengers from his house pushed their way through the crowd to bring him the crushing news that his daughter was dead and there was no need to trouble the Master any further. How far they were from knowing the power of the Lord! Quickly, Jesus assures the stricken father: "Do not fear, only believe."

We can well imagine that the people immediately sensed that something else dramatic was about to happen and that they crowded nearer. But Jesus would not have it so. He took only the three witnesses—Peter, James, and John—with Him to Jairus's house, where there was the usual commotion caused by death. People, perhaps professional mourners, were already weeping and loudly lamenting the death of the child. Jesus sternly forbade such signs of hopeless grief. He knew, after all, that the child was not dead, but only asleep.

"And they laughed at Him." How hard it is for us to believe in the almighty power of the Son of God! How easily we forget it when sorrow strikes deep into our hearts! So Jesus asserted His authority. He took only the parents of the child and His three disciples into the death chamber, not, as we know now, to increase their grief, but to fill them with overwhelming joy by taking the girl by the hand, bidding her arise, giving her back to her parents, alive and fully restored to health. He commanded them to give her something to eat. But Jesus made it clear that He was not doing this for the sake of notoriety but so they would believe that He had come to defeat death.

Prayer

Lord, help our unbelief. Make us ashamed of the littleness of our faith. Reading what we read, knowing what we know, our faith should be strong and our hearts should be without fear— yet sorrow, sin, and death so easily rob us of the joy of believing. Today, we learn once more that we need but touch the hem of Your garment, need only draw near to You in faith, and even before we call, You will answer. Let not even death take from us the assurance that You are mightier than death and that those who believe in You shall never die. Amen.

A PROPHET WITHOUT HONOR IN HIS OWN COUNTRY; A TEACHER OF TEACHERS

Mark 6:1–13

WE now come to the third preaching tour of the Lord. Some sections of the country, particularly Capernaum, had heard His message again and again. From this time on, He did not spend so much time there. But He was going to give His hometown another chance to hear the saving Gospel. Jesus determined, too, that it was time for His apostles to have some practical experience in the work for which He was training them.

Jesus Rejected at Nazareth

He went away from there and came to His hometown, and His disciples followed Him. And on the Sabbath He began to teach in the synagogue, and many who heard Him were astonished, saying, "Where did this man get these things? What is the wisdom given to Him? How are such mighty works done by His hands? Is not this the carpenter, the son of Mary and brother of James and Joses and Judas and Simon? And are not His sisters here with us?" And they took offense at Him. And Jesus said to them, "A prophet is not without honor, except in his hometown and among his relatives and in his own household." And He could do no mighty work there, except that He laid His hands on a few sick people and healed them. And He marveled because of their unbelief.

And He went about among the villages teaching.

Jesus Sends Out the Twelve Apostles

And He called the twelve and began to send them out two by two, and gave them authority over the unclean spirits. He charged them to take nothing for their journey except a staff—no bread, no bag, no money in their belts—but to wear sandals and not put on two tunics. And He said to them, "Whenever you enter a house, stay there until you depart from there. And if any place will not receive you and they will not listen to you, when you leave, shake off the dust that is on your feet as a testimony against them." So they went out and proclaimed that people should repent. And they cast out many demons and anointed with oil many who were sick and healed them.

After leaving Capernaum, Jesus revisited His own country, the scene of His childhood. What memories must have come to Him of the happy youth He had spent in and near Nazareth! He remembered them all, the young men who grew up with Him and whose joys and sorrows He shared, the older people who watched Him grow into manhood. Surely He had reason to hope that for the sake of old acquaintance they would hear Him gladly. There must have been many people there that Sabbath Day in the synagogue when He stood before them as their teacher, people who wanted to hear what their famous countryman had to say.

Jesus did not seek honor or accolades—He longed to bring them the knowledge of their salvation! And His sermon did make a deep impression, but not the one He sought. Indeed, many were astonished at His doctrine, the undeniable wisdom He displayed, and the great deeds He was reported to have done. But was there not a certain envy connected with their astonishment? After all, He was just like them. In fact, He came from a carpenter family. They knew His family well, so they were offended because they believed He tried to be more than they. He understood their attitude. "A prophet is not without honor, except in his hometown and among his relatives and in his own household." Deeply disappointed because of their unbelief, Jesus could do nothing more for them. If men will not believe in Him, all His wisdom and might will do them no good. He is not the loser; they are. So all He could do was heal a few sick folks, who gladly and willingly accepted Him, and teach in the villages nearby. But the unbelief of His countrymen did make Him wonder.

All this did not change the plan Jesus had mapped out for the evangelization of the world. He called the Twelve to Him. To reach as many as possible with the saving Gospel and to give the apostles experience and training for their future work, He sent them out by twos on their first missionary journey. To establish and accredit them as His messengers, He gave them supernatural gifts, such as power over unclean spirits that were sure to try to hinder their work. They were to give freely, as they had received freely. At the same time, the principle was to be upheld that the laborer is worthy of his hire. They were to take nothing along for their journey but the essentials. Wherever they went, they were to establish their residence or headquarters at a home where their message was received in faith. They were told not to waste too much time on those who closed their hearts to their message. The fate of any community that rejected them would be sadder and more awful than that of Sodom and Gomorrah. But the Lord would be the judge of that.

So the apostles went out in His name and boldly proclaimed repentance wherever they went. No real good can be done by all our witnessing unless people first know and acknowledge their sins, otherwise even the sweetest and most eloquent Gospel message will be met with bored indifference. And the power of the Lord went with His messengers. Demons could not withstand them, and sickness had to yield to their ministrations. Although the Church and its Gospel have been established in the world these many centuries, and we do not need such supernatural gifts to prove it, the power of the Gospel message is still the same everywhere.

Prayer

O Lord, how can we ever thank You for making such blessed provision for the proclamation of the saving Gospel to the ends of the world, particularly for establishing the ministry of the Word and Sacraments in our midst! Forgive us when we have been unmindful of such blessings, and help us to make more diligent use of them. Keep us from indifference and opposition to the truth, so that it may work in us repentance and faith and the joy of our salvation, and that such fruits of faith may be brought forth to glorify Your name. Amen.

THE HERALD MEETS HIS KING
Mark 6:14–29

THIS seems a sad story of the untimely death of one of the noblest men God ever created, going down to defeat, as it seemed, before the machinations of an ungodly, bloodthirsty woman and because of the cowardly weakness of a man who thought himself powerful enough to defy the voice of his conscience. But in truth, John the Baptist, whose work was finished, went to his God and into the eternal presence of the Savior, whose coming he had proclaimed and whose way he had prepared.

The Death of John the Baptist

King Herod heard of it, for Jesus' name had become known. Some said, "John the Baptist has been raised from the dead. That is why these miraculous powers are at work in him." But others said, "He is Elijah." And others said, "He is a prophet, like one of the prophets of old." But when Herod heard of it, he said, "John, whom I beheaded, has been raised." For it was Herod who had sent and seized John and bound him in prison for the sake of Herodias, his brother Philip's wife, because he had married her. For John had been saying to Herod, "It is not lawful for you to have your brother's wife." And Herodias had a grudge against him and wanted to put him to death. But she could not, for Herod feared John, knowing that he was a righteous and holy man, and he kept him safe. When he heard him, he was greatly perplexed, and yet he heard him gladly.

But an opportunity came when Herod on his birthday gave a banquet for his nobles and military commanders and the leading men of Galilee. For when Herodias's daughter came in and danced, she pleased Herod and his guests. And the king said to the girl, "Ask me for whatever you wish, and I will give it to you." And he vowed to her, "Whatever you ask me, I will give you, up to half of my kingdom." And she went out and said to her mother, "For what should I ask?" And she said, "The head of John the Baptist." And she came in immediately with haste to the king and asked, saying, "I want you to give me at once the head of John the Baptist on a platter." And the king was exceedingly sorry, but because of his oaths and his guests he did not want to break his word to her. And immediately the king sent an executioner with orders to bring John's head. He went and beheaded him in the prison and brought his head on a platter and gave it to the girl, and the girl gave it to her mother. When his disciples heard of it, they came and took his body and laid it in a tomb.

It was now shortly before the Passover in the spring of the year AD 29. Many great and noble deeds had been done by Jesus from Galilee. No wonder His fame had reached the ears of the tetrarch, King Herod, the cruel and wanton ruler of Galilee and land beyond the Jordan. Herod's reaction is remarkable. Like all unbelievers, he was superstitious. He made the statement that this must be John the Baptist risen from the dead. He knew of no other man who could do such mighty deeds. Other rumors had it that this was Elijah or one of the other prophets come back to life. But Herod insisted that it must be John the Baptist, whom he had beheaded.

What fearful thoughts must have passed through Herod's guilty mind! His conscience brought back the memory of those days some months earlier when he had sent out his servants to take the great prophet of the wilderness from the lofty hills and verdant valleys he loved into the dark and dingy dungeon of Herod's castle Machaerus, east of the Dead Sea. Why? Any Jew and any right-thinking man would have told Herod that it was sinful for him to marry his brother Philip's wife, Herodias, but only John had dared to tell him the truth. Herod was enough of a man to admire John's courage. And he might not have done much about it if it hadn't been for the adulterous woman he had married unlawfully. Herodias held a deep grudge against John and determined to have his life. Still, that was going too far even for an unscrupulous man like Herod, whose conscience told him that, after all, John had done no more than his duty in a manly way. For this, Herod could only respect him, as far as he was capable of such feelings. Although John was his prisoner, Herod sought and, to a certain extent, followed his advice in many things. John was even allowed certain liberties, for we know that his disciples had access to him.

But the venomous heart of the enraged Herodias did not allow her to forget her vengeful schemes. At last, she had her opportunity at Herod's birthday celebration. The lords, captains, and chiefs of Galilee were invited. There must have been the typical carousing, excessive eating, and drinking. The crowning event of this worldly affair was a dance by Herodias's daughter, which so aroused the sinful

excitement and enjoyment of Herod and his guests that he pomp-
ously promised her, with an oath, that he would give her whatever
she wanted, up to the half of his kingdom. Here was a chance not to
be taken lightly. The girl quickly consulted her mother. What should
she ask for? Unhesitatingly, the bloodthirsty monster answered, "The
head of John the Baptist." Are we surprised that a heart void of any
true virtue should also know no pity? The girl could hardly wait to
return to the banquet hall to present her gruesome request. Even the
hardened king was shocked. He would have gladly taken back his
promise and recalled his oath, but pride before his guests made him
stick to his word. The executioner got his orders. The man Jesus
Himself called the greatest of all the prophets was neither given, nor
did he need, any time for preparation. Soon his loyal soul was in the
presence of his Lord. The herald met his King.

The executioner delivered the gory head of John to the waiting
damsel, and she took it to her mother, that inhuman monster. They
had their satisfaction—or did they? Remember, sin brings no joy.
Pity the soul that knows no better happiness! But someone present
had some sense of justice, some human feeling left, and the message was brought to the disciples of John. With bleeding hearts, they
took the remains of their beloved teacher and gave him an honorable
burial. So ended the earthly life of one of God's noblemen.

Prayer

*Lord Jesus, we confess that it is one of our greatest weaknesses and
sins that we are often too timid to confess You before men and to
testify against what is wrong and for what is right. How easily
we partake of the sins of others! Give us the faith of Your loyal
friend John the Baptist, and with it the conviction that nothing
the world may do can really harm us because it cannot separate
us from You and Your Father's love. Amen.*

JESUS, THE LORD OVER THE LAWS OF NATURE

Mark 6:30–56

THE heading of this meditation introduces the miracles Jesus performed at this time, just before the second Passover during His ministry, near and on the Sea of Galilee. We recall that during the imprisonment of John the Baptist, Jesus performed many miracles and taught many people in Galilee. But after the death of His forerunner, Jesus tried to withdraw more and more with His apostles to quiet places, where He could train them for their future work as His witnesses. He had no desire for the fame and popularity of a great healer but longed to make Himself known as the true Messiah and Savior of all mankind.

Jesus Feeds the Five Thousand

The apostles returned to Jesus and told Him all that they had done and taught. And He said to them, "Come away by yourselves to a desolate place and rest a while." For many were coming and going, and they had no leisure even to eat. And they went away in the boat to a desolate place by themselves. Now many saw them going and recognized them, and they ran there on foot from all the towns and got there ahead of them. When He went ashore He saw a great crowd, and He had compassion on them, because they were like sheep without a shepherd. And He began to teach them many things. And when it grew late, His disciples came to Him and said, "This is a desolate place, and the hour is now late. Send them away to go into the surrounding countryside and villages and buy themselves something to eat." But He answered them, "You give them something to eat." And they said to Him, "Shall we go and buy two hundred denarii worth of bread and give it to them to eat?"

And He said to them, "How many loaves do you have? Go and see." And when they had found out, they said, "Five, and two fish." Then He commanded them all to sit down in groups on the green grass. So they sat down in groups, by hundreds and by fifties. And taking the five loaves and the two fish He looked up to heaven and said a blessing and broke the loaves and gave them to the disciples to set before the people. And He divided the two fish among them all. And they all ate and were satisfied. And they took up twelve baskets full of broken pieces and of the fish. And those who ate the loaves were five thousand men.

Jesus Walks on the Water

Immediately He made His disciples get into the boat and go before Him to the other side, to Bethsaida, while He dismissed the crowd. And after He had taken leave of them, He went up on the mountain to pray. And when evening came, the boat was out on the sea, and He was alone on the land. And He saw that they were making headway painfully, for the wind was against them. And about the fourth watch of the night He came to them, walking on the sea. He meant to pass by them, but when they saw Him walking on the sea they thought it was a ghost, and cried out, for they all saw Him and were terrified. But immediately He spoke to them and said, "Take heart; it is I. Do not be afraid." And He got into the boat with them, and the wind ceased. And they were utterly astounded, for they did not understand about the loaves, but their hearts were hardened.

Jesus Heals the Sick in Gennesaret

When they had crossed over, they came to land at Gennesaret and moored to the shore. And when they got out of the boat, the people immediately recognized Him and ran about the whole region and began to bring the sick people on their beds to wherever they heard He was. And wherever He came, in villages, cities, or countryside, they laid the sick in the marketplaces and implored Him that they might touch even the fringe of His garment. And as many as touched it were made well.

Having had the thrilling experience of teaching the truth of the Gospel and confirming their word by signs and wonders, the apostles joyfully reported their success to the Master. Jesus knew the strain they had endured. In demanding faithfulness from His disciples, He takes into account their human limitations. He Himself was so truly human that He realized that they all needed a rest. So He suggested that they look for a quiet place away from the crowds, and they did not even have time to eat. Jesus and His apostles boarded their little ship to find that restful place. But it was not to be. People saw them setting out and, guessing where they were going, hurried around the upper part of the sea. The crowd arrived even before they did and surrounded Jesus as soon as they landed. We know from the other accounts that this place was Bethsaida-Julias, where there was much grass in the spring of the year.

And now we have a typical scene of truly messianic activity. Forgotten are all thoughts of rest. Jesus' heart goes out in sincere compassion to these people, who truly were like sheep without a shepherd, as the prophet Ezekiel described in chapter 34. There was only one thing for Jesus to do—show them His shepherd's love. So "He began to teach them many things." What a blessed afternoon that was!

Eventually the mountains to the west began to cast evening shadows across the landscape. The apostles called His attention to the fact that this place was far removed from the cities and markets and that the people should be sent away before dark so they could find something to eat. Jesus, however, suggested that they might consider themselves the hosts to these people. A quick investigation showed that they had at their disposal 200 denarii (a denarius is equal to about 20 cents), but that would not be enough to buy food for so many, even if there had been a place to buy it. Beyond that, the apostles had no other solution. So Jesus took matters in hand. The five small loaves and the two little fish, which a boy had brought, would have to suffice. Obediently, the apostles, under His direction, told the people to sit in groups of fifty or hundreds. All eyes must have been fastened on Jesus in tense expectation. Were they, perhaps, disappointed when they saw Him hold up the five loaves and two small fish? How could that be enough for them all? But while they watched, He spoke in solemn prayer, blessing the food from God's almighty bounty. As the disciples received the loaves and the fish from His hands, distributing them to the hungry thousands, there was an ever new supply awaiting them when they came for more. No one went hungry that evening. Indeed, as the disciples went out at His command to gather any food that remained, there were twelve baskets left over!

But now it was time for everyone to find shelter for the night. Jesus urged His disciples to take the ship and sail to the other side of the lake, while He sent the people away so He might devote the evening hours to undisturbed prayer. Alone on the mountainside, Jesus saw and sympathized with the plight of His disciples as they struggled valiantly to make headway against the wind. In His wisdom, He let them struggle for a while, only to show them—as He often shows us—that He is eager to help in the hour of utmost need. His sudden appearance as He emerged from the shadows of the night, walking on the storm-tossed sea, indeed frightened the apostles, and they cried out. But His encouraging words, telling them not to be afraid, reassured them. They had their Master with them in the ship. The wind stopped, and soon they reached the familiar shore near Capernaum. The happenings of the night and the miracle of the day before left them feeling amazed, but the significance of it all did not come to them immediately.

Jesus had set out to find rest; He returned to greater labors. The people on the shore soon recognized Him and ran to spread the news and to bring the sick to Him. Although He wanted, above all, to heal their souls from sin, He had compassion also on their bodily sufferings and, wherever He went in cities, villages, and open country, He healed them. If they even touched the hem of His garment in faith, they were made whole.

*Jesus, our Savior and Lord, whenever earthly cares oppress us,
let us think of that day on the shores of the Sea of Galilee and
the loaves and fish that multiplied so marvelously under Your
divine blessing. But help us to follow You, not for the loaves that
perish, but for the Bread of Life to feed our souls until we hunger
no more. And when danger and death are near, may Your nearness
bring assurance to our hearts as we hear You say, "It is I. Do not
be afraid." Amen.*

THE FAULTFINDERS FAULTED
Mark 7:1–23

WE have repeatedly noted that while the people gathered around
Jesus by the thousands, the opposition to Him from the religious
leaders grew as well. His popularity was a thorn in their flesh. The
Pharisees and elders in Galilee were in constant communication with
the leaders in Jerusalem. While the Sanhedrin had no governmental
power in Galilee, their influence among the Jews everywhere was
great, so they sent a delegation to Capernaum to investigate this man's
activities and put a stop to them. We see here how they fared.

Traditions and Commandments

Now when the Pharisees gathered to Him, with some of
the scribes who had come from Jerusalem, they saw that
some of His disciples ate with hands that were defiled, that is,
unwashed. (For the Pharisees and all the Jews do not eat unless
they wash their hands, holding to the tradition of the elders,
and when they come from the marketplace, they do not eat
unless they wash. And there are many other traditions that they

observe, such as the washing of cups and pots and copper vessels and dining couches.) And the Pharisees and the scribes asked Him, "Why do Your disciples not walk according to the tradition of the elders, but eat with defiled hands?" And He said to them, "Well did Isaiah prophesy of you hypocrites, as it is written,

" 'This people honors Me with their lips, but their heart is
   far from Me; in vain do they worship Me, teaching as doctrines
   the commandments of men.'
You leave the commandment of God and hold to the tradition
   of men."

And He said to them, "You have a fine way of rejecting the commandment of God in order to establish your tradition! For Moses said, 'Honor your father and your mother'; and, 'Whoever reviles father or mother must surely die.' But you say, 'If a man tells his father or his mother, "Whatever you would have gained from me is Corban" ' (that is, given to God)— then you no longer permit him to do anything for his father or mother, thus making void the word of God by your tradition that you have handed down. And many such things you do."

What Defiles a Person

And He called the people to Him again and said to them, "Hear Me, all of you, and understand: There is nothing outside a person that by going into him can defile him, but the things that come out of a person are what defile him." And when He had entered the house and left the people, His disciples asked Him about the parable. And He said to them, "Then are you also without understanding? Do you not see that whatever goes into a person from outside cannot defile him, since it enters not his heart but his stomach, and is expelled?" Thus He declared all foods clean. And He said, "What comes out of a person is what defiles him. For from within, out of the heart of man, come evil thoughts, sexual immorality, theft, murder, adultery, coveting, wickedness, deceit, sensuality, envy, slander, pride, foolishness. All these evil things come from within, and they defile a person."

The evangelist refers here to one of the many traditions upheld by the Pharisees and followed by the Jews—the very strict ceremonial cleansings demanded by the Law of Moses and by the traditions of the elders. These cleansings were called washings (in the original, the word *baptize* is used), and were generally done "with the fist," as the Greek has it, that is, with the hollow hand pouring water on the person or object to be cleansed. Such pouring or sprinkling signified running water; stagnant water was considered unclean. They would not think of reclining for their meal after returning from the market, where they could so easily become ceremonially unclean, unless they first sprinkled cleansing water on themselves and their tables and the vessels containing their food. It is no wonder that they were scandalized when they saw Jesus' disciples eat without going through all these ceremonies. Naturally, they blamed Jesus for permitting such things. Possibly they were referring to the feeding of the five thousand in the wilderness, where no ceremonial washings had been observed.

Jesus did not allow these men to put Him on the defensive. He was master of the situation. He had the Word of God on His side. Calling them hypocrites, for He could see and judge their hearts, Jesus reminded them of the words of the prophet Isaiah, that such people honor God with their lips while their heart is far from Him and that all their worship is vain as long as they teach as doctrine the commandments of men. God cannot be pleased with an outward show of piety when our hearts are not right toward Him in faith. Man-made traditions and ceremonies are an offense to Him if we set them above His Word.

Next, Jesus openly went on the attack. He accused the Pharisees of invalidating God's Commandments to uphold their own traditions. This was a clear reference to the Fourth Commandment: "Honor your father and your mother." The Law declared that cursing one's parents was a crime worthy of death. Yet the Pharisees had made it easy to circumvent that Law when they said a man could set aside the money needed for the support of his aged parents by dedicating it to some religious purpose approved by their traditions. Thus people may find it far easier to perform ceremonies with a show of piety than to do what the Word of God demands of them.

We can imagine that the people listened to this conversation with interest. Jesus urged them to come closer and hear what He had to say. He used a parable. What a man eats, what enters into him through his mouth does not make him unclean, but the sinful and unclean words that come from his mouth will certainly defile him. Afterward, when they were alone with Him, the disciples asked for further explanation of this parable. Expressing His disappointment that they were slow to understand His plain meaning, He patiently explained that the food we eat has nothing to do with our spiritual health. What we eat is taken care of by the natural processes of digestion and elimination. But what is generated in our heart will make us unclean before God. Our heart is by nature so wicked that out of it proceeds evil thoughts, adulteries, fornications, murders, thefts, covetousness, wickedness, deceit, lasciviousness, an evil and jealous eye, blasphemy, pride, foolishness. What an awful list of sins comes from the natural, sinful heart! This is something we should be concerned about rather than a few outward ceremonies that have no power or influence to change the heart. The most beautiful ritual cannot take the place of the prayer of the truly penitent who prays, "God, be merciful to me, a sinner."

Prayer

Blessed Savior, keep us from piety or religion that consists only of outward forms and ceremonies. Help us not to substitute man-made rules for Your Word and will so clearly revealed in the Bible. Make us aware of the total depravity and corruption of our sinful heart, the fount and source of all that is evil, so we may turn to You in faith for cleansing and healing. Hear us for the sake of Your gracious promises. Amen.

17

LOST SHEEP NOT OF THE HOUSE OF ISRAEL
Mark 7:24–37

JESUS had left the boundaries of the Holy Land only once before—when He had been carried away as a young child to escape the wrath of cruel Herod, who sought to destroy the newborn King. This time, He chose to travel to the north with His disciples, climbing out of the valley of the Sea of Galilee over the mountains until He saw the land of the Phoenicians, a proud and independent people, famed in ancient history. The purpose of this journey was not to carry the Gospel to the heathen world—that was to be the work of His apostles—but to rest and to give His disciples further instructions as to their work and to strengthen them for the task before them. But even here, He found occasion to help souls in need.

The Syrophoenician Woman's Faith

And from there He arose and went away to the region of Tyre and Sidon. And He entered a house and did not want anyone to know, yet He could not be hidden. But immediately a woman whose little daughter had an unclean spirit heard of Him and came and fell down at His feet. Now the woman was a Gentile, a Syrophoenician by birth. And she begged Him to cast the demon out of her daughter. And He said to her, "Let the children be fed first, for it is not right to take the children's bread and throw it to the dogs." But she answered Him, "Yes, Lord; yet even the dogs under the table eat the children's crumbs." And He said to her, "For this statement you may go your way; the demon has left your daughter." And she went home and found the child lying in bed and the demon gone.

Jesus Heals a Deaf Man

Then He returned from the region of Tyre and went through Sidon to the Sea of Galilee, in the region of the Decapolis. And they brought to Him a man who was deaf and had a speech impediment, and they begged Him to lay His hand on him. And taking him aside from the crowd privately, He put His fingers into his ears, and after spitting touched his tongue. And looking up to heaven, He sighed and said to him, "Ephphatha," that is, "Be opened." And his ears were opened, his tongue was released, and he spoke plainly. And Jesus charged them to tell no one. But the more He charged them, the more zealously they proclaimed it. And they were astonished beyond measure, saying, "He has done all things well. He even makes the deaf hear and the mute speak."

The text does not imply that Jesus went into hiding. He certainly was not afraid of His enemies. If He was trying to avoid anything, it was the adulation that was being thrust upon Him. That they had already tried to make Him their king did not flatter Him; He had not come to establish an earthly kingdom, and only a few were attracted by the liberty, the power, the salvation He offered. But, being human, He needed the rest that might come if He were where people did not know Him. His disciples, who were ever on His mind and in His heart, needed so much more understanding of the nature of His kingdom and the character of their work.

Those were the reasons we see Him on His way to the far north and why He sought seclusion. But a Syrophoenician woman found out where He was, came to the place, and fell down before Him with the anxious prayer that He might heal her daughter, who was possessed by a devil. This was truly a remarkable case, not only because a Gentile woman had come to know and believe in Jesus as the promised Messiah, but also because her faith was extraordinarily strong. Here we see how Jesus tests and strengthens faith through trials. First, He seemed to ignore her entirely. Then, when she fell down before Him and pleaded more ardently, His words seemed most unkind: "I was sent only to the lost sheep of the house of

Israel" (Matthew 15:24). In other words, Jesus wasn't there to help *her*. And when she begged for His help, He used an expression that appeared positively cruel: "Let the children be fed first, for it is not right to take the children's bread and throw it to the dogs." But Jesus did want to help her both physically and spiritually. When she made her quick reply—"Yes, Lord; yet even the dogs under the table eat the children's crumbs"—He joyfully praised her faith and said the devil was already driven from her daughter. Every Christian knows, although he sometimes forgets, that faith in the promises of Christ is never disappointed.

From here, Jesus continued northward along the coast of the Mediterranean Sea to Sidon. Turning eastward, He crossed the lower reaches of the Lebanon mountain range, traveling down the Upper Jordan Valley until He reached the region of the Ten Cities, in the neighborhood where He had healed the demoniac. There they brought a man to Him who could not hear or speak, about whom the people were evidently much concerned and whom no human power could help. Although He could have healed him with a word, Jesus used sign language to assure him that He understood and would help. He put a finger into each of the man's ears, touched his tongue with His moistened finger, looked up to heaven, indicating that help must come from above. Then Jesus visibly sighed as a sign of earnest prayer and cried out in His native language, "Ephphatha," that is, "Be opened"—probably the first words the man had ever heard. And, behold, the man could not only hear, but the impediment in his speech was removed, and he could also speak plainly. Although Jesus had taken the man aside to avoid curiosity and asked the others to make no fuss about the miracle, they were so astonished and amazed that they publicized it all the more: "He has done all things well. He even makes the deaf hear and the mute speak." Thus, these pagan people learned at least something about the saving power of God. Who knows how many learned to know Him as their Lord and Savior!

Prayer

Jesus, our Savior divine, how can we ever thank You for bringing us to the true and saving faith! Help us never to doubt but firmly to believe, no matter how great our trials or how distant Your help may appear. Grant us true humility, asking nothing because of any merit or worthiness on our part, but trusting only in Your Word and promise. Whether in joy or sorrow, teach us to believe and to say that You have done all things well. Amen.

HOW IS IT THAT YOU DO NOT UNDERSTAND?
Mark 8:1–21

AFTER His return from Tyre and Sidon, Jesus spent some time in the comparatively remote region of the Ten Cities east of the Sea of Galilee. But even there, He was surrounded by a great number of people who, even when their supply of food ran low, didn't want to leave Him. So Jesus fed them, as He had done before on a similar occasion. Returning to the western shore of the lake, He was encountered not only by His old enemies the Pharisees, who had repeatedly confronted Him, but also by the Sadducees (Matthew 16). These Jewish liberals had little interest in spiritual matters but were getting alarmed about Jesus' possible political influence. Having answered His enemies as they deserved, Jesus returned to the eastern shore. On the way over, He taught His disciples an important lesson.

Jesus Feeds the Five Thousand

In those days, when again a great crowd had gathered, and they had nothing to eat, He called His disciples to Him and said to them, "I have compassion on the crowd, because they have been with Me now three days and have nothing to eat. And if I send them away hungry to their homes, they will faint on the way. And some of them have come from far away." And His disciples answered Him, "How can one feed these people with bread here in this desolate place?" And He asked them, "How many loaves do you have?" They said, "Seven." And He directed the crowd to sit down on the ground. And He took the seven loaves, and having given thanks, He broke them and gave them to His disciples to set before the people; and they set them before the crowd. And they had a few small fish. And having blessed them, He said that these also should be set before them. And they ate and were satisfied. And they took up the broken pieces left over, seven baskets full. And there were about four thousand people. And He sent them away. And immediately He got into the boat with His disciples and went to the district of Dalmanutha.

The Pharisees Demand a Sign

The Pharisees came and began to argue with Him, seeking from Him a sign from heaven to test Him. And He sighed deeply in His spirit and said, "Why does this generation seek a sign? Truly, I say to you, no sign will be given to this generation." And He left them, got into the boat again, and went to the other side.

The Leaven of the Pharisees and Herod

Now they had forgotten to bring bread, and they had only one loaf with them in the boat. And He cautioned them, saying, "Watch out; beware of the leaven of the Pharisees and the leaven of Herod." And they began discussing with one another the fact that they had no bread. And Jesus, aware of this, said to them, "Why are you discussing the fact that you have no bread? Do you not yet perceive or understand? Are your hearts hardened? Having eyes do you not see, and having ears do you not hear? And do you not remember? When I broke the five loaves for the five thousand, how many baskets full of broken pieces did you take up?" They said to Him, "Twelve." "And the seven for the four thousand, how many baskets full of broken pieces did you take up?" And they said to Him, "Seven." And He said to them, "Do you not yet understand?"

Here we read that the popularity of Jesus among the common people was as great as ever. St. Mark tells us that the crowd that came to Him was very large and that many must have come from far away. They were so anxious to hear and see that they did not take time to get something to eat. Perhaps the supplies in the neighborhood were not enough to take care of so many. The condition of the people aroused Jesus' compassion; it was now three days since they had come to Him. He knew how hungry they were and how it felt to be hungry. Had He not fasted forty days in the wilderness? It was too late to send them home because they would faint on the way. Perhaps the disciples thought it was inappropriate to suggest that Jesus repeat the miracle of feeding the five thousand. They merely stated that they saw no way to feed the people there in the wilderness. So the Lord took charge. Arrangements were quickly made for the people to sit on the bare ground, and a quick inventory established the fact that they could account for seven loaves. Giving thanks to God for these blessings, Jesus broke the loaves into smaller pieces and gave them to the disciples, who distributed them, along with a few small fish, to the hungry crowd. And the miracle was that they all had enough to eat and food to spare. After four thousand men, not counting women and children, had eaten, the disciples picked up seven baskets full of leftovers, which surely were welcome refreshment for the people as they made their way home.

On His return to the western shore of the Sea of Galilee, Jesus was immediately confronted by His enemies. The Pharisees had evidently conspired with the Sadducees, with whom they were otherwise not on friendly terms, to challenge Jesus' authority. They demanded a sign from Him. What blindness and foolishness! Had He not already performed signs that no other man, not even their greatest prophets, had performed? But unbelief is always like that; it does not see what it does not want to see.

Their stubborn unbelief wounded and grieved Jesus deeply, but He refused to do something spectacular just to satisfy their foolish demands. If His words and the proof that went with them were not enough, they could expect only one more and greater miracle (see Matthew 16:4). With that, He left them.

With a heavy heart because of the hard-heartedness He had encountered, Jesus returned to the eastern shore of the lake. In their hurry to get away, the disciples had forgotten to bring food. A single loaf was all they had. Now, despite all they had seen just a short while ago, the disciples were still easily distracted by worldly care. When Jesus, still disappointed about His encounter with His enemies, told them to beware of the leaven of the Pharisees and of Herod, special friends of the Sadducees, they totally misunderstood Him. They thought He criticized them for not taking bread with them. Jesus was more than disappointed with them. Did they not have eyes to see and ears to hear? Was their memory so short that they did not remember what had happened a few days before? Even if they had run out of bread, what was their cause for worry? Almost bitterly He asked, "Do you not yet perceive or understand?" So, it finally dawned on them that He spoke of the false teachings of the Pharisees and Sadducees. How little the warning is understood in our day, that even a pinch of false doctrine is liable to penetrate deeply before we are aware of it and it does irreparable harm.

Prayer

Forgive us, dear Lord, when we fail to trust in Your providing care. Let us receive Your blessings with thankful hearts. But more than that, help us that our foolish and sinful hearts may not break out in open opposition and enmity against You and Your Word. Bear with us when we are slow to understand that the only thing that matters is that we are preserved from error and false doctrine of every kind. Keep us in true faith and a godly life until our end. We ask it for the sake of Your divine promises. Amen.

19

WHO DO PEOPLE SAY THAT I AM?
Mark 8:22–38

IN today's Scripture reading, the narrative takes a definite step forward in the developments that led to the suffering and death of our Savior. The people were far from comprehending the fact that Jesus was the promised Messiah in every sense of the word. But first of all, He had to bring His disciples to this knowledge. The confession Peter made in the name of all the apostles shows that real progress had been made in that direction. Gradually, they had to learn that His kingdom could be established only through His suffering and death and that it would always be a kingdom under the cross, a kingdom of spiritual and eternal values.

Jesus Heals a Blind Man at Bethsaida

And they came to Bethsaida. And some people brought to Him a blind man and begged Him to touch him. And He took the blind man by the hand and led him out of the village, and when He had spit on his eyes and laid His hands on him, He asked him, "Do you see anything?" And he looked up and said, "I see men, but they look like trees, walking." Then Jesus laid His hands on his eyes again; and he opened his eyes, his sight was restored, and he saw everything clearly. And He sent him to his home, saying, "Do not even enter the village."

Peter Confesses Jesus as the Christ

And Jesus went on with His disciples to the villages of Caesarea Philippi. And on the way He asked His disciples, "Who do people say that I am?" And they told Him, "John the Baptist; and others say, Elijah; and others, one of the prophets." And He asked them, "But who do you say that I am?"

Peter answered Him, "You are the Christ." And He strictly charged them to tell no one about Him.

Jesus Foretells His Death and Resurrection

And He began to teach them that the Son of Man must suffer many things and be rejected by the elders and the chief priests and the scribes and be killed, and after three days rise again. And He said this plainly. And Peter took Him aside and began to rebuke Him. But turning and seeing His disciples, He rebuked Peter and said, "Get behind Me, Satan! For you are not setting your mind on the things of God, but on the things of man."

And calling the crowd to Him with His disciples, He said to them, "If anyone would come after Me, let him deny himself and take up his cross and follow Me. For whoever would save his life will lose it, but whoever loses his life for My sake and the gospel's will save it. For what does it profit a man to gain the whole world and forfeit his soul? For what can a man give in return for his soul? For whoever is ashamed of Me and of my words in this adulterous and sinful generation, of him will the Son of Man also be ashamed when He comes in the glory of His Father with the holy angels."

Crossing the northern end of the Sea of Galilee, Jesus and the apostles came to the region of Bethsaida, to the area where He had fed the five thousand. Some people brought to Jesus a blind man, whom He healed in a rather extraordinary manner. He could easily have healed him with a word. But Jesus had His own way of dealing with each individual, even as He deals with us as He sees best, owing us no explanation. But we can readily see His purpose in leading this man out of the town, away from the people, who were miracle-hungry and so slow to understand His real purposes. Touching the man's eyes with His spit, laying His hands on him and speaking to him, Jesus restored the man's eyesight gradually. First, he could see people walking, appearing in his blurred vision as trees. Then, laying His hands on the man's eyes again, Jesus told the man to look up and, behold, his eyesight was fully restored. Because the Lord at this time did not want the notoriety that thoughtless and emotional people were forcing upon Him, He told the man to go directly to his house and not back into the town, where the miracle could not be hidden. To this day, we should remember that the Messiah came to help and save us, not to satisfy our curiosity and longing for excitement and attention.

Leaving the deep-lying Sea of Galilee behind, Jesus and His disciples traveled upward past the shallow Lake Huleh, about thirty miles into the foothills of the Lebanon Mountains toward Philippi, the capital city of the tetrarch, Philip. This was a region of outstanding natural beauty, such as we might choose for a vacation, but it was not for rest that Jesus made this journey. He knew the time for leading His apostles to a better and deeper knowledge of Himself and His kingdom was growing short. As they traveled, Jesus put the question to them, "Who do people say that I am?" The answer showed that the people admired Him in many ways and compared Him with some of their greatest prophets, that they even considered Him a possible reincarnation of this or that prophet. But they seemed to be farther away than ever from the conviction that He was the Messiah Himself. When He then put the matter squarely before them—"But who do you say that I am?"—Peter promptly and beautifully answered, "You are the Christ." What sweet comfort that must have been to the Lord to know that at least those nearest Him were beginning to see more clearly why He came into the world! But they had much to learn before they had the right understanding, so Jesus imposed strict silence upon them. Let us not be too surprised that people today show so little understanding of the character of Christ and His kingdom.

What else could Jesus do but teach these men and prepare them for what was soon to happen? Once before He had publicly referred to His suffering and death (John 2:18–22), but the disciples brushed it aside as something that could not happen. We do that too with many things we do not want to accept, no matter how plain the words are. So Jesus openly and emphatically, in the clearest possible terms, told them about His impending suffering, death, and resurrection.

They were shocked. Peter took Him aside and rebuked Him—He must not say such things! But Jesus was agitated. This was the eternal counsel of God for the salvation of the world; was it to be cast aside? He glared at His shocked apostles and with holy wrath denounced Peter's well-meant words as coming from the father of lies, from Satan himself. What would Christ say today to those who claim to be His messengers but still deny the need of His suffering and death for the salvation of the world?

Drawing in people who were nearby, Jesus now taught them all an unforgettable lesson. Following Jesus means a life of self-denial, crossbearing, self-forgetfulness. To gain the world and lose your soul is a poor exchange indeed. To be rejected on the great Day of Judgment is the supreme tragedy. To be acknowledged as His own before God and the holy angels must be anticipated as the crowning glory of our life. God grant that He may not be ashamed of us on that day!

Prayer

Lord Jesus, open the eyes of my spirit, that I may see You in all the power and glory of Your saving might. As I consider the enormity of my sin and the greatness of Your grace, grant that I may believe that only Your suffering and death in my place could atone for me and gain for me life and salvation. Hear me for Your name's sake. Amen.

THIS IS MY BELOVED SON; LISTEN TO HIM

Mark 9:1–13

IT was a fine confession that Peter had made: "You are the Christ."
Those who come to this conviction find that it has not come to them
from flesh and blood, but from the Holy Spirit who has revealed it to
them. In less than a week, Peter and the other two who were closest
to Jesus were to hear this eternal, saving truth confirmed from heaven
by the voice of the Father on the Mount of Transfiguration.

And He said to them, "Truly, I say to you, there are some
standing here who will not taste death until they see the kingdom of God after it has come with power."

The Transfiguration

And after six days Jesus took with Him Peter and James and
John, and led them up a high mountain by themselves. And He
was transfigured before them, and His clothes became radiant,
intensely white, as no one on earth could bleach them. And
there appeared to them Elijah with Moses, and they were talking with Jesus. And Peter said to Jesus, "Rabbi, it is good that
we are here. Let us make three tents, one for You and one for
Moses and one for Elijah." For he did not know what to say, for
they were terrified. And a cloud overshadowed them, and a
voice came out of the cloud, "This is My beloved Son; listen to
Him." And suddenly, looking around, they no longer saw anyone with them but Jesus only.

And as they were coming down the mountain, He charged
them to tell no one what they had seen, until the Son of Man
had risen from the dead. So they kept the matter to themselves, questioning what this rising from the dead might mean.
And they asked Him, "Why do the scribes say that first Elijah

must come?" And He said to them, "Elijah does come first to restore all things. And how is it written of the Son of Man that He should suffer many things and be treated with contempt? But I tell you that Elijah has come, and they did to him whatever they pleased, as it is written of him."

Often, as He spoke about His impending suffering and death, Jesus also spoke about His second coming in glory. Such is the case in this instance, when He earnestly assured His apostles that some of those present would see the beginning of the coming of the kingdom of God with power. It was only few days later when some of them had a foretaste of that heavenly glory.

They may still have been in the region of Caesarea Philippi, in the foothills of the Lebanon Mountains, when Jesus took Peter, James, and John away from the rest of His disciples and was transfigured before them. He was the same man they knew so well, yet here He stood in transcendent glory! His otherwise plain garments shone with supernatural brilliance. No human effort could have produced such purity and splendor. And there were two other men, also in heavenly brightness, whom they recognized as Elijah and Moses, talking with Jesus about the impending momentous events that would mean so much to the world, to all of us. No wonder the poor sons of earth were overcome by such almost unbearable glory. Arousing himself, still hardly knowing what he was saying, Peter, wishing for nothing more than that this experience of heavenly bliss might last indefinitely, suggested that they build three tents, one for Jesus, one for Moses, and one for Elijah. But while Peter was still groping for words, a cloud came over them, and the Father's voice was heard from heaven, saying: "This is My beloved Son; listen to Him." Truly, the Father had spoken in these last days through the Son (Hebrews 1:2). It is unreasonable and foolish not to pay attention to His testimony. Who else could reveal the inmost thoughts of Father than He who is at the right hand of the Father? Suddenly, the apostles looked around, and the other two men had disappeared. They saw Jesus only.

This vision also, like some of the recent miracles, was not for immediate publication. Jesus knew that after His resurrection, the knowledge of what had happened on the mount would have greater meaning to His disciples. At this time, though, it would only have aroused false hopes. But the three, while they said nothing about the vision to anyone else, could not but wonder among themselves what Jesus might have meant by His words. They had not yet learned that the Christ must first die before He would enter into His glory.

But the appearance of Elijah had reminded them of the Jewish prophecy that Elijah would come as a forerunner of the Messiah and bring back the pot of manna and the rod of Aaron and otherwise make preparation for the coming of the Messiah. How did that reconcile with Jesus' saying that the Son of Man must first suffer and die? He had to assure them that Elijah had already come and that what His enemies did to him, according to their evil will, was in keeping with the prophecy. The mystery of the suffering was to their minds still unsolved, but they understood that He spoke of John the Baptist (Malachi 4:5).

Prayer

Lord Jesus, You deeply humbled Yourself to become obedient unto death, even the death of the cross, to make full atonement for our sins. Let us not forget that You are the beloved Son of the eternal Father, mighty to help and to protect those who seek and abide in Your presence, and let us at last share in Your glory in heaven. Amen.

21

"I BELIEVE; HELP MY UNBELIEF!"
Mark 9:14–29

THE most essential thing in all the world is to learn to say, "I believe." For without faith in the one true God and Jesus Christ, whom He sent, there is no salvation. By the grace of God, a child can say it. Without the Holy Spirit, the wisest man on earth does not even know what it means to believe. The disciples had made a fine confession of their faith not long before. Now we see how their faith failed them in a crucial moment. What could we expect of the poor, troubled father in our text? May the Lord teach us all to believe!

Jesus Heals a Boy with an Unclean Spirit

And when they came to the disciples, they saw a great crowd around them, and scribes arguing with them. And immediately all the crowd, when they saw Him, were greatly amazed and ran up to Him and greeted Him. And He asked them, "What are you arguing about with them?" And someone from the crowd answered Him, "Teacher, I brought my son to You, for he has a spirit that makes him mute. And whenever it seizes him, it throws him down, and he foams and grinds his teeth and becomes rigid. So I asked Your disciples to cast it out, and they were not able." And He answered them, "O faithless generation, how long am I to be with you? How long am I to bear with you? Bring him to Me." And they brought the boy to Him. And when the spirit saw Him, immediately it convulsed the boy, and he fell on the ground and rolled about, foaming at the mouth. And Jesus asked his father, "How long has this been happening to him?" And he said, "From childhood. And it has often cast him into fire and into water, to destroy him. But if You can do anything, have compassion on us and help us." And Jesus said to him, " 'If you can'! All things are possible for one who believes." Immediately the father of the child cried out and said, "I believe; help my unbelief!" And when Jesus saw that a crowd came running together, He rebuked the unclean spirit, saying to it, "You mute and deaf spirit, I command you, come out of him and never enter him again." And after crying out and convulsing him terribly, it came out, and the boy was like a corpse, so that most of them said, "He is dead." But Jesus took him by the hand and lifted him up, and he arose. And when He had entered the house, His disciples asked Him privately, "Why could we not cast it out?" And He said to them, "This kind cannot be driven out by anything but prayer."

Jesus, with Peter, James, and John, had been on the Mount of Transfiguration. This most singular experience lifted the disciples far above the sordid things of this world. They had a foretaste of heaven. To a lesser degree, we, too, have moments when we feel the nearness of God, when in the Word and Sacraments God reveals to us His surpassing love. But the return to the realities of life in this world is unavoidable.

As the little group came down from the heights, they saw that the other disciples were in the midst of an agitated crowd. Front and center were the scribes, who were sharply questioning the disciples and taking advantage of their apparent inability to heal a demon-possessed boy whose father had brought him to Jesus to be healed. In the absence of the Lord, the disciples had vainly tried to drive out the demon that was harassing the child. Before the scribes could answer Jesus about why they were arguing with the disciples, the stricken father poured out his tale of woe. His son, deprived of the ability to hear and speak and suffering from epileptic seizures, had from early childhood been terribly troubled by a demon who would cast him to the ground, trying to destroy him by throwing him into fire and into water. How the father hoped Jesus would do what the disciples could not—heal his child! He did not say like the leper, "Lord, if You will" (Matthew 8:2; Mark 1:40) but, "If You *can.*" Mildly, the Lord corrects him and points out his lack of faith. "All things are possible for one who believes."

Faith that takes God at His Word and lays hold of His almighty power can never fail. It can truly move mountains. Deeply moved, the father exclaims, "I believe; help my unbelief!" This man feels and deplores the weakness of his faith, but he goes straight to the only One who can make up for his lack of faith, who can help him to believe. When we go to Him where He may be found—in His Word—we find that our own weak faith is strengthened in the hour of need. See how soon the time of need and sorrow was over for the troubled soul of that father! Before the curious crowd could grow still larger, the Lord rebuked the wicked spirit, commanding it with authority to leave the child forever. As always, the voice of the Master demanded obedience. Although the demon cried out in anger and gave the helpless body of the boy a final wrench so vicious that he appeared to be dead, Jesus took him by the hand and restored him to life and health.

When they were alone in the house, the chagrined disciples asked Jesus why they were unable to drive out the evil spirit, probably thinking of the power He had given them when He sent them out (Mark 6:13; Luke 9:6). But their power failed because their faith had failed. They should have prayed and fasted, seeking help from above. They must have been overconfident, relying too much on themselves. Strength comes to us in the measure that we ask for it.

Prayer

Our Lord and Savior, we pray You to have patience with us. Help us not to wait until the trouble that surrounds us is so great that we can hardly see Your presence for our tears. May we rather come and learn of Your grace and power to help and to save, so that when Satan assails us and our loved ones, we may not doubt but believe, so that the mountains of difficulties and the depth of despair may not rob us of the certainty that You are mightier than Satan and sorrow. We, too, pray, "I believe; help my unbelief!" Amen.

THE GREATEST IN CHRIST'S KINGDOM
Mark 9:30–50

HOW hard it is for people to understand the nature of Christ's kingdom! No one knew that better than the Lord Himself. As time was growing short, He seized every opportunity to teach His disciples what it was and what it was not. He gave them three lessons, according to today's text. First, they had to learn the lesson of service, for service counts, not greatness. Then, they had to learn not to despise anyone who was His. Finally, the kingdom requires self-denial and self-discipline. What wonderful lessons for us to learn as well!

Jesus Again Foretells Death, Resurrection

They went on from there and passed through Galilee. And He did not want anyone to know, for He was teaching His disciples, saying to them, "The Son of Man is going to be delivered into the hands of men, and they will kill Him. And when He is killed, after three days He will rise." But they did not understand the saying, and were afraid to ask Him.

Who Is the Greatest?

And they came to Capernaum. And when He was in the house He asked them, "What were you discussing on the way?" But they kept silent, for on the way they had argued with one another about who was the greatest. And He sat down and called the twelve. And He said to them, "If anyone would be first, he must be last of all and servant of all." And He took a child and put him in the midst of them, and taking him in His arms, He said to them, "Whoever receives one such child in My name receives Me, and whoever receives Me, receives not Me but Him who sent Me."

Anyone Not Against Us Is for Us

John said to Him, "Teacher, we saw someone casting out demons in Your name, and we tried to stop him, because he was not following us." But Jesus said, "Do not stop him, for no one who does a mighty work in My name will be able soon afterward to speak evil of Me. For the one who is not against us is for us. For truly, I say to you, whoever gives you a cup of water to drink because you belong to Christ will by no means lose his reward.

Temptations to Sin

"Whoever causes one of these little ones who believe in Me to sin, it would be better for him if a great millstone were hung around his neck and he were thrown into the sea. And if your hand causes you to sin, cut it off. It is better for you to enter life crippled than with two hands to go to hell, to the unquenchable fire. And if your foot causes you to sin, cut it off. It is better for you to enter life lame than with two feet to be thrown into hell. And if your eye causes you to sin, tear it out. It is better for you to enter the kingdom of God with one eye than with two eyes to be thrown into hell, 'where their worm does not die and the fire is not quenched.' For everyone will be salted with fire. Salt is good, but if the salt has lost its saltiness, how will you make it salty again? Have salt in yourselves, and be at peace with one another."

The time of Jesus' ministry on earth was drawing to an end. With deep emotion and solemn emphasis, He laid before His disciples the whole plan of our salvation. He had to be delivered into the hands of His enemies, had to die, and would rise again on the third day. There was no other way to save mankind but by His suffering and death. But His disciples were still far from understanding this, and it seems strange that they did not have the courage to ask Him about it.

Jesus came to Capernaum for the last time. Alone with His disciples, He asked what they had been arguing about on the way. They felt guilty and, therefore, had nothing to say. Persisting in their foolish dreams about an earthly kingdom, they had argued about who would be the greatest in this kingdom on earth. So Jesus gave them another much-needed lesson. The kingdom of Christ is not like the kingdoms of this world, and that is not an element of weakness, but of strength. The first and greatest is the one who puts himself last and whose ambition is to serve others. How beautifully Jesus illustrated this lesson! Gathering a little boy in His arms, Jesus said that receiving such a little one in His name and showing him love and care is a greater act than ruling a kingdom, for the Lord considers such a service as if it were done to the Lord Himself.

A comment John made gave Jesus occasion for another lesson. While the disciples were out on their preaching tour, they met a man who was exorcizing demons in Jesus' name, although he was not one of the apostles. For that reason, the apostles told the man to stop his activities. Jesus said this was mistaken zeal. The man evidently was a true believer who was trying to serve the Master as well as the apostles did. He was not one of those Jesus talked about when He said, "Whoever is not with Me is against Me" (Matthew 12:30). Though not an apostle, he was a follower of Jesus. We must be careful not to condemn and reject others as non-Christians simply because they do not happen to be in our group. God alone can judge the heart. The important thing was that this man was a servant of Christ. In this case, Jesus emphasized that if anyone would give a follower of Christ as little as a cup of water to drink and do it in His name and because he belongs to Christ, his deed would certainly be rewarded.

The last lesson Jesus gives is the hardest. Whether still thinking of the man John had tried to discourage or referring to the child who may still have been resting in His arms, Jesus earnestly and almost vehemently warns against giving offense to the weak, putting a stumbling block in their way, and leading them astray by word or example. It would be better for the person who gives offense that a millstone were hanged about his neck and he were drowned in the sea. How marvelous the love of Christ for the weak and helpless! How deep His anger against those who would harm anyone He has saved! And thus, with great eloquence, He warns all not to use their

God-given gifts in the service of sin. He does not literally demand the cutting off of hands or feet; mutilation of the body will not eliminate sin of the heart. But He does expect His disciples to practice the strictest self-discipline and self-denial, lest they be cast into the eternal fire of hell. Are we not the salt of the earth? Then rather than let sin rule in us, let us instead work to counteract the rottenness of our world. To be the salt of the earth and to be at peace with one another is our ideal.

Prayer

Jesus, our Lord and Master, we are reminded that Your kingdom is not one of pride and outward greatness, but of service. It is not a matter of outward show and efforts, but of following You. It requires something we can never do on our own: to conquer our sinful flesh and its unholy desires and to come over entirely to Your side, the cause of truth and holiness. Therefore, we ask You to grant us true repentance and a living faith, that through us Your will may be done and Your kingdom come. Amen.

MARRIAGE AND CHILDREN
Mark 10:1–16

JESUS' ministry in Galilee had come to a close. Capernaum, Bethsaida, and Chorazin had not made the most of His visits. There is always an end to the opportunity to hear and believe. Then, it is too late. Jesus made His way toward Jerusalem knowing what awaited Him there. Beyond the Jordan, He was kept busy enough. The people flocked to Him, and He gave them what they needed. He would have denied His own nature if He had not healed them. He would have been unfaithful to His office if He had not given them the bread of life. There He gave them, and the world, instruction concerning the oldest institution of God, marriage, and pointed out the highest privilege of the child—to share His love and saving grace.

Teaching about Divorce

And He left there and went to the region of Judea and beyond the Jordan, and crowds gathered to Him again. And again, as was His custom, He taught them.

And Pharisees came up and in order to test Him asked, "Is it lawful for a man to divorce his wife?" He answered them, "What did Moses command you?" They said, "Moses allowed a man to write a certificate of divorce and to send her away." And Jesus said to them, "Because of your hardness of heart he wrote you this commandment. But from the beginning of creation, 'God made them male and female.' 'Therefore a man shall leave his father and mother and hold fast to his wife, and the two shall become one flesh.' So they are no longer two but one flesh. What therefore God has joined together, let not man separate."

And in the house the disciples asked Him again about this matter. And He said to them, "Whoever divorces his wife and marries another commits adultery against her, and if she divorces her husband and marries another, she commits adultery."

Let the Children Come to Me

And they were bringing children to Him that He might touch them, and the disciples rebuked them. But when Jesus saw it, He was indignant and said to them, "Let the children come to Me; do not hinder them, for to such belongs the kingdom of God. Truly, I say to you, whoever does not receive the kingdom of God like a child shall not enter it." And He took them in His arms and blessed them, laying His hands on them.

Here is another instance where the Pharisees tried to set a trap for Jesus. We know that society of that time set a low estimate on women. Despite the Law of Moses, it was easy for a man to take advantage of his wife. And the Jewish leaders did not help by their disputes about the meaning of such passages as Deuteronomy 24:1–4. When Jesus asked them about the issue, they felt they were justified in their liberal interpretation of the law that a man need only write his wife a certificate of divorce and send her away for any cause sufficient in his eyes. Jesus pointed out that Moses acted as a civil lawgiver and made allowance for the hardness of their hearts to avoid greater harm. But He goes right back to the original intention and wording of the law as it was laid down when God created the man and the woman and said that a man was to leave his father and his mother to enter into the holy and inviolate union with his wife unto one flesh, concluding, "What therefore God has joined together, let not man separate." Thus the Lord put His divine stamp of approval on marriage as a lifelong union between man and wife.

How the Pharisees reacted to this we are not told, but the disciples, when they were alone in the house with Jesus, could not help but show how deeply they were influenced by the teaching of their former leaders. They still seemed to feel that a man was at a disadvantage if he could not rid himself of an undesirable wife. But Jesus insisted that it was the will and intention of God that neither the man nor the woman should put away a spouse and marry another, unless it would be, as we learn from Matthew 19:9, that one or the other had been guilty of sexual immorality.

Children have always played an important part in God's plans for the human race. We all know Christ's words, "See that you do not despise one of these little ones" (Matthew 18:10). Even the apostles had to be given this warning. When mothers brought their children to Jesus so He could bless them, the apostles, perhaps in well-meant but ill-advised concern for His welfare, tried to interfere. With the strongest signs of disapproval, the Lord set them right. He most assuredly will not allow anyone to come between Him and one of His little ones. How we should appreciate these words: "Let the children come to Me; do not hinder them, for to such belongs the kingdom of God"! Moreover, we are positively told that no one has any claim superior to that of a child. God grants faith to them as well as to us. In fact, their way of taking the Word of the Lord as it is in simple faith is an example to all. There is no way to God and heaven but by such faith. "And He took them in His arms and blessed them, laying His hands on them." Were those particular children the only ones entitled to that blessing? Certainly not. His Word, particularly in Holy Baptism, still powerfully claims and blesses all children who are brought to Him. May we not withhold this blessing!

Prayer

Heavenly Father, who from the very beginning blessed the state of holy matrimony and would have it honored by all, help that this sacred ordinance may not be violated or desecrated in any way. Since sin has entered our hearts, renew us daily by Your Holy Spirit as Your redeemed children to live a chaste and decent life in word and deed. Help us to love and honor our spouse, that Your holy institution of marriage may bring glory to You and benefit us as well. May we strive earnestly to bring up our children in the nurture and admonition of the Lord, doing all in our power to bring them to the waiting arms of their Redeemer, that He may bless them with His grace and mercy. Hear us for the sake of Your divine promises. Amen.

24
YOU CANNOT GIVE CHRIST ANYTHING BECAUSE YOU OWE HIM EVERYTHING
Mark 10:17–31

ONE fundamental mistake people make is that they act as though they are doing the Lord a favor when they offer Him their services. They forget that it is altogether a privilege if He allows us to serve Him, whether that service is with our money, our time, or our talents. Even then, Jesus takes nothing without giving first the reward of His grace so we are always indebted to Him and bound to Him by bonds of eternal gratitude.

The Rich Young Man

And as He was setting out on His journey, a man ran up and knelt before Him and asked Him, "Good Teacher, what must I do to inherit eternal life?" And Jesus said to him, "Why do you call Me good? No one is good except God alone. You know the commandments: 'Do not murder, Do not commit adultery, Do not steal, Do not bear false witness, Do not defraud, Honor your father and mother.' " And he said to Him, "Teacher, all these I have kept from my youth." And Jesus, looking at him, loved him, and said to him, "You lack one thing: go, sell all that you have and give to the poor, and you will have treasure in heaven; and come, follow Me." Disheartened by the saying, he went away sorrowful, for he had great possessions.

And Jesus looked around and said to His disciples, "How difficult it will be for those who have wealth to enter the kingdom of God!" And the disciples were amazed at His words. But Jesus said to them again, "Children, how difficult it is to enter the kingdom of God! It is easier for a camel to go through the eye of a needle than for a rich person to enter the kingdom of God." And they were exceedingly astonished, and said to Him, "Then who can be saved?" Jesus looked at them and said, "With man it is impossible, but not with God. For all things are possible with God." Peter began to say to Him, "See, we have left everything and followed You." Jesus said, "Truly, I say to you, there is no one who has left house or brothers or sisters or mother or father or children or lands, for My sake and for the gospel, who will not receive a hundredfold now in this time, houses and brothers and sisters and mothers and children and lands, with persecutions, and in the age to come eternal life. But many who are first will be last, and the last first."

There is something fascinating about this young man of wealth and influence (according to Luke, he was a ruler of the synagogue), because he was so evidently in earnest. As Jesus went on

His way—remember it was the way that brought Him nearer and nearer to the cross—the man ran to Him, knelt before Him, and in deep humility asked, "Good Teacher, what must I do to inherit eternal life?" What was meant as a sincere compliment did not satisfy Jesus; the man had to have a much deeper knowledge of the Lord. Since doing good works was the only way the man could think of to inherit eternal life, the fast answer to his question was taken from the Law. Only God is good, but the man did not think for a moment that Jesus was God in the real sense of the word. Jesus reminds the young man of the demands of the Law, which he knew well enough, or thought he did. His reply shows clearly that he did not understand the Law in its real meaning, for he claimed he had kept all God's commands from his youth. With love and pity, the Lord looked on the young man. How He longed to bring him to a better knowledge and the way to salvation! The test was a simple one. Did he really love his Lord enough to give up all he had, let the poor have the benefit of it, and take up his cross and follow Jesus? What an opportunity for the man to be happy forever! But he was not equal to it. To give up his wealth was asking too much. He went away sorrowful. The kingdom did not lose anything when it lost him, but he lost everything when he lost the kingdom.

With a heavy heart, Jesus looked at His disciples and called their attention to the fact of how hard it is for a rich man to enter the kingdom of God. The disciples were surprised. Like so many of us, they thought it was an advantage to be rich. Jesus explained that there is nothing wrong with being rich, for wealth is a gift of God. But the trouble occurs when we place our trust in our riches instead of trusting in God alone. We lose God and His kingdom when our possessions get in the way. Jesus emphasizes that it is easier for a camel to go through the eye of a needle than for a rich man to enter the kingdom of God. More astonished than ever, the disciples wondered how anyone could be saved under such circumstances. And again, Jesus reminded them that what is impossible for man is possible for God. He alone can save by His redeeming grace.

Always outspoken, Peter said, "See, we have left everything and followed You." Was Peter in danger of claiming some merit or reward for what he and the other apostles had done? With great kindness, Jesus assured them that what they had done in faith would not be taken lightly by Him. Forsaking all for His and the Gospel's sake would, in His infinite mercy, be rewarded a hundredfold in this world and in the world to come. But He reminds them and us that in serving Him, we must expect persecutions. We must remain faithful to Him, for "many who are first will be last, and the last first." Pride may cause us to lose everything.

Prayer

Lord Jesus, teach us to know that in You, and in You alone, our heart will find true riches and lasting contentment. May Your gifts ever be received with thankful hearts. Let them not come between us and the Giver, that we may not fail with humble hearts to seek first Your kingdom and righteousness, trusting only in Your grace and power to save. Amen.

SALVATION THROUGH THE CROSS, GREATNESS IN SERVICE, HEALING BY FAITH

Mark 10:32–52

THERE are three important lessons in this passage. Jesus' coming suffering and death is made ever clearer and stronger. He is drawn to the cross, although He dreads it, because He knows what it will cost to redeem the world. The apostles are still dreaming of an earthly kingdom of greatness and power. They must still learn the fundamental lesson that in His kingdom, greatness is measured by humility and service. And blind Bartimaeus must teach us that healing and help comes to us by faith in Christ's almighty Word.

Jesus Foretells His Death a Third Time

And they were on the road, going up to Jerusalem, and Jesus was walking ahead of them. And they were amazed, and those who followed were afraid. And taking the twelve again, He began to tell them what was to happen to Him, saying, "See, we are going up to Jerusalem, and the Son of Man will be delivered over to the chief priests and the scribes, and they will condemn Him to death and deliver Him over to the Gentiles. And they will mock Him and spit on Him, and flog Him and kill Him. And after three days He will rise."

The Request of James and John

And James and John, the sons of Zebedee, came up to Him and said to Him, "Teacher, we want You to do for us whatever we ask of You." And He said to them, "What do you want Me to do for you?" And they said to Him, "Grant us to sit, one at Your right hand and one at Your left, in Your glory." Jesus said to them, "You do not know what you are asking. Are you able to drink the cup that I drink, or to be baptized with the baptism with which I am baptized?" And they said to Him, "We are able." And Jesus said to them, "The cup that I drink you will drink, and with the baptism with which I am baptized, you will be baptized, but to sit at My right hand or at My left is not Mine to grant, but it is for those for whom it has been prepared." And when the ten heard it, they began to be indignant at James and John. And Jesus called them to Him and said to them, "You know that those who are considered rulers of the Gentiles lord it over them, and their great ones exercise authority over them. But it shall not be so among you. But whoever would be great among you must be your servant, and whoever would be first among you must be slave of all. For even the Son of Man came not to be served but to serve, and to give His life as a ransom for many."

Jesus Heals Blind Bartimaeus

And they came to Jericho. And as He was leaving Jericho with His disciples and a great crowd, Bartimaeus, a blind beggar, the son of Timaeus, was sitting by the roadside. And when he heard that it was Jesus of Nazareth, he began to cry out and say, "Jesus, Son of David, have mercy on me!" And many rebuked him, telling him to be silent. But he cried out all the more, "Son of David, have mercy on me!" And Jesus stopped and said, "Call him." And they called the blind man, saying to him, "Take heart. Get up; He is calling you." And throwing off his cloak, he sprang up and came to Jesus. And Jesus said to him, "What do you want Me to do for you?" And the blind man said to him, "Rabbi, let me recover my sight." And Jesus said to him, "Go your way; your faith has made you well." And immediately he recovered his sight and followed Him on the way.

At various times, Jesus had talked about His impending death, but never with such clarity and in such detail as on this occasion. Read the passage again, and you will see that it is a summary of His great Passion. But note also that He foretells His triumphant resurrection. Yet none of this makes the impression on the disciples that might have been expected. They still held fast to their dreams of an earthly kingdom of power. James and John reveal their ambition along these lines. Matthew tells us that they bring their request before the Lord through their mother, Salome, Jesus' aunt (Matthew 20:20–21), perhaps because they thought that their relationship as His cousins gave them greater claim. They aspired to nothing less than the seats of honor in His kingdom, one on His right hand and the other on His left.

A wise teacher, Jesus did not lose patience with them. They were not prepared to understand what was involved. This much He tells them: they did not know what they were asking. Without realizing what was involved, they readily agreed to His terms. Jesus emphasized that they would, indeed, drink of the cup of sorrow and be baptized with a baptism that would test their faith to the utmost.

And as to the seats of honor in His kingdom, of which they as yet had no real conception, these would be given to those for whom they were prepared, according to the will of His heavenly Father.

The other ten disciples were indignant about James and John's request, so the Lord called them together for a much-needed lesson in humility and service. They were to learn that the rule in His kingdom did not correspond to the practice among the kingdoms of this world, where the one who lords it over others and makes his authority felt is considered to be great. According to Jesus' own example, our ambition must be to serve one another in love. The Lord considers him the greatest who humbles himself and becomes the least of all in his own estimation, even as He willingly gave His life for the salvation of all.

They now entered Jericho, where Jesus healed two blind men. Mark identifies one of them as Bartimaeus, who sat at the roadside begging. Sensing the commotion caused by the passing of so many people who were following Jesus and His disciples, Bartimaeus, who evidently had heard of Jesus and had come to know Him as the promised Savior, insistently called out to Him for mercy. The man is an example for us because he would not let others discourage him but kept on with his cry. Jesus would not ignore him. When the people saw His interest in Bartimaeus, they changed their attitude and assured the beggar that he had every reason to take comfort. So the man cast off his coat and came forward when Jesus called. What a meeting between a beggar and the King! For the sake of the people, that they might understand the nature of the case and hear the man's confession, Jesus asked Bartimaeus what he wanted Him to do. When he answered from the depth of his heart, "Rabbi, let me recover my sight," Jesus' reply came clear and strong, "Go your way; your faith has made you well."

For thus it is and ever will be: faith in Christ's mercy will never be put to shame. In an instant, the man's sight was restored fully, and gratefully he followed his new Master.

Prayer

What a privilege, Lord Jesus, to know You by faith as the Lamb
who willingly bears the sins of the world! In such knowledge we
find our salvation. Help us to understand better and better the
true nature of Your kingdom. Take from us all foolish pride and
selfishness, and let us learn humility. Give us the spirit of willing
service. In all our need, give us faith in Your mercy, and let
us experience Your saving help in every time of need. Amen.

"YOUR KING IS COMING"

Mark 11:1–14

DURING the long history of the world, many a king has made a
triumphant entry into his royal city, but none like the one we read
about today. The others came in proud triumph of some great victory, bringing with them the spoils of their conquest. This King
came in humility and with the full knowledge that He was facing a
shameful death and apparent defeat. Yet it was the way to the greatest victory ever won, the victory over the powers of darkness, sin,
Satan, death, and hell. Knowing all this, we greet Him again with
the joyful greeting: "Hosanna! Blessed is He who comes in the name
of the Lord! . . . Hosanna in the highest!"

The Triumphal Entry

Now when they drew near to Jerusalem, to Bethphage and
Bethany, at the Mount of Olives, Jesus sent two of His disciples and said to them, "Go into the village in front of you, and
immediately as you enter it you will find a colt tied, on which
no one has ever sat. Untie it and bring it. If anyone says to you,
'Why are you doing this?' say, 'The Lord has need of it and will

send it back here immediately.' "And they went away and found a colt tied at a door outside in the street, and they untied it. And some of those standing there said to them, "What are you doing, untying the colt?" And they told them what Jesus had said, and they let them go. And they brought the colt to Jesus and threw their cloaks on it, and He sat on it. And many spread their cloaks on the road, and others spread leafy branches that they had cut from the fields. And those who went before and those who followed were shouting, "Hosanna! Blessed is He who comes in the name of the Lord! Blessed is the coming kingdom of our father David! Hosanna in the highest!"

And He entered Jerusalem and went into the temple. And when He had looked around at everything, as it was already late, He went out to Bethany with the twelve.

Jesus Curses the Fig Tree

On the following day, when they came from Bethany, He was hungry. And seeing in the distance a fig tree in leaf, He went to see if He could find anything on it. When He came to it, He found nothing but leaves, for it was not the season for figs. And He said to it, "May no one ever eat fruit from you again." And His disciples heard it.

It meant so much to the disciples, this entry into Jerusalem on the Sunday preceding His death. They left Bethany that morning and came as far as Bethphage, where, according to the Lord's command, they brought to Him that donkey and its unbroken colt so all details of the prophecy concerning that day might be fulfilled. The disciples must have had high expectation that now, at last, Jesus would go public as the long expected King and Messiah. After all, did He not again show His authority and omniscience when He told two of them to requisition this colt on which He would make His triumphant entry into the city? Eagerly, they threw their garments across the back of the beast for Him to sit on and also spread some on the ground before Him.

Word quickly spread among the people of Jerusalem and the countless visitors who had come to the feast that the famous Jesus of

Nazareth was coming with a crowd of Galilean followers. Soon the road was clogged with people who were eager to outdo one another in their zeal to greet with their glad hosannas the One who came in the name of the Lord. Some knew this was the fulfillment of the prophecy concerning their King and Savior, but many were merely carried away by the enthusiasm of the crowd. The emotion and the lip service with which so many greet Christ today when in a festive mood is not enough. That is not what our Savior expects of us. We cannot forget the sad complaint of Jesus as He wept over Jerusalem because it knew not the time of His visitation and, therefore, would not escape doom and utter destruction (Luke 19:41–44). He cannot save the proud because they will not be saved.

It is easy to imagine how quickly the day passed while the procession slowly wound its way through the Kidron Valley and the narrow streets of the ancient city. At the temple, Jesus probably caught a glimpse of the activity that was being carried on in the name of religion but was alien to its true spirit. The jealousy and anger of the Pharisees was evident, but He would deal with them later. As the evening shadows fell, He returned to Bethany with the Twelve.

Early Monday morning on their walk back from Bethany, Jesus took note of a fig tree beside the road. Hungry, He looked for fruit on it, but the tree was entirely barren. Impressively, He utters His sentence on the unfruitful tree, a fit emblem of the hypocrites of His day: "May no one ever eat fruit from you again." Although the Lord almost always uses His divine power to bless and to save, He can and will use it to curse and to destroy—something He made clear to His disciples the next day.

Prayer

Lord Jesus, we are reminded today that You came to seek and to save the lost. We need not look for another helper; neither do we look for You to come again before You come to judge the world in righteousness. Help us to greet You without hypocrisy and to receive You by sincere faith, not with mere lip service but with humble repentance and the joy that comes to every believing heart. Hear us for Your mercy's sake. Amen.

THE IMPORTANCE OF FAITH AND THE UNREASONABLENESS OF UNBELIEF

Mark 11:15–33

THE evangelist here gives us an account of what happened on Monday of Holy Week and begins a brief record of the events of that memorable Tuesday, often called the busiest day in the life of Jesus, when He taught the people and His disciples from early morning until late at night. We can summarize Mark's account as a lesson on faith and a warning to the leaders of the Jews not to harden their hearts against the truth, which they could not deny but would not accept.

Jesus Cleanses the Temple

And they came to Jerusalem. And He entered the temple and began to drive out those who sold and those who bought in the temple, and He overturned the tables of the moneychangers and the seats of those who sold pigeons. And He would not allow anyone to carry anything through the temple. And He was teaching them and saying to them, "Is it not written, 'My house shall be called a house of prayer for all the nations'? But you have made it a den of robbers." And the chief priests and the scribes heard it and were seeking a way to destroy Him, for they feared Him, because all the crowd was astonished at His teaching. And when evening came they went out of the city.

The Lesson from the Withered Fig Tree

As they passed by in the morning, they saw the fig tree withered away to its roots. And Peter remembered and said to Him, "Rabbi, look! The fig tree that you cursed has withered." And Jesus answered them, "Have faith in God. Truly, I say to you, whoever says to this mountain, 'Be taken up and thrown into the sea,' and does not doubt in his heart, but believes that what he says will come to pass, it will be done for him. Therefore I tell you, whatever you ask in prayer, believe that you have received it, and it will be yours. And whenever you stand praying, forgive, if you have anything against anyone, so that your Father also who is in heaven may forgive you your trespasses."

The Authority of Jesus Challenged

And they came again to Jerusalem. And as He was walking in the temple, the chief priests and the scribes and the elders came to Him, and they said to Him, "By what authority are You doing these things, or who gave You this authority to do them?" Jesus said to them, "I will ask you one question; answer Me, and I will tell you by what authority I do these things. Was the baptism of John from heaven or from man? Answer Me." And they discussed it with one another, saying, "If we say, 'From heaven,' He will say, 'Why then did you not believe him?' But shall we say, 'From man'?"—they were afraid of the people, for they all held that John really was a prophet. So they answered Jesus, "We do not know." And Jesus said to them, "Neither will I tell you by what authority I do these things."

On Sunday afternoon, the Lord had already glimpsed what was happening in the temple in connection with the preparations for the approaching festival. When He returned the next morning, He immediately went into action. Three years earlier, He had protested and taken vigorous action against the desecration of the temple (John 2:13–16). But the temple courts were again open for the business of buying and selling and exchanging the money of foreign visitors. This commerce took place in connection with the bringing of offerings as demanded by the Law, but it was also an opportunity for avaricious hawkers to abuse the system. In righteous anger, Jesus drove out the offenders and would not allow the sacred courts to be disturbed and defiled by having them used as a common marketplace. As always, Jesus maintained His position by referring to the Scriptures that the Lord's house should be a house of prayer, not a place for crooked business. The angry response of the scribes and priests did not affect Him. And although this incident made them even more determined to destroy Him, they couldn't act immediately and arrest Him on the spot because they were afraid of the people, who were deeply moved by the power of His teachings.

When evening came, Jesus and His apostles went back to Bethany. As they returned to Jerusalem Tuesday morning, they saw that the fig tree Jesus had cursed the day before was dead, withered down to its roots. Peter couldn't resist calling attention to the phenomenon. What struck them was the power of Jesus and His Word. So Jesus used this opportunity for a lesson on faith. Earnestly, He told them that nothing is impossible for the believer. Faith, which must always conform to the will of God and must have implicit confidence in the power of His promises, can and will even move mountains. Jesus calls attention to the power of prayer, of which we make far too little use. Let us not belittle His promise, so definite and far-reaching, that "Whatever you ask in prayer, believe that you have received it, and it will be yours." At the same time, He knew it was important to reinforce the need of a forgiving, loving spirit. He who will not forgive cuts himself off from the forgiving love of his Father in heaven.

Hardly had the Lord arrived in the temple when an official delegation of the Sanhedrin confronted Him. They were representatives of the leading classes, Sadducees, Pharisees, and prominent laymen. They questioned His authority to teach publicly, to receive the adoration of the people (including children), to cleanse the temple, and so on. Jesus did not resent their questions, but He refused to be frightened by their arrogance. He was ready to answer them, but they were first to clear up another matter. They had recently questioned the authority of John the Baptist, disregarding his credentials and the fact that John, so beloved by the people, had pointed to Jesus as the Christ, the Lamb of God, who takes away the sin of the world. The Pharisees and Sadducees owed Jesus and the people an answer to the question of whether John's Baptism was from heaven or from man. That raised a dilemma. If they said that John's Baptism was from heaven, as thousands of people believed, Jesus would demand to know why they had rejected John. If they said John's Baptism was from man, they would offend the people, who believed John was a great prophet. Shamefaced but without remorse, they answered, "We do not know." So Jesus left them with another sting in their guilty souls, saying, "Neither will I tell you by what authority I do these things." What a fatal thing it is to deny the truth when it is presented so plainly!

Prayer

Lord Jesus, forgive us the littleness of our faith. We have every rea-
son in the world to believe in You and Your promises, which are so
plain and true and have never deceived those who take them as
they are. Teach us to pray with faith and confidence, knowing it is
in Your power to give us far above all that we ask or think. Above
all things, let us not shut our hearts against the truth, lest we
harden ourselves against it, and it rise up to condemn us. Hear us
for Your name's sake. Amen.

WICKEDNESS AND CUNNING CANNOT STAND BEFORE THE TRUTH
Mark 12:1–17

WHEN Jesus entered the temple on that last Tuesday of His public ministry, He knew all about the now-or-never plot of the Jews
to destroy Him, but He had nothing to fear. He knew they would
kill Him before the week was out, but it was not going to be at the
sacrifice of His authority or with the suppression of the truth. His
enemies would have their way, but it would bring them no satisfaction or triumph. Every deeply conceived scheme and cleverly

set trap would come to naught before His divine wisdom. And He never failed to hold out a helping hand to anyone who might be won by the truth.

The Parable of the Tenants

And He began to speak to them in parables. "A man planted a vineyard and put a fence around it and dug a pit for the wine-press and built a tower, and leased it to tenants and went into another country. When the season came, he sent a servant to the tenants to get from them some of the fruit of the vineyard. And they took him and beat him and sent him away empty-handed. Again he sent to them another servant, and they struck him on the head and treated him shamefully. And he sent another, and him they killed. And so with many others: some they beat, and some they killed. He had still one other, a beloved son. Finally he sent him to them, saying, 'They will respect my son.' But those tenants said to one another, 'This is the heir. Come, let us kill him, and the inheritance will be ours.' And they took him and killed him and threw him out of the vineyard. What will the owner of the vineyard do? He will come and destroy the tenants and give the vineyard to others. Have you not read this Scripture:

" 'The stone that the builders rejected has become the cornerstone;
   this was the Lord's doing, and it is marvelous in our eyes'?"

And they were seeking to arrest Him but feared the people, for they perceived that He had told the parable against them. So they left Him and went away.

Paying Taxes to Caesar

And they sent to Him some of the Pharisees and some of the Herodians, to trap him in His talk. And they came and said to Him, "Teacher, we know that You are true and do not care about anyone's opinion. For You are not swayed by appearances, but truly teach the way of God. Is it lawful to pay taxes to Caesar, or not? Should we pay them, or should we not?" But, knowing their hypocrisy, He said to them, "Why put Me to the test? Bring me a denarius and let Me look at it." And they brought one. And He said to them, "Whose likeness and inscription is this?" They said to Him, "Caesar's." Jesus said to them, "Render to Caesar the things that are Caesar's, and to God the things that are God's." And they marveled at Him.

This is one of the incomparable parables Jesus told that day: a man planted a vineyard and fitted it out completely, with a hedge to keep out intruders, a pit for the wine when the juice was pressed out, and a tower for the laborers and for storage. He was not anxious about a harvest because it would take several years before the vines would yield fruit. So the man went on a journey and left the vineyard in the care of tenants. In time, he sent a messenger to collect what was his, but the tenants beat him and sent him away empty-handed. Others he sent were treated even more roughly, and some were even killed. Even for the master's only and beloved son, the tenants had no respect—they killed him and threw his body out of the vineyard, boldly claiming the vineyard as their own. Could there be any question about the well-deserved fate of such wicked tenants? In Matthew's account, the Jews themselves had to give the answer that such wicked men should certainly be destroyed and the vineyard given to others (Matthew 21:41).

It would have been interesting to watch the faces of the Jews as they listened to this story. It was unmistakable and clear that Jesus meant the Jewish nation as a whole. God had entrusted His vineyard to them, made them a separate nation, all His own, and blessed them as no other people had ever been blessed. But when God sent to them His prophets to ask for what was due to Him as their Lord, they abused and killed one after the other and were even now plotting to kill God's only-begotten and beloved Son in their disobedient and rebellious spirit. They would have stoned Jesus to death then and there, but they were afraid of the crowd's reaction. And so, instead of repenting of their sin, they left Him and went on their way, heaping sin upon sin upon their own heads, as is always the way with those who are confronted with the undeniable truth and still refuse to believe.

With almost inconceivable boldness, the Jews went on the offensive. This time the Pharisees had a question but were wise enough not to come in person. To appear to be completely neutral and harmless, they sent some of their smartest pupils along with the Herodians (who were friendly to the Romans) to have a difficult question answered. They figured that if Jesus answered one way, the Jews would be deeply offended; if He answered the other way, the Herodians could report Him to the governor as an enemy of the state. The question was this: "Is it lawful to pay taxes to Caesar, or not?" They insisted on an answer, which they felt they could expect since they flattered Him as being so sincere and honest and truthful and fearless.

How could they ever have hoped to deceive a man like Jesus? He answered them in such a dramatic, straightforward manner that there could be no comeback. He asked to see one of the coins used to pay the Roman tax. Then He asked about the image and superscription on the coin. On one side was an image of Tiberius, the Roman emperor, along with an inscription, and there was another inscription on the back. There was no denying the image and superscription on the coin used to pay taxes to the Roman government. The strictest pro-Roman could not find fault with the injunction, "Render to Caesar the things that are Caesar's;" nor could the most devout Jew say he could expect anybody to do more than to give "to God the things that are God's." For all times we must consider this statement the clearest presentation of the separation of church and state. The two kingdoms have separate domains, and both must be given their respective tribute. No wonder the questioners and the people marveled at Jesus' wisdom and let the matter rest.

Prayer

O Lord Jesus Christ, may Your love for us not be wasted because of our unbelief or callousness and indifference. Help us gladly to hear and learn the lessons Your wisdom and grace would teach us. May we as Your stewards render You faithful service. And while we work and pray for the welfare of the country in which we live, let us seek first Your kingdom and Your righteousness, until we are all united in Your kingdom of glory everlasting. Amen.

29

JESUS, THE TEACHER SENT FROM GOD

Mark 12:18–44

WITH treacherous lips and false hearts, the Pharisees had said it: "[You] . . . truly teach the way of God" (Mark 12:14). Questions that the Sadducees and Pharisees discussed by the hour and were never able to decide were answered by Jesus in a few words, and all of them knew His answers were true. But when He tried to arouse their interest in more important matters, they would not listen to Him, nor would they learn. No one is so hopelessly ignorant as the man who refuses to learn.

The Sadducees Ask about the Resurrection

And Sadducees came to Him, who say that there is no resurrection. And they asked Him a question, saying, "Teacher, Moses wrote for us that if a man's brother dies and leaves a wife, but leaves no child, the man must take the widow and raise up offspring for his brother. There were seven brothers; the first took a wife, and when he died left no offspring. And the second took her, and died, leaving no offspring. And the third likewise. And the seven left no offspring. Last of all the woman also died. In the resurrection, when they rise again, whose wife will she be? For the seven had her as wife."

Jesus said to them, "Is this not the reason you are wrong, because you know neither the Scriptures nor the power of God? For when they rise from the dead, they neither marry nor are given in marriage, but are like angels in heaven. And as for the dead being raised, have you not read in the book of Moses, in the passage about the bush, how God spoke to him, saying, 'I am the God of Abraham, and the God of Isaac, and the God of Jacob'? He is not God of the dead, but of the living. You are quite wrong."

The Great Commandment

And one of the scribes came up and heard them disputing with one another, and seeing that He answered them well, asked Him, "Which commandment is the most important of all?" Jesus answered, "The most important is, 'Hear, O Israel: The Lord our God, the Lord is one. And you shall love the Lord your God with all your heart and with all your soul and with all your mind and with all your strength.' The second is this: 'You shall love your neighbor as yourself.' There is no other commandment greater than these." And the scribe said to Him, "You are right, Teacher. You have truly said that He is one, and there is no other besides Him. And to love Him with all the heart and with all the understanding and with all the strength, and to love one's neighbor as oneself, is much more than all whole burnt offerings and sacrifices." And when Jesus saw that he answered wisely, He said to him, "You are not far from the kingdom of God." And after that no one dared to ask Him any more questions.

Whose Son Is the Christ?

And as Jesus taught in the temple, He said, "How can the scribes say that the Christ is the son of David? David himself, in the Holy Spirit, declared,

" 'The Lord said to my Lord, Sit at My right hand,
   until I put Your enemies under Your feet.'

David himself calls Him Lord. So how is He his son?" And the great throng heard Him gladly.

Beware of the Scribes

And in His teaching He said, "Beware of the scribes, who like to walk around in long robes and like greetings in the marketplaces and have the best seats in the synagogues and the places of honor at feasts, who devour widows' houses and for a pretense make long prayers. They will receive the greater condemnation."

The Widow's Offering

And He sat down opposite the treasury and watched the people putting money into the offering box. Many rich people put in large sums. And a poor widow came and put in two small copper coins, which make a penny. And He called His disciples to Him and said to them, "Truly, I say to you, this poor widow has put in more than all those who are contributing to the offering box. For they all contributed out of their abundance, but she out of her poverty has put in everything she had, all she had to live on."

Many of the leaders of the people, even priests, were Sadducees who were like today's modernists who pose as the foremost representatives of the Church. They denied the fundamental teachings of God's Word. They believed in no resurrection, no life hereafter, no angels or spirits. They rejected all of the Old Testament except the five books of Moses, and in these they found nothing but a system of outward morality. They evidently thought it an easy matter to make this young rabbi, Jesus, appear ridiculous before the people. They reminded Jesus of the Law of Moses, which held that if a man died without children, his brother "must take the widow and raise up offspring for his brother." They posed the possibility that a man would die without children and that his six surviving brothers would all, in succession, marry his widow, who would survive them all yet would remain childless. They argued how ridiculous it would be if all seven men would claim her as their wife after the resurrection.

Without hesitation, Jesus responded. He told them how silly and ignorant they were, not knowing the Scriptures and the power of God. First, they should have known that marriage will not exist in heaven. The institution of marriage was established for this life only. In the life to come, men will be like the angels of God. They should also have known from Moses that there is a resurrection; why else would God say to Moses, hundreds of years after the patriarchs were dead, that He was the God of Abraham, Isaac, and Jacob? He is not a God of the dead, but of the living. That silenced the Sadducees.

Now the Pharisees, after listening to this discussion, thought they had a chance to embarrass Jesus by asking Him about a matter on which they were never able to agree. It was the much-discussed question about which of the commandments was the greatest. They chose one of their ablest members as their representative and thought they could easily ensnare Jesus in technicalities, for they had figured out that there were 613 ordinances in the law, as many as there were letters in the Hebrew decalogue.

It never occurred to them that Jesus' answer was the one demanded by the Law itself. The Law is a unit. Its supreme and only demand is love: "You shall love the Lord your God with all your heart and with all your soul and with all your mind and with all your strength," and "You shall love your neighbor as yourself." The scribe who had questioned Him could not deny that Jesus had answered correctly. In fact, he elaborated a little on this summary of the Law and pointed out that such love means more than "all whole burnt offerings and sacrifices." The words of Jesus had made a deep impression on him, and Jesus encouragingly remarked that the man was not far from the kingdom of God. Did this man become one of His followers? So decisive was Jesus' victory that the quibbling and nagging on the part of His enemies had to stop.

Then Jesus asked something far more important than any debate about the Law. What about Christ? Whose Son is He? It was easy to say, "David's." But if David called Him Lord, was He not more than a mere man, the true God-man in one person? Again we read that the people heard this gladly.

Very earnestly Jesus now warned the people against the scribes and Pharisees, against their pride, hypocrisy, and greed. (Read Matthew 23 for a fuller account of His deeply stirring words.) Jesus also gave an example of stewardship at its best, without pride or selfishness—the widow with her two coins. She gave all she could, and she gave from her heart; it was a part of her worship, an act of faith.

Prayer

Our Lord Jesus, when questions arise and doubts assail us, when
there is an honest desire to know the truth or when the enemies would ridicule Your Word and our faith, help us, that we
may search the Scriptures for the answer and that Your Word may
mean more to us than all human wisdom, which often is nothing
but foolishness and a vain attempt to avoid the truth. Take from
us all pride and other sins, and make our faith sincere. Hear us
for the sake of Your divine compassion. Amen.

THE END OF THE WORLD WILL COME: BE READY
Mark 13:1–13

THE unforgettable Tuesday of Holy Week was drawing to a close.
For the last time, Jesus stood before a crowd of representatives of the
chosen people of the Old Testament, declaring that His time among
them was at an end, that another day was coming when even His
enemies would have to greet Him as their King, when He would
come in the name of the Lord. The next great drama in the history
of the world would be its end.

Jesus Foretells Destruction of the Temple

And as He came out of the temple, one of His disciples said
to Him, "Look, Teacher, what wonderful stones and what wonderful buildings!" And Jesus said to him, "Do you see these
great buildings? There will not be left here one stone upon
another that will not be thrown down."

Signs of the Close of the Age

And as He sat on the Mount of Olives opposite the temple, Peter and James and John and Andrew asked Him privately, "Tell us, when will these things be, and what will be the sign when all these things are about to be accomplished?" And Jesus began to say to them, "See that no one leads you astray. Many will come in My name, saying, 'I am He!' and they will lead many astray. And when you hear of wars and rumors of wars, do not be alarmed. This must take place, but the end is not yet. For nation will rise against nation, and kingdom against kingdom. There will be earthquakes in various places; there will be famines. These are but the beginning of the birth pains.

"But be on your guard. For they will deliver you over to councils, and you will be beaten in synagogues, and you will stand before governors and kings for My sake, to bear witness before them. And the gospel must first be proclaimed to all nations. And when they bring you to trial and deliver you over, do not be anxious beforehand what you are to say, but say whatever is given you in that hour, for it is not you who speak, but the Holy Spirit. And brother will deliver brother over to death, and the father his child, and children will rise against parents and have them put to death. And you will be hated by all for My name's sake. But the one who endures to the end will be saved."

The disciples must have been somewhat discouraged by all of the warnings and forebodings Jesus gave them. They could not imagine that all of these things would come to pass. As true Israelites, they took pride in the temple above all things. It was one of the wonders of the ancient world, and Herod had started to rebuild it more than forty years before. As they were passing through the temple gates, one of the disciples called the Lord's attention to the massive buildings and the stones, which, according to historian Josephus, measured about forty by twenty by fourteen feet. Briefly, but definitely, Jesus told His disciples that not one of these massive stones would remain upon the other in the great destruction to come.

As they, a little later, paused on the Mount of Olives across from the city, where they could see the magnificent temple glittering in the rays of the setting sun, Peter, James, John, and Andrew asked Jesus when these things would be fulfilled. What He had said was beyond their comprehension, but they dared not doubt Him. Solemnly and impressively, Jesus told them what they had to know to be prepared for the end to come. First, He warned them against the deceivers who would come during the confusion and uncertainty of the last days and who would even call themselves the Christ. Wars and rumors of wars would be prevalent. Nations and kingdoms would rise up against one another in endless strife. Famines and earthquakes would be additional signs and reminders of the end to come.

These things would be only the beginning of their anxiety and distress. But the end will not come until the Gospel has been preached among all nations, for the Lord was deeply concerned about giving all people an opportunity for repentance and salvation. So they would have no illusions about the work ahead of them, Jesus tells His disciples how the Gospel will be opposed. He predicts cruel persecutions for His sake, persecutions that will give His enemies no satisfaction but will only sting their conscience. In all this, Jesus promises to stand by them. The Gospel testimony is the main thing, and the Gospel is His own. Therefore, He promises them His divine assistance when they stand before rulers and kings so the Holy Spirit would give them the right words at the right time. The New Testament proves the truth of this in accounts of the occasions when the apostles were brought before the highest tribunal of the Jews or when Paul stood before the supreme court in Rome.

At the same time, Jesus says here that the Gospel would show its divisive power. You must either be for it or against it. No wonder, then, that the closest family ties would break in deadly hatred: brother would be against brother, father against son, child against parent. For His name's sake, His followers would be able to bear this because they would not dare love anyone more than Him. Unreasoning, unjust hatred is hard to bear. But there is only one thing that counts—our salvation. It is far more important to be ready for the end than to figure out the day and hour when it comes.

Prayer

O Lord of truth and love, let us have no illusions about the world in which we live, for it is desperately wicked and unalterably opposed to the Gospel. Since it is therefore doomed to destruction, help us to come boldly and be separate, testifying against all error and sin and proclaiming Your blessed Gospel as the only hope of the world, so we may not perish with the unbelievers but have our souls be saved in the end. Amen.

THE COMING OF THE SON OF MAN
Mark 13:14–37

TWO things should be noted in connection with today's reading. One is that the Bible, which gives the Lord's own account of what will happen, reveals nothing about another coming of Christ before Judgment Day. The other is that in Jesus' presentation of these matters, He speaks of the close connection between the judgment over Jerusalem and the judgment of the world. In fact, the final rejection of Jerusalem and Israel is considered to be the beginning of the judgment to come upon all men at the end of the world. This again leaves no room for another coming in between.

The Abomination of Desolation

"But when you see the abomination of desolation standing where he ought not to be (let the reader understand), then let those who are in Judea flee to the mountains. Let the one who is on the housetop not go down, nor enter his house, to take anything out, and let the one who is in the field not turn back to take his cloak. And alas for women who are pregnant and for those who are nursing infants in those days! Pray that it may not happen in winter. For in those days there will be such tribulation as has not been from the beginning of the creation that God created until now, and never will be. And if the Lord had not cut short the days, no human being would be saved. But for the sake of the elect, whom He chose, He shortened the days. And then if anyone says to you, 'Look, here is the Christ!' or 'Look, there He is!' do not believe it. For false christs and false prophets will arise and perform signs and wonders, to lead astray, if possible, the elect. But be on guard; I have told you all things beforehand.

The Coming of the Son of Man

"But in those days, after that tribulation, the sun will be darkened, and the moon will not give its light, and the stars will be falling from heaven, and the powers in the heavens will be shaken. And then they will see the Son of Man coming in clouds with great power and glory. And then He will send out the angels and gather His elect from the four winds, from the ends of the earth to the ends of heaven.

The Lesson of the Fig Tree

"From the fig tree learn its lesson: as soon as its branch becomes tender and puts out its leaves, you know that summer is near. So also, when you see these things taking place, you know that He is near, at the very gates. Truly, I say to you, this generation will not pass away until all these things take place. Heaven and earth will pass away, but My words will not pass away.

No One Knows That Day or Hour

"But concerning that day or that hour, no one knows, not even the angels in heaven, nor the Son, but only the Father. Be on guard, keep awake. For you do not know when the time will come. It is like a man going on a journey, when he leaves home and puts his servants in charge, each with his work, and commands the doorkeeper to stay awake. Therefore stay awake—for you do not know when the master of the house will come, in the evening, or at midnight, or when the rooster crows, or in the morning—lest he come suddenly and find you asleep. And what I say to you I say to all: Stay awake."

Here Jesus gives His disciples a sign of the approaching judgment over Jerusalem, the "abomination of desolation," of which the prophet Daniel had spoken (Daniel 11:31; 12:11), when their sacred temple will fall into heathen hands and the sacrifices would come to an end. When that happens, they are to know that the end is inevitable. They should then let nothing delay them in their flight. There would be no time to save their belongings. With divine tenderness, He spoke of the sad plight of expectant and nursing mothers. For the sadness and suffering of those days would be without parallel in the history of the world and would be unbearable unless the Lord would shorten those days for the sake of His chosen children. In addition, they should not be misled by false christs and false prophets, even if such people performed wonders and signs by which even the elect might be seduced, if that were possible.

In the prophetic vision of one to whom time meant nothing, the Lord now predicted what would happen when the judgment is extended over all the world. The signs He describes are not the preliminary signs mentioned before but will be connected with the end of all things. Sun, moon, and stars will cease to function and will be involved in the general destruction of the present world because the force that holds them in place will be dissolved. Then the great moment will be at hand when the Son of Man will come in the clouds with power and great glory. Far more momentous will that day be than when God, by His almighty Word, created the heaven and the earth. Then there were no witnesses. On the Last Day, all eyes will see Him and the eternal destiny of all humankind will be sealed.

Jesus is speaking here to His beloved ones, whose frailty He knew only too well. For their comfort and ours, He promises that wherever His elect might be—scattered over all the earth or rested for centuries in forgotten graves—His holy angels will gather them into His blessed presence. The signs of the coming judgment should be to them like the welcome signs of an approaching summer. The very fact that "this generation," meaning the Jewish people, would remain throughout the centuries should be a reminder that these prophecies would surely be fulfilled. For although heaven and earth will eventually pass away, His words will remain forever true.

But a word of warning was offered and we should never forget it. The day and hour of His coming is not revealed. The angels do not know it. Even Jesus, in His state of humiliation, was not aware of it. It is the Creator's secret. Therefore, we are not to give in to a feeling of superficial security, but must watch and pray always. A little parable drives home this thought: a master, taking a far journey, telling no one when he will return, expects all his servants to attend to their work with all diligence and be ready for his return at any time, lest he find them faithless. Again sounds forth the warning for all to hear and heed: Watch!

Prayer

Help us, Lord Jesus, to be alert and wide awake for Your coming, lest You find us asleep and unaware and it is too late to prepare for the great judgment. Give us faithfulness in watchfulness and in prayer, that we may escape the terrors of the end of the world and enter into Your presence with joy. Amen.

DARK PLOTTINGS CANNOT TURN THE SAVIOR FROM THE PATH OF LOVE AND OBEDIENCE

Mark 14:1–16

WHAT a contrast we have before us! The Jews, more than ever determined to destroy Jesus, are overjoyed that Judas, with his greed and growing contempt for his Master, is willing to play right into their hands. Although Jesus was fully aware of such treachery, He did not shrink from His path of duty. He directed His disciples to prepare for His last Passover, which would give Him an opportunity to celebrate and institute the great feast of the New Testament Church.

The Plot to Kill Jesus

It was now two days before the Passover and the Feast of Unleavened Bread. And the chief priests and the scribes were seeking how to arrest Him by stealth and kill Him, for they said, "Not during the feast, lest there be an uproar from the people."

Jesus Anointed at Bethany

And while He was at Bethany in the house of Simon the leper, as He was reclining at table, a woman came with an alabaster flask of ointment of pure nard, very costly, and she broke the flask and poured it over His head. There were some who said to themselves indignantly, "Why was the ointment wasted like that? For this ointment could have been sold for more than three hundred denarii and given to the poor." And they scolded her. But Jesus said, "Leave her alone. Why do you trouble her? She has done a beautiful thing to Me. For you always have the poor with you, and whenever you want, you can do good for them. But you will not always have Me. She has done what she could; she has anointed My body beforehand for burial. And truly, I say to you, wherever the gospel is proclaimed in the whole world, what she has done will be told in memory of her."

Judas to Betray Jesus

Then Judas Iscariot, who was one of the twelve, went to the chief priests in order to betray Him to them. And when they heard it, they were glad and promised to give him money. And he sought an opportunity to betray Him.

The Passover with the Disciples

And on the first day of Unleavened Bread, when they sacrificed the Passover lamb, His disciples said to Him, "Where will You have us go and prepare for You to eat the Passover?" And He sent two of His disciples and said to them, "Go into the city, and a man carrying a jar of water will meet you. Follow him, and wherever he enters, say to the master of the house, 'The Teacher says, Where is My guest room, where I may eat the Passover with My disciples?' And he will show you a large upper room furnished and ready; there prepare for us." And the disciples set out and went to the city and found it just as He had told them, and they prepared the Passover.

The enemies of Jesus did not have the courage to take a straightforward course in their opposition to the truth because they could not proceed with a clean conscience. See how the Pharisees, while preparing for the great feast of the Passover, which was connected with the Feast of Unleavened Bread and which they intended to observe with every manifestation of piety and holiness, were nevertheless plotting the death of One whose innocence they could not deny. But even as they planned, they were cowards enough to fear the people and therefore intended to wait until after the feast.

Here St. Mark inserts something that happened the previous Saturday evening to show how Judas was led to abandon every lingering feeling of loyalty to his Master and to cast his lot with the enemy. It was in Bethany, where Jesus was the honored guest in the house of Simon (who was healed from the dread disease of leprosy, no doubt by the Lord Himself), where a woman, Mary of Bethany, brought in a box of very rare and precious ointment and anointed her beloved Savior. She did this with a deep understanding of the high office of her Lord as the promised King and Priest and with a premonition of His impending death. According to St. John's account, it was Judas who suggested to the other disciples that this was an extravagance, a sinful waste, that the money the ointment cost might have been given to the poor. He, as treasurer, hoped to lay his hands on the money himself, for he was greedy. But Jesus valiantly stood up for Mary. He recognized her deed as an act of faith, a good work. He pointed out that they would always have the poor with them and could help them at any time, but Him they would not always have with them. In fact, the time was near when they would lay His body in the grave, and He accepted Mary's service as an act anticipating the anointing of His body for burial. So highly did He think of this act of faith and love that He predicted that Mary's kindness would be spoken of wherever the Gospel would be preached. What a mighty incentive for us to honor the Lord with acts of love—such as beautifying our churches and church services—that may not directly answer a need but nevertheless honor the Savior.

Driven by the evil that was taking possession of him more and more, Judas now went to the chief priests and offered to betray Jesus for a fair price. Greed had gotten the upper hand in him. We can imagine how glad the Jews were to receive such help from unexpected quarters. The traitor now watched his opportunity to deliver the Lord into their hands. What a fearful thing to let sin become one's master!

Thursday dawned. The disciples reminded the Lord that it was time to buy and kill the Passover lamb so they might keep the feast that evening. Perhaps they were worried about finding a room where they might eat the Passover meal, for such rooms must have been at a great premium. But this was a small matter for the wisdom and authority of the Lord. He sent two of His disciples with instructions for finding such a room. It would be a sign to them when they met a man carrying a pitcher of water—indeed an unusual sight, for that was definitely woman's work. They would follow this man to a house where the landlord, evidently a disciple, would willingly place at their disposal a large upper room furnished and prepared. It happened just as Jesus predicted, so the disciples could buy and get ready all that was needed for the Passover, not realizing what a momentous evening it would be.

Prayer

Lord Jesus, have mercy on us in our weakness and proneness to sin, lest our evil nature gain the upper hand and we be turned from You, our only hope and salvation, and be lost in darkness and despair. May Your unchanging grace be our hope and refuge now and evermore. Amen.

THE TREACHEROUS HEART OF JUDAS, THE FAITHFUL HEART OF JESUS, THE DECEITFUL HEART OF PETER

Mark 14:17–31

ONCE again we turn our attention to Judas. His treacherous heart led him deeper and deeper into the meshes of sin into which Satan had entangled him. And all the more, we admire the faithfulness of the heart of Jesus, who continued to warn His erring disciples with all kindness. We, too, are the objects of Christ's faithful concern. For our benefit, He instituted the Sacrament of His body and blood for the remission of sins. For our benefit, the weakness of Peter, whose deceitful heart led to deadly danger, is recorded.

And when it was evening, He came with the twelve. And as they were reclining at table and eating, Jesus said, "Truly, I say to you, one of you will betray Me, one who is eating with Me." They began to be sorrowful and to say to Him one after another, "Is it I?" He said to them, "It is one of the twelve, one who is dipping bread into the dish with me. For the Son of Man goes as it is written of Him, but woe to that man by whom the Son of Man is betrayed! It would have been better for that man if he had not been born."

Institution of the Lord's Supper

And as they were eating, He took bread, and after blessing it broke it and gave it to them, and said, "Take; this is My body." And He took a cup, and when He had given thanks He gave it to them, and they all drank of it. And He said to them, "This is My blood of the covenant, which is poured out for many. Truly, I say to you, I will not drink again of the fruit of the vine until that day when I drink it new in the kingdom of God."

Jesus Foretells Peter's Denial

And when they had sung a hymn, they went out to the Mount of Olives. And Jesus said to them, "You will all fall away, for it is written, 'I will strike the shepherd, and the sheep will be scattered.' But after I am raised up, I will go before you to Galilee." Peter said to Him, "Even though they all fall away, I will not." And Jesus said to him, "Truly, I tell you, this very night, before the rooster crows twice, you will deny Me three times." But he said emphatically, "If I must die with You, I will not deny You." And they all said the same.

The evening that would come to mean so much to all true believers had arrived. One thing threatened to mar it—the traitor was there. The Lord did not resent Judas's presence, but He was deeply concerned about His erring and wandering sheep. With great earnestness, Jesus declared that one of His closest friends who was now eating with Him would betray Him. One of the Twelve, one who ate from the same dish, was to know that Jesus was aware of his deceitfulness and sin. No wonder they were so disturbed and dismayed. Everyone doubted himself, and with troubled and distressed heart, one after the other asked, "Is it I?" The answer was intended to be a final warning to Judas before it was too late. This was tactfully done in such a way that the others, except perhaps Peter and John, did not know who Jesus was talking about. Judas knew, of course, even as the traitor of today must know, that Satan was about to claim him as his own. The death of the Lord was predetermined and long predicted. Not only Judas's sin but our sin made it necessary. But that does not mitigate the sin of the traitor. It would have been better for him if he had never been born rather than to suffer the eternal pangs of a lost soul. With that last warning ringing in his ears, Judas went into the night.

Because of His compassionate heart, Jesus went out to all the lost children of men. On that last night among His apostles, His thoughts were of His children everywhere and the need of strengthening their faith and keeping them faithful to the last or until He comes again. The supper was ended. The last Passover of the Old Testament had been celebrated. The time of fulfillment was come. Jesus' death, by which He would atone for the sins of the world, was imminent. To bring the fruits of that atoning death to His believing children, He instituted the New Testament Sacrament of His true body and blood. He took the bread, blessed it, broke it, and gave it to them, saying, "Take; this is My body." He took the cup, the wine, and speaking the words of thanksgiving, He gave it to them all to drink of it, saying, "This is My blood of the covenant, which is poured out for many." He confirms that His blood was shed for all, that His death was not to benefit only a few, such as the disciples then present, but a mighty host of believers until the end of time. His words are clear. No amount of rationalizing can change the fact that the almighty and all-wise Son of God, our Redeemer, here promises that His body and blood are truly present in, with, and under the bread and wine as a divine pledge of our redemption. He brought the blessed Supper to a conclusion by promising a happy reunion at the marriage feast in heaven.

After ending the celebration with the singing of a psalm, the little group left the Upper Room and proceeded to the Mount of Olives. Sorrowfully, Jesus predicted that this night they would all be offended because of Him. The Shepherd would be struck down, and the sheep would be scattered. But He added the consoling promise that after His resurrection, He would meet them in Galilee. Here the weakness of Peter's heart revealed itself. Rather boastfully, Peter maintained that while it was quite conceivable that others might fail the Lord, he himself would never lose faith. Although Jesus specifically predicted that Peter would deny Him three times that very night, Peter's foolish self-confidence moved him to declare most emphatically that he was ready even to die with Him. What else could the others do but make the same heedless declaration? Not boasting, but praying, not pride, but a humble reliance on God will help us in the hour of trial.

Prayer

Forgive us, O Lord, if we are sometimes foolish with pride and disregard the dangers that threaten our souls. What is even more important, help us, that no treachery and falseness comes between us and Your saving love. Above all, teach us to find consolation and strength in Your Word and Sacrament, the revelation of Your faithful heart. Amen.

THE LORD MAKES READY TO MEET THE TRAITOR AND DEATH

Mark 14:32–52

FOREVER sacred in the memory of every true believer is the little garden of olive trees, Gethsemane, whose very dust was hallowed by the drops of blood that fell from the holy brow of the only sinless Man who ever walked ground once cursed by God. In another garden, no longer worthy to be called Paradise, the first man sinned and brought death to all children. In this garden, the sinless Son of God, in the humility of human flesh and blood, wrestled with the powers of sin, Satan, death, and hell and still remained the Holy One who earned for us a paradise, where righteousness and peace will forever reign in the hearts of those who trust in His redeeming grace.

Jesus Prays in Gethsemane

And they went to a place called Gethsemane. And He said to His disciples, "Sit here while I pray." And He took with Him Peter and James and John, and began to be greatly distressed and troubled. And He said to them, "My soul is very sorrowful, even to death. Remain here and watch." And going a little farther, He fell on the ground and prayed that, if it were possible, the hour might pass from Him. And He said, "Abba, Father, all things are possible for You. Remove this cup from Me. Yet not what I will, but what You will." And He came and found them sleeping, and He said to Peter, "Simon, are you asleep? Could you not watch one hour? Watch and pray that you may not enter into temptation. The spirit indeed is willing, but the flesh is weak." And again He went away and prayed, saying the same words. And again He came and found them sleeping, for their eyes were very heavy, and they did not know what to answer

Him. And He came the third time and said to them, "Are you still sleeping and taking your rest? It is enough; the hour has come. The Son of Man is betrayed into the hands of sinners. Rise, let us be going; see, My betrayer is at hand."

Betrayal and Arrest of Jesus

And immediately, while He was still speaking, Judas came, one of the twelve, and with him a crowd with swords and clubs, from the chief priests and the scribes and the elders. Now the betrayer had given them a sign, saying, "The one I will kiss is the man. Seize Him and lead Him away under guard." And when he came, he went up to Him at once and said, "Rabbi!" And he kissed Him. And they laid hands on Him and seized Him. But one of those who stood by drew his sword and struck the servant of the high priest and cut off his ear. And Jesus said to them, "Have you come out as against a robber, with swords and clubs to capture Me? Day after day I was with you in the temple teaching, and you did not seize Me. But let the Scriptures be fulfilled." And they all left Him and fled.

A Young Man Flees

And a young man followed Him, with nothing but a linen cloth about his body. And they seized him, but he left the linen cloth and ran away naked.

Leaving the other disciples near the entrance of the garden, Jesus took with Him Peter, James, and John, not only to be witnesses of His suffering, but to keep watch and pray with Him. The burden of the sins of the world, for which He was now to begin His great suffering, was so heavy and grievous that even the little human sympathy and prayerful assistance they might have given Jesus would have been deeply appreciated, for His soul was "very sorrowful, even to death." The depth of sorrow and pain we are permitted to see is beyond our human comprehension. Three times Jesus pours out His soul in agonized prayer to His dear heavenly Father, pitifully pleading that if it were possible, He who can do all things might take this cup away and let this hour pass by. Nevertheless, in the holiness of His perfect obedience, Jesus submits to the will of His heavenly Father. As time goes on, He thinks less of the comfort His disciples might have been to Him and more of their souls' welfare. If they only would watch and pray that the trials and temptations that were coming upon them might not overwhelm them. But even Peter, although personally and directly appealed to, could not be moved to watch with Him one hour. Jesus generously acknowledged the willingness of the spirit of His dear apostle but deplored the weakness of his flesh. So sleepy were they all that their mumbling answers made no sense. Finally Jesus gave up every attempt to enlist them in His holy vigil and aroused them with the announcement that the fatal hour of His capture was at hand, for He knew that He was betrayed into the hands of His ungodly enemies. He went out to meet them as they were led on by the wretched traitor.

And so they meet face-to-face, the Lord from heaven, in lowly form but untouched by sin, and one of the saddest victims of Satan's cunning and cruelty—Judas, "one of the twelve." Being one of Christ's own is no guarantee against falling away from Him. "Therefore let anyone who thinks that he stands take heed lest he fall" (1 Corinthians 10:12). It must have been small comfort to Judas that he came at the head of a great multitude of soldiers and servants armed with swords and spears, that he was hired by the Council of the Jews. There was no satisfaction in taking captive someone who could, with a word, strike them all to the ground but who made no effort to defend Himself. There could have been nothing but bitterness in the kiss of feigned friendship that was the sign and seal of Judas's betrayal.

And so the Lord of life was ready to keep His appointment with death. Willingly, Jesus allowed them to lay their wicked hands on Him and take Him away. Peter's weak attempt to defend the Master with his sword was promptly repudiated. All satisfaction His enemies might have felt in taking Him was spoiled by the Lord's pointing out that their swords and spears were a vain show of power. They were cowards to come out in this way when they could, if they had a righteous cause, have taken Him openly in the temple while He was teaching. The only reason they could bind Him now and lead Him away was because it was so ordained in the council of God and was His will. Seeing that their Master was giving Himself up, all the prideful courage and faithfulness of the apostles deserted them. They fled into the night. There was one young man who, perhaps, aroused from his sleep, wrapped a sheet about himself when he saw and heard the commotion and ventured a little too near. As the soldiers tried to lay hands on him, he dropped his covering and disappeared into the darkness. And Jesus was left alone in the hands of His enemies. Truly, there is no guarantee of our faithfulness to Him, but His faithfulness to us will never fail.

Prayer

Lord Jesus, forgive us all our lack of watchfulness and prayerful devotion to You. Forgive us if we ever fail to stand by You in the hour of temptation and trial. But let Your faithfulness to us be our constant consolation as we remember Your prayer and perfect obedience in the hour of darkest trial and Your willingness to give Yourself into shame and death for us and our salvation. Lord, have mercy on us. Amen.

WHAT HURT MORE?
Mark 14:53–72

AS we begin our meditation on Christ's great suffering, let us keep this thought in mind. Great, indescribably great, were the sufferings that came upon the innocent Lamb of God at the hands of His own nation, the chosen people of God. But far deeper were the sorrow and hurt to His soul because of the faithlessness of His own friends and the sin of God's children and for whom He, the sinless Son of God, had to suffer shame, sorrow, and death.

Jesus Before the Council

And they led Jesus to the high priest. And all the chief priests and the elders and the scribes came together. And Peter had followed Him at a distance, right into the courtyard of the high priest. And he was sitting with the guards and warming himself at the fire. Now the chief priests and the whole Council were seeking testimony against Jesus to put Him to death, but they found none. For many bore false witness against Him, but their testimony did not agree. And some stood up and bore false witness against Him, saying, "We heard Him say, 'I will destroy this temple that is made with hands, and in three days I will build another, not made with hands.' "Yet even about this their testimony did not agree. And the high priest stood up in the midst and asked Jesus, "Have You no answer to make? What is it that these men testify against You?" But He remained silent and made no answer. Again the high priest asked Him, "Are You the Christ, the Son of the Blessed?" And Jesus said, "I am, and you will see the Son of Man seated at the right hand of Power, and coming with the clouds of heaven." And the high priest tore his garments and said, "What further witnesses do we need? You have heard His blasphemy. What is your decision?" And they all condemned Him as deserving death. And some began to spit on Him and to cover His face and to strike Him, saying to Him, "Prophesy!" And the guards received Him with blows.

Peter Denies Jesus

And as Peter was below in the courtyard, one of the servant girls of the high priest came, and seeing Peter warming himself, she looked at him and said, "You also were with the Nazarene, Jesus." But he denied it, saying, "I neither know nor understand what you mean." And he went out into the gateway and the rooster crowed. And the servant girl saw him and began again to say to the bystanders, "This man is one of them." But again he denied it. And after a little while the bystanders again said to Peter, "Certainly you are one of them, for you are a Galilean." But he began to invoke a curse on himself and to swear, "I do not know this man of whom you speak." And immediately the rooster crowed a second time. And Peter remembered how Jesus had said to him, "Before the rooster crows twice, you will deny Me three times." And he broke down and wept.

To the leaders of the Jews, the news of Jesus' arrest in the garden must have been almost too good to be true. But if it was a victory for them, there certainly was to be no satisfaction in their triumph. In the meanwhile, messengers hurried through the dark streets to call together the members of the Sanhedrin for an informal meeting at the palace of the high priest. If anywhere in the world, one certainly should have expected justice and a fair trial before this highest tribunal of the chosen people of God. But far from it. Realizing that they had a poor cause or no cause at all, these men of high degree stooped so low that, from the very outset, they looked about for false witnesses to fix upon Jesus some semblance of guilt so they could pass the sentence of death with some pretense of right. All to no avail.

Finally, two men came forward who seemed to have an accusation that might carry some weight. They referred to something Jesus said, early in His ministry, when He challenged the Jews to destroy "this temple," meaning His body, and in three days He would raise it up. But they dismally failed to make the charge stick that He had threatened or commanded to destroy the sacred temple at Jerusalem. When Jesus met the confused babbling of these false witnesses with the absolute silence of dignified innocence, even after the high priest demanded an answer, the chairman of the Council, in utter despair and fury, put Jesus under a most solemn oath and demanded an answer to the question "Are You the Christ, the Son of the Blessed?" That was a different matter. To keep silence now would have amounted to a denial. Promptly and firmly Jesus declared, "I am." Thank God for that solemn testimony to the truth on which our whole salvation rests. But He significantly added that while He now submitted to their judgment, since the will of God had to be carried out, the time would come when they would stand before His tribunal, "seated at the right hand of Power, and coming with the clouds of heaven." Now, here was something. With indescribable horror, His enemies see the fulfillment of these words of the Judge of the living and the dead. In vain was the pompous show of unrighteous indignation on the part of the high priests and the rest of the Council members in calling this blasphemy and declaring Jesus to be guilty of death.

We might want to ignore the following scene. It shows human nature at its worst. Evil-hearted, foul-mouthed, cruel servants, like their masters, taking advantage of an innocent prisoner, mocked Him, beat Him, and wickedly abused Him. What a picture of the depths of depravity to which human nature can sink. Conversely, behold the patience of the innocent, holy Son of God, who willingly turned His cheek toward the blows. What a perfect atonement for us!

We are not spared another sad picture as we meditate on the words of our text. The figure who plays so sad a part is that of our "valiant" friend Peter. After shamelessly deserting his Lord, he is seen dimly in the shadows, following at a distance. With some of his old zeal and courage returning, but without a true knowledge of his own heart, least of all with watchfulness and prayer, he even manages to gain entrance to the palace of the high priest. What now? Does he boldly confess his Lord, ready to share with Him prison and death, as he had so rashly promised just hours before? Far from it! Peter mingles with the enemies of his Lord, doing everything to make it appear as though he were one of them, even as many do today. In his zeal to be one of the crowd, he outdoes them in his boast that he has nothing to do with this Jesus of Nazareth. The taunt of a woman, the doorkeeper, is enough to make him deny his Lord the first time. Even the first rooster crow does not bring Peter to his senses by reminding him of Jesus' warning. The insistent taunting and teasing of the servants bewildered him so that he denied a second and a third time with blasphemous oaths and curses. Where was his courage? Where was even his faith? How little it takes to extinguish the weak faith we have, unless we are constantly on our guard, watching and praying. Only the Savior's endless mercy, as revealed to Peter that night in Jesus' searching but loving look, can bring a fallen disciple to sorrowful but saving repentance.

Prayer

Lord Jesus, let Your divine patience be our hope and comfort. You patiently suffered injustice, shame, and pain to bear with Your erring disciple and not to cast him off. Let that be our consolation when temptation has been too strong for us. Help us to watch and pray so we do not enter into temptation. And when we fall, lift us up again and help us to follow You in faith and humility all the remaining days of our life. We ask it for Your mercy's sake. Amen.

THE LORD OF LIFE CONDEMNED TO DEATH
Mark 15:1–19

THE scene before us is a story that stirs the imagination of men of all ages and times! That hall of polished stone, the seat of the highest court of God's own people, had been witness to the guilt of many a cringing criminal. There, the sinless Son of God must stand trial and be condemned to death. The judgment hall of the proconsul of the worldwide empire of Rome was the very place where the famous sense of justice for which the Roman rulers were renowned might be expected to triumph over the injustice of the bloodthirsty leaders of a conquered people. Yet that very hall was to be stained with the blood of the only Holy One among all the children of men. There, the sentence was pronounced that made angels halt their songs in stunned silence and unchained the passions of hell: "Crucify Him!"

Jesus Delivered to Pilate

And as soon as it was morning, the chief priests held a consultation with the elders and scribes and the whole Council. And they bound Jesus and led Him away and delivered Him over to Pilate. And Pilate asked Him, "Are You the King of the Jews?" And He answered him, "You have said so." And the chief priests accused Him of many things. And Pilate again asked Him, "Have You no answer to make? See how many charges they bring against You." But Jesus made no further answer, so that Pilate was amazed.

Pilate Delivers Jesus to Be Crucified

Now at the feast he used to release for them one prisoner for whom they asked. And among the rebels in prison, who had committed murder in the insurrection, there was a man called Barabbas. And the crowd came up and began to ask Pilate to do as he usually did for them. And he answered them, saying, "Do you want me to release for you the King of the Jews?" For he perceived that it was out of envy that the chief priests had delivered Him up. But the chief priests stirred up the crowd to have him release for them Barabbas instead. And Pilate again said to them, "Then what shall I do with the man you call the King of the Jews?" And they cried out again, "Crucify Him." And Pilate said to them, "Why, what evil has He done?" But they shouted all the more, "Crucify Him." So Pilate, wishing to satisfy the crowd, released for them Barabbas, and having scourged Jesus, he delivered Him to be crucified.

Jesus Is Mocked

And the soldiers led Him away inside the palace (that is, the governor's headquarters), and they called together the whole battalion. And they clothed Him in a purple cloak, and twisting together a crown of thorns, they put it on Him. And they began to salute Him, "Hail, King of the Jews!" And they were striking His head with a reed and spitting on Him and kneeling down in homage to Him.

Only for the sake of appearance and to give the whole matter the guise of regularity and justice was the Council of the Jews summoned in the early morning of that famous Friday to meet in special session. The sentence was a foregone conclusion. Guilty. The fettered prisoner is hurried through the narrow winding streets of the ancient city, where His ancestor David had established the national capital. Now David's greater Son must die, and there was only one person in that city who could confirm and execute that sentence, the Roman governor.

Jesus stands before Pilate. Many accusations are uttered, most of them not worth consideration. But one seemed to have some weight: His claim to be a king. There might have been something to that, although Pilate could hardly have worried about the matter when he looked at the humble prisoner. Calmly and with dignity, Jesus explained that He was the King of those who know and love the truth, the worldly, cynical heathen shrugged the whole matter off. As to all the other accusations, the Lord had only one response, silence, no matter how hard the judge tried to have Him commit Himself. No wonder Pilate marveled. He'd never had such a prisoner brought before him. As Pilate grew more and more alarmed about the situation, he searched for a way out of the dilemma either to condemn an evidently innocent man or to offend the powerful leaders of the Jews. Pilate was relieved to be reminded of a Jewish custom that at the time of the feast, he was expected to release to them a prisoner of their choice.

He remembered that a notorious prisoner was in jail at the time—Barabbas, a leader in a recent insurrection, a murderer. Pilate could think of no greater contrast than a despicable criminal against the evidently innocent and harmless Teacher. Why not place them side by side? Surely the people would have such sense of justice and decency that they would ask for Jesus' release. He even suggested to the people that this would be the proper choice, since he had found no fault in Jesus. But the chief priests were masters in mob psychology. They persuaded the crowd to ask for Barabbas. And when Pilate weakly and helplessly asked, "Then what shall I do with the man you call the King of the Jews?" the fatal answer, born of bitter hatred, was the demand, "Crucify Him!" Like wild beasts, the deluded people thirsted for the blood of their King.

But what about Pilate? No amount of charity can in any way excuse his despicable weakness. He knew and had declared that Jesus was innocent and Barabbas was guilty. Yet he released the guilty and condemned the innocent. But herein lies a deep and comforting lesson: Barabbas is a representative of the human race. The sinless Son of God is condemned in our stead that we might be declared innocent and free from all condemnation, if only we believe in Him who died for the ungodly. But how we are filled with shame and remorse when we see Him condemned to be crucified, scorned, and mocked by vile soldiers and servants. His very holiness and innocence are ridiculed, and His rightful claim to be a King was made the subject of foul jesting! We worship Him on bended knee and are proud to acclaim Him our Lord and God, our King and Savior.

Prayer

Heartless scoffers did surround Thee,
Treating Thee with shameful scorn
And with piercing thorns they crowned Thee.
All disgrace Thou, Lord, hast borne,
That as Thine Thou mightest own me
And with heav'nly glory crown me.
Thousand, thousand thanks shall be,
Dearest Jesus, unto Thee. Amen.
(LSB 420:4)

CHRIST'S CRUCIFIXION AND DEATH

Mark 15:20–37

OUR meditation on the crucifixion and death of our Lord is, in some respects, like the memory of the death of our loved ones, only infinitely more sacred. The wound is always there. Who can forget the horror of that crime of the ages when men took the Son of God and nailed His body to the cursed tree of the cross to let Him die? It hurts bitterly to know that our sins nailed Him there. But we marvel at His love and the love of the Father who sent Him, for it was His will to lift the curse from us and reconcile us to Himself. Who would deny that His will is good, though far beyond our human understanding?

And when they had mocked Him, they stripped Him of the purple cloak and put His own clothes on Him. And they led Him out to crucify Him.

The Crucifixion

And they compelled a passerby, Simon of Cyrene, who was coming in from the country, the father of Alexander and Rufus, to carry His cross. And they brought Him to the place called Golgotha (which means Place of a Skull). And they offered Him wine mixed with myrrh, but He did not take it. And they crucified Him and divided His garments among them, casting lots for them, to decide what each should take. And it was the third hour when they crucified Him. And the inscription of the charge against Him read, "The King of the Jews." And with Him they crucified two robbers, one on His right and one on His left. And those who passed by derided Him, wagging their heads and saying, "Aha! You who would destroy the temple and rebuild it in three days, save Yourself, and come down from the cross!" So also the chief priests with the scribes mocked Him to one another, saying, "He saved others; He cannot save Himself. Let the Christ, the King of Israel, come down now from the cross that we may see and believe." Those who were crucified with Him also reviled Him.

The Death of Jesus

And when the sixth hour had come, there was darkness over the whole land until the ninth hour. And at the ninth hour Jesus cried with a loud voice, "Eloi, Eloi, lema sabachthani?" which means, "My God, My God, why have You forsaken Me?" And some of the bystanders hearing it said, "Behold, He is calling Elijah." And someone ran and filled a sponge with sour wine, put it on a reed and gave it to Him to drink, saying, "Wait, let us see whether Elijah will come to take Him down." And Jesus uttered a loud cry and breathed His last.

The farce in the judgment hall had come to an end; what followed was bitter reality. They took from Him the purple robe, put on Him His own clothes, and led Him out to be crucified. The heart of the evangelist must have bled when he wrote this, but he uses no wordy embellishment to paint a gruesome picture to arouse human sympathy. He records the facts and lets them speak for themselves. We do not need the addition of legends or traditions regarding the Via Dolorosa. It is enough to know that Jesus went forth, bearing His cross and the sins of the world. It is enough to know that the physical suffering alone of that sleepless night, to say nothing of His spiritual agony, was beyond human endurance. That is where Simon of Cyrene came in. On him they laid the cross of Jesus. They forced him to bear it. We can well imagine that Simon objected most strenuously, but in the end he had to carry the cross. And a blessed cross it became to him. Only God knows what thoughts filled Simon's mind as he looked upon the bleeding back and watched the labored steps of the silent man before him. Could he fail to notice that this was not an ordinary criminal? Would it not have been natural for him to stay and see and hear what happened on Calvary? We have all reason to believe that this incident led to Simon's conversion, and that he and his family were blessed by the saving knowledge of their Savior. Let us not resent it if we must bear the cross after Jesus; it can only be a blessing to us.

At last, the fateful hill is reached. There is no other more famous—Golgotha, "Place of a Skull," a well-known place of execution outside the city gates. It was the custom to give condemned criminals a stupefying drink of wine blended with myrrh to deaden somewhat the almost unbearable pain of crucifixion. But Jesus would not take it. That was not the cup the Father had given Him to drink. There was to be no escape from His cup of suffering until He had drained it to the dregs. And so He hung there in the heat of the day. Even His few garments they had taken from Him, dividing what could be divided, gambling for the rest. An insignificant detail? Even this was predicted in Psalm 22:18.

We must not overlook the superscription on the cross, the reason for His execution. There it was, in three languages, for all witnesses to read and ponder: "The King of the Jews." Was that a crime? Despite strenuous objections, there it was and it remains today His rightful title. And what of it if He was placed among criminals, one on the right hand and the other on the left? That is where, according to the will of God, He belonged—in our place, that we might one day be seated on His right hand in His kingdom. And what did it matter that they reviled Him and mocked Him? Using the very words of the prophecy of Psalm 22, the people, the priests, and even one of the thieves on the cross completed the picture the prophet of old had painted.

And then God Himself spoke. That darkness from high noon until the middle of the afternoon was from the Creator. There was no natural cause for that darkness, such as a solar eclipse, which never occurs during a full moon, as at Passover. No, that darkness marked the darkest hour in the history of mankind, when in Christ all men died. The sin of the first man and that of all his children was being avenged by the justice of a holy God, avenged on His own Son, our Substitute and Savior (Romans 5:6–21). What a fearful price

God paid for our transgression! His own Son cried out, "My God, My God, why have You forsaken Me?" In thus tasting the agonies and horrors of hell and still maintaining His filial love and rendering willing obedience to the death, Jesus atoned for the disobedience that would otherwise cast all people into the hopelessness of eternal despair.

The foolish scoffing of those who stood by, as though He were calling for Elijah to help Him, does not detract from the glory and blessed meaning of that scene. The work of our redemption was finished indeed when Jesus committed His soul into the hands of His Father, bowed His head, and died.

Prayer
O Lord Jesus:
Your cross I place before me;
Its saving pow'r restore me,
Sustain me in the test.
It will, when life is ending,
Be guiding and attending
My way to Your eternal rest. Amen. (LSB 453:7)

GOD THE FATHER'S ONLY SON NOW IS BURIED YONDER
Mark 15:38–47

THE burial of Jesus is part of the Passion story. We speak of it as the last stage in the history of Christ's humiliation when we speak the Apostles' Creed. To die and be buried is a consequence of sin. Jesus was no sinner, and the prophecy said He would not see corruption. Still, He was the Sin-bearer and as such allowed Himself to be buried, as we are. But what a difference between His death and burial! He died in shame, surrounded by scoffers and enemies. At His burial, loving friends took charge. Gentle hands prepared His body and laid it in the tomb of a rich man, as foretold by the prophet Isaiah (53:9). Certainly, the gloom that enveloped the cross was beginning to be dispelled by the first rays of Easter joy.

And the curtain of the temple was torn in two, from top to bottom. And when the centurion, who stood facing Him, saw that in this way He breathed His last, he said, "Truly this man was the Son of God!"

There were also women looking on from a distance, among whom were Mary Magdalene, and Mary the mother of James the younger and of Joses, and Salome. When He was in Galilee, they followed Him and ministered to Him, and there were also many other women who came up with Him to Jerusalem.

Jesus Is Buried

And when evening had come, since it was the day of Preparation, that is, the day before the Sabbath, Joseph of Arimathea, a respected member of the Council, who was also himself looking for the kingdom of God, took courage and went to Pilate and asked for the body of Jesus. Pilate was surprised to hear that He should have already died. And summoning the centurion, he asked him whether He was already dead. And when he learned from the centurion that He was dead, he granted the corpse to Joseph. And Joseph bought a linen shroud, and taking Him down, wrapped Him in the linen shroud and laid Him in a tomb that had been cut out of the rock. And he rolled a stone against the entrance of the tomb. Mary Magdalene and Mary the mother of Joses saw where He was laid.

Of the signs that accompanied and followed the death of Jesus, St. Mark mentions only one, the rending of the veil of the temple. He makes no application or explanation of that remarkable happening, when suddenly, perhaps before the very eyes of the priests preparing for the evening sacrifice, the heavy veil that hung between the

Holy Place and the Most Holy Place of the temple was torn as by an unseen hand from the top to the bottom, exposing to all the Most Holy Place, which even the high priest was allowed to enter only once a year (and then only after making a sacrifice for himself in order to be prepared to stand in the very presence of God, conscious of the fact that he was the mediator between God and the people). This sign could mean only one thing—the days of the sacrifices were over, and the great High Priest of all God's people had come and made the sacrifice to end all sacrifices so all people now have free access to the Father through Him.

The Gospel writer also records the effect that Jesus' death had on the centurion, who had stood under the cross and likely had been present at the trial in the judgment hall. He may have even witnessed Jesus' arrest in the garden. This much is certain—the centurion saw and heard enough to bring him to the conviction he freely and publicly confessed, that Jesus was the Son of God. Truly a wonderful conviction and a surprising confession! From the mouth of a rough soldier we have the first public testimony to the divine-human nature of Him who died on the cross.

Mark reports, to their everlasting honor, the faithfulness of the group of women who did not forsake the Lord in His shame and death, although they were obliged to remain at a distance. That they had followed Him and served Him in the happy days gone by was an act of faith that shone more brightly than that of His disciples when the great hour of need had come. Let us not despise or think little of the faith of those who keep themselves in the background. In the hour of trial, the last may become first. How true that was in the case of the two men who were so prominent at the burial of Jesus! The sun was rapidly sinking in the west. That meant that the preparations for the burial of Jesus' body had to be rushed. First, permission had to be secured to take the body from the cross. Here, the influential position of Joseph of Arimathea served a good purpose. He boldly went to Pilate and asked for the body of Jesus, whom he had begun to love and honor as the Savior, but whom he had not found the strength of faith to confess. Pilate must have been surprised that a member of the very court that had condemned Jesus should turn out to be His friend. So as soon as the centurion confirmed that Jesus had died, permission was readily granted. Elsewhere we read that Nicodemus, a Pharisee and also a member of the Council, joined Joseph in furnishing the linen shroud and a large portion of the spices and ointments that the Jews customarily used at burials. Thus, the body of our Lord was laid in the clean, new tomb of Joseph, who was nearby, to await the resurrection morn. At least some of the faithful women stood near to see where His body was laid so they could come after the close of the Sabbath to fully anoint Him. Until then, they buried their hopes with Jesus' body. A dead Master is no Master at all. But the scene was soon to change.

Prayer

O Ground of faith, Laid low in death,
Sweet lips, now silent sleeping!
Surely all that live must mourn
Here with bitter weeping.
O blest shall be Eternally
Who oft in faith will ponder
Why the glorious Prince of Life
Should be buried yonder.
O Jesus blest, My Help and Rest,
With tears I now entreat Thee:
Make me love Thee to the last,
Till in heaven I greet Thee. Amen.
(TLH 167:5–7)

39

HALLELUJAH! JESUS LIVES!
Mark 16

WITHOUT this chapter, all that was written and said in previous chapters would be meaningless as far as our salvation is concerned. As St. Paul says, "If Christ has not been raised, your faith is futile and you are still in your sins." But triumphantly, he adds, "But in fact Christ has been raised from the dead, the firstfruits of those who have fallen asleep" (1 Corinthians 15:17, 20).

The Resurrection

When the Sabbath was past, Mary Magdalene and Mary the mother of James and Salome bought spices, so that they might go and anoint Him. And very early on the first day of the week, when the sun had risen, they went to the tomb. And they were saying to one another, "Who will roll away the stone for us from the entrance of the tomb?" And looking up, they saw that the stone had been rolled back—it was very large. And entering the tomb, they saw a young man sitting on the right side, dressed in a white robe, and they were alarmed. And he said to them, "Do not be alarmed. You seek Jesus of Nazareth, who was crucified. He has risen; He is not here. See the place where they laid Him. But go, tell His disciples and Peter that He is going before you to Galilee. There you will see Him, just as He told you." And they went out and fled from the tomb, for trembling and astonishment had seized them, and they said nothing to anyone, for they were afraid.

[Some of the earliest manuscripts do not include 16:9–20.]

Jesus Appears to Mary Magdalene

Now when He rose early on the first day of the week, He appeared first to Mary Magdalene, from whom He had cast out seven demons. She went and told those who had been with

Him, as they mourned and wept. But when they heard that He was alive and had been seen by her, they would not believe it.

Jesus Appears to Two Disciples

After these things He appeared in another form to two of them, as they were walking into the country. And they went back and told the rest, but they did not believe them.

The Great Commission

Afterward He appeared to the eleven themselves as they were reclining at table, and He rebuked them for their unbelief and hardness of heart, because they had not believed those who saw Him after He had risen. And He said to them, "Go into all the world and proclaim the gospel to the whole creation. Whoever believes and is baptized will be saved, but whoever does not believe will be condemned. And these signs will accompany those who believe: in My name they will cast out demons; they will speak in new tongues; they will pick up serpents with their hands; and if they drink any deadly poison, it will not hurt them; they will lay their hands on the sick, and they will recover."

So then the Lord Jesus, after He had spoken to them, was taken up into heaven and sat down at the right hand of God. And they went out and preached everywhere, while the Lord worked with them and confirmed the message by accompanying signs.

We can imagine how slowly the hours of that Sabbath passed, while the disciples, both the men and the women, sat behind closed doors in deepest dejection. The news was almost too much to bear. Their Lord and Master was dead. It must have been at least some comfort to the women that they could do something for Jesus by anointing His body. So as soon as Saturday evening came, when the Sabbath was over, they went out to buy the necessary spices. Very early the next morning, they were on their way, arriving at the grave as the sun rose. They thought of the heavy stone that sealed the front of the tomb. How could they hope to move it? But as they came near, they saw that the stone was already rolled away. With apprehension, the women, except for Mary Magdalene who immediately ran to tell the disciples, drew near the tomb, only to be frightened by the appearance of an angel in a long white garment who delivered an almost unbelievable message: "Do not be alarmed. You seek Jesus of Nazareth, who was crucified. He has risen; He is not here. See the place where they laid Him. But go, tell His disciples and Peter that He is going before you to Galilee. There you will see Him, just as He told you."

What would you have done upon hearing such an entirely unexpected message? Perhaps just what they did—they hurried as fast as possible to tell the story, their tumultuous thoughts unable to grasp the full impact of the angel's words. Stupefied, mystified, "they said nothing to anyone, for they were afraid."

Mark briefly alludes to what John records in more detail. Jesus appeared to weeping Mary Magdalene, who was bound to Him with the strongest bonds of gratitude and love because He had driven seven devils out of her. She served as His faithful Easter messenger to those disciples who still mourned and wept and were unable to believe her report. Mark also touches on the beautiful story of how Jesus, on the afternoon of that day, appeared to two disciples on their way to Emmaus, revealing Himself to them at the supper table. These two also had difficulty in convincing others that their Lord had truly risen from the dead. This point may well be considered. The disciples were not at all disposed to believe that He had risen. Surely they would not have invented this story to deceive others.

The appearance of the Lord to the apostles, as they were gathered behind closed doors, first to the ten on Easter night and then to the eleven the following Sunday, was of great importance. For it was on that occasion that He conferred on them and those with them the Office of the Keys, the power to forgive and to retain sins in His name, which is still the power and function of the Church.

Finally, Mark refers to the meeting in Galilee, for which Jesus had long before made an appointment with His disciples. It was on that occasion that He gave them the final great commission to go into all the world and proclaim the Gospel to every person. The simple Gospel preaching will bring salvation to those who repent and believe, while those who do not believe will be damned. As a sign and seal of salvation, the Savior also commanded them to baptize all nations, young and old, all people without distinction, while they receive the Gospel of their redemption. He also equipped His messengers with divine credentials, giving them power over demons, the gift of tongues, immunity against dangers, and the miraculous power to heal diseases. By all these signs, the Gospel has been established in all the world, and there truly is no reason anyone should seek further proof—as long as we do not close our hearts to its power and blessing.

And so the time came when Jesus would visibly depart from the earth and return to heaven. Once more He gathered His apostles on Mount Olivet. Blessing them, He was received up into heaven to take His rightful place at the right hand of God the Father to rule and fulfill all things as the Head of His Church and to prepare our place for us for the glorious day when He will come to take us home to be with Him forevermore. Gladly and with holy determination, His disciples went forth to fulfill His command. Faithfully and abundantly, Christ kept His promises as they carried the Gospel to the ends of the earth. What a grand work for us to carry on!

Prayer
Crown Him the Lord of heav'n,
Enthroned in worlds above,
Crown Him the king to whom is giv'n
The wondrous name of Love.
Crown Him with many crowns
As thrones before Him fall;
Crown Him, ye kings, with many crowns,
For He is king of all. Amen.
(LSB 525:5)

MEDITATIONS FOR
THE GOSPEL ACCORDING TO
SAINT LUKE

A GENTILE PHYSICIAN BECOMES AN EVANGELIST
Colossians 4:14

Luke the beloved physician greets you, as does Demas.

WHEN we approach the third Gospel in our daily Bible readings and devotions, we must again admire and praise the wonderful and unmerited grace of God shown in the selection of the holy writers of His Book. Matthew, the first evangelist, was a publican in Galilee, and Jesus called him as His apostle when he sat in his toll booth (Matthew 9:9). Mark, the second evangelist, was a young Jewish man, the son of a Christian woman living in Jerusalem, who later become a disciple of Peter and Paul (Acts 12:12, 25; 1 Peter 5:1–3). And the third evangelist was by birth a Gentile and by profession a physician. His name was Luke, a name derived from the Latin word for light and meaning "belonging to or connected with light." He may have been, as the Church Fathers assume, a native of Antioch, where Paul's missionary activities were headquartered (Acts 13:2; 14:26; 15:35–36). That he was a Gentile we learn from Colossians 4:10–14, where some of Paul's companions and fellow workers are mentioned as being of the circumcision, while others were not, and Luke is classed with the latter. As a Greek, he received a good education, as appears from his elegant style and literary ability (see, for instance, Luke 1:1–4; Acts 17:22–31; 20:18–35; 24:10–21; 26:2–29). With regard to the Book of Acts, also written by him, Luke has been called "a historian of the first order" and his Gospel "the most beautiful book ever written."

As stated above, Luke was a physician, which is evident from his familiarity with medical terminology and practice and his very accurate and detailed reports of cases of sickness, as compared with the other evangelists (see, for instance, Luke 4:38; 5:12; 6:6; 7:2; 8:42; 10:30–37; 16:20–22; Acts 28:8). He was probably Paul's physician, since the apostle calls him "the beloved physician"

(Colossians 4:14). But, above all, he was Paul's highly esteemed companion and coworker (Colossians 4:14; Philemon 24; 2 Timothy 4:11). In Acts, Luke describes Paul's work and travels and what happened to him after his conversion (Acts 8:1; 9:1–30; 11:25–30; 12:25; chapters 13–28). But in this description, we note a difference not to be overlooked. At the beginning, Luke speaks of Saul, or Paul, in the third person when recording the events. But later he uses the plural "we." This indicates clearly that Luke was Paul's companion on these travels. We conclude from these passages that he joined Paul on his second missionary journey (AD 49–51) at Troas in Asia Minor and traveled with him to Philippi in Macedonia (Acts 16:10–17). He also accompanied Paul on his third missionary journey (AD 52–55) and even into his captivity in Caesarea and Rome. According to Acts 20:5–15, Luke traveled with Paul from Philippi via Miletus to Jerusalem (Acts 21:1–18); finally from Caesarea in Palestine to Rome (Acts 27:1–28:16; Colossians 4:14). These events occurred in the years 57–58, and Luke was their trustworthy recorder. He was also with Paul during the apostle's second captivity in Rome, occurring in AD 66 or 67 and ending with his martyrdom in 68. This is all we know of Luke's life and activities.

Prayer

Lord Jesus, You came into the world as the Savior for all men, as a light to lighten the Gentiles and as the glory of Your people Israel. You called Your evangelists from the Jewish people and from a Gentile nation in order to present Your saving Gospel to Jews and Gentiles. We thank You that You have given the third evangelist, St. Luke, to Your Church. Help us to walk in his footsteps as faithful witnesses to the Gospel truth, as willing fellow laborers to the ministers of Your Church, as whole-hearted missionaries, bringing the light to those who walk in darkness and dwell in the land of the shadow of death. Amen.

THE THIRD GOSPEL
Luke 1:1–3

Dedication to Theophilus

Inasmuch as many have undertaken to compile a narrative of the things that have been accomplished among us, just as those who from the beginning were eyewitnesses and ministers of the word have delivered them to us, it seemed good to me also, having followed all things closely for some time past, to write an orderly account for you, most excellent Theophilus . . .

IN the preceding meditation, we considered the life and the work of St. Luke, the third evangelist. Now we approach his book and consider its origin and purpose.

As we have read, Luke was not one of the apostles that Jesus called. However, trustworthy information from faithful and accurate historians and Church Fathers indicates that he, like Mark, wrote his Gospel in a certain dependency on the apostle Paul. This assumption becomes more reasonable when we acknowledge Luke's close connection with St. Paul extending over a number of years and note the "Pauline character" in the two books written by Luke. We note his terminology in presenting the doctrine of justification and his use of the word *justify* (see 18:14; Acts 13:38–39). He emphasizes the saving grace of Christ, the universality of the Gospel message, that Jesus is also the Savior of the Gentiles (see 2:11, 30–32; 4:25–27; 9:1–6; 10:1–20; 14:21–23; 24:46–47). We also note that Luke's record of the Lord's Supper agrees with Paul's wording (compare 22:19–20 and 1 Corinthians 11:23–25 with Matthew 26:26–28 and Mark 14:22–24). The general acceptance of this Gospel by the Early Church confirms the assumption.

Furthermore, it is clear from the book itself that Luke wrote his Gospel for Gentile Christians. It is dedicated to Theophilus, who is otherwise not known to us, but undoubtedly was a prominent man, probably a high Roman official (see 1:3–4, "most excellent";

Acts 1:1), and Luke describes to him localities in Palestine in a more detailed way (see 1:26; 4:31; 24:13; Acts 1:12), while usually omitting details with regard to other countries, particularly Italy (Acts 28:12–15). He does not emphasize that Christ is the Messiah promised in the Old Testament (compare Matthew's Gospel), but rather that He is the Savior of all mankind. While not stressing the false Jewish interpretation of the Law (see again Matthew's Gospel), he often portrays Christ as a friend to the lowly and poor in spirit (see 1:52–53; 2:7–8; 4:18–19; 6:20–21; 12:15–21, 33; 16:19–31); kind to women, who were so often despised and treated contemptuously (see 7:11–15; 8:2–3; 10:38–42; 23:27–28); and attentive to the very poorest people (see 7:36–50; 19:1–10; 23:39–43, 49). This is also very clear from the parables of Jesus, which Luke records in chapter 15 and in 18:9–14. The Italian poet Dante called Luke the "writer of the gentleness of Christ," and twentieth-century author Doremus A. Hayes described Luke's Gospel as "the most beautiful book ever written." Every reader will agree and will love the book more as he reads it. It may well be called the Gospel of the Compassionate Savior. The symbol of the evangelist as handed down by the Early Church and placed at the head of these devotions is the winged steer, the symbol of sacrifice, because St. Luke again and again refers to Christ's work of salvation and atonement for the sins of the world.

Regarding the time and place of writing, we assume that the Gospel was written after Matthew's and Mark's books (see Luke 1:1), but before the year 70, since neither in the book itself nor in the Acts of the Apostles do we find any indication that the destruction of Jerusalem, although prophesied, had occurred (see 19:43–44; 21:20, 24; 23:28–30). The place of writing may have been Antioch, probably the home of Luke, or Caesarea in Palestine, where Luke had journeyed with Paul (Acts 24–26), but more probably it was Rome, where Luke was in Paul's company during the apostle's first and second captivity (Acts 28:16, 30–31; Colossians 4:14; Philemon 24; 2 Timothy 4:11). The book itself bears witness to its author in the unique introduction (1:1–4), repeated to some extent in Acts 1:1.

In its presentation of the life of Christ, the book follows the synoptic arrangement, which we noted when studying Matthew and Mark. After recording Jesus' birth and infancy and the story of His forerunner, John the Baptist (chs. 1–3), the book is divided into three parts: The first tells of Jesus' activity in Galilee, consisting of preaching and performing miracles (4:1–9:50). Then follows a long section covering His last journey to Jerusalem, but recording a number of discourses and parables, some of which undoubtedly were spoken at an earlier date (9:51–18:30). And in the third part, we find the story of Christ's last works in Jerusalem, of His Passion and death, of His resurrection and ascension (18:31–24:53). Throughout we perceive a masterly presentation in beautiful language, a frequent reference to data of world history (1:5; 2:1–2; 3:1–2), so the reader might know the "certainty concerning the things" in which he has been instructed (1:4). In both of his books, Luke is a historian of the first order and his writings are read and studied with great interest.

Prayer

Lord Jesus, we thank You that You have given us this record of Your life and work on earth for the salvation of mankind. And as we begin to consider this beautiful Gospel of St. Luke and read it day by day, help us to see our Savior in Your great work of redemption and to take to heart what You have done for us. Amen.

THE INTRODUCTION
Luke 1:1–4

BY His apostle St. Paul, the Lord admonishes us: "Let the word of Christ dwell in you richly" (Colossians 3:16). There is good reason for this admonition. While we live in this world, we are surrounded on all sides with temptations, and our own human nature is always inclined more to evil than to good. Our only protection is the divine Word.

Nor is our attitude toward life to be merely preventative; we must not be satisfied if we can manage to abstain from gross sin and self-evident wickedness. The Lord does not want such futile service. Our Savior, who served us and suffered on the cross to save us, deserves better from us. But again, when we start out this way of service to the Lord, we are ignorant by nature; we know how to do evil but we don't know how to do good. We must be taught, and the only means of instruction is the Word of God. Scripture is "able to make you wise for salvation through faith in Christ Jesus. All Scripture is breathed out by God and profitable for teaching, for reproof, for correction, and for training in righteousness, that the man of God may be competent, equipped for every good work" (2 Timothy 3:15–17). Moreover, we make our way through this life with a dark future; with no way of knowing what is ahead, we need light to keep us from stumbling and falling; and the lamp to our feet and the light to our path is the Word of God (Psalm 119:105).

Therefore, God's people have, throughout all of history, been diligent students of the Scriptures. The Jews in Old Testament times had the Holy Writings, the Law and the Prophets, which they read regularly in the Sabbath services. This was custom in the Lord's day (Luke 4:16).

Is our need for protection, instruction, and enlightenment less today than in the past? Is the world growing better? Is human nature improving? Only a man who is blind to his surroundings and to the condition of his own heart could harbor such illusions. The Bible is as necessary today as it ever was. With a prayer to God, therefore, that He may bless our meditations, we begin our reading of St. Luke's Gospel.

Dedication to Theophilus

Inasmuch as many have undertaken to compile a narrative of the things that have been accomplished among us, just as those who from the beginning were eyewitnesses and ministers of the word have delivered them to us, it seemed good to me also, having followed all things closely for some time past, to write an orderly account for you, most excellent Theophilus, that you may have certainty concerning the things you have been taught.

Luke, the writer of this Gospel, was a physician (Colossians 4:14), educated, cultured, and well qualified for the task "to write an orderly account" of the facts on which our faith rests. There were earlier accounts of the life and work of Christ. As the original disciples of the Lord were one by one taken away, it became necessary to fix the history of the Lord in writing. But these earlier accounts were fragmented and incomplete; Luke intends to give a complete record of all Jesus "began to do and teach, until the day when He was taken up" (Acts 1:1–2). On the strength of diligent inquiry from eyewitnesses, men who knew by their own experience that these things were true, Luke was ready to write. And by the Holy Spirit's inspiration, he delivered the most extensive narrative of Christ's life and work.

Here we can be reminded that what His Church needs, the Lord supplies in due time. And He always finds those who, like Luke, are equipped for the work and ready to put all their gifts and faculties in His service. The will of God is still done in His Church.

From the description given to Theophilus ("most excellent"), we conclude that he was a man of high rank among the Romans; a man of Gentile origin. Therefore, Luke's Gospel is directed primarily to Gentile readers; he emphasizes that although Jesus was sent to the Jews, He is the Savior of all people. The Lord provides for all the needs of all His children. If only you look for it, you will find in His Word the answer to your questions and instruction for your particular need and your unique circumstances.

Luke presents a declaration of facts. That is what sets Christianity apart from all other religions: it is not a system of philosophy, difficult to understand for all except the highly educated; rather, it rests on a series of facts summed up in the story of Christ, having their center in the person of God the Son. And because it is factual, it can never be altered; it cannot be misunderstood; and it is absolutely certain. Our faith cannot rest on uncertainties. Thank God that we know these things are certain, that we have the testimony of trustworthy eyewitnesses. They had nothing to gain by telling these things; they would have had a more comfortable life had they kept silent, but they braved persecution and death in the most cruel form, testifying that these things are true. Their Gospels are the foundation stones on which rest our faith and hope.

Prayer
Dear Lord, we thank You that You have given us Your Holy Word. Grant us Your grace that we may find in it strength and comfort to run the race You have set before us and, in the power of Your Spirit, to persevere to the end, for Jesus' sake. Amen.

THE BEGINNING OF A NEW ERA

Luke 1:5–25

WHENEVER the Lord aimed to do something extraordinary for His people, He prepared them for it by prophecy and preliminary signs and wonders. When the time was come that Israel was to be delivered from the bondage of Egypt, God sent Moses and Aaron, who with signs and wonders gradually gained the confidence of the Hebrews and moved Pharaoh to let Israel go.

It is not surprising, therefore, that the beginning of the New Testament era was signalized with miraculous events. Angels appeared to announce the birth of Messiah's forerunner and of Christ Himself. John was born of elderly parents who had long ago given up the hope of having a son. Jesus was born of a virgin. Zechariah became mute and didn't speak again until his son was born. Christ's birth was proclaimed by an angel and angel choirs sang His welcome. All this was to show that God walked on the earth and to call on people to note His footsteps. May the wondrous deeds of God move us to observe these events with adoration and receive the message of the Gospel. To this end, we read this section of St. Luke's first chapter.

Birth of John the Baptist Foretold

In the days of Herod, king of Judea, there was a priest named Zechariah, of the division of Abijah. And he had a wife from the daughters of Aaron, and her name was Elizabeth. And they were both righteous before God, walking blamelessly in all the commandments and statutes of the Lord. But they had no child, because Elizabeth was barren, and both were advanced in years.

Now while he was serving as priest before God when his division was on duty, according to the custom of the priesthood, he was chosen by lot to enter the temple of the Lord and burn incense. And the whole multitude of the people were praying outside at the hour of incense. And there appeared to him an angel of the Lord standing on the right side of the altar of incense. And Zechariah was troubled when he saw him, and fear fell upon him. But the angel said to him, "Do not be afraid, Zechariah, for your prayer has been heard, and your wife Elizabeth will bear you a son, and you shall call his name John. And you will have joy and gladness, and many will rejoice at his birth, for he will be great before the Lord. And he must not drink wine or strong drink, and he will be filled with the Holy Spirit, even from his mother's womb. And he will turn many of the children of Israel to the Lord their God, and he will go before Him in the spirit and power of Elijah, to turn the hearts of the fathers to the children, and the disobedient to the wisdom of the just, to make ready for the Lord a people prepared."

And Zechariah said to the angel, "How shall I know this? For I am an old man, and my wife is advanced in years." And the angel answered him, "I am Gabriel. I stand in the presence of God, and I was sent to speak to you and to bring you this good news. And behold, you will be silent and unable to speak until the day that these things take place, because you did not believe my words, which will be fulfilled in their time." And the people were waiting for Zechariah, and they were wondering at his delay in the temple. And when he came out, he was unable to speak to them, and they realized that he had seen a vision in the temple. And he kept making signs to them and remained mute. And when his time of service was ended, he went to his home.

After these days his wife Elizabeth conceived, and for five months she kept herself hidden, saying, "Thus the Lord has done for me in the days when He looked on me, to take away my reproach among people."

Luke the historian was careful to state the exact time this happened: when Herod was king of Judea. But there was another reason this is mentioned: Jacob had prophesied "The scepter shall not depart

from Judah, nor the ruler's staff from between his feet, until tribute comes to him" (Genesis 49:10). This Herod, whom history has
named the Great, was not a Jew, but an Idumean (Edomite), who
owed his position entirely to the favor of Rome (the Roman sen-
ate had given him his title). The time had come when the Prince
of Peace was to appear, since an Edomite usurper ruled the Land of
Promise and could raise and depose the high priest. The burden of
the angel's message, therefore, was the fulfillment of the prophecy of
Malachi (4:5–6). Zechariah's son, who was to be called John ("the
Lord gives grace"), was the messenger of the Lord and prepared the
people for the coming Messiah. God's promises never fail; the people of God waited four thousand years for the fulfillment.

In those depraved days, Zechariah and Elizabeth were models
of sincere piety. Diligently and persistently, they called on God in
prayer. It is much more difficult to wait quietly than to go forward
when the call is to act. But God listened, and we, too, are heard.

How long had Zechariah and Elizabeth waited and prayed!
And at last—isn't it ironic?—at last the angel announced the fulfillment, but Zechariah would not believe. We cry to the Lord; we
anxiously wait for His answer; and then, when the call comes to
go forward into the land of promise, our faith fails us; we limp and
stumble when we should run and not be weary. O Lord, increase
our faith!

Such unbelief deserves chastisement. Yet the Lord is gracious
even when He chastises. His promise is that all trials will come to an
end when they have accomplished their purpose. Let us learn the lesson to bow under the chastening rod and never doubt that all things
work together for good for those who love God.

Prayer

*Teach us, O Lord, that all Your promises are sure and will be ful-
filled when Your good time is come. Teach us to patiently wait and
to persevere in faith and in prayer; in the end, the consummation
of all our hopes in the blessed life that You have promised us will
be fulfilled. For Jesus' sake. Amen.*

THE ANNUNCIATION
Luke 1:26–38

THE time had come for the promise of the Savior, first given in Eden soon after the fall into sin, to be fulfilled. The first man, Adam, had by his transgression brought judgment and condemnation and death on all men. "The last Adam," "the second man," as Paul called Him in 1 Corinthians 15:45, 47, was to annul what the first Adam had done wrong and to restore what he had lost—righteousness and life (Romans 5:12–19). How much greater than the old Adam is the New Adam!

The first Adam came directly from God's creative hand: "the LORD God formed the man of dust from the ground and breathed into his nostrils the breath of life" (Genesis 2:7). We should not be surprised that when the New Adam was born, the creative hand of God again intervened—He was born of a virgin. Only blind and stubborn unbelief can take offense at the story told in this text.

Birth of Jesus Foretold

In the sixth month the angel Gabriel was sent from God to a city of Galilee named Nazareth, to a virgin betrothed to a man whose name was Joseph, of the house of David. And the virgin's name was Mary. And he came to her and said, "Greetings, O favored one, the Lord is with you!" But she was greatly troubled at the saying, and tried to discern what sort of greeting this might be. And the angel said to her, "Do not be afraid, Mary, for you have found favor with God. And behold, you will conceive in your womb and bear a son, and you shall call His name Jesus. He will be great and will be called the Son of the Most High. And the Lord God will give to Him the throne of His father David, and He will reign over the house of Jacob forever, and of His kingdom there will be no end."

And Mary said to the angel, "How will this be, since I am a virgin?"

And the angel answered her, "The Holy Spirit will come upon you, and the power of the Most High will overshadow you; therefore the child to be born will be called holy—the Son of God. And behold, your relative Elizabeth in her old age has also conceived a son, and this is the sixth month with her who was called barren. For nothing will be impossible with God." And Mary said, "Behold, I am the servant of the Lord; let it be to me according to your word." And the angel departed from her.

Here begins the story of the life of Jesus. Tradition has it that Mary herself told it to St. Luke. The believer will be content with receiving the simple story of the girl God chose to become the mother of His Son. We can be sure that the same Power of the Most High who overshadowed Mary inspired the words of the evangelist and gave us the authentic story of the incarnation. A multitude of legends stemmed from the words of the Gospel; they should be set aside, as it is pointless to try to be wise beyond the words of Scripture.

Calmly and quietly, without pomp and show, the Divine entered into the world of man. The Son of Mary would be called the Son of the Highest, in a specific and restricted sense. If Jesus is not God, it is meaningless to celebrate Christmas, foolish to call Him Savior and Redeemer. God in the flesh is the miracle of miracles and the greatest mystery. We cannot understand it, but thank God that we don't need to; we only need believe it. And to strengthen our faith, we hear again all the signs that Jesus is the Son of God.

Such a simple but sure faith was the outstanding characteristic of Mary. Isn't it remarkable that the Scriptures tell us so little of her personal history? It is evidence of divine wisdom that foresaw the danger of magnifying the Virgin beyond her due. She was blessed among women; but her highest blessedness was not that Jesus was her Son, but that He was her Savior. How many women have called Mary blessed and desired to be like her! What prevents them? Mary's greatest acclaim is that she stood in the foremost ranks of those who hear the Word of God and keep it. And her greatest blessedness now is that she is in heaven because she trusted her Son to save her from her sins.

The message of the angels is for us too. God will give Jesus the throne of David, the kingdom of the house of Jacob, which shall never end. That kingdom is the Church of the New Testament. We need never fear for the future of that Church. There will always be a Church. There may be dark days, but the days were also dark for Jesus, His disciples, and the early Christians. In the late Middle Ages, it seemed as though the true Church was rapidly disappearing. Christians are still having a hard time in some countries today. Moreover, what the Lord said is coming true: the love of many who call themselves Christians is diminishing, but this is not true of all Christians. There is still a Church; and no matter what conditions are in the world, Christianity is doing its work, quietly, without much fuss. And when the Lord's time is come, the Church Militant will become the Church Triumphant, His kingdom of glory that will never end.

Prayer

We thank You, dear Lord, for the revelation of Your grace in Your Son, Jesus Christ, for the establishment of Your kingdom of grace here on earth, and for the promise that this kingdom will endure while the world stands. Keep us in Your Church, we pray, until our course is run and we reach our goal—Your kingdom of glory above, for Jesus' sake. Amen.

MARY VISITS ELIZABETH

Luke 1:39–56

WHEN God made His first covenant with His chosen people, the attending circumstances struck terror in the hearts of the Israelites. When the people saw the Lord descending on Mount Sinai in a dark cloud with thunder and lightning and the terrifying blasts of a supernatural trumpet, when they finally heard the voice of God Himself speaking, they fled and said to Moses: "You speak to us, and we will listen; but do not let God speak to us, lest we die" (Exodus 20:19).

But when God made His new covenant with His people, they greeted it with songs of praise. How plainly that indicates the different natures of the two covenants! The first was the covenant of the Law. That, too, was to lead the people of God to the way of salvation in that it was the teacher to bring them to Christ (Galatians 3:24). It was not a perfect covenant (Hebrews 8:7); it could show only that they were not able to keep it and, therefore, that they needed a Savior. So even then God promised them a new covenant (Jeremiah 31:31), a covenant that would bring a better hope and by which we draw closer to God (Hebrews 7:19). It was fitting that Mary responded with her Magnificat, her song of praise, which has been incorporated into the liturgy of the Christian Church. Her song is now our song.

Mary Visits Elizabeth

In those days Mary arose and went with haste into the hill country, to a town in Judah, and she entered the house of Zechariah and greeted Elizabeth. And when Elizabeth heard the greeting of Mary, the baby leaped in her womb. And Elizabeth was filled with the Holy Spirit, and she exclaimed with a loud cry, "Blessed are you among women, and blessed is the fruit of your womb! And why is this granted to me that the mother of my Lord should come to me? For behold, when the sound of your greeting came to my ears, the baby in my womb leaped for joy. And blessed is she who believed that there would be a fulfillment of what was spoken to her from the Lord."

Mary's Song of Praise: The Magnificat

And Mary said,

"*My soul magnifies the Lord,*
and my spirit rejoices in God my Savior,
for He has looked on the humble estate of His servant.
For behold, from now on all generations will call me blessed;
for He who is mighty has done great things for me,
and holy is His name.
And His mercy is for those who fear Him
from generation to generation.
He has shown strength with His arm;
He has scattered the proud in the thoughts of their hearts;
He has brought down the mighty from their thrones
and exalted those of humble estate;
He has filled the hungry with good things,
and the rich He has sent away empty.
He has helped His servant Israel,
in remembrance of His mercy,
as He spoke to our fathers,
to Abraham and to his offspring forever."

And Mary remained with her about three months and returned to her home.

Note the many quotations from the Old Testament in Mary's song. She cites the songs of Hannah, Miriam, and Deborah, and almost a dozen psalms. This shows how familiar she was with the Scriptures. There was the source of her marvelous faith, a faith for which Elizabeth rightly called her blessed; she recognized the contrast between the faith of the Virgin and the unbelief of her own husband. And while so many in Israel misunderstood and misinterpreted the prophecies of the Old Testament, Mary, because of her diligent and faithful study of the Holy Writings, knew of the spiritual hopes of Israel; she understood correctly the promise of the Seed of the woman, of the Child of the virgin. Her joy was based on the fact that God was her Savior. She, too, needed His salvation, and she praised God that He was now sending Him who would save her, and, of course, all the suffering, sinning world around her.

All praise of God must culminate in praise for His sending His Son. God's holiness and power are evident in all His dealings with us—in His creative work, in His providential care for all His creation, in His judgments on people and nations. Twenty centuries have gone by since Mary sang her song, bringing countless examples to show that God still resists the proud and gives grace to the humble. Sooner or later, His judgment will fall on all who trust in their own might or wisdom or virtue, while His blessing rests on those whose hope is in His promises of grace and mercy manifested in the coming of the Savior.

So Mary's song is still our song. She had a special reason for her praise of God that no other mortal can share, but the wide scope of her thanksgiving applies to us as well. We lay in the depths of error, of foolishness and sin, but God looked upon our lowliness and raised us up with a mighty salvation. Never was there a greater manifestation of the power and holiness of God than in the incarnation of His Son to completely bear our sin and to redeem the whole world from the results of its wickedness.

And still, the almighty God is doing great things to individuals and to communities and to whole nations. Mary stood on the threshold of the New Testament Church; we stand well within that kingdom. We see it in the history of the past, and we see it proved all around us every day—His mercy is on those who fear Him. He can win the soul that has fallen to the deepest degradation and raise it to a height of excellence that is fit company of the saints in glory. He has done this not to single isolated souls, but to ten thousand times ten thousand souls. And this power of God is still active in changing the character of families, of communities, of whole nations, by bringing them to His Son, the Savior of the world.

Mary was so highly honored by God that all generations call her blessed; yet it led her only to honor and adore the power and grace of God. Should not our souls be so filled with the majesty and the goodness of our God that we break into songs of praise to God our Savior, that we honor Him with our lips, our lives, and our active service in His kingdom?

Prayer

O God, whose mercy is everlasting and whose love is beyond compare, grant us Your grace to trust wholly in Your promises. Grant that we never stray from Your ways. And keep us steadfast in love and obedience to Your Word. For the sake of Jesus, our God and Savior. Amen.

THE DAWN OF THE NEW COVENANT
Luke 1:57–80

AFTER Noah and his family had spent long months in the ark, Moses tells us "God remembered Noah" (Genesis 8:1). He sent a strong wind to take the waters from the earth, and soon the ark settled on Ararat. Gradually, the waters receded. Noah and his family left the ark and made an altar to the Lord so they could worship Him and thank Him for preserving them. God made a new covenant with Noah and blessed him.

Four thousand years had slowly dragged their way into eternity after the great catastrophe—the fall into sin—that had made man the captive of sin and Satan. God had promised to send a Savior to redeem the world from sin and its consequences after that great catastrophe. And the promise was repeated by many prophets. The last of them, Malachi, spoke of the messenger who would prepare the way for the immediate coming of Messiah. Four hundred dreary years had passed since Malachi spoke. During most of that time, Israel had groaned under the yoke of foreign enemies. In those dark days, when even the voice of prophecy was silent, pious hearts had watched and waited and prayed for the promised Messiah, and longing eyes had wearily searched the horizon for His appearing.

Why the long delay? For such a great event, extensive preparations were necessary. Read the history of those four thousand years, and you will find that all the great nations took part in preparing the world for the coming of the Savior. In fact, all history has meaning and significance only when we view it in the light of Christmas.

But now the fullness of the time was come: God remembered His people. Here, Luke tells us of the messenger who would precede the great Lord and Savior.

The Birth of John the Baptist

Now the time came for Elizabeth to give birth, and she bore a son. And her neighbors and relatives heard that the Lord had shown great mercy to her, and they rejoiced with her. And on the eighth day they came to circumcise the child. And they would have called him Zechariah after his father, but his mother answered, "No; he shall be called John." And they said to her, "None of your relatives is called by this name." And they made signs to his father, inquiring what he wanted him to be called. And he asked for a writing tablet and wrote, "His name is John." And they all wondered. And immediately his mouth was opened and his tongue loosed, and he spoke, blessing God. And fear came on all their neighbors. And all these things were talked about through all the hill country of Judea, and all who heard them laid them up in their hearts, saying, "What then will this child be?" For the hand of the Lord was with him.

Zechariah's Prophecy

And his father Zechariah was filled with the Holy Spirit and prophesied, saying,

"Blessed be the Lord God of Israel,
for He has visited and redeemed His people
and has raised up a horn of salvation for us
in the house of His servant David,
as He spoke by the mouth of His holy prophets from of old,
that we should be saved from our enemies
and from the hand of all who hate us;
to show the mercy promised to our fathers
and to remember His holy covenant,
the oath that He swore to our father Abraham, to grant us
that we, being delivered from the hand of our enemies,
might serve Him without fear,
in holiness and righteousness before Him all our days.
And you, child, will be called the prophet of the Most High;
for you will go before the Lord to prepare His ways,
to give knowledge of salvation to His people
in the forgiveness of their sins,
because of the tender mercy of our God,
whereby the sunrise shall visit us from on high
to give light to those who sit in darkness and in the shadow of death,
to guide our feet into the way of peace."
And the child grew and became strong in spirit, and he was
in the wilderness until the day of his public appearance to Israel.

The tongue that had been tied by unbelief was loosed and immediately broke into a song of praise that swelled into a grand missionary hymn. Zechariah was the last of the Old Testament prophets, so his song echoed the past in the language of Old Testament prophets: the God of Israel was now fulfilling His promises, "that we, being delivered from the hand of our enemies, might serve Him without fear, in holiness and righteousness before Him all our days." But Zechariah was not dreaming of a deliverance from Rome and the founding of a new Jewish kingdom. This newborn son of his was to prepare the Messiah's way by preaching about the salvation of His people by the remission of their sins; to give the light to those who sit in darkness and in the shadow of death that will guide their feet to the way of peace. Yes, sin was the real enemy of Israel; and the salvation for which the patriarchs had waited and of which the prophets had foretold was the redemption from sin and death, which follows sin. And because most of Israel had a false notion of this salvation and had substituted for it a carnal patriotism, John was to prepare them by telling them that their real misery was not the loss of the scepter to Rome but enslavement by sin, and that salvation was not temporal liberation but forgiveness of sin.

It was prophecy; and by the power of the Holy Spirit, Zechariah saw it fulfilled. Since the herald of the New Testament day was born, the work of the Messiah was as good as completed and redemption accomplished. And the sacred story proves that Zechariah was not deceived. The accomplishment of the Savior's work is history. All God's promises have been fulfilled to the last letter.

But God has given other promises. In fact, our whole way through this life is paved with promises of God, promises for every age and every experience. He has promised us strength in weakness, light in darkness, comfort in sorrow, support in temptation, help in the hour of need, and life in the hour of death. God has not changed; His promises are as certain as ever. We can go our way with the solemn assurance that the mountains may depart and the hills be removed, but His kindness will not depart from us and the covenant of His peace will not be removed.

Prayer

O God of truth, we thank You that You have faithfully fulfilled Your promises to deliver us out of the hand of our enemies, sin, death, and the devil. We pray that You prepare us by Your Holy Word, that the Son of righteousness with healing in His wings may shine into our hearts and give us light in this dark world, to guide our feet into the way of peace, to serve You without fear, in holiness and righteousness before You, all the days of our life. Amen.

THE FULLNESS OF TIME

Luke 2:1–7

Let the earth now praise the Lord,
Who has truly kept His word
And at last to us did send
Christ, the sinner's help and friend.

What the fathers most desired,
What the prophets' heart inspired,
What they longed for many a year,
Stands fulfilled in glory here. (LSB 352:1–2)

LUKE 2 takes us to the threshold of a new era. It is the center of the world's history, the great divide. All events in the history of mankind are dated either before or after this chapter. All the streams of ancient history flow to this place; all the rivers of modern history flow from it. But more than this, it is the threshold of the New Testament, the dividing line between the two covenants. We stand on the spot on which the straining eyes of patriarchs and prophets and kings were focused, looking forward, and to which the eyes of all generations and races of God's people look back: Bethlehem. We see the most amazing miracle of all times: the incarnation of the Son of God. Let us hear the evangelist's simple account of this supreme revelation of God.

The Birth of Jesus Christ

In those days a decree went out from Caesar Augustus that all the world should be registered. This was the first registration when Quirinius was governor of Syria. And all went to be registered, each to his own town. And Joseph also went up from Galilee, from the town of Nazareth, to Judea, to the city of David, which is called Bethlehem, because he was of the house and lineage of David, to be registered with Mary, his betrothed, who was with child. And while they were there, the time came for her to give birth. And she gave birth to her first-born son and wrapped Him in swaddling cloths and laid Him in a manger, because there was no place for them in the inn.

The exact date of this event is not known, but that does not matter. It happened in the fullness of time, when God had determined that the time was right for the appearance of the Savior. Luke the historian indicates the place in the course of human events where this birth must be set. There is the closest possible relation between world history and Church history because there is one Lord over all who controls both. The ancient prophecy read that Messiah would be born in Bethlehem. But Mary lived in Nazareth in Galilee. Did she and Joseph wonder at times how that prophecy could be fulfilled? Nevertheless, at the right time the great Lord of history took a hand in the matters of men. Caesar Augustus thought he was upsetting the world by his arbitrary decree that everybody return to his home town for the census. But the Roman emperor was an unwitting yet official agent in the kingdom of God. It was the free act of a free man; but the Lord of nations, who rules the destinies of nations for the benefit of His Church, took the threads of the web out of mortal hands and in silence brought His plan to fruition.

Bethlehem! After all the long ages, it was still that village's chief claim to fame that David, the greatly loved king, had been born there. The kingdom of David had been conquered and dismembered, the people led away into a captivity from which relatively few returned. The royal house had saved little besides family records. This representative of past royalty, Joseph, was a carpenter; Mary was equally humble. But now a new honor was coming to Bethlehem, and the two travelers who knew this looked with new interest at the village and regarded with renewed awe the wonderful ways of God, who had brought them there at this time.

Imagine their disappointment when they found no room in the inn; they had to take refuge in a cave that served as a stable for the beasts of burden of the travelers who stayed at the inn. And there, in deepest poverty, was born the Lord of all the world—the Creator of the universe cast out of all but the smallest corner of His creation.

The people of Bethlehem did not know who they had turned away. It is still so. What the few did in ignorance, a majority does today in willful rejection. Even of those who are called by His name, how many have no room for the true Child of Bethlehem, the Savior sent by God! And that is true of all men. In their pride, they ask God which commandment they have broken. They do not want to know that they owe God ten thousand talents of obedience while they offer Him the few pennies of an outwardly respectable life— and they can't pay even that!

Oh, how people rob themselves of all that has eternal value by crowding out the Lord and giving the Child of Bethlehem no room in their inn!

Prayer

Welcome to earth, O noble Guest,
Through whom the sinful world is blest!
You came to share my misery
That You might share Your joy with me.

Ah, dearest Jesus, holy Child,
Prepare a bed, soft, undefiled,
A quiet chamber set apart
For You to dwell within my heart. Amen.
(LSB 358:8, 13)

OH, COME, LET US ADORE HIM
Luke 2:8–20

WHEN God created the world, when He laid the foundations of the earth and laid the measures and stretched the line upon it and fastened the foundations and laid the cornerstone, then the morning stars sang together and all the sons of God shouted for joy (Job 38:4–7). On the evening of the sixth day, God looked back over all His creative work and, behold, it was very good (Genesis 1:31). But there are no songs of joy in the third chapter of Genesis. Man was cast out of paradise, and the angel with the flaming sword was placed at the entrance to keep hidden the tree of life. Sin had entered and spoiled all the good creation of God. The only rejoicing was in the pits of hell.

But there came another day. Again the gates of heaven open, pouring forth all the hosts of angels, and they join in the most marvelous chorus ever heard. A new thing had entered, again to change entirely the history of men; and all of heaven rang with joy. That is the story St. Luke tells in this text.

The Shepherds and the Angels

And in the same region there were shepherds out in the field, keeping watch over their flock by night. And an angel of the Lord appeared to them, and the glory of the Lord shone around them, and they were filled with fear. And the angel said to them, "Fear not, for behold, I bring you good news of great joy that will be for all the people. For unto you is born this day in the city of David a Savior, who is Christ the Lord. And this will be a sign for you: you will find a baby wrapped in swaddling cloths and lying in a manger." And suddenly there was with the angel a multitude of the heavenly host praising God and saying,

"Glory to God in the highest,
and on earth peace among those with whom He is pleased!"

When the angels went away from them into heaven, the shepherds said to one another, "Let us go over to Bethlehem and see this thing that has happened, which the Lord has made known to us." And they went with haste and found Mary and Joseph, and the baby lying in a manger. And when they saw it, they made known the saying that had been told them concerning this child. And all who heard it wondered at what the shepherds told them. But Mary treasured up all these things, pondering them in her heart. And the shepherds returned, glorifying and praising God for all they had heard and seen, as it had been told them.

God had sent His Son to remove all the harm caused by the fall into sin; and God Himself now makes known the glorious tidings of the Savior's coming. The angel immediately stresses the meaning of this event: "Fear not . . . For unto you is born . . . a Savior." That is the message of the Gospel. Men fear God and everything that reminds them of God because they have a bad conscience. Now the cause of a bad conscience is removed. The Savior is born, the One who shall redeem the souls of all mankind from the great curse of humanity— sin. That is the message of this first New Testament preacher, the angel. And it is the substance of the angels' song. "Glory to God in the highest" for conceiving and carrying out this great plan of salvation, this great work that restored peace on earth. There is peace between God and man because the cause of enmity is taken away. There is peace in man's conscience because there is no longer reason for men to so desperately fear God and His wrath; their sin is atoned for. And there is peace even between man and man, if only they accept the salvation offered by this Savior, for no man can harbor enmity against another if both kneel at this manger and with a whole heart worship Him who lies there. A new era is ushered in on earth, an era of "peace among those with whom He is pleased." The angel keeping the gate of Paradise is removed, and the way to God and heaven is again open.

This message comes to us as often as we read or hear it. What is our response? We say with the shepherds: "Let us go over to Bethlehem." We know the manger where the divine Child is cradled today and where we may find Him—His Gospel. There we kneel in simple faith and ask no silly questions of "Why this way?" and "Why not another way?" This is God's way of leading us back to our first estate, and glory be to Him for His wisdom and love and omnipotence that brought to pass this thing He has made known to us.

It is a wonderful story, and to this day all who hear it wonder. Sadly, with so many that's the end of it. The shepherds undoubtedly remembered, but they eventually died and the story was forgotten— except by a few. "Mary treasured up all these things, pondering them in her heart." And that is the way to true blessedness. Life goes on; the shepherds return to their everyday life—yet it was not the same. What they found and saw in Bethlehem made all the difference. Our lives, too, depend on what we have seen in Bethlehem. If our eyes are opened to see God's own Savior there, we find on earth peace despite wars and terrible losses, and we are active in the service of the Savior, spreading the message of God's good will among men.

The Lord promises that the day will come when we see the Child of Bethlehem on His throne and around Him the ten thousand times ten thousand, and thousands of thousands, and again there will be an angel chorus. May we be among them to join our voices to theirs when they sing:

Prayer
"Worthy is the Lamb who was slain, to receive power and wealth and wisdom and might and honor and glory and blessing"
(Revelation 5:11–12). Amen.

THE NAME ABOVE EVERY NAME
Luke 2:21–32

PAUL, in his letter to the Philippians, wrote of the exaltation of Christ after His work of redemption is finished. In token of His exaltation, God "bestowed on Him the name that is above every name, so that at the name of Jesus every knee should bow, in heaven and on earth and under the earth, and every tongue confess that Jesus Christ is Lord, to the glory of God the Father" (Philippians 2:9–11). The greatest name and the sweetest name of our Lord is the name Jesus; and why shouldn't it be? It was given by God Himself, and the names God gives are always appropriate and significant. We read today about when the name was given and how, at the same time, He began to do what the name signifies.

And at the end of eight days, when He was circumcised, He was called Jesus, the name given by the angel before He was conceived in the womb.

Jesus Presented at the Temple

And when the time came for their purification according to the Law of Moses, they brought Him up to Jerusalem to present Him to the Lord (as it is written in the Law of the Lord, "Every male who first opens the womb shall be called holy to the Lord") and to offer a sacrifice according to what is said in the Law of the Lord, "a pair of turtledoves, or two young pigeons." Now there was a man in Jerusalem, whose name was Simeon, and this man was righteous and devout, waiting for the consolation of Israel, and the Holy Spirit was upon him. And it had been revealed to him by the Holy Spirit that he would not see death before he had seen the Lord's Christ. And he came in the Spirit into the temple, and when the parents brought in the child Jesus, to do for Him according to the custom of the Law, he took Him up in his arms and blessed God and said,

"Lord, now You are letting Your servant depart in peace,
    according to Your word;
for my eyes have seen Your salvation
    that You have prepared in the presence of all peoples,
a light for revelation to the Gentiles, and for glory to Your people Israel."

At the annunciation, God had told Mary what to name this Child, and to Joseph the Lord gave the reason: "She will bear a son, and you shall call His name Jesus, for He will save His people from their sins" (Matthew 1:21). No name was ever given that promised more and no name has ever disappointed less, for He is the name—Jesus, the Savior. At the very time when He received His name, He began the work for which He had come into the world. Later, when John hesitated to baptize Him, Jesus said, "Let it be so now, for thus it is fitting for us to fulfill all righteousness" (Matthew 3:15). So here, in today's reading, Jesus was circumcised, not because He needed this Old Testament sacrament, the symbol of putting off the old Adam, but because here, at the beginning of His earthly life, He was "born under the law, to redeem those who were under the law" (Galatians 4:4–5).

There were two things the Law of God required: perfect fulfillment of all its demands and punishment for all transgressions of those demands. Here Jesus began His obedience to the Law of God, which He fulfilled perfectly for us throughout all of His earthly life, including the moment when on Calvary's hill He cried out, "It is finished!" He is the Savior, and that is the salvation of which Simeon spoke when he took the Child in his arms, the redemption for which all the pious souls in Jerusalem had been looking all these many years. Like a sentinel on a city wall, waiting and watching, Simeon announced that the night was past and the light had come, so he asked to be relieved from his post on the watchtower he had occupied for so long and he welcomed the Redeemer, whose coming marked the end of waiting and the beginning of fulfillment.

Our life, like Simeon's, is one of watchful waiting. We, too, are promised that at the end we will see the Christ. That alone can give us peace; we know the Savior and are sure that at the journey's end we will see Him face-to-face. So we make our way through all the varied business of life; sometimes it is pleasant, sometimes it is grievous. We run our race: some finish early, for some the road seems endless; one by one our companions drop out. Life can be very lonely in old age. Peace, the assurance of security come what may, can be found only in Him who has taught us to pray in all confidence, "Our Father, who art in heaven." We know we are not asking in vain when we join in the psalmist's prayer: "Do not cast me off in the time of old age; forsake me not when my strength is spent" (Psalm 71:9).

But beyond all that, our eyes are fixed on the end of the journey. Death, to many, is the most gruesome word in their vocabulary. But to anyone who with the eyes of faith has seen the Christ of God, death is the portal to a better life, a life of utter fulfillment of all hopes, and on that portal shines the name Jesus, Savior. Anyone who knows Jesus as Savior is ready to say with Simeon, "Lord, now You are letting Your servant depart in peace, according to Your word; for my eyes have seen Your salvation."

Prayer

Jesus! Name of priceless worth
To the fallen of the earth
For the promise that it gave,
"Jesus shall His people save."

Jesus! Only name that's giv'n.
Under all the mighty heaven
Whereby those to sin enslaved
Burst their fetters and are saved.

Jesus! Name of wondrous love,
Human name of God above;
Pleading only this, we flee
Helpless, O our God, to Thee. Amen. (LSB 900:3, 5—6)

9

THE SHADOW OF THE CROSS
Luke 2:33–40

SIMEON had sung his swan song: "Lord, now You are letting Your servant depart in peace, according to Your word; for my eyes have seen Your salvation" (Luke 2:29–30). For him there is nothing else to look forward to, nothing else he desires but to die in peace; and with the Christ Child in his arms, he is assured of that. But for others, life must go on. What will it bring, particularly to those present at this occasion? The coming of the Christ is the culmination of four thousand years of prophecy and promise. Surely it will have an effect on everything from this point forward. Simeon has already stated God's intention: God has "prepared in the presence of all peoples, a light for revelation to the Gentiles, and for glory to Your people Israel" (Luke 2:31–32). How will men receive this salvation? That is the subject of the following verses.

And His father and His mother marveled at what was said about Him. And Simeon blessed them and said to Mary His mother, "Behold, this child is appointed for the fall and rising of many in Israel, and for a sign that is opposed (and a sword will pierce through your own soul also), so that thoughts from many hearts may be revealed."

And there was a prophetess, Anna, the daughter of Phanuel, of the tribe of Asher. She was advanced in years, having lived with her husband seven years from when she was a virgin, and then as a widow until she was eighty-four. She did not depart from the temple, worshiping with fasting and prayer night and day. And coming up at that very hour she began to give thanks to God and to speak of Him to all who were waiting for the redemption of Jerusalem.

The Return to Nazareth

And when they had performed everything according to the
Law of the Lord, they returned into Galilee, to their own town
of Nazareth. And the child grew and became strong, filled with
wisdom. And the favor of God was upon Him.

The shadow of the cross falls clearly across this text. It is, of course,
nothing new. The prophets had foretold all that Simeon announced.
But it is the first hint in New Testament times of the opposition that
the Messiah will encounter among men, and the fulfillment began
almost at once. Between the presentation of the Christ Child in the
temple and the return of the Holy Family to Nazareth was the flight
into Egypt and the slaughter of the innocent children in Bethlehem
(Matthew 2:13–23). Hardly had Simeon's words been spoken when
the powers of darkness began their work against the Savior, a work
that culminated in the crucifixion.

But it did not end there. Down through the ages, men have spoken against Him. They do so today; they deny His divine Sonship,
His virgin birth, His miracles. But the chief offense is His cross;
they will not believe that He suffered and died and rose again for all
mankind. There are many who will not recognize even the Christ
of Bethlehem, although the polite world stands admiringly at the
manger at Christmastime. The closer we come to Good Friday, the
more are the ranks depleted until only a few believers remain to
stand under the cross.

And so to this day it is chiefly the cross of Christ that reveals
what is in men's hearts. People go along unconcerned. They crowd
into the churches on Christmas Day, but they turn away from the
cross. More than that, they become incoherent, enraged, and blasphemous at this foolishness of the cross.

But, like Simeon, we must see the shadow of the cross falling on
the manger. The cross alone gives meaning to the life of the Child
in that manger. The Christ of Bethlehem would be of little value
were it not for the Christ of Calvary. It is the Christ born of the
Virgin Mary, suffered under Pontius Pilate, crucified, dead, and buried, risen again on the third day, ascended into heaven, and seated

at the Father's right hand to come again as the judge of all living and dead. It is this Christ, the Savior; and only those who accept Him as He is are ready with Simeon to depart in peace. Christ stands as the Great Divider between "those who are perishing" and those "who are being saved" (1 Corinthians 1:18).

That the greater part of the world rejects Christ is not pleasant to His followers. The sword that pierced Mary's soul when she heard Simeon's prophecy was fulfilled in her Son's life and death, and it painfully wounds the hearts of Christians too. Perhaps even more so because Christians also encounter the same opposition and persecution that Jesus suffered. What is there for us to do? Like pious Anna, we can give thanks to the Lord that He has opened our eyes to see the Christmas miracle in all its true significance, and then we can go out and speak to others of the salvation that God has prepared for all people.

To much of this world, Christmas has only a sentimental value; the manger might as well be empty. They sing Christmas melodies, but they mean nothing. Thank God that for us the manger is not empty. We see there the entire counsel of God for our salvation; and Christ is to us not a sign that is spoken against, but the Son of God, worshiped and adored, our Savior.

Prayer

O Christ, who perfectly fulfilled the Law on our behalf, let us ever live under the shadow of Your cross and depart in Your peace. Keep us ever steadfast in Your Word and Sacraments that we may honor and praise You forevermore. Amen.

MY FATHER'S BUSINESS

Luke 2:41–52

BETWEEN yesterday's reading and this one, there is a gap of about twelve years. No doubt all of us who love Jesus have felt the desire to know more of His boyhood. How interesting and instructive, we think, if we could read how this holy boy spent His days, how He got along with His friends, what were His pastimes. It was, no doubt, in answer to such questions that there developed, in the early centuries of the Christian era, so-called childhood gospels, the telling of strange experiences on the way to and from Egypt, of miracles performed by the boy Jesus for the amusement of His playmates, of the magical influence wielded by the water in which He was bathed, the towels He used, the bed on which He slept. All of these accounts are counterfeit; to give credit to them does not indicate love for Jesus but contempt of God's Word. God in His wisdom has denied us a detailed account of the Savior's boyhood. He expressly tells us (John 2:11) that the miracle of Cana was the beginning of Jesus' miracles. The text before us today relates the only known event of Christ's youth, after the return from Egypt.

The Boy Jesus in the Temple

Now His parents went to Jerusalem every year at the Feast of the Passover. And when He was twelve years old, they went up according to custom. And when the feast was ended, as they were returning, the boy Jesus stayed behind in Jerusalem. His parents did not know it, but supposing Him to be in the group they went a day's journey, but then they began to search for Him among their relatives and acquaintances, and when they did not find Him, they returned to Jerusalem, searching for Him. After three days they found Him in the temple, sitting among the teachers, listening to them and asking them questions. And all who heard Him were amazed at His understanding and His answers. And when His parents saw Him, they were astonished. And His mother said to Him, "Son, why have You treated us so? Behold, Your father and I have been searching for You in great distress." And He said to them, "Why were you looking for Me? Did you not know that I must be in My Father's house?" And they did not understand the saying that He spoke to them. And He went down with them and came to Nazareth and was submissive to them. And His mother treasured up all these things in her heart.

And Jesus increased in wisdom and in stature and in favor with God and man.

There is a wealth of information in this story, but the overall theme is the first recorded words of Jesus: "Why were you looking for Me? Did you not know that I must be in My Father's house?" Some versions say "about My Father's business." This is the keynote of Jesus' entire life on earth. It puts His own divine seal on the word of the angel (Luke 1:32): "He will be great and will be called the Son of the Most High." Mary had said, "Your father and I have been searching for You in great distress." Jesus answered that He was going about His Father's business. They, of course, knew this, but this is the first recorded statement that Jesus, too, knew who His true Father was and what His work on earth was to be.

And that remained His deliberate decision: "We must work the works of Him who sent Me" (John 9:4). And in the end He would say, "I glorified You on earth, having accomplished the work that You gave Me to do" (John 17:4). To a Jewish boy, a visit to Jerusalem was one of the highlights of his life. But to the boy Jesus, the city had only one attraction—the divine "must" of being about the Father's business. Not a "must" of unwilling constraint, however. What He means is that it is impossible for Him to not be about His Father's business. So Jesus spent His time in the temple. When the other pilgrims left the city, He returned to the temple. It was not strange that Mary and Joseph found Him there. It was strange that they did not look for Him there first; it was His true earthly home.

Even when they returned to Nazareth, He was about His Father's business: He was subject to His parents, and that was part of His work to fulfill the Law for us.

And so it is that this statement of Jesus will be the motto of those who in Christ are the children of God. He is their Father too. And their vocation in life is to be about the Father's business. "The Father's business" is not only the building and spreading of His Church on earth; it is that. But even the commonest duty, the most mundane task, is the Father's business if we do it in obedience to His will. What a blessed transformation of our life! We are doing God's business not only when we go to His temple and take our children there, when we bring them up in the nurture and admonition of the Lord so that they too can serve Him. But when we also remain conscious of that divine "must," then all the petty and paltry and wearisome duties of our daily life will cease to be trivial, and the factory and mill will be the Father's house as well as the temple, and being subject to parents and employers will mean doing the will of the Father in heaven.

The psalmist expresses the highest wish of a child of God when he says, "One thing have I asked of the LORD, that will I seek after: that I may dwell in the house of the LORD all the days of my life" (Psalm 27:4). The Father's house, even here on earth, has many mansions, and if we are intent on doing the Father's business, we will be in one of the rooms of His house wherever we go. May we live our lives so that when they are ended, we may say that we accomplished the work that He gave us to do. And in His own good time, the Father will call us home to sit at His table and we will dwell in the house of the Lord forever.

Prayer

Almighty God, who gave Your only Son to be for us both a sacrifice for sin and an example of godly life, give us grace that we may always most thankfully receive this His inestimable benefit and also daily endeavor to follow the blessed steps of His most holy life; through the same Jesus Christ, Your Son, our Lord. Amen.

11

A VOICE IN THE WILDERNESS
Luke 3:1–20

MALACHI, the last of the prophets, introduced the Messiah as saying, "Behold, I send My messenger, and he will prepare the way before Me" (Malachi 3:1). And Zechariah, the father of John the Baptist, had applied that prophecy to his newborn son: "And you, child, will be called the prophet of the Most High; for you will go before the Lord to prepare His ways" (Luke 1:76). Thirty years had passed since that day. The pious old priest and his wife were dead. Most of the witnesses of the wonderful things recorded in the previous chapters of St. Luke's Gospel had also passed away and the events were old news. John had withdrawn from society and had grown to manhood in the desert. There he had prepared, no doubt, for his future work under the special direction of God. But now the time had come for John to step forward and to do that for which God had sent him, St. Luke relates:

John the Baptist Prepares the Way

In the fifteenth year of the reign of Tiberius Caesar, Pontius Pilate being governor of Judea, and Herod being tetrarch of Galilee, and his brother Philip tetrarch of the region of Ituraea and Trachonitis, and Lysanias tetrarch of Abilene, during the high priesthood of Annas and Caiaphas, the word of God came to John the son of Zechariah in the wilderness. And he went into all the region around the Jordan, proclaiming a baptism of repentance for the forgiveness of sins. As it is written in the book of the words of Isaiah the prophet,

"The voice of one crying in the wilderness: 'Prepare the way of the Lord,
make His paths straight.
Every valley shall be filled,
  and every mountain and hill shall be made low,

and the crooked shall become straight,
  and the rough places shall become level ways,
and all flesh shall see the salvation of God.'"

He said therefore to the crowds that came out to be baptized by Him, "You brood of vipers! Who warned you to flee from the wrath to come? Bear fruits in keeping with repentance. And do not begin to say to yourselves, 'We have Abraham as our father.' For I tell you, God is able from these stones to raise up children for Abraham. Even now the axe is laid to the root of the trees. Every tree therefore that does not bear good fruit is cut down and thrown into the fire."

And the crowds asked him, "What then shall we do?" And he answered them, "Whoever has two tunics is to share with him who has none, and whoever has food is to do likewise." Tax collectors also came to be baptized and said to him, "Teacher, what shall we do?" And he said to them, "Collect no more than you are authorized to do." Soldiers also asked him, "And we, what shall we do?" And he said to them, "Do not extort money from anyone by threats or by false accusation, and be content with your wages."

As the people were in expectation, and all were questioning in their hearts concerning John, whether he might be the Christ, John answered them all, saying, "I baptize you with water, but He who is mightier than I is coming, the strap of whose sandals I am not worthy to untie. He will baptize you with the Holy Spirit and with fire. His winnowing fork is in His hand, to clear His threshing floor and to gather the wheat into His barn, but the chaff He will burn with unquenchable fire."

So with many other exhortations he preached good news to the people. But Herod the tetrarch, who had been reproved by him for Herodias, his brother's wife, and for all the evil things that Herod had done, added this to them all, that he locked up John in prison.

Luke the historian again points out exactly where the events he is about to relate fit into world history. He lists the current rulers in government and the leaders in the Jewish church. But he has another reason for this careful account. In no other way could he so effectively characterize the spirit of the times. The successor of Caesar Augustus on the imperial throne was his stepson Tiberius, whose name in history has become a synonym for cruelty and tyranny. His governors in Jewish lands were men like Pilate and the bad brood of vicious Herod, the murderer of Bethlehem's children. The highest place in the Jewish church was illegally held by Caiaphas, who shared the honor in the mind of the people with his father-in-law, Annas; neither of them was fit to hold any office among the people of God. All the old glory was gone. All the world, and Israel in particular, had become a barren wilderness.

Into this wilderness stepped John with the call, "Prepare the way of the Lord." And how was that to be accomplished? By repentance, by a complete change of heart and mind, which is not merely external but is proved genuine by its fruit, a total change of life. That was John's message to one and all, to high and low, to people in general and to each one in particular.

As John preceded Christ, so must his message still be heard to prepare the way of Christ into our hearts. Jesus comes as the Savior of sinners; He comes to remove that wall of partition that sin has raised between us and our God. But the Jews in Jesus' day wanted no such Savior. They believed they were guaranteed entrance into the kingdom of God because they were Abraham's descendents. In the same way, our own heart, our human nature, does not feel the need of a Savior from sin. In the same way, we need the preaching of John to bring us to our senses so we can see sin in its true nature—rebellion against God that results only in death and damnation.

True, the Law alone can never bring salvation; only the Gospel of Christ can do that. So John pointed his hearers to the mightier One who would come after him. Both must go together. The way into the Kingdom is through repentance to faith in the Savior, Jesus Christ.

John's message of repentance is not pleasant for any of us. As a result of his message, John was imprisoned and beheaded. But a gentler message cannot save us. The Lord's command to His disciples was that repentance and remission of sins should be preached in His name among all nations (Luke 24:47). Let us open our hearts to the message of John. Repentance is still the only means of preparing the way for the Savior.

Prayer

Stir up our hearts, we beseech You, almighty God, to heed the message of John the Baptist so we may prepare the way for the Lord by sincere repentance and in true faith receive the Lamb of God, who takes away the sin of the world, that we may continue in the confession of His name to the end and finally, with John and all the saints, receive the crown of victory and glory, for Jesus' sake. Amen.

SON OF GOD AND SON OF MAN
Luke 3:21–38

"ALL Scripture is breathed out by God," says St. Paul, and "profitable for teaching, for reproof, for correction, and for training in righteousness" (2 Timothy 3:16). Not a single word of Scripture was written in vain. This does not mean, however, that all Scripture passages are of equal importance for that purpose. What the Bible tells us of Jesus Christ is evidently more important than the record, say, of King Jehoahaz (2 Chronicles 36:1–3). Nor is the purpose for which God inspired it equally obvious in every passage. Some passages are so clear that we use them as proof texts in our catechism and commit them to memory. Others are not so clear why God included them in His revealed Word. Such is the genealogy of the Lord Jesus recorded in Matthew 1 and here in Luke 3. When we come to this list of names in our Bible reading, we are apt to skip over them and go on to the next chapter. But God had His purpose when He moved Luke to set down in words the human family tree of Jesus; and perhaps we will recognize that purpose a little more clearly as we consider Jesus' genealogy in the context.

Now when all the people were baptized, and when Jesus also had been baptized and was praying, the heavens were opened, and the Holy Spirit descended on Him in bodily form, like a dove; and a voice came from heaven, "You are My beloved Son; with You I am well pleased."

The Genealogy of Jesus Christ

Jesus, when He began His ministry, was about thirty years of age, being the son (as was supposed) of Joseph, the son of Heli, the son of Matthat, the son of Levi, the son of Melchi, the son of Jannai, the son of Joseph, the son of Mattathias, the son of Amos, the son of Nahum, the son of Esli, the son of Naggai, the son of Maath, the son of Mattathias, the son of Semein, the son of Josech, the son of Joda, the son of Joanan, the son of Rhesa, the son of Zerubbabel, the son of Shealtiel, the son of Neri, the son of Melchi, the son of Addi, the son of Cosam, the son of Elmadam, the son of Er, the son of Joshua, the son of Eliezer, the son of Jorim, the son of Matthat, the son of Levi, the son of Simeon, the son of Judah, the son of Joseph, the son of Jonam, the son of Eliakim, the son of Melea, the son of Menna, the son of Mattatha, the son of Nathan, the son of David, the son of Jesse, the son of Obed, the son of Boaz, the son of Sala, the son of Nahshon, the son of Amminadab, the son of Admin, the son of Arni, the son of Hezron, the son of Perez, the son of Judah, the son of Jacob, the son of Isaac, the son of Abraham, the son of Terah, the son of Nahor, the son of Serug, the son of Reu, the son of Peleg, the son of Eber, the son of Shelah, the son of Cainan, the son of Arphaxad, the son of Shem, the son of Noah, the son of Lamech, the son of Methuselah, the son of Enoch, the son of Jared, the son of Mahalaleel, the son of Cainan, the son of Enos, the son of Seth, the son of Adam, the son of God.

Luke's account of Christ's Baptism is very short; the other Gospels give us more details. But there is a reason why Luke inserts the Lord's genealogy just at this place, immediately after His Baptism. This account of Jesus' Baptism stresses chiefly the testimony of God the Father Himself to His deity: "You are My beloved Son; with You I am well pleased." He is "very God of very God." Then Luke proves He is also "very man," by citing the names of the fathers "according to the flesh, is the Christ" (Romans 9:5). And as such, as Son of God and Son of Man, Jesus is our Redeemer. He became man so He could be our substitute and could suffer and die for us. But no mere man could bear the sins of all mankind and suffer the punishment due to those sins, nor could he offer a sacrifice of infinite value, worth more than anything we could do. So here is God's own accreditation of Jesus as our divine Redeemer. Father and Son and Holy Ghost had planned our redemption in eternity, and now they unite in carrying it out to its completion. Our redemption is assured and heaven is opened to us. In Christ, God acknowledges us as His children, and if we are His children, then we are heirs of His eternal riches (Romans 8:17).

John the Baptist testifies (John 1:29–34) that God's testimony at the Baptism of Jesus was proof that Jesus of Nazareth was the Son of God, the Redeemer promised by God throughout four thousand years of prophecy. And here in the divine record that cannot be denied or recalled, we have the firm assurance that Jesus is the God-man, the Savior indeed, the very Savior we need.

Prayer

O Lord God, heavenly Father, we give You thanks that of Your great goodness and mercy You sent Your only-begotten Son to become incarnate and to redeem us from sin and everlasting death. We ask You to enlighten our hearts by Your Holy Spirit that we may evermore yield You sincere thanks for Your grace and may comfort ourselves with the same in all time of tribulation and temptation; through the same Jesus Christ, Your Son, our Lord. Amen.

THE OPENING BATTLE
Luke 4:1–13

THE fall of Adam had chiefly two fatal consequences for us, his children. Our first parents, in sinning, lost the image of God, that perfect righteousness and holiness in which they had been created. And they fell into the power of the devil; they could no longer withstand and overcome the temptation of Satan. Now, what Adam did not have, he could not bequeath to his children; therefore, to this day we are born not in the image of God but as sinful and servants of the devil. When God in His love and mercy sent us a Savior, His work again was chiefly twofold: He had to save us from sin and its punishment, death (which He did by His holy life and by His innocent suffering and death). And He had to redeem us from the power of the devil; He had to defeat this "strong man, fully armed" (Luke 11:21) and make it possible for us to overcome him. That meant battle against the tempter; and this battle began as soon as Jesus entered upon His public ministry. The opening battle scene is described in our text.

The Temptation of Jesus

And Jesus, full of the Holy Spirit, returned from the Jordan and was led by the Spirit in the wilderness for forty days, being tempted by the devil. And He ate nothing during those days. And when they were ended, He was hungry. The devil said to Him, "If You are the Son of God, command this stone to become bread." And Jesus answered him, "It is written, 'Man shall not live by bread alone.' " And the devil took Him up and showed Him all the kingdoms of the world in a moment of time, and said to Him, "To You I will give all this authority and their glory, for it has been delivered to me, and I give it to whom I will. If You, then, will worship me, it will all be Yours." And Jesus answered him, "It is written,

> " 'You shall worship the Lord your God,
>   and Him only shall you serve.' "

And he took Him to Jerusalem and set Him on the pinnacle of the temple and said to Him, "If You are the Son of God, throw Yourself down from here, for it is written,

> " 'He will command His angels concerning you,
>   to guard you,'

and

> " 'On their hands they will bear you up,
>   lest you strike your foot against a stone.' "

And Jesus answered him, "It is said, 'You shall not put the Lord your God to the test.' " And when the devil had ended every temptation, he departed from Him until an opportune time.

At the very moment Satan was cast out of heaven, he became the tempter. His sole purpose is seducing men into sin. And the great purpose for which the Son of God was manifested was to destroy the works of the devil (1 John 3:8). It was for the very purpose of meeting the devil in open battle that the Holy Spirit led Jesus into the wilderness. He was to undo the harm that had come to men at the hand of the tempter. But Satan came with a deliberate purpose too—to seduce the Second Adam as he had seduced the first and, therefore, sabotage the entire work of redemption from the very beginning. If the devil had succeeded in his evil design, the human race would have remained in his power for all eternity.

He didn't, of course. The Son of God defeated the tempter. But He did not kill him or rob him of all his power. To this day, "the devil prowls around like a roaring lion, seeking someone to devour" (1 Peter 5:8). In His wise design, God allows him to approach us with his seductions. But we are not alone in the wilderness. He gives us the same weapon He used to defeat the tempter—His Word. And God stands by our side in His Word with His almighty help. Moreover, in the temptation of Jesus, we have examples of the way the devil tempts us to this day, so that, forewarned, we can be forearmed.

The hard task of breadwinning brings with it many a suggestion of dishonest ways of gaining wealth. Satan tries to make us impatient and encourages us to help ourselves in wrong and sinful ways instead of waiting until God, in His good time, fulfills His promises. He tempts us to leave the straight path of duty, faithfulness, loyalty to truth, and conviction so we can gain stature or some temporal success. In every case, let us remember that God arms us well. "One little word can fell him" *(LSB* 656:3). Clad in the full armor of God, with the shield of faith, the helmet of salvation, and the sword of the Spirit (which is the Word of God), we are always able to stand against the wiles of the devil. And when God, at times, takes us into the solitude of the wilderness, when by sickness or other circumstances He removes us from the business of everyday life, shuts the door behind us, and draws the curtains closed, then, if we are wise, we will use that time for spiritual renewal and strengthening. And may we always remember that our great High Priest, who was tempted just like we are, yet was without sin, can easily be moved by our weakness. Let us come boldly to His throne of grace with our prayers that we may receive mercy and find grace to help in time of need (Hebrews 4:15–16).

Prayer

O Lord Jesus Christ, who fasted forty days and forty nights in the wilderness and overcame all the temptations of the devil, we thank You that out of love for us You were in all ways tempted, as we are. Yet You remained without sin and, as our merciful High Priest, can be moved with compassion for our weaknesses. We pray that You give us grace to steadfastly resist the allurements of sin, that the desires of our flesh are subdued to the Spirit, so we may ever obey Your godly leadings in righteousness and true holiness, to Your honor and glory. Amen.

THE PROPHET IN HIS OWN COUNTRY

Luke 4:14–30

"HE came to His own, and His own people did not receive Him," so St. John describes the reception given to the long-promised Savior by His own nation (John 1:11). Referring to the inestimable privileges enjoyed by the Jews, St. Paul asks, "Then what advantage has the Jew?" (Romans 3:1). He answers, "Much in every way. To begin with, the Jews were entrusted with the oracles of God" (v. 2). They alone, of all the people of the world, had the revelation of God's holy will. They alone knew of the coming of Messiah and His blessed work. Through thousands of years, they looked for Him. Their worship services and all the sacrifices in the temple were symbols of Him and His work. Then He came to them, His own people, and they rejected Him. Today's text speaks of Christ's first public appearance in His hometown, Nazareth.

Jesus Begins His Ministry

And Jesus returned in the power of the Spirit to Galilee, and a report about Him went out through all the surrounding country. And He taught in their synagogues, being glorified by all.

Jesus Rejected at Nazareth

And He came to Nazareth, where He had been brought up. And as was His custom, He went to the synagogue on the Sabbath day, and He stood up to read. And the scroll of the prophet Isaiah was given to Him. He unrolled the scroll and found the place where it was written,

"The Spirit of the Lord is upon me,
  because He has anointed me
to proclaim good news to the poor.

He has sent me to proclaim liberty to the captives
and recovering of sight to the blind,
to set at liberty those who are oppressed,
to proclaim the year of the Lord's favor."

And He rolled up the scroll and gave it back to the attendant and sat down. And the eyes of all in the synagogue were fixed on Him. And He began to say to them, "Today this Scripture has been fulfilled in your hearing." And all spoke well of Him and marveled at the gracious words that were coming from His mouth. And they said, "Is not this Joseph's son?" And He said to them, "Doubtless you will quote to Me this proverb, 'Physician, heal yourself.' What we have heard you did at Capernaum, do here in your hometown as well." And He said, "Truly, I say to you, no prophet is acceptable in his hometown. But in truth, I tell you, there were many widows in Israel in the days of Elijah, when the heavens were shut up three years and six months, and a great famine came over all the land, and Elijah was sent to none of them but only to Zarephath, in the land of Sidon, to a woman who was a widow. And there were many lepers in Israel in the time of the prophet Elisha, and none of them was cleansed, but only Naaman the Syrian." When they heard these things, all in the synagogue were filled with wrath. And they rose up and drove Him out of the town and brought Him to the brow of the hill on which their town was built, so that they could throw Him down the cliff. But passing through their midst, He went away.

Especially noteworthy in this account is the sentence, "And as was His custom, He went to the synagogue on the Sabbath day." Jesus worshiped regularly in God's house, and He took an active part in the service. An example for us. Not only an example, however. In His human nature, Jesus felt the need of the inspiration, the comfort, and the strength that comes from worship of God, especially worship together with other children of God. Do not we need this infinitely more than He?

But the main point of this text is the Lord's sermon and its reception. He selected a portion of Isaiah in which the prophet describes the gracious work of the Messiah; then He applied it to Himself: "Today this Scripture has been fulfilled in your hearing." On this subject, Jesus spoke at length, revealing the purpose of His coming—to seek and to save those who were lost. The assembled people wondered at His gracious words; they admired the way He spoke. But then it dawned on them what Jesus' words meant for them: were they the poor who needed good tidings; the brokenhearted, sin-sick souls who needed healing; the captives of sin and the devil whom He was to deliver? And did He say that they were blind and did not recognize their need and its help, that they were bruised and helpless in their affliction? That hit at their national vice: self-righteousness. They grew indignant and challenged His Messiahship: wasn't He the son of Joseph, the carpenter? And to discredit Him, they dragged in a childish objection: Were not they, the people of His hometown, just as good as the people of Capernaum? Why hadn't He performed miracles for them? In response, Jesus shows them the other side of the Gospel: it is preached for salvation, but whoever does not receive it in humble confession of sin and his own helplessness signs his own death warrant.

Were these Nazarenes sinners above all others? Luther once called the Gospel a cause of tumult. Oh, men may admire the gracious words until they grasp the implication that they are the lost, the poor, the blind, the sick captives that Jesus came to save. Then their prideful hearts rebel, and while they can no longer harm Him physically, they cast Him out of their heart.

St. Paul later pronounced the fulfillment of Christ's threat on the Jews: "It was necessary that the word of God be spoken first to you. Since you thrust it aside and judge yourselves unworthy of eternal life, behold, we are turning to the Gentiles" (Acts 13:46). The warning still applies. This is the time of the Lord and we are the people of God. He comes to save us. His Gospel is preached to us for our salvation. But if we reject it, the blessing will pass us by and, in the end, the Gospel itself will be taken from us and given to others who will welcome its message.

Prayer

O Lord, help us to overcome the pride of our own heart, to kneel in humble penitence and confession of our sin and spiritual helplessness lest we fall underYour wrath and condemnation. Lead us evermore to rely wholly and alone on the merits of Your Son, Jesus Christ, our Savior, that when He returns in the clouds of heaven to judge all men, we may be found His own and be with Him in His kingdom forever. For Jesus' sake we ask it. Amen.

THE GREAT PHYSICIAN
Luke 4:31–44

NAZARETH did not know the day of her visitation; consequently, she cast out the Savior. And the day her people tried to throw Jesus off that high cliff was, as far as we know, the last time He ever came to Nazareth. He left the highlands of Galilee and went to Capernaum, a city on the shores of the Sea of Galilee. It was the center of trade for all of Palestine, located on "the way of the sea" (Isaiah 9:1), the great caravan road that led from the East to the Mediterranean. It was well suited to be the center of His ministry. And reports of His preaching and His miracles were carried not only throughout the Holy Land but into Gentile lands as well. Capernaum was, moreover, the home of Peter and of the Lord's early disciples. So Jesus chose this city as "His own city" (Matthew 9:1), where so many of His great deeds were done that later He could say, "And you, Capernaum, will you be exalted to heaven? You will be brought down to Hades. For if the mighty works done in you had been done in Sodom, it would have remained until this day" (Matthew 11:23). Today's reading describes a typical day of the Lord's ministry in Capernaum.

Jesus Heals a Man with an Unclean Demon

And He went down to Capernaum, a city of Galilee. And He was teaching them on the Sabbath, and they were astonished at His teaching, for His word possessed authority. And in the synagogue there was a man who had the spirit of an unclean demon, and he cried out with a loud voice, "Ha! What have You to do with us, Jesus of Nazareth? Have You come to destroy us? I know who You are—the Holy One of God." But Jesus rebuked him, saying, "Be silent and come out of him!" And when the demon had thrown him down in their midst, he came out of him, having done him no harm. And they were all amazed and said to one another, "What is this word? For with authority and power He commands the unclean spirits, and they come out!" And reports about Him went out into every place in the surrounding region.

Jesus Heals Many

And He arose and left the synagogue and entered Simon's house. Now Simon's mother-in-law was ill with a high fever, and they appealed to Him on her behalf. And He stood over her and rebuked the fever, and it left her, and immediately she rose and began to serve them.

Now when the sun was setting, all those who had any who were sick with various diseases brought them to Him, and He laid His hands on every one of them and healed them. And demons also came out of many, crying, "You are the Son of God!" But He rebuked them and would not allow them to speak, because they knew that He was the Christ.

Jesus Preaches in Synagogues

And when it was day, He departed and went into a desolate place. And the people sought Him and came to Him, and would have kept Him from leaving them, but He said to them,

"I must preach the good news of the kingdom of God to the other towns as well; for I was sent for this purpose." And He was preaching in the synagogues of Judea.

When Matthew relates this same story, he speaks of the healing of the sick as fulfillment of Isaiah 53:4: " 'He took our illnesses and bore our diseases' " (Matthew 8:17). Jesus spoke of Himself as the Physician (Luke 5:31) of the soul, who calls sinners to repentance. And so He called on those He healed to recognize that their real trouble lay deeper, that their real illness was sin (e.g., the man who was paralyzed with palsy [Matthew 9:2]). We may be sure that He did this when He spoke to those afflicted with diverse diseases who were brought to Him that day in Capernaum.

Sin delivers us into the power of the devil. To be sure, this man "who had the spirit of an unclean demon" was an extreme case. The devil had taken control of the man's body, made him his slave, and used his voice as his own to utter unholy words. But it is true of all of us that we are by nature in the power of the devil, because we are the servants of sin. And Jesus, who came to destroy the works of the devil, is first of all the Physician of the soul, the Savior from sin. Disease and all the ills to which flesh is heir are the result of sin; and Jesus is the true Healer of all diseases, those of body and mind as well as those of the soul. When illness strikes us or our loved ones, we should do as the people in Capernaum did: go to Jesus; He will hear and He will heal.

Perhaps, you say, that you have not found Him as accommodating. Your illness was not cured or when you took someone to Jesus, He did not meet you at the city gate or at the grave to raise them from death. Well, the Lord always delivers from the power of the devil and makes our soul safe for eternity, and that is vital. But He has three ways of helping in bodily ailments. He may restore us to health. He often does. Do we always remember that it is He who heals us, and do we thank Him for His blessing, like Peter's mother-in-law did, by arising and serving Him? He may give us strength and courage to bear the cross. Do we always remember that Jesus gives us that strength? Do we always recognize that bearing the cross is our way of serving Him and so wrest a blessing from the very cross? Or He may let us die—and for a Christian, that's the best help of all! Jesus has told us, "I go to prepare a place for you . . . that where I am you may be also" (John 14:2–3). And in that last hour, He takes us by the hand and says, Come, for all things are now ready. And we shall rise and worship Him.

Jesus is the Great Physician; He always helps—perhaps not in the way we desire or expect, but always in His way, and that is the best way.

Prayer

Blessed Lord Jesus, who in the days of Your earthly life had compassion on all those who suffered under the blows and the fiery darts of the evil one, we pray that You stand by us with Your power when Satan assails us in body, mind, or soul. Help us to bear the cross, to patiently await the time of Your help, and when that time comes, deliver us from all the evil that our sins have brought upon us, that we may serve You in joy and gratitude, here in time and hereafter in eternity. We ask it for Your love's sake. Amen.

CHRIST'S FISHERMEN
Luke 5:1–11

ALL of Jesus' miracles were proof of His divine power and, therefore, credentials of His divine mission. To the Jews He said, "If I am not doing the works of My Father, then do not believe Me; but if I do them, even though you do not believe Me, believe the works" (John 10:37–38). But many of His miracles were, at the same time, symbols and illustrations of divine truths. The cleansing of lepers was a symbol of the cleansing of sinners from the spiritual leprosy of sin; the stilling of the storm on Galilee a symbol of the stilling of all the storms that rage against His Church; the raising of Lazarus a symbol of the spiritual raising of the sinner to a new spiritual life. In some cases, the Lord Himself stamps the miracle with a symbolic purpose. It is so in the story before us today, Peter's wonderful catch of fish.

Jesus Calls the First Disciples

On one occasion, while the crowd was pressing in on Him to hear the word of God, He was standing by the lake of Gennesaret, and He saw two boats by the lake, but the fishermen had gone out of them and were washing their nets. Getting into one of the boats, which was Simon's, He asked him to put out a little from the land. And He sat down and taught the people from the boat. And when He had finished speaking, He said to Simon, "Put out into the deep and let down your nets for a catch." And Simon answered, "Master, we toiled all night and took nothing! But at Your word I will let down the nets." And when they had done this, they enclosed a large number of fish, and their nets were breaking. They signaled to their partners in the other boat to come and help them. And they came and filled both the boats, so that they began to sink. But when Simon Peter saw it, he fell down at Jesus' knees, saying, "Depart from me, for I am a sinful man, O Lord." For he and all who were with him were astonished at the catch of fish that they had taken, and so also were James and John, sons of Zebedee, who were partners with Simon. And Jesus said to Simon, "Do not be afraid; from now on you will be catching men." And when they had brought their boats to land, they left everything and followed Him.

Usually the Lord performed miracles when someone in need cried out for help. Not so here. We would be at a loss to account for the why of this miracle were it not for what Jesus said to Peter: "from now on you will be catching men." That puts the whole story in a different light. We see that the Lord had intended this miracle for their instruction. In the miracle that preceded this command, the

Lord had given them a picture of the work for which He was calling them. They were fishermen, so they knew what His call implied.
Fishing as a profession was hard work; and they knew what their job
was to be: not to sit on thrones and tell others what to do, but to get
out and work. That was one reason why Jesus chose so many of His
apostles from this one group of men. They were used to hard work;
the storms on the sea made the Galilean fishermen hardy.

In a broader sense, that scene on the shores of the sea shows us
the duty of the whole Church, of all of us who are members of the
Church. The Lord's order to Peter is a type of the later command
to "go into all the world and proclaim the gospel to the whole creation" (Mark 16:15). To be sure, not all of us can make that our
life's profession. For one reason, there are not enough boats; some
of us must stay at home to build boats and make nets and raise provisions for those who go out. But the command to launch out into
the deep and let out the net of the Gospel is directed at all of us. So
many of us are satisfied if we have our own church; there we set our
net and return every Sunday morning to see whether the fish have
been wise enough to come into it. But that is not really fishing. Any
boy with a hook and line would know better; he goes where the fish
are. And the sea before us is not, like the Sea of Galilee, twelve miles
long and six miles wide; it's the whole wide world; that is where we
should cast our net.

It isn't easy today to carry out that order. Some of the Lord's
fishermen died on duty; some were burned, some were eaten by
cannibals. What of it? Some who were cannibals are now not only
Christians, but missionaries. There is the Lord's command and His
promise: "let down your nets for a catch." And every sincere disciple of the Lord will say with Peter: "At Your word I will let down
the nets."

How about us? Are we always afraid that the Church in her mission work is getting too far off shore? Do we hamper the work by
not supplying the necessary means? Do we keep the Lord's fishermen so busy trying to keep us safe in the net that they have no time
to go out to catch others? When we examine ourselves, no doubt all

of us will find reason to sink into the dust and say with Peter, "I am a sinful man, O Lord." May we also find courage to say with him, "But at Your word," to forsake all, if need be, and to follow Him.

Prayer

Take, my soul, thy full salvation;
Rise o'er sin and fear and care;
Joy to find in every station,
Something still to do or bear.
Think what Spirit dwells within thee,
What a Father's smile is thine,
What a Savior died to win thee;
Child of heaven, shouldst thou repine?

Haste, then, on from grace to glory,
Armed by faith and winged by prayer;
Heaven's eternal day's before thee,
God's own hand shall guide thee there,
Soon shall close the earthly mission,
Swift shall pass thy pilgrim days,
Hope soon change to glad fruition,
Faith to sight, and prayer to praise. Amen.
(TLH 423:5, 6)

TEACHING THROUGH ADVERSITY
Luke 5:12–26

JESUS taught us to pray: "Our Father who art in heaven." He tells us to regard God as our heavenly Father, to look to Him for all we need for body and soul, for help and relief in all the ills that strike

us. "As a father shows compassion to his children," says the psalmist, "so the LORD shows compassion to those who fear Him" (Psalm
103:13). But the unbeliever says, "Don't talk to me of God as a loving Father. Look around you at what is happening to people. How
can a loving Father do that to His children?" And groaning under
a burden of cross and affliction, a Christian is tempted to have similar thoughts. For example, war not only devastates the earth and
causes the death of millions, but it also leaves a heritage of misery
and suffering for untold millions for many years to come. Accidents,
sickness, famine, and natural disaster bring suffering and heartache to
many. And the Christian heart cries out, "Why does God do this?"
As always, there is instruction in the divine Word. The text before
us should teach us a few lessons.

Jesus Cleanses a Leper

While He was in one of the cities, there came a man full of
leprosy. And when he saw Jesus, he fell on his face and begged
Him, "Lord, if You will, You can make me clean." And Jesus
stretched out His hand and touched him, saying, "I will; be
clean." And immediately the leprosy left him. And He charged
him to tell no one, but "go and show yourself to the priest, and
make an offering for your cleansing, as Moses commanded, for
a proof to them." But now even more the report about Him
went abroad, and great crowds gathered to hear Him and to be
healed of their infirmities. But He would withdraw to desolate
places and pray.

Jesus Heals a Paralytic

On one of those days, as He was teaching, Pharisees and
teachers of the law were sitting there, who had come from
every village of Galilee and Judea and from Jerusalem. And the
power of the Lord was with Him to heal. And behold, some
men were bringing on a bed a man who was paralyzed, and
they were seeking to bring him in and lay him before Jesus,
but finding no way to bring him in, because of the crowd, they
went up on the roof and let him down with his bed through the
tiles into the midst before Jesus. And when He saw their faith,

He said, "Man, your sins are forgiven you." And the scribes and the Pharisees began to question, saying, "Who is this who speaks blasphemies? Who can forgive sins but God alone?" When Jesus perceived their thoughts, He answered them, "Why do you question in your hearts? Which is easier, to say, 'Your sins are forgiven you,' or to say, 'Rise and walk'? But that you may know that the Son of Man has authority on earth to forgive sins"—He said to the man who was paralyzed—"I say to you, rise, pick up your bed and go home." And immediately he rose up before them and picked up what he had been lying on and went home, glorifying God. And amazement seized them all, and they glorified God and were filled with awe, saying, "We have seen extraordinary things today."

Both of these men were driven to Christ by their affliction. Nobody alive today could be in a more desperate situation than this leper. Leprosy is a malady that causes progressive decay of the body: the face and other members of the body are gradually destroyed until the body literally falls to pieces. Note that this man was "full of leprosy"; the disease had reached a very advanced stage. He had heard of Jesus and had come to the conviction that He was the Messiah of God. He fell down, worshiped Him, and called Him Lord. That was faith. Yet, even in His extreme need, He said: "Lord, if You will." That was the fruit of faith.

Similarly, it was the utter hopelessness of his condition that brought the paralytic to Jesus, but it was not merely his physical illness. He also knew he was spiritually sick. During his long illness, he had plenty of time to examine his life, and he had come to the conviction that not his illness, but that which lay behind and caused it—sin—was his real trouble. The omniscient Savior saw that in his heart, and He saw the faith that prompted both the sick man and his bearers to come to Christ.

God allows sickness and other misfortunes to fall on His children. And in every case, it is His voice telling us to stop what we are doing and get our bearings, like a loving parent who sometimes has to curb the desires of his young and impulsive sons and daughters.

In the rush of life, whether pressed by need or impelled by success, we are so apt to forget the essentials, and the Lord in His love for us calls a halt. There is a spiritual palsy, hidden and far more serious and fatal than any physical illness. Often it is manifested in a leprosy that decays more than the body, that destroys the soul for all eternity. The cure of this disease that is sin can be hindered by our stubbornness. So the Lord lays us flat on our back and tells us, "Take a look at yourself."

When God deals with us this way, let us follow His lead: first to recognize our deepest malady and the cure we need more than bodily health or food or drink, forgiveness of our sin; then to recognize the Great Physician of the soul who has earned forgiveness for us with His precious blood. And when we have gone this far under His guidance, we will also see that sickness and other misfortunes may be blessings in disguise. And while we cry to Him for help, knowing that His will toward us is always good and gracious, we will say, "Lord, if You will!" Thy will, not mine, be done!

Prayer

Our Father in heaven, who in Your wisdom, sometimes permits suffering and distress to fall upon us, teach us to know that whatever You ordain is best for us, that all things in the end must work for our good, and that You chasten Your children lest they be condemned with the world. Give us patience in affliction, teach us to pray, grant us humility to submit to Your will. And when Your good time has come, grant us relief from all our troubles here in this life, and in the end in eternity deliver us from all evil, for Jesus' sake. Amen.

18
PHARISEES
AND PUBLICANS
Luke 5:27–39

THERE could hardly be a greater contrast than the one between the Pharisees and the publicans. The Pharisees were the eminently respectable people, the strictest sect among the Jews. So anxious were they to keep the laws given them by Moses that they added countless regulations to them. They did far more than the law demanded lest they inadvertently fail to do enough. The publicans were the collectors of taxes for the Roman government. The Jews who undertook this job for the hated Romans were despised by their countrymen. Publicans were usually men of the basest type, notorious sinners who defrauded the people by charging more than the legal tax and keeping the difference for themselves, thereby getting rich with other people's money. They were put out of the synagogue and became outcasts. No good Jew would have anything to do with them.

We find Jesus dealing with both Pharisees and publicans in this text.

Jesus Calls Levi

After this He went out and saw a tax collector named Levi, sitting at the tax booth. And He said to him, "Follow Me." And leaving everything, he rose and followed Him.

And Levi made Him a great feast in his house, and there was a large company of tax collectors and others reclining at table with them. And the Pharisees and their scribes grumbled at His disciples, saying, "Why do you eat and drink with tax collectors and sinners?" And Jesus answered them, "Those who are well have no need of a physician, but those who are sick. I have not come to call the righteous but sinners to repentance."

A Question about Fasting

And they said to Him, "The disciples of John fast often and offer prayers, and so do the disciples of the Pharisees, but Yours eat and drink." And Jesus said to them, "Can you make wedding guests fast while the bridegroom is with them? The days will come when the bridegroom is taken away from them, and then they will fast in those days." He also told them a parable: "No one tears a piece from a new garment and puts it on an old garment. If he does, he will tear the new, and the piece from the new will not match the old. And no one puts new wine into old wineskins. If he does, the new wine will burst the skins and it will be spilled, and the skins will be destroyed. But new wine must be put into fresh wineskins. And no one after drinking old wine desires new, for he says, 'The old is good.'"

Here St. Luke relates the calling of Levi, who is known to us as Matthew (Matthew 9:9), the writer of the first Gospel. He was a publican, but Jesus made him one of His apostles. To Jesus, no profession in itself is dishonorable. It is not the work a man does in the business of life that makes him worthy or unworthy, but the way in which he does his work. To the Pharisees, though, it was an offense that Jesus chose one of His apostles from this despised class. And when Matthew, out of gratitude, held a feast for Jesus and invited many of his former associates to meet his new Master, the Pharisees' indignation boiled over in open criticism when Jesus attended that feast.

The Lord's answer to them is the whole Gospel in a nutshell. He came to save sinners; therefore, He must go where the sinners are to be found. It doesn't do the one stray sheep any good that the shepherd stays with the ninety-nine who are already safe; the shepherd must seek the lost. It doesn't do sick people any good that the doctor keeps company with those who are well; the doctor has to treat the sick. So by their own judgment, Jesus is where He should be—in the company of sinners. Calling them to repentance is His business.

But there is more in Jesus' answer. In holy irony, He says: if you are whole, if you are righteous, I have nothing for you. He emphasizes this in two parables. It will not do to patch an old garment with a new piece of cloth; the patch will shrink, tear loose, and make the original tear worse; besides the new patch will not match the old. New wine, still fermenting, must not be put into old, worn-out wineskins, for it will burst them. Jesus means that the teachings of the Pharisees and His exclude each other. The two cannot be united. Nor can a part of the old teaching be kept by the person who comes to follow Him. Jesus does not merely refer to the additions they had made to the original law, but to the entire way of life and the way of salvation as they taught it. They taught salvation by man's own works. That's an old worn-out garment, says Jesus, worn out since that sad day in Eden when Adam fell into sin. Discard it for the new one He offers: salvation through His work.

That's the lesson for us: Do not imagine that you can remain a self-righteous Pharisee and still be a Christian. Either you are ill or you are well. You either need a doctor or you don't. If you still think your own life will save you, wholly or in part, then Jesus has nothing for you. He came to save sinners, publicans who have nothing of which they might boast before God.

It is not easy to discard the old. People love the old, smooth, intoxicating wine of self-flattery, and the Lord's way of putting them on a level with publicans and sinners hurts their pride. But there alone lies our salvation.

Prayer

O Lord, help us to overcome our natural pride. Lead us to recognize our true spiritual face in the mirror of Your holy Law, that we might learn to know our sinful state, acknowledge it in true repentance, and accept the help Your grace offers us in the Gospel through the merits of Your Son, our Savior. In Jesus' name we ask it. Amen.

19

THE LORD OF
THE SABBATH
Luke 6:1–11

WHEN Jesus came to be baptized, John objected. He thought *he* should be baptized by Jesus. But Jesus told him, "Let it be so now, for thus it is fitting for us to fulfill all righteousness" (Matthew 3:15). And that was the rule of His entire earthly life. He held Himself bound to fulfill the Law that God had given to His people. From His first visit to the temple to His last Passover, He obeyed perfectly the Law of God. And He directed His followers to do so as well; the Sermon on the Mount gives sufficient evidence of that. But He did not feel bound to keep all that the teachers of Israel at that time taught as God's Law. He rejected the many regulations they had added to the Law as mere rules from men. Particularly had they surrounded the Sabbath command with a large number of additional injunctions, and it is perhaps natural that the first clash between the Pharisees and Jesus came on the keeping of the Sabbath. Of this we read in the text:

Jesus Is Lord of the Sabbath

On a Sabbath, while He was going through the grainfields, His disciples plucked and ate some heads of grain, rubbing them in their hands. But some of the Pharisees said, "Why are you doing what is not lawful to do on the Sabbath?" And Jesus answered them, "Have you not read what David did when he was hungry, he and those who were with him: how he entered the house of God and took and ate the bread of the Presence, which is not lawful for any but the priests to eat, and also gave it to those with him?" And He said to them, "The Son of Man is lord of the Sabbath."

A Man with a Withered Hand

On another Sabbath, He entered the synagogue and was teaching, and a man was there whose right hand was withered. And the scribes and the Pharisees watched Him, to see whether He would heal on the Sabbath, so that they might find a reason to accuse Him. But He knew their thoughts, and He said to the man with the withered hand, "Come and stand here." And He rose and stood there. And Jesus said to them, "I ask you, is it lawful on the Sabbath to do good or to do harm, to save life or to destroy it?" And after looking around at them all He said to him, "Stretch out your hand." And he did so, and his hand was restored. But they were filled with fury and discussed with one another what they might do to Jesus.

The Pharisees had added thirty-nine regulations to the Sabbath commandment of Moses, as well as a vast number of smaller rules. One of the regulations of Moses was that reaping and threshing of grain was forbidden on the Sabbath, and from this the Pharisees argued that plucking the grain was reaping, and rubbing it in their hands was threshing. The followers of two great teachers even kept up a controversy as to whether the comforting of the sick was allowed on the Sabbath day. The exact distance was prescribed that a man might walk on a Sabbath without breaking the Law.

Jesus knew the Pharisees were spying on Him, and when they confronted His disciples, He answered for them. But in His reply, He does not attempt to discuss their rules with them; He goes back to the original Law and God's purpose in giving it. From David's example, Jesus deduces the truth that it is no sin to break the letter of the Sabbath commandment in an emergency. Then He forces them, by their silence, to admit that it is lawful to do good on the Sabbath.

God's Law was never meant to be a burden to man, but to confer a blessing. So the Sabbath commandment was to provide rest from daily labor and time for spiritual needs, for study of God's Word and will, and practicing it in deed and action. "The Sabbath was made for man," Jesus told the Pharisees (Mark 2:27), "not man for the Sabbath."

The requirements of the Old Testament Sabbath law have been repealed in the New Testament. But God still wants us to set aside time for contemplation and study of His Word, although God leaves it to us to decide what time of day and what day of the week we set aside for that purpose. Jesus Himself makes it clear what He expects of us on the day of rest; and He is the Lord of the Sabbath. He went to the synagogue on that day when the children of God met to hear His Word; and He performed works of love on that day. He shows by His example that neither they who insist on a mere mechanical observance of all kinds of external rites, often going far beyond the Word of God, nor they who despise all observance of the day are fulfilling God's command.

And that confronts us with this question: How are we observing the day that Christians by common consent have made the day of rest? Like the Pharisees, who were satisfied with a mere outward observance of the day? As a matter of convenience, resting on that day? As a matter of habit, going to church on that day? Or are we looking for the blessing that the Lord of the Sabbath intended to confer on His people by giving that commandment? The blessing is there; it is there for us unless we willfully deprive ourselves of it.

Prayer

Lord God, heavenly Father, we pray that You govern and guide us by Your Holy Spirit that we may with all our heart hear and receive Your Word and truly sanctify the Lord's Day, to the end that we may be sanctified by Your Word, that we may put all our confidence and hope in Jesus Christ, Your Son, amend our lives in accordance with Your Word, and avoid all offense, until by grace for Christ's sake we shall enter into that eternal rest that remains to the people of God and be saved forever. Amen.

FOUNDING OF THE KINGDOM
Luke 6:12–19

THE Son of God came into the world to seek and save what was lost. To accomplish this, it was necessary first of all to redeem lost mankind. This He did with His holy precious blood and with His innocent suffering and death. But this alone was not enough. The accomplished redemption had to be brought to man and made his own. What you do not know cannot do you any good. The Gospel of redemption had to be made known to lost sinners. Jesus Himself preached this Gospel while He was on earth. At the same time, He made provision for the future when He would no longer walk the earth in the flesh. He established His kingdom on earth, His Church, for the express purpose of spreading the Good News, giving to each and every person the command to "go into all the world and proclaim the gospel to the whole creation" (Mark 16:15). Today's Scripture reading tells us of the first steps Jesus took to organize His kingdom among men.

The Twelve Apostles

In these days He went out to the mountain to pray, and all night he continued in prayer to God. And when day came, He called His disciples and chose from them twelve, whom He named apostles: Simon, whom He named Peter, and Andrew His brother, and James and John, and Philip, and Bartholomew, and Matthew, and Thomas, and James the son of Alphaeus, and Simon who was called the Zealot, and Judas the son of James, and Judas Iscariot, who became a traitor.

Jesus Ministers to a Great Multitude

And He came down with them and stood on a level place, with a great crowd of His disciples and a great multitude of people from all Judea and Jerusalem and the seacoast of Tyre and Sidon, who came to hear Him and to be healed of their diseases. And those who were troubled with unclean spirits were cured. And all the crowd sought to touch Him, for power came out from Him and healed them all.

Jesus here appoints His ambassadors, the men who are to be in charge of His work after He has withdrawn His visible presence. They are to represent Him on earth and see to it that the work of maintaining and spreading His kingdom among men continues until He returns. He chose twelve men, all different. Membership in the Kingdom is not restricted to one or a few classes or groups of people because the Lord has work in His kingdom for all kinds of people. He, the omniscient Son of God, who knows the very heart of man, chooses them. On His resurrection day, He reminded them of this day on the mountainside: "As the Father has sent Me, even so I am sending you" (John 20:21).

Jesus called them "so that they might be with Him" (Mark 3:14). He did not send them out to preach to all the world without instruction. He kept them with Him for a long time so they could hear His preaching and witness His great miracles, His last suffering, His resurrection, and His ascension. He patiently and diligently taught them and carefully prepared them for their future vocation. What a wonderful training that was for them: three years of day-to-day association with Him; three years of study with the Son of God as their teacher! It was a most solemn act when Jesus appointed His first messengers to sinful mankind; how solemn He indicated when He spent the preceding night in prayer.

So, although this brief text records little more than the appointment of the apostles, it carries a number of important lessons for us. To this day, the Lord gives to His Church teachers and leaders for the work He has designed for her. He, the Lord Himself, chooses them, although He does so now through the voice of the Church. Do we always remember that? When we hear our pastors preach the Word, do we receive it "not as the word of men but as what it really is, the word of God" (1 Thessalonians 2:13)? Do we let our personal likes and dislikes of the men who proclaim the Word interfere with the reception of their message? Above all, do we follow the example of our divine Master in praying for them? What a rebuke His example is for our listless, oft forgotten prayers! Would there not be more abundant fruits of their work, more blessing of their message on our own hearts and others, more results of our mission work, if there were more diligent following of Christ's example and the admonition of His apostles: "brothers, pray for us, that the word of the Lord may speed ahead and be honored, as happened among you" (2 Thessalonians 3:1)?

Prayer

Almighty and gracious God, the Father of our Lord Jesus Christ, who commanded us to pray that You send workers to Your harvest, of Your infinite mercy give us true teachers and ministers of Your Word and put Your saving Gospel in their hearts and on their lips, that they may truly fulfill Your command and preach nothing contrary to Your holy Word, that we, being warned, instructed, nurtured, comforted, and strengthened by Your heavenly Word, may do those things that are pleasing to You and profitable to us; through Jesus Christ, Your Son, our Lord. Amen

21
THE CITIZENS OF THE KINGDOM
Luke 6:20–26

JESUS had appointed His apostles. They were to be His representatives on earth, to spread the Gospel of His kingdom, to train others who were to continue His work until the most remote corners of the earth would resound with the Gospel and everywhere people would gather under the cross and praise Him as their Savior and King.

After He selected His apostles, Jesus immediately began to train them. The rest of this chapter contains a summary of the Sermon on the Mount, recorded at greater length in Matthew (chs. 5, 6, and 7). The Lord's purpose in this sermon is not to tell the people how they may become His disciples; His aim is to tell those who are already His disciples how to live. Let us hear the first part of this sermon.

The Beatitudes

And He lifted up His eyes on His disciples, and said:

"Blessed are you who are poor, for yours is the kingdom of God.
"Blessed are you who are hungry now, for you shall be satisfied.
"Blessed are you who weep now, for you shall laugh.
"Blessed are you when people hate you and when they exclude you and revile you and spurn your name as evil, on account of the Son of Man! Rejoice in that day, and leap for joy, for behold, your reward is great in heaven; for so their fathers did to the prophets.

Jesus Pronounces Woes

"But woe to you who are rich, for you have received your consolation.
"Woe to you who are full now, for you shall be hungry.
"Woe to you who laugh now, for you shall mourn and weep.
"Woe to you, when all people speak well of you, for so their fathers did to the false prophets."

This description of the citizens of the Kingdom should be of the utmost interest to us as we compare it to ourselves.

"Blessed are you who are poor." The people to whom Jesus was speaking were mostly poor. The rich, with a few notable exceptions, were His enemies, who joined the multitude that surrounded Him only with hostile intentions. But the Lord is here speaking of the poor in spirit, or the spiritually poor, those who know they have nothing to bring before God, but are poor, miserable sinners.

"Blessed are you who are hungry now." Since they are spiritually poor, they hunger and thirst after righteousness (Matthew 5:6), a righteousness that will avail before God and save them from His wrath.

"Blessed are you who weep now." They weep and mourn over their sins and their inability to lead a life free from evil, although they strive to do so. But the time will come when they will laugh and be glad, when they are fulfilled and satisfied, when they partake of all the riches of the kingdom of God, and so they are blessed, truly blessed.

Such is the disciple of Christ. And this is not merely an ideal, a dream we can never achieve and, therefore, need not attempt. No, this is essential. So Jesus adds a triple woe.

"Woe to you who are rich." Again, most of the rich people in those days were proud, living extravagantly and letting the poor, like Lazarus, pine away at their door, and shortchanging the wages of the poor (James 5:4). But here the Lord speaks of those who think they are spiritually rich and have nothing to fear in God's judgment.

"Woe to you who are full now," who find no fault, nothing lacking in their life, but think themselves perfect.

"Woe to you who laugh now," who find their joy and satisfaction in the things of this world. All these will have a dread awakening in the world to come.

There is, then, a clear line of division between the children of God and the children of the world. Christians live a different life, so obviously that others notice and resent it. They hate them and persecute them in various ways, they call them narrow-minded and bigoted, and they withdraw from them. This is not pleasant, but Christians keep in mind that it is inevitable. It is to them a sign that they are walking the way their Master has gone before them. Woe to them if that line of division is ever removed, if all men speak well of them; this is never a sign that the world is getting better, but is always a sign that they are deteriorating, that they are no longer confessing Christ and living their faith as they should.

Persecution, suffering ill treatment of varied description, is the trademark of true discipleship of Christ. The day is coming when that will change. Until then we bear it, pray to God for courage and strength, and praise Him because we have been found worthy of bearing the name "Christian."

Prayer

Almighty and most merciful God, because we endure sufferings and death with our Lord Jesus Christ before we enter with Him into eternal glory, we ask that You grant us grace at all times to subject ourselves to Your holy will and to continue steadfast in the true faith until the end of our lives. Let us at all times find peace and joy in the blessed hope of the resurrection of the dead and of the glory of the world to come, through Jesus Christ, Your Son, our Lord. Amen.

THE BASIC LAW OF THE KINGDOM
Luke 6:27–38

SINCE the days of St. Paul, the accusation has been raised against those who preach justification by faith without the deeds of the Law that they discourage good works and encourage an ungodly life. This is the meanest slander. All Christians who have found full forgiveness and justification by faith in the Savior do good works as a matter of course. A true Christian must do good works, not because of a legal necessity, but because he cannot do otherwise. It is an essential characteristic of all those who have become members of Christ's kingdom that they love their fellow men and do works of love. So the Lord now, having described the citizens of the Kingdom, speaks of the basic law of the Kingdom.

Love Your Enemies

"But I say to you who hear, Love your enemies, do good to those who hate you, bless those who curse you, pray for those who abuse you. To one who strikes you on the cheek, offer the other also, and from one who takes away your cloak do not withhold your tunic either. Give to everyone who begs from you, and from one who takes away your goods do not demand them back. And as you wish that others would do to you, do so to them.

"If you love those who love you, what benefit is that to you? For even sinners love those who love them. And if you do good to those who do good to you, what benefit is that to you? For even sinners do the same. And if you lend to those from whom you expect to receive, what credit is that to you? Even sinners lend to sinners, to get back the same amount. But love your enemies, and do good, and lend, expecting nothing in return, and your reward will be great, and you will be sons of the Most High, for He is kind to the ungrateful and the evil. Be merciful, even as your Father is merciful.

Judging Others

"Judge not, and you will not be judged; condemn not, and you will not be condemned; forgive, and you will be forgiven; give, and it will be given to you. Good measure, pressed down, shaken together, running over, will be put into your lap. For with the measure you use it will be measured back to you."

In the previous passage, Jesus explained what treatment Christians must expect from their enemies. Now He tells them, and all the world, how Christians respond to such treatment. The Christian weapon to fight hate is love. That is the keynote: love. Love to God above all; that is the source of all good in man. And then love to fellow men. Not only to friends; it's merely human to love those who love us, to do good to those who do good to us, to lend to those what we hope to receive. No, followers of Christ also love their enemies, do good to those who hate them, bless those who curse them, and pray for those who spitefully use them. That's more than human; that's Christian.

The Lord makes His meaning even clearer in the practical examples He cites. Love will show itself in patient endurance of evil, assault, robbery, and persistent begging. The terms the Lord uses are so strong that we instinctively try to soften them. But He means just what He says—true love knows no limits. The world insists on its rights and fights for them; a Christian must not flare up at every affront, but suffer the wrong. True love will influence and determine our general attitude toward our neighbor, showing mercy when he is afflicted, not judging him harshly when evil tongues sully his name, not condemning him, but rather forgiving his faults. All in all, the Christian is to live by the Golden Rule: "And as you wish that others would do to you, do so to them." That is an infallible guide and so easily understood. In every case, all we need ask is, What would I wish for myself?

What a magnificent program! What a paradise the earth would be if we would always use the same yardstick to measure the conduct of our neighbor and ourselves! How this world and the Church would be revolutionized if we would all follow the Lord's directive! But who is able to do so? Not flesh and blood. But true disciples are no longer flesh born of the flesh; they are reborn of the Spirit; they are children of the Highest, and so they take on the character of their Father. True to this ancestry, they strive to follow the example of their Father and of their Lord and Master Jesus Christ. Could there be anything more perfect than the compassion of God for the sinner or the love of the Savior toward others? Is there anything greater than following that example and trying to resemble God Himself?

And how very much the Lord wants us to do so. For that reason, He promises a high reward. Not that we should conduct ourselves this way for the sake of the reward, but God knows our frailty and He knows how many things may happen in a lifetime to dampen our zeal in striving for this high ideal. May we not disappoint Him!

Prayer

*Dear heavenly Father, send us Your Holy Spirit to help us over-
come our flesh with all its passions and vices, to give us patience
to endure and strength to strive ever more to be like Him who
is our perfect example. Forgive us when we forget, and never let
us lose sight of Your presence and Your protection. Go with us
through this life and preserve us in faith and love for the life to
come, when in Your presence we finally reach perfection, for Jesus'
sake. Amen.*

INSTRUCTION AND WARNING FOR WORKERS IN THE KINGDOM

Luke 6:39–49

JESUS outlines a difficult program for His disciples in the Sermon
on the Mount: love your enemies; judge not; condemn not. Is it
possible for flesh and blood to do that? To what are we more prone
than to hit back when we are struck, if possible a little harder than
we receive? to condemn and judge when people act contrary to what
we think is right and proper? This is not just a difficult program; it
is, in fact, an impossible program without help. So the Lord, in the
conclusion of His sermon, tells us how we may be enabled to follow His directions.

He also told them a parable: "Can a blind man lead a blind
man? Will they not both fall into a pit? A disciple is not above
his teacher, but everyone when he is fully trained will be like
his teacher. Why do you see the speck that is in your brother's eye, but do not notice the log that is in your own eye? How
can you say to your brother, 'Brother, let me take out the speck

that is in your eye,' when you yourself do not see the log that is in your own eye? You hypocrite, first take the log out of your own eye, and then you will see clearly to take out the speck that is in your brother's eye.

A Tree and Its Fruit

"For no good tree bears bad fruit, nor again does a bad tree bear good fruit, for each tree is known by its own fruit. For figs are not gathered from thornbushes, nor are grapes picked from a bramble bush. The good person out of the good treasure of his heart produces good, and the evil person out of his evil treasure produces evil, for out of the abundance of the heart his mouth speaks.

Build Your House on the Rock

"Why do you call Me 'Lord, Lord,' and not do what I tell you? Everyone who comes to Me and hears My words and does them, I will show you what he is like: he is like a man building a house, who dug deep and laid the foundation on the rock. And when a flood arose, the stream broke against that house and could not shake it, because it had been well built. But the one who hears and does not do them is like a man who built a house on the ground without a foundation. When the stream broke against it, immediately it fell, and the ruin of that house was great."

The Savior insists on active Christianity. He said it before and He repeats it here. He wants us to be leaders of the blind, to show the true way of life to those who do not know it, to bring them to the only Savior and so to build His kingdom. But only the seeing can lead the blind. You must know before you can teach.

What must you know? First of all your own faults, your own sin. He who would correct the sins and weaknesses of others must have knowledge of his own sinful condition and have diligently worked to change that condition. He who tries to teach others while he himself remains uninformed is a hypocrite.

How can that be accomplished? There's no use treating the symptoms of a disease while the real cause of the ailment is not touched. The seat of all evil in man is his heart. You must be good before you can do good. And so the real core of this text is verse 45: "The good person out of the good treasure of his heart produces good, and the evil person out of his evil treasure produces evil, for out of the abundance of the heart his mouth speaks."

Jesus illustrates this truth in the parable of the good and the corrupt tree. The tree must be good before it can produce good fruit. Yes, there are those who call to the Lord but do not do the things He says. They are hypocrites. There are people who neither say, "Lord, Lord," nor do His will. Others say, "Lord, Lord," and claim to be Christians but do not live accordingly. And there are still others who want to do right and shun wrong but refuse to confess His name and unite with His Church. They all are outside of the kingdom of God. Both must go together: confession and a thorough change of heart, will, and conduct. The Lord does not mention repentance in so many words, but the meaning of His admonition is this: repent and then amend your life.

How can a man make his heart good? The answer is, he can't. "Can the Ethiopian change his skin or the leopard his spots?" (Jeremiah 13:23). But here, too, Jesus offers help. He speaks of the man who hears His saying and does it; he is safe because He builds and rests on Christ's Word. Christ is in that Word; and when He comes and enters the heart, this old sinful house becomes a temple of God. And He keeps it safe against the storms and floods of doubt, temptation, and the fear of death. The day is coming when every other house will fall. The man who builds his spiritual life on ceremonies and rites, on sentiment and emotions, will fail in the end. No matter how sound the superstructure, his foundations are weak; his house will fall, and the ruin of that house will be great. But when heaven and earth pass away, he who does the will of God lives forever.

Prayer

Grant us grace, dear heavenly Father, that we may learn to know our own sinfulness, flee for help to Him who has redeemed us, and find in His Word both pardon for our sin and strength for a new life. And then help us remember our own faults and shortcomings when we deal with others so we are patient and forgiving toward them and so both they and we are led to seek our salvation in the only Savior, Jesus Christ, Your Son, our Lord. Amen.

A GREAT FAITH

Luke 7:1–10

ONCE when Jesus came back to the country where He had spent His childhood, "He marveled because of their unbelief" (Mark 6:6). And as we read of the Lord's experiences with His own countrymen, we, too, marvel. They were the "sons of the kingdom" (Matthew 8:12), God's chosen nation. The Lord God had given them His own revelation, His Word, with all the promises of the Messiah. Surely they were privileged. Paul wrote of "my kinsmen according to the flesh. They are Israelites, and to them belong the adoption, the glory, the covenants, the giving of the law, the worship, and the promises. To them belong the patriarchs, and from their race, according to the flesh, is the Christ who is God over all, blessed forever" (Romans 9:3–5). Yet they were stubborn in their unbelief. No wonder Jesus marveled!

Once more, and only once more in the Bible, are we told that Jesus marveled. This time the object of His marveling was not an Israelite, but a Gentile, and this time He marveled at a great faith. Let us read the story of the Roman centurion.

Jesus Heals a Centurion's Servant

After He had finished all His sayings in the hearing of the people, He entered Capernaum. Now a centurion had a servant who was sick and at the point of death, who was highly valued by him. When the centurion heard about Jesus, he sent to Him elders of the Jews, asking Him to come and heal his servant. And when they came to Jesus, they pleaded with Him earnestly, saying, "He is worthy to have You do this for him, for he loves our nation, and he is the one who built us our synagogue." And Jesus went with them. When He was not far from the house, the centurion sent friends, saying to Him, "Lord, do not trouble Yourself, for I am not worthy to have You come under my roof. Therefore I did not presume to come to You. But say the word, and let my servant be healed. For I too am a man set under authority, with soldiers under me: and I say to one, 'Go,' and he goes; and to another, 'Come,' and he comes; and to my servant, 'Do this,' and he does it." When Jesus heard these things, He marveled at him, and turning to the crowd that followed Him, said, "I tell you, not even in Israel have I found such faith." And when those who had been sent returned to the house, they found the servant well.

Why did Jesus marvel at this man's faith? Most conspicuous was the centurion's humility. There is a strange disagreement in the text. The Jewish elders who bring the centurion's petition to Jesus say, "He is worthy to have You do this for him, for he loves our nation, and he is the one who built us our synagogue." He did not hate the Jews, as so many Romans did, nor was he filled with that overbearing pride and arrogance the Romans usually exhibited toward conquered nations. He was a model ruler. He did not despise the religion of the Jews. On the contrary, he had evidently adopted their faith and worshiped the God of Israel with them. Another fine trait of his is evident in the text: he loved his servant. This is even more praiseworthy, as the servant was a slave, commonly regarded as a mere chattel, on a par with cattle and hardly the equal of a good horse. Yes, the elders seem to be right: he was worthy.

But the centurion himself says: "I am not worthy to have You come under my roof." So initially he did not approach Jesus personally, but sent the elders to plead for him, a Gentile. Additionally, he shows a most remarkable knowledge of Christ. He believes that the Lord need not come under his roof to heal the servant, that He is able to perform the miracle from a distance. And he believes that the Lord will help; what he has previously heard of Him has convinced him of that. He looks for no sign, not even Jesus' presence. His word is enough.

Does not the faith of the centurion put many of us to shame? We come to the Lord in the hour of need. Do we come in the same spirit of this man: Lord, I am not worthy? Do we say with Daniel, "We do not present our pleas before You because of our righteousness, but because of Your great mercy" (Daniel 9:18)? Or is there deep down in our heart a feeling of indignation that such pain and affliction has come upon us, who have always been good Christians, have gone to church and Communion regularly, and have done much work in the Kingdom? Should not the Lord feel a certain obligation to help us when we ask? And what a poor thing our faith often is! We pray because we have been taught it is our duty. We pray, and we doubt. We pray, and we haven't much hope that we are heard. It isn't often that the Lord has reason to marvel at the greatness of our faith!

Let us learn the lesson: the centurion's faith was great in its confession of unworthiness and great in its absolute confidence in the power and mercy of the Lord. Go, and do likewise!

Prayer

Oh, for a faith that will not shrink
Tho' pressed by many a foe;
That will not tremble on the brink
Of poverty or woe;

That will not murmur nor complain
Beneath the chast'ning rod,
But in the hour of grief or pain
Can lean upon its God;

Lord, give us such a faith as this;
And then, whate'er may come,
We'll taste e'en now the hallowed bliss
Of an eternal home. Amen. (TLH *396:1, 2, 6)*

HELP OF
THE HELPLESS

Luke 7:11–17

IT wasn't at all an unusual thing that Luke describes here. He takes us to the city of Nain to meet a funeral procession. That wasn't the first nor the last corpse carried through that city gate; eventually, the people carrying that body would, themselves, be carried out in the same way. Since our first parents listened to the wily serpent, funerals have been the history of men. One generation must always carry another to the grave. We have all gone out to the silent city of the dead to place a new citizen of that realm into his last earthly resting place. That is nothing unusual. And yet this time it was an unusual thing. They started out to carry a dead man to the tomb, but they didn't reach the tomb. At the city gate they met a Man who laid His hand on the bier, and the whole procession stopped right there. They had gone out to bury a dead man; they turned and brought him back alive. We have never been in such a procession. If we had, we would have exclaimed, "Who is this man who calls people back from the dead?" Let us join them at the gates of Nain.

Jesus Raises a Widow's Son

Soon afterward He went to a town called Nain, and His disciples and a great crowd went with Him. As He drew near to the gate of the town, behold, a man who had died was being carried out, the only son of his mother, and she was a widow,

and a considerable crowd from the town was with her. And
when the Lord saw her, He had compassion on her and said to
her, "Do not weep." Then He came up and touched the bier, and
the bearers stood still. And He said, "Young man, I say to you,
arise." And the dead man sat up and began to speak, and Jesus
gave him to his mother. Fear seized them all, and they glorified
God, saying, "A great prophet has arisen among us!" and "God
has visited His people!" And this report about Him spread
through the whole of Judea and all the surrounding country.

It seemed too late when they came to that city gate. While there
was life, that widow hoped; but now it was too late. Already they
could see the dark opening of the tomb. Then Jesus came, and Jesus
is never too late. Jesus is always on time. It may seem to us as though
He is too late. We wait day after day. Hope wanes and we begin to
doubt. But He always comes at the right time—not when we think
it is right but when He knows it is right. The trouble with us is that
our eyes are often so dimmed with tears that we see nothing but our
affliction and think of nothing but our sorrows. If that widow had
only lifted her eyes, she could have seen Him coming afar off; but
she saw nothing but that bier and its sad burden.

"And when the Lord saw her, He had compassion on her."
Truly there was cause for compassion. The dead man was young and
the best years of life would have been ahead of him. But death does
not wait until we are old enough. He was an only son. But death does
not care whether we are an only son or have five brothers. A mother,
though, does care. She was a widow, and with her son's death, she
lost every means of support. There was cause for compassion, and
Jesus shows His compassion when He says, "Do not weep."

And so He is ever compassionate. He left His throne on high
to come into our misery to redeem us from our sin and all its consequences. And still He comes. He sits by our side when we watch
by the sickbed, when we hear the breath come slower and feel the
pulse weaken. And He says, "Do not weep." He meets us when we
carry our dead out through the city gates. And He says, "Do not
weep." You say you did not see Him, did not hear His voice. Are

you sure you looked for Him? Were your ears open and receptive? Or are you so blinded by tears and so hardened by woe that you do not see Him until He lays His hand on the bier and by His power captures your attention?

"Then He came up and touched the bier, and the bearers stood still." That was the touch of divine power! At that city gate was a meeting of two kings: one wants to get out, the other wants to get in. The king of terror, who for ages has ruled on earth and has collected his tribute in every land and city and house; and the King of love, the Prince of life, who is victorious. "He said, 'Young man, I say to you, arise.'" A mighty word! We kneel and worship.

But it shouldn't end there. To be sure, this mother and her son never forgot that day. From that moment forward, they trusted in the Lord and His help and power. And that is the lesson for us. How often have we felt the mighty hand of the Lord! When we thought it was too late and help was impossible, He shamed our weak faith and proved that it is never too late for Him. While we were still worrying, He had already solved the problem and opened a way out of all our troubles. Should not that teach us never again to doubt His power and love?

It's more than two thousand years since that memorable day in Nain, but the story is repeated every day. Jesus Christ is our ever-present help in trouble. And when our last and greatest need comes and we are carried out through the city gate, He will say, "Arise!" and death will be swallowed up in His victory. But He may not meet us at the moment we are carried through the city gate. Jairus's daughter was raised from her death bed and Lazarus after four days in the grave. Be assured, however, that neither of them knew how much time had elapsed. His time is always the right time. When His great day dawns, Jesus will say, "Arise!" and we will sit up and begin to speak and sing His praises, and He will deliver us to our mothers, to all our loved ones. And there will be no more parting.

Prayer
Lord, help us all to that end! Amen.

"ARE YOU THE ONE WHO IS TO COME?"

Luke 7:18–35

ON the threshold of the New Testament stands a remarkable figure—John the Baptist. He attracted the attention of the people in a variety of ways: he lived in the desert, he wore a coat of camel's hair, and he ate locusts and wild honey. This lifestyle was not a bizarre erratic notion; it had a purpose. God wanted John to attract attention because he was sent to prepare the way for the Messiah. This office John zealously fulfilled, although it cost him his freedom and, ultimately, his life.

The last time Luke mentions John, it is to relate that Herod had cast him into prison because he had rebuked Herod about Herodias, his brother Philip's wife, with whom he was living in adultery. But even in prison, John did not forget his great office. This we read in today's passage:

Messengers from John the Baptist

The disciples of John reported all these things to him. And John, calling two of his disciples to him, sent them to the Lord, saying, "Are You the one who is to come, or shall we look for another?" And when the men had come to Him, they said, "John the Baptist has sent us to You, saying, 'Are You the one who is to come, or shall we look for another?' " In that hour He healed many people of diseases and plagues and evil spirits, and on many who were blind He bestowed sight. And He answered them, "Go and tell John what you have seen and heard: the blind receive their sight, the lame walk, lepers are cleansed, and the deaf hear, the dead are raised up, the poor have good news preached to them. And blessed is the one who is not offended by Me."

When John's messengers had gone, Jesus began to speak to the crowds concerning John: "What did you go out into the wilderness to see? A reed shaken by the wind? What then did you go out to see? A man dressed in soft clothing? Behold, those who are dressed in splendid clothing and live in luxury are in kings' courts. What then did you go out to see? A prophet? Yes, I tell you, and more than a prophet. This is he of whom it is written,

" 'Behold, I send My messenger before your face,
who will prepare your way before you.'

I tell you, among those born of women none is greater than John. Yet the one who is least in the kingdom of God is greater than he." (When all the people heard this, and the tax collectors too, they declared God just, having been baptized with the baptism of John, but the Pharisees and the lawyers rejected the purpose of God for themselves, not having been baptized by him.)

"To what then shall I compare the people of this generation, and what
are they like? They are like children sitting in the marketplace and
calling to one another,
" 'We played the flute for you, and you did not dance;
we sang a dirge, and you did not weep.'

For John the Baptist has come eating no bread and drinking no wine, and you say, 'He has a demon.' The Son of Man has come eating and drinking, and you say, 'Look at Him! A glutton and a drunkard, a friend of tax collectors and sinners!' Yet wisdom is justified by all her children."

The Lord Himself explains the object of this text when He says: "Blessed is the one who is not offended by Me." That was the trouble with John's disciples; they were offended because people now came to Jesus and no longer to John (John 3:26). They would not follow their master's direction to leave him and follow Christ. They expected a different messiah, one who would parade in regal pomp and send his lightning to rid his land and his people of their enemies.

John took the only effective way to cure such offense: he sent them to Jesus, and Jesus proved to them that He was indeed the Messiah because His deeds and His preaching corresponded with the image of Him that the prophets had drawn.

People are still offended by Christ. They want a different master. Not that their objections are reasonable. They are like the crabby children in this parable who refuse to play with others; whether they play wedding or they play funeral, they object; they always want something else. Tell them of Jesus' love and forgiveness, and they cannot see why He does not do away with all the wicked people on earth. Tell them of the judgment that is sure to come upon all who despise Him, and they are offended by His intolerance and harshness. Above all, they do not want such a Savior; the Gospel of the crucified is foolishness to them; the idea that they must take salvation as a free gift of His grace without any merit on their part is an insult to their pride.

But why go so far to find people who take offense in Christ! Our own heart often troubles us with doubts about Him and His Word. Why, if He truly loves us, should the cross be such a heavy burden? We hear or read that some learned scientist has found mistakes in the Bible and discredited it, and we are worried.

What should we do? Follow the example of John: send everyone who has concerns, including our own heart, to Christ Himself. Search the Scriptures. That will settle all doubts.

A story is told of a Jewish pawnbroker to whom a widow brought her last possession, a New Testament. He gave her a few pennies and then with a few cronies sat down to read and laugh at that fable of Jesus of Nazareth. But the more they read, the less they laughed; and when they got to Calvary, they stopped altogether. Then the pawnbroker went back and reread the story, this time without laughing. And when he came to Calvary the second time, he stood under the cross with tears. Then he went to a Christian pastor and asked for Baptism in the name of Jesus of Nazareth. Is the story true? We do not know. But this we do know: if ever you doubt the true Messiahship of Jesus Christ, go to Him and ask Him your questions. He will give you the answer.

Prayer

Thrice blessed every one
Who heeds the proclamation
Which John the Baptist brought,
Accepting Christ's salvation.
He who believes this truth
And comes with love unfeigned
Has righteousness and peace
In fullest measure gained.

Oh, grant, Thou Lord of Love,
That we receive, rejoicing,
The word proclaimed by John,
Our true repentance voicing;
That gladly we may walk
Upon our Savior's way
Until we live with Him
In His eternal day. Amen. (TLH 272:4, 5)

THE TWO DEBTORS

Luke 7:36–50

"BLESSED is the one whose transgression is forgiven, whose sin is covered. Blessed is the man against whom the LORD counts no iniquity," sings David in Psalm 32:1–2. Forgiveness of sin is the greatest possible blessing. Nothing on earth exceeds it. And without forgiveness, nothing on earth has real value. "Riches do not profit in the day of wrath," said Solomon (Proverbs 11:4). And the Prophet Ezekiel tells us, "They cast their silver into the streets, and their gold is like an unclean thing. Their silver and gold are not able to deliver them in the day of the wrath of the LORD. They cannot satisfy their hunger or fill their stomachs with it. For it was the stumbling block of their iniquity" (Ezekiel 7:19). More than anything else, therefore, we should seek the assurance that all our iniquities are pardoned. And that, above all, should engage our praises and kindle our love for our Lord that He forgives all our sins and heals all our diseases (Psalm 103:3). This the Lord would have us take to heart as we hear the beautiful story Luke has recorded for us in today's text.

A Sinful Woman Forgiven

One of the Pharisees asked Him to eat with him, and He went into the Pharisee's house and took His place at the table. And behold, a woman of the city, who was a sinner, when she learned that He was reclining at table in the Pharisee's house, brought an alabaster flask of ointment, and standing behind Him at his feet, weeping, she began to wet His feet with her tears and wiped them with the hair of her head and kissed His feet and anointed them with the ointment. Now when the Pharisee who had invited Him saw this, he said to himself, "If this man were a prophet, He would have known who and what sort of woman this is who is touching Him, for she is a sinner." And Jesus answering said to him, "Simon, I have something to say to you." And he answered, "Say it, Teacher."

"A certain moneylender had two debtors. One owed five hundred denarii, and the other fifty. When they could not pay, he cancelled the debt of both. Now which of them will love him more?" Simon answered, "The one, I suppose, for whom he cancelled the larger debt." And He said to him, "You have judged rightly." Then turning toward the woman He said to Simon, "Do you see this woman? I entered your house; you gave Me no water for My feet, but she has wet My feet with her tears and wiped them with her hair. You gave Me no kiss, but from the time I came in she has not ceased to kiss My feet. You did not anoint My head with oil, but she has anointed My feet with ointment. Therefore I tell you, her sins, which are many, are forgiven—for she loved much. But he who is for-given little, loves little." And He said to her, "Your sins are forgiven." Then those who were at table with Him began to say among themselves, "Who is this, who even forgives sins?" And He said to the woman, "Your faith has saved you; go in peace."

"Simon, I have something to say to you," Jesus says to His host, kindly, lovingly. Yet there is a rebuke in the statement: if only you were not so blind, Simon! If only you would recognize the things that bring you peace!

A woman of notoriously bad character had entered Simon's house. She knelt to anoint Jesus, but before she could open her jar, her heart overflowed into her eyes, and the hot tears fell on His feet. Flustered, she tried to undo the results of this accident, but found nothing with which to dry His feet but her hair. And ashamed that she had inflicted an indignity where she had meant an honor, she kissed His feet. The Pharisee was scandalized. He thought that either Jesus did not know she was a bad woman and, if so, He could not be a prophet; or He did know and He was a bad man because He tolerated it.

Simon had not spoken a word, but Jesus responded to him with the parable of the two debtors. And this has a lesson for us too. We all belong to the one or the other class. Some live a respectable life, others fling all caution to the wind and live in sin and vice. God wants us to lead a respectable life; Jesus plainly states that men like Simon owe God less than gross sinners. But the point here is that in the final accounting, neither of the two debtors could pay. We can't even pay the smallest debt to God. And bankrupt is bankrupt, whether the debt is small or great. On the Last Day, it will not be a question of how much or how little we owe: it's all a question of forgiveness.

And now the application. Jesus told Simon that this woman, by her great love, showed that she had found forgiveness of her great debt with God. Simon showed Jesus no love, so he could draw his own conclusion. And Jesus says to us, Where are the evidences of your love for My Word; love for My kingdom, My Church; love for the work of My kingdom, missions at home and abroad?

Simon had invited Jesus to be his guest, and Jesus rewarded him by giving him this loving warning. We ask Jesus to be our guest daily. May the Holy Spirit lead us to take to heart this warning and act accordingly.

Prayer

Gracious Lord and Savior, who by Your holy life and innocent suffering and death has canceled our debt and earned for us God's full and free pardon, teach us to know this and in firm faith hold fast to the assurance that by Your work we are at peace with God and we are His dear children. Keep us from self-righteousness and from ingratitude so we do not lose the treasure You gained for us at so high a price. We ask it for Your mercy's sake. Amen.

THE PARABLE OF THE SOWER
Luke 8:1–15

WE read today one of the well-known parables of Jesus, the parable of the sower. Jesus Himself explained it to His disciples, introducing His explanation with the words: "To you it has been given to know the secrets of the kingdom of God, but for others they are in parables, so that 'seeing they may not see, and hearing they may not understand.'" That sounds as though He did not want everyone to understand and derive benefit from the parable. And that seems to agree with our experience. Some people are quickly moved by the Word of God, some are not moved at all. Some are deeply impressed; aroused from their sin, they rejoice in their salvation and are comforted in distress. Others who hear the same Word remain cold and indifferent. Does the reason lie with God? Doesn't He want them to be saved? Jesus tells this parable to explain why the seed so often brings no fruit.

Women Accompanying Jesus

Soon afterward He went on through cities and villages, proclaiming and bringing the good news of the kingdom of God. And the twelve were with him, and also some women who had been healed of evil spirits and infirmities: Mary, called Magdalene, from whom seven demons had gone out, and Joanna, the wife of Chuza, Herod's household manager, and Susanna, and many others, who provided for them out of their means.

The Parable of the Sower

And when a great crowd was gathering and people from town after town came to Him, He said in a parable: "A sower went out to sow his seed. And as he sowed, some fell along the path and was trampled underfoot, and the birds of the air devoured it. And some fell on the rock, and as it grew up, it withered away, because it had no moisture. And some fell among thorns, and the thorns grew up with it and choked it. And some fell into good soil and grew and yielded a hundredfold." As He said these things, He called out, "He who has ears to hear, let him hear."

The Purpose of the Parables

And when His disciples asked Him what this parable meant, He said, "To you it has been given to know the secrets of the kingdom of God, but for others they are in parables, so that 'seeing they may not see, and hearing they may not understand.' Now the parable is this: The seed is the word of God. The ones along the path are those who have heard; then the devil comes and takes away the word from their hearts, so that they may not believe and be saved. And the ones on the rock are those who, when they hear the word, receive it with joy. But these have no root; they believe for a while, and in time of testing fall away. And as for what fell among the thorns, they are those who hear, but as they go on their way they are choked by the cares and riches and pleasures of life, and their fruit does not mature. As for that in the good soil, they are those who, hearing the word, hold it fast in an honest and good heart, and bear fruit with patience.

We note first that it is not the sower's fault that not all seed grows. He goes to great trouble to spread his seed over all the field, and he wants it to grow. God's seed is the best that can be found; it is the divine Word. To this day, Jesus is the sower, although the Word is proclaimed by men. "The one who hears you hears Me," He says (Luke 10:16). Through His Law, He plows the soil, showing men their sin and the resulting wrath of God. He convinces them that they need a Savior. Then, in the Gospel, He tells them who this Savior is; He takes them to Bethlehem, to Calvary, and to the empty tomb on Easter morn. The seed is the best, and the sower is faithful.

Then why no fruit? The fault lies in the field. A part of the field is hard. The Word doesn't go deeper than a superficial memory and so many things pass over—vain thoughts, sinful thoughts—that the seed is crushed. We do not like the preacher or the way he preaches. We are so busy applying the Word to our neighbor that we forget to apply it to ourselves. Behind it all is the devil. He doesn't care what we think as long as we do not let the Word sink into our heart. And then come the birds, casual acquaintances and companions. With coaxing and mockery, they take the last bit of the seed away.

There is the rocky ground, where the seed is quick to sprout and quick to dry out. There are times when the Word makes a deep impression on our heart—confirmation day, wedding day, times when God's help is obvious—and our heart is aflame for Christ. But other things happen—misfortune, sickness, and death—and we begin to doubt God's love. Or the preacher strikes a sore spot in our heart, and we are indignant and stay away.

And there is the bane of all gardeners: weeds. We hear the Word and believe it and want to follow it. But at the same time other thoughts trouble us: worries about the next day or next month or next year, or the desire to accumulate riches and live beyond the worry for daily bread, or craving the pleasures others enjoy. And weeds always grow faster than the grain; the good seed is choked and forgotten.

It seems as though the Word of Christ faces insurmountable odds. It is almost sure to fail. But praise God, the sower, Jesus, is faithful and the seed is mighty. Every barren field can become fruitful. In fact, even the good ground of which Jesus speaks is not naturally good. No, all hearts are hard and rocky and thorny. But by the grace of God, if they submit to this Word and apply it to their own heart and life, they will become fertile soil.

"He who has ears to hear, let him hear." Every time we hear or read His Word, Jesus the great sower comes to us to make good ground of our heart. But its a dangerous thing to trifle with the Gospel. Pharaoh did that and was lost. The Pharisees did that and were lost. Let us take warning and receive the Lord's Word whenever He brings it to us.

Prayer

Almighty God, Your Word is cast
Like seed into the ground;
Now let the dew of heav'n descend
And righteous fruits abound.

Let not the sly satanic foe
This holy seed remove,
But give it root in ev'ry heart
To bring forth fruits of love.

Let not the world's deceitful cares
The rising plant destroy,
But let it yield a hundredfold
The fruits of peace and joy.

So when the precious seed is sown,
Life-giving grace bestow
That all whose souls the truth receive
Its saving pow'r may know. Amen. (LSB 577)

CHRIST'S MOTHER AND BROTHERS
Luke 8:16–25

THERE is a close connection between the previous passage and this one. In a parable, Jesus had told His disciples that not all who hear the Gospel will accept it and so be saved by it. In fact, a great number of hearers, for various reasons, reject it. Only those who hear it rightly will carry away the blessing. So in this text, He utters a warning to take heed how we hear the Word. He expresses the close relationship between Himself and the true hearers of the Word. And finally, St. Luke tells of an event that mirrors the life of a disciple of Christ.

A Lamp Under a Jar

"No one after lighting a lamp covers it with a jar or puts it under a bed, but puts it on a stand, so that those who enter may see the light. For nothing is hidden that will not be made manifest, nor is anything secret that will not be known and come to light. Take care then how you hear, for to the one who has, more will be given, and from the one who has not, even what he thinks that he has will be taken away."

Jesus' Mother and Brothers

Then His mother and His brothers came to Him, but they could not reach Him because of the crowd. And He was told, "Your mother and Your brothers are standing outside, desiring to see You." But He answered them, "My mother and My brothers are those who hear the word of God and do it."

Jesus Calms a Storm

One day He got into a boat with His disciples, and He said to them, "Let us go across to the other side of the lake." So they set out, and as they sailed He fell asleep. And a windstorm came down on the lake, and they were filling with water and were in danger. And they went and woke Him, saying, "Master, Master, we are perishing!" And He awoke and rebuked the wind and the raging waves, and they ceased, and there was a calm. He said to them, "Where is your faith?" And they were afraid, and they marveled, saying to one another, "Who then is this, that He commands even winds and water, and they obey Him?"

It was, no doubt, one of the tragedies of Christ's human life that His close relatives, with the exception of His mother, did not believe in Him during His lifetime. This is expressly stated of His brothers in John 7:5 (they may have been his true brothers, sons of Mary and Joseph, or perhaps they were His cousins). We are not told what they wanted on this occasion; perhaps they wanted to interfere with His work as they did at another time (Mark 3:21). But we are told that they used their relationship to interrupt Him and tried to persuade Mary to join them. But Jesus took the opportunity to point out that there is a much closer relationship to Him than that of genealogy: "My mother and My brothers are those who hear the word of God and do it."

What a blessed relationship, to be a brother or sister to Christ! It is the fulfillment of a Christian's highest hope and desire, this most intimate communion with our Savior. But it is a communion shared by only those who rightly hear the Word of God, so the Lord warns, "Take care then how you hear." And, remembering the parable of the sower, we understand what He means: those who hear the Word rightly are, therefore, the brothers of Christ who "in an honest and good heart," having heard the Word, keep it, and bring forth fruit with patience.

This blessed relationship also carries with it a stern responsibility of letting the blessed light of the Gospel shine to others. And the man who takes his Christianity seriously will himself gain from it. He will grow in knowledge of the divine Word, in steadfast faith and love, and in patient submission to his Lord's will; he will trust in His final help.

For not even this close companionship with Jesus will turn this world into a paradise. Travelers tell us that the Sea of Galilee is one of the most beautiful spots on earth. But storms quickly rise on that sea, so violent, so sudden and surprising as to render even experienced fishermen helpless. The story St. Luke tells us here is a reflection of the Christian's life. The enemies of our soul will not permit us to go our way calmly and in peace. The Lord knows that, and so He had His apostle tell us "that through many tribulations we must enter the kingdom of God" (Acts 14:22). Even then the Lord intends our good. When the storms roar and the waves rim high, He wants us to do what these disciples did: come to Him in prayer and trust implicitly in His love and in His power and willingness to help.

And to this day, when His time comes, the Lord stretches out His hand and rebukes the wind and the raging waters, and there is a great calm. When in church we hear His Word, when at home in the family circle or alone in our room we read our Bible, when in little or great needs we kneel and pour out the desires of our heart, He comes to us; and while He may lovingly rebuke us because our faith is so weak and we waver in our trust, in the end He calms whatever storm is threatening us and safely takes us to the shore.

Prayer

Jesus, Savior, pilot me
Over life's tempestuous sea;
Unknown waves before me roll,
Hiding rock and treach'rous shoal.
Chart and compass come from Thee.
Jesus, Savior, pilot me.

As a mother stills her child,
Thou canst hush the ocean wild;
Boist'rous waves obey Thy will
When Thou say'st to them, "Be still!"
Wondrous Sovereign of the sea,
Jesus, Savior, pilot me

When at last I near the shore
And the fearful breakers roar
Twixt me and the peaceful rest,
Then, while leaning on Thy breast,
May I hear Thee say to me,
"Fear not, I will pilot thee." Amen. (LSB 715)

THE BLESSING OF AFFLICTION

Luke 8:26–39

WHEN the sisters of Lazarus sent notice to Jesus that their brother was sick, Jesus said, "This illness does not lead to death. It is for the glory of God, so that the Son of God may be glorified through it" (John 11:4). It is one of the answers to the question we humans ask perhaps more frequently than any other: Why? Why must this or that happen? It is so difficult to understand that God could love us and still let cross and affliction rest heavy upon us and at times grind our faces in the dust. Add to this that the devil uses such affliction as a launching pad for his most poisonous darts: "If you really were a child of God," he says, "such things would not happen to you." This text offers help in such times.

Jesus Heals a Man with a Demon

Then they sailed to the country of the Gerasenes, which is opposite Galilee. When Jesus had stepped out on land, there met Him a man from the city who had demons. For a long time he had worn no clothes, and he had not lived in a house but among the tombs. When he saw Jesus, he cried out and fell down before Him and said with a loud voice, "What have You to do with me, Jesus, Son of the Most High God? I beg You, do not torment me." For He had commanded the unclean spirit to come out of the man. (For many a time it had seized him. He was kept under guard and bound with chains and shackles, but he would break the bonds and be driven by the demon into the desert.) Jesus then asked him, "What is your name?" And he said, "Legion," for many demons had entered him. And they begged Him not to command them to depart into the abyss. Now a large herd of pigs was feeding there on the hillside, and they begged Him to let them enter these. So He gave them permission. Then the demons came out of the man and entered the pigs, and the herd rushed down the steep bank into the lake and were drowned.

When the herdsmen saw what had happened, they fled and told it in the city and in the country. Then people went out to see what had happened, and they came to Jesus and found the man from whom the demons had gone, sitting at the feet of Jesus, clothed and in his right mind, and they were afraid. And those who had seen it told them how the demon-possessed man had been healed. Then all the people of the surrounding country of the Gerasenes asked Him to depart from them, for they were seized with great fear. So He got into the boat and returned. The man from whom the demons had gone begged that he might be with Him, but Jesus sent him away, saying, "Return to your home, and declare how much God has done for you." And he went away, proclaiming throughout the whole city how much Jesus had done for him.

This Gerasene man was most terribly afflicted by not only one, but a legion—thousands—of devils who had taken possession of him. His physical suffering was great, but far greater was the mental and spiritual suffering; and that did not cease when the intermittent spells of mania were over. In fact, when in such lucid moments he reflected on his condition, he must have been driven to the verge of despair. The devil had taken firm possession of him and intended to stay there until the man went to his eternal damnation.

But now One who was stronger had come and taken his spoil away. The man was not only freed from the devil's power but he also became a devoted follower of the Son of God and saw no greater joy in life than to go with Him and serve Him. But the Lord denied his request to join Him and His disciples. There was other work for this man to do, work for which his experience had specially prepared him. He could speak from personal experience of the power of Satan and of the dangers that threatened the human soul through his temptations. And he could also speak from personal conviction of the greater power of the Savior and of His almighty help. And the man promptly and gratefully seized the opportunity and became a missionary for Christ.

Does not all this point to one of the reasons why the Lord permits afflictions of many kinds to come upon us? He wants us to realize fully our own weaknesses and turn to Him for help in every need. He wants us to appreciate that help when we receive it. And then He wants us to go home and tell of the great things God has done to us.

How fortunate this man was despite his previous misery; or rather, his misery was a stepping-stone to later happiness. To the Gerasene people, however, their possessions, the result of worldly success, proved a stumbling block. Their hearts were attached to their swine; they valued them higher than this man's soul and well-being. And their loss grieved them so deeply that, rather than risk more loss, they asked Jesus to leave. And Jesus, who had disregarded Peter's cry, "Depart from me" (Luke 5:8), because it was really a plea for help, complied with this request because He saw the people's sin and impenitent spirit. He left, and that was their last chance. He never returned to that region.

"For the Lord disciplines the one He loves, and chastises every son whom He receives." It is for discipline that you have to endure. God is treating you as sons. For what son is there whom his father does not discipline? . . . For the moment all discipline seems painful rather than pleasant, but later it yields the peaceful fruit of righteousness to those who have been trained by it" (Hebrews 12:6–7, 11).

Prayer

Almighty God, You despise not the sighing of the afflicted, nor do You disdain the desire of the sorrowful. Consider, then, our prayer that we bring before You in our great troubles and graciously hear us, that all those evils that the devil or man work against us may be brought to naught and through the counsel of Your bountiful goodness may be destroyed. Therefore, we, being hurt by no temptations, may give thanks to You in Your Church and evermore praise You for the sake of Your beloved Son, Jesus Christ, our Lord and Savior. Amen.

WHAT A FRIEND WE HAVE IN JESUS
Luke 8:40–56

TODAY's text records two of Christ's great miracles. John states the reasons these miracles were recorded, "These are written so that you may believe that Jesus is the Christ, the Son of God, and that by believing you may have life in His name" (John 20:31). At the time, Jesus' miracles were done to convince people that His Word was truth so they might acknowledge Him as their Savior and find life in His name. And that is the lesson for us as well. But this account had another purpose. To every individual comes the day of affliction. He may be ever so proud and self-sufficient, but the day comes when he needs help, and then how great is his misery if he does not know where to find it! Not every man knows, and many are wrecked on the shoals and rocks of bodily and spiritual affliction. There is only One who can help in every need. This lesson assures us of the Friend in life, in death, and after death.

Jesus Heals a Woman and Jairus's Daughter

Now when Jesus returned, the crowd welcomed Him, for they were all waiting for Him. And there came a man named Jairus, who was a ruler of the synagogue. And falling at Jesus' feet, he implored Him to come to his house, for he had an only daughter, about twelve years of age, and she was dying.

As Jesus went, the people pressed around Him. And there was a woman who had had a discharge of blood for twelve years, and though she had spent all her living on physicians, she could not be healed by anyone. She came up behind Him and touched the fringe of His garment, and immediately her discharge of blood ceased. And Jesus said, "Who was it that touched Me?" When all denied it, Peter said, "Master, the crowds surround You and are pressing in on You!" But Jesus said, "Someone touched Me, for I perceive that power has gone out from Me." And when the woman saw that she was not hidden, she came trembling, and falling down before Him declared in the presence of all the people why she had touched Him, and how she had been immediately healed. And He said to her, "Daughter, your faith has made you well; go in peace."

While He was still speaking, someone from the ruler's house came and said, "Your daughter is dead; do not trouble the Teacher any more." But Jesus on hearing this answered him, "Do not fear; only believe, and she will be well." And when He came to the house, He allowed no one to enter with Him, except Peter and John and James, and the father and mother of the child. And all were weeping and mourning for her, but He said, "Do not weep, for she is not dead but sleeping." And they laughed at Him, knowing that she was dead. But taking her by the hand He called, saying, "Child, arise." And her spirit returned, and she got up at once. And He directed that something should be given her to eat. And her parents were amazed, but He charged them to tell no one what had happened.

It was personal crisis that brought Jairus to Jesus. He was no doubt aware of all the other miracles Jesus had performed in Capernaum (Luke 4, 5, and 7), but only when his own daughter was stricken did he come to the Great Healer. Only great personal affliction brought this woman to Jesus. She had gone to many doctors; they had taken all her money. And Mark adds that she "suffered much under many physicians" (Mark 5:26). If we have read about the cures the doctors of that time prescribed for their patients, we can imagine the life the poor woman must have led for those twelve years. Eventually, the doctors would not even try to cure her because she had no money. Then she thought of Jesus.

God uses affliction as a means to drive us to Jesus. Even we who have known Jesus, His power, and His love since childhood are apt to store this knowledge in our mind and not act upon it. While there are other helpers, we forget the true Helper. Only when we have spent our last penny and stand at Wit's End Corner do we make our way to Jesus. What a blessing for us that our God does not lose patience but continues to lead us to see that Jesus is our Great Helper so we go to Him in our need.

When we go, we will find Him. But we must go in faith. The faith of these two was weak; Jairus thought Jesus must come to his house and lay His hand on his child; the woman's faith was mixed with the superstition that touching His garment might cure her. But it doesn't matter whether faith is weak or strong, as long as it is faith that reaches out to Jesus for help. The Lord can make the weak faith grow.

Jesus is our friend in life, in death, and after death. Are we still afraid of the grave? Of this little girl, He said, "She is not dead but sleeping." They that sleep will rise again when the morning dawns. So He said, "This is the will of My Father, that everyone who looks on the Son and believes in Him should have eternal life, and I will raise him up on the last day" (John 6:40). He robs the dark chamber of its gloom by speaking to us. As long as a child hears his mother's voice and knows she is near, he is not afraid in a dark room. And while we hear the Lord speak and know He is near us, who is afraid? So, then, "if we live, we live to the Lord, and if we die, we die to the Lord. So then, whether we live or whether we die, we are the Lord's" (Romans 14:8).

Prayer

I need Thy presence ev'ry passing hour;
What but Thy grace can foil the tempter's pow'r?
Who like Thyself my guide and stay can be?
Through cloud and sunshine, O abide with me.
Hold Thou Thy cross before my closing eyes;
Shine through the gloom, and point me to the skies;
Heav'n's morning breaks, and earth's vain shadows flee;
In life, in death, O Lord, abide with me. Amen. (LSB 878:2, 6)

THE SENDING OF THE TWELVE APOSTLES
Luke 9:1–9

SINCE the miracle of Cana, where He turned water into wine, Jesus had preached and worked chiefly in Galilee. The center of His activity and the place He made His home was Capernaum on the shores of the Sea of Tiberias (Galilee). This Galilean ministry of Jesus was now rapidly coming to a close. What followed was the slow, unrelenting journey to Jerusalem that ended in His death. Outwardly, His Galilean ministry had been a success. Vast crowds had met Him wherever He appeared and welcomed Him with positive enthusiasm; they heard Him gladly. But Jesus was not deceived. The success, He knew, was superficial. There were a few faithful souls, but the crowds were fickle. Today they shouted, "Hosanna!" Tomorrow they would desert Him. They would reappear the next day to shout, "Crucify Him!" So it would ever be. To prepare His followers for this, He told them the parable of the sower (Luke 8:1–15). All that, however, did not deter Him from trying to the very end to save them. So Luke, in this ninth chapter, tells of the last weeks of Christ's activity in Galilee.

Jesus Sends Out the Twelve Apostles

And He called the twelve together and gave them power and authority over all demons and to cure diseases, and He sent them out to proclaim the kingdom of God and to heal. And He said to them, "Take nothing for your journey, no staff, nor bag, nor bread, nor money; and do not have two tunics. And whatever house you enter, stay there, and from there depart. And wherever they do not receive you, when you leave that town shake off the dust from your feet as a testimony against them." And they departed and went through the villages, preaching the Gospel and healing everywhere.

Herod Is Perplexed by Jesus

Now Herod the tetrarch heard about all that was happening, and he was perplexed, because it was said by some that John had been raised from the dead, by some that Elijah had appeared, and by others that one of the prophets of old had risen. Herod said, "John I beheaded, but who is this about whom I hear such things?" And he sought to see Him.

Jesus had traveled all over Galilee and had performed many miracles. Again and again the Gospels report that His fame spread throughout all the land (Matthew 4:24; 9:26; Mark 1:28; Luke 4:14, 37; 5:15). It is hardly possible that there were people in Galilee who had not heard of Jesus and His message. Nevertheless, before He left that region, Jesus sent out the Twelve to preach the kingdom of God. It was not merely a practice trip for the apostles to gain experience for the future under His supervision. The Lord's objective was to send His Gospel into every nook and corner of the land so no one might have the excuse of ignorance.

But more. Soon Jesus was going to His death and the end of His visible activity on earth. But the work of spreading His Church was to go on, and that work would be continued by His apostles and the ministers they would train. Oh, the Lord thought not only of those who lived in His day but also of all sinners throughout all time who needed His redemption. And that means us. He died for all and brought full salvation for all, but all that would have no benefit for us if He had not made provision to have this blessed message brought to our knowledge. The Lord leaves nothing half done. Even before the work of redemption was finished, He established the ministry of the Gospel that extended the invitation to the end of the world: "Come, for everything is now ready" (Luke 14:17). He is the perfect Savior, and calmly we may entrust ourselves to Him, confident that He who began a good work in us will bring it to completion at the day of Jesus Christ (Philippians 1:6).

In the instructions Jesus gave to the Twelve, we find, on the one hand, directions to the preachers of the Gospel, and on the other, indications of what the hearers should do for the preachers. "Those who proclaim the gospel should get their living by the gospel" (1 Corinthians 9:14). They should be completely dependent upon the people they serve. And we who are served by them accordingly are obligated to provide for them. If we do not, we not only show a woeful lack of gratitude for the precious message they bring us from the Lord but we also are guilty of gross disobedience to God's will. The Lord will not overlook this but will call us to account for our neglect.

So the Lord provides for our soul; He has left nothing undone. What is our reaction? There are always some who will receive the Gospel gladly to their salvation. Others, like Herod, will hear it only because their evil conscience fills them with fear and they dare not entirely break with the Church. The Gospel, the message of peace, will serve only to rob them of peace. But that is their fault entirely.

Prayer

Lord Jesus, we thank You for the blessed message of Your Gospel, in which You have come to us to bring us Your redemption and salvation. We pray You, give power to this Word that it may open ever wider the doors of our hearts to receive You and to honor You as our only Savior from our own sinful condition and the well-deserved wrath of God. For Your love's sake we ask it. Amen.

"HE CARES FOR YOU"

Luke 9:10–17

WHEN Jesus had fed the five thousand with five loaves and two fishes, John tells us, He knew "that they were about to come and take Him by force to make Him king" (John 6:15). Such a king they would have welcomed, as they believed he would supply them with all they needed to support them without work or worry on their part. The world would welcome such a king today. But Jesus, on that occasion, eluded the searching multitude. He did not come to be a bread king for an idle people, so they crucified Him. And today He tells the world, "My kingdom is not of this world" (John 18:36). Christians must work as hard as others and often get less for it. So the world will not have Him. And yet Jesus is our Bread King. And that is the lesson in today's reading.

Jesus Feeds the Five Thousand

On their return the apostles told Him all that they had done. And He took them and withdrew apart to a town called Bethsaida. When the crowds learned it, they followed Him, and He welcomed them and spoke to them of the kingdom of God and cured those who had need of healing. Now the day began to wear away, and the twelve came and said to Him, "Send the crowd away to go into the surrounding villages and countryside to find lodging and get provisions, for we are here in a desolate place." But He said to them, "You give them something to eat." They said, "We have no more than five loaves and two fish—unless we are to go and buy food for all these people." For there were about five thousand men. And He said to His disciples, "Have them sit down in groups of about fifty each." And they did so, and had them all sit down. And taking the five loaves and the two fish, He looked up to heaven and said a blessing over them. Then He broke the loaves and gave them to the disciples to set before the crowd. And they all ate and were satisfied. And what was left over was picked up, twelve baskets of broken pieces.

This story is recorded in all four Gospels. In addition, two of the evangelists tell the parallel story of the feeding of the four thousand. The Church has included both texts in the oldest list of Sunday Gospels. Why? Evidently because we need this lesson so greatly. On other occasions, Jesus warned against gluttony, drunkenness, and greed. We, too, need that warning; we need it even more. The other danger is less; we often lack the means. But this is our trouble. We worry. What will we eat? What will we drink? What will we wear? If we have no job, we worry about finding one, and if we have a job, we worry whether it will last and yield enough for us and ours. If we have enough for a week, we worry about next month and next year. If conditions in the land are bad, we think we have reason to worry; and if they are good, we are sure it cannot last—it's the calm before the storm and, oh, how it will blow when it starts! Why is this lesson is so hard to learn?

When Jesus looked on this crowd and told His disciples, "Give them something to eat," they answered, "We have no more than five loaves and two fish—unless we are to go and buy food for all these people." They could think only of the bread and the cash in hand; they left the almighty God, the Son at their side, entirely out of their logic. Despite their experience on this occasion, they did no better when the need arose again. Jesus confronted them with their dullness, "'Why are you discussing the fact that you have no bread? Do you not yet perceive or understand? Are your hearts hardened? Having eyes do you not see, and having ears do you not hear? And do you not remember? When I broke the five loaves for the five thousand, how many baskets full of broken pieces did you take up?' They said to Him, 'Twelve.' 'And the seven for the four thousand, how many baskets full of broken pieces did you take up?' And they said to Him, 'Seven.' And He said to them, 'Do you not yet understand?' " (Mark 8:17–21).

Oh, how often do we give the Lord cause to lose patience with us! But we must learn, just as His disciples had to learn. It took some time and numerous trips into the wilderness before they learned to say with full confidence, "[cast] all your anxieties on Him, because He cares for you" (1 Peter 5:7). "He who did not spare His own Son but gave Him up for us all, how will He not also with Him graciously give us all things?" (Romans 8:32). So we must also learn, and with most of us it takes considerable drilling. That is why He allows need and affliction to enter the individual life and depressions and famines into a land.

Surely the little boy who gave Jesus his five loaves (John 6:9) and saw Him multiply them to feed five thousand never forgot what he saw. No doubt he also told it to many skeptics. And we? Cannot we point to times when we sat down in dull gloom and wasted much precious time in worrying? And that's all the good it did us; it did not advance us one inch. And when the time came, we found that in the meantime the Lord had provided. Perhaps not in the miraculous way He provided for Israel—bread did not rain from heaven and quails did not fly into the pot, but somehow we got food. Our clothes and shoes wore out, but somehow we always got new clothes and new shoes.

How is it that you do not understand, O you of little faith? We are in Christ's school; will we ever graduate? ever learn enough that He can advance us into a higher class? May He never lose patience with us! May He continue to teach us!

Prayer

Almighty God, our heavenly Father, whose mercies are new every morning and who abundantly provides for all our wants of body and soul, although we have in no way deserved Your goodness. Give us, we pray, Your Holy Spirit that we may heartily acknowledge Your merciful goodness toward us, give thanks for all Your benefits, and serve You in willing obedience; through Jesus Christ, Your Son, our Lord. Amen.

34

JESUS FORETELLS HIS PASSION

Luke 9:18–27

THE feeding of the five thousand had aroused a great expectation among the people, and now they wanted to take Jesus by force to make Him king. But the enthusiasm soon died out when Jesus frustrated this plan and withdrew to a remote mountain to be alone. That enthusiasm turned into intense bitterness on the part of many, culminating in numerous attacks (John 6:22-71). To escape the growing opposition that was reaching a dangerous level (for His time was not yet come), Jesus left the populous districts of Galilee and, with His disciples, went north toward Caesarea Philippi. With this text, we enter a new period in Jesus' life. He was about to start on that last journey to Jerusalem. It was time to prepare His disciples for what was to happen in that city. And He did so in this lesson.

Peter Confesses Jesus as the Christ

Now it happened that as He was praying alone, the disciples were with Him. And He asked them, "Who do the crowds say that I am?" And they answered, "John the Baptist. But others say, Elijah, and others, that one of the prophets of old has risen." Then He said to them, "But who do you say that I am?" And Peter answered, "The Christ of God."

Jesus Foretells His Death

And He strictly charged and commanded them to tell this to no one, saying, "The Son of Man must suffer many things and be rejected by the elders and chief priests and scribes, and be killed, and on the third day be raised."

Take Up Your Cross and Follow Jesus

And He said to all, "If anyone would come after Me, let him deny himself and take up his cross daily and follow Me. For whoever would save his life will lose it, but whoever loses his life for My sake will save it. For what does it profit a man if he gains the whole world and loses or forfeits himself? For whoever is ashamed of Me and of My words, of him will the Son of Man be ashamed when He comes in His glory and the glory of the Father and of the holy angels. But I tell you truly, there are some standing here who will not taste death until they see the kingdom of God."

While Jesus had previously alluded to His passion, this was the first time He spoke of it so plainly. Why not earlier? Because the disciples were not ready to hear it. The years they spent with Jesus were the time of their preparation, and He took the normal course in their instruction: He taught them first things first before proceeding to more difficult concepts that presupposed other knowledge. Up to this time, He had, by word and miracle, taught them who He was. That they knew now; they passed their examination. Despite all the false ideas other people had about Him, their confession was that Jesus was "The Christ of God." Now they were ready for the next part of their training: to learn why He came into the world, what His office was. Now, lest they fall into the other error and draw false conclusions from His divinity, He told them there would be no campaign against the Romans, no great restoration of David's kingdom on earth. On the contrary, "The Son of Man must suffer many things and be rejected by the elders and chief priests and scribes, and be killed." He pointed out the necessity of His cross, His suffering and death. God in His wisdom had determined how to redeem sinners, but to accomplish that, His own Son must suffer the cross.

And all who follow Him must bear their cross. That, too, is a "must," although in an altogether different way. There is no atoning power in our cross; Christ's cross is all-sufficient. But the cross is the badge of all followers of Christ. Whoever does not bear that badge is no Christian and has no part in Christ or in what He earned for mankind. "Whoever would save his life will lose it." Peter tried to save his life by avoiding the suffering that threatened him. So a man may save his earthly life with all its joys and pleasure, but lose the eternal life to come, for that belongs only to those who deny themselves and take up their cross daily and follow in the path of the Son of God. They lose this earthly life, it is true. While they live, they live not for themselves but for Him who died for them and rose again. They have given up the control of their life, life itself, its beginning, its entire course, its end, to Christ. It is no longer theirs. Let Him do with it what He pleases. They lose their life. But they find something vastly more precious: the life that has no end; the life in Christ here on earth, the life in glory everlasting after this earth has passed away. They find it; they do not earn it—Christ earned it by His cross. But they find it surely, for Christ gives it as surely as He suffers us to bear our cross after Him.

The Lord reduces it to a simple problem of profit and loss. "What does it profit a man if he gains the whole world and loses or forfeits himself?" Men who strive for the things of this world can gain only a small treasure. But suppose their highest ambitions could be fulfilled; suppose they could gain the whole world, all its wealth and power and pleasure and glory—what would they gain from it if they should lose their soul? The answer is zero. When a man dies, all this slips away, and if he hasn't the true life, he loses all.

Let us glorify Him who chose the cross to gain for us the life that never ends. And then, in love and gratitude, let us take up our cross daily and follow Him.

Prayer

The Son of God goes forth to war
A kingly crown to gain.
His blood-red banner streams afar;
Who follows in His train?
Who best can drink His cup of woe,
Triumphant over pain,
Who patient bears his cross below—
He follows in His train.

A noble army, men and boys,
The matron and the maid,
Around the Savior's throne rejoice,

In robes of light arrayed.
They climbed the steep ascent of heav'n
Through peril, toil, and pain.
O God, to us may grace be giv'n
To follow in their train! Amen. (LSB 661:1, 4)

35

THE TRANSFIGURATION OF CHRIST
Luke 9:28–36

LUKE has brought us to a period in the life of the Lord's disciples when gradually an intense depression was beginning to overshadow the little company. Their Master's enemies were gathering ever closer around Him, determined to crush Him. And more was to come. Not only did Jesus make no efforts to thwart their evil plans but He also actually seemed to invite danger as day by day they drew nearer to Jerusalem, the headquarters of His foes. His own prophecies foreshadowed a time of suffering and danger for Him and for them, which would end, for Him, in a violent death. And while these prophecies prepared them for the coming catastrophe and so lessened the shock, they also increased their despondency. It was partly for the purpose of strengthening their confidence in Him and the ultimate success of His work that Jesus now took three of them and made them witnesses of His transfiguration.

The Transfiguration

Now about eight days after these sayings He took with Him Peter and John and James and went up on the mountain to pray. And as He was praying, the appearance of His face was altered, and His clothing became dazzling white. And behold, two men were talking with Him, Moses and Elijah, who appeared in glory and spoke of His departure, which He was about to accomplish at Jerusalem. Now Peter and those who were with Him were heavy with sleep, but when they became fully awake they saw His glory and the two men who stood with Him. And as the men were parting from Him, Peter said to Jesus, "Master, it is good that we are here. Let us make three tents, one for You and one for Moses and one for Elijah"—not knowing what he said. As he was saying these things, a cloud came and overshadowed them, and they were afraid as they entered the cloud. And a voice came out of the cloud, saying, "This is My Son, My Chosen One; listen to Him!" And when the voice had spoken, Jesus was found alone. And they kept silent and told no one in those days anything of what they had seen.

This marvelous event was quite significant for Jesus, for His disciples, and for us. First, for Jesus Himself: He was entering a new period of His earthly life, the last period, and He knew what it would bring. All His life He had seen the cross at the end, but now it stood more distinctly and in all its horrors. Now, God the Son was a true man, and His human nature shrank from the shame and suffering of such an end. That fact never altered His purpose or shook His resolve, but we should never doubt that His suffering was real as the last weeks of His life were at hand. It was even greater than we can imagine when we foresee pain and suffering because Jesus saw what no man could see, that His cross was the result of sin and the wrath of almighty God that would assail Him with all its indescribable horrors. His sinless nature shrank in terror; He needed strengthening.

And He got it. In Gethsemane, when His suffering was approaching its climax, "there appeared to Him an angel from heaven, strengthening Him" (Luke 22:43). Here on the Mount of Transfiguration, His Father in heaven sent two of the great heroes of faith who had already departed in the hope of His work and were enjoying the fruits of it. Moses and Elijah "appeared in glory and spoke of His departure, which He was about to accomplish at Jerusalem." Isn't that a strange way of speaking—to accomplish death? We suffer death; there is nothing we can do about it. Jesus accomplished His death; the greatest part of His work was to die for our sins. That blessed purpose of His death they held up to Him, and this served to strengthen Him for the battle. And as in the beginning of His public ministry when He was baptized, His Father publicly acknowledged Him as His Son and accredited His work as the accomplishment of His eternal will: "a voice came out of the cloud, saying, 'This is My Son, My Chosen One; listen to Him!'" And so strengthened, Jesus came down from the hill and a few weeks later went to Gethsemane and Calvary. He drank the cup His Father gave Him, every bitter drop of it. And when the eternity of those last six hours of agony was past, He turned the cup and it was empty, and He said, "It is finished," He had accomplished His death at Jerusalem.

Peter explained what this wonderful experience meant to the three apostles who were present, "For we did not follow cleverly devised myths when we made known to you the power and coming of our Lord Jesus Christ, but we were eyewitnesses of His majesty. For when He received honor and glory from God the Father, and the voice was borne to Him by the Majestic Glory, 'This is My beloved Son, with whom I am well pleased,' we ourselves heard this very voice borne from heaven, for we were with Him on the holy mountain" (2 Peter 1:16–18). John, too, referred to Jesus' transfiguration when he wrote, "we have seen His glory, glory as of the only Son from the Father" (John 1:14). They knew by what they had heard and seen that Jesus was the true Son of God. And they, too, needed that strengthening. In the weeks to come, when they saw Him helpless in the hands of His enemies, nailed to the cross, dying that most shameful death, their faith in their Master was sorely tried. But the memory of what they saw and heard kept their faith from total extinction. And it was for that reason that Jesus took them onto the holy mount.

So He cared for His own then. And He cares for His own today. He knows when the river of our life will encounter rapids and waterfalls, when great peril and pain are on our horizon, straining our faith and patience to the utmost. To prepare us for that, He takes us into the holy mount of His Word to see His glory. Let us ever follow His leading. He will never fail us. He will be with us in the darkest hour and lead us to the sunshine on the other side.

Prayer

We thank You, O Lord, that in Your Word You have given us a neverfailing fount of strength and comfort. Make us diligent searchers in Your Word and enlighten our hearts to understand its teachings so we may rightly apply it to our life. Let not the wiles of Satan rob us of this light, but let it shine in this dark world until the night is over and the eternal day dawns. In Jesus' name. Amen.

THE RETURN TO THE VALLEY
Luke 9:37–50

WHILE Peter was with James, John, and Jesus on the mountain, he ecstatically exclaimed, "Master, it is good that we are here. Let us make three tents, one for You and one for Moses and one for Elijah" (Luke 9:33). It was a foretaste of the bliss of heaven. But neither Jesus nor His apostles could remain on the holy mount; they had work to do down in the valley—Jesus to accomplish His death at Jerusalem, to go to the Father, as He said to the Twelve, by way of Gethsemane and Calvary, and so to redeem the world. And the apostles were to carry on the work of bringing a lost world back to God by proclaiming the Gospel of the finished redemption. No, they could not remain where Peter said was so good to be, so they went down the hill and again met the people. Neither can we remain on whatever holy mount the Lord in His love permits us to ascend. There are hours when we, too, say with Peter, "Master, it is good that we are here"—hours of prayer, of meditation on God's promises and blessings, of communion with God. "Let me stay here," we pray, "never to go back into the everyday world." But the Lord still has work for us to do, so we go back into the valley. What do we find there, and how shall we meet it? Let us learn a lesson from the text.

Jesus Heals a Boy with an Unclean Spirit

On the next day, when they had come down from the mountain, a great crowd met Him. And behold, a man from the crowd cried out, "Teacher, I beg You to look at my son, for he is my only child. And behold, a spirit seizes him, and he suddenly cries out. It convulses him so that he foams at the mouth, and shatters him, and will hardly leave him. And I begged Your disciples to cast it out, but they could not." Jesus answered, "O faithless and twisted generation, how long am I to be with you and bear with you? Bring your son here." While he was coming, the demon threw him to the ground and convulsed him. But Jesus rebuked the unclean spirit and healed the boy, and gave him back to his Father. And all were astonished at the majesty of God.

Jesus Again Foretells His Death

But while they were all marveling at everything He was doing, Jesus said to His disciples, "Let these words sink into your ears: The Son of Man is about to be delivered into the hands of men." But they did not understand this saying, and it was concealed from them, so that they might not perceive it. And they were afraid to ask Him about this saying.

Who Is the Greatest?

An argument arose among them as to which of them was the greatest. But Jesus, knowing the reasoning of their hearts, took a child and put him by His side and said to them, "Whoever receives this child in My name receives Me, and whoever receives Me receives Him who sent Me. For he who is least among you all is the one who is great."

Anyone Not Against Us Is For Us

John answered, "Master, we saw someone casting out demons in Your name, and we tried to stop him, because he does not follow with us." But Jesus said to him, "Do not stop him, for the one who is not against you is for you."

Again we meet one of those most miserable people, this time a young boy who was possessed by the devil. The poor father came to ask Jesus for help, but Jesus had gone away to the mountain so he made his request to the disciples who remained in the valley. But these disciples were powerless; the evil spirit defied them. When Jesus heard that, He cried out, "O faithless and twisted generation, how long am I to be with you and bear with you?" That Jesus did not exempt the disciples from this indictment we learn from Matthew's account (Matthew 17:19–21): When they asked Jesus, "Why could we not cast it out?" He answered, "Because of your little faith. For truly, I say to you, if you have faith like a grain of mustard seed, you will say to this mountain, 'Move from here to there,' and it will move, and nothing will be impossible for you." Their faith was weak and wavering and mixed with pride and conceit. So while all who witnessed it were still amazed at the miracle, they began to bicker among themselves as to who among them would be greatest in Christ's kingdom. They were already distributing crowns and thrones to themselves, and in that frame of mind, trusting in their own power, they had attempted to attack the devil. But Satan can be defeated only by the power of God, by faith in Him and prayer to Him.

The old evil foe still means deadly woe to all of us. And let no one believe that the devil is interested only in the bigger picture, in great mass movements against the kingdom of Christ. He actively pursues Christians in the various mind-sets and superstitions that lead thousands away from the Lord, and his aim is always to destroy the individual soul. Every Christian will suffer from his attacks. And the only defense we have is faith in the Savior and prayer for His almighty help. Therefore, we, too, must plead with the father of the boy, "I believe; help my unbelief!" (Mark 9:24). Our faith is so weak that defeat seems to stare us in the face.

Thank God, when we are "tossed about With many a conflict, many a doubt, Fightings and fears within, without" (*LSB* 570:3), we are not left helpless or dependent on our own puny strength. Satan, the murderer from the beginning, has only one goal in mind today: to destroy all creatures of God. But Christ comes to destroy the works of the devil; the power of evil ends where Jesus steps in. His help is ours for the asking. Not, perhaps, as soon as we cry; our faith may need to be refined in the fire of affliction. We may need to learn lessons of humility, love, charity, and tolerance. But when His time comes, He will rebuke the unclean spirit, heal our wounds, and restore us, body and soul, to our Father.

Prayer

O faithful Lord, You who are the fount of all that is good, defend us against the evil designs of the devil to hurt our bodies and destroy our souls. Teach us to seek and find help in prayer. Keep us in the faith until we reach its consummation in Your kingdom of glory. For Jesus' sake. Amen.

37

A LESSON IN DISCIPLESHIP
Luke 9:51–62

BECOMING a disciple of Christ is a matter of conviction, faith, and trust. A disciple of Christ or, in other words, a true Christian, is one who has come to knowledge of his sin and his absolute need of a Savior; to the conviction that Jesus Christ—born in Bethlehem, suffered under Pontius Pilate, crucified and died and buried, risen again on the third day—is that Savior; and to the faith and trust that, unworthy though he is, this Jesus Christ is his Savior. But discipleship is a matter of growth. The old man, corrupt by deceitful desires, must be put off and the new man, created in the image of God in righteousness and true holiness, must be put on. That cannot be done in a moment. Moreover, true discipleship is intensely active in following Christ, and that has to be learned. Jesus imparts a few lessons in true discipleship in today's passage.

A Samaritan Village Rejects Jesus

When the days drew near for Him to be taken up, He set His face to go to Jerusalem. And He sent messengers ahead of Him, who went and entered a village of the Samaritans, to make preparations for Him. But the people did not receive Him, because His face was set toward Jerusalem. And when His disciples James and John saw it, they said, "Lord, do You want us to tell fire to come down from heaven and consume them?" But He turned and rebuked them. And they went on to another village.

The Cost of Following Jesus

As they were going along the road, someone said to Him, "I will follow You wherever You go." And Jesus said to him, "Foxes have holes, and birds of the air have nests, but the Son of Man has nowhere to lay His head." To another He said, "Follow Me." But he said, "Lord, let me first go and bury my father." And Jesus said to him, "Leave the dead to bury their own dead. But as for you, go and proclaim the kingdom of God." Yet another said, "I will follow You, Lord, but let me first say farewell to those at my home." Jesus said to him, "No one who puts his hand to the plow and looks back is fit for the kingdom of God."

The first lesson is a warning against the spirit of vengeance. The people in this village in Samaria denied Jesus lodging for the night. The Samaritans were half pagan, a mixture of the Jews left in the country when Shalmaneser led the ten tribes into captivity in Assyria and the heathen he brought in to occupy the land (2 Kings 17). They were bitterly hostile to the Jews; and because they knew that Jesus claimed to be the Messiah of the Jews and saw that He was on the way to Jerusalem, they refused Him hospitality. But when His disciples proposed to destroy them by fire from heaven, citing the example of Elijah (2 Kings 1:10, 12), Jesus refused. This was no criticism of Elijah. God is just, and under certain conditions His servants must pronounce His wrath and judgment on godless people. But Jesus says it is not fitting that His disciples should harbor the spirit of vengeance; their desire must be to help and to save souls.

Then three men approached Jesus, all willing to follow Him, but each had a private concern that interfered with his discipleship. The first man was too hasty. He wanted to follow Jesus but he did not consider the cost, which is evident from Jesus' answer. The disciple must be willing to share the Master's circumstances, which meant he would have nowhere to sleep. The second man was too slow. Before He would follow the Lord's command, he must bury his father. Jesus tells him that His disciples must be ready to set aside all earthly desires and duties when God's command and the interest of His kingdom demand it. The third man was halfhearted. He wanted to divide his heart between Christ and his friends. Jesus says that cannot work. The man who sets his hands to the plow and lets his eyes wander in other directions will never plow straight furrows because he is distracted.

Do we need these lessons? Who does not? How hard it is to give one's whole heart to Jesus! We say, Lord, I will follow You. But we reserve a corner of our heart for other things, for private feelings and desires, for earthly considerations, for what our heart considers duty toward family and friends, for pleasures and associations that keep us from following Christ altogether.

Paul writes, "Brothers, I do not consider that I have made it my own. But one thing I do: forgetting what lies behind and straining forward to what lies ahead, I press on toward the goal for the prize of the upward call of God in Christ Jesus" (Philippians 3:13–14).

And there is the example of Jesus; He knew all the horrible details yet "He set His face to go to Jerusalem."

Luke doesn't give the result of Jesus' answer to these men. Did these men willingly, gladly set aside their own wishes or did they disappoint the Lord? We do not know, but each and every one of us can consider the question: If we were in their place, what would we do? Follow our own desires or follow Christ?

Prayer

Take, my soul, thy full salvation;
Rise o'er sin and fear and care;
Joy to find in every station,
Something still to do or bear.
Think what Spirit dwells within thee,
What a Father's smile is thine,
What a Savior died to win thee;
Child of heaven, shouldst thou repine?

Haste, then, on from grace to glory,
Armed by faith and winged by prayer;
Heaven's eternal day's before thee,
God's own hand shall guide thee there.
Soon shall close thy earthly mission,
Swift shall pass thy pilgrim days,
Hope soon change to glad fruition,
Faith to sight, and prayer to praise. Amen.
(TLH 423:5–6)

"THE KINGDOM IS COME NIGH"

Luke 10:1–16

SOMEONE once said that God's desire to save us is much greater than our desire to be saved. That is true, and it is a most marvelous truth. Our presence in heaven cannot add to His bliss and glory. Yet His desire to bring us into heaven is so great that it appears as though He could not enjoy the full bliss of heaven without us. So great is His love that He spared not His own Son but delivered Him up for us all. And now He spares no effort to bring all men to the knowledge of this finished redemption. How can any man doubt God's serious intention to save us? How sure should we feel of God's grace toward us, how sure that we are safe in His hand, and that nothing and nobody will be able to pluck us out of His hand! May this lesson help to strengthen us in that faith!

Jesus Sends Out the Seventy-Two

After this the Lord appointed seventy-two others and sent them on ahead of Him, two by two, into every town and place where He Himself was about to go. And He said to them, "The harvest is plentiful, but the laborers are few. Therefore pray earnestly to the Lord of the harvest to send out laborers into His harvest. Go your way; behold, I am sending you out as lambs in the midst of wolves. Carry no moneybag, no knapsack, no sandals, and greet no one on the road. Whatever house you enter, first say, 'Peace be to this house!' And if a son of peace is there, your peace will rest upon him. But if not, it will return to you. And remain in the same house, eating and drinking what they provide, for the laborer deserves his wages. Do not go from house to house. Whenever you enter a town and they receive you, eat what is set before you. Heal the sick in it and say to them, 'The kingdom of God has come near to you.' But whenever you enter a town and they do not receive you, go into its streets and say, 'Even the dust of your town that clings to our feet we wipe off against you. Nevertheless know this, that the kingdom of God has come near.' I tell you, it will be more bearable on that day for Sodom than for that town.

Woe to Unrepentant Cities

"Woe to you, Chorazin! Woe to you, Bethsaida! For if the mighty works done in you had been done in Tyre and Sidon, they would have repented long ago, sitting in sackcloth and ashes. But it will be more bearable in the judgment for Tyre and Sidon than for you. And you, Capernaum, will you be exalted to heaven? You shall be brought down to Hades.

"The one who hears you hears Me, and the one who rejects you rejects Me, and the one who rejects Me rejects Him who sent Me."

Jesus was on His last journey to Jerusalem. His time on earth was rapidly drawing to a close; and still there were many in Israel who had not come to Him to seek their salvation in Him. It is true that they were all waiting for the Messiah, but they did not yet believe that Jesus was the Messiah. They waited for the kingdom of God, but they had to be told that now, since His appearance in the flesh, the kingdom was near. Jesus had already sent out the Twelve. Now He expanded that missionary effort and sent out seventy-two men on that same errand: "say to them, 'The kingdom of God has come near to you.' "

We catch the note of urgency throughout the instructions He gave them: they are about the King's business, and His business requires haste. The time is getting short, so He spreads His net of love farther and wider. This whole journey of the Lord offers Israel a last chance, a final opportunity for decision. Let them come now before it is too late.

That He is anxious for all to come to faith is evident from the instructions He gives: the disciples are to travel light to reach as many people as possible. They must not unduly antagonize people; they must be courteous but not waste time on mere social formalities. They should expect the people to whom they preach to supply their needs, but they must not expect more than they need. He promises to bless their work and to bless the people who receive their message and further their work. He tells them frankly that they will meet opposition and that their enemies are strong and ruthless. Moreover, they are helpless in their own strength; they must put their trust in the Lord. But He will not fail them. Let no man doubt that in them the Lord Himself goes forth and speaks; and whatever is done to them He will consider as done to Him. He pronounces a dreadful curse on those who will not receive His Word. Not that the disciples are to execute that curse; they may safely leave that to Him. But the terrible sentence that fell on the ancient cities that despised His Word and His servants is a guarantee that those who reject Him now will not escape the wrath of God.

There is much food for serious thought for all of us in this text. Messengers of Christ come to us with that same proclamation. The kingdom of God is come to you; come, for all things are now ready! How do we receive them? As Christ's ambassadors? Or do we pass them by, neglect them, perhaps even despise and oppose them? The ancient blessing still goes with their message—but so does the curse!

Furthermore, to us who have opened our heart to the Savior now comes the same command given to the seventy-two. We must go forth, each in the way the Lord has set before us, to tell others that the kingdom of God is come. The field is still so great and the laborers are still few. Mission work should expand today as in the day of the Lord. As the mustard seed grows and the leaven diffuses in the dough, the influence it exerts among people will also increase; and we are all responsible for that, each in his or her own sphere and in his or her own way. And if the King's business in the time of today's reading required haste, how much more so today when conditions in world and Church indicate that the day is far spent. The night comes when no one can work.

Prayer

Up! The ripening fields ye see.
Mighty shall the harvest be;
But the reapers still are few,
Great the work they have to do.

Lord of Harvest, let there be
Joy and strength to work for Thee
Till the nations far and near
See Thy light and learn Thy fear. Amen. (TLH 507:5–6)

ARE OUR NAMES WRITTEN IN HEAVEN?

Luke 10:17–22

WHEN Jesus sent out the seventy-two disciples, He warned them, "Behold, I am sending you out as lambs in the midst of wolves" (Luke 10:3). The same warning is given to us. The Lord does not want to deceive us; we must expect trouble and persecution. The opposition differs at different times. Sometimes it takes the form of bloody persecution and Christians die. Other times our enemies show their spite by heaping scorn on our heads and making our lives miserable. This world has never been and never will be a paradise for Christians. Yet there is joy in the Christian's life, a joy far greater than any the world can know, a joy that more than compensates us for our sorrow. This text tells us of that side of the Christian life.

The Return of the Seventy-Two

The seventy-two returned with joy, saying, "Lord, even the demons are subject to us in Your name!" And He said to them,

"I saw Satan fall like lightning from heaven. Behold, I have given you authority to tread on serpents and scorpions, and over all the power of the enemy, and nothing shall hurt you. Nevertheless, do not rejoice in this, that the spirits are subject to you, but rejoice that your names are written in heaven."

Jesus Rejoices in the Father's Will

In that same hour He rejoiced in the Holy Spirit and said, "I thank You, Father, Lord of heaven and earth, that You have hidden these things from the wise and understanding and revealed them to little children; yes, Father, for such was Your gracious will. All things have been handed over to Me by My Father, and no one knows who the Son is except the Father, or who the Father is except the Son and anyone to whom the Son chooses to reveal Him."

The disciples returned from their mission trip with joy, chiefly because even the devils were subject to them through His name. And Jesus joins them in their rejoicing. He tells them that this is how it will be in the future, "I have given you authority to tread on serpents and scorpions, and over all the power of the enemy, and nothing shall hurt you." It is the same promise Paul gave to the Romans, "The God of peace will soon crush Satan under your feet" (Romans 16:20). Satan's agents are the worst serpents and scorpions that Christ's disciples have to contend with, far more dangerous than natural creatures with poison that threatens natural life. And it is a far greater victory to tread upon delusions, deceptions, and spiritual falsehoods than upon such poisonous creatures. Christ's disciples have power over all of them in His name, and these evil things will not be able to harm them.

We have the same reason for rejoicing. It is not easy work that the Lord expects of His children on earth. The old evil foe is still active. Wherever we plant the banner of the cross, he sets up his golden calf. And he means deadly woe. This is not a light skirmish; it's a battle to the death. Moreover, subtle deception and great might are his powerful weapons in this war. Today he likes to persuade people that there is no devil; when he does, he attacks unhindered. He tempts us through family and friends, just as he tempted Jesus through Peter. He paints sin in innocent colors and attacks us when we are weakest. And he has millions of people who willingly or unknowingly assist him in seducing Christians. And who are we? David facing Goliath. Yet in the name of the Lord, David killed Goliath. Luther would go to Worms although there were as many devils there as tiles on the rooftops. The Lord would have us be as reckless. There is something profoundly grand in Jesus' promise "nothing shall hurt you." To be sure, the power is not ours. "I have given you authority," Jesus says. The valiant One, sent by God Himself, fights for us. Therefore, the entire world may be filled with devils eager to devour us, but we tremble not, we fear no ill—they will not overpower us.

"Nevertheless," Jesus says, "rejoice that your names are written in heaven." There is a certain danger in the joy over what we do, even in the name of Jesus. Pride or self-confidence may enter the heart. So even as we rejoice when by our work souls are saved, let us rejoice because our "names are written in heaven." Not all names are written there; only the names of those who are washed of their filth and purged of their guilt (Isaiah 4:3–4). And there is only one way of washing away sin: "the blood of Jesus his Son cleanses us from all sin" (1 John 1:7). When in faith we accept Christ and His merits, our names are written in heaven.

Why is that so great a cause for joy? Daniel says, "Your people shall be delivered, everyone whose name shall be found written in the book" (12:1). And in Hebrews 12:22–24, we read, "But you have come to Mount Zion and to the city of the living God, the heavenly Jerusalem, and to innumerable angels in festal gathering, and to the assembly of the firstborn who are enrolled in heaven, and to God, the judge of all, and to the spirits of the righteous made perfect, and to Jesus, the mediator of a new covenant." Oh, surely, "rejoice that your names are written in heaven."

Like the seventy-two, we will one day be asked to give an account. It is well if we, too, can rejoice, "Lord, even the demons are subject to us in Your name!" or if we can say that we have helped spread the Gospel on earth. But let us beware of pride. There was an old preacher who was highly complimented on an excellent sermon. He answered, "That's exactly what the devil told me when I came down from the pulpit." For the sake of our own soul, it is most important that we have the right answer to the question, "Is your name written in heaven?"

Prayer

Lord, write my name, I pray Thee,
Now in the Book of Life
And with all true believers
Take me where joys are rife.
There let me bloom and flourish,
Thy perfect freedom prove,
And tell, as I adore Thee,
How faithful was Thy love. Amen. (TLH 407:5)

THE GOOD SAMARITAN
Luke 10:23–37

THERE are two ways to heaven. One is the way of the Law, summarized in the Ten Commandments; the other way is our Lord Jesus Christ. The first way, however, is blocked and impossible for us; it requires perfect fulfillment of the Law, and this is beyond our power since the fall into sin. But the Law is by nature planted in the human heart. That is why every person naturally assumes that is the way to gain God's favor and blessing. If he is to be saved, he must, first of all, be convinced that the way of the Law is impossible in man's present state. With that perspective, Jesus told the story of the Good Samaritan to the scribe and had it recorded for us.

Then turning to the disciples He said privately, "Blessed are the eyes that see what you see! For I tell you that many prophets and kings desired to see what you see, and did not see it, and to hear what you hear, and did not hear it."

The Parable of the Good Samaritan

And behold, a lawyer stood up to put Him to the test, saying, "Teacher, what shall I do to inherit eternal life?" He said to him, "What is written in the Law? How do you read it?" And he answered, "You shall love the Lord your God with all your heart and with all your soul and with all your strength and with all your mind, and your neighbor as yourself." And He said to him, "You have answered correctly; do this, and you will live."

But he, desiring to justify himself, said to Jesus, "And who is my neighbor?" Jesus replied, "A man was going down from Jerusalem to Jericho, and he fell among robbers, who stripped him and beat him and departed, leaving him half dead. Now by chance a priest was going down that road, and when he saw him he passed by on the other side. So likewise a Levite, when he came to the place and saw him, passed by on the other side. But a Samaritan, as he journeyed, came to where he was, and when he saw him, he had compassion. He went to him and bound up his wounds, pouring on oil and wine. Then he set him on his own animal and brought him to an inn and took care of him. And the next day he took out two denarii and gave them to the innkeeper, saying, 'Take care of him, and whatever more you spend, I will repay you when I come back.' Which of these three, do you think, proved to be a neighbor to the man who fell among the robbers?" He said, "The one who showed him mercy." And Jesus said to him, "You go, and do likewise."

This scribe was evidently provoked that Jesus called His disciples blessed because they saw the deeds and heard the words of the Messiah. So he tempted Jesus with his question; would He have a different answer than Moses had given them? Jesus led him to answer his own question and then advised, "Do this, and you will live." That implied that until then, the scribe had not kept Moses' Law. The scribe understood and in defense he suggested that Jesus had a different concept of who his neighbor was. But Jesus explained with the perfect example of true neighborly love.

There is in the Samaritan's heart the genuine motive for all deeds of love: compassion. The priest and Levite perhaps knew better than the Samaritan what should be done, but they passed by the injured man. They either had no compassion or other considerations outweighed whatever pity they felt. Perhaps they worried about the danger from lurking bandits to anyone tarrying in the neighborhood, the loss of time, the labor it would involve, the cost, and so on. Yet the Samaritan, with or without these same worries, acted according to the Golden Rule: "Whatever you wish that others would do to you, do also to them, for this is the Law and the Prophets" (Matthew 7:12). He helped as long as there was a need and did not expect the innkeeper to continue what he began. And all this was not for a friend, not just for a perfect stranger, but for one of his bitterest enemies, a Jew.

The scribe understood the lesson well. He also understood what Jesus meant when He said, "Go, and do likewise." And the scribe had no response because he knew he failed to meet the requirements of the Law as Jesus taught it. Did he draw the right conclusion? Did he now ask Jesus: how, then, may I be saved, if my works fail me? We do not know. But the lesson Jesus teaches here is that our attempts to keep the Law cannot save us; our own works will condemn us. But what we cannot do God has done for us: "God sent forth His Son, born of woman, born under the law, to redeem those who were under the law, so that we might receive adoption as sons" (Galatians 4:4–5). That is the only salvation for us, the way of the Gospel of Jesus Christ.

Like the apostles, we also hear and see the things that prophets and kings of old desired vainly to see and to hear. We know Him who for our salvation was made flesh. He is with us in His Word.

And we know that in Him we have all we need for time and for eternity. And now we are free from the Law because we have become His own and live under Him in His kingdom. Therefore, this story of the Good Samaritan has another meaning for us: it is the perfect example of life in His kingdom, a life of service to our neighbor, to all who need our help in any way. And it is well that we compare our life with the pattern the Lord here presents to us. And when we find that we fall short, let us go to Him who is the great and perfect Good Samaritan, for it is there alone that we find the comfort we will never be able to attain on our own: perfect fulfillment of God's Law. With Christ, we will find help to do better in the future.

Prayer

Dear Father in heaven, we thank You that You have sent us a Savior, Your Son, Jesus Christ, to redeem us from our sin and the punishment we justly deserved. To us, who had by our transgressions of Your Law barred the way to You and heaven, He has opened a new way to attain eternal blessedness through faith in His merits. Grant us grace to accept His redemption with a true heart, and by Your Holy Spirit enable us to bring forth the fruits of gratitude to You and our Savior in love toward You and to our neighbor, and in all things to follow the example of our Good Samaritan, our Lord Jesus Christ. In His name we ask it. Amen.

ONE THING IS NEEDFUL

Luke 10:38–42

IN our previous meditation, we found Jesus surrounded by many people, His disciples and many others, some friendly, others hostile; and He told them all what they needed most. Today we find Him in a quiet home with His closest friends, and again He tells them what they needed most. There is a place for Jesus in every situation and every life, and He always brings His blessing. These friends of Jesus, Lazarus and his sisters, Martha and Mary, lived in Bethany, a village just outside Jerusalem. Jesus loved them and usually visited their home when He was in the neighborhood (for instance, during the week before His Passion). When they were in need, their first thought was to send for Jesus, as was the case when Lazarus was sick (John 11:3). It is a beautiful example of loving friendship. Let us accompany Jesus to this home and see what happened there.

Martha and Mary

Now as they went on their way, Jesus entered a village. And a woman named Martha welcomed Him into her house. And she had a sister called Mary, who sat at the Lord's feet and listened to His teaching. But Martha was distracted with much serving. And she went up to Him and said, "Lord, do you not care that my sister has left me to serve alone? Tell her then to help me." But the Lord answered her, "Martha, Martha, you are anxious and troubled about many things, but one thing is necessary. Mary has chosen the good portion, which will not be taken away from her."

When Jesus arrived at the house, both sisters welcomed Him and made Him comfortable. But after the greetings were over and Jesus sat down to speak, Mary left her sister, her work, and her other cares and sat down to listen to Him. Martha kept on working. She loved Jesus, and it was for Him that she was working. No doubt she would have preferred to sit and listen to Him, too, but she thought she could not because of all of the work to do. So she became provoked at her sister and at Jesus for permitting Mary, as she thought, to shirk her part of the work.

What did Jesus say to her? Kindly, tenderly He said, "Martha, Martha, you are anxious and troubled about many things, but one thing is necessary." He does not chide her for working but for being troubled about so many things while there is really only one thing worth fixing her mind on. She was distracted, thinking now of this, now of that, and so she missed that one essential thing. Not Mary. She, too, served, but when it came to the choice, she knew of only one thing that was supreme in her heart: the one thing needful, the Word of Jesus.

Let us apply this to our own life. Are we ever too busy to listen to the words of Jesus? too busy to read the Scriptures? too busy for prayer? too busy to get ready for church services? Are the various excuses offered for not attending church valid? Business is so pressing that we have no time, or business is so poor that we must work night and day to make ends meet, telling ourselves that when times change, we will come. Just like Martha! Later, when dishes were washed and the dough was set for tomorrow's baking, then she, too, would sit at Jesus' feet. Of course we are busy. Every man worth his salt will keep busy if he has the opportunity. Are we ever too busy to eat? We may occasionally miss a meal, but rarely are we so busy that we miss two meals in succession. Feed your soul; that is the *one thing that is necessary*.

This applies as well to much that is loosely called "church work." Martha was not amusing herself, nor was she working for herself— she was serving Jesus. Yet Jesus reproved her, kindly, but decidedly. Although she did what she did for Jesus, it wasn't the right thing at the right time. Her service would have been good had she not thereby neglected something vastly better and more important. She saw in Jesus only the guest, and she wanted to provide for Him. But there are two ways of serving the Lord: one is to bring Him our efforts, offerings, and labors; the other is to let Him feed and bless and serve us by His Word—this is the *one thing that is necessary*.

St. Luke does not tell us what Martha did after hearing Jesus' reply, but no doubt she, too, sat to listen to Him. When He was done, both of the sisters likely served Him with grateful hearts. And we can assume that Martha was thankful, indeed, that she did so because a few days later her brother lay dead and she found comfort not in serving but in remembering her Lord's teaching. What Jesus said to the two sisters on this occasion is not recorded, but would not

He, the Omniscient, knowing the shadow that would soon fall on them, prepare them for that blow? How much Martha would have missed had she failed to listen to Jesus! How much we may miss if we fail to attend one church service! Perhaps our Great Friend had a special message for us on that day to prepare us for something that is coming!

"Mary has chosen the good portion, which will not be taken away from her." These words would be a fine epitaph!

Prayer

One thing's needful; Lord, this treasure
*   Teach me highly to regard.*
All else, though it first give pleasure,
*   Is a yoke that presses hard!*
Beneath it the heart is still fretting and striving,
No true, lasting happiness ever deriving.
This one thing is needful; all others are vain—
I count all but loss that I Christ may obtain!

How were Mary's thoughts devoted
*   Her eternal joy to find*
As intent each word she noted,
*   At her Savior's feet reclined!*
How kindled her heart, how devout was its feeling,
While hearing the lessons that Christ was revealing!
All earthly concerns she forgot for her Lord
And found her contentment in hearing His Word.

Therefore You alone, My Savior,
*   Shall be all in all to me;*
Search my heart and my behavior,
*   Root out all hypocrisy.*
Through all my life's pilgrimage, guard and uphold me,
In loving forgiveness, O Jesus enfold me.
This one thing is needful; all other are vain—
I count all but loss that I Christ may obtain! Amen.
(LSB 536:1–2, 5)

42

SECRETS OF CHRISTIAN PRAYER

Luke 11:1–13

TODAY Jesus speaks to us of the greatest privilege that we poor mortals enjoy—that we may at any time come into the presence of God and tell Him what is troubling us and ask Him for the help we need. Do we always do this and value it as the great privilege that it is? If the president of our country invited us to talk with him about the needs of our nation, would we consider it a privilege and an honor? Consider that the great Creator of the universe invites us to come and talk over our private and public needs with Him and promises that He will listen and do what is best for us—not what someone else thinks best, but what He knows is best. But let's admit that we forget or are sometimes ashamed to pray. And the reason for this, whether or not we confess it, is that often we lack the faith that God will surely hear and answer our prayer. We pray because we have been taught to do so and we are accustomed to it; and then we are disappointed because our prayers are not answered. St. James tells us why, "You ask and do not receive, because you ask wrongly, to spend it on your passions" (James 4:3). We must learn better how to pray. Let us now go to Jesus' classroom and have Him teach us how to pray.

The Lord's Prayer

Now Jesus was praying in a certain place, and when He finished, one of His disciples said to Him, "Lord, teach us to pray, as John taught his disciples." And He said to them, "When you pray, say:

"Father, hallowed be Your name. Your kingdom come. Give us each day our daily bread, and forgive us our sins,

for we ourselves forgive everyone who is indebted to us.
And lead us not into temptation."

And He said to them, "Which of you who has a friend will go to him at midnight and say to him, 'Friend, lend me three loaves, for a friend of mine has arrived on a journey, and I have nothing to set before him'; and he will answer from within, 'Do not bother me; the door is now shut, and my children are with me in bed. I cannot get up and give you anything'? I tell you, though he will not get up and give him anything because he is his friend, yet because of his impudence he will rise and give him whatever he needs. And I tell you, ask, and it will be given to you; seek, and you will find; knock, and it will be opened to you. For everyone who asks receives, and the one who seeks finds, and to the one who knocks it will be opened. What father among you, if his son asks for a fish, will instead of a fish give him a serpent; or if he asks for an egg, will give him a scorpion? If you then, who are evil, know how to give good gifts to your children, how much more will the heavenly Father give the Holy Spirit to those who ask Him!"

When the disciples asked Jesus to teach them to pray, He complied with their request, in the first place, by teaching them a model prayer, the Lord's Prayer. It is the best of all prayers; how could it be otherwise when the Son of God Himself composed and taught it? And it is the best prayer that even the Son of God could offer us. It is all-comprehensive; there is nothing that is not included in these petitions. And so it is the best model for all other prayers in which we take our personal and private needs to God.

Then Jesus teaches us three secrets of successful prayer. The first is perseverance. He tells the story of the persistent beggar and wants us to draw this conclusion: if that selfish friend yields to dogged requests when he is asked at the most inopportune time by a perfect stranger when the need is very slight, how much more will your heavenly Father yield to your persevering prayer when He is always pleased to hear you, when there is no inconvenient time with Him, when there is no midnight when He is sleeping, when He loves you, and when your need is so great. So pray on!

The second lesson is this: be absolutely confident that God will hear you. That is probably the hardest lesson to learn and why we do not persist in prayer. We grow impatient and give up after a few attempts. The reason is secret unbelief. God will sometimes let us get in such desperate situations that prayer is the only thing left with any hope of getting us out. Jesus gives us the thrice-repeated promise that our prayer will be heard and answered. Surely that is enough!

There remains, however, the fact that sometimes even persistent praying seems to go unanswered. So Jesus teaches us another lesson: God gives us no useless or harmful or deadly gifts, although we at times ask for them in our ignorance. God is our Father; we are His children and, childlike, we sometimes ask foolishly. A child likes nothing better than a shiny object that is, in reality, a sharp knife. Some children cry for the moon. Some ask for a car when they still need a tricycle. God knows what is best when it is best. When God's divine knowledge does not agree with our wishes, let us not be stubborn children and cry our heart out because we do not get exactly what we foolishly desire.

"He who can pray is blessed always." We all should pray. It's our greatest privilege. But can we? Prayer is an art that must be learned and requires much practice. Let Jesus teach us to pray; we will never regret it.

Prayer

Lord God, our heavenly Father, who by Your Son promised to give us whatsoever we shall ask in His name, we ask that You grant us by the power of Your Holy Spirit that we may make requests of You in faithful prayer and desire what is pleasing to You and profitable for us, lifting up holy hands without wrath or doubt and being firmly assured that You will hear our prayer; through Jesus Christ, Your Son, our Lord. Amen.

THE TWO KINGDOMS
Luke 11:14–28

CHRIST has many enemies. In His days on earth, there were those who persecuted Him and finally brought Him to the cross. There were false friends who forsook Him and betrayed Him and sold Him for thirty pieces of silver. Those who on one day cried, "Hosanna to the Son of David!" and a few days later, "Crucify Him!" This was so true that John later wrote, "He came to His own, and His own people did not receive Him" (John 1:11). So today Christ still has many enemies, and at first glance they seem to be of many different kinds. Some openly despise and reject Him; some are indifferent; some waver back and forth between Him and the world; some fear to confess Him; and some are hypocrites who say, "Lord, Lord," but do not do the will of the Father. There are many kinds of enemies, yet fundamentally they belong in one class. Christ divides all men into two kingdoms when He says, "Whoever is not with Me is against Me." Both are presented in this text.

Jesus and Beelzebul

Now He was casting out a demon that was mute. When the demon had gone out, the mute man spoke, and the people marveled. But some of them said, "He casts out demons by Beelzebul, the prince of demons," while others, to test Him, kept seeking from Him a sign from heaven. But He, knowing their thoughts, said to them, "Every kingdom divided against itself is laid waste, and a divided household falls. And if Satan also is divided against himself, how will his kingdom stand? For you say that I cast out demons by Beelzebul. And if I cast out demons by Beelzebul, by whom do your sons cast them out? Therefore they will be your judges. But if it is by the finger of God that I cast out demons, then the kingdom of God has come upon you. When a strong man, fully armed, guards his own palace, his goods are safe; but when one stronger than he attacks him and overcomes him, he takes away his armor in which he trusted and divides his spoil. Whoever is not with Me is against Me, and whoever does not gather with Me scatters.

Return of an Unclean Spirit

"When the unclean spirit has gone out of a person, it passes through waterless places seeking rest, and finding none it says, 'I will return to my house from which I came.' And when it comes, it finds the house swept and put in order. Then it goes and brings seven other spirits more evil than itself, and they enter and dwell there. And the last state of that person is worse than the first."

True Blessedness

As He said these things, a woman in the crowd raised her voice and said to Him, "Blessed is the womb that bore You, and the breasts at which You nursed!" But He said, "Blessed rather are those who hear the word of God and keep it!"

Jesus had healed a man who was blind, could not speak, and was possessed by a devil (Matthew 12:22). All had seen the miracle; it could not be denied. But there were people who simply would not believe one good thing about this Jesus. They even accused Him of being in league with the devil. They were actually sorry that the poor man had been healed because they would have preferred it had Jesus failed. But the deed was done, and because of it, they could not deny His power; therefore, they ascribed it to the devil rather than give Jesus His due honor. There are people today who claim that Jesus did His miracles merely by making people believe they saw what actually they did not see. Such people may be members, even pastors, of so-called Christian churches. They will not confess that Jesus is Christ, the Son of the living God, co-Creator.

"Others, to test Him, kept seeking from Him a sign from heaven." These people were not satisfied with the signs Jesus did.

Such people who always want something new, and when they do not get it, they use that as an excuse for unbelief. They want signs that suit them, but they won't get them. If they do not believe the first-hand accounts of the four evangelists, they would not believe their own eyes. They would not have believed had they been present when this blind man was healed. They would not believe under any circumstances. "Whoever is not with Me is against Me."

"The people marveled." Their hearts were moved. They admired Jesus. But their response was only superficial. Some people shed tears every Good Friday. They see young people pledge their life to their Savior at the confirmation altar, and they are moved. They feel the touch of God's hand at the deliverance from danger and they make the finest resolutions. Then comes the deadly monotony of daily life and their heart congeals again. But the more often that happens, the harder the heart becomes. You cast out the devil once and go to sleep, but he will come back with many companions and again take possession. And it will be harder to cast him out the second time.

Was no one in that group for Jesus? There was one, a woman who blessed the mother of Christ because she had such a Son. Jesus said yes, His mother was blessed, but "Blessed rather are those who hear the word of God and keep it." Even Mary was blessed only because she was of that category, because she kept everything she learned about Jesus in her heart. And every individual may have Mary's same blessing. If we hear the Word of Christ and keep it, believe it, and set the trust of our heart on its promises, then are we with Christ. And then we are blessed. If we do not, then neither old nor new signs will do us any good. And if we could see Christ bodily and touch Him with our hands as the disciples did, Judas included, it would earn us nothing. The plea of those who are truly in the kingdom of Christ is this: "Jesus, Thy blood and righteousness My beauty are, my glorious dress; Midst flaming worlds, in these arrayed, With joy shall I lift up my head" (*LSB* 563:1). Can we say that?

Prayer

*Lord Jesus, we thank You that You have overcome our evil foe
and wrested us from his power and dominion. Grant us the aid
of Your Holy Spirit that we may withstand and overcome all the
devil's attacks and temptations. Keep us steadfast in the faith
that we may abide in Your kingdom here on earth and in the
end enter Your everlasting kingdom of glory. Amen.*

SIGNS AND EVIDENCES
Luke 11:29–36

IN their confrontation with Jesus related in the previous section,
the Pharisees had asked for a sign from heaven. Jesus refused to give
them such a sign, but that does not mean He was unwilling to give
them proof of His divine mission. He was not willing to perform
miracles on command just to satisfy the wishes of individuals. Jesus
had given them ample proof that He was sent by God and, therefore,
that His Word was the truth. (The greatest sign, of course, was still
in the future.) The veracity of His Word is what Jesus speaks about
here, and what He declares to them, and to us, in most impressive
language, is the importance of heeding His testimony and acting
upon it.

The Sign of Jonah

When the crowds were increasing, He began to say, "This
generation is an evil generation. It seeks for a sign, but no
sign will be given to it except the sign of Jonah. For as Jonah
became a sign to the people of Nineveh, so will the Son of Man
be to this generation. The queen of the South will rise up at the
judgment with the men of this generation and condemn them,

for she came from the ends of the earth to hear the wisdom of Solomon, and behold, something greater than Solomon is here. The men of Nineveh will rise up at the judgment with this generation and condemn it, for they repented at the preaching of Jonah, and behold, something greater than Jonah is here.

The Light in You

"No one after lighting a lamp puts it in a cellar or under a basket, but on a stand, so that those who enter may see the light. Your eye is the lamp of your body. When your eye is healthy, your whole body is full of light, but when it is bad, your body is full of darkness. Therefore be careful lest the light in you be darkness. If then your whole body is full of light, having no part dark, it will be wholly bright, as when a lamp with its rays gives you light."

Jesus called the people who were facing Him an evil generation, and despite the many signs He had already given them, they demanded more. They wanted signs according to their own specification; otherwise they would not believe. Doesn't this apply to our time and our generation as well? They want what they call logical proof, visible demonstration of the truth of Christianity and its power. Let Christianity erase poverty, prevent wars, and create peace and harmony, then they will, perhaps, consider its claims.

What can we do? Argue and debate, compromise, adapt the essentials of our faith, the doctrine of the cross of Christ, and change it to a social Gospel, a mere effort to improve conditions here on earth? Jesus said the only sign that will be given these unbelievers is that of the prophet Jonah, that is, the resurrection of Christ (see Matthew 12:40). That will be the last call extended to them. If they reject that, too, there is no help for them, and all those who had been led to repentance and acceptance of God's truth by far lesser testimonies would rise up in judgment against them.

This is written as a warning. What will the great Judge say when He compares what the men of Nineveh did and the little they received with the great abundance of testimony granted to us? Or when the Queen of Sheba, who made faithful use of her meager opportunities, is called to face us who do not have to travel thousands of miles to hear One who is far greater than Solomon? Will He not condemn us who have had the Gospel since childhood, who have the Church at our very door, if we seek something else?

In the second part of the text, Jesus speaks of the evidence of the faith that is within us. In the Sermon on the Mount, He summarized this in the well-known passage, "Let your light shine before others, so that they may see your good works and give glory to your Father who is in heaven" (Matthew 5:16). A light will send out its rays unless it is artificially restricted, and if that happens, the light is useless. If, with the eye of our soul, we have seen the light of the Gospel of Christ, then this light will enlighten our whole being. It will give us true knowledge of God's good and gracious will toward us as He has revealed it in our Savior, Jesus Christ. If this light, however, is shining in our soul, it cannot do anything but cast its beams in all directions. It will extend its influence on our every thought, word, and action. In other words, if in true faith we have received the Word of Christ, it will show its evidences in our life. We will live according to this Word. We will be ready and zealous for every good work.

The question involved in this discourse of the Lord is directed to us: What are the evidences of our faith? Is the light of the knowledge of Jesus Christ, our Savior, not only shining within us, but also shedding its rays around us in truly Christian conduct, in works of Christian love and charity? Are we, above all, zealous in drawing others into this light? Are we active in mission work? Are we personally trying to bring others to that Savior whom we have found? Do we support the missionary work carried on by our church body and congregation?

Our own conscience must give the answer to these questions. The Lord warns us that if these evidences are lacking, we should examine ourselves to see whether the light of faith is still shining in our heart. Good works are not the light; faith is the light. But a light must shine and throw out its rays; and faith without good works is impossible.

Prayer

O Lord, who caused the light of the knowledge of Jesus Christ, our Savior, to shine into our hearts, we praise You for Your grace that has called us out of darkness into Your marvelous light. Establish us, we ask You, in the faith of Your Son, and grant us the power of Your Holy Spirit to walk in this light, so that by our service others may be brought to this light, that Your glory may be extended and Your kingdom be expanded throughout the earth. In the name of Jesus, hear our prayer. Amen.

WARNING AGAINST HYPOCRISY
Luke 11:37–54

TODAY we read that the Lord condemned the Pharisees and the scribes of Israel in scathing terms. The Pharisees were a religious sect among the Jews. St. Paul, who was a Pharisee before his conversion, says they were the strictest sect of the Jewish religion (Acts 26:5). In the days of the Maccabeans, when adherence to the laws of Moses was punishable by torture and death, the Pharisees formed a party to maintain the Law, and down to the time of Jesus they insisted on obedience to all Mosaic laws to the minutest detail. The scribes (also called lawyers) were the religious teachers of the Jews; they studied the Scriptures and imparted the results of their study to the people. The object of both parties seems praiseworthy. Why did Jesus condemn them?

Woes to the Pharisees and Lawyers

While Jesus was speaking, a Pharisee asked Him to dine with him, so He went in and reclined at table. The Pharisee was astonished to see that He did not first wash before dinner. And the Lord said to him, "Now you Pharisees cleanse the outside of the cup and of the dish, but inside you are full of greed and wickedness. You fools! Did not He who made the outside make the inside also? But give as alms those things that are within, and behold, everything is clean for you.

"But woe to you Pharisees! For you tithe mint and rue and every herb, and neglect justice and the love of God. These you ought to have done, without neglecting the others. Woe to you Pharisees! For you love the best seat in the synagogues and greetings in the marketplaces. Woe to you! For you are like unmarked graves, and people walk over them without knowing it."

One of the lawyers answered Him, "Teacher, in saying these things You insult us also." And He said, "Woe to you lawyers also! For you load people with burdens hard to bear, and you yourselves do not touch the burdens with one of your fingers. Woe to you! For you build the tombs of the prophets whom your fathers killed. So you are witnesses and you consent to the deeds of your fathers, for they killed them, and you build their tombs. Therefore also the Wisdom of God said, 'I will send them prophets and apostles, some of whom they will kill and persecute,' so that the blood of all the prophets, shed from the foundation of the world, may be charged against this generation, from the blood of Abel to the blood of Zechariah, who perished between the altar and the sanctuary. Yes, I tell you, it will be required of this generation. Woe to you lawyers! For you have taken away the key of knowledge. You did not enter yourselves, and you hindered those who were entering."

As He went away from there, the scribes and the Pharisees began to press Him hard and to provoke Him to speak about many things, lying in wait for Him, to catch Him in something He might say.

The invitation of the Pharisee to dine with Him gave Jesus the opportunity to teach a lesson. Jesus omitted the customary washing before the meal, and when He was criticized for this, He in return exposed their faults. They stressed outward purity but did not touch the evil in the heart. They paid tithes on the smallest vegetables that grew in their garden but neglected the really important virtues. They were ambitious and proud, seeking honor among men. When a scribe interrupted Jesus, He included them in His arraignment. They imposed upon the people with all kinds of precepts and ordinances that they themselves did not observe. They built monuments to the prophets but denied their teaching. They claimed to be the only teachers of religion, yet they taught the people a false religion. Jesus sums up all their wickedness by pointing out their hypocrisy.

Hypocrisy is a most atrocious sin because it is deliberate sin against better knowledge. The hypocrite knows what is right. He tries to make people believe he is doing right, while he consciously and deliberately does what he knows is wrong. Therefore, the Lord, who was tender and loving toward all other sinners, no matter how deeply they had fallen, could castigate these hypocrites in such harsh terms. He is Himself the truth; He comes from the God of truth; He preaches the religion of truth; and He has no mercy for those who choose a life of deceit.

Phariseeism has not died out in the course of time. Hypocrisy is a very prevalent sin. Worse than that, hypocrisy is born into us all. Even the best Christian will find this weed growing in his heart. We must fight it all the days of our life. If we do not, if we fall asleep on the battlefront, it will overpower us and gain dominion over us. Unless we are very watchful, this insidious sin will occupy our heart before we are aware of it. There is reason for the oft-repeated warning against hypocrisy in Scripture. How many of Jesus' parables are aimed at this detestable sin! His woe still stands against all those who practice it.

Let us examine our hearts for any signs of hypocrisy, and if we find them, let us go to Him who has bled and died to cleanse us from all sin. And then, with His help, let us cleanse our heart from this filth and live uprightly before God and men.

Prayer

O Lord, to whom the most secret thoughts of our heart are known, open our eyes, we pray You, by Your holy Law that we, too, may see and acknowledge our failings. Let not sin overpower us, but grant us grace to root it out of our heart and life. And where we fail because of our weakness, forgive us for the sake of Him who bore all our sins on the cross, our Lord and Savior, Jesus Christ. Amen.

FEAR NOT!
Luke 12:1–12

THE experience related in the previous lesson, Jesus' clash with the hypocritical Pharisees and scribes and His severe denunciation of hypocrisy, quite naturally led to the admonitions and promises in today's text. Jesus warns against all hypocrisy, urges a frank and bold confession of His name and Word, and assures His disciples that they do not stand alone in a hostile world. He Himself is watching over them and taking note of their confession; their heavenly Father protects them; the Holy Spirit guides and leads them. So the message of this passage is "Fear not." Do Christians today need the admonition and comfort of these words? Who could doubt it?

Beware of the Leaven of the Pharisees

In the meantime, when so many thousands of the people had gathered together that they were trampling one another, He began to say to His disciples first, "Beware of the leaven of the Pharisees, which is hypocrisy. Nothing is covered up that will not be revealed, or hidden that will not be known. Therefore whatever you have said in the dark shall be heard in the light, and what you have whispered in private rooms shall be proclaimed on the housetops.

Have No Fear

"I tell you, My friends, do not fear those who kill the body, and after that have nothing more that they can do. But I will warn you whom to fear: fear Him who, after He has killed, has authority to cast into hell. Yes, I tell you, fear Him! Are not five sparrows sold for two pennies? And not one of them is forgotten before God. Why, even the hairs of your head are all numbered. Fear not; you are of more value than many sparrows.

Acknowledge Christ Before Men

"And I tell you, everyone who acknowledges Me before men, the Son of Man also will acknowledge before the angels of God, but the one who denies Me before men will be denied before the angels of God. And everyone who speaks a word against the Son of Man will be forgiven, but the one who blasphemes against the Holy Spirit will not be forgiven. And when they bring you before the synagogues and the rulers and the authorities, do not be anxious about how you should defend yourself or what you should say, for the Holy Spirit will teach you in that very hour what you ought to say."

Hypocrisy is like leaven; it will soon permeate the whole existence of those who allow it to find even a tiny place in their heart. It will pollute every word and deed; it will not remain hidden. Hypocrisy must have no place in the Christian life, says the Lord. Christians have nothing to hide, nor should they be inclined to cover up their convictions. Why should we be ashamed to have anyone know that we pray, that we go to church, that we read our Bibles? Why be ashamed to wear a crucifix or hang religious artwork on our walls? Friends who regard such things with a pitying smile, perhaps even sneer at them, are not good friends, and we are better off without them.

Yes, a frank confession of Christ or our Christian convictions may cause trouble for us, especially when it provokes us to part ways with such friends or perhaps condemn their way of life. Even then, Pharisees and scribes were beginning to plot against the life of Jesus. So we can expect to encounter criticism, more or less vicious; they will call us intolerant and persecution may even result. But at its worst, such persecution can only harm the body. No one can hurt our soul but God, and so long as He is on our side we need not fear any other power. And when the end comes, and it will come, there will be the Son of God to acknowledge us as His own. Meanwhile, although He is not visibly at our side, He will send His Holy Spirit to assist us in our confession, even giving us the words to speak when we are called upon to defend our faith and life.

It is a wonderful promise. Life is as uncertain for us as it was for the disciples on that day. There was bound to be danger and trouble they did not know, so Jesus assured them of that microscopic care of God. Sparrows surely are not worth much, Jesus says. In Matthew 10:29, Jesus says they are two for a penny; here He makes it less: five for two pennies. Yet not one of them, not even that fifth sparrow, is forgotten before God. He has even counted every hair on your head!

So the Lord assures us, "Fear not; you are of more value than many sparrows." You are His precious child, redeemed by the blood of His own Son. God showed you that unequaled evidence of His love when He gave His only-begotten Son for you. Why would He now deny you that love, that protection and providing care! It is impossible that anything would happen to you that He has not foreknown and permitted. And whatever He permits must be good and in some way profitable for you.

Thousands of God's children can testify to the truth of this promise. There was a man who had far more than the average Christian's share of trouble, who at the time lay in prison, his future about as uncertain as it could be. Yet this man, Paul, looked back at all the experiences of his life and said, "We know." Not we *hope*, but "we know that for those who love God all things work together for good" (Romans 8:28).

If ever our hearts threaten to fail us for fear and for worrying about things that are coming on this earth, let us think of that fifth sparrow and hear the Lord whisper at our side, "Fear not; you are of more value than many sparrows."

Prayer

O Lord, who in Your infinite love cares for the least of Your creatures, defend us from all fear and anxiety for the future; fill our hearts with trust in You and Your Fatherly care that we may fix our mind on that which is to come and, unhampered by the troubles of this world, strive for that better life that You have in store for us. In Jesus' name. Amen.

47 BEWARE OF COVETOUSNESS!
Luke 12:13–21

THE only repetition or duplication in the Decalogue is in the Ninth and Tenth Commandments; both forbid coveting. There is, of course, a difference in the object, but the attitude and action forbidden is the same. Surely that means something. He who gave the Law knows that this is the sin to which we are specially given and against which we must be especially on guard. Although this sin is so prevalent, it is least acknowledged. So the parable the Lord tells us here contains a lesson that we need.

The Parable of the Rich Fool

Someone in the crowd said to Him, "Teacher, tell my brother to divide the inheritance with me." But He said to him, "Man, who made Me a judge or arbitrator over you?" And He said to them, "Take care, and be on your guard against all covetousness, for one's life does not consist in the abundance of his possessions." And He told them a parable, saying, "The land of a rich man produced plentifully, and he thought to himself, 'What shall I do, for I have nowhere to store my crops?' And he said, 'I will do this: I will tear down my barns and build larger ones, and there I will store all my grain and my goods. And I will say to my soul, Soul, you have ample goods laid up for many years; relax, eat, drink, be merry.' But God said to him, 'Fool! This night your soul is required of you, and the things you have prepared, whose will they be?' So is the one who lays up treasure for himself and is not rich toward God."

It is a serious matter to call a man a fool. Jesus uses strong language in reference to it in His Sermon on the Mount (Matthew 5:22), "Whoever says, 'You fool!' will be liable to the hell of fire." We may be sure, therefore, that when the Lord called this man a fool, He uses the term in its fullest sense. The provocation was such a fool among the people to whom Jesus was speaking. He had pushed his way to the front, and when Jesus paused, he interrupted Him and said, "Teacher, tell my brother to divide the inheritance with me." While Jesus spoke of eternal things, this man thought only of his greed and his petty grievance against his brother. So Jesus told the parable of the covetous fool.

Why was he a fool? He was a rich man. Jesus does not say he was dishonest, so we may assume he had acquired his riches honestly. "The hand of the diligent makes rich" (Proverbs 10:4). He was a skillful farmer who knew how to get the most out of his land. True, it is God who provides, but He lets no corn grow where no seed has been planted, nor does He let the untilled acre produce as much as the well-cultivated one. The man was thrifty; he would not let his corn spoil in the field. So he had many admirable qualities.

But in the most important things he was a fool. He had a false view of life, thinking that wealth gives life significance. He provided only for the body, the least important part. And he left God out of his reckoning altogether. "My crops," "my barns," "my grain," he said. But who gave his crop rain and sunshine? Who gave him strength of body, the active brain, and life itself? He hasn't a word to say about God or to God, only about himself. Nor did he think of other people; he is utterly selfish. And finally, he provided only for the shortest part of his existence. "Soul, you have ample goods laid up for many years," he said. But God said, "Fool! This night your soul is required of you." And from that verdict there is no appeal.

Is that selfish, worldly minded man unknown today? Hardly. He is the type of man who is so wrapped up in the temporary concerns of this world that he has no time for the far more important concerns of the soul. When Jesus tells this parable, He in effect asks, Suppose you had all you desire and more; what would you gain in the end? Jesus calls this man a fool and tells us, "Take care, and be on your guard against all covetousness, for one's life does not consist in the abundance of his possessions."

So in this parable the Lord shows us the image of this man and underneath He signs His name: "So is the one who lays up treasure for himself and is not rich toward God." Let us look closely to see if perhaps that is our name as well. It makes a vast difference whether you are merely rich or are rich toward God. How happy the merely rich could be, eating, drinking, being merry, if it were not for one thing: "This night your soul is required of you." It is a familiar story. Man says, Not now; later. God says, Now—in a plane crash, a sinking boat, a car wreck, by sudden heart failure. And to the man in this passage, Jesus says, No matter how much that inheritance means to you, if you have no higher wealth, you are only another fool. And to us, Jesus says, If you know no other thoughts but of your crops, your goods, the things of this life, then you may in other things be very different from this man. You may not die so suddenly; you may die with more or less wealth; but in all essentials you are a fool.

Prayer

Dear heavenly Father, for the sake of our Savior, Jesus Christ, grant us true wisdom that while it is still day we may gather in the true riches that do not fade away when the sun of this life goes down. Let us, in Your Holy Word, find the pardon in the blood of Your Son for all that we have done amiss, comfort in every trial, strength for any battle, and the sure hope that after the night of death there will be the eternal day of bliss with You in heaven. In Jesus' name we ask it. Amen.

48

DO NOT WORRY!
Luke 12:22–34

THE Lord told the parable of the rich fool as a warning against covetousness. But covetousness is not limited to the rich; the beggar may also be covetous. Often the cause of covetousness is worry about the future. Not only the needy worry. The old proverb says, Uneasy lies the head that wears a crown. Why? They fear the loss of what they have. Worry is a common plague. Farmers know there is a worm that infests granaries and gnaws into the wheat kernel and eats out the heart. When the wheat is sold, it has no weight, and when it is ground, there is no flour. Care is such a worm; it bores into the heart and takes all the joy and blessing out of every gift of God. Nor is worry limited to those who do not know the Father in heaven. That is why Jesus addresses this message to His disciples.

Do Not Be Anxious

And He said to His disciples, "Therefore I tell you, do not be anxious about your life, what you will eat, nor about your body, what you will put on. For life is more than food, and the body more than clothing. Consider the ravens: they neither sow nor reap, they have neither storehouse nor barn, and yet God feeds them. Of how much more value are you than the birds! And which of you by being anxious can add a single hour to his span of life? If then you are not able to do as small a thing as that, why are you anxious about the rest? Consider the lilies, how they grow: they neither toil nor spin, yet I tell you, even Solomon in all his glory was not arrayed like one of these. But if God so clothes the grass, which is alive in the field today, and tomorrow is thrown into the oven, how much more will He clothe you, O you of little faith! And do not seek what you are to eat and what you are to drink, nor be worried. For all the nations of the world seek after these things, and your Father knows that you need them. Instead, seek His kingdom, and these things will be added to you.

"Fear not, little flock, for it is your Father's good pleasure to give you the kingdom. Sell your possessions, and give to the needy. Provide yourselves with moneybags that do not grow old, with a treasure in the heavens that does not fail, where no thief approaches and no moth destroys. For where your treasure is, there will your heart be also."

When we hear the Lord tell us in so many different ways not to worry, is not our first thought, That's impossible? Angels may be able to let go of worry, but for a human heart, it is impossible. But in this text, Jesus gives us an unqualified command. He does not say *try* not to worry or don't worry any more than you can help. No. Jesus says, Do not worry at all. Is it possible?

It surely cannot be denied that ours is a careworn generation. The world has never been so rich in material things, never before had so many mechanical appliances and technological advances to make life easier. But the richer the world grows, the more anxious it gets. All the machinery and technology that surround us have multiplied our power enormously and multiplied our cares correspondingly. They increase the speed at which we must move, increase the pressure under which we live. Worry is the bane of modern life. It is worry, not hard work, that wears us out before our time. Is it possible to keep anxiety out of the heart?

There must be a way to make the impossible possible, some way of overcoming worry. Where was Paul when he wrote, "Do not be anxious about anything" (Philippians 4:6)? In prison in Rome, awaiting the trial that would probably end in his death. Once Rome fixed her claws, she did not usually let go without drawing blood. Paul's future was about as dark and threatening as it could be. But calmly he tells his brothers, "Do not be anxious about anything." What was his secret?

Jesus tells us the secret, "Your Father." That's the answer. He points to the birds and the flowers. The birds sing when crops are good and when crops are poor. The lilies are arrayed finer than Solomon in all his glory, yet none of them ever lost sleep because they had nothing to wear or because they were worried about the future. They have a Father. The boy playing out in the field does not suddenly drop bat and ball, lean up against the fence, and worry about tomorrow's breakfast. No, he has a father who provides for him. And Jesus says, "Your Father knows that you need them." He has not promised to do everything for us; He wants us to work; but He has promised to provide for all our needs. Why be foolish and worry when He has already taken the load from us?

Or does it seem as though the Lord's illustrations are poorly chosen? Lilies have no heart; birds have no mind. Can a man who thinks of the future escape worry? Paul wrote thirteen letters that are included in the New Testament, and in all of them not one word indicates that he has a worry or care. How could he do that? "Do not be anxious about anything, but in everything by prayer and supplication with thanksgiving let your requests be made known to God" (Philippians 4:6). Worry is a habit, an evil habit. We must get rid of it. And to do that, we must replace it with that other habit of casting all care on God.

Prayer

*Almighty God, our heavenly Father, whose mercies are new
to us every morning and who, although we have in no way
deserved Your goodness, abundantly provides for all our wants
of body and soul, give us, we pray, Your Holy Spirit, that we
may heartily acknowledge Your merciful goodness toward us,
give thanks for all Your benefits, and serve You in willing
obedience; through Jesus Christ, Your Son, our Lord. Amen.*

BE READY!
Luke 12:35–48

JESUS warned His disciples against worry. It is vain and useless, He
says, and silly. After all, of what value are the things people usually
worry about? There is really only one thing that is worth a little
worry—and even that we should not worry about! That one thing
is that the kingdom of God come to us; or, to put it another way,
that we enter the kingdom of God. "But seek first the kingdom of
God," Jesus says (Matthew 6:33). God indeed wants us to inherit the
Kingdom; "Fear not, little flock, for it is your Father's good pleasure to give you the kingdom" (Luke 12:32). But we may by our
own fault frustrate the good pleasure of our Father and so lose the
Kingdom. Seek that Kingdom, therefore, and do so now because
time is passing and soon it may be too late. That is the Lord's warning in this text: Be ready!

You Must Be Ready

"Stay dressed for action and keep your lamps burning, and
be like men who are waiting for their master to come home

from the wedding feast, so that they may open the door to him at once when he comes and knocks. Blessed are those servants whom the master finds awake when he comes. Truly, I say to you, he will dress himself for service and have them recline at table, and he will come and serve them. If he comes in the second watch, or in the third, and finds them awake, blessed are those servants! But know this, that if the master of the house had known at what hour the thief was coming, he would not have left his house to be broken into. You also must be ready, for the Son of Man is coming at an hour you do not expect."

Peter said, "Lord, are You telling this parable for us or for all?" And the Lord said, "Who then is the faithful and wise manager, whom his master will set over his household, to give them their portion of food at the proper time? Blessed is that servant whom his master will find so doing when he comes. Truly, I say to you, he will set him over all his possessions. But if that servant says to himself, 'My master is delayed in coming,' and begins to beat the male and female servants, and to eat and drink and get drunk, the master of that servant will come on a day when he does not expect him and at an hour he does not know, and will cut him in pieces and put him with the unfaithful. And that servant who knew his master's will but did not get ready or act according to his will, will receive a severe beating. But the one who did not know, and did what deserved a beating, will receive a light beating. Everyone to whom much was given, of him much will be required, and from him to whom they entrusted much, they will demand the more."

The lesson in all of these parables is the same: the Lord will return for judgment, and only those who are ready and waiting for Him when He comes will enter His kingdom. But no one knows when He will return; it may be soon, it may be later. Therefore, we must be ready at all times.

Be ready. This message is evident from the fact that in this passage the Lord calls His disciples His servants. But His disciples, His Christians, are more than that. Jesus tells them, "No longer do I call you servants, for the servant does not know what his master is doing; but I have called you friends, for all that I have heard from My Father I have made known to you" (John 15:15). But they are servants while they live in this world. Servants are ready for their Lord's coming if they faithfully and diligently do the work assigned to them. So we, His Christians, are to wait for His coming, but we are not to be idle. During this time before His return, we are to use the talents He has given us to serve Him, to support, maintain, and spread His kingdom. The servant who is thus employed is ready for his lord's return at any time and he is blessed, for his lord will reward him. Not that he has earned that reward. Being a servant, he owes his lord this service. His reward is one of grace, but this reward will not fail him because that's the kind of master he has.

Jesus assures Peter that the disciples who stand close to Him must above all heed that warning because, knowing His will so well, they have a correspondingly great responsibility. Not that others who know less of the Lord's will are absolved of responsibility. Not to know the will of the Lord is in itself a neglect of duty, a lack of watchfulness.

So the warning comes to us. It is the Lord's will that we live in this world and carry on the business of this life until the end of our days here. But during all this time, we must not forget that we are traveling toward a goal. Therefore, we must not permit the things that surround us to interfere with our journey. It is easy in the competition of this world's business to become so deeply involved that we forget our real business: preparing for the Lord's coming. So Jesus reminds us, first, of the certainty of His coming. Perhaps we will not live to see Him coming in the clouds of heaven; if that is the case then, as Augustine says, death is our Judgment Day. Second, we must remember that the time of His coming is uncertain. Nothing is as certain as death; nothing as uncertain as the hour of death. And at that all-decisive hour, the hour of our death, so shall we be in all eternity.

So let us live in the light of God's Word; a life of faith is always a life of service. So let us pray with David, "O Lord, make me know my end and what is the measure of my days; let me know how fleeting I am!" (Psalm 39:4), and with Moses, "So teach us to number our days that we may get a heart of wisdom" (Psalm 90:12), so that in the end we may say with Simeon, "Lord, now you are letting Your servant depart in peace, according to Your word; for my eyes have seen Your salvation" (Luke 2:29–30).

Prayer
Teach us in watchfulness and prayer
To wait for the appointed hour,
And fit us by Thy grace to share
The triumphs of Thy conquering power. Amen.
(TLH 64:5)

THE SIGN THAT WILL BE SPOKEN AGAINST
Luke 12:49–59

JESUS had warned His disciples against worry and anxiety and the paralyzing effect these feelings have on the spiritual life. In the parables of the watchful servants, He admonished them in all the business of this life to focus on things of eternal value and, therefore, to be prepared for the Lord's return. He had answered Peter's question about whether these parables applied to them, too, by telling him that they did. In fact, the parables applied to them especially, since much would be required of those to whom so much had been given. Now, Jesus bids them to look at the matter from a different angle. His disciples will really have no time to waste on such frivolities as this world's goods. Their lives will not run smoothly and quietly while they wait for their Lord's return. There will be conflict and tumult, and they will be deeply involved in it. This is written for our instruction too. Let us consider the last section of this chapter.

Not Peace, but Division

"I came to cast fire on the earth, and would that it were already kindled! I have a baptism to be baptized with, and how great is My distress until it is accomplished! Do you think that I have come to give peace on earth? No, I tell you, but rather division. For from now on in one house there will be five divided, three against two and two against three. They will be divided, father against son and son against father, mother against daughter and daughter against mother, mother-in-law against her daughter-in-law and daughter-in-law against mother-in-law."

Interpreting the Time

He also said to the crowds, "When you see a cloud rising in the west, you say at once, 'A shower is coming.' And so it happens. And when you see the south wind blowing, you say, 'There will be scorching heat,' and it happens. You hypocrites! You know how to interpret the appearance of earth and sky, but why do you not know how to interpret the present time?

Settle with Your Accuser

"And why do you not judge for yourselves what is right? As you go with your accuser before the magistrate, make an effort to settle with him on the way, lest he drag you to the judge, and the judge hand you over to the officer, and the officer put you in prison. I tell you, you will never get out until you have paid the very last penny."

In this passage, Jesus introduces His disciples to a situation that was apparent then and has been ever since, that wherever Jesus appears, there is division and strife. This situation is to this day one of the chief causes of offense to non–Christians and even to many Christians. But it shouldn't surprise or offend us. Simeon foretold it when the Christ Child was but six weeks old, "Behold, this child is appointed for the fall and rising of many in Israel, and for a sign that is opposed" (Luke 2:34). Even at that early date, the shadow of the cross fell across His path, and so it was throughout His life. At His first appearance in His hometown, Nazareth, a few believed in Him, but the others wanted to throw Him off a cliff. The struggle grew ever more intense until three years later Jesus hung on the cross; a few faithful huddled near, in fear and trembling, but the great majority jeered at Him. So it is today. Ask any missionary—people live in relative peace until the Gospel of Christ is preached, then they divide, for Him or against.

Here Jesus tells us that this must be so. Since the fall of man, there is a terrible union on earth; all people are by nature the slaves of sin and destined for eternal damnation. Jesus came and with His life and death brought redemption to sinners. He offers this redemption to all people. Some accept it, many do not, and there is the division. It seems logical that all people would welcome and gratefully accept their release from bondage and the wrath of God. But the awful thing is that people love sin, and the majority do not want to be removed from their life of sin. So they reject the Savior and even fight against Him. And behind it all is Satan, who does not want his work destroyed.

Thank God for this division! How terrible if Christ, foreseeing this division, had decided not to redeem man, or, foreseeing that so many would not accept the Gospel, had decided it was not worthwhile to have it preached to us! In the face of all opposition, He designed a perfect redemption for us. And even now He is not discouraged by the ingratitude of men but continues to send out His Gospel call into the world. He considers not those who reject and oppose Him and His work, but those who joyfully and gratefully receive Him.

And that leads to the question Where do we stand? God in His grace has given us the truth. We know the Savior. Are we completely on His side? This is a vital question because there can be no compromise nor neutrality. In earthly things, we know very well that there are times when we must decide what is right or wrong; we cannot remain neutral. Let us not be like the Jews of that day who could tell the signs of the weather but could not or would not be convinced by the proof God gave them of Jesus' divinity and mission. With Him is our salvation, no matter how many turn away from Him.

Prayer

Thus my longings, heav'nward tending,
  Jesus, rest alone on Thee.
Help me, thus on Thee depending;
  Savior, come and dwell in me.
Although all the world should forsake and forget Thee,
In love I will follow Thee, ne'er will I quit Thee.
Lord Jesus, both spirit and life is Thy Word;
And is there a joy which Thou dost not afford?
(TLH 366:4)

Therefore You alone, my Savior,
  Shall be all in all to me;
Search my heart and my behavior,
  Root out all hypocrisy.
Through all my life's pilgrimage guard and uphold me,
In loving forgiveness, O Jesus enfold me.
This one thing is needful, all others are vain—
I count all but loss that I Christ may obtain! Amen.
(LSB 536:5)

THE GOODNESS AND THE SEVERITY OF GOD
Luke 13:1–9

ONCE, seeing a man born blind, His apostles asked Jesus, "Rabbi, who sinned, this man or his parents, that he was born blind?" (John 9:2). That is the same reaction many people have when they see victims of misfortune: what did he do to deserve that? There must be a dark secret in his life. And how often does that question rise in our own mind when we suffer: why did that happen to me? Now, one thing we should all know, if we believe what the Word of God teaches, no one suffers as he deserves; it is of the Lord's mercies that we are not all totally consumed (Lamentations 3:22). Neither is it true that one who suffers more also deserves it more than others. In all this there is a mystery in God's providence that is beyond our understanding. Only one thing is sure—God's intentions toward us are good and kind. That is the lesson this text teaches us.

Repent or Perish

There were some present at that very time who told Him about the Galileans whose blood Pilate had mingled with their sacrifices. And He answered them, "Do you think that these Galileans were worse sinners than all the other Galileans, because they suffered in this way? No, I tell you; but unless you repent, you will all likewise perish. Or those eighteen on whom the tower in Siloam fell and killed them: do you think that they were worse offenders than all the others who lived in Jerusalem? No, I tell you; but unless you repent, you will all likewise perish."

The Parable of the Barren Fig Tree

And He told this parable: "A man had a fig tree planted in his vineyard, and he came seeking fruit on it and found none.

> And he said to the vinedresser, 'Look, for three years now I
> have come seeking fruit on this fig tree, and I find none. Cut
> it down. Why should it use up the ground?' And he answered
> him, 'Sir, let it alone this year also, until I dig around it and
> put on manure. Then if it should bear fruit next year, well and
> good; but if not, you can cut it down.' "

People in the crowd told Jesus about that tragedy of the Galilaeans.
Why they did that, we are not told; some people love to bring bad
news. Perhaps they expected a tirade against the rotten government
of Pilate, but the Lord often does not answer as we wish and expect.
Jesus is a masterful preacher; He can use anything He hears for the
edification of His hearers. He forestalls any thoughts of condemnation and turns their thoughts on their own life. Yes, they were
wicked, He says, but not more so than anyone else, not more so
than the people speaking with Him. He tells them that they must
not judge those who are caught in a great catastrophe; judgment
must be left to God. That's His business, and His alone. What they
should do was to apply the lesson to themselves.

And that is its meaning to us. Jesus does not solve for us the
mysteries of God's providence in such tragic events. He does say,
however, that we should ask ourselves how it is that we are still living, that God has held His protecting hand over us while catastrophe
comes to thousands of others? How is it that we must confess, if we
are honest, that God has blessed us richly in spiritual and temporal
things, while others have starved in body and soul? Are we less guilty?
For our self-examination, Jesus tells the parable of the fig tree.

This parable refers directly to Israel, but it has a much wider
meaning. It is our life's story too. God planted us in a church of the
pure Gospel, in a land where we enjoy religious freedom. Did we
deserve this blessing? That's a foolish question. Can we give one reason why we were born here and not in a country where Christians
are persecuted or executed; why our mothers brought us to Baptism
instead of throwing us to the sacred crocodiles? Were we better than
they even before we were born? Why did God do this for us?

In the parable, the owner of the fig tree looked for fruit. He had a right to expect some after all he had done for the fig tree. And God has a right to expect fruit in us. He gave us His Son for a Savior and His Holy Spirit with His Word and grace, and He placed us right in the midst of His garden. Jesus tells us what that fruit is, "Unless you repent, you will all likewise perish." True repentance, with genuine fruits of repentance, a thoroughly godly life, that is the fruit God desires.

But what does the Lord find in us? "Look, for three years now I have come seeking fruit," He says. His patience is great; but note that He counts the years. His patience will eventually end. In fact, we owe it to the great Vinedresser, Jesus Christ, that God still bears with us. "If anyone does sin, we have an advocate with the Father, Jesus Christ the righteous. He is the propitiation for our sins, and not for ours only but also for the sins of the whole world" (1 John 2:1–2). So He grants us one year after another. But He wants fruit; not just the absence of bad fruit, but a yield good fruit. And someday His patience will end.

Jesus intentionally left the parable incomplete. Did that tree finally bear fruit or was it cut down? We do not know. Our life's story is not yet complete either. God has showered all His grace on us. He has looked for fruit from us time after time. And He has prolonged our day of grace. Thank God for the Savior, who has washed away our past sins! Thank God if there has been some fruit in our life! But we must confess that there should be more.

As we meditate on this parable, may the justice of God warn us away from all carelessness and indifference, and may His grace and patient love win us wholly unto Himself and our Savior, Jesus Christ.

Prayer

*O Lord, You are the God of patience and Your mercy is new
to us every morning. We pray that You continue Your grace to us,
that we may repent of our sin, that we find forgiveness in the
blood of Your Son and amend our sinful life and bring forth
the fruits of righteousness, that we may escape Your righteous*

judgment and not forfeit the blessings our Savior has earned for us. For His sake we ask it. Amen.

TRUE OBSERVANCE OF THE LORD'S DAY

Luke 13:10–17

IT is a sad fact that people will misinterpret, misjudge, and abuse whatever God says or does. God gave His Law, and humans regard it as a heavy burden and view Him as a hard, severe judge for demanding and enforcing obedience. The truth is, however, that God in His Law has outlined the truly happy way of life for us. Originally, the Law was the way to attain eternal life. Jesus told the scribe, "Do this, and you will live," when he correctly stated that the core of God's Law is love to God and love to the neighbor (Luke 10:28). That way to heaven was blocked by man's fall into sin; we can no longer keep the Law as God wants it kept. It is still true that the man who walks the way of God's Commandments will be happy in this life. But men continue to misapply God's Law. An example of this was the Sabbath law. The Sabbath was given for man, Jesus said; for man's own sake, God set aside a day of rest. And men promptly made a burden of the Sabbath, as though man was made for the Sabbath. Today's reading shows both that the Jewish teachers abused the Sabbath law and that Jesus taught the true observance of the Sabbath, or the Lord's Day.

A Woman with a Disabling Spirit

Now He was teaching in one of the synagogues on the Sabbath. And there was a woman who had had a disabling spirit for eighteen years. She was bent over and could not fully straighten herself. When Jesus saw her, He called her over and said to her, "Woman, you are freed from your disability." And He laid His hands on her, and immediately she was made straight, and she glorified God. But the ruler of the synagogue, indignant because Jesus had healed on the Sabbath, said to the people, "There are six days in which work ought to be done. Come on those days and be healed, and not on the Sabbath day." Then the Lord answered him, "You hypocrites! Does not each of you on the Sabbath untie his ox or his donkey from the manger and lead it away to water it? And ought not this woman, a daughter of Abraham whom Satan bound for eighteen years, be loosed from this bond on the Sabbath day?" As He said these things, all His adversaries were put to shame, and all the people rejoiced at all the glorious things that were done by Him.

Note, first, that Jesus "was teaching in one of the synagogues on the Sabbath." Jesus went to church on the Lord's Day. That is basic. No matter how the Old Testament Sabbath law has been changed (and God has changed it), this remains: true observance of the Lord's Day requires that we go to the Lord's house and hear His Word. "Remember the Sabbath day, to keep it holy," was God's command (Exodus 20:8). The Sabbath day has been abolished; God no longer requires that we keep the seventh day of the week. St. Paul wrote, "Let no one pass judgment on you in questions of food and drink, or with regard to a festival or a new moon or a Sabbath. These are a shadow of the things to come, but the substance belongs to Christ" (Colossians 2:16–17). The command still stands to keep the Lord's Day holy, but while in the Old Testament God prescribed which day of the week was to be observed, in the New Testament, He leaves the choice of the day to us. But whatever day we choose, it is His will that we keep it holy, "for it is made holy by the word of God and prayer" (1 Timothy 4:5). Primarily, what God requires of us and what we owe to our souls is that we hear, read, believe, and keep the Word of God.

But true observance of the Lord's Day requires more, and that, too, Jesus showed by His example. He healed this poor, suffering woman. The ruler of the synagogue was offended because Jesus did this on the Sabbath. But Jesus exposed his hypocrisy by pointing out that he would never hesitate to water his cattle on the Sabbath, and here was a daughter of Abraham that Satan had tormented for eighteen years. Was not her need far greater? In other words, Jesus says that showing love and providing service to our brothers and sisters are true and God-pleasing ways to observe the Lord's Day. The relief of human sorrow and suffering is always in season, it is appropriate at any hour, and especially so on the Lord's Day. "Religion that is pure and undefiled before God, the Father, is this: to visit orphans and widows in their affliction, and to keep oneself unstained from the world" (James 1:27). And by the prophet Isaiah, the Lord describes the service that pleases Him, "Is it not to share your bread with the hungry and bring the homeless poor into your house; when you see the naked, to cover him, and not to hide yourself from your own flesh?" (Isaiah 58:7).

The Lord's Day is to be a day of rest from the activity of daily life and, chiefly, a day of spiritual rest so that our immortal soul may be renewed, refreshed, and fed. So we should first of all take our soul to the Lord's Table, where He feeds us with food that nourishes us to eternal life. We will always find this in the Lord's house. Indeed, if we are ready to receive, we will find more than we expect. This woman did not expect to meet the Divine Healer when she set out to go to the Lord's house on that Sabbath morning—but He met her there. The Lord always has some special, some personal blessing for us in His house. How much we may miss if we fail to go even one Sunday! But the soul that has been filled with the Lord's treasure cannot possibly keep it all for herself; she must impart some of these riches to others. The miser who keeps everything for himself cannot enjoy what he has; nor is it a blessing for him. The Christian is constrained by his grateful heart to distribute the riches he has received in service to others who are not as fortunate. And that will only increase his own blessings. At the end of such a Sunday, His Master will say, "Well done, good and faithful servant" (Matthew 25:21).

Prayer

O Lord, teach us to love the habitation of Your house and the place where Your glory dwells. May we welcome the day when we can visit Your house to worship You and gladly embrace every opportunity to hear Your Word, to laud, and magnify Your name, to seek strength and comfort for the coming week and the blessed assurance that all our sins are forgiven for the sake of Him who shed His blood for us, our Savior, Jesus Christ. For His sake grant our prayer. Amen.

THE KINGDOM OF GOD
Luke 13:18–35

"THE kingdom of God is not coming with signs to be observed," the Lord told the Pharisees (Luke 17:20). They had asked Him when the kingdom of God would come. Jesus told them that the kind of kingdom they expected, a kingdom like that of David, would never come, nor would it come in the way they expected, in the wake of an army conquering the Romans. The world has always despised the kingdom of God—the Church—because there is so little pomp and splendor about it. They believe that important things make a show in the world. This belief keeps some people from paying attention to the message of the Church. But to know the kingdom of God and to become a member of it is the most important thing in life. Jesus speaks to us today about the kingdom of God.

The Mustard Seed and the Leaven

He said therefore, "What is the kingdom of God like? And to what shall I compare it? It is like a grain of mustard seed that a man took and sowed in his garden, and it grew and became a tree, and the birds of the air made nests in its branches."

And again He said, "To what shall I compare the kingdom of God? It is like leaven that a woman took and hid in three measures of flour, until it was all leavened."

The Narrow Door

He went on His way through towns and villages, teaching and journeying toward Jerusalem. And someone said to Him, "Lord, will those who are saved be few?" And He said to them, "Strive to enter through the narrow door. For many, I tell you, will seek to enter and will not be able. When once the master of the house has risen and shut the door, and you begin to stand outside and to knock at the door, saying, 'Lord, open to us,' then he will answer you, 'I do not know where you come from.' Then you will begin to say, 'We ate and drank in your presence, and you taught in our streets.' But he will say, 'I tell you, I do not know where you come from. Depart from me, all you workers of evil!' In that place there will be weeping and gnashing of teeth, when you see Abraham and Isaac and Jacob and all the prophets in the kingdom of God but you yourselves cast out. And people will come from east and west, and from north and south, and recline at table in the kingdom of God. And behold, some are last who will be first, and some are first who will be last."

Lament over Jerusalem

At that very hour some Pharisees came and said to Him, "Get away from here, for Herod wants to kill you." And He said to them, "Go and tell that fox, 'Behold, I cast out demons and perform cures today and tomorrow, and the third day I finish my course. Nevertheless, I must go on My way today and tomorrow and the day following, for it cannot be that a prophet should perish away from Jerusalem.' O Jerusalem,

Jerusalem, the city that kills the prophets and stones those who are sent to it! How often would I have gathered your children together as a hen gathers her brood under her wings, and you would not! Behold, your house is forsaken. And I tell you, you will not see Me until you say, 'Blessed is He who comes in the name of the Lord!' "

Jesus speaks of the growth of God's kingdom. It began in the world as small as a mustard seed, then it grew mightily, spreading from land to land until today it has reached all parts of the globe. And it grows intensively, as the leaven permeates the whole lump of dough, so the Gospel of the Kingdom enters the heart of a sinner and changes it and makes that person a new creation. Although to the world it seems insignificant, the kingdom of God is a mighty force that silently spreads and gradually conquers and changes whole nations.

Next, Jesus warns His hearers to make sure they have entered this Kingdom. Questions like the one put to Jesus here, whether many or few will be saved, should not worry us much. The important question for us is, Am *I* in God's kingdom? The gate to the Kingdom is narrow, it is the gate of repentance and faith in the Savior, and it's easy to miss. It is not safe to delay, because the time is coming when the gate will be shut and the time of grace will be over. While you are living, you may effectively knock at the door of heaven, but beyond the grave it is too late. There is even a chance that people who could have entered the Kingdom at one time are no longer able to do so. God can, as punishment for long and persistent contempt, close the door before death. And there is nothing more awful than the sentence of eternity!

Those who have entered the Kingdom are *forever* safe. Jesus knew that Herod, with all his power and enmity, could not cut His life one day shorter, and so His Christians know that they may calmly go on their way. No power on earth or in hell can hinder their work or shorten their time as determined for them by God. When their appointed task is done, God will call them to rest.

Oh, our God is a gracious God! He wants everyone to be in His kingdom. Even Jerusalem, with such a black record behind her, was the object of the Savior's solicitous care. No person ever misses the gate of heaven but by his own fault. "How often would I have gathered your children together," Jesus said, "and you would not!" God is not mocked; He is long-suffering. But the time comes when His patience ends and His justice steps in. What a warning for us who are enjoying privileges as great as those given to Jerusalem! We are eating and drinking in His presence, and we hear Him teach in our streets. But what use are we making of these privileges, of His Means of Grace?

Prayer

We thank You, O Father, that in Your mercy You have redeemed us by Your Son and made us members of Your kingdom of grace and heirs of Your kingdom of glory. Guide us by Your Holy Spirit, we pray You, that we many not abuse Your blessings or neglect them until it is too late. Give power to Your Word when we hear it that in contrite and believing hearts we may receive it and by it may be preserved in the faith until we see Him, our Savior, coming to take us to Himself in heaven. In His name we ask it. Amen.

CHRIST'S TABLE TALK
Luke 14:1–14

EVERYONE who reads the Gospels must note how often the Pharisees tried to convict Jesus of transgressing the Sabbath law. It is evident that the Sabbath commandment, and particularly the part that required complete rest on the Sabbath day, stood very high in the list of things taught to the people. Transgressing that commandment by doing any kind of labor was, in their opinion, one of the great sins. Does not Jesus indicate this when, after such a controversy with the Pharisees, He says, "The Son of Man is lord of the Sabbath" (Matthew 12:8)? In other words, even this law, which they held so highly, is subject to the Lord. But, He tells them, there are things that stand higher in God's eyes than the Sabbath rest. God says, "I desire steadfast love and not sacrifice" (Hosea 6:6). In today's text, St. Luke tells us how Jesus, on another occasion, after a similar controversy, taught His hearers a great lesson.

Healing of a Man on the Sabbath

One Sabbath, when He went to dine at the house of a ruler of the Pharisees, they were watching Him carefully. And behold, there was a man before Him who had dropsy. And Jesus responded to the lawyers and Pharisees, saying, "Is it lawful to heal on the Sabbath, or not?" But they remained silent. Then He took him and healed him and sent him away. And He said to them, "Which of you, having a son or an ox that has fallen into a well on a Sabbath day, will not immediately pull him out?" And they could not reply to these things.

The Parable of the Wedding Feast

Now He told a parable to those who were invited, when He noticed how they chose the places of honor, saying to them, "When you are invited by someone to a wedding feast, do not sit down in a place of honor, lest someone more distinguished than you be invited by him, and he who invited you both will come and say to you, 'Give your place to this person,' and then you will begin with shame to take the lowest place. But when you are invited, go and sit in the lowest place, so that when your host comes he may say to you, 'Friend, move up higher.' Then you will be honored in the presence of all who sit at table with you. For everyone who exalts himself will be humbled, and he who humbles himself will be exalted."

The Parable of the Great Banquet

He said also to the man who had invited Him, "When you give a dinner or a banquet, do not invite your friends or your brothers or your relatives or rich neighbors, lest they also invite you in return and you be repaid. But when you give a feast, invite the poor, the crippled, the lame, the blind, and you will be blessed, because they cannot repay you. For you will be repaid at the resurrection of the just."

Jesus was well aware that His enemies were watching Him. Perhaps this sick man was brought to the Pharisee's house for the very purpose of testing Jesus—would He heal him on the Sabbath? Jesus was ready for them when He pointed out that they themselves would not hesitate to rescue an animal on the Sabbath. The Pharisees would not answer Jesus' question, nor could they; how could they question an act of love done to a suffering fellow man?

When they were seated at the table, Jesus told them two parables, one to the guests and one to the host. The first parable teaches humility. Three times the Gospels records Jesus' words, "For everyone who exalts himself will be humbled, and he who humbles himself will be exalted." He, of course, does not only mean that this principle should be observed by guests at the table. This is one of the basic principles of Christian life, and one, sadly, that is often forgotten. Humility is one of the first and foremost Christian graces. More than that, the prophet Micah presented a program for a Christian life when he said, "He has told you, O man, what is good; and what does the Lord require of you but to do justice, and to love kindness, and to walk humbly with your God?" (Micah 6:8). No one can be a Christian and still be proud before God. Only the self-righteous Pharisee is proud before God. He who believes, along with Paul, that he is the foremost among sinners (1 Timothy 1:15) and that he owes all he is and all he can hope for to the grace of God and his Savior cannot be proud. Nor can a sinner who has a true knowledge of himself be proud and arrogant toward others who are in equal condemnation with him and who are equally redeemed with the same Savior's blood.

And right next to humility stands the Christian virtue of unselfishness. He who has learned the spirit of Jesus Christ feeds the poor, helps the needy, and defends those who are in danger of body or soul, not because he expects a return but because he loves them and he loves mercy. He is deeply grateful to his Lord for the blessings of His grace, and he knows that is the only way he can show his thankfulness to the Lord. "Truly, I say to you, as you did it to one of the least of these My brothers, you did it to Me" (Matthew 25:40).

World history offers many examples for the truth of the Word: "God opposes the proud but gives grace to the humble" (1 Peter 5:5). How well are we living this principle?

Prayer

O Lord, who gave us the most perfect example of humility and unselfish service, help us to conquer our natural pride, that we may know our sin and its terrible consequences, that we may see our only hope in Your redemption and in faith accept the salvation freely offered in Your Gospel. Grant us Your gracious assistance that we may follow in Your footsteps so that we may love our brothers and sisters and help and serve them in every need. Do not forsake us, because without You we can do nothing. Amen.

EXCUSES
Luke 14:15–24

THE next section of St. Luke's Gospel shows Jesus in the house of one of the chief Pharisees, where He had gone for a meal on the Sabbath. He had rebuked the guests for their pride in seeking places of honor at the table, and He'd rebuked the host for inviting only those guests from whom he might expect something in return. It was a harsh criticism and not very welcome. We can imagine an embarrassed silence at the table. Then one of the guests, perhaps

to change the subject or ease the tension, said, "Blessed is everyone who will eat bread in the kingdom of God!" In response, the
Lord told one of His most striking parables. This is the subject of
our meditation today.

> When one of those who reclined at table with Him heard
> these things, he said to Him, "Blessed is everyone who will eat
> bread in the kingdom of God!" But He said to him, "A man
> once gave a great banquet and invited many. And at the time
> for the banquet he sent his servant to say to those who had
> been invited, 'Come, for everything is now ready.' But they
> all alike began to make excuses. The first said to him, 'I have
> bought a field, and I must go out and see it. Please have me
> excused.' And another said, 'I have bought five yoke of oxen,
> and I go to examine them. Please have me excused.' And
> another said, 'I have married a wife, and therefore I cannot
> come.' So the servant came and reported these things to his
> master. Then the master of the house became angry and said to
> his servant, 'Go out quickly to the streets and lanes of the city,
> and bring in the poor and crippled and blind and lame.' And
> the servant said, 'Sir, what you commanded has been done, and
> still there is room.' And the master said to the servant, 'Go out
> to the highways and hedges and compel people to come in,
> that my house may be filled. For I tell you, none of those men
> who were invited shall taste my banquet.'"

That guest expressed a pious thought, but it included a note of
national pride: that they, the Jews, would undoubtedly spend eternity in the house of God. Jesus' answer was the parable of the great
banquet. This man sends out his invitations, and presumably they
are accepted, but when the supper is ready, nobody comes. Next,
he sends out his servant to remind the forgetful guests, but one after
another they make excuses and refuse to come. The first application
of the parable was, of course, to the Jews. Through the prophets,
God invited them to the great feast of salvation that He would prepare by His Son, the Messiah. But when the time came, they would
not come. Then John the Baptist came to extend the invitation. And

then came Christ Himself. But Jesus "came to His own, and His own people did not receive Him" (John 1:11). In today's reading, Jesus says that if eating the bread in the kingdom of God is so blessed a thing, why do they not come? Why do they make excuses?

How much like the Jewish nation of that time are we? God still sends out the invitation to His great supper, but few come, and most of them make excuses. The Lord is not referring to declared enemies of the Gospel but to those who know they should come to God's great supper, those who should think more of their soul and their eternal welfare but find reasons to delay or decline.

These are strong arguments. It is perfectly right to look at new investments, to try out new equipment, to enjoy family life. But it is perfectly wrong that these things interfere with the Lord's invitation. It is wrong that our jobs take a higher priority than Gethsemane and Calvary, than the new Jerusalem. It is wrong that our work should make us forget that we have an immortal soul that is worth more than any amount of wealth. It is wrong that we should say, "First, let me enjoy this life; then, when I lie on my deathbed, talk to me of eternity." Jobs, property, and family are legitimate priorities, but they are flimsy excuses if they interfere with the Lord's invitation. God's call may interfere with our wishes but never with our duties. In fact, our duties will be better performed if we seek first the kingdom of God and His righteousness. Our fields will be better tilled, family affairs will run more smoothly, and our emotional life will be healthy if first we answer the call of God.

So the real root of these excuses lies in the will. Our old evil heart does not want God's salvation, so it offers unreasonable excuses. It's unreasonable to say, "I'd rather be rich than go to heaven," but that is what people say when they neglect the spiritual for the earthly. So they become guilty of this shameful ingratitude to God, to His love that provided this feast for us, to the bitter sacrifice of the Lamb of God by which it was provided. It took Christ's agony and tears and blood to prepare this supper. And now He comes in the Gospel and says, "Come, for everything is now ready." Can there be more shameful ingratitude than this, that people should look unmoved at that sacrifice and offer vain and flimsy excuses for why they will not come and accept God's blessings?

Someday all excuses will disappear. Men can deceive their conscience, they can deceive the messengers of the Gospel, but they cannot deceive the Lord when He comes. May we, each of us, do what no man can do for us—lay our hand on our heart and say, "Here I am, Lord."

Prayer

Bless Your Word, we pray, O Lord, and make it powerful in our hearts that we may always heed its call and warning and not by vain excuses set aside its admonitions; that we may gratefully receive and accept the blessings that our Savior has earned for us and now offers us in His kingdom. Feed our soul at Your Table here in time, and grant us a place at Your heavenly table when time is done, for Jesus' sake. Amen.

THE TERMS OF DISCIPLESHIP
Luke 14:25–35

THANK God, there is no entrance fee to the kingdom of Christ! Salvation is free; "the free gift of God is eternal life in Christ Jesus our Lord" (Romans 6:23). And yet the mindful choice to respond to Christ and join His disciples is a very serious matter. When a certain scribe came to Jesus and offered to follow Him wherever He would go, Jesus answered, "Foxes have holes, and birds of the air have nests, but the Son of Man has nowhere to lay His head" (Luke 9:58). And a little later, to another man who first wanted to attend to his family, Jesus said, "No one who puts his hand to the plow and looks back is fit for the kingdom of God" (Luke 9:62). Following Christ will entail grave consequences, and the disciple should be prepared for that. That is the subject of Christ's teaching in today's reading.

The Cost of Discipleship

Now great crowds accompanied Him, and He turned and said to them, "If anyone comes to Me and does not hate his own father and mother and wife and children and brothers and sisters, yes, and even his own life, he cannot be My disciple. Whoever does not bear his own cross and come after Me cannot be My disciple. For which of you, desiring to build a tower, does not first sit down and count the cost, whether he has enough to complete it? Otherwise, when he has laid a foundation and is not able to finish, all who see it begin to mock him, saying, 'This man began to build and was not able to finish.' Or what king, going out to encounter another king in war, will not sit down first and deliberate whether he is able with ten thousand to meet him who comes against him with twenty thousand? And if not, while the other is yet a great way off, he sends a delegation and asks for terms of peace. So therefore, any one of you who does not renounce all that he has cannot be My disciple.

Salt Without Taste Is Worthless

"Salt is good, but if salt has lost its taste, how shall its saltiness be restored? It is of no use either for the soil or for the manure pile. It is thrown away. He who has ears to hear, let him hear."

Jesus knew that too many of the people who followed Him had earthly hopes and desires. They wanted to make Him king because He could feed them with bread and fish in the desert. But the Lord wants no followers under false pretenses, so He warns them—and us—about what every disciple of His must expect.

First, we must be prepared for sacrifice, to give up our dearest and best. Abraham must leave his home and his family. Moses must leave the security of Pharaoh's court. True, not every Christian is called upon to make this sacrifice, but every Christian must be willing to do so. When love of parents and family conflicts with our service to Christ, when self-interest or consideration for our own safety or welfare draws us away from Christ, we must be reminded that the love of Christ and His cause must stand highest in our heart and determine our conduct.

Second, the life of a disciple must have a focus. Every Christian is a builder, with the goal of building a perfect temple in which the triune God may dwell. But this building is costly, and whoever follows Christ should count the cost of building up his soul into a house of God. It requires repentance, self-denial, watchfulness, and continuous holy duties. It may cost reputation and honor among men; it may cost earthly possessions and liberties; it may cost life itself.

Third, the life of a disciple will be a constant battle. We have spiritual enemies who are restless in their opposition. They come well fortified. They meet us face-to-face or they lie in ambush to attack us unawares; they skirmish all around us. Are we able to withstand and overcome the onslaughts of devil, world, and our own flesh?

The Christian life is not a short burst, a sudden decision to follow Christ, and then it is done. No, it is a long process of hard work and constant battle. Like Nehemiah's builders, Christians must live with the trowel in one hand and the sword in the other (Nehemiah 4:17). And a beginning is worth nothing unless it leads to a successful end. God is not served with a tower of Babel, a landmark of a failed builder. It is easy to understand the derision of the world when there are so many ruins, so many half-finished towers in the Church. How can the world respect Christianity when there is so much obvious half-heartedness! But the Lord has set His Church in the midst of a godless world for a purpose, "That they may see your good works and give glory to your Father who is in heaven" (Matthew 5:16). Christians are to be the salt that preserves the world from total decay, the light to lead others along the right way. The Christian who fails to do that is not only no blessing to the world, but is also a curse because he causes the enemies of the Lord to blaspheme (Romans 2:23–24).

What if, after counting the cost and estimating our strength, we find that we lack the requirements for discipleship? Does Jesus say we should just quit or not begin at all? Oh, no! When His disciples asked despairingly, "Who then can be saved?" He answered, "With man this is impossible, but with God all things are possible" (Matthew 19:26). God wants the tower built. God wants the battle fought. And He can and will give all that is needed to do both to the successful end. Jesus, in His love, assures us that we cannot depend on our own strength but can go to that eternal source for all we need to make and keep us His true disciples.

Prayer

Without You, O Lord, we can do nothing. We pray that You send us Your Holy Spirit to give us courage and strength both to sacrifice and to labor and battle for Your kingdom, so that, in the certainty that neither the sufferings nor the hardships of this time are worthy to be compared with the glory that shall be revealed in us, we may gladly follow You, here under the cross and there to eternal victory and bliss. Amen.

57
JESUS SINNERS DOTH RECEIVE
Luke 15:1–10

WHEN Jesus entered Jerusalem on the Sunday before His great suffering, the children hailed Him as the Messiah and sang, "Hosanna to the Son of David!" When the chief priests and scribes wanted Jesus to make them stop, He answered, "Have you never read, 'Out of the mouth of infants and nursing babies you have prepared praise'?" (Matthew 21:16). If men who have reached the age of wisdom and understanding refuse to give the honor due to Him, then children will sing His praises and put them to shame. More than that, the Lord rules in the midst of His enemies, and even they must give glory to God. Balaam set out to curse Israel, but his tongue would not obey and he had to bless (Numbers 23). Caiaphas was the first to give the Jewish Council the terrible advice to put Christ to death, but under God's control he had to express that basic truth of the Gospel on which all our hope rests—that Jesus died for all men (John 11:49–50). We have a similar example of unwilling testimony to the Lord in today's text.

The Parable of the Lost Sheep

Now the tax collectors and sinners were all drawing near to hear Him. And the Pharisees and the scribes grumbled, saying, "This man receives sinners and eats with them."

So He told them this parable: "What man of you, having a hundred sheep, if he has lost one of them, does not leave the ninety-nine in the open country, and go after the one that is lost, until he finds it? And when he has found it, he lays it on his shoulders, rejoicing. And when he comes home, he calls together his friends and his neighbors, saying to them, 'Rejoice with me, for I have found my sheep that was lost.' Just so, I tell you, there will be more joy in heaven over one sinner who repents than over ninety-nine righteous persons who need no repentance.

The Parable of the Lost Coin

"Or what woman, having ten silver coins, if she loses one coin, does not light a lamp and sweep the house and seek diligently until she finds it? And when she has found it, she calls together her friends and neighbors, saying, 'Rejoice with me, for I have found the coin that I had lost.' Just so, I tell you, there is joy before the angels of God over one sinner who repents."

They thought they had said the worst thing that could be said of Jesus, "This man receives sinners." They indicated that He must be as bad as the people He associates with. But Jesus tells them the parable of the lost sheep and the lost coin. What do you expect of a shepherd when one of his sheep has gone astray; of a poor woman when she has lost a coin? They will search for that which is lost until it is found. The sheep and the coins need looking after.

It is the whole Gospel in one sentence, and so we love to sing it, "Jesus sinners doth receive." We praise God for this truth. Nobody else wants sinners. Pharisees say, "God, I thank You that I am not like other men" (Luke 18:11). They despise sinners and want nothing to do with them lest they soil their hands. They don't know what to do with them or how to help them. Nor does God in His holiness receive sinners. Adam and Eve were cast out of Paradise because they sinned. This is what happens to all sinners: they are cast out of the presence of God. That makes the sinner's lot desperate. "There is no distinction: for all have sinned and fall short of the glory of God" (Romans 3:22–23). The sinner has no refuge, no help, no friend.

There is only One: Jesus receives sinners. That's the very reason He came to earth—to save the lost. His very name testifies to that: Jesus, Savior. So we change this slur from the Pharisees a little. "This man receives sinners," they say with contempt. We say with joy, "Jesus receives sinners!" The name God gave to Him before He was born expresses His whole life's work. And now, since He could say, "It is finished," God, too, will receive sinners. Jesus has reconciled us with God. If we come in Jesus' name, God will receive us.

"Jesus receives sinners." Only sinners. The sheep that heedlessly or perhaps in stubbornness and willfulness has run away and can only stray farther into danger, the coin that lies lifeless and hidden in the dust and can do nothing toward being found, sinners who are dead in trespasses and sins and are hostile to God—these He seeks. In His Gospel, Jesus shows them their lost condition and invites them to return. He picks them up out of the mire, the thorns, the pitfalls in which they lie and carries them back to safety.

To the Pharisees, it was offensive that Jesus associated with tax collectors and sinners. The Pharisees, too, were sinners, but they would not admit it. They thought they needed no Savior. They would not let Jesus save them, so they were lost despite His work on their behalf. Jesus seeks such lost sheep, but they will not let Him help them. And that is the saddest thing of all, to be lost when all has been done to save them, lost forever just because they will not take the helping hand Jesus extends.

"Jesus receives sinners." That means me. Jesus has redeemed me, a lost and condemned creature. He purchased and won me from all sins, from death, and the power of the devil. He purchased me with His holy, precious blood and His innocent suffering and death. Now His Holy Spirit calls me by His Gospel, enlightens me with His gifts so I may know my Savior, sanctifies and keeps me in the true faith until the blessed end.

Jesus tells us that there is rejoicing in heaven among the angels whenever a sinner comes to the Savior in humble repentance and faith. How much greater should be our joy that "Jesus receives sinners," that He receives us.

Prayer

I, a sinner, come to Thee
With a penitent confession.
Savior, mercy show to me;
Grant for all my sins remission.
Let these words my soul relieve:
Jesus sinners doth receive.

Jesus sinners doth receive;
Also I have been forgiven;
And when I this earth must leave,
I shall find an open heaven.
Dying, still to Him I cleave:
Jesus sinners doth receive. Amen.
(LSB 609:4, 7)

THE PRODIGAL SON
Luke 15:11–32

THE three parables of this chapter belong together. In the two previous parables, of the lost sheep and of the lost coin, the seeking love of God is pictured to us. Neither the sheep nor the coin can do anything toward their return to safety; it is God who seeks and saves the sinner. In the parable of the prodigal son, Jesus tells us how the sinner returns to God. It is the most beautiful of Christ's parables and has even been called the pearl and crown of all the parables of Scripture. Much more might be said in its praise, but it does not need our praise; every eye can see its beauty. It is a wonderful story. And it's your story and mine, the history of mankind and of every Christian's soul. Let us hear it.

The Parable of the Prodigal Son

And He said, "There was a man who had two sons. And the younger of them said to his father, 'Father, give me the share of property that is coming to me.' And he divided his property between them. Not many days later, the younger son gathered all he had and took a journey into a far country, and there he squandered his property in reckless living. And when he had spent everything, a severe famine arose in that country, and he began to be in need. So he went and hired himself out to one of the citizens of that country, who sent him into his fields to feed pigs. And he was longing to be fed with the pods that the pigs ate, and no one gave him anything.

"But when he came to himself, he said, 'How many of my father's hired servants have more than enough bread, but I perish here with hunger! I will arise and go to my father, and I will say to him, "Father, I have sinned against heaven and before you. I am no longer worthy to be called your son. Treat me as one of your hired servants."' And he arose and came to his father. But while he was still a long way off, his father saw him and felt compassion, and ran and embraced him and kissed him. And the son said to him, 'Father, I have sinned against heaven and before you. I am no longer worthy to be called your son.' But the father said to his servants, 'Bring quickly the best robe, and put it on him, and put a ring on his hand, and shoes on his feet. And bring the fattened calf and kill it, and let us eat and celebrate. For this my son was dead, and is alive again; he was lost, and is found.' And they began to celebrate.

"Now his older son was in the field, and as he came and drew near to the house, he heard music and dancing. And he called one of the servants and asked what these things meant. And he said to him, 'Your brother has come, and your father has killed the fattened calf, because he has received him back safe and sound.' But he was angry and refused to go in. His father came out and entreated him, but he answered his father, 'Look, these many years I have served you, and I never disobeyed your command, yet you never gave me a young goat, that I might celebrate with my friends. But when this son of yours came, who has devoured your property with prostitutes, you killed the fattened calf for him!' And he said to him, 'Son, you are always with me, and all that is mine is yours. It was fitting to celebrate and be glad, for this your brother was dead, and is alive; he was lost, and is found.' "

This is the story of every sinner who turns away from God to go his own way as his wicked heart prompts him. He wants to be independent, not bound by the laws of God and considerations of eternity but free to live his own life. But the soul that is created for God and eternity cannot be satisfied with earthly things. Sooner or later, the veneer of the best this earth can offer wears thin, and the soul that has nothing beyond this world is bankrupt. All he can find or that false friends can offer is nothing but empty, unsatisfying food for a starving soul.

Then the sinner comes to himself. How? It is the remembrance of God's love that moves him. That love that gave even His dearest and best to salvage bankrupt souls moves the sinner to compare his present state with life in his Father's house. It brings him to a realization that he turned his back in contempt on Him who has given so many evidences of His love. And the hard heart softens. "I will go to my Father and confess my wickedness and unworthiness," he says. And he knows that his Father's love cannot have turned into hate; He will not turn him away.

Such trust in God's love is never disappointed. When the son in the parable, conscious of the load of his guilt, approaches the father's house, the father runs to meet him. He embraces him and kisses him before one word of confession is spoken. That is God's unending love to the sinner.

No question will be asked us
How often we have come;
Although we oft have wandered,
It is our Father's home. (*LSB* 915:3)

Through our sins, we forfeited all right to be called God's children, but He takes us back as His sons and daughters, His heirs, with all rights and privileges restored.

That is the way the sinner returns to the Father's house: repentance, confession, faith, and trust in the Father's love. The most serious fault of the elder brother is his blindness to himself. He claims never to have transgressed a commandment of his father, yet in every word he shows that he has never observed the heart of God's Law. Mercy and love are completely unknown to him; he loves neither his brother nor his father. And while Jesus does not complete the story, it is evident that there is a warning in the father's words to the elder brother: he is in danger of losing the father's love.

Prayer

Oh, draw us ever unto Thee,
Thou Friend of sinners, gracious Savior;
Help us that we may fervently
Desire Thy pardon, peace, and favor.
When guilty conscience doth reprove,
Reveal to us Thy heart of love.
May we, our wretchedness beholding,

See then Thy pardoning grace unfolding
And say:"To God all glory be:
My Savior, Christ, receiveth me."Amen.
(TLH 386:5)

59

WISE STEWARDSHIP
Luke 16:1–13

IN the three parables of chapter 15, Jesus told us how the sinner comes to God—God seeks him in his lost and helpless condition; God restores him to his former estate, forgives all his misdeeds, and completely justifies him of all his sins. Although it is not specifically stated in these parables, because it is explained elsewhere in the Bible, all this is for Jesus' sake. In the next parable, Jesus speaks of the life of those who have been brought back to God. He addresses His disciples, all those who have come to Him, all who have left the service of the world and have entered His service. To these He now speaks of their life in His service.

The Parable of the Dishonest Manager

He also said to the disciples, "There was a rich man who had a manager, and charges were brought to him that this man was wasting his possessions. And he called him and said to him, 'What is this that I hear about you? Turn in the account of your management, for you can no longer be manager.' And the manager said to himself, 'What shall I do, since my master is taking the management away from me? I am not strong enough to dig, and I am ashamed to beg. I have decided what to do, so that when I am removed from management, people may receive me into their houses.' So, summoning his master's debtors one by one, he said to the first, 'How much do you owe my master?' He said, 'A hundred measures of oil.' He said to him, 'Take your bill, and sit down quickly and write fifty.' Then he said to another, 'And how much do you owe?' He said, 'A hundred measures of wheat.' He said to him, 'Take your bill, and write eighty.' The master commended the dishonest manager for his shrewdness. For the sons of this world are more shrewd in dealing with their own generation than the sons of light. And I tell you, make friends for yourselves by means of unrighteous wealth, so that when it fails they may receive you into the eternal dwellings.

"One who is faithful in a very little is also faithful in much, and one who is dishonest in a very little is also dishonest in much. If then you have not been faithful in the unrighteous wealth, who will entrust to you the true riches? And if you have not been faithful in that which is another's, who will give you that which is your own? No servant can serve two masters, for either he will hate the one and love the other, or he will be devoted to the one and despise the other. You cannot serve God and money."

This parable may be somewhat puzzling because Jesus says that the rich man commended the unjust steward, but we should note that he is commended not for his crookedness and double-dealing but for his wisdom. When this steward realized that his day of reckoning was coming, he did not deceive himself; he knew he would be deposed and he made provision for the future. And that is the same advice Jesus gives to His disciples: do not deceive yourselves as to what you are and what the future will bring; but make provision for your future security.

We are the Lord's stewards. All that we have is His and we must use it wisely as long as we have it. We must return it when He demands it, and we must be accountable when He calls us. We are the Lord's stewards. If we would only keep this in mind at all times, whoever we are, however much or little we have, whether we have spiritual or material gifts, then what a change would there be in our attitude and our life!

The wise thing is to think ahead. The day of reckoning is coming, and it is folly to think that on that day we will be able to hide our faults or that God will overlook them. No, on that day we shall fail as surely as this unjust steward failed. We need help on that day of judgment, help that is found only in the Savior. He is our Advocate with our heavenly Judge, the propitiation for our sins.

But here Jesus directs our attention to another point. He says, Use the gifts God has entrusted to you in such a way that your works will speak for you in the day of judgment. When we leave this world naked as on the day we entered it, when our soul, without riches, without merits, stands at the door of eternity, what have we then but these works of which the Lord says, "their deeds follow them" (Revelation 14:13). It is true that these works will not open heaven's door for us. Luther said, "I would not give a penny for St. Peter's merits, that he should help me. He cannot help himself, but whatever he has he has from God by faith in Christ." Heaven is God's free gift through faith in Christ. But our letter of recommendation to the great Judge on that day will read, "Truly, I say to you, as you did it to one of the least of these My brothers, you did it to Me" (Matthew 25:40). The prayers and the blessings of those whose friendship we have gained with our wealth will knock at the doors of everlasting life and bear testimony to our faith that was active in love. And when the call comes for us to give an account of our stewardship, they will be there to speak for us, the living proof that we have been disciples and followers of the Lord.

Money is one of the little things in life. It is nothing in God's sight; there is no money in heaven. But it matters tremendously and eternally what we do with our money while we live. Cling to it, worship it, and God will say, "Fool! This night your soul is required of you, and the things you have prepared, whose will they be?" (Luke 12:20). Use it to God's glory, for His kingdom, for His poor and needy children, and He will say, "Well done, good and faithful servant" (Matthew 25:23).

Prayer

Lord, teach us to live our days wisely! Help us to remember always that we are Your stewards, that we may not abuse or waste the goods You have entrusted to us, but rather use them to serve You and our fellow men. Forgive us all our poor stewardship in the past, and grant us the will and the strength to do better today and in the future. Amen.

THE RICH MAN AND POOR LAZARUS
Luke 16:14–31

GOD has made us His stewards, His partners in the work of His kingdom here on earth. All that we are and all that we have is now to be used in service to Him. A lazy partner who does nothing is almost as bad as a dishonest partner. While the latter abuses the gifts he has received, the former wastes them. In this respect, and this respect only, the children of the world can serve as an example to the children of light. Are we as diligent in service to God and His Church as the people of the world are to their selfish life, to serving their desires and pride? The Pharisees, who were listening in, thought Jesus was warning them when He said, "No servant can serve two masters. . . . You cannot serve God and money" (Luke 16:13). So they derided Him and sneered at Him. In response, Jesus told them the parable of the rich man and Lazarus.

The Law and the Kingdom of God

The Pharisees, who were lovers of money, heard all these things, and they ridiculed Him. And He said to them, "You are those who justify yourselves before men, but God knows your hearts. For what is exalted among men is an abomination in the sight of God.

"The Law and the Prophets were until John; since then the good news of the kingdom of God is preached, and everyone forces his way into it. But it is easier for heaven and earth to pass away than for one dot of the Law to become void.

Divorce and Remarriage

"Everyone who divorces his wife and marries another commits adultery, and he who marries a woman divorced from her husband commits adultery.

The Rich Man and Lazarus

"There was a rich man who was clothed in purple and fine linen and who feasted sumptuously every day. And at his gate was laid a poor man named Lazarus, covered with sores, who desired to be fed with what fell from the rich man's table. Moreover, even the dogs came and licked his sores. The poor man died and was carried by the angels to Abraham's side. The rich man also died and was buried, and in Hades, being in torment, he lifted up his eyes and saw Abraham far off and Lazarus at his side. And he called out, 'Father Abraham, have mercy on me, and send Lazarus to dip the end of his finger in water and cool my tongue, for I am in anguish in this flame.' But Abraham said, 'Child, remember that you in your lifetime received your good things, and Lazarus in like manner bad things; but now he is comforted here, and you are in anguish. And besides all this, between us and you a great chasm has been fixed, in order that those who would pass from here to you may not be able, and none may cross from there to us.' And he said, 'Then I beg you, father, to send him to my father's house—for I have five brothers—so that he may warn them, lest they also come into this place of torment.' But Abraham said, 'They have Moses and the Prophets; let them hear them.' And he said, 'No, father Abraham, but if someone goes to them from the dead, they will repent.' He said to him, 'If they do not hear Moses and the

Prophets neither will they be convinced if someone should rise from the dead.' "

This is perhaps the sternest of Christ's parables. Descriptions of the fate of the ungodly after death are very rare in Scripture, but here the Lord gives us a glimpse of hell and of the torment of lost souls. The real object of the parable, however, is to teach us that the abuse of God's gifts has dire consequences. Not much is said about Lazarus; he is presented as the rich man's opportunity, which the latter denied. But there is nothing to tell us why Lazarus went to heaven. We learn why from other Scriptures: Lazarus did not go to heaven because he was poor and sick but because he was a true son of Abraham who sought his salvation in the faith of Abraham. What the rich man did or did not do made no difference for Lazarus; but it made a great difference for the rich man himself.

And that is the lesson Jesus teaches us here. This parable is the conclusion of the previous one. If your faith is active in love, if you make friends through the wealth and the gifts God has given you, then you will be received into the eternal mansions of God. If your faith is not active, it is proof that it is not real faith. And so failure to use your gifts in a God-pleasing way will have dire consequences. If in pride and selfishness you use them only for yourself, to satisfy your own wishes and desires, you will suffer eternally. The rich man was not lost because he was rich (Abraham was rich too), but he was lost because he did not make the right use of his riches. It is not only the evil that men do that condemns them, it is also the good they fail to do. The rich man did not mistreat Lazarus. In fact, no one could say anything evil of him; but his heart was wrong. He failed to help Lazarus.

In the end, Jesus indicates that the man could not even claim ignorance as an excuse. After all, when he asked that Lazarus go to warn his brothers, he meant that if he'd had such a warning from someone who had risen from the dead, then he would not be where he was now. But Abraham points the rich man to the Word of God, where there is sufficient instruction and warning if people are only willing to learn. Signs and miracles will not convert those who are not willing to listen to the Word. Only a short time later, another Lazarus did return from the dead, but this miracle only incited the enemies of the Lord to greater wrath and strengthened their desire to kill Jesus. And now, a greater One than Lazarus has returned from the dead to tell us what we must expect in eternity and to warn us that this present life is our opportunity to prepare for the future life. We must make use of it now before it is forever too late. "He who has ears to hear, let him hear" (Matthew 11:15).

Prayer

O God, who made both rich and poor, preserve us from dire poverty, lest we despair and sin against Your commandments. And preserve us from love of money and from selfish use of the gifts You have given us, lest our earthly possessions become a trap and drag us into damnation. Help us to keep our eyes fixed on our eternal goal and to regard all earthly things as temporary, that they may not hinder us on the way to that home that You have prepared for us through Your Son, our Savior, in whose name we ask it. Amen.

"LORD, INCREASE OUR FAITH"

Luke 17:1–10

THE previous passage recorded another disagreeable experience with the Pharisees. They had again met the Lord's teaching with a sneer. Jesus encourages His disciples by telling them not to be offended when their best and most loving attempts to teach people are met with contempt, derision, and, perhaps, even active opposition and persecution. Unreasonable as it seems, they must make up their minds that preaching Christ's sweet Gospel will evoke the enmity of the unsaved. In today's reading, Jesus explains why that is so, but above all He answers the disciples' plea, "Lord, increase our faith!"

Temptations to Sin

And He said to His disciples, "Temptations to sin are sure to come, but woe to the one through whom they come! It would be better for him if a millstone were hung around his neck and he were cast into the sea than that he should cause one of these little ones to sin. Pay attention to yourselves! If your brother sins, rebuke him, and if he repents, forgive him, and if he sins against you seven times in the day, and turns to you seven times, saying, 'I repent,' you must forgive him."

Increase Our Faith

The apostles said to the Lord, "Increase our faith!" And the Lord said, "If you had faith like a grain of mustard seed, you could say to this mulberry tree, 'Be uprooted and planted in the sea,' and it would obey you.

Unworthy Servants

"Will any one of you who has a servant plowing or keeping sheep say to him when he has come in from the field, 'Come at once and recline at table'? Will he not rather say to him, 'Prepare supper for me, and dress properly, and serve me while I eat and drink, and afterward you will eat and drink'? Does he thank the servant because he did what was commanded? So you also, when you have done all that you were commanded, say, 'We are unworthy servants; we have only done what was our duty.'"

The Lord prepares His disciples for disappointments from those to whom they preach. Since the world is what it is, the Word of the cross will always be a stumbling block and offense to many. But, Jesus warns, be very careful that you do not give people a reason for being offended at your preaching and your life. One who leads others, particularly children or those of weak faith, to sin through words or actions, himself sins grievously. Jesus says it would be better for such a person if he had never been born. One example of this kind of sin is the absence of forgiving love. Our whole life should be one of forgiving love. If someone should sin against us seven times a day or seventy times seven (Matthew 18:22), if he pleads for forgiveness, we should gladly grant it. Our forgiving love must know no end and no limit.

Let us look at our own heart. Is that a superhuman demand? To be able to look inward, something new, something superhuman and divine, must be added to our natural ability. There is only one thing that enables a person to rise above all his natural inclinations and forgive without any limitation: a living faith in the Redeemer. Having received free and boundless forgiveness for his own sins, he therefore has the ability and willingness to extend this same forgiveness to others. Is there a Christian who will not join in the disciples' prayer, "increase our faith"? Do not we all recognize the weakness and imperfection of our faith when we face the standard Jesus sets here? How impatient we are with the weaknesses of others!

Jesus encourages His disciples. True faith can do all things; it can move mountains—including mountains of intolerance and enmity. But it must be true faith, and an essential element of true faith is humility. Pride simply cannot exist in a heart filled with faith. Only the person who does not yet know himself can be proud and boastful. All we are and have we owe to God. He has made us, and He preserves us from day to day. Without His providence, we would immediately return to the dust we come from. We owe it to the Lord God that we are Christians. He called us by the Gospel, enlightened us with His gifts, sanctified and kept us in the one true faith. We are His, and we owe it to Him to live according to His will. Now, if that were possible, if in all things—every moment of our life—we perfectly fulfilled every one of His Commandments, we would still have done our duty only, no more. God owes us nothing. Yet He has promised us a reward. Jesus tells us that the Lord will do for the watchful servants all that the master does not owe them: "He will dress himself for service and have them recline at table, and he will come and serve them" (Luke 12:37). But this is a reward of God's grace and kindness; even with a perfect fulfillment of His Law we earn nothing. "We are unworthy servants; we have only done what was our duty." And no more. How contrite should we be because we know that even our best service to our Lord is so imperfect.

Faith is trust. The better we learn to humble ourselves before our God, to realize and confess that even our best works merit nothing in His sight, the more implicitly we learn to trust in His grace only. And then can we still be hard and unforgiving to those who sin against us? God has forgiven us a debt of millions, and we should be hard against one who owes us pennies? God forbid!

Prayer

Nothing have I, Christ, to offer,
You alone, my highest good.
Nothing have I, Lord, to proffer
But Your crimson-colored blood.
Your death on the cross has death wholly defeated
And thereby my righteousness fully completed;
Salvation's white raiments I there did obtain,
And in them in glory with You I shall reign.

Therefore You alone, my Savior,
Shall be all in all to me;
Search my heart and my behavior,
Root out all hypocrisy.
Through all my life's pilgrimage, guard and uphold me,
In loving forgiveness, O Jesus, enfold me.
This one thing is needful; all others are vain—
I count all but loss that I Christ may obtain! Amen.
(LSB 536:4–5)

ONE IN TEN
Luke 17:11–19

ISAIAH said, "O Lord, in distress they sought You; they poured out a whispered prayer when Your discipline was upon them" (Isaiah 26:16). That is true to this day. When danger threatens or need presses, people find the way to God. When people are confronted with the destruction of hurricanes and earthquakes, terrorist attacks and disasters, the churches are full. People who have never been to church, who haven't attended a worship service in decades, are on their knees. A tragedy is a mighty persuader! But the prophet Isaiah indicates something else: when the anguish is over and the danger has passed, people again forget about God. Gratitude is a rare virtue. "The ox knows its owner," Isaiah says in 1:3, "and the donkey its master's crib, but Israel does not know, My people do not understand." What does the Lord think of such behavior? He tells us in today's reading.

Jesus Cleanses Ten Lepers

On the way to Jerusalem He was passing along between Samaria and Galilee. And as He entered a village, He was met by ten lepers, who stood at a distance and lifted up their voices, saying, "Jesus, Master, have mercy on us." When He saw them He said to them, "Go and show yourselves to the priests." And as they went they were cleansed. Then one of them, when he saw that he was healed, turned back, praising God with a loud voice; and he fell on his face at Jesus' feet, giving Him thanks. Now he was a Samaritan. Then Jesus answered, "Were not ten cleansed? Where are the nine? Was no one found to return and give praise to God except this foreigner?" And He said to him, "Rise and go your way; your faith has made you well."

Two thousand years have passed by since these ten men stood in that village of Samaria, but it might as well be happening now. For three years, Jesus had sought them, but they had avoided Him. But now they call Him "Jesus, Master." Human nature does not change; these people might be Americans instead of Galileans and Samaritans. When misfortune arrives and the cross presses hard, then they can find the Lord, then they meet Him in His Word, then they visit Him in His house. And the Lord is always ready to listen and to lend His aid, no matter how late we come!

Is it right to think of Him only when our need is great and beyond all other help? We wear the badge of Christians, but we are ashamed to confess it before our wise and worldly friends; we are ashamed to speak to our churchless neighbors about their spiritual needs and tell them about our Lord and Savior. Only when the floor gets hot under our feet or the storm threatens to wreck the house do we remember what we owe to our God and what we hope and expect of Him. There is such a thing as waiting too long. There are people who have used their hands for raking in the world's goods so long that even the threat of death does not cause them to fold them in prayer.

Why is it that people act this way, that we, too, are inclined to forget our God until we are in dire need of His help? The second part of today's reading answers that.

When the lepers noticed that they were healed, one of them turned around and gave thanks to Jesus. One out of ten! Jesus sadly asked about the other nine. They had gone on their way; it didn't occur to them to return to Jesus. They had what they wanted and they forgot the One who gave it to them. Jesus put His finger on what they really lacked. To the thankful Samaritan, He said, "Your faith has made you well." He alone had that faith that brings help and salvation. Although the others had also started out on the way of faith, they went astray. They had lost the faith. True faith in the Savior cannot exist with ingratitude.

Where do we stand? Are we with the nine or with the one? There are some who for a time walked with us shoulder to shoulder, but we see them no more; they have gone. And again Jesus sadly asks, "Where are the nine?" Where do we stand? We are always ready to pray, "Give us this day our daily bread," but do we continue, "Oh give thanks to the Lord, for He is good" (Psalm 106:1)? When sickness enters our home, we cry, "Jesus, Master, have mercy on us!" Then, do we return with the Samaritan to thank the Lord for His help? Where is the evidence of our faith in deep gratitude to God for the mercy He has shown us and our country?

Prayer

Dear heavenly Father, who daily cares for us and is an ever-present help in every need, we pray that You awaken our hearts that we may be truly thankful for all Your blessings. Let us not grow apathetic about Your temporal and eternal benefits, but, knowing that Your goodness has provided for all our needs all the days of our life, let us remember in confidence that Your mercy is new every morning, that in perfect trust we may call upon You in every trouble and thank and praise You with a joyous heart. Amen.

THE KINGDOM OF GOD COMES
Luke 17:20–25

JESUS said repeatedly that He found greater faith among those who were not of Israel than among those who regarded themselves the chosen people of God. For instance, of the Roman centurion, He said, "Truly, I tell you, with no one in Israel have I found such faith" (Matthew 8:10). To that poor Canaanite woman, He said, "O woman, great is your faith!" (Matthew 15:28). Naturally, this did not please the Pharisees, who were proud of being Abraham's sons and regarded all others as lesser breeds. Perhaps they were provoked when Jesus publicly praised the Samaritan for his faith in contrast to the nine who had not returned. So, to embarrass Him, they asked when the kingdom of God would come. Although Jesus answered their question, His words are directed mostly to His disciples and, therefore, to us.

The Coming of the Kingdom

Being asked by the Pharisees when the kingdom of God would come, He answered them, "The kingdom of God is not coming with signs to be observed, nor will they say, 'Look, here it is!' or 'There!' for behold, the kingdom of God is in the midst of you."

And He said to the disciples, "The days are coming when you will desire to see one of the days of the Son of Man, and you will not see it. And they will say to you, 'Look, there!' or 'Look, here!' Do not go out or follow them. For as the lightning flashes and lights up the sky from one side to the other, so will the Son of Man be in His day. But first He must suffer many things and be rejected by this generation.

The Pharisees knew about the kingdom of God, of course. All the prophets had spoken of it. John the Baptist had preached, "Repent, for the kingdom of heaven is at hand" (Matthew 3:2). Now Jesus had come. There was much excited expectation among the people as Jesus made His way to Jerusalem. Many people, even His disciples, asked when the Kingdom would come. And Jesus said, It is here! It is not a kingdom that can be seen coming in with the parade of conquering armies with cannons and tanks. This Kingdom is one that Christ established by living and dying for men. And when He bowed His head on the cross, He said, "It is finished." The kingdom of God had come despite all obstacles—despite the devil's temptations, despite rejection and persecution from the Jews, despite crucifixion by the Gentiles. But the very cross is the foundation of this kingdom of God.

The Kingdom came to the Jews in the person, the Word, and the work of Christ. And today, the Kingdom is wherever the King is. He comes to us in His Word and in His Sacraments. Luther says, "When our heavenly Father gives us His Holy Spirit, so that by His grace we believe His holy Word and lead godly lives," then the Kingdom comes to us (Small Catechism, Second Petition). This Kingdom is in our hearts; it is the communion of saints on earth. It is not a mere kingdom of virtue. It is true that no slave of sin can belong to it, but the members of the Kingdom cannot be distinguished by mere goodness. They are saints because Christ's righteousness is given to them by faith.

Jesus gives us this vision of the kingdom of God for our comfort as well as for our instruction. The times are evil and often we look forward with a heavy heart. But Jesus would have us know that we are like travelers walking in the mountains; we see only a small section of the path that God is leading us on. Here, in the spirit, He takes us to the mountaintop, shows us the vast expanse of God's counsel, and says, "The kingdom of God is in the midst of you." You may not always see it; you may at times have to unlearn certain notions. Just like the people in His day, we are apt to look for visible evidence of the Kingdom—large congregations, beautiful churches, honor, influence. This is a mistake. In Bethlehem, in a stable, a little Child is born. He grows up as a carpenter's son, Himself a carpenter. Ignorant fishermen are His disciples. Few of the great and mighty of the time follow Him. Then He dies on the cross, the most despised and rejected of men. Not much glory there! Yet He established the Kingdom that has conquered the world; the only Kingdom that could conquer the world. No other kingdom on earth compares!

The kingdom of God comes! God lets us see some of its power. It has survived all the world wars and is advancing with new strength. Christians show by their lives that the kingdom of God is within them. But even without such obvious evidence, we know that wherever the Word is, there the Kingdom comes. And as surely as we have the Word with us, so surely will the Kingdom come among us and to us.

Prayer

Let Your kingdom come, O Lord, to all those who are yet outside
its blessed bounds. Gather the nations of the earth by Your holy
Gospel into Your Church so they with us may here live under
You in Your kingdom and serve You in everlasting righteousness,
innocence, and blessedness. Above all, O Lord, we thank You that
You have called us into Your kingdom. And we pray that You keep
us as true members of Your kingdom until You come in glory to
take us home to You in heaven. For Your mercy's sake, we ask it.
Amen.

THE DAY OF THE SON OF MAN
Luke 17:26–37

"WATCHMAN, tell us of the night!" That is the song of the
Christian soul while traveling through the night of this life. It is not
only the Pharisee who asks when the kingdom of God will come,
not just the misguided disciples who want to know when He will
restore the kingdom of Israel. Every Christian anxiously waits for
the day of the Lord's reappearing. After all, this world is no paradise
for the Christian. The Lord made it clear to His disciples that while
they are here on this earth, His kingdom is a kingdom of the cross.
But He also told them that the day of redemption, the full revelation
of the kingdom of God, is coming. Now is the time of our captivity.
We long for full and final redemption. That is the encouragement
that Jesus gives to us in today's reading.

Just as it was in the days of Noah, so will it be in the days
of the Son of Man. They were eating and drinking and marrying and being given in marriage, until the day when Noah
entered the ark, and the flood came and destroyed them all.
Likewise, just as it was in the days of Lot—they were eating

and drinking, buying and selling, planting and building, but on the day when Lot went out from Sodom, fire and sulfur rained from heaven and destroyed them all—so will it be on the day when the Son of Man is revealed. On that day, let the one who is on the housetop, with his goods in the house, not come down to take them away, and likewise let the one who is in the field not turn back. Remember Lot's wife. Whoever seeks to preserve his life will lose it, but whoever loses his life will keep it. I tell you, in that night there will be two in one bed. One will be taken and the other left. There will be two women grinding together. One will be taken and the other left." And they said to him, "Where, Lord?" He said to them, "Where the corpse is, there the vultures will gather."

Regarding their life on earth, Jesus had told His disciples, "The days are coming when you will desire to see one of the days of the Son of Man, and you will not see it. And they will say to you, 'Look, there!' or 'Look, here!' Do not go out or follow them" (Luke 17:22–23). Oh, how often, when they were hunted like wild beasts and slaughtered like cattle, how often did the early Christians think of Jesus' miracles and wish for a day, only one day, of His powerful help.

The Kingdom has not changed; it is still a Kingdom of the cross. And oh, how often, when cares multiply and dangers threaten and faith grows small and trust weakens, how often do we wish that the Lord would come in His power and be with us only for a day with His almighty help! And in such days, how dangerous are the false Christs, crying, Here is Christ! Here you will find true happiness! Here is help for all your ills! And when the cross is heavy, we, too, ask—as did the Pharisee—when will the kingdom of God, the kingdom of glory, come? The Lord did not answer the Pharisee. In fact, repeatedly He told His disciples that nobody but God the Father knows the date of that day, and He has not revealed it.

But Jesus tells us very definitely that it is coming. At Sodom, the "fire and sulfur rained from heaven and destroyed them all—so will it be on the day when the Son of Man is revealed." He will come suddenly, and in an instant He will be visible universally. All people will see Him. There will be no need to point Him out and to say, "There He is!" Every person will know who He is and why He is there. He will come in judgment.

Jesus does not describe the judgment here. In this passage, His purpose is a warning: be prepared for that day at all times, no matter where you are or what you are doing. To make His point, He cites two examples from Old Testament history. People lived carelessly in the days of Noah and of Lot. The flood came suddenly, and only eight were saved. Fire fell suddenly from heaven, and only three were saved. So will it be on the day of Jesus' second coming. Utter sensuality will mark the times. Most people will be completely secure in their logic and science and arrogance. The sun rose yesterday and a good many yesterdays before, so they will believe, of course, it will rise tomorrow. And they will ignore the clouds gathering and the fiery dawn rising.

All the typical occupations of life—eating, drinking, marrying, buying, selling, planting, building—are not wrong, but if they distract us from watching for the Lord, they become wrong. To have worldly goods is not wrong, but if, like Lot's wife, we hang our hearts on them, it will cost us our soul. And on the Last Day, everyone is responsible for himself. Close association with good Christians, membership in a church, will not save us. The question will be, What is our attitude toward the Judge? Do we know Him not only as Judge, but as our Savior as well? Do we rejoice that He is coming for our redemption? The world is like a dead, decaying body, close to ultimate destruction. May we look forward to the Last Day without fear, with a holy joy, because for us it will mean the end of all sorrow and trouble, the fulfillment of all our highest hopes.

Prayer

Almighty God, we ask You to grant us grace that we may wait with vigilance for the second coming of Your Son, our Lord, so that when He returns in righteousness and with salvation, He will find us not sleeping in sin but diligent in His service and rejoicing in His praise. Grant that we may enter with Him into

*the marriage supper of the Lamb. We ask this through the merits
of our Savior, Jesus Christ. Amen.*

PRAY WITHOUT CEASING
Luke 18:1–8

ONE of the last admonitions Jesus gave His disciples before His
death was, "Stay awake at all times, praying that you may have
strength to escape all these things that are going to take place, and to
stand before the Son of Man" (Luke 21:36). In the previous chapter
of Luke, Jesus spoke of the need for watchfulness. He will return for
judgment in an instant, and only those who are ready for His second
coming will enter with Him into His kingdom of glory. The door
will be closed forever to all others. Now Jesus speaks of prayer. His
disciples were shocked by the description of conditions on earth at
the time of His return. In those days of tribulation, when Christ's
followers "will desire to see one of the days of the Son of Man, and
you will not see it" (Luke 17:22), when people will again live as
they did in the days of Noah and Lot and the danger of falling away
is greater than ever, how will people endure to the end and still be
saved? Jesus answers: pray always and do not despair. And to impress
that upon us, He tells the parable of the insistent widow.

The Parable of the Persistent Widow

And He told them a parable to the effect that they ought
always to pray and not lose heart. He said, "In a certain city
there was a judge who neither feared God nor respected man.
And there was a widow in that city who kept coming to him
and saying, 'Give me justice against my adversary.' For a while
he refused, but afterward he said to himself, 'Though I neither

fear God nor respect man, yet because this widow keeps bothering me, I will give her justice, so that she will not beat me down by her continual coming.' "And the Lord said, "Hear what the unrighteous judge says. And will not God give justice to His elect, who cry to Him day and night? Will He delay long over them? I tell you, He will give justice to them speedily. Nevertheless, when the Son of Man comes, will He find faith on earth?"

Note that Jesus does not tell this parable to tell us to pray. All God's children pray. God expects it of us, and so prayer might be called a Christian duty. But it is much more than that; you might as well call breathing a duty. But do we pray always and without despair? Do we persevere in prayer? Jesus teaches us an important lesson in this passage.

If we are easily discouraged and do not persist in prayer until we are heard, then our prayer is in vain. Furthermore, every unsuccessful prayer only discourages future efforts. So the Lord tells this rather strange parable of the unjust judge and the widow who persisted in begging him for help. Simply and solely because she pestered him so much, he finally did what she wanted. This is a parable of opposites.

God is not at all like this judge. He is just and merciful, and the prayers of His children are pleasing to Him. But the comparison that Jesus wants us to make is this: if a judge who is unjust, who has no fear of God or regard for mankind, who is altogether unwilling to help someone in need, if this judge is finally persuaded to help the petitioner, how sure should we be that our persistent prayers will finally prevail with our Father in heaven, even if for a while it appears as though He does not answer?

But that is why it is of such importance in our life that we persevere in prayer. God does not always help in the first moment of danger. This widow in her need and oppression is Christ's depiction of the Christian's life on earth. Jesus foretold it: "In the world you will have tribulation" (John 16:33). And our cry for help often seems to go unheard. How many centuries of persecution have swept over the Church of Christ, how many multitudes of prayers sent up to heaven seemed as vain as though there were no God who hears when His children cry. Haven't we had such experiences ourselves? Haven't there been days when we felt what Mary and Martha felt when they sent their message to Jesus—"he whom You love is ill"—and Jesus "stayed two days longer in the place where He was" (John 11:3, 6). They had been so sure that Jesus would come at once, but He delayed until Lazarus had been dead for four days. When God seems deaf to our prayers, we are apt to become impatient. Our faith weakens. We cry out with the disciples in the ship, "Do you not care that we are perishing?" (Mark 4:38). We are tempted to think hard thoughts about our God as though our confidence in Him were misplaced; we are tempted to say, "What is the use of prayer? It's only a waste of time."

We are all subject to this temptation, and the parable in today's reading is meant to bolster us. Jesus says, "Hear what the unrighteous judge says. And will not God give justice to His elect, who cry to Him day and night? Will He delay long over them?" It is unreasonable to suspect that God, who loves us, would deny us what an unjust judge grants the widow. And Jesus adds the triumphant assurance, "I tell you, He will give justice to them speedily." Yes, speedily. It is true that God's clocks do not keep the same time as ours, but His help comes at the earliest moment when God, in His wisdom, has determined that it is beneficial for us. So God's delays are not delays. He is only watching for the most appropriate time to send us help when it will do us the most good.

Oh, it is not exaggeration when Jesus admonishes us to pray always and not despair! That is exactly what He means. No promise is given to the person who lightly taps at God's door and walks away if it does not immediately open. But because so many do just that, Jesus says, "When the Son of Man comes, will He find faith on earth?" (Luke 18:8). Lack of persevering prayer is a sure sign that faith in God's promises has died out and unbelief has taken possession of the heart. May God preserve us from that! And if, in order to teach us to pray, the Lord sends cross and tribulation, let us thank

Him for it, follow His lead, and patiently await His hour when He will surely help.

Prayer

Lord God, our heavenly Father, who by Your Son has promised to give us whatever we ask in His name, we ask that You grant us the power of Your Holy Spirit, that we may make known our requests to You in faithful prayer, desire of You that which is well-pleasing to You and profitable for us, lift up holy hands without wrath or doubt, and be firmly assured that You will hear our prayer, through Jesus Christ, Your Son, our Lord. Amen.

PHARISEE AND PUBLICAN
Luke 18:9–14

IN the preceding parable, Jesus spoke of prayer and unwavering faith in the efficacy of prayer. There were, perhaps, among His hearers some who thought His instruction superfluous, who thought, We know how to pray and we do not lack faith. No matter; Jesus again speaks of prayer, but this time the object is different. Not every prayer is pleasing to God. Prayer reflects the heart of the one who prays. If the heart is not right, the prayer cannot be right. So here Jesus contrasts the two prayers, the two men, their hearts, their characters, and their attitudes toward God. This is one of Jesus' best-known parables, one that we have often heard or read. But we cannot hear it too often because it carries a most important lesson that God's book has for us.

The Pharisee and the Tax Collector

He also told this parable to some who trusted in themselves that they were righteous, and treated others with contempt: "Two men went up into the temple to pray, one a Pharisee and the other a tax collector. The Pharisee, standing by himself, prayed thus: 'God, I thank You that I am not like other men, extortioners, unjust, adulterers, or even like this tax collector. I fast twice a week; I give tithes of all that I get.' But the tax collector, standing far off, would not even lift up his eyes to heaven, but beat his breast, saying, 'God, be merciful to me, a sinner!' I tell you, this man went down to his house justified, rather than the other. For everyone who exalts himself will be humbled, but the one who humbles himself will be exalted."

No two people in the world could be more unalike than the two in this parable. One of them is all the world expects a respectable man to be, the very model of a church member. The Pharisee went to church, the very best church, the temple of the living God. He went there not to buy or sell doves or to exchange money but to pray and worship. And he was not a mere Sabbath worshiper; he practiced what he professed. He was honest in all his dealings with others. He gave a tenth of his income for church, for missions, for charity. The other man lacks all these conspicuous virtues; not one good work is mentioned of him. The tax collector was what we might call a bad man. He was wicked. God knew it. People around him knew it. He himself knew it. He was a sinner.

But Jesus condemned the good man and said that the bad man was justified before God. Why? The Pharisee believed that he was righteous. He came before God with a list of his good works and took his stand on the Law of God. The Law says, "Do this, and you will live" (Luke 10:28). The Pharisee could say he had done all that the Law demands, so he deserved life. But God said, in truth, he was not good enough; he had not kept the Law as it should be kept. Those who have nothing better to offer, will take their reward with the wicked. The tax collector, however, humbly confessed his sinfulness. He proffered no good work. But he appealed to God's mercy, and that put him on an entirely different footing with God than the Pharisee. The Pharisee offered up his good works as evidence and appealed to God's justice. So God dealt with him according to His justice and condemned him because he was far from perfect. The tax collector recognized his sin and wickedness. We are not told here how he came to that knowledge, but we know from other passages that knowledge of sin, repentance, and faith in God's mercy are the work of the Word of God, the Law and the Gospel. So this man had become a penitent sinner. And because he knew his sin, he knew he could expect only God's justice: judgment and condemnation. He knew there was only one avenue of escape for him: to throw himself on God's mercy and to appeal to that mercy for pardon and forgiveness.

For two thousand years, these two men have represented the two types of people in the world. We all, by nature, seek the favor of God. That is the basis of all religions. But most people are like the Pharisee. The German philosopher Max Mueller correctly stated that the essence of all religions except Christianity is "be good." That is the religion of natural man; he wants to be justified by his own works. And that is the religion of our own human nature. Our natural pride rebels against the religion of the tax collector. He did the hardest thing in the world for us to do—let go of all pride in our own merits, every lingering thought that we are not as bad as others, that there is some goodness in us that God can see. But Jesus Christ tells us there is no hope in the attitude of the Pharisee; it leads only to condemnation.

Thank God there is another way, the way of God's mercy. It is the very essence of true Christianity that God is a merciful God and that with Him there is forgiveness through Jesus Christ, who bore our sins and suffered our punishment. That is our only hope, but it is a sure hope. We have Jesus' own assurance of it in this parable. Just like the tax collector, we are sinners. And if we are sinners, then we have tortured to death the Son of God. We could have done nothing worse than that. And now there is only one way of escape for us: to plead with the tax collector, "God, be merciful to me, a sinner!" There is no other way for the worst man, and there is no other way for the best man.

Prayer

I know that, though in doing good
I spend my life, I never could
Atone for all I've done;
But though my sins are black as night,
I dare to come before Thy sight
Because I trust Thy Son.

In Him alone my trust I place,
Come boldly to Thy throne of grace,
And there commune with Thee.
Salvation sure, O Lord, is mine,
And, all unworthy, I am Thine,
For Jesus died for me. Amen.
(TLH 379:4–5)

BE LIKE LITTLE CHILDREN
Luke 18:15–30

IN the parable of the Pharisee and the tax collector, Jesus taught His disciples that the way to justification is not by one's works but by humble appeal to God's mercy. It is a very simple lesson, but it is hard to apply because the old Adam in us is a proud Pharisee. The poison of spiritual pride runs in our veins by nature. Again and again we must be reminded to see ourselves as God sees us, to know that only the mercy of God for Jesus' sake can save us. The way to the kingdom of God is through the dust of Calvary and not through self-righteous pride, but penitent humility is its gate. Christian hearts, then, will welcome a reminder of this lesson in today's reading.

Let the Children Come to Me

Now they were bringing even infants to Him that He might touch them. And when the disciples saw it, they rebuked them. But Jesus called them to Him, saying, "Let the children come to Me, and do not hinder them, for to such belongs the kingdom of God. Truly, I say to you, whoever does not receive the kingdom of God like a child shall not enter it."

The Rich Ruler

And a ruler asked Him, "Good Teacher, what must I do to inherit eternal life?" And Jesus said to him, "Why do you call Me good? No one is good except God alone. You know the commandments: 'Do not commit adultery, Do not murder, Do not steal, Do not bear false witness, Honor your father and mother.' " And he said, "All these I have kept from my youth." When Jesus heard this, He said to him, "One thing you still lack. Sell all that you have and distribute to the poor, and you will have treasure in heaven; and come, follow Me." But when he heard these things, he became very sad, for he was extremely rich. Jesus, seeing that he had become sad, said, "How difficult it is for those who have wealth to enter the kingdom of God! For it is easier for a camel to go through the eye of a needle than for a rich person to enter the kingdom of God." Those who heard it said, "Then who can be saved?" But He said, "What is impossible with men is possible with God." And Peter said, "See, we have left our homes and followed You." And He said to them, "Truly, I say to you, there is no one who has left house or wife or brothers or parents or children, for the sake of the kingdom of God, who will not receive many times more in this time, and in the age to come eternal life."

The story of Jesus blessing the little children is like a ray of sunshine during the last days of His earthly life, as dark and threatening clouds gathered over Him. We have all loved that story since our own childhood. Most important, however, is the truth that Jesus expressed on this occasion: "Whoever does not receive the kingdom of God like a child shall not enter it." The disciples thought Jesus shouldn't be bothered with children. They can come to Him after they've grown up. But, Jesus says, all people should become like little children if they want to enter heaven. Jesus wants to teach humility, and here He points the disciples to young children as an example to follow.

Be like children! They love their parents even when they cannot understand. And their love leads them to believe Father and Mother without question. Try to convince a young child to disagree with what Mother has said, and his simple answer will be, "But Mother said so!" How completely and implicitly children trust their parents! They do not worry about tomorrow because Father and Mother are in control, and it is certain that they will provide!

The necessity of a humble, childlike faith became evident in the story of the rich young ruler. He was a Pharisee at heart; nothing humble about him! He did not seek grace because he was sure he had earned his reward. Mark's version of this event tells us that Jesus, "looking at him, loved him" (Mark 10:21). The young ruler meant well, but his teachers had misled him. So Jesus, lovingly and tenderly, explained what he was missing. Although the man thought he had kept all the Commandments of God, Jesus said he had not even begun to keep the First Commandment—he loved his goods more than God!

The young man left Jesus. He was sorrowful, but he left. Did he ever return? We do not know, but Jesus had taught His disciples another lesson. The evil in our own heart and the temptations that surround us are so great that we cannot possibly save ourselves. Only God's omnipotence can save us. And God, in His mercy, will use His almighty power to save us if we just let Him. There is more. God will reward us a hundredfold for all we sacrifice in His service, not because He owes us anything, but because He is our heavenly Father who loves us!

Do we see ourselves in the first or the second example in the text? In the children who lovingly crowd around the Savior or in the young man who sorrowfully leaves Him? Our children never fear that they might get lost when we take them somewhere because we know where they are and keep them close to us. Our heavenly Father knows all things, and even when our way is dark and stormy, He knows the way home. What's more, He has given us the most overwhelming proof of His love and mercy in sending us His Son to redeem us and open the way to our eternal home for us.

If ever we are tempted to set out on our own way, following the pride or the covetousness of our human heart, may we be reminded of the Savior's words and be like little children and take hold of Father's hand. The darker the night and the rougher the way, the tighter we will cling to that hand!

Prayer

Create in me a clean heart, O God, and renew a right spirit within me! Cleanse me from all natural pride and self-confidence so I do not fall and lose my soul's salvation. I am Your child, purchased and won for Your kingdom by the blood of Your Son. Give me a child's implicit trust in Your fatherly care and the Savior's merits, that nothing may lead me astray, neither love of the things of this present world nor fear of the future. You are my God. In You I trust. Let me not be ashamed. In Jesus' name I ask it. Amen.

68

JESUS OF NAZARETH PASSES BY

Luke 18:31–43

TWICE before, Jesus had spoken to His disciples of His suffering and death (Luke 9:22, 44). They hadn't paid much attention to His words and, so we are told, they did not understand Him. Now Jesus took the Twelve aside and spoke more plainly to them. The reason Jesus did so at this time is revealed in the last verses of the previous text. Peter had said, "See, we have left our homes and followed You" (Luke 18:28). Jesus replied with the marvelous promise, "Truly, I say to you, there is no one who has left house or wife or brothers or parents or children, for the sake of the kingdom of God, who will not receive many times more in this time, and in the age to come eternal life" (Luke 18:29–30). But Jesus did not want them to return to their old error of expecting a glorious earthly kingdom in which they would rule with Him, so He told them now in plain, simple words what would happen to Him in Jerusalem. This is where the Passion story begins, for although St. Luke recorded various incidents that happened on the way, it is clear what the end and object of His journey to Jerusalem is. Let us read as Jesus foretells His Passion and take it to heart.

Jesus Foretells His Death a Third Time

And taking the twelve, He said to them, "See, we are going up to Jerusalem, and everything that is written about the Son of Man by the prophets will be accomplished. For He will be delivered over to the Gentiles and will be mocked and shamefully treated and spit upon. And after flogging Him, they will kill Him, and on the third day He will rise." But they understood none of these things. This saying was hidden from them, and they did not grasp what was said.

Jesus Heals a Blind Beggar

As He drew near to Jericho, a blind man was sitting by the roadside begging. And hearing a crowd going by, he inquired what this meant. They told him, "Jesus of Nazareth is passing by." And he cried out, "Jesus, Son of David, have mercy on me!" And those who were in front rebuked him, telling him to be silent. But he cried out all the more, "Son of David, have mercy on me!" And Jesus stopped and commanded him to be brought to Him. And when he came near, He asked him, "What do you want Me to do for you?" He said, "Lord, let me recover my sight." And Jesus said to him, "Recover your sight; your faith has made you well." And immediately he recovered his sight and followed Him, glorifying God. And all the people, when they saw it, gave praise to God.

At the outset of this final journey of Jesus to Jerusalem, Luke tells us, "When the days drew near for Him to be taken up, He set His face to go to Jerusalem" (Luke 9:51). And Mark, introducing this section of the story, said, "And they were on the road, going up to Jerusalem, and Jesus was walking ahead of them. And they were amazed, and those who followed were afraid" (Mark 10:32). What a picture that brings to mind! Jesus hurrying along that mountain path ahead of them, impelled by the longing clearly expressed in His words, "How great is My distress until it is accomplished!" (Luke 12:50). Lagging behind, the little group of disciples, awed, shrinking from that resolved determination, that more-than-mortal heroism shining in their Master's eyes. Here we are given a glimpse into the very heart of Jesus, and it should make more real to us the sacrifice He made, more deep to us the love that impelled Him. And it should make our love for Him more true and our Christian resolve more firm.

With perfect clarity, Jesus knew what was coming; yet He resolutely set out for Jerusalem. He could have easily escaped His enemies by traveling north instead of south or by using His divine power to foil their plans. But He knew that His death was necessary to accomplish the redemption of mankind. In His love for us, He had the prophets record it in Old Testament Scriptures so men might not despair in their sin but trust in the coming Messiah of God. His love now drove Him into that suffering because that was how the divine plan must be worked out.

Let us not look at this great sacrifice in idle wonder or even turn away from it carelessly out of familiarity. Let us look at it with the conviction that His love in that sacrifice embraces us too. And then let us learn a lesson from that blind man. When he heard that Jesus of Nazareth was passing by, he did not say that he was still young and strong and had many years before him; he did not choose to wait until Jesus came again. The blind man was wiser. He cried out, "Jesus, Son of David, have mercy on me!" until he was heard.

And it was the last time that Jesus passed through Jericho! The blind man did not know it, but it was his last chance. What if he had not insisted on taking it? Jesus of Nazareth is passing by today. Here is our opportunity. "Jesus of Nazareth is passing by" means He is coming, but it also may mean that He is leaving! Will He come again in our lifetime? I do not know; you do not know. All we do know is this: He is here today.

Prayer

Today Your mercy calls us
To wash away our sin.
However great our trespass,
Whatever we have been,
However long from mercy
Our hearts have turned away,
Your precious blood can wash us
And make us clean today.

O all-embracing Mercy,
O ever-open Door,
What should we do without You
When heart and eye run o'er?
When all things seem against us,
To drive us to despair,
We know one gate is open,
One ear will hear our prayer. Amen.
(LSB 915:1, 4)

THE PURPOSE OF CHRIST'S COMING

Luke 19:1–10

JESUS shocked His disciples when He said, "How difficult it is for those who have wealth to enter the kingdom of God! For it is easier for a camel to go through the eye of a needle than for a rich person to enter the kingdom of God." When they in their amazement exclaimed, "Then who can be saved?" He answered, "What is impossible with men is possible with God" (Luke 18:24–27). In the reading for today, Jesus demonstrated that it is possible for divine grace to save even rich men, even those who acquire their riches by unjust means and become slaves of their sin and love of money. The man Jesus saved from his evil ways was a tax collector for the Roman government. He was not what anyone would call a good man. Jews of good character did not take this job for a hated foreign ruler. Tax collectors were usually con artists and extortionists. From his own confession, we know that this man did not get all his riches honestly. In his house now, Jesus spoke that word, so precious to all sinners of all times, that states the entire purpose of His coming in one brief compact sentence. That statement makes this story so beautiful to us.

Jesus and Zacchaeus

He entered Jericho and was passing through. And there was a man named Zacchaeus. He was a chief tax collector and was rich. And he was seeking to see who Jesus was, but on account of the crowd he could not, because he was small of stature. So he ran on ahead and climbed up into a sycamore tree to see Him, for He was about to pass that way. And when Jesus came to the place, He looked up and said to him, "Zacchaeus, hurry and come down, for I must stay at your house today." So he hurried and came down and received Him joyfully. And when they saw it, they all grumbled, "He has gone in to be the guest of a man who is a sinner." And Zacchaeus stood and said to the Lord, "Behold, Lord, the half of my goods I give to the poor. And if I have defrauded anyone of anything, I restore it four-fold." And Jesus said to him, "Today salvation has come to this house, since he also is a son of Abraham. For the Son of Man came to seek and to save the lost."

When the Pharisees said, "This man receives sinners and eats with them" (Luke 15:2), they thought they had said about the worst thing possible of Him. But they could have made it even stronger by saying that Jesus seeks out sinners. Wherever He goes, He seeks souls—Nathanael under a tree, Zacchaeus in a tree, Matthew in his tax collector's booth, a blind beggar at the roadside, the man at Siloam's pool who had been sick for thirty-eight years. He seeks them to save them. That is why He came into the world. He was not born like everyone else, who come into the world without their own volition; He came because He wanted to come. And He came for a purpose. Before He was born, the angel stated this purpose: "He will save His people from their sins" (Matthew 1:21). That is His clear and oft-repeated program: He is come to seek and to save that which was lost.

Who are the lost? Zacchaeus was one. The people of Jericho grumbled because Jesus entered the house of a sinner. If Jesus had had the same misgivings, He would have had to camp in the streets. A few days later, some of the same people who had so scornfully spoken of the tax collector would cry, "Crucify, crucify Him!" in the streets of Jerusalem. Among the apostles, surely His most devoted followers, was one who sold Him for thirty pieces of silver. Another swore a great oath that he did not know Jesus; this was the same man who had heard the voice of God on the hilltop declare, "This is My beloved Son" (Matthew 17:5). At the same time, the rest of the apostles were hiding where it was safe. If those were His most loyal friends, what could be expected of the others? "The Lord looks down from heaven on the children of man, to see if there are any who understand, who seek after God. They have all turned aside;

together they have become corrupt; there is none who does good, not even one" (Psalm 14:2–3).

Jesus said He came to save the lost and He came to save the world; both terms mean the same. This applies to the world today; it applies to us. "For there is no distinction: for all have sinned and fall short of the glory of God" (Romans 3:22–23). Our very righteousness is as filthy rags, stained with selfish motives, evil desires, and dark purposes. The only thing we can truthfully say is, "I am one of the lost." And the only star of hope in a world of night is He who said, "The Son of Man came to seek and to save the lost" (Luke 19:10). He came to give His life as ransom for us, to save us; not try to save us, not help to save us—but to save us completely and ultimately.

This is a wonderful story. Jesus comes to the gates of Jericho, where He heals the blind beggar, then He passes through another place, a town that does not want Him. In that town, He doesn't pause at palace or hut; He doesn't look at the beauty spots of the city, but He goes to the other gate to a certain tree He knows. And there, half ashamed like a little boy, hiding in the foliage, sits a man who has come to the knowledge of his lost condition and whose heart is ready to receive Him. Jesus makes straight for that tree and says, "Zacchaeus, hurry and come down, for I must stay at your house today." And today Jesus comes in His Word, passes through land and city where so many do not want Him, and arrives at the tree where we perch, the tree of pride and arrogance, or the tree of shame and contrition. There Jesus says to us, "Hurry and come down, for I must stay at your house today."

Oh, that we might always be as ready to receive Him as He is to come to us and to save us, as ready as Zacchaeus was to pledge our life to His service in gratitude for His salvation!

Prayer
I lay my sins on Jesus,
The spotless Lamb of God;
He bears them all and frees us

From the accursed load.
I bring my guilt to Jesus
To wash my crimson stains
Clean in His blood most precious
Till not a spot remains. Amen.
(LSB 606:1)

... UNTIL HE COMES
Luke 19:11–28

WHEN, during the Reformation, Luther restored the doctrine of free grace to the Church, he had to defend this truth against the slander that he, in effect, taught men to sin. If justification is by faith alone without good works, so his opponents said, then men will no longer feel any obligation to do good. They accused Luther of teaching that if we but believe, we may sin as much as we please and God in His grace will forgive us. That accusation was not a new one. Even St. Paul, in his day, had to meet it. After outlining the doctrine of free grace in the first five chapters of Romans, he refuted this slander: "What shall we say then? Are we to continue in sin that grace may abound? By no means!" (Romans 6:1–2). But Paul wrote only what he had learned from his Lord and Master Jesus Christ, a truth that Jesus teaches in the parable of the ten minas.

The Parable of the Ten Minas

As they heard these things, He proceeded to tell a parable, because He was near to Jerusalem, and because they supposed that the kingdom of God was to appear immediately. He said therefore, "A nobleman went into a far country to receive for himself a kingdom and then return. Calling ten of his servants, he gave them ten minas, and said to them, 'Engage in business until I come.' But his citizens hated him and sent a delegation after him, saying, 'We do not want this man to reign over us.' When he returned, having received the kingdom, he ordered these servants to whom he had given the money to be called to him, that he might know what they had gained by doing business. The first came before him, saying, 'Lord, your mina has made ten minas more.' And he said to him, 'Well done, good servant! Because you have been faithful in a very little, you shall have authority over ten cities.' And the second came, saying, 'Lord, your mina has made five minas.' And he said to him, 'And you are to be over five cities.' Then another came, saying, 'Lord, here is your mina, which I kept laid away in a handkerchief; for I was afraid of you, because you are a severe man. You take what you did not deposit, and reap what you did not sow.' He said to him, 'I will condemn you with your own words, you wicked servant! You knew that I was a severe man, taking what I did not deposit and reaping what I did not sow? Why then did you not put my money in the bank, and at my coming I might have collected it with interest?' And he said to those who stood by, 'Take the mina from him, and give it to the one who has the ten minas.' And they said to him, 'Lord, he has ten minas!' 'I tell you that to everyone who has, more will be given, but from the one who has not, even what he has will be taken away. But as for these enemies of mine, who did not want me to reign over them, bring them here and slaughter them before me.' "

As a warning to the Jews, Jesus clearly states what will happen to His enemies who reject Him. But He here He speaks primarily to His servants, those who outwardly are His followers. These people may lose their salvation in either of two ways: by trusting in their own works (this Jesus condemned in the parable of the Pharisee and the tax collector) or by being content with a stagnant faith that does not result in a Christian life. The nobleman in this story gave money to his servants and told them to use it, to do business with it. To all His servants, the Lord gives certain gifts—material goods, talents of body or mind, and spiritual gifts—and especially that gift that is most valuable: the Means of Grace, Word and Sacraments. He tells every one of us: until I return, use these gifts according to My instructions to build and expand My kingdom, to help others, and so on. All of His servants receive these gifts; the Lord forgets no one. He gives them freely; we do not earn or deserve them. But He expects us to use them and gives us every opportunity to do so. The seriousness of this instruction is clear in the sentence pronounced on the servant who made no use of his gift.

In this parable, Jesus condemns sins of omission. This servant had done nothing evil with the money; he hadn't cheated others, he hadn't wasted it in careless living. He simply had done nothing with it. The other servants had not worked with equal results, but they both had worked. The Lord knows our caliber; He knows which gifts we can use, and that's the mina we get. He knows our weakness; He knows in what measure we can use His gifts, and He will not deal hard with us if we cannot point to great brilliant achievements. But there is one thing that will disqualify us in His kingdom: if we do not use His gifts according to His will. This is not to say that good works will save us, but a lack of good works can damn us. That rich man in the parable was not accused of doing any wicked thing to Lazarus; he simply did nothing for him and so he woke up in hell. Then he wanted to do missionary work, but it was too late.

The point Jesus makes here is this: His real servants use the gifts they receive, and the one who does not use his gifts and talents for God and His kingdom is not Christ's servant and will be banished from His kingdom. True faith in the Savior brings the fruit of good works; where good works are lacking, there is no true faith.

Does this parable condemn us too? Do we wrap our mina in a handkerchief and hide it in the ground? Even when we do our best, much will be left undone; this the Lord in His love will forgive. But do we try to do our best in the Lord's service?

Prayer

O God, merciful Father, forgive our neglect and our indolence in making use of the gifts and opportunities to further Your work on earth. We are indeed unprofitable servants, and if You should mark iniquities, O Lord, who could stand? Grant us Your grace for Jesus' sake, and strengthen the new man in us so we may make use of the time still given to us, better serve You in Your kingdom here on earth, and retain the blessed inheritance You promises to Your servants. Grant our prayer for Jesus' sake. Amen.

THE COMING
OF THE KING
Luke 19:29–48

TODAY we witness Jesus' triumphal entry into Jerusalem, the most magnificent reception He received in His life on earth. And we note that He wanted it to be that way, so He deliberately prepared for it. When the Pharisees demanded, "Teacher, rebuke Your disciples," Jesus replied, "I tell you, if these were silent, the very stones would cry out." This was how Jesus wanted it so all who were in or near Jerusalem would know about Him and would hear Him hailed as the promised Messiah. Yet, looking down at the city, He weeps and prophesies its destruction. In spirit, we hear a crowd cry, "Crucify Him!" This was Armageddon, the day of decision, for Jerusalem. What would have happened if these people in Jerusalem and Israel had known the things that would bring them peace? We do not know. But we do know that whenever we hear the proclamation, "your King is coming," it is Armageddon, the day of decision, for us. And so let us consider this text today.

When He drew near to Bethphage and Bethany, at the mount that is called Olivet, He sent two of the disciples, saying, "Go into the village in front of you, where on entering you will find a colt tied, on which no one has ever yet sat. Untie it and bring it here. If anyone asks you, 'Why are you untying it?' you shall say this: 'The Lord has need of it.' " So those who were sent went away and found it just as He had told them. And as they were untying the colt, its owners said to them, "Why are you untying the colt?" And they said, "The Lord has need of it." And they brought it to Jesus, and throwing their cloaks on the colt, they set Jesus on it. And as He rode along, they spread their cloaks on the road. As He was drawing near—already on the way down the Mount of Olives—the whole multitude of His disciples began to rejoice and praise God with a loud voice for all the mighty works that they had seen, saying, "Blessed is the King who comes in the name of the Lord! Peace in heaven and glory in the highest!" And some of the Pharisees in the crowd said to Him, "Teacher, rebuke Your disciples." He answered, "I tell you, if these were silent, the very stones would cry out."

Jesus Weeps over Jerusalem

And when He drew near and saw the city, He wept over it, saying, "Would that you, even you, had known on this day the things that make for peace! But now they are hidden from your eyes. For the days will come upon you, when your enemies will set up a barricade around you and surround you and hem you in on every side and tear you down to the ground, you and your children within you. And they will not leave one stone upon another in you, because you did not know the time of your visitation."

Jesus Cleanses the Temple

And He entered the temple and began to drive out those who sold, saying to them, "It is written, 'My house shall be a house of prayer,' but you have made it a den of robbers."

And He was teaching daily in the temple. The chief priests and the scribes and the principal men of the people were seeking to destroy Him, but they did not find anything they could do, for all the people were hanging on His words.

This was the Sunday before Good Friday. During the first part of this week, until Thursday, Jesus again offered His salvation to His people. It was Jerusalem's last chance. That city still stood where David had founded it, but where David's harp had sounded, the Roman sentries now perched. The temple was still there, but when Jesus entered it that day, He had to use a scourge to drive out those who desecrated the holy place. And He had already observed the trenches around the city walls, the Roman soldiers swarming through the breaches, and Roman torches lighting the temple.

When Jesus looks today on the world and on us, does He still weep? There are more Christians in the world than ever before, but how many merely bear the name? There are many large and beautiful churches, but how many empty pews are there? And in the homes, how many who ask Him to enter with as good a conscience even as Zacchaeus? Zacchaeus was a thief, but he could stand and say, not to his fellow men or his pastor, but to the soul-searching eye of the Son of God: from this day forward, there will be nothing in this house that I would hide from You.

Jerusalem did not want the Christ, and God's hand leveled it to the ground. Do we want Him? Or does it sound like the trumpet of Judgment Day when we hear the message, "your King is coming to you" (Matthew 21:5)? He comes to us bringing salvation. There still is not much regal pomp and magnificence about Him as He comes in the Word of the cross, but He comes bringing salvation, the only salvation for the world and for us.

Let us receive Him as our King, as the multitude on Palm Sunday did, but let us not forget as quickly as they did! His coming should have lasting effects on our life, noticeable in better church attendance, more frequent use of His Sacrament, greater interest in the work of His kingdom, and more generous contributions for that work. In the very streets, these effects should be noted in a more sincere confession of His name and a consistent Christian life; in homes in a more diligent study of His Word; on sickbeds in greater patience and submission to His will.

Someday, perhaps soon, He will come to us for the last time to call us home. Will we be prepared to meet Him? That will depend on whether we receive Him now as our Savior and our King.

Prayer

Lord God heavenly Father, we give You hearty thanks that for us poor sinners You ordained and sent Your Son as a righteous King and Savior to redeem Your people from sins, from the power of the devil, and from eternal death. And we most heartily ask You to enlighten and govern us by Your Holy Spirit that we may ever know and confess Christ to be our King and Savior and, firmly trusting in Him alone, receive eternal life through Him, our Lord Jesus Christ. Amen.

THE WICKED TENANTS
Luke 20:1–19

IN the last verses of the previous chapter, St. Luke said, "The chief priests and the scribes and the principal men of the people were seeking to destroy Him, but they did not find anything they could do, for all the people were hanging on His words" (Luke 18:47–48). Jesus had cleansed the temple, driving out the buyers and sellers and money-changers because their business profaned the house of God. But above all, the people had resorted to an altogether false conception of the way to God, as though they could buy their way into His favor by their sacrifices. After Jesus had cast out these desecrators and false teachers, He was in the temple every day that week, teaching about the true way of salvation. But the leaders of Israel, the teachers and rulers determined to preserve their own authority and power, now concluded that something must be done to stop Him. Today we read of their first attempt against the Lord and of His reply.

The Authority of Jesus Challenged

One day, as Jesus was teaching the people in the temple and preaching the gospel, the chief priests and the scribes with the elders came up and said to Him, "Tell us by what authority You do these things, or who it is that gave You this authority." He answered them, "I also will ask you a question. Now tell Me, was the baptism of John from heaven or from man?" And they discussed it with one another, saying, "If we say, 'From heaven,' He will say, 'Why did you not believe him?' But if we say, 'From man,' all the people will stone us to death, for they are convinced that John was a prophet." So they answered that they did not know where it came from. And Jesus said to them, "Neither will I tell you by what authority I do these things."

The Parable of the Wicked Tenants

And He began to tell the people this parable: "A man planted a vineyard and let it out to tenants and went into another country for a long while. When the time came, he sent a servant to the tenants, so that they would give him some of the fruit of the vineyard. But the tenants beat him and sent him away empty-handed. And he sent another servant. But they also beat and treated him shamefully, and sent him away empty-handed. And he sent yet a third. This one also they wounded and cast out. Then the owner of the vineyard said, 'What shall I do? I will send my beloved son; perhaps they will respect him.' But when the tenants saw him, they said to themselves, 'This is the heir. Let us kill him, so that the inheritance may be ours.' And they threw him out of the vineyard and killed him. What then will the owner of the vineyard do to them? He will come and destroy those tenants and give the vineyard to others." When they heard this, they said, "Surely not!" But He looked directly at them and said, "What then is this that is written:

> " 'The stone that the builders rejected has become the
> cornerstone'?
> Everyone who falls on that stone will be broken to pieces,
> and when it falls on anyone, it will crush him."

Paying Taxes to Caesar

The scribes and the chief priests sought to lay hands on Him
at that very hour, for they perceived that He had told this parable against them, but they feared the people.

This delegation consisted of chief priests, scribes, and elders; in other
words, representatives of the Jewish Council. They had the right to
ask anyone in the land for his credentials. But Jesus, in His counterquestion, replied that they would find their answer in their own
view of John the Baptist. Was John God's messenger? If so, then
his testimony at Jesus' Baptism that He was the Son of God was
Christ's credentials from heaven. Since the Council, for its own
wicked reasons, had never taken a public stand on John's position,
Jesus now refused to answer their question. Instead, He gave them a
harsh answer in the parable of the wicked tenants and their punishment. In effect, Jesus revealed their plot to slay the Son of God that
lay behind their series of attacks on Him they were now launching.
Referring to a parable that Isaiah had already used (Isaiah 5:1–7), He
continued it and so told the long history of Israel and her attitude
to God. God had chosen Israel as His people and had richly blessed
them with earthly goods and with His own covenant and revelation. But when He demanded fruits, they despised His messengers,
cast them out, and killed them. And now, they were determined to
do the same to the Son of God. What would be—what must be—
the consequence? In answer, Jesus pointed them to Psalm 118 and
Isaiah 8. They, the builders of Israel, were now rejecting Him on
whom rested their salvation. But whoever rejects Him will himself be rejected; whoever stumbles at this stone or takes offense at
His lowliness will be left without a Savior; whoever defies Him will
lose his soul.

In this parable, Jesus continued to cleanse the temple of God not with a scourge of ropes but with the sword of His Word, exposing their wickedness and foretelling their fate if they persisted in their projects. We know now that they did not heed Jesus' last warnings. In fact, in that very hour they tried to stop Him. There is something appalling in this blindness that in the very moment that they showed clear understanding of the parable, they turned right around and began to fulfill it.

The greater the love, the greater the judgment. Other nations have experienced the result of ingratitude and rejection of God's love. And what about us? God has planted His vineyard among us where the sun of His grace shines brighter than it ever did in the twilight of Israel. Should not the ground of the New Testament, sprinkled with the blood of Christ and warmed by the sun of Pentecost, produce more fruit of holy living? If the Lord were to hold court in our midst today and demand an account for the countless invitations extended to us, for the many witnesses who have told us the Word of God, for all the gracious work of the Spirit on our heart, would He find genuine and rich fruit of repentance? Or would He be disappointed in us too?

Prayer

O Father, God of love,
Now hear my supplication;
O Savior, Son of God,
Accept my adoration;
O Holy Spirit, be
My ever faithful guide
That I may serve You here
And there with You abide. Amen. (LSB 703:5)

TRAPS THAT FAILED

Luke 20:20–40

IT is not unusual for people who hate one another and would do anything to frustrate one another's goals to join in a common cause against a common enemy. The last days of Jesus' life on earth offer an example of the hatred, as well as the love, that unites men. The Pharisees were bitter opponents of the Sadducees, the liberals of that day who were aristocratic worldlings who did not believe in life beyond the grave and sought only enjoyment of earthly life. The Sadducees had only scorn for the Pharisees, who were sticklers for the Law of Moses and boasted of their own holiness. Many of the Pharisees were scribes, the religious teachers of the Jews. Both parties, however, were Jews and, therefore, foes of the Roman conquerors. Here we read that not only do the Pharisees and Sadducees bury their own differences but they also unite with the Herodians, supporters of the Roman authorities (Matthew 22:16), against a common foe, Jesus, who, they feared, was a threat to their power over the people. This passage tells us of two attacks on Jesus.

So they watched Him and sent spies, who pretended to be sincere, that they might catch Him in something He said, so as to deliver Him up to the authority and jurisdiction of the governor. So they asked Him, "Teacher, we know that You speak and teach rightly, and show no partiality, but truly teach the way of God. Is it lawful for us to give tribute to Caesar, or not?" But He perceived their craftiness, and said to them, "Show Me a denarius. Whose likeness and inscription does it have?" They said, "Caesar's." He said to them, "Then render to Caesar the things that are Caesar's, and to God the things that are God's." And they were not able in the presence of the people to catch Him in what He said, but marveling at His answer they became silent.

Sadducees Ask about the Resurrection

There came to Him some Sadducees, those who deny that there is a resurrection, and they asked Him a question, saying, "Teacher, Moses wrote for us that if a man's brother dies, having a wife but no children, the man must take the widow and raise up offspring for his brother. Now there were seven brothers. The first took a wife, and died without children. And the second and the third took her, and likewise all seven left no children and died. Afterward the woman also died. In the resurrection, therefore, whose wife will the woman be? For the seven had her as wife."

And Jesus said to them, "The sons of this age marry and are given in marriage, but those who are considered worthy to attain to that age and to the resurrection from the dead neither marry nor are given in marriage, for they cannot die anymore, because they are equal to angels and are sons of God, being sons of the resurrection. But that the dead are raised, even Moses showed, in the passage about the bush, where he calls the Lord the God of Abraham and the God of Isaac and the God of Jacob. Now He is not God of the dead, but of the living, for all live to Him." Then some of the scribes answered, "Teacher, You have spoken well." For they no longer dared to ask Him any question.

Both attacks recorded here take the form of trick questions. Is it lawful, they ask, according to God's Law, to pay the tax that the Romans are levying? If Jesus said no, the Herodians would deliver Him to Pilate as a rebel. If He said yes, they would hold Him up as a Messiah who supports foreign conquerors instead of rendering them powerless and restoring the kingdom to Israel. Either way, it would be His end. Jesus easily escaped this trap. He pointed out to them that they acknowledged Caesar's rule by using his money and they enjoyed the protection of Caesar's government; therefore, they owed Caesar the tax that made such government possible. Such a position need not interfere with their duties to God. They could, and should, still render God worship and service.

The Sadducees then proposed an absurd case of a woman who successively had seven husbands; whose wife would she be in the hereafter? What this question really meant was, How can there be a resurrection since such situations would be impossible in a future life? Jesus easily solves this problem too. Marriage belongs to earthly life. In eternity, the children of God will be like the angels, who neither marry nor are given in marriage.

Both traps had failed. And in addition to exposing His enemies' duplicity and ignorance in spiritual things, Jesus presented lessons for all Christians of all times. In this world, we live in two kingdoms: that of the state and that of the Church, the kingdom of God on earth. We owe our dues to both. To our government, we owe obedience in all temporal things. To God, we owe obedience in all things He has revealed to us in His Word. The two need not interfere with each other, because they pertain to two entirely different spheres. If they do, if the temporal rulers overstep their bounds and command things contrary to God's Word, then duty to God comes first (Acts 5:29). Just so, it is wrong to apply conditions of this world to those in the world to come because, again, they are different. To conclude that because conditions in this life cannot continue after death there must be no afterlife is a fallacy. On the contrary, the Scriptures from the very beginning, in the Books of Moses, bear unmistakable witness to the resurrection. Before God, all the dead are living. The souls of righteous men, those who were clothed in the righteousness of the Savior when they died, are in the presence of God in eternal happiness. Their bodies are only sleeping. When the great morning comes, God will awaken them again to join souls and bodies in a new blessed eternal life.

Thank God, there are no problems that unbelievers or our own wicked heart may propose for which the Lord does not have the solution. Most problems we, too, can solve if we only study and believe the divine Word. And those that we cannot solve we leave to God. When the time comes, He will disclose them to us too. Until then, we know that, following His guidance in the Bible and trusting in His loving care and protection, we are safe in time and in eternity.

Prayer

We thank You, Lord, that in Your Holy Word You have given us the true revelation of all that we need to know for this life and for eternity. Give us the strength to follow its instruction in our life that we may live quietly and peaceably. Grant us the faith firmly to believe what You have taught us of the blessed life to come, so that, undisturbed by doubts and misgivings, we may firmly set our hopes on Your gracious promises and, when the time comes, calmly close our eyes in death, knowing that You will awaken us again for an eternity of dwelling in the Father's house, where You have gone to prepare a place for us. In Your love, hear us, O Jesus. Amen.

FALSE AND TRUE WORSHIP
Luke 20:41–21:4

CLOSING the previous reading, Luke wrote, "For they no longer dared to ask Him any question" (Luke 20:40). That ended the time in which Jesus permitted His enemies to heckle Him. They no longer tried to set traps for Him because they understood that not only did all their attempts to trick Him through His own words fail, but also the outcome was always humiliating for them—their ignorance of Scripture was exposed and their evil intentions were revealed. In addition, there is here an indication of Christ's power: they could no longer ask Him such questions. Until this time, He had permitted it; now that permission was withdrawn and they were silent. Not that they repented, but because they could not publicly discredit Him, they began instead to make secret plans to use force against Him and to put Him to death. A few of the scribes had responded with, "Teacher, You have spoken well" (Luke 20:39). If not altogether convinced, they were at least led to think about Christ's words. And to lead them farther on the right way as well as to warn the others, Jesus now asks them a question.

Whose Son Is the Christ?

But He said to them, "How can they say that the Christ is David's son? For David himself says in the Book of Psalms,

"'The Lord said to my Lord, Sit at My right hand,
until I make Your enemies Your footstool.'
David thus calls Him Lord, so how is He his son?"

Beware of the Scribes

And in the hearing of all the people He said to His disciples, "Beware of the scribes, who like to walk around in long robes, and love greetings in the marketplaces and the best seats in the synagogues and the places of honor at feasts, who devour widows' houses and for a pretense make long prayers. They will receive the greater condemnation."

Luke 21

The Widow's Offering

Jesus looked up and saw the rich putting their gifts into the offering box, and He saw a poor widow put in two small copper coins. And He said, "Truly, I tell you, this poor widow has put in more than all of them. For they all contributed out of their abundance, but she out of her poverty put in all she had to live on."

There is an air of finality in this text. With this question, Jesus takes leave of His enemies. The great Prophet is done and no longer will teach them. Now the great High Priest goes forth to bring the perfect sacrifice for all mankind's sins before God. What is more, this is the climax of Christ's teaching, the answer to the question, "How can they say that the Christ is David's son?" The standard answer of

Israel's teachers was that the Christ, the Messiah, would be David's son. Jesus did not deny that He was David's son. But could His hearers reconcile that with the fact that David calls Him Lord? The only possible answer was that Christ is both David's son after the flesh and David's Lord because He is also the Son of God. To the scribes, the Messiah was to be David's son, a great earthly ruler who would defeat the Romans and restore David's kingdom. When Jesus told them the truth about Himself, they either did not understand or, when it dawned on them that He claimed to be the Son of God, they decided to kill Him. Jesus here shows them that their conception of the Messiah must be wrong; their answer to the question, Who is Christ? was only half the truth and, therefore, false.

This was the final parting of the ways between Christ and the Jewish teachers. "Unless you believe that I am He you will die in your sin," He had told them (John 8:24). And even today this issue is the dividing line between Christians and unbelievers. It is not merely an academic question for the learned to discuss, interesting but of little practical importance, because our souls' salvation hangs on the right answer. If Christ is not the Son of God, then His claims were false, He was a deceiver, we have no Savior. Praise God that we know the proof is overwhelming—Jesus is David's son and David's Lord; He is true God, begotten of the Father from eternity, and also true man, born of the Virgin Mary; He is our Savior.

To all the people listening, Jesus now pronounced a final warning against the scribes—hypocritical, proud, and covetous, they would receive greater damnation because they should have known better and because, as false teachers, they were leading others to the same end.

With this warning, Jesus rose to leave the temple, but He could not leave the holy place, His Father's house, with a curse. So Jesus' parting word was a blessing. His gaze fell on a widow who was sacrificing her all because love and gratitude to God compelled her. By monetary standards, it was a small gift, but in spiritual value it was the largest gift brought to the temple because it was all she had. In Jesus' eyes, her offering had such vast value because He judges by a different standard than we do. People judge the heart by deeds; the omniscient Son of God judges deeds by the heart. Her love made her willing. She had two small coins. She did not divide them with the Lord, but she gave both. She was poor, but Jesus did not tell her to keep her small offering because she was too poor to give. No—He singled her out and praised her. He read her heart with its love and faith and trust in God.

The widow did not know that the Son of God was watching her, nor did Jesus let her know. Why not? The Lord often seems to pay little attention to those who serve Him—but He still sees. He will not spoil a loving soul by praising too soon, but on the day when all the angels hear it, He will say that He saw the act. And we will bow our heads lower in adoring wonder that the Lord of heaven and earth should acknowledge the trifling things we have done.

Prayer

O Lord, to whom our hearts are an open book and to whom are known our most secret thoughts, forgive us our lack of love and gratitude for all the love You have shown us. Evermore grant us true repentance. Teach us to do better tomorrow than we did today, for Your mercy's sake. Amen.

75

THE BEGINNING OF THE END
Luke 21:5–24

JESUS left the temple and, as the evening fell, He started out toward the street. In this last week before His death, Jesus did not spend the nights in Jerusalem but stayed out on the Mount of Olives or with His friends in Bethany. As they walked through the halls of the magnificent building that had been under construction for fifty years and looked at the huge foundation stones, the forty-foot-tall marble columns on which the roof rested, and the beautiful and costly furnishings that kings and princes had presented to the Lord's sanctuary, the disciples could not help recalling that on the Sunday before Jesus had spoken of the destruction of Jerusalem and the temple. That prompted them to call attention to the beauty and massive construction of the temple—was it possible that all this should be destroyed? In answer, Jesus repeated and extended His prophecy.

Jesus Foretells Destruction of the Temple

And while some were speaking of the temple, how it was adorned with noble stones and offerings, He said, "As for these things that you see, the days will come when there will not be left here one stone upon another that will not be thrown down." And they asked Him, "Teacher, when will these things be, and what will be the sign when these things are about to take place?" And He said, "See that you are not led astray. For many will come in My name, saying, 'I am he!' and, 'The time is at hand!' Do not go after them. And when you hear of wars and tumults, do not be terrified, for these things must first take place, but the end will not be at once."

Jesus Foretells Wars and Persecution

Then He said to them, "Nation will rise against nation, and kingdom against kingdom. There will be great earthquakes, and in various places famines and pestilences. And there will be terrors and great signs from heaven. But before all this they will lay their hands on you and persecute you, delivering you up to the synagogues and prisons, and you will be brought before kings and governors for My name's sake. This will be your opportunity to bear witness. Settle it therefore in your minds not to meditate beforehand how to answer, for I will give you a mouth and wisdom, which none of your adversaries will be able to withstand or contradict. You will be delivered up even by parents and brothers and relatives and friends, and some of you they will put to death. You will be hated by all for My name's sake. But not a hair of your head will perish. By your endurance you will gain your lives.

Jesus Foretells Destruction of Jerusalem

"But when you see Jerusalem surrounded by armies, then know that its desolation has come near. Then let those who are in Judea flee to the mountains, and let those who are inside the city depart, and let not those who are out in the country enter it, for these are days of vengeance, to fulfill all that is written. Alas for women who are pregnant and for those who are nursing infants in those days! For there will be great distress upon the earth and wrath against this people. They will fall by the edge of the sword and be led captive among all nations, and Jerusalem will be trampled underfoot by the Gentiles, until the times of the Gentiles are fulfilled."

Jesus clearly speaks here of two events: the destruction of Jerusalem and the end of the world. But we must remember that this is prophecy; therefore, we should not expect to fully understand every detail. Understanding prophecy is not always possible until the foretold events have taken place; then prophecy and fulfillment can be compared. Again, the disciples apparently thought that the destruction of Jerusalem and of the temple must mean the end of the world, that the two must go together (compare Matthew 24:3). Jesus agrees. The two events go together, but He does not say that there may not be a long period of time between them. After all, what is time to the eternal God! "For a thousand years in Your sight are but as yesterday when it is past, or as a watch in the night" (Psalm 90:4). The destruction of Jerusalem is the beginning of the end, the introduction to the judgment of the world.

The disciples asked when these things would happen and by what signs they would know they were impending. The Lord ignores the "when"; that is not for them to know. But He speaks of the signs portending the destruction of Jerusalem and of the world, connecting the signs in such a way that they apply to both. And so the warning and the promise of the Lord applies to us too.

There will be much religious deceit, attempts to lead Christians astray, and we must be on our guard. There will be much suffering because of wars and of natural calamities, and Christians will not be exempt. But we must not be offended at that because we know that these are signs of the Lord's coming and they should move us to be prepared. There will be persecution by secular rulers and religious leaders. We must not unduly worry how we remain true to our Lord under such conditions because He Himself will be with us and enable us to confess Him before men. Far from it that this should harm His Church—our confession will draw others to Christ. And although the closest bonds of relationship may be dissolved and families may be broken up by religious differences, not even a hair of our head will perish. Yes, we might die, but we will not perish. Death will only usher us into a new and better life.

History tells us how literally the prophecy concerning Jerusalem was fulfilled; how the Romans leveled the city, including the temple, to the ground; how the Christians, warned by the preliminary signs, were saved by taking refuge in the surrounding mountains.

And is not this a pledge, a guarantee, that the remainder of His prophecy will also be fulfilled? "This will be your opportunity to bear witness. Settle it therefore in your minds not to meditate beforehand how to answer, for I will give you a mouth and wisdom, which none of your adversaries will be able to withstand or contradict. You will be delivered up even by parents and brothers and relatives and friends, and some of you they will put to death. You will be hated by all for My name's sake. But not a hair of your head will perish." This is the Lord's promise. May we never forget it! May we always trust in it! It will not fail us!

Prayer

O Lord Jesus Christ, You will come again in majesty to judge the living and the dead and call forth all who sleep in the graves, either to the resurrection of life or to the resurrection of condemnation. We ask You to be gracious to us and to raise us from the death of sin to the life of righteousness, that, when we depart this life, we may rest in You, and, having been found acceptable in Your sight, may on the Last Day be raised up to life everlasting, inherit the kingdom prepared for us from the foundation of the world, and give You glory and praise, world without end. Amen.

THE SECOND COMING OF THE KING

Luke 21:25–38

AS we read in the previous section of this chapter, Jesus did not answer the "when" of His disciples' question regarding the end of the world. They would know that the destruction of Jerusalem was impending when they saw the city surrounded by armies. Then they should escape to the mountains. But of the end of the world He said, "But concerning that day and hour no one knows, not even the angels of heaven, nor the Son, but the Father only" (Matthew 24:36). He left no doubt about the fact of the world's final destruction and of His return to judgment. And in order that every trace of doubt might be removed from their hearts, and ours, Jesus next describes various signs of His return. Upon seeing these, His disciples of all time can be sure that He is coming.

The Coming of the Son of Man

"And there will be signs in sun and moon and stars, and on the earth distress of nations in perplexity because of the roaring of the sea and the waves, people fainting with fear and with foreboding of what is coming on the world. For the powers of the heavens will be shaken. And then they will see the Son of Man coming in a cloud with power and great glory. Now when these things begin to take place, straighten up and raise your heads, because your redemption is drawing near."

The Lesson of the Fig Tree

And He told them a parable: "Look at the fig tree, and all the trees. As soon as they come out in leaf, you see for yourselves and know that the summer is already near. So also, when you see these things taking place, you know that the kingdom of God is near. Truly, I say to you, this generation will not pass away until all has taken place. Heaven and earth will pass away, but My words will not pass away.

Watch Yourselves

"But watch yourselves lest your hearts be weighed down with dissipation and drunkenness and cares of this life, and that day come upon you suddenly like a trap. For it will come upon all who dwell on the face of the whole earth. But stay awake at all times, praying that you may have strength to escape all these things that are going to take place, and to stand before the Son of Man."

And every day He was teaching in the temple, but at night He went out and lodged on the mount called Olivet. And early in the morning all the people came to Him in the temple to hear Him.

St. Peter wrote, "Knowing this first of all, that scoffers will come in the last days with scoffing, following their own sinful desires. They will say, 'Where is the promise of His coming? For ever since the fathers fell asleep, all things are continuing as they were from the beginning of creation'" (2 Peter 3:3–4). Scoffers are with us today, of course. After all, after two thousand years of such talk, there is still no sign of Jesus' second coming. Our own heart, too, is inclined to doubt. An event that can happen only once in history, that, moreover, is placed at the very end of history, of which no man can speak by experience, such an event is naturally an object of doubt. Other events of Christ's life are recorded in history, and only those who will not believe doubt them. But the judgment stands alone in the future, and so doubt and faithlessness have always been amused by it.

For that reason, Jesus made special effort to assure us that the judgment is fact, not fiction. In addition to His oft-repeated prophecy, to His solemn oath that "heaven and earth will pass away, but My words will not pass away," He told us of the signs that will precede His coming: signs in sun, moon, and stars; earthquakes, floods, and tidal waves; wars and rumors of war. True, unbelievers laugh that we believe these to be signs of the end times. These things happen in a perfectly natural way, they say. But who stands behind nature and moves all her forces? If a friend tells us he is coming for a visit but he has a long way to travel so he doesn't set a time but instead will call periodically, when we get his calls, one after another, will we not take them as sure signs that he is on the way? All these signs in nature are the Lord's announcements: He is coming; He is on the way; see to it that His room is ready when He comes!

So Jesus has assured us of the fact of His coming. But why did He hide the day and the hour from us? This, too, He tells us plainly: "But stay awake at all times, praying," He says, "that you may have strength to escape all these things that are going to take place, and to stand before the Son of Man." Oh, the Lord knows how easily we are lulled into sleep by the cares, riches, and pleasures of the world until we do not expect His coming and do not prepare for it. But only those who are ready to meet Him in true repentance and trusting faith in His merits will be able to stand in God's judgment. The signs of His coming are to keep us watchful and waiting. It is not to be a fearful waiting but a joyful one as we greet the signs of spring and summer when the long and hard winter is past.

We do not know when our Lord will return, but we do know that time is passing. We see the signs foretelling His coming, signs that are the beginning of the judgment. When that day comes, history will end—the world's history, the Church's history, and our history; the history of our sin, of our repentance, and of our faith.

Then what's won is won; what's lost is lost. After that there will be no change.

Prayer

Lord God, heavenly Father, who has appointed a day in which heaven and earth will pass away and in which both the living and the dead will be judged by the Son of Man, we humbly ask You to make us diligent in the use of Your Word and enable us, by the grace of Your Holy Spirit, to walk before You in fervent faith and all holy obedience, that with constant watchfulness and prayer we may look for and hasten to the second coming of Your Son and, being judged in the robes of His righteousness, enter with Him into His eternal kingdom. In His name and for His sake. Amen.

PREPARATIONS
Luke 22:1–13

WITH this chapter, we enter the Passion history of the Lord. Jesus had left the glory of His Father to come into this world, which the curse of sin had turned into a vale of tears. He had relinquished the loving service of the angels to take upon Himself the form of a humble servant. Now He prepared to be the ultimate sacrifice to lift the curse from sinful mankind. Jesus steadfastly set toward to Jerusalem, where stood the altar on Calvary's hill. Since Palm Sunday, He had spent the days in the city, the nights with His disciples on the Mount of Olives or with His friends Lazarus, Mary, and Martha in Bethany. Now He would enter the city to celebrate His last Passover. Others were making preparations too. His enemies, who had long planned to put Him to death, were now presented with an opportunity, and they promptly seized it.

The Plot to Kill Jesus

Now the Feast of Unleavened Bread drew near, which is called the Passover. And the chief priests and the scribes were seeking how to put Him to death, for they feared the people.

Judas to Betray Jesus

Then Satan entered into Judas called Iscariot, who was of the number of the twelve. He went away and conferred with the chief priests and officers how he might betray Him to them. And they were glad, and agreed to give him money. So he consented and sought an opportunity to betray Him to them in the absence of a crowd.

The Passover with the Disciples

Then came the day of Unleavened Bread, on which the Passover lamb had to be sacrificed. So Jesus sent Peter and John, saying, "Go and prepare the Passover for us, that we may eat it." They said to Him, "Where will you have us prepare it?" He said to them, "Behold, when you have entered the city, a man carrying a jar of water will meet you. Follow him into the house that he enters and tell the master of the house, 'The Teacher says to you, Where is the guest room, where I may eat the Passover with My disciples?' And he will show you a large upper room furnished; prepare it there." And they went and found it just as He had told them, and they prepared the Passover.

Judas's conference with the chief priests likely took place on Wednesday of Holy Week, only the day before he carried out his evil plan. We are told that Satan now entered into Judas, but it wasn't Satan's first attack. Judas's decision to betray his Lord may have been precipitated by anger because Jesus had exposed his love of money at that supper in Simon the leper's house (John 12:4–6). But that was not the real motive that drove him. As John indicates, Judas had fallen for Satan's seduction long before. His sin was against the ninth commandment: greed. Judas coveted money. People like to think of greed as a minor sin, but see what can come of it! It starts with an unholy desire, with small secret pilferings and dishonesty. Then, more easily than most other sins, it becomes a ruling sin that controls a person's thoughts and actions. We are given a glimpse here of what makes sin so powerful. It is difficult to understand how greed for money could induce Judas to commit such a horrid sin—after all, it was a very small sum of money that he got—until we remember that Satan was active in the deal. This is what makes sin so powerful. Every willful sin opens the heart to the devil. He takes control, and then there is no telling what man might do, because Satan is capable of anything.

The scene in our text changes. Jesus sends two of His disciples to prepare for His last Passover. Again, as on Palm Sunday, Jesus reveals His omniscience. He knew they would meet that man with the water jar, that he would take them to the room where they would celebrate the meal. And He knew even more. The hatred of the Jews, festering for a long time, had reached the climax—they were firmly resolved to kill Him. And Judas's offer of betrayal gave them the means to carry out the plan. Jesus knew it all, knew all that was waiting for Him. Still, He went into the very den of His foes. The culmination of their plans was at the same time the accomplishment of His work on earth, the very reason His Father had sent Him and for which He had come. With full knowledge, but without a moment's hesitation, He went to Jerusalem, to the cross.

"He came to His own, and His own people did not receive Him" (John 1:11). Jesus had to ask for a guest room where He might sit with His disciples. Now, with His work completed and salvation won, He again comes to us in His Word, and again He asks where He would find His disciples. How far must He travel to find a receptive heart? There are many a church with a cross on the spire but where the cross of Calvary is absent, many homes where they close the door in open scorn, where they hide from Him out of fear or where they think they do not need Him; there are many temples of money where they worship the golden calf and have no time for the Savior, many homes where they would not hear His knocking at the door for the noise of reveling or of discord within.

There are many homes where they would seat Him at the head of the table but He would not sit because the air is icy with hypocrisy and self-righteousness.

Let us not judge our neighbor but ask ourselves: Is mine the house where He may find a home? Am I glad to let Him see my life? Would I gladly show Him the pictures on my walls, the books on my shelves, the thoughts of my heart? Even in the capital city of His enemies, Jesus knew where to find a friend. When He comes this way, may He come straight to our home because He knows who says, "Abide with us, for it is toward evening, and the day is far spent" (Luke 24:29).

Prayer

Abide, O dearest Jesus,
Among us with Your grace
That Satan may not harm us
Nor we to sin give place.

Abide, O dear Redeemer,
Among us with Your Word,
And thus now and hereafter
True peace and joy afford.

Abide with Your protection
Among us, Lord, our strength,
Lest world and Satan fell us
And overcome at length.
Abide, O faithful Savior,
Among us with Your love;
Grant steadfastness and help us
To reach our home above. Amen.
(LSB 919:1–2, 5–6)

THE CHOICEST GIFT OF CHRIST'S LOVE
Luke 22:14–23

WHEN the storms howl and ships are wrecked and the air is filled with cries for help, the rescue workers go out on their errands of mercy to save wherever saving is possible. They forget that the storm that wrecked the great ship may even more easily destroy their little nutshell of a boat; they risk their lives to save others. When the firefighter is called to duty where the flames roar and consume and a face appears at a high window, he does not hesitatingly calculate the height or consider that the walls may cave in before he gets there; he raises his ladder despite the danger and risks his life to save another. And we honor such bravery and faithfulness.

Institution of the Lord's Supper

And when the hour came, He reclined at table, and the apostles with Him. And He said to them, "I have earnestly desired to eat this Passover with you before I suffer. For I tell you I will not eat it until it is fulfilled in the kingdom of God." And He took a cup, and when He had given thanks He said, "Take this, and divide it among yourselves. For I tell you that from now on I will not drink of the fruit of the vine until the kingdom of God comes." And He took bread, and when He had given thanks, He broke it and gave it to them, saying, "This is My body, which is given for you. Do this in remembrance of Me." And likewise the cup after they had eaten, saying, "This cup that is poured out for you is the new covenant in My blood. But behold, the hand of him who betrays Me is with Me on the table. For the Son of Man goes as it has been determined, but woe to that man by whom He is betrayed!" And they began to question one another, which of them it could be who was going to do this.

A great majestic mountain scene is apt to enthrall us so much that we overlook details. We see the mighty snowcaps, the tall pines, and the rushing waterfall with the rainbow, but we overlook the flowers at our feet. So it may be in the words of institution of the Lord's Supper. We hear them often, and we think of the prominent features mentioned: the Son of God Himself, the true body and blood of Christ, the purpose to assure every communicant of his pardon from all his sin. But we are apt to overlook the very first phrase: "Our Lord Jesus Christ, on the night when He was betrayed."

This statement reminds us of that night when He instituted His Holy Supper. He told His disciples that this was the last Passover He would eat with them on earth, that there was a special reason why He wanted to celebrate this feast with them. It is evident that Jesus knew what was waiting for Him. He was aware of Judas counting his thirty pieces of silver, of the soldiers arming themselves and lighting the torches. He saw the ropes, the scourge, the cross, the nails. Oh, there were greater storms and hotter flames facing Jesus that night than any man has ever met. Jesus knew He would die not only the most shameful death but also a death more horrible than we can ever imagine because in that death was summed up the wages of all sins of all mankind.

And what does He do? Steadfastly, He looks beyond that death to how He will provide for all His followers until the end of time—a food and a cup to nourish and to strengthen their souls to eternal life. He thought of each individual Christian. His Gospel, too, is universal; every sinner is included. That blessed promise—"whoever believes in Him should not perish but have eternal life" (John 3:16)—does not mention any name because He wanted us to know that He did all this for you and for me. When we come to His Table, we should each know, "This body was given for me; this blood was shed for me; my sins are forgiven."

Jesus knew that within twenty-four hours those awful words of Isaiah would be fulfilled in Him: "He had no form or majesty that we should look at Him, and no beauty that we should desire Him. He was despised and rejected by men; a man of sorrows, and acquainted with grief; and as one from whom men hide their faces He was despised, and we esteemed Him not" (Isaiah 53:2–3). Yet He reaches over His death as though it were nothing, and in His last testament bequeaths to them who caused His death, to you and to me, the most precious inheritance. It is the most sublime example of selfless love the world has known and His Sacrament is the superior gift of magnificent love.

How will we respond? When the rain falls and the sun shines, the earth brings forth fruit. And when the blood of Jesus Christ cleanses our heart from all sin, it must bring forth the fruits of thankfulness in word and deed. A beautiful name of this Sacrament is Holy Communion. While that name refers to the communion between bread and wine and the body and blood of Christ, it indicates also what St. Paul wrote to the Corinthians, "We who are many are one body, for we all partake of the one bread" (1 Corinthians 10:17). Here at this Table, the Lord fosters and nourishes that mutual love that shows that all Christians are the one body of Christ. If our life is not what it should be, if love is lacking in our relationship with our fellow Christians, if there is anything wrong in our home and family life, let us ask ourselves: do we come to seek strength and help here where the Lord offers it and where we all may find it—at His Table?

Prayer

Lord Jesus Christ,
You have prepared
This feast for our salvation;
It is Your body and Your blood,
And at Your invitation
As weary souls, with sin oppressed,
We come to You for needed rest,
For comfort, and for pardon.

Grant that we worthily receive
Your supper, Lord, our Savior,
And, truly grieving for our sins,
May prove by our behavior

That we are thankful for Your grace
And day by day may run our race,
In holiness increasing. Amen. (LSB 622:1, 7)

WARNING AND COMFORT ON THE WAY

Luke 22:24–38

IT is not an easy thing to be faithful to Christ. That formidable trio—the devil, the world, and the flesh—is ever active in keeping us away from the Lord, who has redeemed us and wants to save us, and turning us against Him. And because we have that traitor, our own human nature, in our own camp, it is not an easy thing to remain faithful to Him even after He has made us His own. The account of Jesus' own apostles is evidence enough of that. Surely, if ever there were men favored above all others, it was that group of twelve who were in almost daily personal contact with Jesus for years. And yet, what happened? As a warning, but also for our consolation and encouragement, let us consider what happened in that Upper Room.

Who Is the Greatest?

A dispute also arose among them, as to which of them was to be regarded as the greatest. And He said to them, "The kings of the Gentiles exercise lordship over them, and those in authority over them are called benefactors. But not so with you. Rather, let the greatest among you become as the youngest, and the leader as one who serves. For who is the greater, one who reclines at table or one who serves? Is it not the one who reclines at table? But I am among you as the one who serves.

"You are those who have stayed with Me in My trials, and I assign to you, as My Father assigned to Me, a kingdom, that you may eat and drink at My table in My kingdom and sit on thrones judging the twelve tribes of Israel.

Jesus Foretells Peter's Denial

"Simon, Simon, behold, Satan demanded to have you, that he might sift you like wheat, but I have prayed for you that your faith may not fail. And when you have turned again, strengthen your brothers." Peter said to Him, "Lord, I am ready to go with You both to prison and to death." Jesus said, "I tell you, Peter, the rooster will not crow this day, until you deny three times that you know Me."

Scripture Must Be Fulfilled in Jesus

And He said to them, "When I sent you out with no moneybag or knapsack or sandals, did you lack anything?" They said, "Nothing." He said to them, "But now let the one who has a moneybag take it, and likewise a knapsack. And let the one who has no sword sell his cloak and buy one. For I tell you that this Scripture must be fulfilled in Me: 'And He was numbered with the transgressors.' For what is written about Me has its fulfillment." And they said, "Look, Lord, here are two swords." And He said to them, "It is enough."

Jesus had revealed to His apostles that one of them would betray Him to His enemies. Supplementing the brief account of Luke from the other Gospels, we know that the Lord pointed out Judas and gave him a last warning, whereupon the betrayer left the room and went out into the night. Now, whether it was that this exposure of one of their number led them to debate which of them was least like the betrayer, or whether Jesus' prophecy of His imminent departure suggested the thought that one of them would have to take His place as leader, they again quarreled about which of them should be considered to be the greatest.

How that must have grieved the Lord! After that bitter task of unmasking the traitor and the important task of giving them the testament of His supreme love, our Lord had to hear the remaining apostles express pride and selfish ambition! But the patient Lord, not yet tired of teaching them, gives an example of His great humility. He kneels down and washes their feet, as John tells us (John 13), a service done usually by the humblest slave. And then, calmly but impressively, He tells them again that the way of the world does not prevail in the kingdom of God, where the highest distinction is not pomp and power but unselfish service. They must find their satisfaction in the awareness that they are walking in the way their Lord has walked. And there will be a reward in the glory beyond. The Savior will not forget the least service rendered to His brothers. He keeps a record against the Day of Judgment.

But now evil hours were coming, not just for Him but for them too. Satan would not be satisfied with one victim; each of them would be intensely tempted and tested. Chiefly was Peter threatened. Jesus clearly foretold what would happen. He warned Peter and told him where he should seek and find help—in the intercession of His Lord. But Peter still trusted in his own strength. He had to learn by bitter experience that we mortals can do nothing on our own.

Again Jesus warned them: the golden days when He provided everything they needed were over. In the future, they would be in both spiritual and bodily danger. It would be necessary now for them to protect themselves against danger. Again He referred to His end. He would now fulfill all that was required for the accomplishment of His work. In their love and zeal, the disciples exclaimed, "Look, Lord, here are two swords," meaning they would defend Him against His enemies. Again they had misunderstood. It was not the Father's will that they fight for Him with earthly weapons, so Jesus sighed, "It is enough." He meant that the time would come when they would know better, when the Holy Spirit would come to enlighten them.

It was growing dark, and the powers of darkness were rapidly closing in on Him. His Christians must expect a similar fate. Sometimes our very lives will be in danger. Always there will be

Satan's cohorts threatening our soul. Where is our help? Jesus does not change—as He prayed for Peter, so He intercedes for us. And as His prayer prevailed and Peter returned to serve his Lord anew and better, so His prayer for us is powerful today. When we, in our weakness, fail and fall, let us not, like Judas, go out into the night alone. Instead, let us unfailingly return to Him who is the same loving Savior yesterday, today, and forever.

Prayer

O God, grant us true humility after the likeness of Your Son, who took upon Himself the form of a servant, humbled Himself, and became obedient unto death, even death on the cross, to save us from the consequences of our sin and wickedness. Help us in Your mercy to root out all thoughts of our own worthiness in Your sight, that we may never be lifted up in our own mind and provoke Your wrath but in all lowliness be made partakers of the gifts of Your grace, for the sake of the merits of Your Son, our Lord and Savior, Jesus Christ. Amen.

GETHSEMANE
Luke 22:39–46

JESUS and His disciples left the Upper Room, where they had gathered for supper, and set out for the Mount of Olives. That alone indicates a definite intention on the Lord's part. Jesus knew what Judas had planned; He knew that Judas expected Him to go to Olivet and that there he would attempt to betray Him. Yet knowing all this, Jesus set out for the Mount of Olives. Up to this time, Jesus had evaded His enemies, but now His time had come, so He deliberately went to the place where Judas was leading His captors.

Jesus Prays on the Mount of Olives

And He came out and went, as was His custom, to the Mount of Olives, and the disciples followed Him. And when He came to the place, He said to them, "Pray that you may not enter into temptation." And He withdrew from them about a stone's throw, and knelt down and prayed, saying, "Father, if You are willing, remove this cup from Me. Nevertheless, not My will, but Yours, be done." And there appeared to Him an angel from heaven, strengthening Him. And being in an agony He prayed more earnestly; and his sweat became like great drops of blood falling down to the ground. And when He rose from prayer, He came to the disciples and found them sleeping for sorrow, and He said to them, "Why are you sleeping? Rise and pray that you may not enter into temptation."

The story of mankind began in a garden. In Eden, God had walked with Adam and Eve and talked with them as a father with his children. Man spoiled that beautiful picture; he turned away from God and began his dreary journey into sin and damnation. So paradise was lost. Now, again in a garden, began mankind's way back to God. Again God walked the earth and talked with men in His love; and here in Gethsemane, the Son of God began His great Passion for our redemption. In the end, when He said, "It is finished," paradise was regained.

We cannot even begin to imagine the suffering of Christ that began in the garden. The lost souls in hell might come closer to imagining it. But it wasn't mere terror of death that pressed Him down into the dust. He knew He would die the most cruel form of death, a death that would subject Him to all the infamy of a criminal and brand Him a pretender and deceiver. But here was something infinitely more horrible than death. This was the hour when He who knew no sin was made to be sin for us, the hour when Jesus alone had to face what to us is incomprehensible—meeting and overcoming the appalling burden of human sin. "The Lord has laid on Him the iniquity of us all" (Isaiah 53:6). What depths of accursed wickedness He had to answer for when He agreed to become our Savior! It was the curse of this sin and the wrath of an outraged God that struck terror to His soul. Add to this that now, no doubt, Satan and all his hosts began their final and harshest assault on Him. We can have no comprehension of the suffering that began here and reached its climax in that cry on the cross, "My God, My God, why have You forsaken Me?" (Matthew 27:46).

Jesus sought and found strength in prayer. What an example for us! "Have we trials and temptations? Is there trouble anywhere? We should never be discouraged—Take it to the Lord in prayer" (*LSB* 770:2). If only we would more faithfully follow this example and go into conflicts thus equipped, there would be more victories for us too. That is the way all the great men of God met their troubles—Jacob, Elijah, John the Baptist, Paul, Luther.

It is good for us to go with Jesus to Gethsemane because there we see our sinfulness and our need of a Savior. Jesus did not suffer for Himself, but for us. He is our substitute. Had it not been for our sin, Jesus would not have suffered as He did. And from the depth of His suffering, we may read the horror of what caused it—and what would have been our fate had He not intervened. Also here is assurance for our faith: the conflict of Jesus in the garden ended in victory. At first, it might appear that He did not obtain what He asked for. But He did. He asked that if it were possible, if the Father could find another way, but what He wanted above all was that the Father's will be done. And because Jesus knew that this was the Father's will, that He alone could endure the struggle—His disciples could not even stay awake, much less help Him—it was His will too. And His victory is our victory. Christ has paid our debt. There is no further charge against us in God's court except that we accept Christ's payment. God will not require double payment for our debt; He is just. So while we sorrow for what caused His agony, we rejoice in His victory. And in the Garden of Gethsemane, we see the Garden of Eden reopened to us.

Prayer

O Lord Jesus Christ, true God and true man, who took upon Yourself the sin of the world and in the garden did sweat blood, we give You hearty thanks for Your grace and for all You did for our redemption. We ask You, grant that by the gracious work

*of Your Holy Spirit we may in every temptation comfort ourselves
with Your bitter sufferings and death, and that we may learn to
abhor and to shun sin, and that we may serve you all our days.
Amen.*

BETRAYAL AND DENIAL
Luke 22:47–62

WHEN Jesus arose from His prayer in Gethsemane, the deciding
step was taken. Even after such a prayer of His Son, the Father denied
His petition to take the cup of suffering from Him. Jesus knew it was
necessary. As the Substitute of sinful mankind, He must suffer the
punishment due to sin. Only then can the just God, in mercy, forgive sin. Jesus, then, arose from prayer to proceed rapidly from one
stage of His suffering to the other until it culminated on the cross.
Not the least of His suffering was caused by the actions of His disciples. They all forsook Him and fled. One of them betrayed Him
to His enemies; another denied Him in the face of danger. Despite
all this, they were not horrible exceptions but merely examples of
sins very common to disciples. Let us today look at Judas and Peter,
beat our own breast, and ask, "Is it I, Lord?"

Betrayal and Arrest of Jesus

While He was still speaking, there came a crowd, and the
man called Judas, one of the twelve, was leading them. He
drew near to Jesus to kiss Him, but Jesus said to him, "Judas,
would you betray the Son of Man with a kiss?" And when those
who were around Him saw what would follow, they said,
"Lord, shall we strike with the sword?" And one of them struck
the servant of the high priest and cut off his right ear. But Jesus

said, "No more of this!" And He touched his ear and healed him. Then Jesus said to the chief priests and officers of the temple and elders, who had come out against Him, "Have you come out as against a robber, with swords and clubs? When I was with you day after day in the temple, you did not lay hands on Me. But this is your hour, and the power of darkness."

Peter Denies Jesus

Then they seized Him and led Him away, bringing Him into the high priest's house, and Peter was following at a distance. And when they had kindled a fire in the middle of the courtyard and sat down together, Peter sat down among them. Then a servant girl, seeing him as he sat in the light and looking closely at him, said, "This man also was with Him." But he denied it, saying, "Woman, I do not know Him." And a little later someone else saw him and said, "You also are one of them." But Peter said, "Man, I am not." And after an interval of about an hour still another insisted, saying, "Certainly this man also was with Him, for he too is a Galilean." But Peter said, "Man, I do not know what you are talking about." And immediately, while he was still speaking, the rooster crowed. And the Lord turned and looked at Peter. And Peter remembered the saying of the Lord, how He had said to him, "Before the rooster crows today, you will deny Me three times." And he went out and wept bitterly.

At the gate of the garden, Judas met Jesus and identified Him to his co-conspirators with the sign of intimate friendship—a kiss. Judas's crime has put him beyond the pale of human sympathy. There is a legend of a criminal whose crime was so hateful that everyone who passed his grave threw a stone upon it. So does history regard Judas; the smallest child who hears the story for the first time throws a stone with her little hand and the blackest criminal deems himself a saint beside Judas and with his soiled hand heaves a stone. For the other dark characters in the Passion story, we can find explanations that we can understand. For Judas's crime there can be only one explanation: "Then entered Satan into Judas" (Luke 22:3).

Yes, Satan was on the prowl this night. To the soldiers who came to arrest Him, Jesus said, "This is your hour, and the power of darkness." It is evident that Satan had blinded them when, despite two miracles, they still arrested Jesus. He healed the servant of the high priest, whose ear Peter had cut off in an ill-advised use of one of their two swords. Luke summarizes this account; but from the other Gospels, we know that Jesus, with one word, worked a miracle and again gave evidence of His divine majesty. Yet the soldiers took Him and led Him to the high priest.

And Peter? If ever a man stood high in the Lord's favor, it was Peter. He led the disciples in that glorious confession, "You are the Christ, the Son of the living God," to which Jesus answered, "Blessed are you, Simon Bar-Jonah! For flesh and blood has not revealed this to you, but My Father who is in heaven" (Matthew 16:16–17). And if ever a man fell deep, it was Peter. He knew what he should have done; after all, he had boasted of it. Just a few hours before, Jesus had warned him; how could he forget so quickly? How small the temptation that felled him: the teasing of a few servants and maids! How his sin grew! At first he was fearful, then defiant, then bold and shameless in his sin.

In the end, all sin is alike. Every sin opens the heart to Satan, although the doors through which he enters are different. With Judas it was greed; with Peter it was fear. And so, in reading this story, let us not criticize others, but instead, let us ask, "Is it I, Lord?" True, we cannot literally repeat the crime of Judas, but how many of us betray Him by sitting in the seat of the scornful, repressing our convictions and staying quiet when others scoff and blacken the name of Christ or His Church lest we lose a job or a sale or an acquaintance? How many in the camp of Christ are two-faced—while the weather is fair, we walk with Him, but when the sky grows dark, we run away; when we get into a crowd of unbelievers, we act as they do or at least keep a low profile so as to not draw attention to ourselves? Sometimes we would rather stay by the false fires of the world than be out in the night with Christ. "Is it I, Lord?"

If we are honest, we all must confess, "Lord, it is I!" Then what shall we do? Look to Him on the cross, who looks at us with love and forgiving grace. Even Judas was not lost because he betrayed Jesus, he was lost because he would not accept His love; to the end, the Lord tried to save him. The difference between Judas, who betrayed, and Peter, who denied, was that the one thought only of his wicked deed and went out and hanged himself while the other thought of his loving Savior and went out and wept bitterly. Let us take all our sins, even black betrayal, to Him because "the blood of Jesus His Son cleanses us from all sin" (1 John 1:7).

Prayer

I lay my sins on Jesus,
The spotless Lamb of God;
He bears them all and frees us
From the accursed load.
I bring my guilt to Jesus
To wash my crimson stains
Clean in His blood most precious
Till not a spot remains. Amen. (LSB 606:1)

"DESPISED AND REJECTED BY MEN"
Luke 22:63–71

WHEN Judas left the circle of the apostles assembled for the Passover, it was nighttime. That describes the whole trial of Jesus: it was night. At night, the things that shun the light sneak about, schemes and plots are hatched and carried out; people do things under the cover of night that they would not do during the light of day. By night, Judas made his shameful bargain with the Jewish leaders; by night, he led that armed mob to the garden to arrest Jesus. Had he tried it in daytime, more swords than Peter's might have been drawn to defend Him. By night, Jesus was led to the house of Caiaphas, the high priest. There, a preliminary meeting was held in the apartments of Annas, the former high priest and father-in-law of Caiaphas (John 18:13). Members of the Council who were present agreed on what accusation should be levied against Jesus. Because this night meeting was illegal, the Council met again as soon as the day dawned, perhaps in the same building but in the rooms of Caiaphas. It is this trial that St. Luke now tells us.

Jesus Is Mocked

Now the men who were holding Jesus in custody were mocking Him as they beat Him. They also blindfolded Him and kept asking Him, "Prophesy! Who is it that struck You?" And they said many other things against Him, blaspheming Him.

Jesus Before the Council

When day came, the assembly of the elders of the people gathered together, both chief priests and scribes. And they led Him away to their Council, and they said, "If You are the Christ, tell us." But He said to them, "If I tell you, you will not believe, and if I ask you, you will not answer. But from now on the Son of Man shall be seated at the right hand of the power of God." So they all said, "Are You the Son of God, then?" And He said to them, "You say that I am." Then they said, "What further testimony do we need? We have heard it ourselves from His own lips."

Luke's record of this trial is very brief; more detail is given in the other Gospels. But Luke emphasizes the fact that Jesus, in plain, unmistakable words, claimed to be the Son of God. For that confession, the Council sentenced Him to death. Jesus Himself pointed out that the whole procedure of the Council was unjust. They asked Him to confess and on that confession alone, not on any proof of crimes committed, He was condemned. Even before that, in the preliminary hearing and while they waited for dawn and the rest of the Council to be called into session, the Roman soldiers and servants mistreated and mocked Jesus. Not one member of the Council, which was responsible for the administration of justice among the Jews, protested against this totally unjust procedure.

More than that, when the Council was assembled for official action, they asked Jesus, "If You are the Christ, tell us." That was a legitimate question, and the Council of the Jewish church had a right to ask it. But Jesus pointed out that they were not honest in asking it. He said, "If I tell you, you will not believe, and if I ask you, you will not answer." They had already resolved not to believe anything He said. His whole case was prejudged because they had made up their minds to reject His claim and condemn Him no matter what He said or did. Yet, lest they have the least excuse, He again stated under oath that He is indeed the Son of God. Moreover, after they have put Him to death, they will see Him when He returns in all His divine glory.

They sentenced Him to death, but not because He did anything against human or divine law. All the false witnesses they procured could fix no crime on Him, no two of them could agree to tell the same lie—surely remarkable evidence of His innocence. But they sentenced Him for blasphemy because He claimed to be the Messiah, the Savior of the world, whom they had been expecting for thousands of years.

When that godless band of Korah rebelled against Moses, the earth opened her mouth and devoured them, 250 men (Numbers 16). When King Ahaziah sent his soldiers to take Elijah captive, the Lord twice sent fire from heaven to consume them (2 Kings 1). Here, the Son of God is mocked and spat upon and condemned to death in the greatest mockery of a trial in world history.

Yet it was a perfectly just trial. An invisible court was sitting on the case of Jesus of Nazareth. One higher than Annas and Caiaphas was judge. The Gospel of John tells how Caiaphas proposed this vile plan to the Council: "It is better for you that one man should die for the people, not that the whole nation should perish." But Caiaphas was high priest and so he "prophesied that Jesus would die for the nation, and not for the nation only, but also to gather into one the children of God who are scattered abroad" (John 11:49–53). Yes, there is a higher tribunal than the Council and before that court we are all arraigned. Many witnesses appear against us, but they are not false witnesses. There is the Law of God, which we have not kept. There is Satan, who watches our life more closely than the Jews ever watched Jesus. There are all our sins and transgressions. And divine justice says, "The soul who sins shall die" (Ezekiel 18:20). But One arises in that court and says, "It was expedient, eternally expedient that One Man should die for the people. I am that Man. I am the Lamb of God that takes away the sin of the world. I have borne their griefs and carried their sorrows. I was convicted for their sins, and I died for their atonement. I am He that justifies." And that is our salvation. Let us make that our trust and our consolation in life and in death.

Prayer

Thou, ah! Thou, hast taken on Thee
Bonds and stripes, a cruel rod;
Pain and scorn were heaped upon Thee,
O Thou sinless Son of God!
Thus didst Thou my soul deliver
From the bonds of sin forever.

Thou hast borne the smiting only
That my wounds might all be whole;
Thou hast suffered, sad and lonely,
Rest to give my weary soul;
Yea, the curse of God enduring,
Blessing unto me securing.

Thou hast suffered men to bruise Thee,
That from pain I might be free;
Falsely did Thy foes accuse Thee:
Thence I gain security;
Comfortless Thy soul did languish
Me to comfort in my anguish.
Thousand, thousand thanks shall be,
Dearest Jesus, unto Thee. Amen. (LSB 420:2–3, 5)

"THE RULERS TAKE COUNSEL TOGETHER"

Luke 23:1–12

WHEN Pilate told the Jews, "Take Him yourselves and judge Him by your own law," they answered, "It is not lawful for us to put anyone to death" (John 18:31). Die He must, they were agreed on that, but they didn't have the legal authority to execute the death sentence; only the Roman governor could do that. Therefore, after they had condemned Jesus to death, they were forced to take Him to Pilate to have the sentence confirmed and executed. Then, by the offhand remark of the accusers, Herod was brought into the case. So we have here the Council, the supreme council of the Jews; Pilate, the governor of Judea; and Herod, tetrarch of Galilee, all deliberating what to do with Jesus. It reminds us of that prophecy in Psalm 2:2: "The kings of the earth set themselves, and the rulers take counsel together, against the Lord and against His Anointed."

Jesus Before Pilate

Then the whole company of them arose and brought Him before Pilate. And they began to accuse Him, saying, "We found this man misleading our nation and forbidding us to give tribute to Caesar, and saying that He Himself is Christ, a king." And Pilate asked Him, "Are You the King of the Jews?" And He answered him, "You have said so." Then Pilate said to the chief priests and the crowds, "I find no guilt in this man." But they were urgent, saying, "He stirs up the people, teaching throughout all Judea, from Galilee even to this place."

Jesus Before Herod

When Pilate heard this, he asked whether the man was a Galilean. And when he learned that He belonged to Herod's jurisdiction, he sent Him over to Herod, who was himself in Jerusalem at that time. When Herod saw Jesus, he was very glad, for he had long desired to see Him, because he had heard about Him, and he was hoping to see some sign done by Him. So he questioned Him at some length, but He made no answer. The chief priests and the scribes stood by, vehemently accusing Him. And Herod with his soldiers treated Him with contempt and mocked Him. Then, arraying Him in splendid clothing, he sent Him back to Pilate. And Herod and Pilate became friends with each other that very day, for before this they had been at enmity with each other.

The Jews did not bring Jesus to Pilate because they respected him or the power he represented or because they sought advice. It was a case of necessity. Yet the hand of God is evident in this too. Why did the enemies of Jesus not simply assassinate Him? God did not permit it because His innocence was to be established by the highest court in the land. It was not for His own transgressions that Christ died. Jesus had foretold that He would be delivered to the Gentiles and that He would be crucified, which was the Roman method of execution.

Again, Luke's account is very brief. The Jewish Council knew Pilate would never accept the accusation on which they had condemned Jesus; blasphemy against the Jewish God was not a capital crime under Roman law. So they twisted their accusation to give it a political side: Jesus said He was King of the Jews; in that rebellion, He had incited the people to sedition against Rome. But Pilate, as John tells us, spoke to Jesus and was soon convinced that Jesus was innocent of that crime. He said so.

The casual remark that Jesus came from Galilee suggested an easy way for Pilate to get rid of the case, which was threatening to become troublesome. Pilate sent them to Herod. But Herod's interest in Jesus was based only on curiosity; he hoped to see a miracle and therefore experience a new thrill. But when Jesus refused to satisfy Herod's curiosity, He was sent back to Pilate. This also indicates, however, that Herod found no guilt in Him.

All three—the Jews, Pilate, and Herod—were in the very presence of the Savior. They saw Him, spoke to Him, heard the truth from His own lips. Yet all this only served to increase their disbelief and, therefore, their guilt and condemnation. Isn't that same trial reenacted continually in the world today? Wherever the Gospel is preached or read, men are confronted with the question that Pilate asked the Jews: what should I do with Jesus? And sooner or later every person must answer it.

How does the world answer today? Many still cry, "Crucify Him!" This is usually put in less offensive language; it is expressed in beautiful poetry or in erudite philosophy, but the meaning is still the same: rejection. The crowd of people is indifferent. Like Pilate and Herod, they may be curious but they do not recognize their personal stake in this man, and so they pass Him by and follow false prophets who lead them astray.

Jesus' entire trial was a travesty of justice. The Jews brought Him to Pilate not because they wanted justice done or because they respected him and his advice but because they had already condemned Jesus and wanted to use every means to confirm their sentence. Pilate repeatedly declared Him innocent but finally sentenced Him to death. A travesty, indeed! But God, too, had a voice in this trial, so it is not so much of a travesty after all. Before God's tribunal, Jesus was guilty of all the sins the Jews listed and of many more that they had never heard of because God had imputed all men's sins to Him. He bore all the sin of the world, all our sin. What, then, shall be our answer to Pilate's question? God grant that it be the answer of faith.

Prayer

Jesus, Savior, come to me;
Let me ever be with Thee.
Come and nevermore depart,
Thou who reignest in my heart.

Thou alone, my God and Lord,
Art my Glory and Reward.

Thou hast bled for me and died;
In Thy wounds I safely hide.

Come, then, Lamb for sinners slain,
Come and ease me of my pain.
Evermore I cry to Thee:
Jesus, Jesus, come to me! Amen.
(TLH 356:1, 5–6)

"SUFFERED UNDER PONTIUS PILATE"

Luke 23:13–25

PILATE tried every way possible, except the right way, to get Jesus off his hands. First, he turned to the Jews and said, "Judge Him by your own law" (John 18:31). But they said, "We cannot do that. By our law He should die, but we do not have the power to put Him to death." Then Pilate tried to shift the responsibility to Herod, but Herod would not take it and sent Jesus back. So Pilate had to deal with Jesus after all.

He made several more attempts to escape the decision we read about in today's text. But Pilate was not only an unjust judge who used the law for his own purposes, he was also the type of person who, when brought face-to-face with Jesus, tried to be noncommittal.

> Pilate then called together the chief priests and the rulers and the people, and said to them, "You brought me this man as one who was misleading the people. And after examining Him before you, behold, I did not find this man guilty of any of your charges against Him. Neither did Herod, for he sent Him back to us. Look, nothing deserving death has been done by Him. I will therefore punish and release Him."

Pilate Delivers Jesus to Be Crucified

But they all cried out together, "Away with this man, and release to us Barabbas"— a man who had been thrown into prison for an insurrection started in the city and for murder. Pilate addressed them once more, desiring to release Jesus, but they kept shouting, "Crucify, crucify Him!" A third time he said to them, "Why, what evil has He done? I have found in Him no guilt deserving death. I will therefore punish and release Him." But they were urgent, demanding with loud cries that He should be crucified. And their voices prevailed. So Pilate decided that their demand should be granted. He released the man who had been thrown into prison for insurrection and murder, for whom they asked, but he delivered Jesus over to their will.

Pilate summarized the result of his investigation to the Jews: Jesus was innocent. A just judge would have released Him. But Pilate didn't have the courage to deny the Jews their insistent demands so he offered to compromise, to satisfy their hatred by scourging Jesus. Again an attempt—and what a cruel attempt!—of side-stepping the decision. And although the Jews voiced their disapproval in no uncertain terms, Pilate tried it, as John tells us (ch. 19). He had Jesus scourged. The soldiers set a crown of thorns on His head, beat Him, and mistreated Him in many ways. Then Pilate had Jesus brought before the crowd; perhaps the Jews would be moved with pity when they saw Him. "Behold the man!" Pilate said (John 19:5). But it was in vain. The Jews cried, "Crucify Him!"

Then Pilate thought of another way out. It was an old custom at the Passover for the governor to pardon one prisoner at the wish of the people. Pilate picked the meanest criminal then in prison and set him beside Jesus and gave the crowd the choice. But again the effort failed. Pilate could no longer avoid the decision. He had to decide for or against Jesus. This decision he had in part already made when he began to compromise with his conscience. He offered to do what he considered a little injustice, to scourge Jesus, in order to prevent a great injustice, His crucifixion. He gave the devil his little finger, and Satan rapidly took his hand, his arm, and then the whole man.

No one who comes face-to-face with Christ can take a neutral or compromising position. He that is not with Him is against Him. Nor can any person safely make others the keepers of his conscience and follow the majority. That is the easy way, but it is frequently the wrong way. In religion, because of man's inborn depravity, it is always the wrong way; the majority is always against Christ. Only in heaven will we be able to stand with the majority; there the vote will be unanimous.

Jesus "suffered under Pontius Pilate." The other evangelists tell of the indignities that were inflicted upon the spotless Son of God before and after He was sentenced to death by His judge. But the crowning insult was that the people whom God had chosen as His own preferred Barabbas to the Messiah, who had been so long expected and sent by God. The story of this mob seems almost unbelievable; did none of them remember the miracles of Jesus? It shows what sin can do to the human heart; it drags men down to the most gruesome depths. Everyone today who rejects Christ commits the same sin and even worse because then, at the time of Jesus' trial and crucifixion, His work of redemption was not yet fulfilled and recorded. But today the person who reads the story has both prophecy and fulfillment; his is the greater sin if he rejects it because he knows the full story.

There is deeper meaning still in this dark picture. Good Friday meant disgrace and death for Jesus and life and freedom for Barabbas. And that's exactly what it means for us. We, who are as guilty as Barabbas, are given freedom and life eternal because Jesus Christ, the innocent, was condemned for us.

Prayer

O sacred Head, now wounded,
With grief and shame weighed down,
Now scornfully surrounded
With thorns, Thine only crown.
O sacred Head, what glory,

What bliss, till now was Thine!
Yet, though despised and gory,
I joy to call Thee mine.

What Thou, my Lord, hast suffered
Was all for sinners' gain;
Mine, mine was the transgression,
But Thine the deadly pain.
Lo, here I fall, my Savior!
'Tis I deserve Thy place;
Look on me with Thy favor,
And grant to me Thy grace.

What language shall I borrow
To thank Thee, dearest Friend,
For this Thy dying sorrow,
Thy pity without end?
Oh, make me Thine forever!
And should I fainting be,
Lord, let me never, never,
Outlive my love for Thee! Amen. (LSB 449:1–3)

"WAS CRUCIFIED"
Luke 23:26–33

Behold the Savior of mankind
Nailed to the shameful tree!
How vast the love that Him inclined
To bleed and die for thee! (TLH 176:1)

HE is "like a lamb that is led to the slaughter," so Isaiah had prophesied (53:7). He is "the Lamb of God, who takes away the sin of the

world" (John 1:29). In today's reading, we see Him brought to the altar, where He is sacrificed for the world's sin. It is truly remarkable how briefly and calmly the evangelists record the story of the crucifixion. They limit themselves to the mere reporting of the facts. And that is as it should be because these facts speak in a louder tone than any human voice. Let us follow Jesus on the way to the cross as St. Luke relates it.

The Crucifixion

And as they led Him away, they seized one Simon of Cyrene, who was coming in from the country, and laid on him the cross, to carry it behind Jesus. And there followed Him a great multitude of the people and of women who were mourning and lamenting for Him. But turning to them Jesus said, "Daughters of Jerusalem, do not weep for Me, but weep for yourselves and for your children. For behold, the days are coming when they will say, 'Blessed are the barren and the wombs that never bore and the breasts that never nursed!' Then they will begin to say to the mountains, 'Fall on us,' and to the hills, 'Cover us.' For if they do these things when the wood is green, what will happen when it is dry?"

Two others, who were criminals, were led away to be put to death with Him. And when they came to the place that is called The Skull, there they crucified Him, and the criminals, one on His right and one on His left.

Christian writers call it Via Dolorosa, the way of sorrows, this road along which they led Christ to the cross. Isaiah saw Him walking that way, "despised and rejected by men; a man of sorrows, and acquainted with grief" (Isaiah 53:3). But on all this way, "He has borne our griefs and carried our sorrows; yet we esteemed Him stricken, smitten by God, and afflicted. But He was wounded for our transgressions; He was crushed for our iniquities" (Isaiah 53:4–5).

The evangelists relate only two incidents that happened on the way to Calvary, though legend has added many more. The whole trial, from the early morning session of the Council to the execution of the sentence, was crowded into a few hours because Jesus was crucified at about nine o'clock (Mark 15:25). This adds another point to show the injustice of the trial; Roman law required that there be ten days between sentence and execution; Jesus was crucified within an hour after Pilate sentenced Him.

These two incidents are recorded because they carry a lesson for us. According to custom, Jesus had to carry His own cross. And when He, weakened by suffering and loss of blood, broke down under the load, the soldiers forced Simon of Cyrene to carry it for Him. Simon has become the symbol of all crossbearers. Unexpectedly, unwillingly, he had to bear it. So the cross comes to every Christian, and it seems a grievous load; flesh and blood strain against it; but it is the badge of every true Christian. But in God's hand, the cross becomes a blessing. Mark names the sons of Simon, who were evidently well-known Christians. We conclude that Simon had become a true follower of Christ, whom he met for the first time on the Via Dolorosa when he was compelled to bear His cross. It is never easy to bear the cross, but it is God's way of bringing us nearer to Him.

As the procession made its way to Calvary, they were followed by a number of women who had pity on this man who was to die so horrible a death; they wept and mourned. Jesus appreciated their sympathy, but He is the Savior first, He thinks of the individual's welfare first. Therefore, He tells them to think of the judgment that will fall on those who are causing His death. Christ does not want our sympathy now; He wants us to consider with a penitent heart what caused His suffering and death: our sin. We should not weep for Him but for ourselves. Sin must be grieved for, if not in time, then in eternity. That is the lesson for all of us. The tears of repentance are the tears that please the Lord. Only they who have learned to weep over their sins can understand the Passion of the Lord.

And then they came to Calvary and the soldiers carried out the most horrible deed under the sun. They laid the Son of God upon the cross, bound Him to the wood, placed the great nails, and then, stroke upon stroke, drove them through His hands and feet while the blood flowed. They raised the cross, and the Man of Sorrows hung on nails between heaven and earth. With sacred simplicity, Luke tells us this fact: "There they crucified Him." We follow Luke's example and say but little about it, and we stand under the cross in deep humility. Surely in heaven or on earth there is no more expressive language than is spoken here: "I have loved you with an everlasting love" (Jeremiah 31:3). And blessed are they who understand.

Prayer
See, from His head, His hands, His feet
Sorrow and love flow mingled down!
Did e'er such love and sorrow meet
Or thorns compose so rich a crown?
Were the whole realm of nature mine,
That were a tribute far too small;
Love so amazing, so divine,
Demands my soul, any life, my all. Amen.
(LSB 425:3–4)

"DIED"
Luke 23:34–46

IN our meditation today, we stand on Calvary's hill on Good Friday—the darkest day that ever dawned on the universe; the day marked by God Himself with signs and wonders as the most significant day in world's history. The sun, as though horrified by the spectacle of Calvary, drew a veil over his face, causing a darkness noted in the annals of lands far beyond the confines of Israel. The earth trembled in mourning. Rocks were fractured and graves were opened. And the people who had been so brave when that lone man was nailed to the cross, now, crushed by a nameless dread, pale, and fear-ridden, through dark ways and back alleys, slunk home into

hiding. The day the blackest deed the world ever saw was done—
men had killed their God and Creator.

And yet it was the brightest day in the world's history! God gave
another great sign on this day: the veil in the temple, which separated the Most Holy, God's own throne on earth, from the rest of the
temple, was torn open to the view of all the place, which before no
one was permitted to see except the high priest on the great Day of
Atonement. That is the meaning of Christ's death: the way to God
is again opened to all sinners. Good Friday is the day of our redemption. Let us hear St. Luke's record of Christ's death.

> And Jesus said, "Father, forgive them, for they know not
> what they do." And they cast lots to divide His garments. And
> the people stood by, watching, but the rulers scoffed at Him,
> saying, "He saved others; let Him save Himself, if He is the
> Christ of God, His Chosen One!" The soldiers also mocked
> Him, coming up and offering Him sour wine and saying, "If
> You are the King of the Jews, save Yourself!" There was also an
> inscription over Him, "This is the King of the Jews."
>
> One of the criminals who were hanged railed at Him, saying,
> "Are You not the Christ? Save Yourself and us!" But the other
> rebuked him, saying, "Do you not fear God, since you are under
> the same sentence of condemnation? And we indeed justly, for
> we are receiving the due reward of our deeds; but this man has
> done nothing wrong." And he said, "Jesus, remember me when
> You come into Your kingdom." And He said to him, "Truly, I say
> to you, today you will be with Me in Paradise."

The Death of Jesus

> It was now about the sixth hour, and there was darkness over
> the whole land until the ninth hour, while the sun's light failed.
> And the curtain of the temple was torn in two. Then Jesus,
> calling out with a loud voice, said, "Father, into Your hands I
> commit My spirit!" And having said this He breathed His last.

There are three parts to this text, and Luke connects each one with
a word of the dying Savior. His first word is a prayer; He prays for
those who crucified Him and for those who brought Him to the

cross. They did it out of ignorance; they did not know the Lord of Glory in His guise of a lowly servant. So the Lord prays for them in love and patience. His prayer includes us, for we with our sins caused His death and crucifixion. That is our comfort, that in His dying hour Jesus pleaded for forgiveness for all sins of all sinners, the forgiveness He procured in that very hour.

The people around the cross did not heed this prayer, just as the world today goes by the cross unheeding. The soldiers divided His clothing among them. The Jewish leaders continued their scoffing, blasphemously referring to His miracles and His inability to work a miracle on His own behalf, thereby uttering a great truth—He did not save Himself not because He lacked the power but because the work He had come to do required His death. The soldiers sneered and pointed to the sign Pilate had put on the cross and had refused to change at the demand of the Jews. Neither Pilate nor the Jews knew that in this, too, the governor was prompted by a higher power: that inscription was right, He was the King of the Jews, the promised Messiah.

In all that multitude, there was one who saw more in this than a helpless criminal dying. The patient suffering of Christ, His prayer for His enemies, had deeply impressed the thief who hung on His right. No doubt the sign on the cross reminded him of what he knew about the great King and Savior who was to come. And the Holy Spirit opened his eyes to see both this sufferer and himself in the true light. Against the jeers of the other thief, he confessed his own sin and his faith in the man who was crucified between them. And Jesus extended to him the same grace He offers to all sinners. In Him the doors of paradise are opened for all sinners. Only those who refuse His grace and deprive themselves of the great heritage He has won for them are excluded.

Finally, the text records the last word and the last act of the Redeemer. His last word is a prayer, and it is, as it were, the seal on all His work. "Father, into Your hands I commit My spirit," meaning that Jesus had finished the work the heavenly Father sent Him to do and it was now time to return to Him. And with that prayer, which was at the same time a cry of victory, "He breathed His last." That was the final act of His human life. Voluntarily, of His own accord, He gave up His life. That was the requirement of divine justice; that was the punishment for the world's sin; so the Savior paid the debt.

Calvary shows us the desperate vileness of sin. Even here on earth, the consequences of sin are terrible; it fills our institutions and builds our hospitals and jails and abuses God's beautiful earth. The crucified Son of God on Calvary shows us just how desperately vile sin is. But above all, Calvary speaks of love, a love that passes all understanding. Christ loved us and gave Himself for us. Let us love Him because He first loved us!

Prayer

If my sins give me alarm
And my conscience grieve me,
Let Your cross my fear disarm;
Peace of conscience give me.
Help me see forgiveness won
By Your holy passion.
If for me He slays His Son,
God must have compassion!

Graciously my faith renew;
Help me bear my crosses,
Learning humbleness from You,
Peace mid pain and losses.
May I give You love for love!
Hear me, O my Savior,
That I may in heav'n above
Sing Your praise forever. Amen.
(LSB 440:5–6)

"AND WAS BURIED"

Luke 23:47–56

O darkest woe! Ye tears, forth flow!
> Has earth so sad a wonder?

God the Father's only Son
> Now is buried yonder.

O blest shall be Eternally
> Who oft in faith will ponder

Why the glorious Prince of Life
> Should be buried yonder. (TLH 167:1, 6)

THE Lord was crucified at about nine o'clock in the morning. Six hours of suffering followed, reaching its climax during three hours of darkness, from noon to three o'clock. This physical darkness over all the earth was an emblem of the darkness in the soul of Christ when He plumbed the utmost depth of temporal and eternal tragedy and was forsaken by God—the torture of the damned in hell. At three o'clock, Jesus said, "It is finished!" He commended His soul to His divine Father and died. Today we read what was done to His body after His death. The Romans, in characteristic cruelty, were not concerned about the fate of the remains of crucified men; they were left to the birds and the weather. But Jewish law demanded that dead bodies be buried that day (Deuteronomy 21:23). That is why the death of the two thieves was hastened by breaking their bones (John 19:31), and they were no doubt hastily interred on Calvary. But Luke tells us more of the burial of Christ.

> Now when the centurion saw what had taken place, he praised God, saying, "Certainly this man was innocent!" And all the crowds that had assembled for this spectacle, when they saw what had taken place, returned home beating their breasts. And all His acquaintances and the women who had followed Him from Galilee stood at a distance watching these things.

Jesus Is Buried

Now there was a man named Joseph, from the Jewish town of Arimathea. He was a member of the council, a good and righteous man, who had not consented to their decision and action; and he was looking for the kingdom of God. This man went to Pilate and asked for the body of Jesus. Then he took it down and wrapped it in a linen shroud and laid Him in a tomb cut in stone, where no one had ever yet been laid. It was the day of Preparation, and the Sabbath was beginning. The women who had come with Him from Galilee followed and saw the tomb and how His body was laid. Then they returned and prepared spices and ointments.

Even in death, Jesus found disciples among both Jews and Gentiles. This centurion was in charge of the crucifixion. What he heard and saw of Christ impressed him deeply, and when he saw the supernatural signs that accompanied the death of Jesus, he came to the conclusion expressed in his confession, "Certainly this man was innocent" (Luke 23:47) and "Truly this man was the Son of God!" (Mark 15:39). And surely among the people, who, horror-struck at these signs, now beat their breast and went home, there were some who were led to true repentance and faith in Him whose death they had witnessed.

It is a marvelous example of the power of the cross. Just as Jesus finished His work, human souls began to see the meaning of the cross. The march of the cross had begun, and it continues throughout the centuries to the end of time, gathering souls in the most unexpected places: Simon of Cyrene, the thief on the cross, the captain of the guard on Calvary. His is the last voice we hear from Calvary; shouldn't it urge us on to spread the message of the cross to all lands, to all people?

Next we hear how the death of Jesus made courageous confessors of previously secret disciples of Christ. We find it natural that His apostles fled when they saw Jesus arrested. But others came forward when danger threatened most. This story, too, is repeated again and again in church history. The Gospel of the Crucified, firmly accepted in faith, makes heroes of cowards. It is the power of God in His Word that gives strength to the weak, while the man who is strong in his own imagination fails and flees.

Finally, we are told how the body of Jesus was laid in Joseph's new grave because it was close by and there wasn't much time. The Sabbath began at six o'clock. The faithful women watched carefully how and where Jesus was laid because they had already planned that when the Sabbath was over they would complete the work of love so hastily begun this day. So they prepared spices and ointments— which they never used!

A grave is a place of tears and mourning. No doubt those who loved Jesus wept at His grave. But the time soon came when they regarded this grave with altogether different feelings. And to us today, to all Christians, the grave of Christ is not the sign of ultimate defeat but of eternal victory, for three days later the grave was empty; it had been only a temporary resting place for Him. But as He had died for us, so He was buried for us. The grave is the place where we all, old and young, high and low, rich and poor, will find our last earthly bed. But because Christ lay there and rose again, the grave will not be our final abode. The day will come when our graves will be empty and we will share His victory over death. Oh, death is still the king of terrors and our heart still trembles when we remember that we, too, must return to the dust from which we are taken. But in Jesus' name, who hallowed the grave by His presence, by faith in Him who rose from the dead despite sealed grave and armed guard, in the strength that He gives, we can sing and say, "I would not live alway; no, welcome the tomb; Since Jesus hath lain there, I dread not its gloom. There sweet be my rest till He bids me arise To hail Him in triumph descending the skies" (*TLH* 588:3).

Prayer

Almighty God, who by the death of Your Son, Jesus Christ, has destroyed death and by His rest in the tomb has sanctified the graves of Your saints, we pray You, do not let the thought of death and the grave make us afraid or troubled. Instead, graciously keep us in Your Son in true faith and a good conscience to the end that we may lead a Christian life, prepare for a blessed departure, and finally fall asleep and rest in peace and joy until You open our graves and, by the sound of the trumpet, call us forth again into life, through Jesus Christ, our Lord. Amen.

"THE THIRD DAY HE ROSE AGAIN"
Luke 24:1–12

WE will probably never be able fully to comprehend the utter despair of the hours between Good Friday and Easter Sunday for the disciples of Christ. Our faith rests on the knowledge of centuries. We know that the death of Jesus did not end—did not even interrupt—His work but was the direct road to victory and glory. The eyewitnesses did not know that. Yes, they could have known and should have known because Jesus had told them. But the fact is, they did not know. That His life, so full of miracles and other evidences of goodness ended so in crucifixion and the grave was appalling to them. Their thoughts ran along the same lines, although with an altogether different emotion, as those of the scoffers, who said, "He saved others; He cannot save Himself" (Matthew 27:42). And that thought was absolutely mind-numbing. They were utterly hopeless. We can understand, therefore, that their joy was equally great when they learned that Jesus had risen. They knew now in whom they had believed. Their hopes had not deceived them. He was the Son of God, the Christ, their Savior and Redeemer!

Easter means as much to us as it did to the disciples. Without Easter, the worst fears of the disciples would be fact—we would be hopelessly lost. Should not, then, our joy in the Easter message be as great as theirs? That the echoes of that first Easter Day may again resound in our hearts, let us read St. Luke's account of that day.

The Resurrection

But on the first day of the week, at early dawn, they went to the tomb, taking the spices they had prepared. And they found the stone rolled away from the tomb, but when they went in they did not find the body of the Lord Jesus. While they were perplexed about this, behold, two men stood by them in dazzling apparel. And as they were frightened and bowed their faces to the ground, the men said to them, "Why do you seek the living among the dead? He is not here, but has risen. Remember how He told you, while He was still in Galilee, that the Son of Man must be delivered into the hands of sinful men and be crucified and on the third day rise." And they remembered His words, and returning from the tomb they told all these things to the eleven and to all the rest. Now it was Mary Magdalene and Joanna and Mary the mother of James and the other women with them who told these things to the apostles, but these words seemed to them an idle tale, and they did not believe them. But Peter rose and ran to the tomb; stooping and looking in, he saw the linen cloths by themselves; and he went home marveling at what had happened.

Can you think of anything more sad than these women going out in the gray dawn of Sunday morning to finish the task they had begun so hastily on Friday afternoon when the Sabbath was beginning and the grave had to be closed? Saturday evening, after the end of the Sabbath, they prepared their ointments, and at daybreak, they went to the tomb to perform their work of love. But all their ointments were not needed; the grave was empty! As soon as she saw the open tomb, Mary Magdalene ran back to tell the apostles, "They have taken the Lord out of the tomb, and we do not know where they have laid Him!" (John 20:2). The Lord had made provision that they should immediately have the truth. Two angels gave them the Easter message: "Why do you seek the living among the dead? He is not here, but has risen." They add a little rebuke that they should pass on to the other apostles: You should have known! He told you He would rise!

Luke's account is very brief, merely emphasizing the facts: the empty tomb, the message of the angels (He is risen), and the admonition (Why did you not believe? If you had, you would have avoided most of the misery you have suffered!) And there Luke puts the finger on the most important point for us: whether the death and resurrection of Christ means anything to us depends on whether we believe. First of all, whether we believe the facts. That is why Luke adds that the apostles did not believe the report of the women. Even when Peter saw the empty grave himself, even when the Lord appeared to them, they were slow to believe. They were not credulous fools, ready to believe every idle tale. They were hard to convince, but in the end they were so thoroughly convinced that they suffered and died for their testimony of the crucified and risen Lord. They were the best witnesses, and no man has the slightest reason for unbelief.

But do these facts have any meaning for us? What is it to us that Christ died and rose again? Paul tells us Christ "was delivered up for our trespasses and raised for our justification" (Romans 4:25). The Lord had laid on Jesus Christ the iniquity of us all. He atoned for it and paid our debt to eternal justice. Did He succeed? Here is the answer: the grave is empty; He is risen! He was crucified, buried, and descended into hell laden with our guilt. Then God called Him forth again in a public testimony that He had paid the wages of sin, of our sin. It is true what He said in the moment of His death: "It is finished!"

That is the heart of the Easter Gospel. And the soul that truly holds this message cannot but be filled with Easter faith and joy because it means to us not only that Christ escaped death and the grave, but that His resurrection is the escape from death for us as well. Even when all the things we see around us are gone, we will still have the Easter Gospel. "Because I live, you also will live" (John 14:19). And we, too, will rise on the third day: the first day is our day of preparation, when we suffer and die with Christ; the second is the Sabbath, when we rest in the grave; and the third day is when we rise again to eternal life.

Prayer

Merciful God, heavenly Father, we give You most hearty thanks that You raised Your Son from the dead and from His tomb caused the light of eternal life to shine upon the world. We ask that You fill our hearts with Your Holy Spirit so that we may with joyous faith embrace the atonement made for our sins, be enabled to put away more and more the leaven of malice and wickedness, and serve You in pureness of living and holiness of heart in the fervent hope of life and glory everlasting, through Jesus Christ, Your Son, our Lord. Amen.

GOING TO EMMAUS
Luke 24:13–35

IN the Book of Acts, the first chapter of the second letter to his friend Theophilus, Luke reviews what he had written in this last chapter of his Gospel. He says that Jesus "presented Himself alive to them after His suffering by many proofs, appearing to them during forty days and speaking about the kingdom of God" (Acts 1:3). We are told of eleven such appearances of Jesus after His resurrection. But He never stayed with them for any length of time. As soon as He convinced them that it was He and that He was alive, He disappeared again. His purpose in appearing to them was to convince them of His resurrection, and they had to learn that the relationship between them had changed. From this time forward, they were to know Him not by sight but by faith because His kingdom is not of this world; it is a spiritual kingdom in which men live not by sight, but by faith. Luke is coming to the end of his Gospel, and he relates only two of these appearances in detail; one we read about today.

On the Road to Emmaus

That very day two of them were going to a village named Emmaus, about seven miles from Jerusalem, and they were talking with each other about all these things that had happened. While they were talking and discussing together, Jesus Himself drew near and went with them. But their eyes were kept from recognizing Him. And He said to them, "What is this conversation that you are holding with each other as you walk?" And they stood still, looking sad. Then one of them, named Cleopas, answered Him, "Are you the only visitor to Jerusalem who does not know the things that have happened there in these days?" And He said to them, "What things?" And they said to Him, "Concerning Jesus of Nazareth, a man who was a prophet mighty in deed and word before God and all the people, and how our chief priests and rulers delivered Him up to be condemned to death, and crucified Him. But we had hoped that He was the one to redeem Israel. Yes, and besides all this, it is now the third day since these things happened. Moreover, some women of our company amazed us. They were at the tomb early in the morning, and when they did not find His body, they came back saying that they had even seen a vision of angels, who said that He was alive. Some of those who were with us went to the tomb and found it just as the women had said, but Him they did not see." And He said to them, "O foolish ones, and slow of heart to believe all that the prophets have spoken! Was it not necessary that the Christ should suffer these things and enter into His glory?" And beginning with Moses and all the Prophets, He interpreted to them in all the Scriptures the things concerning Himself.

So they drew near to the village to which they were going. He acted as if He were going farther, but they urged Him strongly, saying, "Stay with us, for it is toward evening and the day is now far spent." So He went in to stay with them. When He was at table with them, He took the bread and blessed and broke it and gave it to them. And their eyes were opened, and they recognized Him. And He vanished from their sight. They said to each other, "Did not our hearts burn within us while He talked to us on the road, while He opened to us the Scriptures?" And they rose that same hour and returned to Jerusalem. And they found the eleven and those who were with them gathered together, saying, "The Lord has risen indeed, and has appeared to Simon!" Then they told what had happened on the road, and how He was known to them in the breaking of the bread.

We could draw a great many lessons from this story, but the main point of the text is Jesus' opening the Scriptures to the two men. That is the turning point. As these men begin to understand Scripture, and more especially the life and work of Christ in the light of Scripture, their sadness departs and they return to Jerusalem rejoicing. The deepest cause of their sadness had not been the mere fact of Jesus' death—not even His death by crucifixion. What was crushing their hearts is expressed in their words, "We had hoped that He was the one to redeem Israel." "We had hoped," they said, with so pathetic a use of the past tense. We hope no more, they say. Dead lay their Master in the grave, and buried with Him were all their hopes that He was the promised Messiah. That ended their dream. He was only another impostor like Theudas and Judas of Galilee before Him (Acts 5:36–37). But Jesus pointed them to the revealed Word of God, where there is a full and clear account of the Messiah's suffering and His victory. Had they only believed, they would have been spared much misery and avoided that false conception of the Messiah's work. They would have realized that this work was infinitely greater than they had believed—not to deliver a small nation from Caesar's rule and taxes but to deliver all nations from Satan's dominion. Then they would have believed Christ's own word that He would rise again, and what they saw on Good Friday could not have brought them such despair. And on Easter morning they would not have gone to the tomb to anoint a dead body but to meet a living Christ.

What a lesson for us! As we walk along the path of life, how much grief we would spare ourselves—how many disappointments, fears of the future, doubts of God's love and the Savior's constant care—if we only had a better knowledge of and a firmer trust in the Word of our God; if we would only and always remember that in His Word, He comes to us and abides with us! How blessed the assurance that there is no time in our life when the risen Lord is not with us—in war and in peace, at work and at rest, in health and in sickness, in life and in death. And when He is with us, all is well. That is the blessing of Easter that we share with these two disciples.

Prayer

Abide with us, Lord Jesus, for it is toward evening, and the day is far spent. Abide in our home and in our heart. Open our eyes to see You, our minds to know You, our hearts to give heed to You and to Your Word. Be our companion on the way of life, and teach us in the perils of the day and in the darkness of the night to trust in Your loving care. Above all, when the evening of our life turns into night, abide with us in that last trial, and keep us safe until we see You face-to-face in our Father's house. Amen.

THE CHURCH'S ONE FOUNDATION
Luke 24:36–49

WHEN we read the resurrection story in the four Gospels, the first chapter of the Acts, and St. Paul's testimony in 1 Corinthians 15:5–8, we cannot fail to note that Jesus went to a great deal of trouble to convince His apostles that He was truly risen. He must have deemed this fact of the utmost importance, and we should see it that way too. Everything in Scripture is divine truth, of course, yet not everything in the Bible is of equal importance. For instance, it is certainly more important to know what the Bible tells us of Jesus Christ than what it tells us of Doeg. And there are certain high points in the life of Christ that are of preeminent importance, so much so that we devote a large part of the church year to their consideration. Such are the birth and the death of Jesus, and such is, above all, His resurrection. No one who is ignorant of the resurrection or who denies it has a true understanding of the life and work of Christ. We may, therefore, say that the foundation on which the Church of Christ, the communion of believers, rests is the resurrection of Christ. The words of Jesus in today's text indicate this.

Jesus Appears to His Disciples

As they were talking about these things, Jesus Himself stood among them, and said to them, "Peace to you!" But they were startled and frightened and thought they saw a spirit. And He said to them, "Why are you troubled, and why do doubts arise in your hearts? See My hands and My feet, that it is I Myself. Touch Me, and see. For a spirit does not have flesh and bones as you see that I have." And when He had said this, He showed them His hands and His feet. And while they still disbelieved for joy and were marveling, He said to them, "Have you anything here to eat?" They gave Him a piece of broiled fish, and He took it and ate before them.

Then He said to them, "These are My words that I spoke to you while I was still with you, that everything written about Me in the Law of Moses and the Prophets and the Psalms must be fulfilled." Then He opened their minds to understand the Scriptures, and said to them, "Thus it is written, that the Christ should suffer and on the third day rise from the dead, and that repentance and forgiveness of sins should be proclaimed in His name to all nations, beginning from Jerusalem. You are witnesses of these things. And behold, I am sending the promise of My Father upon you. But stay in the city until you are clothed with power from on high."

Jesus met His disciples with the common greeting of the time, "Peace to you!" But that greeting meant much more on His lips than a fleeting "Good morning!" or "How do you do?" He said to them, "Peace I leave with you; My peace I give to you" (John 14:27). His peace, the peace He earned—peace with God because He removed the cause of enmity between us and God, sin; peace of conscience that can no longer accuse us because God has forgiven our sin; peace because we are reconciled to Him and are His dear children. That is the peace He gave to His disciples; that is the peace He offers to us—our salvation.

And then Jesus showed them His hands and His feet with the marks of the nails. He asked them for something to eat to convince them that He was their Master, who had been dead but now was alive. And He again opened the Scriptures to them. According to prophecy, this was the way the Messiah was to perform His work—after suffering, He was to rise again. And here He stood before them as living proof that His work was accomplished. His resurrection is the guarantee that the peace He offers is not a fantasy but a divinely attested fact.

To preach this peace between God and mankind, Jesus now sends His disciples out into the world to tell others what they witnessed and to call on them in repentance and faith to accept the fruits of His redemption. They were to establish His Church on earth, the communion of saints who have come to know their own sin and know Him as the Savior from that sin and from death.

It all rests on His resurrection. St. Paul sums it all up when he says, "And if Christ has not been raised, your faith is futile and you are still in your sins" (1 Corinthians 15:17). "And if Christ has not been raised, then our preaching is in vain and your faith is in vain" (1 Corinthians 15:14). No resurrection—no Savior and no salvation. No resurrection—His work ended at the grave, and all the help He could give us would end at the grave. No resurrection—no Gospel; in fact, no revelation of God; the Bible is only a collection of fables. No resurrection—no Church, only a society of deluded fools.

But Paul concludes jubilantly, Jesus Christ is risen from the dead. He is the Savior who can save to the utmost. He has gone beyond the veil to prepare a place for us. And He said, "Because I live, you also will live" (John 14:19). He established His kingdom here on earth, and by His Gospel He draws us into that Church until faith comes to fruition and we inherit our place in His eternal kingdom of glory. Yes, "thanks be to God, who gives us the victory through our Lord Jesus Christ" (1 Corinthians 15:57).

Prayer
Mighty Victor, reign forever,
Wear the crown so dearly won;
Never shall Thy people, never,
Cease to sing what Thou hast done.
Thou hast fought Thy people's foes;
Thou hast healed Thy people's woes. Amen.
(TLH 209:4)

CHRIST'S ASCENSION INTO HEAVEN
Luke 24:50–53

THERE is a parallel between the grave of John the Baptist and the grave of Jesus Christ. Of the former, Matthew says, "And his disciples came and took the body and buried it, and they went and told Jesus" (Matthew 14:12). And that was the end of John's school; his followers separated and met no more. Their master was dead, and there was nothing to hold them together so they disbanded. That other group on Good Friday laid the body of their crucified Master into Joseph's tomb with even greater love but with no more hope. The bond that held them together was gone, and they immediately begin to scatter. Thomas left them. The women came to the grave to perform women's work of anointing the body, but they were left to do this work alone. When Mary Magdalene returned from the grave, she evidently found Peter and John alone, and the two of them ran to the grave. Two of the disciples went home to Emmaus; they saw no point in staying in Jerusalem. In three days, the ties that bound them together were loosening. If Jesus had not risen, nothing could have saved His disciples from the fate of John's disciples. The fact that they again drew together and by their preaching founded the Christian Church is proof positive that Christ was risen. Even when Jesus now finally withdrew to heaven, their work continued. They saw in His ascension the end of His redemptive work, His crowning as Victor, and for them a new era. And so it is. From this perspective, let us consider these last verses of St. Luke's Gospel.

The Ascension

Then He led them out as far as Bethany, and lifting up His hands He blessed them. While He blessed them, He parted from them and was carried up into heaven. And they worshiped Him and returned to Jerusalem with great joy, and were continually in the temple blessing God.

What a difference! Before this, when Jesus spoke of His departure, the disciples were sad (John 16:6). Now He actually was gone from them and they "returned to Jerusalem with great joy, and were continually in the temple blessing God." The reason for this change is that at last their eyes had been opened; they understood and believed what Jesus had told them, "It is to your advantage that I go away" (John 16:7). They saw in Christ's ascension the final and crowning act of His redemptive work, His re-enthronement at the right hand of the Father's majesty.

What if Jesus, after His resurrection, had remained on earth, had lived His allotted time, and had then died like any other man? Then He would not have been the Son of God and His resurrection would have not been fact, but fraud. At any rate, He could not be our Savior; a man who himself falls a victim to death could not save us from death. So with all the other mighty events of Christ's history, there was still something needed to complete it and crown it all.

That finishing touch was His ascension. He returned to heaven. That, too, He foretold: "I came from the Father and have come into the world, and now I am leaving the world and going to the Father" (John 16:28). He came into the world to redeem us; He returned to heaven because His work was done. We were redeemed. The work that was begun on Christmas Day was completed on Ascension Day. It puts the final stamp of certainty on Christ's word, "It is finished!" The disciples realized this and so they "returned to Jerusalem with great joy." And we rejoice with them and all the saints in glory: "Worthy is the Lamb who was slain, to receive power and wealth and wisdom and might and honor and glory and blessing!" (Revelation 5:12).

But the Lord's ascension had its meaning for the future as well. To His disciples, He had said, "Repentance and forgiveness of sins should be proclaimed in His name to all nations, beginning from Jerusalem. You are witnesses of these things" (Luke 24:47–48). He had given them the Great Commission, "Go into all the world and proclaim the gospel to the whole creation" (Mark 16:15). And so, after the promise of the Father had been fulfilled and the Holy Spirit had come upon them, they went out from Jerusalem into all the world.

Someone has called this last chapter of Luke "The Unfinished Chapter." The story of Jesus' life ends here, but His Gospel goes on. Luke himself says that in his Gospel he told of "all that Jesus began to do and teach" (Acts 1:1). He continues in his second treatise, the Acts of the Apostles.

But even that is only the beginning. One generation of disciples after another took up the work and successfully carried out the Great Commission because the ascended and victorious Christ worked through them. So today we rejoice in the conviction that it is His work we are continuing. We do not worry about our success, we leave that to Him, but we are assured of success; because He cannot fail.

At times a wave of melancholy comes over the Christian. Paul says, "My desire is to depart and be with Christ" (Philippians 1:23).

John closes the last book of the Bible with the prayer, "Amen. Come, Lord Jesus!" (Revelation 22:20). But there's still work to do, and so we carry on, sure of His presence with us, rejoicing in the privilege of working for Him, until the evening comes and He Himself calls us home for eternal rest. Amen.

Prayer
King of Glory, reign forever;
Thine an everlasting crown.
Nothing from Thy love shall sever
Those whom Thou hast made Thine own,
Happy objects of Thy grace,
Destined to behold Thy face.

Savior, hasten Thine appearing;
Bring, oh, bring, the glorious day
When, the awe-full summons hearing,
Heaven and earth shall pass away;
Then with golden harps we'll sing,
"Glory, glory, to our King!"Amen.
(TLH 221:5–6)

MEDITATIONS FOR
THE GOSPEL ACCORDING TO
SAINT JOHN

THE DISCIPLE JESUS LOVED
John 21:24

THE writer of the fourth Gospel is St. John the apostle, son of Zebedee and of Salome. Salome was probably a sister of the Virgin Mary, and John, accordingly, a cousin of our Lord. St. John's father, Zebedee, was a master fisherman, a man of some substance, assisted in his business by employees and by his sons James and John. John had probably heard the preaching of John the Baptist before becoming a disciple of Jesus. He is, in all probability, the unnamed disciple to whom, along with Andrew, John the Baptist pointed out Jesus as the Lamb of God, for the very hour of that first meeting is recorded (John 1:39).

John evidently followed Jesus to Galilee after that first meeting and was present at the wedding at Cana (John 2:1–11). It seems, however, that he had not yet been called to permanent fellowship. He returned home and resumed his work as a fisherman, sometimes in partnership with Simon Peter (Luke 5:10). Later, he and his brother James were called to follow Jesus (Matthew 4:21–22) and were appointed apostles (Matthew 10:2).

Among the Twelve, John was one of the three who enjoyed the greatest intimacy with Jesus, being admitted to the raising of Jairus's daughter and to the transfiguration. He was also nearest to our Lord during His agony in Gethsemane. At the Last Supper, he was "reclining at table close to Jesus" (John 13:23). Upon Jesus' arrest, John followed Him to the palace of the high priest, to whom he was known, and he stood near the cross during Jesus' crucifixion. It was to John that Jesus commended His mother, and "from that hour the disciple took her to his own home" (John 19:27). On the morning of Christ's resurrection, John ran with Peter to the empty grave, and on Easter evening, with the other ten, he saw the risen Lord. He also went to Galilee as the Lord had directed, heard His last commandments, and saw Him ascend into heaven.

After Pentecost, we find John active in Jerusalem and in Samaria as Peter's colleague in the first mission work of the Church. He remained in Jerusalem during the first persecution of the Church, and it was in Jerusalem that he met Paul, one of the pillars of the Church, when Paul visited Jerusalem after his first missionary journey.

According to a tradition that goes back to John's own disciples, he spent his latter years in Ephesus, where he probably wrote the Gospel and his three Epistles. The Book of Revelation was written on the nearby island of Patmos, where he had been banished about AD 95 during a persecution of the Christians by the Roman emperor Domitian. Tradition holds that John returned to Ephesus, lived there until after the accession of Emperor Trajan in AD 98, and died there of natural causes.

Jesus called John and his brother James "Boanerges, that is, Sons of Thunder" (Mark 3:17). We can see something of the fiery temper implied by that name in the incident recorded in Luke 9. When a Samaritan village refused to receive Jesus, it was James and John who said, "Lord, do You want us to tell fire to come down from heaven and consume them?" (Luke 9:54). A similar forwardness and vehemence of disposition appear also in their request to Jesus to "sit, one at Your right hand and one at Your left, in Your glory" (Mark 10:37).

In early Christian art, John is usually symbolized by an eagle, indicating the heights to which he rises in proclaiming the glory of our Lord.

Prayer

Blessed Lord, who made the fiery "Son of Thunder" a fit vessel of Your grace and an instrument for the showing of Your glory, grant us Your Spirit, that according to the measure of the gifts You bestow we may likewise wholeheartedly serve You. Amen.

THE FOURTH GOSPEL

John 1:14

"We have seen His glory."

THE Gospel according to St. John is both like and unlike the other three Gospels. John is like them in general outline, that is, it is the same story of Jesus that Matthew, Mark, and Luke told some thirty years earlier: the story of the ministry of Jesus in Galilee and Judea; of His arrest, condemnation, and death; of His resurrection and appearances to His disciples.

But there are striking differences even in the events John records. He omits much that the earlier evangelists had recorded because it would be well known to his readers. Great events including Jesus' Baptism, His temptation, the transfiguration, the institution of the Lord's Supper, and His agony in Gethsemane are known to us only from the other three Gospels. On the other hand, only John adds the conversations of Jesus with Nicodemus and with the Samaritan woman, the raising of Lazarus, Jesus' appearance to Mary Magdalene and to doubting Thomas, the appearance of Jesus to the seven disciples in Galilee, and the reinstatement of Peter.

The differences between St. John and the Synoptics do not end there. St. John's whole treatment is such that his Gospel was early on called "the Spiritual Gospel." Where Matthew portrays Jesus as the promised Messiah; Mark, as the Prophet mighty in deed and word; and Luke, as the Savior of the world, John portrays Him as the eternal Word made flesh. John emphasizes, incomparably, the glory of Christ as of the only-begotten of the Father. Where the other evangelists begin their story chronologically, with the birth, the Baptism, or the public ministry of Jesus, St. John begins in eternity. In his divinely majestic prologue, he sets before us the eternal Word, who was from the beginning, was with God, was God, and became flesh and lived among men as the revelation of God and the creative power of God at work to bring eternal life. The whole of John's Gospel carries out that theme. Jesus is shown particularly through His words and His self-testimony; the miracles John records and treats as "signs" are indications of who and what Jesus is. Thus, the raising of Lazarus serves as the basis of Jesus' testimony of Himself as the giver of eternal life; the miracle is the "sign" that points to the great truth: "I am the resurrection and the life" (John 11:25). Again, the feeding of the five thousand is told much as it is told in the Synoptic Gospels, but it is followed by the great discourse wherein Jesus depicts Himself as the bread of life.

Another striking example of the differences between John and the other Gospels is the record of the last evening Jesus spent with His disciples. John adds a richness and depth to the Passion story not revealed by the other Gospel writers. And all this is written in a style that combines simplicity with majesty, in which, as Luther put it, "every word is a hundredweight."

"In the midst of the congregation shall he open his mouth, and the Lord filled him with the spirit of wisdom and understanding: and clothed him with a robe of glory. *Ps.* It is a good thing to give thanks unto the Lord: and to sing praise unto Thy name, O Thou Most High" (Introit for Saint John the Apostle and the Evangelist's Day; *TLH,* p. 89).

Prayer

Lord Jesus, merciful God, we ask You to cast the bright beams of Your light upon Your Church, that it, being instructed by the doctrines of Your blessed apostle and evangelist St. John, may attain to the light of everlasting life; through Jesus Christ, Your Son, our Lord, who lives and reigns with You and the Holy Spirit, ever one God, world without end. Amen.

Martin H. Franzmann

JESUS, THE SON OF GOD

John 1:1–18

WHO is this man called Jesus? Is it true, as He claimed, that He is the Son of God and Savior of the world?

That was the question people were asking in the city of Ephesus when John was writing his Gospel within their city gates. And that is the question people ask today. Men wanted to know then, even as they want to know now, the great unchanging truths about God, about Christ, about sin, about salvation, and about the life that lies beyond the grave.

If Christ is God and all His words are truth, then all of the riddles that haunt the human soul are solved. Then man has found the answer to his deepest questions, the fulfillment of his highest needs. But, if not, what then?

It was to remove forever the question mark that his contemporaries placed behind the deity of our Savior and to bear witness for all times to His eternal Sonship that John undertook to write this fourth Gospel. "These [things] are written," he tells us, "so that you may believe that Jesus is the Christ, the Son of God, and that by believing you may have life in His name" (John 20:31). That, in one sentence, was John's purpose in writing his Gospel. Let that also be our purpose in reading it: that we may believe that Jesus is the Christ, the Son of God, and that by believing, we may have life in His name.

John introduces his Gospel with a prologue, a preface, of eighteen verses. These verses reach down into the very depths of divine truth, and they do it in language that is so simple, so clear, and so meaningful (most of the words have only one syllable) that all who read it can understand it. God grant us His Holy Spirit as we read these simple words of John's majestic prologue.

The Word Became Flesh

In the beginning was the Word, and the Word was with God, and the Word was God. He was in the beginning with God. All things were made through Him, and without Him was not any thing made that was made. In Him was life, and the life was the light of men. The light shines in the darkness, and the darkness has not overcome it.

There was a man sent from God, whose name was John. He came as a witness, to bear witness about the light, that all might believe through him. He was not the light, but came to bear witness about the light.

The true light, which enlightens everyone, was coming into the world. He was in the world, and the world was made through Him, yet the world did not know Him. He came to His own, and His own people did not receive Him. But to all who did receive Him, who believed in His name, He gave the right to become children of God, who were born, not of blood nor of the will of the flesh nor of the will of man, but of God.

And the Word became flesh and dwelt among us, and we have seen His glory, glory as of the only Son from the Father, full of grace and truth. (John bore witness about Him, and cried out, "This was He of whom I said, 'He who comes after me ranks before me, because He was before me.' ") And from His fullness we have all received, grace upon grace. For the law was given through Moses; grace and truth came through Jesus Christ. No one has ever seen God; the only God, who is at the Father's side, He has made Him known.

Matthew begins his Gospel with Abraham, Mark starts his with the ministry of John the Baptist, and Luke carries us all the way back to Adam. But John takes us behind the veil of time for his beginning. Genesis and John's Gospel have the same opening words, "in the beginning"—"In the beginning, God created the heavens and the earth" and "In the beginning was the Word." John is the only evangelist who speaks of the Savior as "the Word," as the Eternal One through whom the Father speaks and through whom He has made His gracious will known to man. But John is by no means the only Bible penman who speaks of Jesus in the exalted and majestic language of this prologue. The apostle Paul, who had written some thirty years earlier, makes the very same claims for Christ (Colossians 1:11–20).

Jesus is true God, says John. He is eternal: He was "in the beginning." He is omnipotent: "All things were made through Him." He is the only source of all light and life: "In Him was life, and the life was the light of men." Those who do not know Jesus as the true God know neither Jesus nor God. "All may honor the Son, just as they honor the Father. Whoever does not honor the Son does not honor the Father who sent Him" (John 5:23).

"From His fullness we have all received," says John. Christ is the fountainhead of every blessing for the Christian. All that we are, all that we have, we have received of "His fullness." Forgiveness of sins, peace, love, joy, and the blessed assurance of eternal life in heaven through His blood—these, and more, we have received from the limitless treasuries of heaven through the matchless name of Jesus!

Prayer

All hail the pow'r of Jesus' name! Let angels prostrate fall;
Bring forth the royal diadem And crown Him Lord of all.

Hail Him, ye heirs of David's line, Whom David Lord did call,
The God incarnate, man divine, And crown Him Lord of all.

Oh, that with yonder sacred throng We at His feet may fall!
We'll join the everlasting song And crown Him Lord of all.
Amen. (LSB 549:1, 4, 7)

THE GREATEST OF MEN

John 1:19–28

JESUS once said: "Truly, I say to you, among those born of women there has arisen no one greater than John the Baptist. Yet the one who is least in the kingdom of heaven is greater than he" (Matthew 11:11). Alexander the Great added conquest to conquest, until there were no more lands to be conquered; Julius Caesar brought the glory and grandeur that was Rome to its highest pinnacle; Caesar Augustus wielded more power and influence than any man of his day. Yet Jesus says: "Among those born of women there has arisen no one greater than John the Baptist." Why?

We catch a glimpse of the greatness of John the Baptist, both as to his person and as to his purpose, in the following incident, which the evangelist singles out and places near the beginning of his Gospel.

The Testimony of John the Baptist

And this is the testimony of John, when the Jews sent priests and Levites from Jerusalem to ask him, "Who are you?" He confessed, and did not deny, but confessed, "I am not the Christ." And they asked him, "What then? Are you Elijah?" He said, "I am not." "Are you the Prophet?" And he answered, "No." So they said to him, "Who are you? We need to give an answer to those who sent us. What do you say about yourself?" He said, "I am the voice of one crying out in the wilderness, 'Make straight the way of the Lord,' as the prophet Isaiah said."

(Now they had been sent from the Pharisees.) They asked him, "Then why are you baptizing, if you are neither the Christ, nor Elijah, nor the Prophet?" John answered them, "I baptize with water, but among you stands one you do not know, even He who comes after me, the strap of whose sandal

I am not worthy to untie."These things took place in Bethany across the Jordan, where John was baptizing.

There was none greater than John the Baptist because he had been chosen by God for a glorious purpose—to point the Jews of his day (and all people of all time) to the Word that was made flesh and dwelt among them. His credentials, his clear and undisputed claim to greatness, were found in the Book of Isaiah, written some seven hundred years before. There the prophet spoke of John as the forerunner of the Messiah and placed on his lips this message: "In the wilderness prepare the way of the Lord; make straight in the desert a highway for our God" (Isaiah 40:3). John was greater than Alexander, Caesar, or Augustus because of the far nobler and far greater purpose his life was to fill. He was to "bear witness about the light" (John 1:7), to "testify" of the Lord's Messiah, to "bear record" that Jesus is the Christ, the Son of the living God. John was truly great because of the great and glorious Savior that it was his privilege to proclaim.

In this respect, is there essentially much difference between the purpose of John the Baptist and our purpose here on earth? "You will be My witnesses," Jesus says to all of His disciples (Acts 1:8). We, too, are "voices" for the Savior, crying in this wilderness of sin and sorrow: "Make straight in the desert a highway for our God." We, too, will be numbered among the greatest if, like John, we point men to Christ, the eternal Son of God, as "the way, and the truth, and the life" (John 14:6), without whom no one can come to the Father. So great a glory do the Scriptures attach to faithful witnessing for Christ that the prophet Daniel writes by inspiration: "Those who turn many to righteousness [shall shine] like the stars forever and ever" (Daniel 12:3).

John the Baptist bore faithful witness. "This is the testimony of John," says the evangelist. And what a splendid testimony it was! What if we were to read the record of our witnessing for Christ, set down in print? What dodging of the issue, what shaving of the truth, what hiding of our colors, what flagrant, base denial of our Savior would the record show? John the Baptist confessed and denied not. Too often we have denied and confessed not. Pray God that we may be imbued with the spirit of this man John, of whom there is none greater, and that we may learn from him to bear ever more and more courageous witness of our Savior!

Prayer

Dear Lord, I thank You for revealing Your only-begotten Son to me as my personal Savior from sin. Grant that with each passing day I may bring greater glory to His holy name. May my every thought, my every word, and my every deed be acceptable in His sight, and may my very life be a daily witness to His eternal power to save. In Jesus' name. Amen.

JESUS, THE LAMB OF GOD
John 1:29–34

JOHN wrote his Gospel, as he tells us, "that you may believe that Jesus is the Christ, the Son of God, and that by believing you may have life in His name" (John 20:31). But if we are to find eternal life in the name of Jesus, we must believe in more than His eternal Sonship. If we knew Christ only as the almighty and eternal Son of the Highest, at whose name "every knee should bow" (Philippians 2:10), we would not yet have found what the evangelist has promised us: "life in His name." To find life through Christ, we must learn to know Him as the Lamb!

John, of course, was well aware of this, and so he permits the shadow of Calvary to fall across the very first page of his Gospel. Indeed, his entire Gospel moves in the shortening shadow of that cross and carries us swiftly to the doors of the Upper Room and to the unforgettable scene of the crucifixion. As the hero in an ancient tragedy, so the Savior is presented to the readers of John's Gospel, already in His first appearance, as one who is predestined to a tragic fate. "Behold," says John the Baptist, "the Lamb of God, who takes away the sin of the world!" God grant us His Spirit as we now behold that Lamb!

Behold the Lamb of God

The next day he saw Jesus coming toward him, and said, "Behold, the Lamb of God, who takes away the sin of the world! This is He of whom I said, 'After me comes a man who ranks before me, because He was before me.' I myself did not know Him, but for this purpose I came baptizing with water, that He might be revealed to Israel." And John bore witness: "I saw the Spirit descend from heaven like a dove, and it remained on Him. I myself did not know Him, but He who sent me to baptize with water said to me, 'He on whom you see the Spirit descend and remain, this is He who baptizes with the Holy Spirit.' And I have seen and have borne witness that this is the Son of God."

John the Baptist's testimony opens with the call "Behold, the Lamb of God" and closes with the confident assertion "This is the Son of God." Those two statements formed the very heart, the core and center, of his preaching.

The Word was made flesh so it could be "the Lamb." The entire Old Testament pointed toward One who would, once and forever, do in fact what thousands of lambs in the Old Testament had done in symbol—give His life for the sins of the people. Just as the blood of the Passover lamb, sprinkled on the doorposts of God's people, was their pledge of deliverance from Egyptian bondage and their guarantee of safety and protection, so the blood of the coming Redeemer would be the ransom that would free their souls from the bondage of sin and Satan and would guarantee eternal safety in the heavenly mansions.

It was this promised Lamb of whom Isaiah wrote, more than seven hundred years before John the Baptist: "Surely He has borne our griefs and carried our sorrows. . . . He was wounded for our transgressions; He was crushed for our iniquities; upon Him was the chastisement that brought us peace, and with His stripes we are healed" (Isaiah 53:4–5). Jesus, the Son of God, the Word made flesh, is that Lamb! In Him, we have full and free forgiveness of every sin. Our debt, our penalty, our punishment has been paid—paid in His name. He—for us! The Just for the unjust! "Upon Him was the chastisement that brought us peace, and with His stripes we are healed" (Isaiah 53:5). What a glorious, what a blessed study in pronouns: He for us!

And, praise be to God, that "us" includes me! Christ is "the Lamb of God, who takes away the sin of the world!" "He is the propitiation [the reconciliation] for our sins, and not for ours only but also for the sins of the whole world" (1 John 2:2). "God so loved the world, that He gave His only Son, that whoever believes in Him should not perish but have eternal life" (John 3:16). All three of these statements are recorded by John, and they are recorded to show us that the scope of God's love and mercy and the power of Christ's redemption embrace the entire human family. No one is excluded. All are included! And so I, too, can be sure that my sins have been taken away by His blood. With the great apostle, I can place my faith in the sin-atoning Lamb and say: "[He] loved me and gave Himself for me" (Galatians 2:20).

Prayer

Not all the blood of beasts On Jewish altars slain
Could give the guilty conscience peace Or wash away the stain.

But Christ, the heav'nly Lamb, Takes all our sins away;
A sacrifice of nobler name And richer blood than they.

My faith would lay its hand On that dear head of Thine,
While as a penitent I stand, And there confess my sin.

Believing, we rejoice To see the curse remove;
We bless the Lamb with cheerful voice And sing His bleeding love.
Amen. (LSB 431:1–3, 5)

FINDING CHRIST IS FINDING ALL
John 1:35–42

WE are not told that John the Baptist's public sermon pointing to the "Lamb of God, who takes away the sin of the world!" (John 1:29) resulted in any new followers for the Savior. No doubt, his mighty testimony did leave a deep impression on many of the Baptist's followers, but the actual decision to join with Christ, to become His followers, was not reached until some time later.

We are told that on the following day John was standing with only two of his disciples when the Savior passed his way again. Again, John directs them to Jesus as the Lamb of God, but this time with different results. We read:

Jesus Calls the First Disciples

The next day again John was standing with two of his disciples, and he looked at Jesus as He walked by and said, "Behold, the Lamb of God!" The two disciples heard him say this, and they followed Jesus. Jesus turned and saw them following and said to them, "What are you seeking?" And they said to Him, "Rabbi" (which means Teacher), "where are You staying?" He said to them, "Come and you will see." So they came and saw where He was staying, and they stayed with Him that day, for it was about the tenth hour. One of the two who heard John speak and followed Jesus was Andrew, Simon Peter's brother. He first found his own brother Simon and said to him, "We have found the Messiah" (which means Christ). He brought him to Jesus. Jesus looked at him and said, "So you are Simon the son of John? You shall be called Cephas" (which means Peter).

"What are you seeking?" It is significant that the first words of Christ recorded in John's Gospel are a simple question: "What are you seeking?" Simple? Yes, but with what eternal issues these little words were fraught, not only for the two young men who on that day entered into the Savior's company for the first time, but also for all people of all ages who would be confronted with the choice of believing—or not believing—in the Savior. What are you seeking? What do people hope to find in Christ? What does He have to offer?

"Come and you will see." This is the second statement of the Savior recorded by the evangelist. Nine words. Two sentences. But in these few words we have the first unfolding of the Savior's gracious Gospel invitation. "Come and you will see," He says. "Oh, taste and see that the Lord is good! Blessed is the man who takes refuge in Him!" (Psalm 34:8).

"We have found the Messiah." That was the exultant and triumphant shout of the two disciples who were the first to accept the Savior's invitation to come and see. Now their seeking days were over, for they had found Him of whom Moses and the Prophets had written! And thus it has ever been with those who, after the dark night of uncertainty, have found "the light of the knowledge of the glory of God in the face of Jesus Christ" (2 Corinthians 4:6). They have found something beyond the measure of man to evaluate and beyond the language of mortals to describe. In Christ, they have found the clear title to heaven!

And having found Christ, they seek no more. True, they seek to know Him better, to increase in the knowledge of His love and grace and power. (John and Andrew were to learn much more about the Savior during the months that lay ahead.) But having found Christ, they seek nothing else beyond Him.

One of the first to attest to the all-sufficiency of Christ to meet every human need would be the evangelist St. John himself. He was one of the two young men who stood by the roadside that afternoon and heeded the Savior's invitation to "come and see." Much had happened since then—the three years of intimate companionship with the Savior, the unforgettable scene on the Mount of Transfiguration, the unspeakable anguish in Gethsemane, the merciful darkness that shrouded the agony of Calvary, the empty tomb on Easter morning, the visible ascension of the Savior into heaven—John had seen it all. And now, more than fifty years later, the aged John undertakes to write a Gospel to show that this Savior, who had walked with him, who had talked with him, and whose glory he had beheld, was none other than the Son of God. John had seen. John had tasted.

He knew that his Lord was abundantly able to fill his every need.

And can't we say the same? Having found Christ, haven't we found everything?

Prayer

Jesus, Thou art mine forever,
Dearer far than earth to me;
Neither life nor death shall sever
Those sweet ties which bind to Thee.

Thou alone art all my Treasure,
Who hast died that I may live;
Thou conferrest noblest pleasure,
Who dost all my sins forgive.

Lamb of God, I do implore Thee,
Guard, support me, lest I fall.
Let me evermore adore Thee;
Be my everlasting All. Amen.
(TLH 357:1, 3, 6)

JESUS
FINDS PHILIP
John 1:43–51

THIS has been called the "chapter of great finds." And that description fits very well. For again and again we read of people "finding" and of people being "found." Of Andrew, we read that "He first found his own brother Simon and said to him, 'We have found the Messiah'" (which means Christ)' " (John 1:41). Of Philip, we are told that he "found Nathanael and said to him, 'We have found Him of whom Moses in the Law and also the prophets wrote, Jesus of Nazareth, the son of Joseph.'" And of the Savior Himself we read that "He found Philip and said to him, 'Follow Me.'" It is such finding—and being found—of which the following verses speak.

Jesus Calls Philip and Nathanael

The next day Jesus decided to go to Galilee. He found Philip and said to him, "Follow Me." Now Philip was from Bethsaida, the city of Andrew and Peter. Philip found Nathanael and said to him, "We have found Him of whom Moses in the Law and also the prophets wrote, Jesus of Nazareth, the son of Joseph." Nathanael said to him, "Can anything good come out of Nazareth?" Philip said to him, "Come and see." Jesus saw Nathanael coming toward Him and said of him, "Behold, an Israelite indeed, in whom there is no deceit!" Nathanael said to Him, "How do You know me?" Jesus answered him, "Before Philip called you, when you were under the fig tree, I saw you." Nathanael answered Him, "Rabbi, You are the Son of God! You are the King of Israel!" Jesus answered him, "Because I said to you, 'I saw you under the fig tree,' do you believe? You will see greater things than these." And He said to him, "Truly, truly, I say to you, you will see heaven opened, and the angels of God ascending and descending on the Son of Man."

Andrew had told his brother Simon, "We have found the Messiah." He would have spoken more precisely and more correctly if he had said, "The Messiah has found us!" The particle of steel may say, "I have found the magnet," but that will never change the fact that it was the magnet that drew the particle of steel. In the parable of the lost sheep, it was the sheep that was lost and not the shepherd; in the parable of the lost coin, it was the coin that was lost and not the woman who owned it (Luke 15). The sheep could not find the shepherd, and the coin could not find its owner, and so the shepherd went out in search of the sheep, and the woman searched high and low for her coin until she found it!

It is this kind of finding that the evangelist records in John 1:43: "[Jesus] found Philip." Philip was found by his Savior, just as is every sinner who comes to Christ. Luther, in his explanation of the Third Article of the Apostles' Creed, says, "I believe that I cannot by my own reason or strength believe in Jesus Christ, my Lord, or come to Him; but the Holy Spirit has called me by the Gospel" (*Luther's Small Catechism with Explanation,* p. 147). Paul, in speaking of the manner of his coming to the Savior, says he was "apprehended" by the Lord—literally, the word means that he was overtaken by the Lord and "laid hold of," while he was trying to run away. And at the end of his life, as he reflects upon the gracious manner in which the Lord "found" him and took him into His kingdom, Paul wrote to his student Timothy, "[God] saved us and called us to a holy calling, not because of our works but because of His own purpose and grace, which He gave us in Christ Jesus before the ages began" (2 Timothy 1:9). If anyone had asked Paul whether he had found Christ or Christ had found him, there can be no doubt as to how he would have answered.

It is a source of endless comfort to the believer to know that among the millions who crowd the highways and the byways of this topsy-turvy world, his Lord found him, singled him out, and called him as His own. To every one of His believers, the Savior says, personally and individually: "Fear not, for I have redeemed you; I have called you by name, you are Mine" (Isaiah 43:1).

Jesus found Philip. Yes, and what a happy day for Philip! Jesus found me too! What a blessed thought! He is mine, and I am His—because His love found me and took me to be His very own.

> Oh, the height of Jesus' love, Higher than the heav'ns above,
> Deeper than the depths of sea, Lasting as eternity!
> Love that found me—wondrous thought!
> Found me when I sought Him not. (*LSB* 611:2)

Prayer

Blessed Lord Jesus, I thank You with my whole heart that, although I wandered far across the wilderness of sin, Your gracious love found me. Make and keep me ever grateful for Your mercy. Grant that, as Philip was found by You and as he gave his life to You, so I may give myself to You and follow in Your steps. Keep me faithful, blessed Lord, faithful unto death, and grant to me, according to Your promise, the crown of eternal life. Amen.

THE BEGINNING OF MIRACLES
John 2:1–11

THE entire Gospel of John might very well be summed up in that remarkable fourteenth verse of the first chapter: "The Word became flesh and dwelt among us, and we have seen His glory." John and the other disciples were convinced beyond all doubt that Jesus was the Christ, the Son of God, because they had "seen His glory, glory as of the only Son from the Father, full of grace and truth."

And now, what he had learned firsthand, what he had learned through his intimate association with the Savior, John proposes to share with his readers. They, too, are to see the Master's glory so they, too, might believe in Him and be saved. So John begins this second chapter with the story of Jesus turning water into wine, which he calls a "sign," namely, proof that Jesus was in truth God the Son.

It is significant that, consistent with the purpose of his Gospel, John concludes this account with the meaningful remark, "This, the first of His signs, Jesus did at Cana in Galilee, and manifested His glory. And His disciples believed in Him." May we who read, just as those who saw, behold this miracle with believing hearts and learn to trust, to worship, and to adore the mighty Savior who performed it.

The Wedding at Cana

On the third day there was a wedding at Cana in Galilee, and the mother of Jesus was there. Jesus also was invited to the wedding with His disciples. When the wine ran out, the mother of Jesus said to Him, "They have no wine." And Jesus said to her, "Woman, what does this have to do with Me? My hour has not yet come." His mother said to the servants, "Do whatever He tells you."

Now there were six stone water jars there for the Jewish rites of purification, each holding twenty or thirty gallons. Jesus said to the servants, "Fill the jars with water." And they filled them up to the brim. And He said to them, "Now draw some out and take it to the master of the feast." So they took it. When the master of the feast tasted the water now become wine, and did not know where it came from (though the servants who had drawn the water knew), the master of the feast called the bridegroom and said to him, "Everyone serves the good wine first, and when people have drunk freely, then the poor wine. But you have kept the good wine until now." This, the first of his signs, Jesus did at Cana in Galilee, and manifested His glory. And His disciples believed in Him.

Jesus at a wedding! What a welcome, winsome picture! In the first chapter, we are told that Jesus was "the beginning" and that "all things were made through Him" and that "without Him was not any thing made that was made" (1:1–3). Now we are told that He gladly accepted the wedding invitation of a humble villager, entered his home, and mingled freely with the wedding guests.

In a sense, more so than when Jacob spoke the words, this bride and groom could say, after seeing the Savior's miracle, "Surely the Lord is in this place, and I did not know it" (Genesis 28:16). Yes, God was there! "Oh, blest the house, whate'er befall, Where Jesus Christ is all in all! A home that is not wholly His—How sad and poor and dark it is!" (*LSB* 862:1).

Have we invited Jesus into our home? If so, we find Him to be a bountiful provider. Turning the water of want into the wine of plenty for His Christians is still something the Savior does. Is Jesus the "Head of our house, the unseen Guest at every meal"? If so, then we find that He not only comforts us in sorrow and strengthens us in days of stress, but that He also sanctifies our joys and pleasures. He who is happy is twice happy if he knows that Jesus shares his gladness.

And if Jesus is a permanent guest in our home, we need have no fear or worry for the future. He always keeps the best wine until last. The cup that our Lord has given us today may be a bitter one— the cup of sorrow or remorse, of sickness or bereavement. But in His hands He already holds the cup of gladness that, when His hour is come, He will surely place into our hands. On that day—and we have His promise for this—we shall say, "You have kept the good wine until now."

Prayer

O Lord Jesus, who at the wedding feast at Cana blessed the home, we thank You for the gift of Christian parents and for the influence of a Christian family. Keep us ever grateful for these blessings. Abide with us, Lord Jesus, in our hearts and in our family circle. Protect and prosper all Christian families through- out the world, that they might glorify Your name, extend Your kingdom here on earth, and finally be joined in the heavenly family of all of Your redeemed. Amen.

JESUS CLEANSES THE TEMPLE

John 2:12–17

FOR a clear understanding of Jesus' cleansing of the temple, we must know of what the temple needed to be cleansed. The abuses that aroused the righteous wrath of the holy Son of God were chiefly twofold.

Throughout the years, the Jews had been accustomed to pay an annual temple tax. This had to be paid in the sacred coin, the shekel of the sanctuary. When, especially at Passover and on other high festivals, the Jews came from all parts of the world and used this occasion to pay their temple tax, they first had to exchange their foreign money for the sacred coin of the temple. And so bankers, or money-changers, soon established a flourishing business within the precincts of the temple—in the crowded court of the Gentiles. As objectionable as such traffic was within the very shadow of the sanctuary, it became doubly reprehensible when these money-changers resorted to unfair practices, charged exorbitant exchange rates, and turned the business into a racket.

In addition to the proper currency, it was necessary for God's people to bring sacrificial animals for offerings in the temple. Those who came from far away brought money to buy their doves or lambs or oxen within the holy city (Deuteronomy 14:24–26). This, too, gave rise to notorious abuse. Vendors crowded closer and closer to the temple until they were selling within the temple walls. Concessions were sold, monopolies were arranged, and prices were fixed. (One historian tells us that during an earlier reform, a "ceiling price" was set to reduce the price of a pair of pigeons from four dollars to eight cents.) And the members of the priestly family were foremost in gathering the spoils.

But what could be done? Who would be bold enough to tackle this deep-rooted scandal? "The Lord whom you seek will suddenly come to His temple," Malachi had written. "He is like a refiner's fire and like fullers' soap" (3:1–2). In today's reading, we see this prophecy fulfilled:

> After this He went down to Capernaum, with His mother and His brothers and His disciples, and they stayed there for a few days.

Jesus Cleanses the Temple

> The Passover of the Jews was at hand, and Jesus went up to Jerusalem. In the temple He found those who were selling oxen and sheep and pigeons, and the money-changers sitting there. And making a whip of cords, He drove them all out of the temple, with the sheep and oxen. And He poured out the coins of the money-changers and overturned their tables. And He told those who sold the pigeons, "Take these things away; do not make My Father's house a house of trade." His disciples remembered that it was written, "Zeal for Your house will consume Me."

It is difficult to read this passage without thinking of another "cleansing of the temple" that took place about 1,500 years later. Over the years, shameful abuses had crept into the Christian Church. Forgiveness of sins was offered across the table of the money-changer. The Most Holy Place of our blessed religion, the doctrine of full and free salvation without money and without price, had been profaned by a dollar-for-dollar religion of works. Corruption was high and wide and deep. Disapproving voices were raised by priest and prince, by preacher and professor, in public and in private. But all to no avail.

Then suddenly the Lord sent His messenger to His temple. Martin Luther, as one historian puts it, made a scourge of Romans 1:16–17—"The righteous shall live by faith"—and drove out the merchants with their "holy business" and turned the den of thieves into a house of prayer. There is indeed a striking parallel between the racketeering traffic that had all but drowned out the voice of the temple worship in the Savior's day and the merchandising in spiritual matters that had desecrated the Church of God in the days of Martin Luther.

Do not the words of Peter have their application now and at any time: "It is time for judgment to begin at the household of God" (1 Peter 4:17)? Oh, that we all had the same zeal for the house of our Lord that burned in the Savior's heart: "Zeal for Your house has consumed Me" (Psalm 69:9). Let us pray that God might use us to preserve the honor and the good name of His Church.

Prayer

I love Your kingdom, Lord,
The place of Your abode,
The Church our blest Redeemer saved
With His own precious blood.

I love Your Church, O God,
Your saints in ev'ry land,
Dear as the apple of Your eye
And graven on Your hand.

For them my tears shall fall;
For them my prayers ascend;
For them my cares and toils be giv'n
Till toils and cares shall end.
(LSB 651:1, 3–4)

8

CHRIST'S AUTHORITY CHALLENGED

John 2:18–25

WE are still standing with Christ in the temple—the tables have been turned upside down, the Roman coins and Jewish shekels have rolled in all directions, the animals are all astir, and the vendors and money-changers have sought refuge behind the temple colonnades from the wrath of the young Jesus of Nazareth. In the midst of this confusion, we cannot suppress a natural question.

Wasn't this strange behavior for the man who was to become known as the gentle Nazarene? Wasn't it standard practice of Jesus not to use force in an attempt to change men's attitudes (John 18:11, 36)? Has Jesus, perhaps in a moment of weakness, "lost His temper"?

By no means! It would be a false conception to think of Jesus only as the gentle, winsome, soft-spoken Savior. Some of the most scathing, most terrifying, and most burning condemnations ever to be spoken by the lips of man were uttered by the blessed lips of Jesus (Matthew 23:13–33). Christ is the righteous judge, and in His justice He is a consuming fire (Hebrews 12:29). It is, of course, true—and God be praised for this—that to every sinner who comes to Him in penitence and faith, Jesus is, above all else, the compassionate and loving Redeemer. The hand that held the scourge is the same hand that wipes the tear and lifts the burden from the disconsolate and sorrowing.

But when Jesus entered the temple that day, He did not enter it as Savior; He entered it as Judge! The Lord of the temple had suddenly come to rid His house of those who had profaned it. The righteous Judge had come to execute judgment in His court. And so—as on the Mount of Transfiguration and again for one brief moment in Gethsemane—we are permitted to catch a fleeting glimpse of the terrible majesty of Him who is "appointed by God to be judge of the living and the dead" (Acts 10:42).

Small wonder that the vendors and money-changers demanded to know by what authority Jesus had done these things!

> So the Jews said to Him, "What sign do You show us for doing these things?" Jesus answered them, "Destroy this temple, and in three days I will raise it up." The Jews then said, "It has taken forty-six years to build this temple, and will You raise it up in three days?" But He was speaking about the temple of His body. When therefore He was raised from the dead, His disciples remembered that He had said this, and they believed the Scripture and the word that Jesus had spoken.

Jesus Knows What Is in Man

Now when He was in Jerusalem at the Passover Feast, many believed in His name when they saw the signs that He was doing. But Jesus on His part did not entrust Himself to them, because He knew all people and needed no one to bear witness about man, for He Himself knew what was in man.

"Destroy this temple, and in three days I will raise it up." Again, the shadow of Calvary! The evangelist who stood at the foot of the cross could see, perhaps more clearly than the rest, how every word of Jesus was charged not only with a premonition but also with a sure and certain foresight of the tragedy that awaited Him.

These words, we know, were twisted by the Savior's enemies and used against Him on the very day the temple of His body was destroyed (Matthew 26:61; 27:40; Mark 14:58). But to us who believe in Him and who have found our soul's salvation in the destroyed temple of His body, given into death for the remission of our sins, these words are precious comfort because they confirm our faith in Him who, though He knew that the way of salvation was the way of the cross, nevertheless "endured the cross, despising the shame, and is seated at the right hand of the throne of God" (Hebrews 12:2).

This prophecy of the Savior has the same faith-strengthening effect on us as it had on His faithful few. For of them we read: "When therefore He was raised from the dead, His disciples remembered that He had said this, and they believed the Scripture [Psalm 16:10] and the word that Jesus had spoken." We too! At the door of the empty tomb, we believe "the Scripture and the word that Jesus had spoken."

Prayer

O Lord Jesus, I thank You that by Your innocent death and by Your glorious resurrection, You have saved me from the guilt, the power, and the punishment of sin. Keep me ever mindful of this blessed truth and ever grateful for its gracious comfort. Grant me Your Holy Spirit, that in thought and word and deed I may always be

*obedient to Your holy will and may always bring honor and glory
to Your holy name. I ask this, trusting solely in Your mercy. Amen.*

A MIDNIGHT INTERVIEW

John 3:1–13

THE third chapter of John's Gospel tells us the well-known and
well-loved story of a man who "came to Jesus by night" in search of
spiritual knowledge. This man, Nicodemus, was a Pharisee, a leader
in the Jewish church and member of the Council, the supreme court
of the Jewish nation.

Whether or not Nicodemus became a follower of the Savior, we
are not definitely told. There are only two other references to him
in the entire Scripture, and both are in the Gospel of John. When
later the chief priests and Pharisees spoke violently against Jesus, we
read that Nicodemus rose to speak in His defense: "Does our law
judge a man without first giving him a hearing and learning what he
does?" (7:51). And after the crucifixion, we are told that this same
Nicodemus joined Joseph of Arimathea in preparing the Savior's
body for burial (19:38–40). It would seem that the description John
gives of Joseph of Arimathea could also be applied, at least in some
measure, to Nicodemus: "a disciple of Jesus, but secretly for fear of
the Jews" (19:38).

In every era there are those who because of weakness, fear,
or faintheartedness have not taken an open stand for the Savior,
although in their heart of hearts they find in Him their only stay and
hope. They, too, are to be numbered among Christ's followers. Even
a weak faith saves—not because it is weak, but because it is faith. "A
bruised reed He will not break, and a faintly burning wick He will

not quench" (Isaiah 42:3). It is for these hesitating and timid followers of Christ that we pray in the well-known mission hymn:

> Glory then to Jesus, Who, the Prince of light,
> To a world in darkness Brought the gift of sight;
> Praise to God the Father; In the Spirit's love
> Praise we all together Him who reigns above. (LSB 512:7)

God grant us His Holy Spirit as we now read of that memorable interview between Jesus and Nicodemus.

You Must Be Born Again

Now there was a man of the Pharisees named Nicodemus, a
ruler of the Jews. This man came to Jesus by night and said to
Him, "Rabbi, we know that You are a teacher come from God,
for no one can do these signs that You do unless God is with
him." Jesus answered him, "Truly, truly, I say to you, unless one
is born again he cannot see the kingdom of God." Nicodemus
said to Him, "How can a man be born when he is old? Can he
enter a second time into his mother's womb and be born?"
Jesus answered, "Truly, truly, I say to you, unless one is born
of water and the Spirit, he cannot enter the kingdom of God.
That which is born of the flesh is flesh, and that which is born
of the Spirit is spirit. Do not marvel that I said to you, 'You
must be born again.' The wind blows where it wishes, and you
hear its sound, but you do not know where it comes from or
where it goes. So it is with everyone who is born of the Spirit."

Nicodemus said to Him, "How can these things be?" Jesus
answered him, "Are you the teacher of Israel and yet you do
not understand these things? Truly, truly, I say to you, we speak
of what we know, and bear witness to what we have seen, but
you do not receive our testimony. If I have told you earthly
things and you do not believe, how can you believe if I tell you
heavenly things? No one has ascended into heaven except He
who descended from heaven, the Son of Man."

Volumes have been written on these verses. Perhaps all of them could
be condensed into five short words: you must be born again! Christ,

who "knew all people [and] knew what was in man" (2:24–25), knew that the human heart was "deceitful above all things, and desperately sick" (Jeremiah 17:9). He knew that "the intention of man's heart is evil from his youth" (Genesis 8:21) and that the unregenerate heart of man is "dead in the trespasses and sins" (Ephesians 2:1).

And so He does not speak to Nicodemus about the necessity of a reformation, of turning over a new leaf, of getting a new outlook on life. No, the need lies far deeper. "Unless one is born again!" "The natural person does not accept the things of the Spirit of God, for they are folly to him, and he is not able to understand them because they are spiritually discerned" (1 Corinthians 2:14). As little as the blind man can appreciate the glories of the sunset, as little as the deaf man can thrill his heart to the beautiful refrain of an enchanting melody—so little can flesh "born of the flesh" appreciate the beauty and the grandeur of the simplest Gospel promise.

He must be born again. The Spirit of God, working through the water and the Word, must perform that divine operation by which children of men become children of God. This glorious rebirth, says Jesus, is a mystery that surpasses human understanding (John 3:7–8), but it is a fact, attested to by the eternal Son, who has spent endless ages in the bosom of the Father (vv. 11–13). Surely, there can be no higher authority!

Let us thank God daily for having granted us the priceless blessing of the rebirth in Jesus Christ, our Savior, for having opened our eyes to the wonders of His love. "Blessed be the God and Father of our Lord Jesus Christ! According to His great mercy, He has caused us to be born again to a living hope through the resurrection of Jesus Christ from the dead, to an inheritance that is imperishable, undefiled, and unfading, kept in heaven for you" (1 Peter 1:3–4).

Prayer

All that I was, my sin, my guilt, My death, was all mine own;
All that I am I owe to Thee, My gracious God, alone.

The evil of my former state Was mine, and only mine;
The good in which I now rejoice Is Thine, and only Thine.

Thy Word first made me feel my sin, It taught me to believe;
Then, in believing, peace I found, And now I live, I live!

All that I am, e'en here on earth, All that I hope to be,
When Jesus comes and glory dawns, I owe it, Lord, to Thee.
Amen. (TLH 378:1–2, 4–5)

"GOD SO LOVED THE WORLD"
John 3:14–21

WE are still listening to the Savior and Nicodemus in their midnight interview. Jesus has spoken at length on the necessity of being born again. Now He is ready to talk about how this mysterious rebirth is accomplished.

In His unsearchable wisdom, God determined to send us a Savior, who would forever break the shackles of spiritual death and would restore spiritual life and light to the sin-darkened souls of men.

Faith in this Savior, who would suffer and bleed and die for the sins of the world, is the divine method of the rebirth that would change the children of men into the children of God. Now Jesus tells Nicodemus about the person and work of this divine Redeemer—about Himself!

And as Moses lifted up the serpent in the wilderness, so must the Son of Man be lifted up, that whoever believes in Him may have eternal life.

For God So Loved the World

For God so loved the world, that He gave His only Son, that whoever believes in Him should not perish but have eternal life.

For God did not send His Son into the world to condemn the world, but in order that the world might be saved through Him. Whoever believes in Him is not condemned, but whoever does not believe is condemned already, because he has not believed in the name of the only Son of God. And this is the judgment: the light has come into the world, and people loved the darkness rather than the light because their works were evil. For everyone who does wicked things hates the light and does not come to the light, lest his works should be exposed. But whoever does what is true comes to the light, so that it may be clearly seen that his works have been carried out in God.

There is a legend that every time a sinner is converted, the angels in heaven write his name in the margin of a large Bible, opposite the passage that brought him to the light. If that were true, how many millions of the redeemed of all ages would have their names inscribed opposite John 3:16!

A college student read this verse and later wrote: " 'God so loved the world'—that is big enough for me. 'That He gave His only Son'—that is provision enough for me. 'That whoever believes in Him'—that is definite enough for me. 'Should not perish but have eternal life'—that is sure enough for me!"

Can we ever sufficiently thank God for the healing streams of comfort that come into our lives through the divine assurance of John 3:16? When trials beset us, when doubts assail us, when our faith would break beneath the burden of the strain, or when the deepening shadow of death throws an icy chill into our frightened soul—how often has our problem, our difficulty, our doubt, or our anxiety dissolved and disappeared before the warmth of this divine assurance like snow before the April sun!

At the foot of the cross, all problems—sin, sorrow, death, and whatever else plagues the soul of man—find their solution. For "as Moses lifted up the serpent in the wilderness" (so that they who looked at it might live, Numbers 21:4–9), "so must the Son of Man be lifted up" (on the cross), "that whoever believes in Him may have eternal life. For God so loved the world, that He gave His only Son, that whoever believes in Him should not perish but have eternal life."

Christ, and Christ alone, is the Christian's only hope. But in Christ, his every hope is fulfilled. In Christ, he is "born again," is accepted into the Father's family. In Christ, he will not perish. In Christ, he is assured of everlasting life.

Prayer

Therefore my hope is in the Lord
And not in mine own merit;
It rests upon His faithful Word
To them of contrite spirit
That He is merciful and just;
This is my comfort and my trust.
His help I wait with patience. (LSB 607:3)

JOHN THE BAPTIST'S FINAL TESTIMONY

John 3:22–36

A RASH of jealousy had broken out among the disciples of John the Baptist. So why did he stand by complacently, while one after another of his disciples deserted him for this Jesus of Nazareth? Why was it that he did not register an earnest protest, especially now that the disciples of Jesus had begun to baptize and were going up and down the land, as it seemed to John's disciples, in open competition with their master? Their secret jealousy finally found expression. A dispute arose among the followers of John the Baptist and certain Jews concerning the Baptism that was being administered by Jesus' disciples.

When they brought their complaint to John the Baptist, he took the opportunity to give his final recorded testimony to the divine preeminence of Jesus. And what a beautiful testimony it is! We read:

John the Baptist Exalts Christ

After this Jesus and His disciples went into the Judean countryside, and He remained there with them and was baptizing. John also was baptizing at Aenon near Salim, because water was plentiful there, and people were coming and being baptized (for John had not yet been put in prison).

Now a discussion arose between some of John's disciples and a Jew over purification. And they came to John and said to him, "Rabbi, He who was with you across the Jordan, to whom you bore witness—look, He is baptizing, and all are going to Him." John answered, "A person cannot receive even one thing unless it is given him from heaven. You yourselves bear me witness, that I said, 'I am not the Christ, but I have been sent before Him.' The one who has the bride is the bridegroom. The friend of the bridegroom, who stands and hears him, rejoices greatly at the bridegroom's voice. Therefore this joy of mine is now complete. He must increase, but I must decrease."

He who comes from above is above all. He who is of the earth belongs to the earth and speaks in an earthly way. He who comes from heaven is above all. He bears witness to what He has seen and heard, yet no one receives His testimony. Whoever receives His testimony sets his seal to this, that God is true. For He whom God has sent utters the words of God, for He gives the Spirit without measure. The Father loves the Son and has given all things into His hand. Whoever believes in the Son has eternal life; whoever does not obey the Son shall not see life, but the wrath of God remains on him.

John the Baptist is still the same self-effacing servant and faithful herald. He reminds his jealous friends that he had told them before that Jesus was the Christ, and not he! He was merely "the voice of one crying out in the wilderness, 'Make straight the way of the Lord' " (John 1:23). Jesus was that Lord!

John calls himself the friend of the Bridegroom. It was the duty of the friend of the bridegroom to present the bride, a duty that in our day is usually performed by the father of the bride when he answers the pastor's question, "Who gives this bride away?" At this point in the wedding ceremony, the father usually answers, "I do," and then retires to a less prominent position.

In a similar spirit, John the Baptist says here, "I have presented the Bride to her Bridegroom. My task is done, and my joy is complete. Most gladly do I now withdraw so that the beloved Bridegroom may be all in all." Christ was the heavenly Bridegroom who was to bring joy and comfort to the heart of His Bride, the Church. John was content to be the friend of that Bridegroom.

"He must increase, but I must decrease." These are among the most memorable, most tender and endearing words of John the Baptist. A candle consumes itself—grows smaller and smaller—so it can shed light on the path of others. "I must decrease, but He must increase." That is the philosophy of the candle. Said the great apostle Paul, "But whatever gain I had, I counted as loss for the sake of Christ" (Philippians 3:7).

Do we serve our Lord in that spirit? "He must increase, but I must decrease"? Oh, how often our sinful heart has insisted, "He must increase, but I must increase too!" It is not an easy thing to serve our Lord in sincere humility and singleness of heart. Our Savior admonishes, "Let your light shine before others, so that they may see your good works." But why? For what purpose? "That they may see your good works and give glory to your Father who is in heaven" (Matthew 5:16). It is to His glory and not our own that we are to dedicate our every aim and effort. "Whether you eat or drink, or whatever you do, do all to the glory of God," says Paul (1 Corinthians 10:31). May our every thought and action be impelled by that same spirit of humility and devotion to our Lord that moved John the Baptist to exclaim, "He must increase, but I must decrease."

Prayer

Forbid it, Lord, that I should boast
Save in the death of Christ, my God;
All the vain things that charm me most,
I sacrifice them to His blood.

Were the whole realm of nature mine,
That were a tribute far too small;
Love so amazing, so divine,
Demands my soul, my life, my all! Amen.
(LSB 425:2, 4)

WELLS OF LIVING WATER

John 4:1–15

IN the third chapter of John's Gospel, we read Jesus' private interview with Nicodemus. The fourth chapter brings us the account of His private conversation with the Samaritan woman at Jacob's well. The evangelist had good reason for reporting both of these remarkable interviews in great detail. His purpose in writing his Gospel, we will remember, was "that you may believe that Jesus is the Christ, the Son of God, and that by believing you may have life in His name" (John 20:31).

In these two interviews—with Nicodemus and with the woman at the well—we listen to the Lord Himself as He reveals Himself as being, in deed and in truth, "the Christ, the Son of God," and proclaiming that all who believe in Him will "have life in His name." To the public testimony of John the Baptist is added the private testimony of Jesus.

We begin by reading the first half of this memorable interview.

Jesus and the Woman of Samaria

Now when Jesus learned that the Pharisees had heard that Jesus was making and baptizing more disciples than John (although Jesus Himself did not baptize, but only His disciples), He left Judea and departed again for Galilee. And He had to pass through Samaria. So He came to a town of Samaria called Sychar, near the field that Jacob had given to his son Joseph. Jacob's well was there; so Jesus, wearied as He was from His journey, was sitting beside the well. It was about the sixth hour.

A woman from Samaria came to draw water. Jesus said to her, "Give Me a drink." (For His disciples had gone away into the city to buy food.) The Samaritan woman said to Him, "How is it that You, a Jew, ask for a drink from me, a woman of Samaria?" (For Jews have no dealings with Samaritans.) Jesus answered her, "If you knew the gift of God, and who it is that is saying to you, 'Give Me a drink,' you would have asked Him, and He would have given you living water." The woman said to Him, "Sir, You have nothing to draw water with, and the well is deep. Where do You get that living water? Are You greater than our father Jacob? He gave us the well and drank from it himself, as did his sons and his livestock." Jesus said to her, "Everyone who drinks of this water will be thirsty again, but whoever drinks of the water that I will give him will never be thirsty again. The water that I will give him will become in him a spring of water welling up to eternal life." The woman said to Him, "Sir, give me this water, so that I will not be thirsty or have to come here to draw water."

What an appropriate prayer for this woman as she went to bed that night! Christ, the eternal Son of God, the "Word made flesh," had spoken to her despite the barriers that tradition and custom had placed in His way. She was, first of all, a woman, and no Jewish rabbi would be seen in public speaking to a woman. Second, she was a

Samaritan, and no respectable Jew would have any dealings with a native of Samaria. Worst of all, she was a sinful woman, an adulteress, and no self-respecting Jewish teacher would be seen in the company of public sinners (Matthew 9:11)! That is, nobody but Jesus!

To Jesus, these barriers were invitations. They were calls for help, calls for mercy. So He sat down to speak with her. What tact, what winsomeness, what tender kindness gives form to every word the Savior spoke! He sat by the well because He knew He would meet her there. He asked for a drink—from her cup, the unclean cup of a sinful Samaritan woman to show from the outset that His "love unknown has broken ev'ry barrier down" (*LSB* 570:6). He spoke of water and of thirst, something they both had in common, with the purpose of teaching her about a deeper thirst and a far more precious water.

What Jesus did for this poor Samaritan woman He has also done for us! In times past, we were alienated from Israel and strangers to the covenants of promise, having no hope and without God in the world. But now in Christ Jesus, we who once were far off are brought near by the blood of Christ (Ephesians 2:12–13). In His mercy, He has surmounted every barrier our sins had built that would have separated us forever from the fellowship of the saints.

We drink of His "living water"—we hear and believe His precious Gospel—and this has been in us "a spring of water welling up to eternal life." Oh, let us never cease to thank and praise our God for His matchless mercy!

Prayer

I heard the voice of Jesus say,
"Come unto Me and rest;
Lay down, thou weary one, lay down
Thy head upon My breast."
I came to Jesus as I was,
So weary, worn, and sad;
I found in Him a resting place,
And He has made me glad.

I heard the voice of Jesus say,
"Behold, I freely give
The living water; thirsty one,
Stoop down and drink and live."
I came to Jesus, and I drank
Of that life-giving stream;
My thirst was quenched, my soul revived,
And now I live in Him. Amen. (LSB 699:1—2)

THE FORGOTTEN WATER JAR
John 4:16–30

JESUS gained the attention and the interest of the Samaritan woman. But that is not enough. He must also bring her to a deep conviction of her dire need of the living water He offers. He must convince her of her sin because it is the thirsty who values water and the guilty who values pardon. So He shifts the discussion with the sudden and unexpected request: "Go, call your husband, and come here."

Here the conversation takes a serious turn—there is a confession of guilt, followed by an honest inquiry into the Savior's teachings, and then the preaching of the sweetest Gospel in the self-revelation of the Savior as the long-awaited Messiah. It is noteworthy that the clearest revelation of Jesus as the promised Messiah in this Gospel is given not to the Jews, not to the leaders at Jerusalem, but to this unknown Samaritan woman at the well. With this in mind, we read the concluding report of this remarkable interview:

Jesus said to her, "Go, call your husband, and come here." The woman answered Him, "I have no husband." Jesus said to her, "You are right in saying, 'I have no husband'; for you have had five husbands, and the one you now have is not your husband. What you have said is true." The woman said to Him, "Sir, I perceive that You are a prophet. Our fathers worshiped on this mountain, but You say that in Jerusalem is the place where people ought to worship." Jesus said to her, "Woman, believe Me, the hour is coming when neither on this mountain nor in Jerusalem will you worship the Father. You worship what you do not know; we worship what we know, for salvation is from the Jews. But the hour is coming, and is now here, when the true worshipers will worship the Father in spirit and truth, for the Father is seeking such people to worship Him. God is spirit, and those who worship Him must worship in spirit and truth." The woman said to Him, "I know that Messiah is coming (He who is called Christ). When He comes, He will tell us all things." Jesus said to her, "I who speak to you am He."

Just then His disciples came back. They marveled that He was talking with a woman, but no one said, "What do You seek?" or, "Why are You talking with her?" So the woman left her water jar and went away into town and said to the people, "Come, see a man who told me all that I ever did. Can this be the Christ?" They went out of the town and were coming to Him.

Volumes could be written on these few verses. We could speak of the Savior's winning evangelism method. We could speak of His omniscience as shown by His telling the woman everything she ever did (John 4:29). We could speak of her deep conviction of sin in the presence of this mighty Prophet. We could speak of the nature of God as revealed by the Savior's words: "God is spirit, and those who worship Him must worship in spirit and truth." Or we could speak of the dramatic climax reached in the words of Jesus: "I who speak to you am He."

But we do not focus here on these topics. Instead, we fix our attention on one seemingly unimportant detail. We are told that when the woman realized that the man with whom she spoke was none other than the promised Messiah and Savior of the world, she left the water jar at the well and ran into the city to tell her friends. With the water of life bubbling up within her soul, the water in Jacob's well could wait. She had found something of surpassing importance, and it would have made little difference to her if she never saw her water jar again.

Do we feel the same? Having drunk freely of the water of life, do we feel that impulse to run and tell our friends? Do we feel that joy of discovery that refuses to keep silent and that becomes the greater for the sharing? Oh, how often we find ourselves clinging to our earthly water jars—to the chores and duties of our everyday existence—when, instead, we should leave those water jars at the well and run an errand of mercy for the Savior. How often when our hearts have been moved to high resolves by the hearing of the Gospel have we forgotten to run, and have merely stood "while the multitudes are dying And the Master calls for you" (*LSB* 826:4)! No, forgetting the water jar, this woman ran! Too often, remembering our water jars, we forget to run—and the world is the poorer because of it.

In another place, the Savior tells us, "The kingdom of heaven is like a merchant in search of fine pearls, who, on finding one pearl of great value, went and sold all that he had and bought it" (Matthew 13:45–46). Does the kingdom of God mean that much to us? Does the water of life taste that sweet to us? Then let us run and tell others.

Prayer

O Lord Jesus, I thank You with my whole heart for having revealed Yourself to me as the Son of God and Savior of the world. Make me willing and eager to share this unspeakable blessing with everyone I know. Let no earthly consideration keep me from speaking freely to sinners of Your mercy. And receive me finally, with all of Your redeemed, into Your heavenly kingdom. I ask it, precious Savior, trusting only in Your mercy. Amen.

DOING THE
WILL OF GOD
John 4:31–42

JESUS had arrived at Jacob's well at high noon, the sixth hour. Weary, hungry, and thirsty, He seated Himself on the edge of the well while His disciples went into the city to buy food for their midday lunch. It was during this interval, while His disciples were gone, that Jesus had engaged the Samaritan woman in lengthy conversation.

That conversation was now over. The disciples had returned, and the meal was spread. But Jesus seems to have lost His interest in food; at any rate, He is not in as great a hurry to eat as the disciples had expected. Had someone else brought a meal to Him while they were in the city?

Such is the background against which the following story now unfolds.

Meanwhile the disciples were urging Him, saying, "Rabbi, eat." But He said to them, "I have food to eat that you do not know about." So the disciples said to one another, "Has anyone brought Him something to eat?" Jesus said to them, "My food is to do the will of Him who sent me and to accomplish His work. Do you not say, 'There are yet four months, then comes the harvest'? Look, I tell you, lift up your eyes, and see that the fields are white for harvest. Already the one who reaps is receiving wages and gathering fruit for eternal life, so that sower and reaper may rejoice together. For here the saying holds true, 'One sows and another reaps.' I sent you to reap that for which you did not labor. Others have labored, and you have entered into their labor."

Many Samaritans from that town believed in Him because of the woman's testimony, "He told me all that I ever did." So when the Samaritans came to Him, they asked Him to stay with them, and He stayed there two days. And many more believed because of His word. They said to the woman, "It is no longer because of what you said that we believe, for we have heard for ourselves, and we know that this is indeed the Savior of the world."

Jesus says, "I have food to eat that you do not know about." He is still thinking about His conversation with the woman at the well. He speaks figuratively. But what is this "food" He talks about? "My food is to do the will of Him who sent me and to accomplish His work."

The Savior is explaining to His disciples, in other words, how it was that He had momentarily forgotten all about His hunger. He had become so absorbed in His personal mission work, in His conversation with the woman at the well, that for the time being He had felt no sense of need for food. His work was His meat! Doing His Father's will was such a source of inner satisfaction to Him that, after a manner of speaking, He could live on that satisfaction alone. That was His food—doing His Father's will and finishing His Father's work.

Haven't you often heard people say, "I would rather sing than eat" or "I would rather read a good book than eat"? Such statements are, of course, exaggerations, but they do convey the thought that singing or reading may be a rich source of inner satisfaction. As Christians, we are to find just such a source of inner joy and strength in the knowledge that we are doing our Father's will and finishing our Father's work. That is our food that the world does not know, our source of highest joy and satisfaction.

If, like the Savior, we have surrendered our entire life to the gracious leadings of God's will; if, with Him, we have learned to say in every moment of life, "Not My will, but Yours, be done" (Luke 22:42)—then we will have learned that secret source of strength that will enable us to triumph over all of life's adversities. For doing our Father's will will be our meat.

Furthermore, if we, like the Savior, have set ourselves to the task of finishing our Father's work on earth, we will find our appetite for the empty pleasures of this world growing less and less—for doing and finishing our Father's work will be our food.

Have we found this food? God grant us the strength that comes from knowing, doing, following, and loving our Father's will. There lies the secret of our joy and strength.

Prayer

Drawn to the cross, which Thou hast blessed
With healing gifts for souls distressed,
To find in Thee my life, my rest,
Christ crucified, I come.

Thou knowest all my griefs and fears,
Thy grace abused, my misspent years;
Yet now to Thee with contrite tears,
Christ crucified, I come.

Wash me and take away each stain;
Let nothing of my sin remain.
For cleansing, though it be through pain,
Christ crucified, I come.

And then for work to do for Thee,
Which shall so sweet a service be
That angels well might envy me,
Christ crucified, I come. Amen. (LSB *560)*

THE OFFICIAL'S FAITH

John 4:43–54

IS there sickness in our home? a special cross? a son or daughter who has brought grief and heartache into the family circle? "Have we trials and temptations? Is there trouble anywhere?" *(LSB* 770:2). It would be difficult to think of a Christian home into which the cruel hand of sin has not brought some secret sorrow, some pain, or some heartache.

But even these "family crosses" are intended, in the kind providence of God, to work together for our good (Romans 8:28). "For the moment all discipline seems painful rather than pleasant, but later it yields the peaceful fruit of righteousness to those who have been trained by it" (Hebrews 12:11). And the psalmist confessed in later life: "Before I was afflicted I went astray but now I keep Your word. . . . It is good for me that I was afflicted, that I might learn Your statutes" (Psalm 119:67, 71).

The following verses bring us a beautiful example of a "family cross" being used, in God's providence, to bring an entire family to faith in Jesus as the Son of God and to eternal life through His name.

> After the two days He departed for Galilee. (For Jesus Himself had testified that a prophet has no honor in his own hometown.) So when He came to Galilee, the Galileans welcomed Him, having seen all that He had done in Jerusalem at the feast. For they too had gone to the feast.

Jesus Heals an Official's Son

> So He came again to Cana in Galilee, where He had made the water wine. And at Capernaum there was an official whose son was ill. When this man heard that Jesus had come from Judea to Galilee, he went to Him and asked Him to come down and heal his son, for he was at the point of death. So Jesus said to him, "Unless you see signs and wonders you will not believe." The official said to Him, "Sir, come down before my child dies." Jesus said to him, "Go; your son will live." The man believed the word that Jesus spoke to him and went on his way. As he was going down, his servants met him and told him that his son was recovering. So he asked them the hour when he began to get better, and they said to him, "Yesterday at the seventh hour the fever left him." The father knew that was the hour when Jesus had said to him, "Your son will live." And he himself believed, and all his household. This was now

the second sign that Jesus did when He had come from Judea to Galilee.

There are many striking features to this simple story. There is, first, the official's prayer for his son. How many a son, how many a daughter, owe their good fortune in this life and their eternal happiness in the life to come to the faithful prayers of a believing father or mother! And then there is the seeming rebuke of the Savior: "Unless you see signs and wonders you will not believe." The official's faith had to be tried; it had to be tested. Our faith, too, must often be purified of the dross we permit to accumulate. But we may be sure that, even as in the case of the Canaanite woman (Matthew 15:21–28) and of this official, there is always a gracious purpose behind these periods of painful testing.

Judge not the Lord by feeble sense,
But trust Him for His grace;
Behind a frowning providence
Faith sees a smiling face. *(LSB* 765:2)

To the official's persistent and repeated plea, "Sir, come down before my child dies," the Lord finally replies with the glorious assurance: "Go; your son will live." And we read: "The man believed the word that Jesus spoke to him and went on his way." That is Christian faith—relying solely on the simple word of Christ and acting on that word. Someone has said of Abraham that he believed the almost unbelievable promise of God and then obeyed the almost unobeyable command of God. Surely these words apply, at least in a measure, to this nobleman. He believed the almost unbelievable promise, "Your son will live," and then he obeyed the almost unobeyable command, "Go"!

Have we learned to do the same? If so, we shall find that our gracious God will give us beauty for our ashes, the oil of gladness for our mourning, and the garment of praise for our faint spirit (Isaiah 61:3), even as He did for this believing official in his distress. For under the overruling hand of God, the "sickness unto death" of the official's son was transformed into a "sickness unto life—eternal life" for him and his entire family!

Prayer

God moves in a mysterious way
His wonders to perform;
He plants His footsteps in the sea
And rides upon the storm.

His purposes will ripen fast,
Unfolding ev'ry hour;
The bud may have a bitter taste,
But sweet will be the flow'r.

Blind unbelief is sure to err
And scan His work in vain;
God is His own interpreter,
And He will make it plain.

You fearful saints, fresh courage take;
The clouds you so much dread
Are big with mercy and will break
In blessings on your head. Amen. (LSB 765:1, 3–5)

16

JESUS VISITS A HOSPITAL
John 5:1–16

WITH chapter 5 of John's Gospel, we move deeper into the gathering shadows of Calvary. Until now, the evangelist has told us very little about the growing opposition of the Jews to the claims of Jesus. There had been opposition, to be sure, but none so severe that John had thought it necessary to describe it in detail. From now on, however, the evangelist begins to speak in ominous tones about the impending climax. For the first time in his Gospel, he acquaints us with the smoldering desire of Christ's enemies to put the Savior to death.

But why this mounting hatred? John tells us in this and the following chapters. It is significant, for the present, to notice that one of the first demonstrations of open hostility to Christ was occasioned by a bedside visit in a hospital, Bethesda, "the house of mercy." He, whose love and mercy for lost mankind would bring Him to death on Calvary's cross, is hastened on His way of suffering by an act of mercy on a hopeless sufferer.

The Healing at the Pool on the Sabbath

After this there was a feast of the Jews, and Jesus went up to Jerusalem.

Now there is in Jerusalem by the Sheep Gate a pool, in Aramaic called Bethesda, which has five roofed colonnades. In these lay a multitude of invalids—blind, lame, and paralyzed. One man was there who had been an invalid for thirty-eight years. When Jesus saw him lying there and knew that he had already been there a long time, He said to him, "Do you want to be healed?" The sick man answered Him, "Sir, I have no one to put me into the pool when the water is stirred up, and while I am going another steps down before me." Jesus said to him, "Get up, take up your bed, and walk." And at once the man was healed, and he took up his bed and walked.

Now that day was the Sabbath. So the Jews said to the man who had been healed, "It is the Sabbath, and it is not lawful for you to take up your bed." But he answered them, "The man who healed me, that man said to me, 'Take up your bed, and walk.'" They asked him, "Who is the man who said to you, 'Take up your bed and walk'?" Now the man who had been healed did not know who it was, for Jesus had withdrawn, as there was a crowd in the place. Afterward Jesus found him in the temple and said to him, "See, you are well! Sin no more, that nothing worse may happen to you." The man went away and told the Jews that it was Jesus who had healed him. And this was why the Jews were persecuting Jesus, because He was doing these things on the Sabbath.

Of all the places in Jerusalem that Jesus could have visited that day, He chooses to visit a hospital. How totally like Him! "The Son of Man came to seek and to save the lost," He had said (Luke 19:10). "Come to Me, all who labor and are heavy laden, and I will give you rest," was His gracious invitation (Matthew 11:28). But here was a man who couldn't come, and so the Savior came to him. Do we consider it a part of our Christian calling to visit the sick? When were we in a hospital last?

If ever a man needed a friend, it was this man. Thirty-eight years in bed! What an eternity of helplessness it must have seemed to him! "Do you want to be healed?" How foolish that question would have been on the lips of anyone else but the Great Physician! But how loving, how rich with promise it was on the lips of Jesus! Jesus asks no probing questions about the sick man's past. He knew what was in his heart. He knew that this man had no greater desire than to be up and around and to be well again. And so without preliminaries, without the usual introductions, Jesus approaches the man and asks: "Do you want to be healed?" And a moment later: "Get up, take up your bed, and walk." Was there ever power and love like this?

An anxious patient lying on her sickbed turned to her doctor and asked, "Doctor, how long will I have to lie here and suffer?" "Just take it a day at a time," replied the kind and wise physician. Just a day at a time! What a comforting thought for those whom the Lord, in His unsearchable wisdom, has confined to a sickbed of many years or for those who have been otherwise afflicted. God, as it were, breaks their crosses into little pieces and asks them to carry only a piece at a time—day by day. And for each day He portions out the needed strength. "As your days, so shall your strength be" (Deuteronomy 33:25).

At the foot of every Christian sickbed stands the same Savior— "the same yesterday and today and forever" (Hebrews 13:8)—who stood at the bedside of the poor man at Bethesda. Let us become ever more keenly conscious of the Savior's cheering, healing presence in the sickroom of the Christian and of His ability to hallow every hour of illness that comes into our home. He is "the Lord, your healer" (Exodus 15:26). He is the Great Physician. His love has saved our souls; His love will share our sorrows; His love will help us bear our pain; His love can heal our bodies.

Prayer

I lay my wants on Jesus;
All fullness dwells in Him;
He heals all my diseases;
My soul He does redeem.
I lay my griefs on Jesus,
My burdens and my cares;
He from them all releases;
He all my sorrows shares.

I rest my soul on Jesus,
This weary soul of mine;
His right hand me embraces;
I on His breast recline.
I love the name of Jesus,
Immanuel, Christ, the Lord;
Like fragrance on the breezes
His name abroad is poured. Amen. (LSB 606:2–3)

FATHER AND SON
John 5:17–35

JOHN's Gospel is known especially for its lengthy and self-revealing discourses of the Savior. In the third chapter, we heard His long discourse with Nicodemus. In the fourth chapter, we listened to

Him as He spoke at length to the woman at the well. And now in the fifth chapter, we hear Him address Himself to the unbelieving Jews. Some Bible students regard the address that Jesus delivers in this chapter as His formal and official answer to the Council in reply to the charges laid against Him. The charges, we will recall, were primarily that He had broken the Sabbath by His miracle at the pool of Bethesda (John 5:1–16).

As we read the exalted language of the Savior's reply, we are moved to say with the psalmist, "Such knowledge is too wonderful for me; it is high; I cannot attain it" (Psalm 139:6). For in the following words, He reaches deep into the unsearchable mystery of the Godhead to explain the close relationship that exists between Him and His Father. We have in this address one of the clearest claims of the Savior that He is the Son of God. May the Holy Spirit bless these precious words upon our hearts, that we might "believe that Jesus is the Christ, the Son of God, and that by believing [we] may have life in His name" (John 20:31).

But Jesus answered them, "My Father is working until now, and I am working."

Jesus Is Equal with God

This was why the Jews were seeking all the more to kill Him; not only was Jesus breaking the Sabbath, but He was even calling God His own Father, making Himself equal with God.

The Authority of the Son

So Jesus said to them, "Truly, truly, I say to you, the Son can do nothing of His own accord, but only what He sees the Father doing. For whatever the Father does, that the Son does likewise. For the Father loves the Son and shows Him all that He Himself is doing. And greater works than these will He show Him, so that you may marvel. For as the Father raises the dead and gives them life, so also the Son gives life to whom He will. The Father judges no one, but has given all judgment to the Son, that all may honor the Son, just as they honor the Father. Whoever does not honor the Son does not honor the Father who sent Him. Truly, truly, I say to you, whoever hears My word and believes Him who sent Me has eternal life. He does not come into judgment, but has passed from death to life.

"Truly, truly, I say to you, an hour is coming, and is now here, when the dead will hear the voice of the Son of God, and those who hear will live. For as the Father has life in Himself, so He has granted the Son also to have life in Himself. And He has given Him authority to execute judgment, because He is the Son of Man. Do not marvel at this, for an hour is coming when all who are in the tombs will hear His voice and come out, those who have done good to the resurrection of life, and those who have done evil to the resurrection of judgment.

Witnesses to Jesus

"I can do nothing on My own. As I hear, I judge, and My judgment is just, because I seek not My own will but the will of Him who sent Me. If I alone bear witness about Myself, My testimony is not deemed true. There is another who bears witness about Me, and I know that the testimony that He bears about Me is true. You sent to John, and he has borne witness to the truth. Not that the testimony that I receive is from man, but I say these things so that you may be saved. He was a burning and shining lamp, and you were willing to rejoice for a while in his light.

Whole libraries could be written on the deep doctrines and glorious assurances contained in these few verses. We will try to compress them into the simple statement that Jesus is true God, the eternal Son of the Father, and that all who reject Him reject the Father also.

The story is told of an Early Church bishop who bowed respectfully before Emperor Theodosius but refused to bow to his son, Arcadius—at which the emperor, of course, showed great displeasure. But the stalwart Christian replied, "O King, how much more will Jehovah abhor those who reject His Son!" Yes, how much more!

According to John, all should "honor the Son, just as they honor the Father. Whoever does not honor the Son does not honor the Father who sent Him." These are the simple, clear, and unmistakable words of Christ. Without Christ, there is no God. To be without Christ is to be, in the strictest sense, an atheist! How distasteful this passage must be to the unbeliever, to the modernist who would like to pay lip service to Christ but hear nothing of His claim to Sonship with the Father. How embarrassing to all who in their ritual or worship would prefer to delete the name of Christ and be content with more general names for the Deity! To all, Christ here says, "Whoever does not honor the Son does not honor the Father who sent Him."

But how comforting are the claims of Christ to the heart of the Christian! Our Savior is no mere prophet, no mere teacher, no mere human leader. He is "very God of very God." He is the almighty Son of the Most High. He has come from the bosom of the Father. He is the Word made flesh, "True Godhead incarnate, omnipotent Word" *(TLH* 102:4). And He has been appointed by His Father to be the Savior and the Judge of all mankind.

To those who refuse to believe in His name, who refuse to accept Him as the Son of God and Savior of the world, He will be a stern Judge on the day when He returns to judge the living and the dead (Matthew 25:31–46). But to those who honor Him as the only-begotten of the Father and who trust in Him as their Savior and Redeemer, He will be a mighty Deliverer from sin, death, and the powers of hell.

How can we ever sufficiently thank God for the gift of such a Savior!

Prayer

O Lord, I thank You for the revelation of Your dear Son, Jesus Christ, as my divine Redeemer. And I thank and praise You for having brought me to knowledge of Him as my only hope for time and eternity. Grant, I pray You, that I may never dishonor His holy name, but that by word and deed I may extol His glory among my fellow men. I ask it in His name. Amen.

MORE WITNESSES
John 5:36–47

WE cannot read a chapter of John's Gospel without seeing how steadily, how irresistibly, he is leading his readers to the one conclusion that he has set as the aim and object of his book: "that you may believe that Jesus is the Christ, the Son of God, and that by believing you may have life in His name" (20:31).

In chapter 5, he recorded the Savior's long and formal reply to the unbelieving Jews who had challenged His right to heal on the Sabbath. The Savior asserts His right to work on the Sabbath Day by saying that He is the Son of God and therefore is Lord even of the Sabbath. And now to prove that He is indeed the Son of God, He lists a number of "witnesses"—a favorite word in John's Gospel.

The first witness He summons is His Father. Had not His Father testified at His Baptism, "This is My beloved Son" (Matthew 3:17)? His second witness is John the Baptist. "He has borne witness to the truth. . . . He was a burning and shining lamp" (John 5:33, 35). His third witness is His works. "The works that the Father has given Me to accomplish, the very works that I am doing, bear witness about Me that the Father has sent Me." And His final witness is the Old Testament—Moses and the Prophets. They "bear witness about Me."

May God grant us His Holy Spirit as we now read this concluding portion of the Savior's testimony.

"But the testimony that I have is greater than that of John. For the works that the Father has given Me to accomplish, the very works that I am doing, bear witness about Me that the Father has sent Me. And the Father who sent Me has Himself borne witness about Me. His voice you have never heard, His form you have never seen, and you do not have His word abiding in you, for you do not believe the one whom He has sent.

You search the Scriptures because you think that in them you have eternal life; and it is they that bear witness about Me, yet you refuse to come to Me that you may have life. I do not receive glory from people. But I know that you do not have the love of God within you. I have come in My Father's name, and you do not receive Me. If another comes in His own name, you will receive Him. How can you believe, when you receive glory from one another and do not seek the glory that comes from the only God? Do not think that I will accuse you to the Father. There is one who accuses you: Moses, on whom you have set your hope. For if you believed Moses, you would believe Me; for he wrote of Me. But if you do not believe his writings, how will you believe My words?"

When Christ says, "Search the Scriptures . . . they . . . bear witness about Me," we think of two well-known Bible stories. On the afternoon of the first Easter, we see the Savior and two downhearted disciples on the way to Emmaus. As we draw closer, we hear the Savior chide them gently for their lack of understanding when He says, " 'O foolish ones, and slow of heart to believe all that the prophets have spoken! Was it not necessary that the Christ should suffer these things and enter into His glory?' And beginning with Moses and all the Prophets, He interpreted to them in all the Scriptures the things concerning Himself" (Luke 24:25–27).

The second story is that of Philip and the Ethiopian eunuch. We are told that the eunuch had just been reading from Isaiah: "Like a lamb that is led to the slaughter, and like a sheep that before its shearers is silent, so He opened not his mouth" (53:7). And now he turns to Philip and asks, " 'About whom, I ask you, does the prophet say this, about himself or about someone else?' Then Philip opened his mouth, and beginning with this Scripture he told him the good news about Jesus" (Acts 8:34–35.)

Let us read our Bible, not as the scribes and Pharisees, who closed their eyes against the truth, but in order that we might be in the blessed company of Him who is our Lord and Savior and in whose name we shall be able to stand on that great day! "Search the Scriptures," He says. They "bear witness about Me."

Prayer

How precious is the Book Divine, By inspiration giv'n!
Bright as a lamp its doctrines shine To guide our souls to heav'n.

Its light, descending from above Our gloomy world to cheer,
Displays a Savior's boundless love And brings His glories near.

It shows to man his wand'ring ways, And where his feet have trod,
And brings to view the matchless grace Of a forgiving God.

This lamp through all the tedious night Of life shall guide our way
Till we behold the clearer light Of an eternal day. Amen.
(TLH 285:1–3, 6)

ABUNDANT BREAD
John 6:1–14

MARTIN LUTHER, in his explanation of the Fourth Petition of the Lord's Prayer, wrote, "God certainly gives daily bread to everyone without our prayers, even to all evil people, but we pray in this petition that God would lead us to realize this and to receive our daily bread with thanksgiving."

In other words, we are to recognize the label of heaven on every piece of food we eat. It has come to us from our Savior's hand. If that hand would ever withhold its blessing, all the scientific knowledge and all the accumulated skill of men could not produce a single slice of bread to satisfy our gnawing hunger.

How beautifully the psalmist expresses this when he says, "The eyes of all look to You, and You give them their food in due season. You open Your hand; You satisfy the desire of every living thing" (Psalm 145:15–16).

If ever there was a group of people who had every reason to recognize their dependence upon the Savior and to know that it was He who was giving them their daily bread, it was the five thousand who followed Him beyond the Sea of Galilee. The eyes of all looked to Him—and He gave them their food in due season! Do we always see the Savior's hand behind the food we eat? The softening rains of springtime, the welcome warmth of summer, and the ripening rays of the autumn sun—He holds them all in the hollow of His hand; and by the miracle of His providing love, He transforms them into daily bread for all His children, even as beyond the Sea of Galilee He multiplied the loaves and fish.

A striking instance of the Savior's ability and willingness to provide also for the wants of our body is given us in the opening of this sixth chapter of St. John's Gospel.

Jesus Feeds the Five Thousand

After this Jesus went away to the other side of the Sea of Galilee, which is the Sea of Tiberias. And a large crowd was following Him, because they saw the signs that He was doing on the sick. Jesus went up on the mountain, and there He sat down with His disciples. Now the Passover, the feast of the Jews, was at hand. Lifting up His eyes, then, and seeing that a large crowd was coming toward Him, Jesus said to Philip, "Where are we to buy bread, so that these people may eat?" He said this to test him, for He Himself knew what He would do. Philip answered Him, "Two hundred denarii would not buy enough bread for each of them to get a little." One of His disciples, Andrew, Simon Peter's brother, said to Him, "There is a boy here who has five barley loaves and two fish, but what are they for so many?" Jesus said, "Have the people sit down." Now there was much grass in the place. So the men sat down, about five thousand in number. Jesus then took the loaves, and when

He had given thanks, He distributed them to those who were seated. So also the fish, as much as they wanted. And when they had eaten their fill, He told His disciples, "Gather up the leftover fragments, that nothing may be lost." So they gathered them up and filled twelve baskets with fragments from the five barley loaves left by those who had eaten. When the people saw the sign that He had done, they said, "This is indeed the Prophet who is to come into the world!"

In the Savior's question addressed to Philip, "Where are we to buy bread?" we have an excellent example of the way in which God sometimes "tests" His children in order to accomplish His good and gracious purpose. By permitting Philip to measure his limited resources against the tremendous need of the moment, Jesus impresses Philip with the utter hopelessness of their present "bread problem" without the Savior's help. We may be sure Philip's appreciation of the Savior's miracle was the greater because of this "testing."

And in our own lives, how often have we learned, as Philip learned here, that "man's extremity is God's opportunity"?

Andrew's reply, "But what are they for so many?" is typically human. His arithmetic is right, but he is figuring without the Savior. Many a Christian family, as they take stock of their budget at the end of the month, become gratefully aware of the Savior's multiplying hand as they balance the columns—"How did we go so far on so little!" Five loaves and two fish with the Savior's blessing are worth more than all the riches in the world without His benediction!

We are told that Jesus prayed before He broke bread. If the Son of heaven addressed prayers of thanks to heaven for the food He ate, how much more should we fold our hands in prayer before and after every meal!

In asking His disciples to "gather up the leftover fragments," the Savior has given us an example of God-pleasing frugality and thrift. Nothing, not even the crumbs of the abundant bread He had supplied, was to be wasted. Are we exercising a careful, conscientious stewardship of all the blessings He has given us?

A BREAD KING?
John 6:15–27

IN every age, there have been those who failed to grasp the true spiritual nature of the Savior's kingdom. For instance, we read that immediately after Jesus fed the five thousand, there were some who wanted to make Him their king. Surely, they thought, a man who could convert scarcity into plenty and poverty into wealth would be the ideal head of their government.

Even the disciples of Jesus were not free from a purely bread-and-butter conception of the Savior's kingdom here on earth. After all, didn't they ask Him even at so late a date as the day of His ascension, "Lord, will You at this time restore the kingdom to Israel?" (Acts 1:6).

Two thousand years have not succeeded in erasing this fundamental error. To many, Christ is still a "bread king" and nothing more. They look to Him to solve almost every problem except the one that, above all others, He came to earth to solve: the sin problem!

They appeal to the Savior for solutions to the problems of economics, politics, morals, and international relations, but they refuse to listen to what He has to say about sin, forgiveness, and eternal life in heaven through faith in His atoning blood. To them, the Savior is a "social" savior, His Gospel a "social" gospel, and His kingdom a kingdom of mere externals.

Just what Jesus thought of such a notion about His kingdom is clearly seen from the following verses:

> Perceiving then that they were about to come and take Him by force to make Him king, Jesus withdrew again to the mountain by Himself.

Jesus Walks on Water

> When evening came, His disciples went down to the sea, got into a boat, and started across the sea to Capernaum. It was now dark, and Jesus had not yet come to them. The sea became rough because a strong wind was blowing. When they had rowed about three or four miles, they saw Jesus walking on the sea and coming near the boat, and they were frightened. But He said to them, "It is I; do not be afraid." Then they were glad to take Him into the boat, and immediately the boat was at the land to which they were going.

I Am the Bread of Life

> On the next day the crowd that remained on the other side of the sea saw that there had been only one boat there, and that Jesus had not entered the boat with His disciples, but that His disciples had gone away alone. Other boats from Tiberias came near the place where they had eaten the bread after the Lord had given thanks. So when the crowd saw that Jesus was not there, nor His disciples, they themselves got into the boats and went to Capernaum, seeking Jesus.
>
> When they found Him on the other side of the sea, they said to Him, "Rabbi, when did You come here?" Jesus answered them, "Truly, truly, I say to you, you are seeking Me, not because you saw signs, but because you ate your fill of the loaves. Do not labor for the food that perishes, but for the food that endures to eternal life, which the Son of Man will give to you. For on Him God the Father has set His seal."

"Following Christ" does not necessarily make one His disciple. The Jews who were eager to make Christ their king surely went to great pains to "follow" Him—they hired a boat and crossed the Sea of Galilee—but they were following a Christ of their own imagination. How different was the Christ of their imagination from the Christ of the third, fourth, and fifth chapters of St. John's Gospel— the Christ who had told Nicodemus that He would have to be lifted up upon the cross for the sins of all mankind, the Christ who had spoken to the woman at the well about the precious water of life, and the Christ who had told the unbelieving Jews at Jerusalem that He was the Son of God, coequal with the Father. That was not the kind of Christ they thought they were following. "You are seeking Me . . . because you ate your fill of the loaves." That was the kind of leader they were after!

"Do not labor for the food that perishes, but for the food that endures to eternal life, which the Son of Man will give to you." These are words that we well might ponder. How similar to the Savior's words on another occasion: "Seek first the kingdom of God" (Matthew 6:33), or His words to Martha, who indeed was laboring "for the food that perishes": "One thing is necessary" (Luke 10:42).

Have we, in our own lives, learned to place proper value on "the food that perishes" and "the food that endures to eternal life"? The "loaves" have great attraction also for the Christian. We are in danger of overestimating the importance of things that have value only for this life and of underestimating the importance of things that have value for the life to come. Let us be constantly on our guard: the scales of our lives, the weights and measures by which we judge the enduring worth of things, need daily testing!

Prayer

Jesus, Thou art mine forever, Dearer far than earth to me;
Neither life nor death shall sever Those sweet ties which bind to Thee.

Thou alone art all my Treasure, Who hast died that I may live;
Thou conferrest noblest pleasure, Who dost all my sins forgive.

Jesus, Thou art mine forever; Never suffer me to stray.
Let me in my weakness never Cast my priceless pearl away.

Lamb of God, I do implore Thee, Guard, support me, lest I fall.
Let me evermore adore Thee; Be my everlasting All. Amen.
(TLH 357:1, 3, 5–6)

THE BREAD OF LIFE
John 6:28–51

TODAY we read about food. With every forward step of science, we see more clearly in what a marvelous manner our heavenly Father has cared for the physical needs of His children: in His infinite wisdom, He has placed into the food He provides us exactly those ingredients that are needed to support our body and life.

Similarly, but in an unspeakably more sublime manner, He has provided for the needs of our soul. He has given us a spiritual bread, a "bread that comes down from heaven," that will meet our every need. *Jesus is that bread!* "I am the bread of life; whoever comes to Me shall not hunger, and whoever believes in Me shall never thirst."

We who believe in Christ have experienced the blessed truth of that promise. There is no need in our spiritual life that Jesus cannot fill, no wish that He cannot satisfy. Peace of mind, peace of conscience, assurance of the love of God, and eternal fellowship with Him in heaven—these are the immeasurable gifts that have become ours through Jesus, our "bread of life" that has come down from heaven. What precious food! And how perfectly adapted to our needs! "Sir, give us this bread always"—this is the thought the Savior now develops:

Then they said to Him, "What must we do, to be doing the works of God?" Jesus answered them, "This is the work of God, that you believe in Him whom He has sent." So they said to Him, "Then what sign do You do, that we may see and believe You? What work do You perform? Our fathers ate the manna in the wilderness; as it is written, 'He gave them bread from heaven to eat.' " Jesus then said to them, "Truly, truly, I say to you, it was not Moses who gave you the bread from heaven, but My Father gives you the true bread from heaven. For the bread of God is He who comes down from heaven and gives life to the world." They said to Him, "Sir, give us this bread always."

Jesus said to them, "I am the bread of life; whoever comes to Me shall not hunger, and whoever believes in Me shall never thirst. But I said to you that you have seen Me and yet do not believe. All that the Father gives Me will come to Me, and whoever comes to Me I will never cast out. For I have come down from heaven, not to do My own will but the will of Him who sent me. And this is the will of Him who sent Me, that I should lose nothing of all that He has given Me, but raise it up on the last day. For this is the will of My Father, that everyone who looks on the Son and believes in Him should have eternal life, and I will raise Him up on the last day."

So the Jews grumbled about Him, because He said, "I am the bread that came down from heaven." They said, "Is not this Jesus, the son of Joseph, whose father and mother we know? How does He now say, 'I have come down from heaven'?" Jesus answered them, "Do not grumble among yourselves. No one can come to Me unless the Father who sent Me draws Him. And I will raise him up on the last day. It is written in the Prophets, 'And they will all be taught by God.' Everyone who has heard and learned from the Father comes to Me—not that anyone has seen the Father except He who is from God; He has seen the Father. Truly, truly, I say to you, whoever believes has eternal life. I am the bread of life. Your fathers ate the manna in the wilderness, and they died. This is the bread that comes down from heaven, so that one may eat of it and not die. I am

the living bread that came down from heaven. If anyone eats
of this bread, he will live forever. And the bread that I will give
for the life of the world is My flesh."

As in chapters 3–5, in which John records the highly instructive discourses of the Savior with Nicodemus, the woman at the well, and
with the unbelieving Jews, in this chapter John has preserved for us
one of the most beautiful of Christ's discourses. Let us look at it a
bit more closely.

We have here the first great "I am" of the Savior. "I am the
bread of life." Later, He was to say, "I am the light of the world"
(John 8:12); "I am the door" (10:7, 9); "I am the good shepherd"
(10:11, 14); "I am the way, and the truth, and the life" (14:6). We
notice that it is John who records all of the Savior's astounding "I
am" statements. Why? To reinforce the purpose of his Gospel: to
establish the divine Sonship of the Savior.

When God spoke to Moses from the burning bush, He said, "I
AM WHO I AM. . . . Say this to the people of Israel, 'I AM has sent me
to you'" (Exodus 3:14). As the only-begotten Son, who has come
from the bosom of the Father, Jesus now applies that sublime and
"unspeakable" name of the Father to Himself because it is His name
too. Christ is the eternal and the great "I AM"! But He reveals the
good and gracious purpose of God when He adds to that majestic
name His tender attributes: "I am the bread of life"; "I am the good
shepherd"; and so forth.

Notice, too, how frequently in this and other chapters Jesus uses
such expressions as "I have come down from heaven" and "I am the
bread that came down from heaven." No other person could speak
like that. You and I were born. Jesus "came down from heaven."
He is the eternal Word made flesh.

At least six different times in this brief section, Jesus refers to the
resurrection of the body and eternal life in heaven. He is still speaking
to the delegation of Jews who had come across the Sea of Galilee to
make Him their "bread king," and He wishes to impress them with
the fact that His kingdom is not of this world, but that His purpose
on earth is to save immortal souls for heaven.

But we would miss the glorious comfort of this chapter if we did not remind ourselves that the precious bread of life, of whom this chapter speaks, is ours in fullest measure. Let us turn to it again and again for spiritual nourishment and for strength to bear the burdens of the day. Our only hope for time and for eternity is in the blessed name of Jesus.

> It makes the wounded spirit whole
> And calms the heart's unrest;
> 'Tis manna to the hungry soul
> And to the weary, rest. *(LSB 524:2)*

Prayer

O Lord Jesus, I thank You that You are the bread of my life. Grant that I may come to You daily for the assurance of my forgiveness and for renewed strength to resist the temptations of the devil, the world, and my flesh. Grant that by Your Holy Spirit I may be enabled to lead a life acceptable in Your sight, O Lord, my Savior and Redeemer. Amen.

WILL YOU ALSO GO AWAY?
John 6:52–71

IT has always been the same. Whenever the Church has descended from high-sounding generalities and has "got down" to the real fundamentals of the Christian faith—repentance and salvation through the blood of Christ—there have been those who handed in their resignation. "I quit." "I resign."

Jesus, too, had to experience this. The "church supper Christians" who had followed Him across the Sea of Galilee were indeed willing to listen to Him for a while. But when He came to that part in His sermon where He said, "Unless you eat the flesh of the Son of Man and drink His blood, you have no life in you," they had heard all they wanted to hear. Even some of His disciples thought Jesus had become a little strong; they said, "This is a hard saying; who can listen to it?" "After this many of His disciples turned back and no longer walked with Him."

The stream always divides at the cross. Pious Simeon had said, "This child is appointed for the fall and rising of many in Israel, and for a sign that is opposed . . . so that thoughts from many hearts may be revealed" (Luke 2:34). The following verses show us how "the thoughts from many hearts" were revealed by the Savior's preaching of the cross on this occasion.

The Jews then disputed among themselves, saying, "How can this man give us His flesh to eat?" So Jesus said to them, "Truly, truly, I say to you, unless you eat the flesh of the Son of Man and drink His blood, you have no life in you. Whoever feeds on My flesh and drinks My blood has eternal life, and I will raise him up on the last day. For My flesh is true food, and My blood is true drink. Whoever feeds on My flesh and drinks My blood abides in Me, and I in him. As the living Father sent Me, and I live because of the Father, so whoever feeds on Me, he also will live because of Me. This is the bread that came down from heaven, not like the bread the fathers ate and died. Whoever feeds on this bread will live forever." Jesus said these things in the synagogue, as He taught at Capernaum.

The Words of Eternal Life

When many of His disciples heard it, they said, "This is a hard saying; who can listen to it?" But Jesus, knowing in Himself that His disciples were grumbling about this, said to them, "Do you take offense at this? Then what if you were to see the Son of Man ascending to where He was before? It is the Spirit who gives life; the flesh is no help at all. The words that I have spoken to you are spirit and life. But there are some of you who do not believe." (For Jesus knew from the beginning who those were who did not believe, and who it was who would betray Him.) And He said, "This is why I told you that no one can come to Me unless it is granted him by the Father."

After this many of his disciples turned back and no longer walked with Him. So Jesus said to the Twelve, "Do you want to go away as well?" Simon Peter answered Him, "Lord, to whom shall we go? You have the words of eternal life, and we have believed, and have come to know, that You are the Holy One of God." Jesus answered them, "Did I not choose you, the Twelve? And yet one of you is a devil." He spoke of Judas the son of Simon Iscariot, for he, one of the Twelve, was going to betray Him.

What did Jesus mean when He said, "Unless you eat the flesh of the Son of Man and drink His blood, you have no life in you"? That He was not referring to the Lord's Supper is evident from the fact that the Sacrament had not yet been instituted—as well as from the fact that He here makes the eating and drinking of His flesh and blood absolutely necessary for salvation, which the Lord's Supper is not.

The only essential to salvation is faith—faith in the broken body and shed blood of Jesus, broken and shed for the forgiveness of our sins. And that is what the Savior says in this passage: "unless you eat the flesh of the Son of Man and drink His blood, you have no life in you." Eating and drinking in the above verses, then, mean simply *believing*.

But the Jews in general, and some of Christ's disciples in particular, would have none of this doctrine. And so they left. "Do you want to go away as well?" We can almost hear the Savior's loving heart beat against His breast as He puts the fateful question. One by one His listeners had been turning their backs on Him, and now—"Do you want to go away as well?"

Simon Peter answered, "Lord, to whom shall we go? You have the words of eternal life, and we have believed, and have come to know, that You are the Holy One of God." Peter was sure! Of what was he sure? "That You are the Holy One of God." And being sure of that, Peter was sure that there was nothing else in all the world that could make up for his loss if he would ever lose his Savior.

Blessed Peter! Peter was the spokesman for the Twelve; may he be our spokesman too. With him, we take our stand at our Savior's side and say, "Lord, to whom shall we go? You have the words of eternal life, and we have believed, and have come to know, that You are the Holy One of God."

Prayer

O from our sins, Lord turn Your face;
Absolve us through Your boundless grace.
Be with us in our anguish still;
Free us at last from ev'ry ill.

So we with all our hearts each day
To You our glad thanksgiving pay,
Then walk obedient to Your Word,
And now and ever praise You, Lord. Amen.
(LSB 615:5–6).

CHRIST'S UNBELIEVING BROTHERS

John 7:1–13

EVER since the uproar that had followed His healing of the helpless man at the pool of Bethesda, Jesus had avoided further contact with the Jews of Judea, for "His hour had not yet come" (John 7:30). Instead of carrying on His ministry in or near the capital city, we read that He "went about in Galilee."

Six months had passed, and the Jewish Feast of Booths, their annual harvest festival, was at hand. And so the unbelieving brothers of Jesus (they may have been cousins, half brothers, or stepbrothers) take this occasion to taunt and jeer Him.

They say in effect, "If You are really all that You claim to be, now is Your opportunity to go to Jerusalem and to do something big, something sensational, to convince the people of Your claims. No one who is looking for the public recognition of the Jews will hide himself here in far-off Galilee."

The Savior, however, was not to be stampeded into any rash act by His unbelieving brethren (see Matthew 4:5–7). He chides them gently but firmly. He tells them, "Your time is always here. The world cannot hate you, but it hates Me because I testify about it that its works are evil."

And so His brethren go up to the city without Him. But we read that, a little while later, the Savior Himself goes to the city also, but in a manner different from the one they had suggested (alone and "not publicly but in private") and for a different purpose: to proclaim His doctrine. That is, in brief, what John tells us in the following verses.

Jesus at the Feast of Booths

After this Jesus went about in Galilee. He would not go about in Judea, because the Jews were seeking to kill Him. Now the Jews' Feast of Booths was at hand. So His brothers said to Him, "Leave here and go to Judea, that Your disciples also may see the works You are doing. For no one works in secret if he seeks to be known openly. If You do these things, show Yourself to the world." For not even His brothers believed in Him. Jesus said to them, "My time has not yet come, but your time is always here. The world cannot hate you, but it hates Me because I testify about it that its works are evil. You go up to the feast. I am not going up to this feast, for My time has not yet fully come." After saying this, He remained in Galilee.

But after His brothers had gone up to the feast, then He also went up, not publicly but in private. The Jews were looking for Him at the feast, and saying, "Where is He?" And there was much muttering about Him among the people. While some said, "He is a good man," others said, "No, He is leading the people astray." Yet for fear of the Jews no one spoke openly of Him.

That some of Jesus' closest relatives did not believe in Him is almost unthinkable to us. Yet the Holy Spirit tells us in words that are clear and unmistakable: "For not even His brothers believed in Him." Some of us may have near and dear ones who do not believe. Perhaps the fault is ours. Perhaps we have failed in our duty of witnessing for the Savior. But if we have been leading the kind of life that Christ expects of us and have been testifying to our relatives of the truth of Christ's Gospel and have been carrying their needs to the throne of grace in prayer, then we may draw comfort from the knowledge that "not even His brothers believed in Him"—despite His testimony and His spotless, sinless, holy life.

But we may find even greater encouragement in the knowledge that Jesus' unbelieving brothers did not remain unbelievers. Some of them, perhaps all of them, became entirely different persons after the Savior's resurrection and joined Mary, the mother of Jesus, in her worship of the Lord (Acts 1:14). The power of unbelief is great; the power of God's grace in Christ is even greater.

Let us continue to pray, to plead, to implore—to storm the gates of heaven—on behalf of any unbelieving brothers and sisters who might be numbered among those who are dear to us, knowing that God's promise still stands sure: "The prayer of a righteous person has great power as it is working" (James 5:16).

Prayer
O Christ, our true and only light,
Enlighten those who sit in night;
Let those afar now hear Your voice
And in Your fold with us rejoice.

Fill with the radiance of Your grace
  The souls now lost in error's maze;
Enlighten those whose inmost minds
  Some dark delusion haunts and blinds.

Shine on the darkened and the cold;
  Recall the wand'rers to Your fold.
Unite all those who walk apart;
  Confirm the weak and doubting heart,

That they with us may evermore
  Such grace with wond'ring thanks adore
And endless praise to You be giv'n
  By all Your Church in earth and heav'n. Amen.
(LSB 839: 1–2, 4–5)

UNBELIEF IN THE TEMPLE
John 7:14–31

THE Feast of Booths, which lasted a whole week, was now in full swing. For a day or two, the Savior had kept Himself in the background, lest He stir up a turmoil prematurely. But when the festival was about half over, perhaps on the third or fourth day, He went to the temple to teach. That most of the Jews in the temple were in no mood to accept Christ and His message is clearly evident from the incidents John records in the remainder of this seventh chapter of his Gospel.

About the middle of the feast Jesus went up into the temple and began teaching. The Jews therefore marveled, saying, "How is it that this man has learning, when He has never studied?" So Jesus answered them, "My teaching is not Mine, but

His who sent Me. If anyone's will is to do God's will, he will know whether the teaching is from God or whether I am speaking on My own authority. The one who speaks on his own authority seeks his own glory; but the one who seeks the glory of Him who sent Him is true, and in Him there is no falsehood. Has not Moses given you the law? Yet none of you keeps the law. Why do you seek to kill Me?" The crowd answered, "You have a demon! Who is seeking to kill you?" Jesus answered them, "I did one work, and you all marvel at it. Moses gave you circumcision (not that it is from Moses, but from the fathers), and you circumcise a man on the Sabbath. If on the Sabbath a man receives circumcision, so that the law of Moses may not be broken, are you angry with Me because on the Sabbath I made a man's whole body well? Do not judge by appearances, but judge with right judgment."

Can This Be the Christ?

Some of the people of Jerusalem therefore said, "Is not this the man whom they seek to kill? And here He is, speaking openly, and they say nothing to Him! Can it be that the authorities really know that this is the Christ? But we know where this man comes from, and when the Christ appears, no one will know where He comes from." So Jesus proclaimed, as He taught in the temple, "You know Me, and you know where I come from? But I have not come of My own accord. He who sent Me is true, and Him you do not know. I know Him, for I come from Him, and He sent Me." So they were seeking to arrest Him, but no one laid a hand on Him, because His hour had not yet come. Yet many of the people believed in Him. They said, "When the Christ appears, will He do more signs than this man has done?"

From His unbelieving brethren in Galilee, Jesus had come to His unbelieving countrymen in Jerusalem. What a lonely, solitary figure it is that John reveals to us in this seventh chapter! "He was in the world, and the world was made through Him, yet the world did not know Him. He came to His own, and His own people did not receive Him" (John 1:10–11). "He was despised and rejected by men" (Isaiah 53:3).

Let us look at this dialogue in the temple a little more closely. "How is it that this man has learning, when He has never studied?" they ask. He is not a licensed preacher! He has no diploma from our rabbinical schools! How is it that He teaches in the temple?

"My teaching is not Mine, but His who sent Me," replied Jesus. He was, indeed, a licensed preacher. Had Jesus not come from the school of His Father, and had not His Father accredited Him with a divine diploma: "This is My beloved Son, with whom I am well pleased; listen to Him" (Matthew 17:5; see also 3:17)? "No, My teaching is not Mine," He says, "but His who sent Me." "No one has ever seen God; the only God, who is at the Father's side, He has made Him known" (John 1:18). Christ is the heaven-taught and heaven-sent Teacher!

Such a claim, of course, again brought up the question of the Savior's origin. Was He sent by God? Was He really the promised Messiah? "No!" said the Jews. "But we know where this man comes from, and when the Christ appears, no one will know where He comes from."

To this, Jesus replies with one of those rare instances of irony recorded in the Gospels: "You know Me, and you know where I come from?" As much as to say, "You do, do you?"—"I have not come of My own accord. He who sent Me is true, and Him you do not know. I know Him, for I come from Him, and He sent Me."

What a reply! And what an effect! It was the same effect that the faithful preaching of the Word always has. To some it was a savor of life unto life, to others a savor of death unto death. For we read that immediately some "were seeking to arrest Him, but no one laid a hand on Him, because His hour had not yet come." And of others, we read that they "believed in Him. They said, 'When the Christ appears, will He do more signs than this man has done?' "

Do we see how the evangelist in chapter after chapter of his Gospel has preserved particularly those incidents and statements from the life of our blessed Lord that will confirm our faith in His

Messiahship, His divine Sonship, and His all-embracing, all-redeeming Saviorhood? Oh, let us thank God for this unspeakably precious revelation! With the small number of believers in the temple that day and with the great unnumbered throng of the faithful of all ages, let us say with hearts full of faith: "We have believed, and have come to know, that You are the Holy One of God" (John 6:69).

Prayer

O Lord Jesus, You have revealed the loving heart of Your Father
to sinful men, and we thank You for this glorious revelation.
Teach us evermore to know and do Your will. Grant that, trusting
solely in Your mercy and Your merit, we may be numbered among
those who dwell before Your presence throughout the endless ages.
We ask this, relying on Your promise. Amen.

CAPTIVES OF CHRIST
John 7:32–53

THIS appearance of Christ in the temple in the midst of the Feast of Booths had created a stir. His fearless preaching, His bold teaching, and His astounding claims had become the talk of the city. Could this be, indeed, "that Prophet"? "Yes!" said some. "No!" said others. "So there was a division among the people over Him."

At this point, the chief priests and Pharisees decided that the moment had come for them to intervene with a strong hand. The moment had come for them to put an end to the activities of this presumptuous impostor! And so they call the officers of the temple police and send them to arrest Jesus as a disturber of the peace and as a perverter of the people.

Did these temple guards return with their prisoner bound and tied as the chief priests had expected? The evangelist unfolds the story:

Officers Sent to Arrest Jesus

The Pharisees heard the crowd muttering these things about Him, and the chief priests and Pharisees sent officers to arrest Him. Jesus then said, "I will be with you a little longer, and then I am going to Him who sent Me. You will seek Me and you will not find Me. Where I am you cannot come." The Jews said to one another, "Where does this man intend to go that we will not find Him? Does He intend to go to the Dispersion among the Greeks and teach the Greeks? What does He mean by saying, 'You will seek Me and you will not find Me,' and, 'Where I am you cannot come'?"

Rivers of Living Water

On the last day of the feast, the great day, Jesus stood up and cried out, "If anyone thirsts, let him come to Me and drink. Whoever believes in Me, as the Scripture has said, 'Out of his heart will flow rivers of living water.'" Now this He said about the Spirit, whom those who believed in Him were to receive, for as yet the Spirit had not been given, because Jesus was not yet glorified.

Division Among the People

When they heard these words, some of the people said, "This really is the Prophet." Others said, "This is the Christ." But some said, "Is the Christ to come from Galilee? Has not the Scripture said that the Christ comes from the offspring of David, and comes from Bethlehem, the village where David was?" So there was a division among the people over Him. Some of them wanted to arrest Him, but no one laid hands on Him.

The officers then came to the chief priests and Pharisees, who said to them, "Why did you not bring Him?" The officers answered, "No one ever spoke like this man!" The Pharisees

answered them, "Have you also been deceived? Have any of
the authorities or the Pharisees believed in Him? But this
crowd that does not know the law is accursed." Nicodemus,
who had gone to Him before, and who was one of them, said
to them, "Does our law judge a man without first giving him
a hearing and learning what he does?" They replied, "Are you
from Galilee too? Search and see that no prophet arises from
Galilee."

They went each to his own house.

Those who had been sent to arrest the Savior returned as *captives*
of His eloquence. "Why did you not bring Him?" demanded the
priests. "No one ever spoke like this man!" replied the police. In a
sense, they had brought the Savior with them. There lingered in their
hearts the unforgettable picture of One who "was teaching them as
one who had authority, and not as their scribes" (Matthew 7:29).
They had not laid hold of Jesus, but Jesus had laid hold of them!

The fanatical Saul had set out on the road to Damascus "breathing threats and murder against the disciples of the Lord" (Acts 9:1).
It was his avowed intention and inflexible purpose to search out
the followers of Christ and "bring them bound to Jerusalem" (9:2).
Instead, Saul was brought "bound" into Damascus, bound by the
exalted and glorified Christ, whom he had seen while on the way.
Paul had, indeed, been arrested, "apprehended," by the Savior,
whose work he had set out to bring to naught.

And even so it has been down through the ages. Again and again,
it has been true that those who came to scoff remained to pray—
happy prisoners of the overpowering grace of Jesus!

And now notice the weak retort of the Pharisees—in reply to
the testimony of the temple guards. "Have you also been deceived?
Have any of the authorities or the Pharisees believed in Him? But
this crowd that does not know the law is accursed." Surely, there
was more heat than light in that answer! They had nothing to say,
and so they said it loudly. "You illiterate policemen! Are you going
to let yourselves be taken in by this 'impostor'? Have any of the educated Pharisees believed on Him?"

But just a minute! There was a Pharisee who believed in Him. Nicodemus, the man who had come to Jesus by night (John 3), raised a timid, but nevertheless honest, voice in defense of the Savior. "Does our law judge a man without first giving him a hearing and learning what he does?" Here was an earnest plea for fair play. But fair play was not to be our Savior's lot. He who knew no sin was to be made sin for us, "that in Him we might become the righteousness of God" (2 Corinthians 5:21).

One more remark before we close our meditation on this important seventh chapter. We cannot escape the sense of tragic disappointment that breathes through its closing sentence. What was the upshot of the Savior's brilliant and forceful testimony in the temple at this Feast of Booths? Did the multitudes spread their garments in His way, strew His path with palm branches, and exult, "Hosanna to the Son of David!" They did nothing of the kind. The chilling epitaph John places at the end of this chapter reads simply, "They went each to his own house."

"O Jerusalem, Jerusalem, the city that kills the prophets and stones those who are sent to it! How often would I have gathered your children together as a hen gathers her brood under her wings, and you would not!" (Matthew 23:37). God grant that we may recognize the glorious opportunities of this, our day of grace!

Prayer

Today Your mercy calls us To wash away our sin.
However great our trespass, Whatever we have been,
However long from mercy Our hearts have turned away,
Your precious blood can wash us And make us clean today. Amen.
(LSB 915:1)

WHERE MISERY MET MERCY

John 8:1–11

IT was the morning after the Feast of Booths. The Pharisees were smarting under the rebuffs of the past few days and were determined to trap Jesus at all costs. Into the silence of the temple, where He sat teaching, they brought a woman who had been "caught in adultery." And with all the deceit and cunning for which they were known, they confronted Jesus with the question, "Now in the Law Moses commanded us to stone such women. So what do You say?"

Here was an airtight dilemma, they thought. If Jesus said she should not be stoned, then the Jews would reject Him as their Messiah, for Moses had expressly commanded that an adulteress be put to death (Leviticus 20:10). But if He said she should be stoned, then the Pharisees could deliver Him to the Roman authorities, for the Roman government had decreed that the Jews could put no man to death (John 18:31). At last, they thought, they had Him cornered—and in the presence of a host of witnesses who had gathered in the temple.

Before we read the record of how Jesus handled this delicate situation, let us notice the heartless fiendishness and the mean hypocrisy of the Pharisees. They showed their heartlessness by exposing this wretched woman and dragging her into the temple to serve their purpose in a clever scheme they concocted. And they show their mean hypocrisy by forgetting all about the man in the case (whom they probably knew) and who, if they were serious in quoting the Law of Moses, should have suffered the same punishment as the woman. But they were not as serious that morning as they were clever—and so they confront the Savior with a difficult dilemma. And how did He solve it? We read:

The Woman Caught in Adultery

But Jesus went to the Mount of Olives. Early in the morning
He came again to the temple. All the people came to Him, and
He sat down and taught them. The scribes and the Pharisees
brought a woman who had been caught in adultery, and placing her in the midst they said to Him, "Teacher, this woman
has been caught in the act of adultery. Now in the Law Moses
commanded us to stone such women. So what do You say?"
This they said to test Him, that they might have some charge
to bring against Him. Jesus bent down and wrote with His
finger on the ground. And as they continued to ask Him, He
stood up and said to them, "Let him who is without sin among
you be the first to throw a stone at her." And once more He
bent down and wrote on the ground. But when they heard it,
they went away one by one, beginning with the older ones,
and Jesus was left alone with the woman standing before Him.
Jesus stood up and said to her, "Woman, where are they? Has
no one condemned you?" She said, "No one, Lord." And Jesus
said, "Neither do I condemn you; go, and from now on sin no
more."

"Let him who is without sin among you be the first to throw a stone
at her." By that one sentence, Jesus accomplished three important
purposes. First, He avoided the trap that had been so cleverly set and
turned the tables on His enemies. Second, He preached a sermon
of withering law to the hypocritical and self-righteous Pharisees, of
whom we read that they left the temple one by one. And, finally,
by this brief but brilliant sentence the Savior preached the sweetest Gospel to this sinful woman. By that one sentence, she knew
that Jesus was her friend. In that one sentence, misery and mercy
had met!

Do we see a picture of ourselves in this sinful woman? The case
against us is just as complete and convicting as it was against her.
"There is not a righteous man on earth who does good and never
sins" (Ecclesiastes 7:20). And the Law is clear too: "The soul who sins
shall die" (Ezekiel 18:4). If the Law were to exact its just demands,

there would indeed be no hope for us. "If You, O Lord, should mark iniquities, O Lord, who could stand?" (Psalm 130:3).

That is where Christ comes in. He who alone had power to execute the sentence caused the sentence to be pronounced upon Himself. "He was wounded"—scourged, beaten, crucified—"for our transgressions" (Isaiah 53:5). And now from the blessed lips of Him who holds the keys of hell and of heaven, we hear the precious words of pardon: "Neither do I condemn you; go, and from now on sin no more."

With all forgiven sinners of all ages, we can exult in the words of St. Paul: "There is therefore now no condemnation for those who are in Christ Jesus" (Romans 8:1). And again: "Who shall bring any charge against God's elect? It is God who justifies. Who is to condemn? Christ Jesus is the one who died—more than that, who was raised—who is at the right hand of God, who indeed is interceding for us" (Romans 8:33–34).

Prayer

Just as I am and waiting not
To rid my soul of one dark blot,
To Thee, whose blood can cleanse each spot,
O Lamb of God, I come, I come.
Just as I am, Thou wilt receive,
Wilt welcome, pardon, cleanse, relieve;
Because Thy promise I believe,
O Lamb of God, I come, I come. Amen.
(LSB 570:2, 5)

THE LIGHT
OF THE WORLD

John 8:12–20

IT was still the morning after the Feast of Booths. On the last day of the feast, as a climax to the weeklong celebration, two immense oil-fed candelabra would throw a flood of light throughout the temple court. This was to symbolize the pillar of fire by which God had guided the children of Israel through the darkness of the wilderness (Exodus 13:21).

It was on the morning after this great celebration—when the great lights had gone out and the people of Jerusalem had returned to the routine of their everyday existence—that Jesus stood up in the temple and cried out, "I am the light of the world. Whoever follows Me will not walk in darkness, but will have the light of life."

With this background, there could be no doubt in the minds of the Jews as to what Jesus meant. He was the light that had been pre-figured in Old Testament symbols. He was the light of the world, the "light of the Gentiles," the light that had been promised of old (Isaiah 42:6; 49:6; 60:1–3; Luke 2:32; John 1:9).

That the Jews understood full well that Jesus was claiming to be the Son of God and promised Messiah is evident from their bitter response, which John recorded in the remainder of this eighth chapter. We read first only a brief section:

I Am the Light of the World

Again Jesus spoke to them, saying, "I am the light of the world. Whoever follows Me will not walk in darkness, but will have the light of life." So the Pharisees said to Him, "You are bearing witness about Yourself; Your testimony is not true." Jesus answered, "Even if I do bear witness about Myself, My testimony is true, for I know where I came from and where I am going, but you do not know where I come from or where I am going. You judge according to the flesh; I judge no one. Yet even if I do judge, My judgment is true, for it is not I alone who judge, but I and the Father who sent Me. In your Law it is written that the testimony of two people is true. I am the one who bears witness about Myself, and the Father who sent Me bears witness about Me." They said to Him therefore, "Where is Your Father?" Jesus answered, "You know neither Me nor My Father. If you knew Me, you would know My Father also." These words He spoke in the treasury, as He taught in the temple; but no one arrested Him, because His hour had not yet come.

We have here another of the Savior's great "I am" statements. We have already heard Him say, in the sixth chapter of this Gospel, "I am the bread of life" to soul-hungry men. Here He says, "I am the light of the world" to men who are stumbling in darkness.

How the world is groping for light! Darkness covers the earth, and deep darkness envelops the people! One by one the candles of man's reason have been lighted and lifted, but one by one they have sputtered and gone out, leaving the darkness deeper than before. Philosophy, science, education, "religion" so called—one after the other has held forth bright promise, but all have only contributed their ashes to the darkness that covers the people. None of them has produced the light of life!

In the midst of these broken lamps and melted candles, our blessed Lord towers heavenward as that "true light, which enlightens everyone" (John 1:9). "In Him was life, and the life was the light of men" (1:4). His Gospel is the pillar of light that will lead us through the darkness of this present wilderness into the Promised Land above. "Your word," O Christ, "is a lamp to my feet and a light to my path" (Psalm 119:105).

Prayer

I heard the voice of Jesus say, "I am this dark world's light.
Look unto Me; thy morn shall rise And all thy day be bright."
I looked to Jesus, and I found In Him my star, my sun;
And in that light of life I'll walk Till trav'ling days are done.
(LSB 699:3)

Even so may it be, Lord Jesus! Amen.

28

EITHER–OR

John 8:21–30

HOW often have we heard, "It makes no difference what you believe, as long as you are sincere"! This is the same thing as saying, "You may believe that Jesus is the Son of God, or you may not; you may believe that He died to pay the penalty for your sins, or you may not; you may believe that He arose again on the third day, or you may not—as long as you are sincere in what you believe (or in what you don't believe), God will reward your good intentions."

It seems strange, does it not, that men never think that way in other fields of endeavor—in science, medicine, law, or even in the domestic arts of cooking and baking. Where is the pastry chef who believes a cake recipe that reads, "Use any ingredients you may have and in any proportion you prefer. It makes no difference, as long as you are sincere in your intentions."

It does make a difference! Men are saved and men are lost because of what they believe or what they do not believe. It is either-or: salvation through faith in Christ or damnation because of a lack of such faith. This is clearly brought out in the following words of Jesus. He is still addressing the unbelieving Jews in the temple.

> So He said to them again, "I am going away, and you will seek Me, and you will die in your sin. Where I am going, you cannot come." So the Jews said, "Will He kill Himself, since He says, 'Where I am going, you cannot come'?" He said to them, "You are from below; I am from above. You are of this world; I am not of this world. I told you that you would die in your sins, for unless you believe that I am He you will die in your sins." So they said to Him, "Who are You?" Jesus said to them, "Just what I have been telling you from the beginning. I have much to say about you and much to judge, but He who sent Me is true, and I declare to the world what I have heard from Him." They did not understand that He had been speaking to them about the

Father. So Jesus said to them, "When you have lifted up the Son of Man, then you will know that I am He, and that I do nothing on My own authority, but speak just as the Father taught Me. And He who sent Me is with Me. He has not left Me alone, for I always do the things that are pleasing to Him." As He was say-ing these things, many believed in Him.

We notice in these words two tremendous claims of the Savior. One is His increasingly emphatic claim to divine Sonship. The other is His increasingly clear insistence that without Him there is no salvation.

Christ's claims leave us no choice. He is either the eternal Son of the Highest, or He is the greatest fraud of the ages. What ordi-nary mortal would ever dare to say, "You are from below; I am from above. You are of this world; I am not of this world"? Before such a claim, we must either fall down with Thomas and say, "My Lord and my God!" (John 20:28), or we must rise up with the Jews and say, "You have a demon!" (7:20). It is either–or. Where do we stand? Praise God if you have taken your stand with Simon Peter and with those for whom he was spokesman and have said, "We have believed, and have come to know, that You are the Holy One of God" (6:69).

And now the other claim of Jesus: "Unless you believe that I am He you will die in your sins." Can anyone claim to be a follower of this Christ and yet say that it makes no difference what a man believes as long as he is sincere? Here is something that every man must believe or reject—and in his believing or rejecting, he settles his destiny for time and for eternity.

Christ is God! Together with the Father and the Holy Spirit, He is the great "I AM" (Exodus 3:14). That is what He claimed. And what is more, He claimed, "Unless you believe that I am He you will die in your sins." There is the great either–or of human destiny. The question of Pilate is still the question of the ages: "What shall I do with Jesus?" (Matthew 27:22).

The Jews in the temple that day answered the challenge by tak-ing up stones to throw at Jesus. Let us reply by strewing the Savior's path with the garments of praise and the palms of thanksgiving. Let us enthrone Him within our hearts as our eternal King and our divine Redeemer.

Prayer

Enter now my waiting heart,
Glorious King and Lord most holy.
Dwell in me and ne'er depart,
Though I am but poor and lowly.
Ah, what riches will be mine
When Thou art my guest divine!
My hosannas and my palms
Graciously receive, I pray Thee;
Evermore, as best I can,
Savior, I will homage pay Thee,
And in faith I will embrace,
Lord, Thy merit through Thy grace. Amen.
(LSB 350:2–3)

MADE FREE BY THE SON
John 8:31–59

SIN is the greatest of tyrants. That is why the Bible again and again refers to those who are still in the power of sin as being slaves—bound in cruel bondage by a wicked taskmaster. You have heard the expression, "He is the slave of drink." In a similar sense, all men are by nature the slaves of sin; they are sold under its power and utterly incapable of purchasing their freedom.

Jesus says, for example, "Everyone who commits sin is a slave to sin." Paul writes, "Do you not know that if you present yourselves to anyone as obedient slaves, you are slaves of the one whom you obey?" (Romans 6:16). From this bondage there is only one escape, and that is through the redemption, the emancipation, that has been won for us by Jesus Christ, our Savior.

"But when the fullness of time had come, God sent forth His Son, born of woman, born under the law, to redeem those who were under the law, so that we might receive adoption as sons" (Galatians 4:4–5). Christ assumed our human nature, says the writer to the Hebrews, in order to "deliver all those who through fear of death were subject to lifelong slavery" (Hebrews 2:15).

"He breaks the pow'r of canceled sin; He sets the pris'ner free," we sing in the well-known hymn *(LSB 528:4)*. And that is the claim that Jesus now makes for Himself in the following paragraphs:

The Truth Will Set You Free

So Jesus said to the Jews who had believed in Him, "If you abide in My word, you are truly My disciples, and you will know the truth, and the truth will set you free." They answered Him, "We are offspring of Abraham and have never been enslaved to anyone. How is it that You say, 'You will become free'?"

Jesus answered them, "Truly, truly, I say to you, everyone who commits sin is a slave to sin. The slave does not remain in the house forever; the son remains forever. So if the Son sets you free, you will be free indeed. I know that you are offspring of Abraham; yet you seek to kill Me because My word finds no place in you. I speak of what I have seen with My Father, and you do what you have heard from your father."

You Are of Your Father the Devil

They answered Him, "Abraham is our father." Jesus said to them, "If you were Abraham's children, you would be doing the works Abraham did, but now you seek to kill Me, a man who has told you the truth that I heard from God. This is not what Abraham did. You are doing the works your father did." They said to Him, "We were not born of sexual immorality. We have one Father—even God." Jesus said to them, "If God were your Father, you would love Me, for I came from God and I am here. I came not of My own accord, but He sent me. Why do you not understand what I say? It is because you cannot bear to hear My word. You are of your father the devil, and your will is to do your father's desires. He was a murderer from the beginning, and has nothing to do with the truth, because there is no truth in him. When he lies, he speaks out of his own character, for he is a liar and the father of lies. But because I tell the truth, you do not believe Me. Which one of you convicts Me of sin? If I tell the truth, why do you not believe Me? Whoever is of God hears the words of God. The reason why you do not hear them is that you are not of God."

Before Abraham Was, I Am

The Jews answered Him, "Are we not right in saying that You are a Samaritan and have a demon?" Jesus answered, "I do not have a demon, but I honor My Father, and you dishonor Me. Yet I do not seek My own glory; there is One who seeks it, and He is the judge. Truly, truly, I say to you, if anyone keeps My word, he will never see death." The Jews said to Him, "Now we know that You have a demon! Abraham died, as did the prophets, yet You say, 'If anyone keeps My word, he will never taste death.' Are You greater than our father Abraham, who died? And the prophets died! Who do You make yourself out to be?" Jesus answered, "If I glorify Myself, My glory is nothing. It is My Father who glorifies Me, of whom you say, 'He is our God.' But you have not known Him. I know Him. If I were to say that I do not know Him, I would be a liar like you, but I do know Him and I keep His word. Your father Abraham rejoiced that he would see My day. He saw it and was glad." So the Jews said to Him, "You are not yet fifty years old, and have You seen Abraham?" Jesus said to them, "Truly, truly, I say to you, before Abraham was, I am." So they picked up stones to throw at Him, but Jesus hid Himself and went out of the temple.

In one of His bitterest encounters with His enemies, the Savior gives us one of the most forceful testimonies of His eternal Sonship: "Truly, truly, I say to you" (this was the usual form of an oath), "before Abraham was, I am." Abraham had lived about two thousand years before the birth of Christ. And yet the Savior says (and these are His exact words), "Before Abraham was, I am."

Here we have the clearest instance of Jesus taking the exalted name of Yahweh (Exodus 3:14) and applying it to Himself. Abraham was, but "I am," Jesus says. Men may come and men may go, but Christ goes on forever, "the same yesterday and today and forever" (Hebrews 13:8). He is the eternal, never-changing, great "I am." What a comfort for us to know that He, who on Calvary's cross died to pay the debt of all mankind, was the eternal, unchangeable, omnipotent, and omnipresent Son of God. Surely, His blood will avail. His death in the sinner's stead must be sufficient. If this Son sets us free, we will be free indeed.

Prayer

Thy work alone, O Christ, Can ease this weight of sin;
Thy blood alone, O Lamb of God, Can give me peace within.

Thy love to me, O God, Not mine, O Lord, to Thee,
Can rid me of this dark unrest And set my spirit free.

Thy grace alone, O God, To me can pardon speak;
Thy pow'r alone, O Son of God, Can this sore bondage break.

I bless the Christ of God, I rest on love divine,
And with unfalt'ring lip and heart I call this Savior mine. Amen.
(LSB 567:3–6)

WHO SINNED?

John 9:1–12

IS it true that if a man suffers much, he must have sinned much? There are those who are always ready to point the finger of accusation and say, "Surely, he must have been a great sinner, or else the Lord would not have afflicted him so grievously."

It is true that all suffering is the result of sin. When sin entered into the world, it brought with it its ugly retinue of sickness and suffering and grief and heartache. In that sense, suffering is the result of sin. For had there been no sin, there would be no suffering.

But it is wrong to assume that every specific instance of suffering is the result of a specific instance of sin. Job's friends tried to prove that his great misfortunes were the result of his great sins, but the purpose of the entire Book of Job is to show that his friends were wrong.

Job was not a great sufferer because he was a great sinner. His sufferings were sent him by a gracious God, not as punishments, but as a necessary means to achieve a gracious purpose. In the following verses, we see this principle beautifully illustrated in the life of a man who was blind from birth.

Jesus Heals a Man Born Blind

As [Jesus] passed by, He saw a man blind from birth. And His disciples asked Him, "Rabbi, who sinned, this man or his parents, that he was born blind?" Jesus answered, "It was not that this man sinned, or his parents, but that the works of God might be displayed in him. We must work the works of Him who sent Me while it is day; night is coming, when no one can work. As long as I am in the world, I am the light of the world." Having said these things, He spat on the ground and made mud with the saliva. Then He anointed the man's eyes with the mud and said to him, "Go, wash in the pool of Siloam" (which means Sent). So he went and washed and came back seeing.

The neighbors and those who had seen him before as a beggar were saying, "Is this not the man who used to sit and beg?" Some said, "It is he." Others said, "No, but he is like him." He kept saying, "I am the man." So they said to him, "Then how were your eyes opened?" He answered, "The man called Jesus made mud and anointed my eyes and said to me, 'Go to Siloam and wash.' So I went and washed and received my sight." They said to him, "Where is He?" He said, "I do not know."

Are we laboring under a severe handicap, a cross under whose burden we have become faint and weary? Let us remember that in God's hands, a cross is but a lever by which He raises His children to closer fellowship with Him and to greater usefulness to their fellow men.

Nearer, my God, to Thee, Nearer to Thee.
E'en though it be a cross That raiseth me. (*TLH* 533:1)

The blind man in our Gospel may not have known it, but he was soon to learn that his blindness had a purpose—"that the works of God might be displayed in him." But for his blindness, it is probable that he may never have believed in the Savior. But for his blindness, the ninth chapter of John's Gospel, which has brought comfort to millions, would never have been written. But for his blindness, he would never have been able to testify to his friends and neighbors of the love and power of the Son of God, who had restored sight to his eyes and light to his soul.

It was the blind John Milton who wrote, "My vision Thou hast dimmed that I may see Thyself—Thyself alone!" William Moon, a blind man who published the Gospel in raised type in nearly two hundred languages and dialects, once told an audience, "When I became blind as a young boy, people consoled my mother because of the 'heavy dispensations' with which I was afflicted. They were wrong. God gave me blindness as a talent to be used for His glory. Without blindness I should never have been able to see the needs of the blind."

Have we learned to look on our crosses as talents, as gifts of God we are to consecrate and dedicate to His glory? Our crosses, too, have come to us "that the works of God might be displayed" in us. Let us pray that we exercise a faithful stewardship over the crosses that, in God's mercy and wisdom, He sees fit to send us. Let every cross be dedicated to the greater glory of our God and to the greater welfare of our fellow men.

Prayer

Drawn to the cross, which Thou hast blessed
   With healing gifts for souls distressed,
To find in Thee my life, my rest, Christ crucified, I come.

Thou knowest all my griefs and fears, Thy grace abused,
   my misspent years;
Yet now to Thee with contrite tears, Christ crucified, I come.

Wash me and take away each stain; Let nothing of my sin remain.
For cleansing, though it be through pain, Christ crucified, I come.

And then for work to do for Thee, Which shall so sweet a service be
That angels well might envy me, Christ crucified, I come. Amen.
(LSB 560)

"I WAS BLIND, NOW I SEE"

John 9:13–41

IT is a sign of the perversity of the human heart that with each succeeding act of mercy from Jesus, the enmity of His opponents became greater and more intense. His healing of the blind man on the Sabbath was the occasion for another outburst of anger and indignation by the Pharisees. In the following verses, we see how they bring the former blind man and his parents to trial in an effort to disprove the Savior's miracle and how finally, in despair, they excommunicate the man from membership in the Jewish synagogue. Truly, the Pharisees were blind, but the blind man saw!

They brought to the Pharisees the man who had formerly been blind. Now it was a Sabbath day when Jesus made the mud and opened his eyes. So the Pharisees again asked him how he had received his sight. And he said to them, "He put mud on my eyes, and I washed, and I see." Some of the Pharisees said, "This man is not from God, for He does not keep the Sabbath." But others said, "How can a man who is a sinner do such signs?" And there was a division among them. So they said again to the blind man, "What do you say about Him, since he has opened your eyes?" He said, "He is a prophet."

The Jews did not believe that he had been blind and had received his sight, until they called the parents of the man who had received his sight and asked them, "Is this your son, who you say was born blind? How then does he now see?" His parents answered, "We know that this is our son and that he was born blind. But how he now sees we do not know, nor do we know who opened his eyes. Ask him; he is of age. He will speak for himself." (His parents said these things because they feared the Jews, for the Jews had already agreed that if anyone should confess Jesus to be Christ, he was to be put out of the synagogue.) Therefore his parents said, "He is of age; ask him."

So for the second time they called the man who had been blind and said to him, "Give glory to God. We know that this man is a sinner." He answered, "Whether He is a sinner I do not know. One thing I do know, that though I was blind, now I see." They said to him, "What did He do to you? How did He open your eyes?" He answered them, "I have told you already, and you would not listen. Why do you want to hear it again? Do you also want to become His disciples?" And they reviled him, saying, "You are His disciple, but we are disciples of Moses. We know that God has spoken to Moses, but as for this man, we do not know where He comes from."The man answered, "Why, this is an amazing thing! You do not know where He comes from, and yet He opened my eyes. We know that God does not listen to sinners, but if anyone is a worshiper of God and does His will, God listens to him. Never since the world began has it been heard that anyone opened the eyes of a man born blind. If this man were not from God, He could do nothing." They answered him, "You were born in utter sin, and would you teach us?" And they cast him out.

Jesus heard that they had cast him out, and having found him He said, "Do you believe in the Son of Man?" He answered, "And who is He, sir, that I may believe in Him?" Jesus said to him, "You have seen Him, and it is He who is speaking to you." He said, "Lord, I believe," and he worshiped Him. Jesus said, "For judgment I came into this world, that those who do not see may see, and those who see may become blind." Some of the Pharisees near Him heard these things, and said to Him, "Are we also blind?" Jesus said to them, "If you were blind, you would have no guilt; but now that you say, 'We see,' your guilt remains."

One sentence in particular in the former blind man's testimony stands out above all others. "Whether He is a sinner I do not know. One thing I do know, that though I was blind, now I see." In other words, When it comes to long and logical arguments, I am no match for you Pharisees. There are many questions I cannot answer. But there is one thing I do know—and all your arguments will never change that fact! Yesterday I was blind! And today I can see!

Do we see a lesson in this? We are living in a day when many of the precious truths of our Bible are being called into question. How can you prove that there is a God, that the world was created in six days, that the Bible has been given by inspiration, that Jesus is the Son of God, that His death on Calvary's cross was in the place of sinners, that salvation is free to all who believe? These and a thousand other questions are hurled at the believing Christian by an unbelieving world in an attempt to shake his faith in God's promises.

Is it necessary that the humble Christian be able to answer every question an unbelieving world puts to him? Not at all! There come times when we must answer in the simple words of the former blind man. "Whether He is a sinner I do not know. One thing I do know, that though I was blind, now I see."

There are certain things that the Christian knows by experience and that are not at all dependent on skillful arguments and logical deductions (1 Corinthians 2:9–16). He may not know how it was possible for God to become man, but he does know that the God-man, Jesus Christ, has shone into his heart and has given him the light of the glory of God. He may not know how it was possible for the death of the Son of God to redeem his life from destruction, but he does know that a heavenly and indescribable peace has flooded his soul ever since he learned to believe that "the blood of Jesus His Son cleanses us from all sin" (1 John 1:7).

These things he knows. He cannot explain them, nor are they any longer open to argument. Like the former blind man, he refuses to be robbed of his clear convictions by the idle, academic speculations of a world that is hostile to his Savior. "Whether this be so, or that be so, I do not know. But this I do know: that whereas I was sold under sin, unable to purchase my release, Jesus Christ has brought me fullest freedom. Whereas once "I was blind, now I see."

Prayer

Jesus, the very tho't of Thee With sweetness fills the breast;
But sweeter far Thy face to see And in Thy presence rest.

Nor voice can sing, nor heart can frame, Nor can the mem'ry find
A sweeter sound than Thy blest name, O Savior of mankind!

O Hope of ev'ry contrite heart, O Joy of all the meek!
To those who fall, how kind Thou art,
How good to those who seek!

But what to those who find? Ah! this
Nor tongue nor pen can show;
The love of Jesus, what it is, None but His loved ones know. Amen.
(TLH 350:1—4)

"I AM THE DOOR"
John 10:1–10

WE are told that the ancient city of Troy had only one gate. You either entered the city by that gate, or you did not enter it at all! Similarly, there is but one entrance to the city of God, and that entrance is Jesus!

"I am the door. If anyone enters by Me, he will be saved." There are those, of course, who do not like the narrowness of such a claim. They prefer to believe there are many doors and many entrances, all leading into the same sheepfold. But we have our Savior's word for it: there is but one door into the safety of the fold, and He is that door!

"I am the way, and the truth, and the life," Jesus told His disciples later. "No one comes to the Father except through Me" (John 14:6). And that His disciples fully understood Him is evident from the words of Peter after the Savior's ascension into heaven: "And there is salvation in no one else, for there is no other name under heaven given among men by which we must be saved" (Acts 4:12). Truly, there is no other way! That is the lesson Jesus now seeks to impress upon His listeners.

I Am the Good Shepherd

"Truly, truly, I say to you, he who does not enter the sheepfold by the door but climbs in by another way, that man is a thief and a robber. But he who enters by the door is the shepherd of the sheep. To him the gatekeeper opens. The sheep hear his voice, and he calls his own sheep by name and leads them out. When he has brought out all his own, he goes before them, and the sheep follow him, for they know his voice. A stranger they will not follow, but they will flee from him, for they do not know the voice of strangers." This figure of speech

Jesus used with them, but they did not understand what He was saying to them.

So Jesus again said to them, "Truly, truly, I say to you, I am the door of the sheep. All who came before Me are thieves and robbers, but the sheep did not listen to them. I am the door. If anyone enters by Me, he will be saved and will go in and out and find pasture. The thief comes only to steal and kill and destroy. I came that they may have life and have it abundantly."

These words bring both a sharp warning and a sweet comfort. A sharp warning to those who would teach a salvation that does not have Christ as "the door." And a sweet comfort to those who have already found in Christ "the way, and the truth, and the life" (John 14:6) and have come to the Father by Him.

"If anyone enters by Me, he will be saved and will go in and out and find pasture." That means he will be rescued from the clutches of sin, death, and the power of the devil and will enjoy the safety and protection of a loving and forgiving God.

He "will go in and out." That means he will have perfect freedom. To be brought into the sheepfold of the Master is not to be confined or to be imprisoned, but it is as a son freely comes in and goes out of the Father's house. Perfect freedom is the happy lot of every member of the sheepfold.

"He will . . . find pasture." That means every want of body and soul will be abundantly provided for by the Shepherd of the fold. "I am the bread of life," says Jesus (John 6:35). "He makes me lie down in green pastures," says David (Psalm 23:2). "I came that they may have life and have it abundantly," says the Savior.

We who have entered by the Door, have we not experienced the glorious truth of all these promises? As we look back to the day when we passed through the Door into the promised land of God's kingdom of grace, must we not say with ancient Joshua: we know in our hearts that "not one word has failed of all the good things that the Lord your God promised concerning you. All have come to pass for you; not one of them has failed" (Joshua 23:14).

Prayer

Jesus, my Truth, my Way, My sure, unerring Light,
On Thee my feeble soul I stay, Which Thou wilt lead aright.

Give me to trust in Thee; Be Thou my sure Abode;
My Horn and Rock and Buckler be, My Savior and my God.

Myself I cannot save, Myself I cannot keep;
But strength in Thee I surely have, Whose eyelids never sleep.

My soul to Thee alone Now, therefore, I commend.
Thou, Jesus, having loved Thine own, Wilt love me to the end.
Amen. (TLH 433:1, 4–6)

"I AM THE GOOD SHEPHERD"

John 10:11–18

FEW verses of the Bible are more beautiful, more intimate, and more consoling to the heart of the Christian than those that picture our Savior as the Good Shepherd. The following verses give us such a picture.

Jesus had just spoken of Himself as the door to the sheepfold, as the One by whom we gain entrance into the fold. But He is more than the door—He is the owner, the keeper, the tender of the flock. He is the Shepherd!

I am the good shepherd. The good shepherd lays down His life for the sheep. He who is a hired hand and not a shepherd, who does not own the sheep, sees the wolf coming and leaves the sheep and flees, and the wolf snatches them and scatters them. He flees because he is a hired hand and cares nothing for the sheep. I am the good shepherd. I know My own and My own know Me, just as the Father knows Me and I know the

Father; and I lay down My life for the sheep. And I have other sheep that are not of this fold. I must bring them also, and they will listen to My voice. So there will be one flock, one shepherd. For this reason the Father loves Me, because I lay down My life that I may take it up again. No one takes it from Me, but I lay it down of My own accord. I have authority to lay it down, and I have authority to take it up again. This charge I have received from My Father.

Jesus tells us three important things about Himself as the Good Shepherd. First, the Good Shepherd lays down His life for the sheep. Because He is the Good Shepherd, because the sheep are His own, given Him by the Father from all eternity, and because He cares for the sheep, He lays down His life so the sheep might live. And He does so willingly: "I lay it down of My own accord."

How touchingly these words were fulfilled during the hours of the first Maundy Thursday and the first Good Friday. "Having loved His own who were in the world, He loved them to the end" (John 13:1). "I will strike the shepherd," the Lord had said through the prophet Zechariah (Matthew 26:31; see Zechariah 13:7). In Gethsemane, the Shepherd was smitten, and on Calvary He laid down His life so that we, the sheep of His fold, might go free (Isaiah 53:4–8).

Second, the Savior tells us that there is a beautiful intimacy between the Good Shepherd and His sheep. "I know My own and My own know Me." So close is this intimacy between the Shepherd and the sheep that Jesus compared it to the intimate and loving relationship that exists between Himself and His Father.

How often have we experienced the heartwarming comfort of this close communion with the tender Shepherd! "I am Jesus' little lamb, Ever glad at heart I am" is the confession of the oldest member of the flock as well as of the youngest. "For my Shepherd gently guides me, Knows my need and well provides me, Loves me ev'ry day the same, Even calls me by my name" (LSB 740:1)—how often have our fears, our worries, and our anxieties been put to rest by that simple sweet assurance!

And third, the Good Shepherd thinks also of the "other sheep" who are not of the Jewish fold. As He speaks of His death for the sheep, He thinks of the wide extent of its blessings. He would lay down His life for the sins of the world—including the Gentile world. They are the "other sheep" He must still bring in. No—we are the other sheep!

Jesus had us in mind when He said He must still bring them in! Can we ever sufficiently thank Him for this, for His all-encompassing mercy? We are in the fold today, not because of any superior wisdom or merit of our own, but only because the omniscient Shepherd from all eternity and in His measureless mercy decided "I must bring them also."

Prayer

I was a wandering sheep, I did not love the fold;
I did not love my Shepherd's voice, I would not be controlled.
I was a wayward child, I did not love my home;
I did not love my Father's voice, I loved afar to roam.

The Shepherd sought His sheep, The Father sought His child;
They followed me o'er vale and hill, O'er deserts waste and wild;
They found me nigh to death, Famished and faint and lone;
They bound me with the bands of love, They saved the wand'ring one.

Jesus my Shepherd is: 'Twas He that loved my soul;
'Twas He that washed me in His blood, 'Twas He that made me whole.
'Twas He that sought the lost, That found the wand'ring sheep,
'Twas He that brought me to the fold, 'Tis He that still doth keep.
Amen. (Horatius Bonar, 1808–89)

34

"THEY WILL NEVER PERISH"

John 10:19–42

IT is a remarkable fact that some of the most precious words of Christ were spoken while He was engaged in bitter conflict with His enemies. Thus, for instance, the following verses that describe a heated encounter between Jesus and the unbelieving Jews contain the ever-beautiful, ever-powerful, and ever-consoling words of Christ to His believers: "My sheep hear My voice, and I know them, and they follow Me. I give them eternal life, and they will never perish, and no one will snatch them out of My hand" (John 10:27–28).

The scene of the incident is in the temple. Suddenly the Savior is surrounded by a group of hostile Jews. Literally, they "gathered around Him" as a cordon of police surrounds a dangerous suspect, preventing His escape. They want Him to give them a clear-cut answer, one that will leave no doubt in their minds whatsoever. Is He the Christ? Or is He not?

The answer Jesus gives them is plainer than they asked for. Yes, He says, I am the Messiah. But I am more than you mean by that term. I am the Son of God, of one essence with the Father: "I and the Father are one." But He also tells them that He knows they will not accept His claim. And the reason they would not believe Him is not to be found in any lack of evidence, but in the fact that they are not His sheep and therefore are not willing to hear and believe His voice.

May God grant us believing hearts as we now read the story.

There was again a division among the Jews because of these words. Many of them said, "He has a demon, and is insane; why listen to Him?" Others said, "These are not the words of one who is oppressed by a demon. Can a demon open the eyes of the blind?"

I and the Father Are One

At that time the Feast of Dedication took place at Jerusalem. It was winter, and Jesus was walking in the temple, in the colonnade of Solomon. So the Jews gathered around Him and said to Him, "How long will You keep us in suspense? If You are the Christ, tell us plainly." Jesus answered them, "I told you, and you do not believe. The works that I do in My Father's name bear witness about Me, but you do not believe because you are not part of My flock. My sheep hear My voice, and I know them, and they follow Me. I give them eternal life, and they will never perish, and no one will snatch them out of My hand. My Father, who has given them to Me, is greater than all, and no one is able to snatch them out of the Father's hand. I and the Father are one."

The Jews picked up stones again to stone Him. Jesus answered them, "I have shown you many good works from the Father; for which of them are you going to stone Me?" The Jews answered Him, "It is not for a good work that we are going to stone You but for blasphemy, because You, being a man, make Yourself God." Jesus answered them, "Is it not written in your Law, 'I said, you are gods'? If He called them gods to whom the word of God came—and Scripture cannot be broken—do you say of Him whom the Father consecrated and sent into the world, 'You are blaspheming,' because I said, 'I am the Son of God'? If I am not doing the works of my Father, then do not believe Me; but if I do them, even though you do not believe Me, believe the works, that you may know and understand that the Father is in Me and I am in the Father." Again they sought to arrest Him, but He escaped from their hands.

He went away again across the Jordan to the place where John had been baptizing at first, and there He remained. And many came to Him. And they said, "John did no sign, but everything that John said about this man was true." And many believed in Him there.

Much could be written about this section: there is the clear claim of the Savior not only to divine Sonship but also to literal unity and equality with the Father. And there is the clear evidence that the Jews fully understood His claim because they picked up stones to kill Him (the punishment for blasphemy, Leviticus 24:16), saying, "You, being a man, make Yourself God." We do not dwell on these thoughts, as important as they are. Instead, we focus our attention on the beautiful words of assurance that Christ addresses to His Christians in the midst of this discourse, and on the basis of these words we answer a most important question.

How can I be sure that I will continue in the faith until the end? I know that I am a believer today, firm in the faith of my Savior, but how can I be sure that I will be a believer tomorrow? Above all, what assurance do I have that I will trust in the Savior when my feet are wandering through the valley of the shadow? These are questions that have entered the heart of every child of God at one time or another.

Fortunately, God Himself has answered them for us. He has answered them in every Gospel promise. As perfect as God's love is, the Gospel offer is also perfect. His love could not permit Him to offer me a salvation that would not "wear." No, His love goes all the way: not only my coming to faith, but also my continuing in the faith and my dying in the faith are part of His plan for me.

"They will never perish," says Jesus, "and no one will snatch them out of My hand." "By God's power [you] are being guarded through faith for a salvation," says Peter (1 Peter 1:5). Not we, but God does the keeping. And He keeps us through faith—faith nurtured through His Word, faith strengthened by the Sacrament. What a blessed promise: "They will never perish!" God has promised to sustain the arms of my faith; and He has given me His pledge that the strong arms of His love will never let me go! I will never perish.

Prayer

Dearest Jesus, gracious Lord, we come before You with repentant hearts and thanksgiving that we are washed clean through the waters of Baptism in Your name. Let us be forever in Your merciful keeping, shielded from harm and strengthened in faith. Amen.

35

A MODEL PRAYER
John 11:1–19

JUST outside Jerusalem, about two miles from the city limits, lay the little town of Bethany. Here was the home of Mary and Martha and their brother Lazarus—a home where Jesus was a frequent and welcome guest (Luke 10:38; John 12:1).

Things were happening in Bethany that would have a tremendous effect upon the lives of many people. The divine plan, which would bring the Savior to His cross, was rapidly unfolding. The death of Lazarus set the stage for the "greatest" of Jesus' miracles, and the "greatest" of His miracles set the stage for His greatest suffering—His death by crucifixion. It was at Bethany that the shadows of Calvary began to lengthen with a quickened pace.

God grant us grace that we may find a precious blessing as we read this beloved story.

The Death of Lazarus

Now a certain man was ill, Lazarus of Bethany, the village of Mary and her sister Martha. It was Mary who anointed the Lord with ointment and wiped His feet with her hair, whose brother Lazarus was ill. So the sisters sent to Him, saying, "Lord, he whom You love is ill." But when Jesus heard it He said, "This illness does not lead to death. It is for the glory of God, so that the Son of God may be glorified through it."

Now Jesus loved Martha and her sister and Lazarus. So, when He heard that Lazarus was ill, He stayed two days longer in the place where He was. Then after this He said to the disciples, "Let us go to Judea again." The disciples said to Him, "Rabbi, the Jews were just now seeking to stone You, and are You going there again?" Jesus answered, "Are there not twelve hours in the day? If anyone walks in the day, he does not stumble, because he sees the light of this world. But if anyone walks in the night, he stumbles, because the light is not in him." After saying these things, He said to them, "Our friend Lazarus has fallen asleep, but I go to awaken Him." The disciples said to Him, "Lord, if he has fallen asleep, he will recover." Now Jesus had spoken of his death, but they thought that He meant taking rest in sleep. Then Jesus told them plainly, "Lazarus has died, and for your sake I am glad that I was not there, so that you may believe. But let us go to him." So Thomas, called the Twin, said to his fellow disciples, "Let us also go, that we may die with Him."

I Am the Resurrection and the Life

Now when Jesus came, He found that Lazarus had already been in the tomb four days. Bethany was near Jerusalem, about two miles off, and many of the Jews had come to Martha and Mary to console them concerning their brother.

Lazarus was sick. What anxiety, what care, what heartache can a siege of sickness bring into a family circle! Only those who have anxiously stroked the feverish brow of a dear one, as the clock ticks off the endless minutes that finally blend into eternity, can know the anguish that tore the heart of Mary and Martha as they saw their brother waste away and linger at the entrance to the valley of the shadow. But Mary and Martha knew there was still one hope! And so they sent word to Jesus, saying, "Lord, he whom You love is ill."

> Have we trials and temptations?
> Is there trouble anywhere?
> We should never be discouraged—
> Take it to the Lord in prayer. *(LSB* 770:2)

Notice the simplicity of their prayer. They do not tell Jesus what to do. Nor do they prescribe the how or the when. They do not even ask Him to help or cure their brother. They are content merely to inform Him of the fact that "Lord, he whom You love is ill." It was enough that Jesus had been informed of their plight. Could He know and still withhold His help? Notice, too, that their plea is not "he who loves You" but "he whom You love." They claim no merit for Lazarus. Their only plea is the love of Jesus.

Thy love to me, O God,
Not mine, O Lord, to Thee. *(LSB* 567:4)

But why did Jesus wait? Why did He delay His answer to their prayer? We can even assume that Lazarus had died before the message of his sickness reached Him. Jesus delayed only two days, and when He arrived at Bethany, Lazarus had been dead four days already. But why a delay of even two days?

"That the Son of God may be glorified through it." In His divine omniscience, Jesus timed His miracle of mercy so there could be no doubt as to its reality. Lazarus must first be buried—there must be no doubt as to the fact of physical death—and then He would come and raise him up.

Can there be any doubt that the faith of Mary and Martha and of their believing friends was the stronger and the purer for this brief delay? And dare we doubt that similar delays in the answers to our prayers have an equally good and gracious purpose?

Prayer

O Lord Jesus, teach us to come to You in every hour of trial and trouble. Grant that in trusting faith we may rest ourselves on You and on Your never-ending mercy. In Your own time and in Your own way, give us those things that are needful for our soul and body, and take us at last to You in heaven. We ask it, trusting only in Your mercy. Amen.

THE RESURRECTION OF LAZARUS

36

John 11:20–46

LAZARUS had died. Four days had passed. We can well imagine that Mary and Martha must have said to themselves over and over again, "If only Jesus had been here, this thing would never have happened." Small wonder that, when the Lord arrived and Martha ran out to meet Him, her first words were "Lord, if You had been here, my brother would not have died"—and small wonder that, when Mary came running to Him several moments later, she greeted Him with the identical words: "Lord, if You had been here, my brother would not have died." That was all they had been thinking, so it was natural that it should be the first thing they said: "If You had been here!"

But now their Lord was there. Was He too late? Let us read the blessed record.

So when Martha heard that Jesus was coming, she went and met Him, but Mary remained seated in the house. Martha said to Jesus, "Lord, if You had been here, my brother would not have died. But even now I know that whatever You ask from God, God will give You." Jesus said to her, "Your brother will rise again." Martha said to Him, "I know that he will rise again in the resurrection on the last day." Jesus said to her, "I am the resurrection and the life. Whoever believes in Me, though he die, yet shall he live, and everyone who lives and believes in Me shall never die. Do you believe this?" She said to Him, "Yes, Lord; I believe that You are the Christ, the Son of God, who is coming into the world."

Jesus Weeps

When she had said this, she went and called her sister Mary, saying in private, "The Teacher is here and is calling for you."

And when she heard it, she rose quickly and went to Him. Now Jesus had not yet come into the village, but was still in the place where Martha had met Him. When the Jews who were with her in the house, consoling her, saw Mary rise quickly and go out, they followed her, supposing that she was going to the tomb to weep there. Now when Mary came to where Jesus was and saw Him, she fell at His feet, saying to Him, "Lord, if You had been here, my brother would not have died." When Jesus saw her weeping, and the Jews who had come with her also weeping, He was deeply moved in His spirit and greatly troubled. And He said, "Where have you laid him?" They said to Him, "Lord, come and see." Jesus wept. So the Jews said, "See how He loved him!" But some of them said, "Could not He who opened the eyes of the blind man also have kept this man from dying?"

Jesus Raises Lazarus

Then Jesus, deeply moved again, came to the tomb. It was a cave, and a stone lay against it. Jesus said, "Take away the stone." Martha, the sister of the dead man, said to Him, "Lord, by this time there will be an odor, for he has been dead four days." Jesus said to her, "Did I not tell you that if you believed you would see the glory of God?" So they took away the stone. And Jesus lifted up His eyes and said, "Father, I thank You that You have heard Me. I knew that You always hear Me, but I said this on account of the people standing around, that they may believe that You sent Me." When He had said these things, He cried out with a loud voice, "Lazarus, come out." The man who had died came out, his hands and feet bound with linen strips, and his face wrapped with a cloth. Jesus said to them, "Unbind him, and let him go."

The Plot to Kill Jesus

Many of the Jews therefore, who had come with Mary and had seen what He did, believed in Him, but some of them went to the Pharisees and told them what Jesus had done.

Could there be anything more comforting to the heart of the Christian than the words we have just read? The glories of our precious Savior seem to crowd the verses as we read them. We see in Him, first of all, our compassionate Redeemer, and then the mighty and majestic God who is the resurrection and the life.

Our compassionate Redeemer! Behold Him weeping as He walks along the road that leads from the village out to the place of burial. He who was "in the beginning" (John 1:1), He by whom "all things were made" (1:3), He who "upholds the universe by the word of His power" (Hebrews 1:3)—He weeps hot tears of sorrow and compassion as He beholds the misery and anguish not only of Mary and of Martha but also of all of humankind. His heart beats fast, His spirit groans, His throat is choked, His eyes run over.

What a blessed assurance to know that this sympathetic Savior is even now at the right hand of God, making intercession for us! "For we do not have a high priest who is unable to sympathize with our weaknesses, but one who in every respect has been tempted as we are, yet without sin. . . . For because He Himself has suffered when tempted, He is able to help those who are being tempted" (Hebrews 4:15; 2:18). Christ has plumbed the depths of human misery. He knows our sorrows and He has mingled His tears with ours to assure us of His tender and divine compassion.

But our Savior has more than compassion—He has power! He has power over all our enemies, even our final enemy, death. In this chapter of John's Gospel, He both claims and demonstrates that power. He claims it when He speaks those never-to-be-forgotten words to Martha: "I am the resurrection and the life. Whoever believes in Me, though he die, yet shall he live, and everyone who lives and believes in Me shall never die." And He demonstrates His power over death when He speaks the life-giving words "Lazarus, come out," and "the man who had died came out."

It was this almighty Savior who stood at the deathbed of our sainted fathers and mothers and loved ones who are now asleep in Jesus. What a comfort to know that they are safe in His keeping! And what an unspeakably precious assurance to know that this same

Jesus will someday stand at their grave and at ours, just as He did at the tomb of Lazarus, and will call us to be with Him in His eternal kingdom! God grant us that ever-blessed reunion through Jesus Christ, our Savior.

Prayer

Jesus, I live to Thee,
The Loveliest and Best;
My life in Thee, Thy life in me,
In Thy blest love I rest.

Jesus, I die to Thee
Whenever death shall come;
To die in Thee is life to me
In my eternal home.

Whether to live or die,
I know not which is best;
To live in Thee is bliss to me,
To die is endless rest.

Living or dying, Lord,
I ask but to be Thine;
My life in Thee, Thy life in me,
Make heav'n forever mine. Amen.
(TLH 591:1–4)

ONE MAN MUST DIE FOR THE PEOPLE

John 11:47–57

THE resurrection of Lazarus had such a tremendous effect upon the people that the chief priests and Pharisees called a special meeting of the Jewish Council. Something must be done! The Passover was just a few days off, and Jerusalem would be crowded. If the populace would make a demonstration and perhaps hail Jesus as the promised Messiah and King of the Jews, the Romans would march against the city to quell the uprising. And, more important, the members of the Council would lose their positions because they would have shown themselves incapable of handling the situation.

It was not that the chief priests and Pharisees could any longer deny Jesus' miracles—they were now compelled to admit them—but they were determined to deny the Savior. Their hearts had been hardened. And so they call their hurried meeting not to study the validity of Jesus' latest miracle, not to examine the evidence as to whether or not He was indeed the Messiah—but to discuss ways and means of getting rid of Him. Let us read the record of their meeting.

> So the chief priests and the Pharisees gathered the Council and said, "What are we to do? For this man performs many signs. If we let Him go on like this, everyone will believe in Him, and the Romans will come and take away both our place and our nation." But one of them, Caiaphas, who was high priest that year, said to them, "You know nothing at all. Nor do you understand that it is better for you that one man should die for the people, not that the whole nation should perish." He did not say this of his own accord, but being high priest that year he prophesied that Jesus would die for the nation, and not for the nation only, but also to gather into one the children of

God who are scattered abroad. So from that day on they made plans to put Him to death.

Jesus therefore no longer walked openly among the Jews, but went from there to the region near the wilderness, to a town called Ephraim, and there He stayed with the disciples.

Now the Passover of the Jews was at hand, and many went up from the country to Jerusalem before the Passover to purify themselves. They were looking for Jesus and saying to one another as they stood in the temple, "What do you think? That He will not come to the feast at all?" Now the chief priests and the Pharisees had given orders that if anyone knew where He was, he should let them know, so that they might arrest Him.

We marvel at the irony of the words of Caiaphas: "It is better for you that one man should die for the people, not that the whole nation should perish." To the ears of his fellow conspirators and partners in crime, these words simply meant this: it is to our advantage that this man be put out of the way so He doesn't gather too large a following and the Romans come and destroy us. It is better that Jesus suffer now than that we all suffer later!

But what an indescribably glorious meaning these words of the scoundrel high priest convey to the ears and to the heart of the believer! It is better that Jesus suffer now than that we all suffer later—that is the very heart of the Gospel message. "God shows His love for us in that while we were still sinners, Christ died for us" (Romans 5:8). "For our sake [God] made Him to be sin who knew no sin, so that in Him we might become the righteousness of God" (2 Corinthians 5:21). "Christ redeemed us from the curse of the law by becoming a curse for us" (Galatians 3:13). "Christ died for our sins in accordance with the Scriptures" (1 Corinthians 15:3). "He was wounded for our transgressions; He was crushed for our iniquities; upon Him was the chastisement that brought us peace, and with His stripes we are healed" (Isaiah 53:5).

Truly, it is better for us, infinitely better, that Jesus suffered then because now we may go free. One man, the God-man Christ Jesus, died for the people. And now the people need not perish. We are those people! Can we ever sufficiently thank our Savior for this His matchless mercy?

Prayer

"Create in me a clean heart, O God, and renew a right spirit within me. Cast me not away from Your presence, and take not Your Holy Spirit from me. Restore to me the joy of Your salvation, and uphold me with a willing spirit"(Psalm 51:10–12). Amen.

MARY ANOINTS HER SAVIOR
John 12:1–11

TO Mary, Martha, and their brother Lazarus, it was "six days before the Passover." To Jesus, it was the day before Palm Sunday and six days before Good Friday. Although He knew that at Jerusalem a price had been offered for His capture, Jesus nevertheless set out on the journey from Ephraim toward the Holy City. He knew that the hour He had often spoken about to His friends had come; and so, conscious of all that would befall Him during these six final, tragic days, He goes up to Jerusalem.

But just outside the city limits lies the little village of Bethany, the home of Mary and Martha and their brother Lazarus, whom the Savior had recently restored to life. He must spend the Sabbath evening with them before entering the city on the following morning. It is this visit with His Bethany friends that the evangelist now records.

Mary Anoints Jesus at Bethany

Six days before the Passover, Jesus therefore came to Bethany, where Lazarus was, whom Jesus had raised from the dead. So they gave a dinner for Him there. Martha served, and Lazarus was one of those reclining with Him at table. Mary therefore took a pound of expensive ointment made from pure nard, and anointed the feet of Jesus and wiped His feet with her hair. The house was filled with the fragrance of the perfume. But Judas Iscariot, one of His disciples (he who was about to betray Him), said, "Why was this ointment not sold for three hundred denarii and given to the poor?" He said this, not because he cared about the poor, but because he was a thief, and having charge of the moneybag he used to help himself to what was put into it. Jesus said, "Leave her alone, so that she may keep it for the day of My burial. For the poor you always have with you, but you do not always have Me."

The Plot to Kill Lazarus

When the large crowd of the Jews learned that Jesus was there, they came, not only on account of Him but also to see Lazarus, whom He had raised from the dead. So the chief priests made plans to put Lazarus to death as well, because on account of him many of the Jews were going away and believing in Jesus.

Let us look more closely at this Bethany visit. We see that Lazarus joined the rest of the company at the supper table. He who had been alive, who had been dead, and who had been made alive again, takes his accustomed place at the table. There could be no doubt about Jesus' miracle of raising Lazarus from the dead.

Small wonder that many people walked the two miles from Jerusalem to the home in Bethany, not so much to see Jesus as to see Lazarus! Could it really be that a man who had been dead had been made alive again? And if so, must not this Jesus of Nazareth be the Son of God? It is no surprise that the chief priests discussed whether it was necessary for them to put Lazarus to death again! Whenever the evidence gets too strong for the willful unbeliever, he sets out to destroy the evidence!

But we must return to the supper scene at Bethany. After Jesus and His friends had eaten and were still reclining on their couches, Mary opened a box of costly and sweet-smelling ointment and anointed Jesus' feet, drying them with her hair. This was her way of showing her love, her gratitude, and her devotion to the Savior.

We need not linger long on the hypocritical objection of Judas, who suddenly developed a soft heart for the poor and asked why this ointment had not been sold and the money given to the under-privileged. Judas was a man of a mean and stingy heart. It would have been far better for him if he had spent more of his money on the Savior—perhaps he would not later have had to throw his silver pieces all over the temple floor!

Jesus commends Mary for this act of love. Have we learned to pour out our costliest gifts at His feet? Have our children learned to open their money banks for the cause of missions? Have Father and Mother learned to dig deep into their bank accounts to give gener-ously as a sign of affection and devotion to their Savior? Mary gave of her best; her heart could not be satisfied with less. God grant that our devotion to the Savior be as fervent and as deep as that of Mary.

Prayer

Take my life and let it be
Consecrated, Lord, to Thee;
Take my moments and my days,
Let them flow in ceaseless praise.

Take my love, my Lord, I pour
At Thy feet its treasure store;
Take myself, and I will be
Ever, only, all, for Thee. Amen.
(LSB 783:1, 6)

39

JESUS' ENTRY INTO JERUSALEM
John 12:12–19

IT was Sunday morning. Jesus and His disciples had taken leave of their Bethany friends and were well on their way to Jerusalem. The news that Jesus was approaching created a stir within the city—the great Prophet of Nazareth who had restored dead Lazarus to life was soon to enter the city gates!

Seized by a sudden spell of enthusiasm (which, alas, was only for the moment), the multitudes thronged through the city gates and hurried along the open road to meet the approaching Savior. It is this triumphal entry into the Holy City the evangelist now describes.

The Triumphal Entry

The next day the large crowd that had come to the feast heard that Jesus was coming to Jerusalem. So they took branches of palm trees and went out to meet Him, crying out, "Hosanna! Blessed is He who comes in the name of the Lord, even the King of Israel!" And Jesus found a young donkey and sat on it, just as it is written, "Fear not, daughter of Zion; behold, your king is coming, sitting on a donkey's colt!"

His disciples did not understand these things at first, but when Jesus was glorified, then they remembered that these things had been written about Him and had been done to Him. The crowd that had been with Him when He called Lazarus out of the tomb and raised him from the dead continued to bear witness. The reason why the crowd went to meet Him was that they heard He had done this sign. So the Pharisees said to one another, "You see that you are gaining nothing. Look, the world has gone after Him."

Before Jesus enters into His deepest humiliation, He is given a hint of the homage that men will someday give Him at the final revelation of His glory (Philippians 2:9–11). To carry and to wave a palm branch was a token of royal honor to a victorious king returning home from battle. And so the jubilant throngs line the road, swinging their palms, and shouting, "Hosanna! Blessed is He who comes in the name of the Lord." Unwittingly, they give Jesus the honor due Him as the promised Savior and Messiah, for these very words, taken from Psalm 118, were spoken in prophecy of Him!

Small wonder that five days later Pilate asked Jesus, "Are You the King of the Jews?" (John 18:33), and that the mocking superscription of His cross read, "Jesus of Nazareth, the King of the Jews." But Pilate didn't need to fear that the King who entered Jerusalem that day had come to unseat him from his power because this was the lowly King of whom the prophet Zechariah had foretold: "Rejoice greatly, O daughter of Zion! Shout aloud, O daughter of Jerusalem! Behold, your king is coming to you; righteous and having salvation is He, humble and mounted on a donkey, on a colt, the foal of a donkey" (Zechariah 9:9).

The King who entered Jerusalem on Palm Sunday amid the acclaim of the people could truthfully say to Pilate on Good Friday, "You say that I am a king" (John 18:37). But He could also add, "My kingdom is not of this world" (18:36). His was a kingdom of grace, a kingdom of hearts. It was human hearts that He had come to conquer and to win as trophies for His eternal kingdom.

And still today, Jesus, the King of kings and Lord of lords, does not march at the head of great legions to take great cities captive. He comes quietly, without pomp and circumstance, through the preaching of His Word, and knocks at the doors of human hearts. That is where He seeks to establish and expand His blessed kingdom of grace.

Has Christ entered the city of our heart? Have we flung wide the portals to receive our royal Guest? And having received Him, have we enthroned Him as our Lord and King? God grant it. And to this end, may we always pray:

Prayer

Redeemer, come and open wide
My heart to Thee; here, Lord, abide!
O enter with Thy grace divine;
Thy face of mercy on me shine.

Thy Holy Spirit guide us on
Until our glorious goal is won.
Eternal praise and fame
We offer to Thy name. Amen.
(LSB 341:5–6)

40
JESUS PREACHES TO THE GREEKS
John 12:20–36

JERUSALEM was the converging point for travelers from many countries, so it is no surprise that "among those who went up to worship at the feast were some Greeks." These Greeks had no doubt heard about the mighty wonder-worker already before they came to the capital city, but now that they were in Jerusalem, they noticed that the city was all astir with rumors and reports about the man from Galilee.

And so it is only natural that the Greeks search for the disciples and, having found them, arrange for an interview with their Master. They wanted to talk to the man who was the talk of the city. And, as the story unfolds, we see that the man who was the talk of the city wanted to talk to them.

Some Greeks Seek Jesus

Now among those who went up to worship at the feast were some Greeks. So these came to Philip, who was from Bethsaida in Galilee, and asked him, "Sir, we wish to see Jesus." Philip went and told Andrew; Andrew and Philip went and told Jesus. And Jesus answered them, "The hour has come for the Son of Man to be glorified. Truly, truly, I say to you, unless a grain of wheat falls into the earth and dies, it remains alone; but if it dies, it bears much fruit. Whoever loves his life loses it, and whoever hates his life in this world will keep it for eternal life. If anyone serves Me, he must follow Me; and where I am, there will My servant be also. If anyone serves Me, the Father will honor him.

The Son of Man Must Be Lifted Up

"Now is My soul troubled. And what shall I say? 'Father, save Me from this hour'? But for this purpose I have come to this hour. Father, glorify Your name." Then a voice came from heaven: "I have glorified it, and I will glorify it again." The crowd that stood there and heard it said that it had thundered. Others said, "An angel has spoken to Him." Jesus answered, "This voice has come for your sake, not Mine. Now is the judgment of this world; now will the ruler of this world be cast out. And I, when I am lifted up from the earth, will draw all people to Myself." He said this to show by what kind of death He was going to die. So the crowd answered Him, "We have heard from the Law that the Christ remains forever. How can You say that the Son of Man must be lifted up? Who is this Son of Man?" So Jesus said to them, "The light is among you for a little while longer. Walk while you have the light, lest darkness overtake you. The one who walks in the darkness does not know where he is going. While you have the light, believe in the light, that you may become sons of light."

Jesus reminds His disciples and the Greeks in His audience of the necessity of His cross and also of the necessity of our crosses. As it is necessary for the grain of wheat to fall into the ground and apparently decay and die before it can bring forth new life, so must the Son of God be laid low in death before He could achieve the ultimate goal and purpose for which He had come into the world: the salvation of all mankind, both Jew and Gentile.

And the hour of that death, He says, is now at hand. By that death, in the place of sinners, He would redeem the entire human family. "When I am lifted up from the earth," on the cross, [I] "will draw all people to Myself." That was the first point of His discourse.

And the second was like it. In a similar way, we Christians must lose our life if we are to find it. "Whoever loves his life loses it, and whoever hates his life in this world will keep it for eternal life." The early Christians who denied their faith in order to escape the lions saved their life in this world but lost it in the death eternal; but the martyr who dared to confess his faith in Christ lost his life in this world but kept it in the life eternal.

It is not probable that we will have to lose our lives in the same way as did the early Christians. But we will have to stand ready at all times to lose it for the Savior's sake.

Yes, in a sense we lose our life for the Savior every day. We lose it in unselfish service to our Lord and to our fellow men. "If anyone serves Me, he must follow Me," said Jesus, and then He walked straight toward Calvary. Are we willing to follow Him in such a path of service? Are we willing to "follow until it hurts," to "obey until it hurts," to "give until it hurts"?

The great apostle Paul said, "But whatever gain I had, I counted as loss for the sake of Christ. Indeed, I count everything as loss because of the surpassing worth of knowing Christ Jesus my Lord. For His sake I have suffered the loss of all things and count them as rubbish, in order that I may gain Christ" (Philippians 3:7–8).

Paul "suffered the loss of all things." But He found Christ. He lost his life, but in that loss he found something even more precious than life itself: eternal salvation through his Lord and Savior. Have we similarly lost our lives for Jesus?

Prayer

Jesus, I my cross have taken,
All to leave and follow Thee;
Destitute, despised, forsaken,
Thou from hence my All shalt be.
Perish ev'ry fond ambition,
All I've sought or hoped or known;
Yet how rich is my condition!
God and heav'n are still mine own.

Man may trouble and distress me,
'Twill but drive me to Thy breast;
Life with trials hard may press me,
Heav'n will bring me sweeter rest.
Oh, 'tis not in grief to harm me
While Thy love is left to me;
Oh, 'twere not in joy to charm me
Were that joy unmixed with Thee. Amen.
(TLH *423:1, 4)*

41

JESUS' FINAL PUBLIC APPEAL

John 12:37–50

THE evangelist is about to close the first great section of his Gospel. The remainder of his written record will be devoted to the never-to-be-forgotten scenes in the Upper Room on Maundy Thursday, to the dark and doleful events of Good Friday, and to the glorious events of Easter Sunday and the weeks following.

But before closing this first section, John gives a brief summary of the effects of Jesus' public ministry until this point. Alas! The overwhelming majority of the Jews did not believe in Him. And, while it was true that some of the leaders were inclined to accept Him as the Jews' Messiah, none of them had the courage to come out boldly and say so. Measured by all human standards, Jesus' ministry had been a failure.

Against this background, John now records the final public appeal of Jesus, delivered in the temple sometime during Holy Week. God grant us believing hearts as we read this last appeal of the Savior.

The Unbelief of the People

When Jesus had said these things, He departed and hid Himself from them. Though He had done so many signs before them, they still did not believe in Him, so that the word spoken by the prophet Isaiah might be fulfilled:

"Lord, who has believed what he heard from us,
and to whom has the arm of the Lord been revealed?"

Therefore they could not believe. For again Isaiah said,

"He has blinded their eyes and hardened their heart,
lest they see with their eyes, and understand with their
heart, and turn, and I would heal them."

Isaiah said these things because he saw His glory and spoke of Him. Nevertheless, many even of the authorities believed in Him, but for fear of the Pharisees they did not confess it, so that they would not be put out of the synagogue; for they loved the glory that comes from man more than the glory that comes from God.

Jesus Came to Save the World

And Jesus cried out and said, "Whoever believes in Me, believes not in Me but in Him who sent Me. And whoever sees Me sees Him who sent Me. I have come into the world as light, so that whoever believes in Me may not remain in darkness. If anyone hears My words and does not keep them, I do not judge him; for I did not come to judge the world but to save the world. The one who rejects Me and does not receive My words has a judge; the word that I have spoken will judge him on the last day. For I have not spoken on My own authority, but the Father who sent Me has Himself given Me a command-ment—what to say and what to speak. And I know that His commandment is eternal life. What I say, therefore, I say as the Father has told Me."

John introduces this final appeal of Jesus with the words "Jesus cried out and said." Literally, "He cried aloud." The compassion-ate Redeemer is eager to give His unbelieving countrymen a final opportunity to believe in Him. Before the week would end, He would be nailed to the cross, but they must have one more oppor-tunity to hear His words of pleading and of warning.

And what was it that He said? He gave them a brief summary of everything He had already told them. He is the Son of God. He and the Father are one. He who has seen Him has seen the Father. He that believes in Him believes in the Father also.

Jesus had "come into the world as light, so that whoever believes in Me may not remain in darkness." These are almost the same words that He had spoken in the temple only a few weeks before: "I am the light of the world. Whoever follows Me will not walk in dark-ness, but will have the light of life" (John 8:12).

But if any man rejects the Light, refuses to see Jesus as the Son of God and Savior of the world, his judgment is sure. He will be judged by the very words that Christ has spoken. For His words are not His words only but they are also the words of His Father who has sent Him.

What a terrible warning, not only to the Jews of Christ's day, but also to all people of all time! He that spurns Christ and His Gospel thereby condemns himself. On the last day, it will be the word of Christ that will render the judgment: those who have rejected it will themselves be rejected, and those who have accepted it will them-selves be accepted. Truly, says the Savior, "The word that I have spoken will judge him on the last day."

Have we accepted that Word? Oh, let us cherish that Word in believing hearts so it might always be "a fragrance from life to life," and never "a fragrance from death to death" (2 Corinthians 2:16). "For the word of the cross is folly to those who are perishing, but to us who are being saved it is the power of God" (1 Corinthians 1:18). Yes, the Gospel of Christ "is the power of God for salvation to everyone who believes" (Romans 1:16).

Prayer

As I pray, dear Jesus, hear me;
Let Your words in me take root.
May Your Spirit e'er be near me
That I bear abundant fruit.
May I daily sing Your praise,
From my heart glad anthems raise,
Till my highest praise is given
In the endless joy of heaven. Amen.
(LSB 589:4)

JESUS WASHES HIS DISCIPLES' FEET
John 13:1–17

WHEN the Lord appeared to Moses in the burning bush, He said, "Take your sandals off your feet, for the place on which you are standing is holy ground" (Exodus 3:5). These words might very well be written above the doorway to the Upper Room, which we are about to enter. For we are about to stand on "holy ground."

The earthly life of our Savior had extended over a period of more than thirty years. The three busy years of His public ministry had been crowded with intense activity. And yet John chooses to devote almost one-fourth of his entire Gospel to only one night of the Savior's life! Why?

We must remember the purpose of John's Gospel: "that you may believe that Jesus is the Christ, the Son of God, and that by believing you may have life in His name" (John 20:31). No one who beholds the gracious Savior in the Upper Room on the night of His betrayal, who traces His every act and hangs on His every word, can escape the inevitable conclusion: this is the Son of God! On that night, above all others, our blessed Lord revealed Himself in all the tenderness, all the beauty, and all the majestic dignity of the world's divine Redeemer.

John should know! For it was he who "was reclining at the table close to Jesus" in this most solemn night. How fortunate for us that he who was closest to the Savior's bleeding heart on the night before His crucifixion should have written down, for all men of all time, an intimate and accurate record of all that the Savior said and did. It is that record we now read.

Jesus Washes the Disciples' Feet

Now before the Feast of the Passover, when Jesus knew that His hour had come to depart out of this world to the Father, having loved His own who were in the world, He loved them to the end. During supper, when the devil had already put it into the heart of Judas Iscariot, Simon's son, to betray Him, Jesus, knowing that the Father had given all things into His hands, and that He had come from God and was going back to God, rose from supper. He laid aside His outer garments, and taking a towel, tied it around His waist. Then He poured water into a basin and began to wash the disciples' feet and to wipe them with the towel that was wrapped around Him. He came to Simon Peter, who said to Him, "Lord, do You wash my feet?" Jesus answered him, "What I am doing you do not understand now, but afterward you will understand." Peter said to Him, "You shall never wash my feet." Jesus answered him, "If I do not wash you, you have no share with Me." Simon Peter said to Him, "Lord, not my feet only but also my hands and my head!" Jesus said to him, "The one who has bathed does not need to wash, except for his feet, but is completely clean. And you are clean, but not every one of you." For He knew who was to betray Him; that was why He said, "Not all of you are clean."

When He had washed their feet and put on His outer garments and resumed His place, He said to them, "Do you understand what I have done to you? You call Me Teacher and Lord, and you are right, for so I am. If I then, your Lord and Teacher, have washed your feet, you also ought to wash one another's feet. For I have given you an example, that you also should do just as I have done to you. Truly, truly, I say to you, a servant is not greater than his master, nor is a messenger greater than the one who sent him. If you know these things, blessed are you if you do them."

In the closing hours of His life, Jesus must still teach His faithful few a lesson in humility. It had been only a few days before that a quarrel had arisen among them as to which of them was the greatest (Matthew 20:20–28). And so, after they have eaten their supper, Jesus lays aside His outer garments, takes a towel and girds Himself (the usual attire of a slave), and washes His disciples' feet.

The lesson He taught them on this night must have burned in their hearts forever after. No doubt, Simon Peter could still see his Lord kneeling down before him when he wrote almost thirty years later: "Clothe yourselves, all of you, with humility toward one another, for 'God opposes the proud but gives grace to the humble' " (1 Peter 5:5). Yes, it was the proud, haughty, and self-reliant Simon Peter who later learned to admonish to humility.

Have we learned as much? "If you know these things, blessed are you if you do them," says Jesus. Oh, it is so hard to be humble, so easy to be proud. It is so hard to serve, so easy to be served. Our wicked heart rebels against humility with every fiber of its being. And yet our Savior says, "I have given you an example, that you also should do just as I have done to you."

Let us pray daily and strive daily for true humility of heart, knowing that it is our Savior's will that we be humble, and knowing that if we ask anything according to His will, He will grant it to us.

Prayer

Prayer

*O Lord, thank You for sending Your Son into the world and
through Him giving us the commandment to love one another.
Grant, through the power of His holy Passion, that we may live in
obedience to His command, that we may follow His example, and
that finally, trusting solely in His merits, we may stand before
His throne in glory. In Jesus' name. Amen.*

JUDAS, THE TRAITOR
John 13:18–30

IN Psalm 41:9, we read: "Even my close friend in whom I trusted,
who ate my bread, has lifted his heel against me." To accept the
invitation to eat bread with a superior was regarded as a token of
undying loyalty. And to betray the superior at whose table one had
eaten was one of the lowest forms of treachery. Small wonder that
Jesus refers to this passage of the Old Testament as He now proceeds
to reveal the identity of His betrayer.

I am not speaking of all of you; I know whom I have chosen.
But the Scripture will be fulfilled, "He who ate My bread has
lifted his heel against Me." I am telling you this now, before it
takes place, that when it does take place you may believe that
I am He. Truly, truly, I say to you, whoever receives the one I
send receives Me, and whoever receives Me receives the one
who sent Me."

One of You Will Betray Me

After saying these things, Jesus was troubled in His spirit,
and testified, "Truly, truly, I say to you, one of you will betray

Me." The disciples looked at one another, uncertain of whom
He spoke. One of His disciples, whom Jesus loved, was reclining at table close to Jesus, so Simon Peter motioned to him
to ask Jesus of whom He was speaking. So that disciple, leaning back against Jesus, said to Him, "Lord, who is it?" Jesus
answered, "It is he to whom I will give this morsel of bread
when I have dipped it." So when He had dipped the morsel,
He gave it to Judas, the son of Simon Iscariot. Then after He
had taken the morsel, Satan entered into him. Jesus said to
him, "What you are going to do, do quickly." Now no one at
the table knew why He said this to him. Some thought that,
because Judas had the moneybag, Jesus was telling him, "Buy
what we need for the feast," or that he should give something
to the poor. So, after receiving the morsel of bread, he immediately went out. And it was night.

"And it was night." It was night in the city of Jerusalem, and it was
night in the soul of Judas. Of his own free will, he walked out of
the light and into the night because he preferred the darkness. How
true were the words of the Savior to Nicodemus: "And this is the
judgment: the light has come into the world, and people loved
the darkness rather than the light because their works were evil.
For everyone who does wicked things hates the light and does not
come to the light, lest his works should be exposed" (John 3:19–
20). The man who had spent three years in the company of "the
light of the world" has now forever drawn the curtains of his soul
against that light!

But how did Judas get that way? Did he not have the same
opportunity to be numbered among the Savior's "own" (John 13:1)
as did Peter and John and the other disciples? Indeed, he did. But
consciously and willingly, he trampled that blessed opportunity
underfoot. Oh, it was only a "little" sin that started Judas on the
path away from the light and into the darkness, but little sins have
a way of becoming big sins when they go unrepented day after day
and year after year. Surely Judas never thought, on the day that he
became one of Christ's disciples, that his "innocent" love of money

would grow to such uncontrollable proportions that the day would come when he would sell his Savior (and his soul!) for thirty pieces of silver!

Let us do a little soul-searching. John Bunyan tells us that, long after he had become a Christian, he could not eat a meal nor stoop to pick up a pin or chop a stick without hearing the voice of the tempter say, "Sell Christ for this or sell Christ for that; sell him, sell him" (*Grace Abounding to the Chief of Sinners* [The Religious Tract Society, 1905; Project Gutenberg, 1996], http://www.gutenberg.org/dirs/etext96/gacos10h.htm [accessed April 15, 2009]).

And isn't it true that the same tempter comes to us again and again with the same suggestion? Sell Christ for a moment of pleasure! Sell Christ for material gain! Sell Christ for public acclaim! Sell Christ for a life of comfort! Sell Christ for a high-salaried position! Sell Him! Sell Him! Isn't it true that in one form or another these sly suggestions of the evil one assail us again and again and are almost always present with us?

Let us beware of sinful ambition, of covetousness, of the love of money, of the love of ease and pleasure, for "it is through this craving that some have wandered away from the faith and pierced themselves with many pangs" (1 Timothy 6:10). Let the fate of Judas be our constant warning!

Prayer

O God, my faithful God,
True fountain ever flowing,
Without whom nothing is,
All perfect gifts bestowing:
Give me a healthy frame,
And may I have within
A conscience free from blame,
A soul unstained by sin.

Lord, let me win my foes
With kindly words and actions,
And let me find good friends
For counsel and correction.

Help me, as You have taught,
To love both great and small
And by Your Spirit's might
To live in peace with all. Amen.
(LSB 696:1, 4)

CHRIST GLORIFIED
John 13:31–38

JUDAS had left the Upper Room. An atmosphere of uneasiness and gloomy foreboding seems to have settled upon the disciples. They knew that an order for the arrest of their Master had been issued by the leaders of Jerusalem (John 11:57); they had heard from Jesus' lips that one of their very circle was about to betray Him (13:21); and they could sense from His solemn attitude as He sat at the meal with them that events were rapidly leaping toward a climax.

If ever a group of men needed encouragement, it was the Eleven as they sat alone with their Master on the night of His betrayal. And if ever a group of men was given encouragement, it was these Eleven in the Upper Room that night. John, the very John who had leaned on Jesus' bosom as they reclined at supper that night, recorded the beautiful words of comfort and encouragement that the Savior addressed to them. Not only this chapter, but also chapters 14–17 of his Gospel are devoted to Jesus' parting words in the Upper Room that night. May God grant us grace that we may find strength and comfort for our souls as we listen to these words from the lips of the Master.

A New Commandment

When He had gone out, Jesus said, "Now is the Son of Man glorified, and God is glorified in Him. If God is glorified in Him, God will also glorify Him in Himself, and glorify Him at once. Little children, yet a little while I am with you. You will seek Me, and just as I said to the Jews, so now I also say to you, 'Where I am going you cannot come.' A new commandment I give to you, that you love one another: just as I have loved you, you also are to love one another. By this all people will know that you are My disciples, if you have love for one another."

Jesus Foretells Peter's Denial

Simon Peter said to Him, "Lord, where are You going?" Jesus answered him, "Where I am going you cannot follow Me now, but you will follow afterward." Peter said to Him, "Lord, why can I not follow You now? I will lay down my life for You." Jesus answered, "Will you lay down your life for Me? Truly, truly, I say to you, the rooster will not crow till you have denied Me three times."

Within twelve hours, the Savior would be nailed to the cross. And yet He says, "Now is the Son of Man glorified." Again and again throughout His life, He had pointed to His death as the culmination of His purpose here on earth (John 3:14; 8:28; 12:32). It was on the cross that His divine glory was to be fully revealed—both His glory and the glory of His Father! That is why, on the eve of His crucifixion, the almighty Son of heaven could say, "Now is the Son of Man glorified."

"A new commandment I give to you, that you love one another." The Latin word for "commandment" is *mandatum*. And so from this commandment we have our "Maundy" Thursday. It is the day on which our blessed Lord gave us the new commandment that we love one another—new because of the new motivation from which this love should spring—"as I have loved you." The motivation for Christian love down through the centuries has found its source in the scenes of Maundy Thursday and Good Friday. "In this is love, not that we have loved God but that He loved us and sent His Son to be the propitiation for our sins. Beloved, if God so loved us, we also ought to love one another" (1 John 4:10–11). That was how John worded this "new commandment" of His Savior almost sixty years later.

"By this all people will know that you are My disciples, if you have love for one another." What a test of discipleship! "Behold, how they love one another," men said of the early Christians. Can that be said of our family? of our congregation? of our church body? Can people tell that we have been with Christ by the kindliness of our manner, by the humility of our bearing, by the solicitude we show for our brother's welfare?

Prayer

Father, who through Your Son have given us the commandment to love one another, grant us an abundant measure of Your Spirit, that we might love our fellow men even as You have loved us. In Jesus' name. Amen.

HEART TROUBLE
John 14:1–14

HEART trouble! That was the Great Physician's diagnosis of what really ailed His sorrowing disciples. He had just told them that He would soon leave them and they could not follow where He was going. The thought of separation after many months of intimate companionship, and especially after this never-to-be-forgotten night of tender fellowship, was a source of grief and pain to them.

Their hearts were troubled. And so, in His infinite wisdom and compassion, Jesus chose words to soothe their sorrows and silence all their fears. Luther says of the words we are about to read: "Here we find the best and most comforting sermon preached by Christ while on this earth . . . a jewel and treasure not purchasable with the world's goods" (AE 24:7). May God grant us believing hearts that this treasure, which cannot be purchased with gold and silver, may be ours by simple, trusting faith.

I Am the Way, and the Truth, and the Life

"Let not your hearts be troubled. Believe in God; believe also in Me. In My Father's house are many rooms. If it were not so, would I have told you that I go to prepare a place for you? And if I go and prepare a place for you, I will come again and will take you to Myself, that where I am you may be also. And you know the way to where I am going." Thomas said to Him, "Lord, we do not know where You are going. How can we know the way?" Jesus said to him, "I am the way, and the truth, and the life. No one comes to the Father except through Me. If you had known Me, you would have known My Father also. From now on you do know Him and have seen Him."

Philip said to Him, "Lord, show us the Father, and it is enough for us." Jesus said to him, "Have I been with you so long, and you still do not know Me, Philip? Whoever has seen Me has seen the Father. How can you say, 'Show us the Father'? Do you not believe that I am in the Father and the Father is in Me? The words that I say to you I do not speak on My own authority, but the Father who dwells in Me does His works. Believe Me that I am in the Father and the Father is in Me, or else believe on account of the works themselves.

"Truly, truly, I say to you, whoever believes in Me will also do the works that I do; and greater works than these will he do, because I am going to the Father. Whatever you ask in My name, this I will do, that the Father may be glorified in the Son. If you ask Me anything in My name, I will do it."

Heart trouble! Who among God's children has not had his share of heart troubles! Who among us has not had his share of anxious, trying hours; hours of sickness, perhaps hours of death; sleepless nights;

friendless, lonely hours; moments when that lump within our throat began to swell and that teardrop in our eye refused to be concealed; hours when our debts seemed greater than our God, hours when our enemies seemed closer than our Savior; days when our heart, indeed, was troubled, and we cried to God for help.

It was then that the divine prescription of our Savior for hearts in trouble provided the only healing balm. "Let not your hearts be troubled," He says. But He also tells us why: "In My Father's house are many rooms. ... And if I go and prepare a place for you, I will come again and will take you to Myself, that where I am you may be also."

All sorrows, all heartaches, all disappointments, all bereavements, and all heart troubles lose their bitterness in the sweetness of the Savior's tender promise: "I will come again." I will come again to turn your sorrows into joy, your heartaches into gladness, and your bereavements into heavenly reunions in My Father's house above.

In the healing light of that heavenly assurance, our Divine Physician has given us the cure for all our griefs and sorrows. He whose love brought Him to Calvary's cross to open the doors of His Father's house to a world that had spurned His every pleading— He will come again to lead us, His children, across the threshold into the eternal mansions, prepared by Him for all who love Him. What a glorious promise! What a heavenly prospect! Let us find daily strength and joy in that sublime assurance.

Prayer
What is the world to me
With all its vaunted pleasure
When You, and You alone,
Lord Jesus, are my treasure!
You only, dearest Lord,
My soul's delight shall be;
You are my peace, my rest.
What is the world to me!
(LSB 730:1)

THE PROMISE OF THE HELPER

John 14:15–26

JESUS comforted His troubled disciples with the assurance that He would come again to receive them to Himself. But what about the time that would elapse between now and then, between that first Maundy Thursday and the glorious day of Christ's return? Would they be left alone? Would they be left to face a hostile world on their own, without the guidance, without the assurance, without the strength of the Savior's power and presence?

No, He made provision for this need also. He would send them another Strengthener, "another Helper." "Another" indicates that, in some respects, the mission of the coming Helper would be similar to His own: to guide, to teach, to strengthen, and to defend those whom the Father had entrusted to His care.

But let us read this remarkable and consoling promise of "another Helper."

Jesus Promises the Holy Spirit

"If you love Me, you will keep My commandments. And I will ask the Father, and He will give you another Helper, to be with you forever, even the Spirit of truth, whom the world cannot receive, because it neither sees Him nor knows Him. You know Him, for He dwells with you and will be in you.

"I will not leave you as orphans; I will come to you. Yet a little while and the world will see Me no more, but you will see Me. Because I live, you also will live. In that day you will know that I am in My Father, and you in Me, and I in you. Whoever has My commandments and keeps them, he it is who loves Me. And he who loves Me will be loved by My Father, and I will love him and manifest Myself to him." Judas (not Iscariot) said to Him, "Lord, how is it that You will manifest Yourself to us,

and not to the world?" Jesus answered him, "If anyone loves
Me, he will keep My word, and My Father will love him, and
We will come to him and make Our home with him. Whoever
does not love Me does not keep My words. And the word that
you hear is not Mine but the Father's who sent Me.

"These things I have spoken to you while I am still with you.
But the Helper, the Holy Spirit, whom the Father will send
in My name, He will teach you all things and bring to your
remembrance all that I have said to you."

A most remarkable passage! Notice, first, how Jesus, on the eve of
His return to the Father's house, speaks clearly of the other two persons of the Holy Trinity who await His arrival there. He says, "I
will ask the Father, and He will give you another Helper, to be with
you forever, even the Spirit of truth." The Son will pray the Father
to send the Holy Spirit. Three persons. Again He speaks of "the
Helper, the Holy Spirit, whom the Father will send in My name,"
clearly revealing all three persons of the Godhead.

But what does He say about this Helper? That He will "be with
you forever." The gift of the Holy Spirit is the New Testament
gift to all Christians. All Christians have a share in the blessings of
the Comforter and can exult with Martin Luther when he says: "I
believe that I cannot by my own reason or strength believe in Jesus
Christ, my Lord, or come to Him; but the Holy Spirit has called me
by the Gospel, enlightened me with His gifts, sanctified and kept
me in the true faith" (*Luther's Small Catechism with Explanation,* p.
147). This is the Helper who is to abide with us forever, "the Spirit
of truth, whom the world cannot receive, because it neither sees
Him nor knows Him. You know Him, for He dwells with you and
will be in you."

But more: "He will teach you all things and bring to your
remembrance all that I have said to you." The glorious fulfillment
of this precious promise is before our eyes at this very moment.
We are reading the exact words the Lord Jesus spoke in the Upper
Room that night because the Holy Spirit brought them to John's
memory some sixty years later and prompted him to write them

in his Gospel. We have the complete inspired record of the New Testament because the Holy Spirit of God inspired the penman to write down "all that I have said to you." It is a mark of the Savior's tender concern not only for the Eleven, but also for all who were to believe in Him through their word, that on His last night on earth He arranged for the preservation—in the sacred pages of the Bible—of all He said and did.

Are we always sufficiently conscious of this New Testament gift of the Holy Spirit? And are we always sufficiently grateful for its blessings? Let us implore our heavenly Father for an ever greater measure of the blessings of this Comforter.

Prayer

Holy Spirit, light divine,
Shine upon this heart of mine;
Chase the shades of night away,
Turn the darkness into day.

Let me see my Savior's face,
Let me all His beauties trace;
Show those glorious truths to me
Which are only known to Thee.

Holy Spirit, joy divine,
Cheer this saddened heart of mine;
Yield a sacred, settled peace,
Let it grow and still increase.

Holy Spirit, all divine,
Dwell within this heart of mine;
Cast down ev'ry idol throne,
Reign supreme, and reign alone. Amen.
(LSB 496:1–2, 4–5)

"MY PEACE I GIVE TO YOU"
John 14:27–31

IN the face of His departure, Jesus had consoled the hearts of His despondent disciples with two glorious assurances. First, He was leaving them only temporarily: He was going to prepare a place for them; He would come again and receive them unto Himself. Second, until such a time as they would meet again face-to-face, He was sending them "another Helper" (v. 15), the Holy Spirit, who would guide, uphold, and strengthen them until the moment of His return.

These assurances should soothe their troubled spirits, should stay their hearts in peace. Having their almighty Savior at their side and His comforting and sustaining Spirit within their hearts, the future could hold nothing of which they need be afraid. Their hearts could be kept in perfect peace.

That is the thread of the Savior's thought as He now continues.

> Peace I leave with you; My peace I give to you. Not as the world gives do I give to you. Let not your hearts be troubled, neither let them be afraid. You heard Me say to you, "I am going away, and I will come to you." If you loved Me, you would have rejoiced, because I am going to the Father, for the Father is greater than I. And now I have told you before it takes place, so that when it does take place you may believe. I will no longer talk much with you, for the ruler of this world is coming. He has no claim on Me, but I do as the Father has commanded Me, so that the world may know that I love the Father. Rise, let us go from here.

"Peace I leave with you; My peace I give to you." There is a tender beauty concealed in the two verbs of this familiar sentence of the Savior. "Peace I bequeath to you" would perhaps be an accurate translation of the first half of His statement. The Master was about to die. What could He leave behind as an everlasting token of His love for those whom the Father had given to His care? What was it they needed? What was it for which their hearts ached and for which their souls yearned? Peace! And so His last bequest is suited to their foremost need. "Peace I bequeath to you."

And then He continues, in seeming repetition: "My peace I give to you." The word *peace* was the usual wish of farewell. But Jesus wants them to know that with Him it was far more than a mere wish. "My peace I give to you"—"I impart My peace to you." It was within His power actually to give peace to their troubled hearts, and He was doing just that.

It was not to be a spurious or counterfeit peace. "My peace I give to you," He says. "Not as the world gives do I give to you." The world may cry for peace where there is none, but when the Son of God grants peace to a human heart, all conflict ceases. His is the peace "which surpasses all understanding" (Philippians 4:7). "Therefore, since we have been justified by faith, we have peace with God through our Lord Jesus Christ," says Paul (Romans 5:1).

With this precious gift of abiding peace assured to them, the Savior repeats the words He had addressed to them before: "Let not your hearts be troubled, neither let them be afraid."

Is our heart troubled? Is our heart afraid? The peace of Christ, the assurance of a loving and forgiving and providing Father, revealed to us by our blessed Savior, will drive our fears away. Let us rest our hearts in that assurance. "And the peace of God, which surpasses all understanding, will guard your hearts and your minds in Christ Jesus" (Philippians 4:7).

Prayer

Jesus, priceless treasure,
Fount of purest pleasure,
Truest friend to me,
Ah, how long in anguish
Shall my spirit languish,

Yearning, Lord, for Thee?
 Thou art mine,
 O Lamb divine!
I will suffer naught to hide Thee;
Naught I ask beside Thee.

In Thine arms I rest me;
Foes who would molest me
Cannot reach me here.
Though the earth be shaking,
Ev'ry heart be quaking,
Jesus calms my fear.
 Lightnings flash
 And thunders crash;
Yet, though sin and hell assail me,
Jesus will not fail me.

Hence, all fear and sadness!
For the Lord of gladness,
Jesus, enters in.
Those who love the Father,
Though the storms may gather,
 Still have peace within.
 Yea, whate'er I here must bear,
Thou art still my purest pleasure,
Jesus, priceless treasure! Amen.
(LSB 743:1–2, 6)

48

"I AM THE VINE; YOU ARE THE BRANCHES"

John 15:1–11

WE Christians are not always sufficiently mindful of the "mystic sweet communion" that exists between our blessed Lord and His believers. Indeed, we sometimes find ourselves imagining that since His ascension into heaven, our Lord is separated from His loved ones by the vast, unmeasured distances that separate the planets. Christ is *there*, we say; and we are *here*; while the truth of the matter is that both Christ and we are *here*!

Jesus knew His faithful few would soon be grieved by such a painful sense of separation. They would feel that the intimate tie that had bound them to their Lord had been broken. And so, on the eve of His departure, He assures them that, in a sense, their association in the future will be even more intimate than it was before. The relationship of Master and disciple was soon to take on the indescribably more intimate, more abiding, and more satisfying relationship of the vine and its branches. That is the relationship Jesus now describes.

I Am the True Vine

I am the true vine, and My Father is the vinedresser. Every branch in Me that does not bear fruit He takes away, and every branch that does bear fruit He prunes, that it may bear more fruit. Already you are clean because of the word that I have spoken to you. Abide in Me, and I in you. As the branch cannot bear fruit by itself, unless it abides in the vine, neither can you, unless you abide in Me. I am the vine; you are the branches. Whoever abides in Me and I in him, he it is that bears much fruit, for apart from Me you can do nothing. If anyone does not abide in Me he is thrown away like a branch and withers; and the branches are gathered, thrown into the fire, and burned. If you abide in Me, and My words abide in you, ask whatever you wish, and it will be done for you. By this My Father is glorified, that you bear much fruit and so prove to be My disciples. As the Father has loved Me, so have I loved you. Abide in My love. If you keep My commandments, you will abide in My love, just as I have kept My Father's commandments and abide in His love. These things I have spoken to you, that My joy may be in you, and that your joy may be full.

Books could be written on these few paragraphs. We must limit ourselves to sentences. The world knows no relationship as intimate, as beautiful, and as comforting as the mystic union that exists between Christ and His believers. Jesus says, "I am the vine; you are the branches." Notice He does not say, "I am the root." He is the whole vine, and to be a part of that vine is to be a part of Christ. This is the same thought Paul expresses when he says that all Christians are members of Christ's Body (1 Corinthians 12:12). Can there be any thought of separation or of absence from His love and power when He tells us that we are a part of Him?

"Whoever abides in Me and I in him, he it is that bears much fruit." The branch that is part of the living vine brings forth fruit in abundance. And what is this fruit? Paul groups it into a beautiful cluster of nine: "The fruit of the Spirit is love, joy, peace, patience, kindness, goodness, faithfulness, gentleness, self-control" (Galatians 5:22–23). This is the fruit of Christian character that identifies the branch as belonging to the vine. Is this the fruit we bear?

Notice the two laws of fruit-bearing that Jesus lays down: pruning and abiding. Pruning—by God. Abiding—by us. The good branches, says Jesus, are pruned so they might bring forth still more and better fruit. Has God found it necessary to "prune" us, to cut away the dead twigs we allowed to grow? If so, it was so our fruit might be the better.

And the other law of fruit-bearing is "abiding." The branch that falls from the vine will bring no fruit to perfection. "Whoever abides in Me and I in him, he it is that bears much fruit." Are we abiding? When did we attend the Lord's Supper last? How often do we hear

His Word? Do we speak to Christ on the way to work? and again when our tasks are finished? Remember, abiding in the vine is the fundamental law of fruit-bearing.

Prayer

Chief of sinners though I be,
Jesus shed His blood for me,
Died that I might live on high,
Lives that I might never die.
As the branch is to the vine,
I am His, and He is mine.

O my Savior, help afford
By Your Spirit and Your Word!
When my wayward heart would stray,
Keep me in the narrow way;
Grace in time of need supply
While I live and when I die. Amen. (LSB 611:1, 5)

"IF THE WORLD HATES YOU"

John 15:12–25

THE disciples were well aware that they were hated by the leaders of the Jews. After all, they were the associates of the very Man whose arrest had already been ordered. Being a friend of Jesus, they knew, was not the popular thing in Jerusalem that night. Had not the blind man been cast out of the synagogue for being His friend? Had not the life of Lazarus been endangered because of his relation to the Savior? Could they expect better treatment?

But now that Jesus speaks of leaving them, the hatred of the unbelieving Jews must have suddenly become much more real, much more threatening to them. What if Jesus leaves them—will they be able to face the hatred of a hostile world? The omniscient and compassionate Savior knows their hearts, and so He has a word to say about the hatred of the world. He would forewarn them and, thus, forearm them.

"This is My commandment, that you love one another as I have loved you. Greater love has no one than this, that someone lay down his life for his friends. You are My friends if you do what I command you. No longer do I call you servants, for the servant does not know what his master is doing; but I have called you friends, for all that I have heard from My Father I have made known to you. You did not choose Me, but I chose you and appointed you that you should go and bear fruit and that your fruit should abide, so that whatever you ask the Father in My name, He may give it to you. These things I command you, so that you will love one another.

The Hatred of the World

"If the world hates you, know that it has hated Me before it hated you. If you were of the world, the world would love you as its own; but because you are not of the world, but I chose you out of the world, therefore the world hates you. Remember the word that I said to you: 'A servant is not greater than his master.' If they persecuted Me, they will also persecute you. If they kept My word, they will also keep yours. But all these things they will do to you on account of My name, because they do not know Him who sent Me. If I had not come and spoken to them, they would not have been guilty of sin, but now they have no excuse for their sin. Whoever hates Me hates My Father also. If I had not done among them the works that no one else did, they would not be guilty of sin, but now they have seen and hated both Me and My Father. But the word that is written in their Law must be fulfilled: 'They hated Me without a cause.'"

As long as we Christians remain in this world, we are in enemy territory. And as long as we "bear on [our] body the marks of Jesus" (Galatians 6:17), we cannot look for anything else but hatred from the world of sinful men in which we live. That is the clear statement of the Savior. "If you were of the world, the world would love you as its own; but because you are not of the world, but I chose you out of the world, therefore the world hates you." And on another occasion, He said, "You will be hated by all for My name's sake" (Matthew 10:22).

But we are in good company when we endure the world's enmity. Our blessed Lord was the first to taste its venomous fury. Almost the entire Gospel of St. John is the record of the world's hate for the sinless Son of God and of His love for that hating world. Therefore, He says, "If the world hates you, know that it has hated Me before it hated you. . . . A servant is not greater than his master." Our intimate communion with the Savior, which He described by the relationship of the vine and the branches, demands that we are in fellowship with Him in His suffering. What a precious glory to share the hatred of a godless world with the eternal King of glory! If it is true that we can judge a man by the enemies he has, what a badge of honor it is to have the same enemies as the holy and spotless Son of God!

Or do we have no enemies? "Woe to you, when all people speak well of you," says Jesus (Luke 6:26). If we stand for the things Jesus stood for, we are bound to have enemies. The world will have nothing to do with a religion that claims that Jesus is God, that claims salvation can come only through trusting faith in His blood, that claims "there is salvation in no one else" (Acts 4:12). As long as we cling to these and other teachings of the Savior, we will incur the scorn, the ridicule, and the opposition of a world that has set itself against these very doctrines. If the sinful world is not our enemy, then it is high time that we ask ourselves if Jesus Christ is our Friend. "Remember the word that I said to you: 'A servant is not greater than his master.' If they persecuted Me, they will also persecute you." Those are the words of our Master.

Prayer

Jesus, I my cross have taken,
All to leave and follow Thee;
Destitute, despised, forsaken,
Thou from hence my All shalt be.
Perish ev'ry fond ambition,
All I've sought or hoped or known;
Yet how rich is my condition!
God and heav'n are still mine own.

Let the world despise and leave me,
They have left my Savior, too.
Human hearts and looks deceive me;
Thou art not, like them, untrue.
And while Thou shalt smile upon me,
God of wisdom, love, and might,
Foes may hate and friends may shun me;
Show Thy face, and all is bright.

Man may trouble and distress me,
'Twill but drive me to Thy breast;
Life with trials hard may press me,
Heav'n will bring me sweeter rest.
Oh, 'tis not in grief to harm me
While Thy love is left to me;
Oh, 'twere not in joy to charm me
Were that joy unmixed with Thee. Amen.
(TLH 423:1–2, 4)

"IT IS TO YOUR ADVANTAGE THAT I GO"

John 15:26–16:15

PERSECUTION was to be the inevitable lot of Jesus' disciples. Yes, the time would come when those who would raise their hand to kill His followers would think they were doing God a service. But where would the Eleven—weak, timid, and fearful as they were that night—where would they ever get the courage to face their inevitable ordeal with fortitude, boldness, and joy? Again Jesus promises them "the Helper." The Holy Spirit, whom He would send them from the Father, would pour light and power and courage into their doubting hearts; He would enable them to bear bold and courageous witness; He would support their preaching by convicting the world "concerning sin and righteousness and judgment"; and He would guide them into all truth.

In today's reading, Jesus reveals these purposes of the Helper.

"But when the Helper comes, whom I will send to you from the Father, the Spirit of truth, who proceeds from the Father, He will bear witness about Me. And you also will bear witness, because you have been with Me from the beginning.

"I have said all these things to you to keep you from falling away. They will put you out of the synagogues. Indeed, the hour is coming when whoever kills you will think he is offering service to God. And they will do these things because they have not known the Father, nor Me. But I have said these things to you, that when their hour comes you may remember that I told them to you.

The Work of the Holy Spirit

"I did not say these things to you from the beginning, because I was with you. But now I am going to Him who sent

Me, and none of you asks Me, "Where are You going?" But because I have said these things to you, sorrow has filled your heart. Nevertheless, I tell you the truth: it is to your advantage that I go away, for if I do not go away, the Helper will not come to you. But if I go, I will send Him to you. And when He comes, He will convict the world concerning sin and righteousness and judgment: concerning sin, because they do not believe in Me; concerning righteousness, because I go to the Father, and you will see Me no longer; concerning judgment, because the ruler of this world is judged.

"I still have many things to say to you, but you cannot bear them now. When the Spirit of truth comes, He will guide you into all the truth, for He will not speak on His own authority, but whatever He hears He will speak, and He will declare to you the things that are to come. He will glorify Me, for He will take what is Mine and declare it to you. All that the Father has is Mine; therefore I said that He will take what is Mine and declare it to you."

The coming of the Helper was conditional; it was dependent upon Jesus' departure. "I tell you the truth," He says, "If I do not go away, the Helper will not come to you." It was necessary for the Christ to carry out the full program of redemption by His suffering, death, resurrection, and ascension before the Pentecost gift of the Holy Spirit could be given. For it was the glorious message of redemption that the Holy Spirit was to apply to the hearts of men. That is why it was necessary Jesus suffer before the Helper could come.

And praise be to His name, Jesus kept His promise: "But if I go, I will send Him to you." It was but ten days after His ascension into heaven that He poured out His Holy Spirit upon His faithful few who were assembled at Jerusalem. And what a difference did that first Pentecost make (Acts 2)! The Helper had come! And from an unknown room in the city of Jerusalem, there issued forth a little group of men—fearless, bold, courageous man—who were soon to turn the world upside down for Christ.

Let us never forget that this same Holy Spirit attends and gives power to all faithful Gospel preaching to this very day. Through the preaching of the Word and our hearing of it, He still convicts the world of unbelief, He still bears witness to the only righteousness that avails in the sight of God (the righteousness that is ours by faith in Christ), and He still proclaims the judgment whereby Christ has forever overcome the powers of darkness. To this day, the Holy Spirit gives persuasive power to the sermon of the humblest preacher who preaches the Gospel of our Savior.

Do we pray for the gift of the Holy Spirit for our pastor every time he preaches? Do we pray that the Holy Spirit would bring the light of the Gospel into the hearts of those who have not yet learned to know their Savior? And do we pray for the warming, cheering, and enlightening influence of the Helper in our own lives? Let us do so now.

Prayer

Come, Holy Spirit, come!
Let Thy bright beams arise;
Dispel the sorrow from our minds,
The darkness from our eyes.

Revive our drooping faith,
Our doubts and fears remove,
And kindle in our breasts the flame
Of never-dying love.

Convince us of our sin,
Then lead to Jesus' blood,
And to our wond'ring view reveal
The mercies of our God. Amen.
(TLH 225:1–3)

51

"A LITTLE WHILE"
John 16:16–22

WHEN Philip Melanchthon, Luther's friend, lay on his deathbed, he asked that a Bible be brought and that the Gospel of John, chapters 14–17, be read. In the sweet assurance of those chapters, he was ready to close his eyes in death. No one will ever be able to count the unnumbered throngs who have found strength for life and comfort in death in just these chapters. And if these four chapters are so rich in comfort, what can we say about the seven verses we read today? Let us read these words with reverence for the One who spoke them, with gratitude for the fact that He did speak them, and with joy because of the unspeakable comfort they bring.

Your Sorrow Will Turn into Joy

"A little while, and you will see Me no longer; and again a little while, and you will see Me." So some of His disciples said to one another, "What is this that He says to us, 'A little while, and you will not see Me, and again a little while, and you will see Me'; and, 'because I am going to the Father'?" So they were saying, "What does He mean by 'a little while'? We do not know what He is talking about." Jesus knew that they wanted to ask Him, so He said to them, "Is this what you are asking yourselves, what I meant by saying, 'A little while and you will not see Me, and again a little while and you will see Me'? Truly, truly, I say to you, you will weep and lament, but the world will rejoice. You will be sorrowful, but your sorrow will turn into joy. When a woman is giving birth, she has sorrow because her hour has come, but when she has delivered the baby, she no longer remembers the anguish, for joy that a human being has been born into the world. So also you have sorrow now, but I will see you again, and your hearts will rejoice, and no one will take your joy from you."

A little while! When Jesus spoke these words, He was referring, of course, to the sorrow of Good Friday and to the holy joy of Easter. The little while of sadness is followed by an eternity of bliss.

In a sense, the life of the Christian is a swift succession of many little whiles. We experience sorrow, but our sorrows are separated from our joys by little whiles. "For a brief moment I deserted you," He says, "but with great compassion I will gather you" (Isaiah 54:7). "Weeping may tarry for the night, but joy comes with the morning," He says through David the psalmist (Psalm 30:5).

And life itself is but "a little while" in the calendar of God's eternity. Life's little while of sorrow will soon be swallowed up in the endless ages of pure delight in heaven. Lazarus spent a little while in the company of dogs, but he is spending an eternity of bliss in Abraham's bosom. The thief spent a little while suspended on the cross, but his sorrow has been turned into the endless joy of paradise. Of these sorrows and joys Paul writes, "The sufferings of this present time are not worth comparing with the glory that is to be revealed to us" (Romans 8:18).

Let us, then, accept these little whiles of pain and sorrow as preludes to a perfect day. We have our Savior's promise: Our sorrows will be turned into joy; our cloudy days into days of sunshine; our little whiles of doubt, trial, loneliness, and sadness shall be turned into eternal ages of joy and glory in the company of heaven.

His promise to all Christians of all times is this: "I will see you again, and your hearts will rejoice, and no one will take your joy from you."

Prayer

My Jesus, as Thou wilt;
Oh, may Thy will be mine!
Into Thy hand of love
I would my all resign.
Thro' sorrow or thro' joy
Conduct me as Thine own
And help me still to say,
My Lord, Thy will be done.

My Jesus, as Thou wilt.
Tho' seen thro' many a tear,
Let not my star of hope
Grow dim or disappear.
Since Thou on earth hast wept
And sorrowed oft alone,
If I must weep with Thee,
My Lord, Thy will be done.

My Jesus, as Thou wilt.
All shall be well for me;
Each changing future scene
I gladly trust with Thee.
Thus to my home above
I travel calmly on
And sing in life or death,
My Lord, Thy will be done. Amen. (TLH 420:1, 3, 5)

52

CHRIST'S LAST WORDS TO HIS DISCIPLES

John 16:23–33

NO one can read Jesus' farewell address to His disciples without noticing what great emphasis He placed on prayer (John 14:13–14; 15:16; 16:23–24). He knew that His visible presence was soon to be withdrawn from them, so He reminds them again and again of the intimate fellowship that will continue to exist between them and His Father and Himself even after He is gone—the intimate fellowship of prayer.

He encourages them to pray by repeated and emphatic promises that their prayers will be heard. And He reminds them of the three essentials of every truly Christian prayer:

It must be directed to the God of the Bible—"the Father." It must be prayed in the name of Jesus—"in My name." And it must be prayed in faith (Matthew 21:22). Do our prayers follow this?

The words we are about to read are the last words Jesus addressed to His disciples before the familiar scenes of the Garden of Gethsemane. God grant us His Spirit as we read them.

> "In that day you will ask nothing of Me. Truly, truly, I say to you, whatever you ask of the Father in My name, He will give it to you. Until now you have asked nothing in My name. Ask, and you will receive, that your joy may be full.

I Have Overcome the World

> "I have said these things to you in figures of speech. The hour is coming when I will no longer speak to you in figures of speech but will tell you plainly about the Father. In that day you will ask in My name, and I do not say to you that I will ask the Father on your behalf; for the Father Himself loves you, because you have loved Me and have believed that I came from God. I came from the Father and have come into the world, and now I am leaving the world and going to the Father."

> His disciples said, "Ah, now You are speaking plainly and not using figurative speech! Now we know that You know all things and do not need anyone to question You; this is why we believe that You came from God." Jesus answered them, "Do you now believe? Behold, the hour is coming, indeed it has come, when you will be scattered, each to his own home, and will leave Me alone. Yet I am not alone, for the Father is with Me. I have said these things to you, that in Me you may have peace. In the world you will have tribulation. But take heart; I have overcome the world."

"I have overcome the world!" And the next day He was to die upon a cross! What a glorious thought this is: "I have overcome the world!" By His substitutionary death upon the cross, He has over-come, He has gained victory over all the enemies of our soul: sin, death, and the power of the devil.

And His victory is our victory. That is why He says to His dis-ciples and to us: "But take heart; I have overcome the world." The fruits of His victory—forgiveness of sins, life, and salvation—are ours. What a marvelous triumph! What precious spoils our Captain has wrested from the hands of our enemy and thrown into our lap! With the apostle Paul, we can exclaim, " 'O death, where is your victory? O death, where is your sting?' The sting of death is sin, and the power of sin is the law. But thanks be to God, who gives us the victory through our Lord Jesus Christ" (1 Corinthians 15:55–57).

But Christ did not only win the victory for us, He also "won the peace." "I have said these things to you, that in Me you may have peace. In the world you will have tribulation. But take heart; I have overcome the world." The Christian has a twofold life—in the world and in Christ. And therefore he has a twofold experi-ence—in the world, tribulation; in Christ, peace. Haven't we often experienced the sweet comfort of this truth? In the world, tribula-tion, but in Christ, peace?

What a kind farewell and comforting last word Christ leaves to His disciples. Have we experienced the tender kindness of these words and the reassuring comfort of their promise? God grant it for Jesus' sake.

Prayer

O God, the coming of whose Son into our hearts brings victory, grant to us the peace that the world cannot give. Grant that in the midst of tribulation we may rest in the quiet assurance of Your love and find our only joy and hope in You. Give all men every-where that peace that surpasses all understanding and which is to be found only in the merits of Jesus Christ, Your Son, our only Savior. Amen.

THE PRAYER OF JESUS ON THE NIGHT OF HIS BETRAYAL
John 17:1–5

IT is universally felt that, in some wonderful sense, chapter 17 of John's Gospel is the Most Holy Place of the Sacred Scriptures. Here we stand, as it were, in the holy presence of God the Father and God the Son and listen to the Son as He communes with God the Father. Here we have what has come to be known as the High Priestly Prayer of Jesus, addressed to His Father on behalf of His friends on the eve of His crucifixion.

In our meditation on this passage, we see that the petitions that welled from the Savior's heart and found expression in this prayer of prayers flowed in three distinct movements. He opens His prayer with a plea on behalf of Himself, then continues with a petition on behalf of His disciples, and closes with a prayer for all believers of all times. It is the first third of His High Priestly Prayer that we now read.

The High Priestly Prayer

When Jesus had spoken these words, He lifted up His eyes to heaven, and said, "Father, the hour has come; glorify Your Son that the Son may glorify You, since You have given Him authority over all flesh, to give eternal life to all whom You have given Him. And this is eternal life, that they know You the only true God, and Jesus Christ whom You have sent. I glorified You on earth, having accomplished the work that You gave Me to do. And now, Father, glorify Me in Your own presence with the glory that I had with You before the world existed."

Having completed His farewell address to His disciples, Jesus lifts His eyes toward heaven and begins His Priestly Prayer. "Father,"

He says. And six times in His prayer He repeats this intimate and loving salutation. He was not praying to a God who was far off, to a God who was unknown, to a God who held Himself aloof from the affairs of men. He was praying to someone He knew, someone He knew intimately and affectionately: "Father."

"The hour has come." The hour that had been appointed before the world's beginning, on which all history had converged, on which the destiny of the human family hung—that hour had come! Judas and his band were already on their way. The hour for the suffering of the Son of God in the place of sinners had come!

And for what does the Savior pray in the face of that dreadful hour? "Glorify Me in Your own presence with the glory that I had with You before the world existed." Jesus knew the way back to the glory He had with His Father "before the world existed" lay through Gethsemane and Calvary. He knew that it was through His Passion, death, and resurrection that He was to glorify His Father. He knew that the work of redemption was the crowning glory of the heavenly counsel. And so He prays that the work of redemption might now be accomplished. The hour has come—and He prays His Father that the stupendous plan they had agreed upon for this supremely momentous hour might be carried out as planned.

"Father, the hour has come; glorify Your Son." That is the summary of the first part of our Savior's High Priestly Prayer. Thank God that prayer was answered! For in the suffering, death, and resurrection of our blessed Lord lies our salvation. The Father has glorified the Son. The Son has glorified the Father. And we all—unworthy as we are—have received grace and mercy because of the greatness of their glory!

Prayer
Lord God, heavenly Father, I thank You for giving Your only-
begotten Son into death that I might have life. Grant that,
as Your Son glorified Your name while here on earth, I, too,
may live and die to the honor and the glory of Your holy name.
For Jesus' sake. Amen.

JESUS PRAYS FOR HIS APOSTLES
John 17:6–19

AS we read the High Priestly Prayer of Christ, we are impressed by the frequent repetition of the pronouns *I* and *You* and *they*. "I have manifested Your name to the people whom You gave Me out of the world. Yours they were" is just one of the many beautiful lines of this prayer, in which Jesus pours out His heart to His Father on behalf of His friends.

They, You, and *I.* In these three words, we find the blessed meaning and the full glory of the Savior's priestly office. He is the eternal mediator between the Father and the sinner. Throughout the endless ages, He stands before the Father's throne, and the burden of His changeless plea is ever, only *they* and *You* and *I* (see Romans 8:34; 1 Timothy 2:5; 1 John 2:1). "I have manifested Your name to the people whom You gave Me." Are we always sufficiently conscious of and grateful for the merciful and mighty intercession of our Savior?

Let us now listen to Him as, on the night of His betrayal, He pleads with His heavenly Father on behalf of His apostles.

> "I have manifested Your name to the people whom You gave Me out of the world. Yours they were, and You gave them to Me, and they have kept Your word. Now they know that everything that You have given Me is from You. For I have given them the words that You gave Me, and they have received them and have come to know in truth that I came from You; and they have believed that You sent Me. I am praying for them. I am not praying for the world but for those whom you have given Me, for they are Yours. All Mine are Yours, and Yours are Mine, and I am glorified in them. And I am no longer in the world, but they are in the world, and I am coming to You. Holy Father,

keep them in Your name, which You have given Me, that they may be one, even as We are one. While I was with them, I kept them in Your name, which You have given Me. I have guarded them, and not one of them has been lost except the son of destruction, that the Scripture might be fulfilled. But now I am coming to You, and these things I speak in the world, that they may have My joy fulfilled in themselves. I have given them Your word, and the world has hated them because they are not of the world, just as I am not of the world. I do not ask that You take them out of the world, but that You keep them from the evil one. They are not of the world, just as I am not of the world. Sanctify them in the truth; Your word is truth. As You sent Me into the world, so I have sent them into the world. And for their sake I consecrate Myself, that they also may be sanctified in truth.

For three years, Jesus had "kept" His disciples; He had watched over them, protected them, and preserved them. Now He was going to leave them. And so, as a mother who is to be absent from her little ones for a while commends them to the safekeeping of their father, so Jesus in His High Priestly Prayer commends His faithful few to the watchful care and guidance of their Father in heaven. "Holy Father, keep them in Your name. . . . While I was with them, I kept them in Your name, which You have given Me."

He does not ask that the Father take them out of this world—for He has specific work for them to do. But Jesus asks that God preserve them from the evil one. To be immediately taken to heaven would, indeed, seem to be the most blessed lot for the Christian, but then the world would be robbed of the power of the Christian's testimony, God would be robbed of a precious tool that He fashioned for the building of His kingdom, and the Christian himself would be robbed of the benefits that come from faithful service to his Lord in the face of opposition. No, says the Savior, "I do not ask that You take them out of the world, but that You keep them from the evil one." In the world—but not of the world!

And to this end, He asks the Father to consecrate them, to set them apart, to dedicate them for time and for eternity to the high and holy purpose for which He had called them. "Sanctify them in the truth; Your word is truth." We see in these words the tender care and eager solicitude of the Good Shepherd, who only a few days before had said, "My sheep hear My voice, and I know them, and they follow Me. I give them eternal life, and they will never perish, and no one will snatch them out of My hand. My Father, who has given them to Me, is greater than all, and no one is able to snatch them out of the Father's hand" (John 10:27–29). Into that Father's hand He now commends them.

This intimate plea of the Son was addressed to the heart of His Father on behalf of a handful of frightened, timid, weak, and wavering disciples. Can we read these words without a thrill of assurance surging through our hearts? That Savior is our Savior. His Father is our Father. We are forever safe in their keeping. With fearless Paul, who had staked his all on this assurance of his Savior, we, too, can say: "The Lord will rescue me from every evil deed and bring me safely into His heavenly kingdom. To Him be the glory forever and ever. Amen" (2 Timothy 4:18).

Prayer

Myself I cannot save,
Myself I cannot keep;
But strength in Thee I surely have,
Whose eyelids never sleep.

My soul to Thee alone
Now, therefore, I commend.
Thou, Jesus, having loved Thine own,
Wilt love me to the end. Amen.
(TLH 433:5–6)

JESUS PRAYS FOR HIS CHURCH
John 17:20–26

IT is a wonderful thought, and it is just as true as it is wonderful, that Jesus was thinking of you and me when He uttered the closing petitions of His High Priestly Prayer—the real Lord's prayer! For after He had pleaded with His Father for the continued safety of His faithful few, His vision swept across the coming ages, as it were, and He could see the countless throngs who were yet to believe in Him through the Word of His disciples. These, too, would have to be kept; these, too, would have to be sanctified; these, too, would have to be preserved unto His heavenly kingdom. And so He includes these, too, in His prayer of intercession.

God grant us His grace as we now read the closing sentences of our Redeemer's prayer.

"I do not ask for these only, but also for those who will believe in Me through their word, that they may all be one, just as You, Father, are in Me, and I in You, that they also may be in Us, so that the world may believe that You have sent Me. The glory that You have given Me I have given to them, that they may be one even as We are one, I in them and You in Me, that they may become perfectly one, so that the world may know that You sent Me and loved them even as You loved Me. Father, I desire that they also, whom You have given Me, may be with Me where I am, to see My glory that You have given Me because You loved Me before the foundation of the world. O righteous Father, even though the world does not know You, I know You, and these know that You have sent Me. I made known to them Your name, and I will continue to make it known, that the love with which You have loved me may be in them, and I in them."

In the concluding words of His prayer, the Savior throws the doors of His Church open to the Gentiles—to all who would believe in Him as a result of the apostles' preaching, as a result of their spoken and written word. It is just as though our blessed Lord pointed His finger to each of us and said, "For you I am praying; I am praying for you!"

Again and again, the Savior asks that "they may be one." In Christ, all believers are united. In Him, we are one Body (Romans 12:5). So close is this fellowship of believers that Jesus compares it to the communion that exists between His Father and Himself: "even as We are one." Are we always aware of the close ties that bind all believers into a fellowship of faith and love? And does this awareness find expression in our lives?

> Blest be the tie that binds
> Our hearts in Christian love;
> The fellowship of kindred minds
> Is like to that above. (*LSB* 649:1)

And what rivers of comfort have flowed from that tender and familiar line of the Savior's prayer: "Father, I desire that they also, whom You have given Me, may be with Me where I am, to see My glory that You have given Me"! "Father, I desire. . . ." What divine authority and assurance! Only the equal Son could address the equal Father in this way. It is the Savior's will—His gracious but mighty will—that we be with Him.

To be with Christ—that is heaven. "My desire is to depart and be with Christ, for that is far better" says Paul (Philippians 1:23).

> "Forever with the Lord!"
> Amen! so let it be.
> Life from the dead is in that word,
> 'Tis immortality. (*TLH* 616:1)

To behold His glory—what ecstasy of bliss! That is the bliss the Son has asked the Father that you and I should have.

> We know not, oh, we know not
> What joys await us there:

The radiancy of glory,

The bliss beyond compare! (*LSB* 672:1)

It was many years later that the aged John, remembering this prayer and promise of his Savior, wrote to his "little children": "we know that when He appears we shall be like Him, because we shall see Him as He is" (1 John 3:2).

Let us learn to cherish this seventeenth chapter of St. John. Let us read it again and again. Let us go to it for comfort, for assurance, for joy, for spiritual communion with our Savior, and for its glorious promise of eternal life with Christ in heaven.

Prayer

I know that my Redeemer lives
And ever prays for me;
A token of His love He gives,
A pledge of liberty.

I find Him lifting up my head;
He brings salvation near;
His presence makes me free indeed,
And He will soon appear.

Jesus, I hang upon Thy Word:
I steadfastly believe
Thou wilt return and claim me, Lord,
And to Thyself receive. Amen.
— Charles Wesley

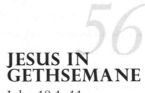

JESUS IN GETHSEMANE
John 18:1–11

DEAR to the heart of every Christian are those sacred hours of the Lenten season when he meditates upon the Passion and death of his Lord and Savior. Gethsemane, the high priest's palace, the courts of Pilate and Herod, Gabbatha, and Golgotha—all are rich with blessed memory for the heart of the believer.

In our meditations on John's Gospel, we have come to his account of the Passion of our Lord. Perhaps more than any other disciple, John was close to Jesus throughout most of the closing hours of His life—in the Upper Room, in Gethsemane, in the high priest's court, and at the foot of the cross. John was an eyewitness of most of the things he describes. That is why in the midst of his description of the crucifixion he assures us, "He who saw it has borne witness—his testimony is true" (John 19:35).

It is the account of this eyewitness of our Savior's sufferings that we are about to read.

> Jesus, I will ponder now
>> On Your holy passion;
> With Your Spirit me endow
>> For such meditation.
> Grant that I in love and faith
>> May the image cherish
> Of Your suff'ring, pain, and death
>> That I may not perish. (*LSB* 440:1)

Betrayal and Arrest of Jesus

When Jesus had spoken these words, He went out with His disciples across the Kidron Valley, where there was a garden, which He and His disciples entered. Now Judas, who betrayed Him, also knew the place, for Jesus often met there with His disciples. So Judas, having procured a band of soldiers and some officers from the chief priests and the Pharisees, went there with lanterns and torches and weapons. Then Jesus, knowing all that would happen to Him, came forward and said to them, "Whom do you seek?" They answered Him, "Jesus of Nazareth." Jesus said to them, "I am He." Judas, who betrayed Him, was standing with them. When Jesus said to them, "I am He," they drew back and fell to the ground. So He asked them again, "Whom do you seek?" And they said, "Jesus of Nazareth." Jesus answered, "I told you that I am He. So, if you seek Me, let these men go." This was to fulfill the word that He had spoken: "Of those whom you gave Me I have lost not one." Then Simon Peter, having a sword, drew it and struck the high priest's servant and cut off his right ear. (The servant's name was Malchus.) So Jesus said to Peter, "Put your sword into its sheath; shall I not drink the cup that the Father has given Me?"

One great fact stands out in every detail of the Passion story: our Savior died because He wanted to! John took great pains throughout his Gospel to show that with every step of His life Jesus consciously and deliberately walked toward His death on the cross. Already to Nicodemus Jesus had said, "As Moses lifted up the serpent in the wilderness, so must the Son of Man be lifted up" (John 3:14). To the unbelieving Jews He had intimated a few days before that His death would be by crucifixion (12:32–33). When He left Galilee for the last time, He told His disciples He was going to Jerusalem to suffer and to die, but He would arise again (Luke 18:31–33).

And now, throughout this first chapter of the Passion story, the evangelist shows us that the Good Shepherd was, indeed, laying down His life for the sheep as a free and voluntary act (John 10:18). Jesus does not wait for Judas to betray Him—He steps forward and reveals Himself. His captors need not come to Him—He comes to them. When, overwhelmed by a flash of His majestic power and splendor, His captors fall to the ground, He does not take this opportunity to escape. Instead, He restores power to the hands that are soon to lay hold of Him. As complete master of the situation, He directs that He be taken prisoner but that His disciples should go free. And when Simon Peter attempts to intervene, Jesus asks, "Shall I not drink the cup that the Father has given Me?"

O blessed truth! The fact that Jesus Christ, the God-man, suffered and died voluntarily, willingly, in the sinner's place gives His Passion its redeeming power. The Good Shepherd laid down His life for the sheep (John 10:18). "The Son of Man came," He says, "to give His life as a ransom for many" (Matthew 20:28; Mark 10:45). What unspeakable love! Surely, "greater love has no one than this, that someone lay down his life for his friends" (John 15:13).

> A Lamb goes uncomplaining forth,
> The guilt of sinners bearing;
> And, laden with the sins of earth,
> None else the burden sharing;
> Goes patient on, grows weak and faint,
> To slaughter led without complaint,
> That spotless life to offer,
> He bears the stripes, the wounds, the lies,
> The mockery, and yet replies,
> "All this I gladly suffer." (*LSB* 438:1)

Prayer

O Lord Jesus, You willingly took my sin upon Your sinless soul and suffered and died that I might go free. Grant that Your cross may be my comfort in life and my strength in death. Grant that, looking to You, I may run with patience the race set before me and hereafter obtain the end of my faith, even an eternal crown in heaven. I am trusting only in Your mercy. Amen.

PETER'S DENIAL
John 18:12–27

THE record of Simon Peter's behavior throughout the entire Passion story is indeed a sorry one. When Jesus first told the disciples He would have to suffer and die, Peter objected so violently that Jesus had to censure him with the severe rebuke, "Get behind Me, Satan!" (Matthew 16:23). When He predicted that all of the disciples would be offended because of Him, it was Peter who blurted out the proud boast: "Even if I must die with You, I will not deny You!" (Matthew 26:35).

When our Lord was in the sweat and tears of His dreadful agony in the Garden of Gethsemane, Peter was sound asleep—despite Jesus' warning to watch and pray. When "the hour" had come and Jesus was ready to deliver Himself into the hands of His enemies, Peter made one final gesture in defense of his Master, for which he had to be rebuked. And when finally he saw that his Lord would be taken prisoner, he fled into the darkness of the garden to save his own life. What a record!

Despite this unenviable record, there is something about Simon Peter that attracts us, something that may even cause us to prefer him to most of the other disciples. What is it? Perhaps it is the realization that Peter is so much like us. His weaknesses are our weaknesses. His temptations are our temptations. And in many instances his failures are our failures. With this in mind, let us read the tragic account of Peter's denial of his Master and see ourselves in Peter's place.

Jesus Faces Annas and Caiaphas

So the band of soldiers and their captain and the officers of the Jews arrested Jesus and bound Him. First they led Him to Annas, for he was the father-in-law of Caiaphas, who was high priest that year. It was Caiaphas who had advised the Jews that it would be expedient that one man should die for the people.

Peter Denies Jesus

Simon Peter followed Jesus, and so did another disciple. Since that disciple was known to the high priest, he entered with Jesus into the court of the high priest, but Peter stood outside at the door. So the other disciple, who was known to the high priest, went out and spoke to the servant girl who kept watch at the door, and brought Peter in. The servant girl at the door said to Peter, "You also are not one of this man's disciples, are you?" He said, "I am not." Now the servants and officers had made a charcoal fire, because it was cold, and they were standing and warming themselves. Peter also was with them, standing and warming himself.

The High Priest Questions Jesus

The high priest then questioned Jesus about His disciples and His teaching. Jesus answered him, "I have spoken openly to the world. I have always taught in synagogues and in the temple, where all Jews come together. I have said nothing in secret. Why do you ask Me? Ask those who have heard Me what I said to them; they know what I said." When He had said these things, one of the officers standing by struck Jesus with his hand, saying, "Is that how you answer the high priest?" Jesus answered him, "If what I said is wrong, bear witness about the wrong; but if what I said is right, why do you strike Me?" Annas then sent Him bound to Caiaphas the high priest.

Peter Denies Jesus Again

Now Simon Peter was standing and warming himself. So they said to him, "You also are not one of His disciples, are you?" He denied it and said, "I am not." One of the servants of the high priest, a relative of the man whose ear Peter had cut off, asked, "Did I not see you in the garden with Him?" Peter again denied it, and at once a rooster crowed.

Simon Peter is our brother. And, sad to say, in some respects we take after him very much. We all are in possession of a heart that is only too prone to be as overconfident and self-reliant as was

Peter. We all can so easily forget the wisdom of Solomon, who said, "Pride goes before destruction, and a haughty spirit before a fall" (Proverbs 16:18). We all can so easily forget the admonition of St. Paul: "Let anyone who thinks that he stands take heed lest he fall" (1 Corinthians 10:12).

But let us profit by Peter's experience. Let us never go where we know in advance we might be tempted to deny our Savior. Let us never mingle too intimately with the children of the world. Let us never keep company with them on their level. Because again and again, directly or indirectly, openly or insidiously, the question will be put to us: "You also are not one of His disciples, are you?" Then our weak and wicked heart will be tempted to yield to the promptings of Satan, and we will either deny our Savior or, just as bad, make apologies for Him.

No, it is better to stand alone in the cold than to warm ourselves in the company of Christ's enemies. "Lead us not into temptation," we pray. Then surely we must beware so we lead ourselves into temptation. "Blessed is the man who walks not in the counsel of the wicked, nor stands in the way of sinners, nor sits in the seat of scoffers," says the psalmist (Psalm 1:1). Notice the progress of those three verbs. First we walk with the ungodly, then we stand with them, and then we sit (we make our permanent abode) with them.

Luke tells us that no sooner had Peter uttered his third denial than "the Lord turned and looked at Peter. . . . And he went out and wept bitterly" (22:61–62). Tears of repentance, tears of faith. Let us pray God that we, too, may weep tears of repentance over our repeated base denials and, like Simon Peter, we, too, may be welcomed back into the fold of our forgiving Savior.

Prayer

In the hour of trial, Jesus, plead for me
Lest by base denial I depart from Thee.
When Thou seest me waver, With a look recall
Nor for fear or favor Suffer me to fall. Amen.
(TLH 516:1)

58

"SUFFERED UNDER PONTIUS PILATE"

John 18:28–40

THE name of Pontius Pilate will live forever in infamy! For many centuries, Christian people have repeated his name every time they recite the words of the Apostles' Creed: "Suffered under Pontius Pilate."

But how did Pilate come to enter the Passion story? The trial before the Jewish court had been completed. The chief priests and leaders of the people had decreed that Jesus (because He had declared Himself to be the Son of God) was guilty of blasphemy and was therefore deserving of death (Matthew 26:63–66). But the Jews were not permitted to put anyone to death without the approval of the Roman authorities (John 18:31), so during the early morning hours, perhaps still before dawn, they dragged Jesus through the city streets to the court of the Roman governor, Pontius Pilate. The verdict of the Jews was to be confirmed by the representative of Rome.

It is this trial that the evangelist describes.

Jesus Before Pilate

Then they led Jesus from the house of Caiaphas to the governor's headquarters. It was early morning. They themselves did not enter the governor's headquarters, so that they would not be defiled, but could eat the Passover. So Pilate went outside to them and said, "What accusation do you bring against this man?" They answered him, "If this man were not doing evil, we would not have delivered Him over to you." Pilate said to them, "Take Him yourselves and judge Him by your own law." The Jews said to him, "It is not lawful for us to put anyone to death." This was to fulfill the word that Jesus had spoken to show by what kind of death He was going to die.

My Kingdom Is Not of This World

So Pilate entered his headquarters again and called Jesus and said to Him, "Are you the King of the Jews?" Jesus answered, "Do you say this of your own accord, or did others say it to you about Me?" Pilate answered, "Am I a Jew? Your own nation and the chief priests have delivered You over to me. What have You done?" Jesus answered, "My kingdom is not of this world. If My kingdom were of this world, My servants would have been fighting, that I might not be delivered over to the Jews. But My kingdom is not from the world." Then Pilate said to Him, "So You are a king?" Jesus answered, "You say that I am a king. For this purpose I was born and for this purpose I have come into the world—to bear witness to the truth. Everyone who is of the truth listens to My voice." Pilate said to Him, "What is truth?"

After he had said this, he went back outside to the Jews and told them, "I find no guilt in Him. But you have a custom that I should release one man for you at the Passover. So do you want me to release to you the King of the Jews?" They cried out again, "Not this man, but Barabbas!" Now Barabbas was a robber.

What sham, what hypocrisy, what hollow mockery is evident throughout this sorry account! The Jews could not enter the court of the heathen governor "so that they would not be defiled." But they thought nothing of killing the Prince of Life! When Pilate asked for a formal charge against the prisoner, they replied with a sneer: "If this man were not doing evil, we would not have delivered Him over to you." Can we imagine such a charge being given a hearing in any court today? And when Pilate finally rendered his verdict, "I find no guilt in Him," does he dismiss the case and release the prisoner? Not at all. Surely, there was never a "trial" less worthy of the name.

Notice the fateful conversation between the hard and callous practical man of the world and the kind and tender man of the other world! "Are you the King of the Jews?" Pilate thought that perhaps

Jesus claimed to be an earthly king. Such views regarding the Messiah were held by the Jews of Christ's day and are still held by the Jews today. But Jesus brushes aside all such misconceptions. His kingdom is not of this world; it is not a physical kingdom, not built and defended by earthly means. He tried to get Pilate to see that His was a spiritual kingdom, found only in the hearts of those who believe the truth of His Gospel.

But proud, carnal, skeptical Pilate had no taste for things that were spiritual. And as for truth—he had long since given up the hope of ever finding what was true. And so with a shrug of his shoulder he turns his back to the fountain of truth and utters the sneering taunt, "What is truth?" Truly, "The natural person does not accept the things of the Spirit of God, for they are folly to him, and he is not able to understand them because they are spiritually discerned" (1 Corinthians 2:14).

Thank God that we are members of the Savior's kingdom! We have heard His voice, and we have learned the truth. Do we love that truth? Do we follow that truth? Do we find our highest joy, our deepest comfort, our only hope for time and for eternity, in the assurance of that blessed truth?

Prayer

Blessed Lord, since You have caused all Holy Scriptures to be written for our learning, grant that we may so hear them, read, mark, learn, and inwardly digest them that we may embrace and ever hold fast the blessed hope of everlasting life; through Jesus Christ, Your Son, Our Lord, who lives and reigns with You and the Holy Spirit, one God, now and forever. Amen.
(LSB Collect for Proper 10, Series A)

59

"BEHOLD THE MAN! BEHOLD YOUR KING!"

John 19:1–16

THERE is perhaps no more pathetic picture of the Savior than Albrecht Dürer's painting that bears the title "Behold the Man!" From beneath the thorn-encircled brow of the suffering "Man of Sorrows" there comes the anguished look of the man who had patiently borne the cruel buffetings of His tormentors. It is the face of the man whom Pilate led out to the Jewish people and then—half in pity, half in scorn—exclaimed, "Behold the man!"

But it is also the picture of the man whom Pilate several minutes later led out to the same people and said, "Behold your King!" Pilate may have sneered as he said it, but he never uttered words more true. The "Man of Sorrows" was indeed the King of kings and Lord of lords. Pilate may not have know it and the Jews may have refused to believe it, but before them stood the long-awaited King of Zion, "Wonderful Counselor, Mighty God, Everlasting Father, Prince of Peace" (Isaiah 9:6).

May God grant us believing hearts that as we behold the man, we may also behold our King; that as we see the Suffering Servant, we may also see the glorious Lord, the Author, the Captain, the King of our salvation!

Jesus Delivered to Be Crucified

Then Pilate took Jesus and flogged Him. And the soldiers twisted together a crown of thorns and put it on His head and arrayed Him in a purple robe. They came up to Him, saying, "Hail, King of the Jews!" and struck Him with their hands. Pilate went out again and said to them, "See, I am bringing Him out to you that you may know that I find no guilt in Him." So Jesus came out, wearing the crown of thorns and the purple robe. Pilate said to them, "Behold the man!" When the chief priests and the officers saw Him, they cried out, "Crucify Him, crucify Him!" Pilate said to them, "Take Him yourselves and crucify Him, for I find no guilt in Him." The Jews answered him, "We have a law, and according to that law He ought to die because He has made Himself the Son of God." When Pilate heard this statement, he was even more afraid. He entered his headquarters again and said to Jesus, "Where are You from?" But Jesus gave him no answer. So Pilate said to Him, "You will not speak to me? Do You not know that I have authority to release You and authority to crucify You?" Jesus answered him, "You would have no authority over Me at all unless it had been given you from above. Therefore he who delivered Me over to you has the greater sin."

From then on Pilate sought to release Him, but the Jews cried out, "If you release this man, you are not Caesar's friend. Everyone who makes himself a king opposes Caesar." So when Pilate heard these words, he brought Jesus out and sat down on the judgment seat at a place called The Stone Pavement, and in Aramaic Gabbatha. Now it was the day of Preparation of the Passover. It was about the sixth hour. He said to the Jews, "Behold your King!" They cried out, "Away with Him, away with Him, crucify Him!" Pilate said to them, "Shall I crucify your King?" The chief priests answered, "We have no king but Caesar." So he delivered Him over to them to be crucified.

There may be no better comment on this text than the immortal words of Bernard of Clairvaux:

Prayer
O sacred Head, now wounded,
With grief and shame weighed down,
Now scornfully surrounded
With thorns, Thine only crown.
O sacred Head, what glory,

What bliss, till now was Thine!
Yet, though despised and gory,
I joy to call Thee mine.

What Thou, my Lord, hast suffered
Was all for sinners' gain;
Mine, mine was the transgression,
But Thine the deadly pain.
Lo, here I fall, my Savior!
'Tis I deserve Thy place;
Look on me with Thy favor,
And grant to me Thy grace.

What language shall I borrow
To thank Thee, dearest Friend,
For this Thy dying sorrow,
Thy pity without end?
O make me Thine forever!
And should I fainting be,
Lord, let me never, never,
Outlive my love for Thee. Amen.
(LSB 450:1, 3, 5)

"IT IS FINISHED"
John 19:16b–30

AS we look back over the centuries to the cross of Christ and think of the untold blessings that have streamed upon the world from that little knoll outside the city of Jerusalem, and as we think of the millions upon millions who since that day have made pilgrimages to the Holy City just to see the spot where our Lord was crucified, our heart almost freezes within us to think that within arm's length of that stupendous scene at that tremendous moment there was a gambling game!

Viewed from our perspective, it seems unbelievable that men, in their ignorance and blindness, could be rolling dice within the shadow of what was at once the greatest tragedy and the greatest triumph of all history. And yet, what do we find in the world today? Within earshot of heaven's gracious call, we see men and women immersed in their empty trivialities, selling eternal gain for a cast of dice! Oh, that they would look up from their worthless pursuits, from their purposeless preoccupations, to see the face of the Crucified One, who is so close to everyone and whose tender Gospel call is meant for all! In Him, and in Him alone, is their only hope of eternal profit.

In the midst of another busy day, let us now look up into the face of our Suffering Savior as we see Him completing the glorious work of our redemption.

The Crucifixion

So they took Jesus, and He went out, bearing His own cross, to the place called The Place of a Skull, which in Aramaic is called Golgotha. There they crucified Him, and with Him two others, one on either side, and Jesus between them. Pilate also wrote an inscription and put it on the cross. It read, "Jesus of Nazareth, the King of the Jews." Many of the Jews read this inscription, for the place where Jesus was crucified was near the city, and it was written in Aramaic, in Latin, and in Greek. So the chief priests of the Jews said to Pilate, "Do not write, 'The King of the Jews,' but rather, 'This man said, I am King of the Jews.'" Pilate answered, "What I have written I have written."

When the soldiers had crucified Jesus, they took His garments and divided them into four parts, one part for each soldier; also His tunic. But the tunic was seamless, woven in one piece from top to bottom, so they said to one another, "Let us not tear it, but cast lots for it to see whose it shall be." This was to fulfill the Scripture which says,

> "They divided My garments among them,
> and for My clothing they cast lots."

So the soldiers did these things, but standing by the cross of Jesus were His mother and His mother's sister, Mary the wife of Clopas, and Mary Magdalene. When Jesus saw His mother and the disciple whom He loved standing nearby, He said to His mother, "Woman, behold, your son!" Then He said to the disciple, "Behold, your mother!" And from that hour the disciple took her to his own home.

The Death of Jesus

After this, Jesus, knowing that all was now finished, said (to fulfill the Scripture), "I thirst." A jar full of sour wine stood there, so they put a sponge full of the sour wine on a hyssop branch and held it to His mouth. When Jesus had received the sour wine, He said, "It is finished," and He bowed His head and gave up His spirit.

"It is finished." Blessed words! When, just a week before, Jesus had told His disciples of His coming Passion, He had said, "See, we are going up to Jerusalem, and everything that is written about the Son of Man by the prophets will be accomplished" (Luke 18:31–33). Again and again throughout the Passion record we read the familiar refrain, "All this has taken place that the Scriptures of the prophets might be fulfilled" (Matthew 26:56).

And now, in almost His last word from the cross, the Savior proclaims: "It is finished." All that had been prophesied about the coming Lamb of God—in script, in symbol, and in prophecy—had been fulfilled. All that had been written by the prophets concerning the Son of Man had been accomplished. The work of redemption had been completed. The work His Father had given Him to do had been finished (John 4:34). All righteousness had been fulfilled (Matthew 3:15). The old evil foe had been met and faced and conquered! In a most glorious, sublime, and heavenly sense, our Savior could exclaim in His final moments on the cross, "It is finished."

Do we sufficiently appreciate the divine comfort those words express? Our salvation is complete. Our sins have been fully atoned. Our punishment has been fully suffered. Our debt has been fully paid. The pains and pangs of hell, which we earned, have been borne in all their bitter fury! The bitter dregs of the cup of damnation have been drunk. The Lamb has brought the perfect sacrifice for all the sins of all the world, for your sins and for mine!

> Mark that miracle of time,
> God's own sacrifice complete.
> "It is finished!" hear Him cry. (*LSB* 436:3)

"There is therefore now no condemnation for those who are in Christ Jesus" (Romans 8:1). For "when Christ had offered for all time a single sacrifice for sins, He sat down at the right hand of God," and "where there is forgiveness of [sins], there is no longer any offering for sin" (Hebrews 10:12, 18). Therefore "Christ is the end of the law for righteousness to everyone who believes" (Romans 10:4).

With Paul, grateful for the complete redemption that we have in Jesus Christ, our Savior, let us take our stand at the foot of Calvary's cross and exclaim, "I have been crucified with Christ. It is no longer I who live, but Christ who lives in me. And the life I now live in the flesh I live by faith in the Son of God, who loved me and gave Himself for me" (Galatians 2:20).

Prayer

Not all the blood of beasts
On Jewish altars slain
Could give the guilty conscience peace
Or wash away the stain.

But Christ, the heav'nly Lamb,
Takes all our sins away;
A sacrifice of nobler name
And richer blood than they.

My faith would lay its hand
On that dear head of Thine,

While as a penitent I stand,
And there confess my sin.

My soul looks back to see
The burden Thou didst bear
When hanging on the cursed tree;
I know my guilt was there.

Believing, we rejoice
To see the curse remove;
We bless the Lamb with cheerful voice
And sing His bleeding love. Amen.
(LSB 431:1–5)

"O SORROW DREAD! GOD'S SON IS DEAD!"

John 19:31–42

FROM the earliest times, there have been those who denied the resurrection of our Savior from the dead. Some have tried to deny His resurrection by contending that Jesus never really died, that He was taken from the cross before the stream of life had ebbed away, and that He was nursed back to health by His friends.

All four evangelists give the lie to any such preposterous denial. But John, especially, heaps evidence upon evidence to establish the incontrovertible fact of the death of Jesus. Let us consider the witnesses he summons as we read the concluding verses of the account of our Savior's Passion.

Jesus' Side Is Pierced

Since it was the day of Preparation, and so that the bodies would not remain on the cross on the Sabbath (for that Sabbath was a high day), the Jews asked Pilate that their legs might be broken and that they might be taken away. So the soldiers came and broke the legs of the first, and of the other who had been crucified with Him. But when they came to Jesus and saw that He was already dead, they did not break His legs. But one of the soldiers pierced His side with a spear, and at once there came out blood and water. He who saw it has borne witness—his testimony is true, and he knows that he is telling the truth—that you also may believe. For these things took place that the Scripture might be fulfilled: "Not one of His bones will be broken." And again another Scripture says, "They will look on Him whom they have pierced."

Jesus Is Buried

After these things Joseph of Arimathea, who was a disciple of Jesus, but secretly for fear of the Jews, asked Pilate that he might take away the body of Jesus, and Pilate gave him permission. So he came and took away His body. Nicodemus also, who earlier had come to Jesus by night, came bringing a mixture of myrrh and aloes, about seventy-five pounds in weight. So they took the body of Jesus and bound it in linen cloths with the spices, as is the burial custom of the Jews. Now in the place where He was crucified there was a garden, and in the garden a new tomb in which no one had yet been laid. So because of the Jewish day of Preparation, since the tomb was close at hand, they laid Jesus there.

The Jews had begun Good Friday with close observance of their religious ritual—they refused to enter Pilate's court "so that they would not be defiled, but could eat the Passover" (John 18:28). Now they ended the day with a similar diabolical hypocrisy. So that the Sabbath not be defiled, they asked Pilate to break Jesus' legs to hasten His death and to have Him taken from the cross. And all in order to sanctify the holy day! Let us beware of empty religious formalism!

Hardened criminals who think nothing of murder have been known to refrain from eating meat on Friday. Truly, the human heart has always been known for its straining at gnats and swallowing camels (Matthew 23:24).

But even the fiendish hypocrisy of Christ's enemies was used by God to serve a purpose. It was used to establish the fact of His death beyond the possibility of question. The testimony of the Roman soldiers, the acquiescence of the Jewish leaders, the pierced side, the flowing blood and water, the emphatic testimony of John the evangelist himself ("He who saw it has borne witness"), the ointments, the linen grave clothes, and the burial all bear incontestable testimony to the death of our beloved Savior.

Indeed, the Lamb who had been brought to the slaughter had been "cut off out of the land of the living" (Isaiah 53:8). The Lamb of God, who by His death was to take away the sin of the world, had entered death—and had atoned for the sin of all mankind.

> O sorrow dread!
> God's Son is dead!
> > But by His expiation
> Of our guilt upon the cross
> > Gained for us salvation. (*TLH* 167:2)

"They laid Jesus there." Him of whom John told us in his first chapter that He was at the beginning and that "in Him was life" and that "all things were made through Him"—Him they laid into a grave! The almighty and everlasting Lord, who had said of Himself that He was the Resurrection and the Life—Him they laid in Joseph's tomb!

> Has earth so sad a wonder?
> God the Father's only Son
> Now is buried yonder. (*LSB* 448:1)

But this, too, must be "that the Scriptures of the prophets might be filled" (Matthew 26:56). By resting in the tomb, our blessed Lord and Savior has hallowed our graves and made them peaceful resting places for our bodies until the day of resurrection. He has robbed our grave of all its terrors. "O death, where is your victory? O death, where is your sting? . . . But thanks be to God, who gives us the victory through our Lord Jesus Christ" (1 Corinthians 15:55, 57).

Prayer

Lord Jesus, who, our souls to save,
Didst rest and slumber in the grave,
Now grant us all in Thee to rest
And here to live as seems Thee best.

Give us the strength, the dauntless faith,
That Thou hast purchased with Thy death,
And lead us to that glorious place
Where we shall see Thee face to face.

O Lamb of God, who once wast slain,
We thank Thee for Thy bitter pain.
Oh, let us share Thy death, that we
May enter into life with Thee! Amen.
  —George Werner

62

THE EMPTY TOMB
John 20:1–10

THE twentieth chapter of St. John's Gospel brings us the glorious story of the world's first Easter. Since that memorable morning in the garden, Easter has been a day of rejoicing throughout the Christian Church. Mournful Lenten hymns give way to festive resurrection melodies. The sorrowful strains of "O Sacred Head, Now Wounded" fade in the distance, and the jubilant notes of "Awake, My Heart, with Gladness" swell in a mighty crescendo wherever the message of the Easter angel is proclaimed. For Easter is a day of triumph and a day of gladness. It is the day of our Savior's resurrection!

But why is the story of the resurrection such a source of joy and comfort to us? Because it is conclusive evidence that Christ is the Son of God and that His doctrine is the truth; that God the Father has accepted the sacrifice of His Son for the reconciliation of the world; and that all believers will rise unto life eternal. These are the three keynotes of all true Easter joy. May the Holy Spirit grant us this blessed assurance as we now read John's account of the wonderful resurrection morning.

The Resurrection

Now on the first day of the week Mary Magdalene came to the tomb early, while it was still dark, and saw that the stone had been taken away from the tomb. So she ran and went to Simon Peter and the other disciple, the one whom Jesus loved, and said to them, "They have taken the Lord out of the tomb, and we do not know where they have laid Him." So Peter went out with the other disciple, and they were going toward the tomb. Both of them were running together, but the other disciple outran Peter and reached the tomb first. And stooping to look in, he saw the linen cloths lying there, but he did not go in. Then Simon Peter came, following him, and went into the tomb. He saw the linen cloths lying there, and the face cloth, which had been on Jesus' head, not lying with the linen cloths but folded up in a place by itself. Then the other disciple, who had reached the tomb first, also went in, and he saw and believed; for as yet they did not understand the Scripture, that He must rise from the dead. Then the disciples went back to their homes.

Mark tells us in his Gospel that Mary Magdalene had set out for the tomb of Jesus along with the other women. But no sooner had she seen from a distance that the stone had been rolled away from the grave than she turned and ran back into the city to tell John and Peter. Notice, she did not tell the disciples that Christ had arisen. No, she comes running, breathless, with the excited report: "They have taken the Lord out of the tomb, and we do not know where they have laid Him." Impetuous and devoted Mary seems to have been the feminine counterpart of impetuous and devoted Simon Peter.

And now a remarkable footrace is on between the younger John and the older Simon Peter. They run, as fast as their feet can carry them, out to the garden tomb. John arrives at the grave first, but, hesitant and cautious, he does not enter. Peter comes soon after him and, as we would expect of Simon Peter, he boldly enters the sepulcher.

Now notice how careful and explicit John is in his description of exactly what they found. The linen cloths in which Jesus' body had been wrapped were lying in neat and careful order. At the head of the grave, lay the cloth that had been placed around His head—still neatly wrapped and lying by itself. Here was conclusive proof that Jesus' wrapped body had not been carried away by grave steal-ers. Here was conclusive proof, too, that His body had not been unwrapped by violent hands, for all was left in perfect order. But more! Here was conclusive proof that the glorified and heavenly body of the majestic Savior had issued forth through the grave lin-ens that, still wrapped, lay there as empty shells. Clearly, a miracle had taken place. The omnipotent and omnipresent Christ had bro-ken through the closed walls of the sepulchre! And so we read that after John had closely examined the startling evidence, "he saw"; his eyes were opened and "he believed."

Do we believe? Remember the purpose of John's Gospel: "These are written so that you may believe that Jesus is the Christ, the Son of God, and that by believing you may have life in His name" (John 20:31). God grant us a sure and abiding faith in Jesus, our risen and glorified Redeemer.

Prayer
"Christ the Lord is ris'n today!"
Saints on earth and angels say;
Raise your joys and triumphs high;
Sing, ye heav'ns, and earth, reply.

Vain the stone, the watch, the seal;
Christ hath burst the gates of hell.
Death in vain forbids His rise;
Christ has opened paradise. Amen.
(LSB 469:1, 3)

63

JESUS APPEARS TO MARY MAGDALENE

John 20:11–18

OF all the characters in the great Easter drama, Mary Magdalene is the most lonely and most disconsolate. She was with the first women to approach the sepulchre "while it was still dark," but as soon as she saw that the stone was rolled away, she left the company of women and fled into the city. To Peter and John, she exclaimed, "They have taken the Lord out of the tomb, and we do not know where they have laid Him" (John 20:2). Poor Mary! She had come to a hasty conclusion, based on only partial evidence—always a dangerous procedure, but especially in matters of religious faith and life.

Peter and John, as we have heard, rushed to the grave, examined the evidence, and then hurried back into the city. Meanwhile, Mary went her weary way, alone, out of the city and back to the garden to indulge her uncontrollable grief in tears of bitter sorrow. The other women had heard the thrilling Easter message and were already spreading the happy news in the city. Peter and John had come and gone. But Mary lingered at the empty grave of her beloved. That is where John now takes up the thread of the Easter story.

Jesus Appears to Mary Magdalene

But Mary stood weeping outside the tomb, and as she wept she stooped to look into the tomb. And she saw two angels in white, sitting where the body of Jesus had lain, one at the head and one at the feet. They said to her, "Woman, why are you weeping?" She said to them, "They have taken away my Lord, and I do not know where they have laid Him." Having said this, she turned around and saw Jesus standing, but she did not know that it was Jesus. Jesus said to her, "Woman, why are you weeping? Whom are you seeking?" Supposing Him to be the gardener, she said to Him, "Sir, if You have carried Him away, tell me where You have laid Him, and I will take Him away." Jesus said to her, "Mary." She turned and said to Him in Aramaic, "Rabboni!" (which means Teacher). Jesus said to her, "Do not cling to Me, for I have not yet ascended to the Father; but go to My brothers and say to them, 'I am ascending to My Father and your Father, to My God and your God.'" Mary Magdalene went and announced to the disciples, "I have seen the Lord"—and that He had said these things to her.

Have you ever noticed that the more we think about our griefs and sorrows, the more similar the words become in which we express them? Mary Magdalene had her own version of the Easter message, and it seems she was determined to stick to it. Her words to the angels are almost identical with the lament that earlier in the morning she had brought to John and Peter: "They have taken away my Lord, and I do not know where they have laid Him." Mary was obsessed with only one thought: the empty tomb could mean nothing else than that "they have taken away my Lord."

Mary had no eyes for angels, no ears for angel messengers, no discernment for the neatly placed face cloth and orderly arranged grave clothes that had sent John and Peter back into the city with the joyful news of the resurrection. No, to Mary, everything that morning could mean only one thing: "They have taken away my Lord, and I do not know where they have laid Him."

How often have we acted just like Mary! We have hugged our sorrows to our bosom until even angels could not comfort us. We have recited our griefs over and over again until, like Mary, we have memorized them into a depressing, melancholy refrain—and all the while the glorious fact of Christ's power and love and comfort has remained hidden from our eyes!

But Mary's eyes were soon to be opened. Her sorrow was to be assuaged.

"Mary." It was the voice of her Master! "My sheep hear My voice, and I know them, and they follow Me," Jesus had said (John 10:27). Here was a wounded sheep who had heard her Shepherd's voice. And in that voice, which called her by her name (see Isaiah 43:1), was all the sweet assurance for which her aching soul had hungered. They have not taken Him away. He is not dead. He lives! He lives!

> He lives, all glory to His name!
> He lives, my Jesus, still the same;
> Oh, the sweet joy this sentence gives:
> I know that my Redeemer lives! (*LSB* 461:8)

May the joy of Mary Magdalene be our joy in life and in death. In every trial, in every trouble, may we hear the sweetly reassuring voice of our divine Redeemer: "Fear not, for I have redeemed you; I have called you by name, you are Mine" (Isaiah 43:1).

Prayer

I know that my Redeemer lives;
What comfort this sweet sentence gives!
He lives, He lives, who once was dead;
He lives, my ever-living head.

He lives to bless me with His love;
He lives to plead for me above;
He lives my hungry soul to feed;
He lives to help in time of need.

He lives to silence all my fears;
He lives to wipe away my tears;

He lives to calm my troubled heart;
He lives all blessings to impart.

He lives, all glory to His name!
He lives, my Jesus, still the same;
Oh, the sweet joy this sentence gives:
I know that my Redeemer lives! Amen. (*LSB 461:1, 3, 5, 8*)

JESUS AND THOMAS

John 20:19–31

DID it ever occur to us that there is real comfort in the fact that our Lord's closest friends at first refused to believe the Easter message? When the women reported the joyful tidings to the sorrowing band of Jesus' disciples, we are told that "these words seemed to them an idle tale, and they did not believe them" (Luke 24:11). Of Thomas, we are told that he was even more stubborn in his refusal to accept the resurrection miracle.

What was it that finally converted this melancholy group of unbelievers into the later band of joyful and courageous witnesses? Why the sudden transformation that enabled Simon Peter, for instance, to stand up a few weeks later and to say to a hostile multitude: "This Jesus God raised up, and of that we all are witnesses" (Acts 2:32)? Surely, there must have been many and convincing proofs of the fact of the resurrection. How else to explain the unanimous testimony of all these erstwhile unbelievers?

It is one of these clear and unmistakable proofs of the Savior's resurrection the evangelist now records. God grant us His Holy Spirit as we read this marvelous witness to the Easter miracle.

Jesus Appears to the Disciples

On the evening of that day, the first day of the week, the
doors being locked where the disciples were for fear of the
Jews, Jesus came and stood among them and said to them,
"Peace be with you." When He had said this, He showed them
His hands and His side. Then the disciples were glad when they
saw the Lord. Jesus said to them again, "Peace be with you. As
the Father has sent Me, even so I am sending you." And when He
had said this, He breathed on them and said to them, "Receive
the Holy Spirit. If you forgive the sins of any, they are forgiven
them; if you withhold forgiveness from any, it is withheld."

Jesus and Thomas

Now Thomas, one of the Twelve, called the Twin, was not
with them when Jesus came. So the other disciples told him,
"We have seen the Lord." But he said to them, "Unless I see in
His hands the mark of the nails, and place my finger into the
mark of the nails, and place my hand into His side, I will never
believe."

Eight days later, His disciples were inside again, and Thomas
was with them. Although the doors were locked, Jesus came
and stood among them and said, "Peace be with you." Then He
said to Thomas, "Put your finger here, and see My hands; and
put out your hand, and place it in My side. Do not disbelieve,
but believe." Thomas answered Him, "My Lord and my God!"
Jesus said to him, "Have you believed because you have seen
Me? Blessed are those who have not seen and yet have believed."

The Purpose of This Book

Now Jesus did many other signs in the presence of the disciples, which are not written in this book; but these are written
so that you may believe that Jesus is the Christ, the Son of God,
and that by believing you may have life in His name.

Someone has said that the exclamation of believing Thomas, "My
Lord and my God," is the climax sentence of St. John's Gospel. And
well we might agree for two reasons.

John was writing to answer questions that people of his day were asking: Who is Jesus? Is He the Son of God? From chapter to chapter, John has been enumerating incident after incident and adding "sign" to "sign," and miracle to miracle, and discourse to discourse—all for the purpose of building up within his reader the growing and assured conviction that this man called Jesus is indeed the Son of God and Savior of the world. How natural, then, that he chose this clear, concise, convincing statement of Thomas for the climax of his Gospel. "My Lord and my God!" This Jesus of Nazareth, whose life, suffering, death, and resurrection John has recorded, is both Lord and God! This, indeed, was the climax of the Gospel according to St. John.

But there is another reason for considering this the crowning sentence of St. John's Gospel. And that is the position he has given it—right at the climax of his account. Immediately after this incident, the Gospel of John hastens to its close. His purpose has been accomplished. He has portrayed and exalted his divine Redeemer as the Alpha and Omega, the First and the Last, the Word made flesh, the omnipotent and eternal Son of the Highest—his Lord and his God. And so he goes right from the glorious, climactic confession of Thomas to the verse that sums up the entire purpose of his writing, the verse that forms the end of the main section of his Gospel: "Now Jesus did many other signs in the presence of the disciples, which are not written in this book; but these are written so that you may believe that Jesus is the Christ, the Son of God, and that by believing you may have life in His name."

Do we now believe? Do we say of Jesus, as did Thomas, "My Lord and my God"? God grant it!

Prayer
All hail the pow'r of Jesus' name!
Let angels prostrate fall;
Bring forth the royal diadem
And crown Him Lord of all.

Hail Him, ye heirs of David's line,
Whom David Lord did call,
The God incarnate, man divine,
And crown Him Lord of all.

Let ev'ry kindred, ev'ry tribe,
On this terrestrial ball
To Him all majesty ascribe
And crown Him Lord of all.

Oh, that with yonder sacred throng
We at His feet may fall!
We'll join the everlasting song
And crown Him Lord of all. Amen.
(LSB 549:1, 4, 6–7)

JESUS AT THE SEA OF TIBERIAS

John 21:1–14

ALTHOUGH John has brought his Gospel to its climax in the concluding verses of chapter 20, he is not quite ready to lay his pen aside. There is one more memorable incident he would like to leave with his readers and to preserve for all Christians of all times.

And so in a postscript, as it were, he devotes his concluding chapter to a beautiful description of the risen Lord's appearance to the disciples at the Sea of Tiberias—the Sea of Galilee. God grant us His Spirit as we read this remarkable account.

Jesus Appears to Seven Disciples

After this Jesus revealed Himself again to the disciples by the Sea of Tiberias, and He revealed Himself in this way.

Simon Peter, Thomas (called the Twin), Nathanael of Cana in
Galilee, the sons of Zebedee, and two others of His disciples
were together. Simon Peter said to them, "I am going fishing."
They said to him, "We will go with you." They went out and
got into the boat, but that night they caught nothing.

Just as day was breaking, Jesus stood on the shore; yet the
disciples did not know that it was Jesus. Jesus said to them,
"Children, do you have any fish?" They answered Him, "No."
He said to them, "Cast the net on the right side of the boat,
and you will find some." So they cast it, and now they were
not able to haul it in, because of the quantity of fish. That disciple whom Jesus loved therefore said to Peter, "It is the Lord!"
When Simon Peter heard that it was the Lord, he put on his
outer garment, for he was stripped for work, and threw himself into the sea. The other disciples came in the boat, dragging
the net full of fish, for they were not far from the land, but
about a hundred yards off.

When they got out on land, they saw a charcoal fire in place,
with fish laid out on it, and bread. Jesus said to them, "Bring
some of the fish that you have just caught." So Simon Peter
went aboard and hauled the net ashore, full of large fish, 153
of them. And although there were so many, the net was not
torn. Jesus said to them, "Come and have breakfast." Now
none of the disciples dared ask Him, "Who are You?" They
knew it was the Lord. Jesus came and took the bread and gave
it to them, and so with the fish. This was now the third time
that Jesus was revealed to the disciples after He was raised
from the dead.

John's chief purpose for adding this postscript to his Gospel is given
us in the concluding words, "This was now the third time that Jesus
was revealed to the disciples after He was raised from the dead." In
other words, John was eager to add just one more mighty witness
to the fact of the Savior's resurrection. But in doing so He has also
given us one more insight into the mind of our Savior with regard
to His children.

"I am going fishing," said Simon Peter. "We will go with you," said the rest. And all unknown to them, their Lord decided to go fishing too. He wanted to be with them while they were engaged in their customary occupation. Unseen by us, our Lord is with us while we are occupied with our daily business. All of our labor, at home or at work, is hallowed by the presence and approval of our Savior. Christ has placed the stamp of dignity on any form of labor that is performed to the glory of God and to the welfare of our fellow men. And so we find Him, the holy Son of God, the resurrected and glorified Redeemer, concerned with the catch of fish of these poor Galilean fishermen. What comfort!

And it is Christ who blesses our daily labors and grants success to our undertakings. Without Christ there would have been no catch of fish that morning in Galilee, but with Him there was more than enough. "The eyes of all look to You, and You give them their food in due season. You open Your hand; You satisfy the desire of every living thing" (Psalm 145:15–16). Do we always sufficiently realize this? And when we see the hand of the Lord in our many blessings, do we, like Simon Peter, rush to fall down and worship Him?

What a beautiful picture for the final chapter of John's Gospel! Christ, the glorified Redeemer, the host of His disciples! With His own pierced hands, He starts the fire, roasts the fish, toasts the bread, serves the breakfast, and waits on His tired and hungry friends. And yet that is exactly what He is doing for us every day of our lives. The eternal Savior is the eternal host, the bountiful provider, who day after day prepares the food and sets the table for mankind. Oh, that we might always know it and receive His bounties with thanksgiving!

Prayer

When all Thy mercies, O my God,
My rising soul surveys,
Transported with the view,
I'm lost In wonder, love, and praise.

Ten thousand precious gifts
My daily thanks employ;
Nor is the least a cheerful heart
That tastes those gifts with joy.

Thro' ev'ry period of my life
Thy goodness I'll pursue
And after death, in distant worlds,
The glorious theme renew.

Through all eternity to Thee
A joyful song I'll raise;
But, oh! eternity's too short
To utter all Thy praise. Amen. (TLH 31:1–3, 5)

"DO YOU LOVE ME?"
John 21:15–19

JESUS had already appeared to Simon Peter on Easter Sunday and had assured him that all was forgiven, reinstating him as one of His apostles (Mark 16:7; Luke 24:34; 1 Corinthians 15:5). But it was still necessary for Peter to be confirmed in his faith and love for the Savior, and this confirmation was to take place in the presence of other disciples of the Lord. For the disgrace of Peter's threefold denial in the night before the crucifixion had become a matter of public knowledge.

And so, after the disciples had been refreshed by a hearty breakfast, the Savior proceeds to the main purpose of His presence there that morning. Peter was to be publicly questioned, confirmed, and commissioned. God grant us believing hearts as we now read the

touching record of our Savior's interview with His fallen but penitent and believing disciple.

Jesus and Peter

When they had finished breakfast, Jesus said to Simon Peter,
"Simon, son of John, do you love Me more than these?" He
said to Him, "Yes, Lord; You know that I love You." He said to
him, "Feed My lambs." He said to him a second time, "Simon,
son of John, do you love Me?" He said to Him, "Yes, Lord; You
know that I love You." He said to him, "Tend My sheep." He said
to him the third time, "Simon, son of John, do you love Me?"
Peter was grieved because he said to him the third time, "Do
you love Me?" and he said to Him, "Lord, You know everything;
You know that I love You." Jesus said to him, "Feed My sheep.
Truly, truly, I say to you, when you were young, you used to
dress yourself and walk wherever you wanted, but when you
are old, you will stretch out your hands, and another will dress
you and carry you where you do not want to go." (This He said
to show by what kind of death he was to glorify God.) And
after saying this He said to him, "Follow Me."

Three questions! Three answers! Three commands!—"Do you love
Me?" "Yes, Lord; You know that I love You." "Feed My lambs …
tend My sheep . . . feed My sheep." How forcefully this deliberate
repetition must have reminded Simon Peter of the previous warning of his Lord, "Before the rooster crows twice, you will deny Me
three times" (Mark 14:30) and of the shameful fulfillment of that
prediction in the court of the palace of the high priest!

But, by the grace of God, Peter was permitted to match his
tragic threefold denial with a glorious threefold confession of his
faith and love and loyalty to his Master. Three times, in the presence
of witnesses, he assures his risen Lord of his heart's affection—and
this time not as the proud and boastful, self-reliant braggart of several weeks ago, but as the humbled, chastened, self-effacing disciple
of his Lord.

"Lord, You know everything; You know that I love You." As
much as to say, "Lord, You know me better than I know myself.

Look into my crushed and humbled heart, and there (not in any words that I might say) You will find proof of my burning love for You."

At this point, as after his third denial, no doubt "the Lord turned and looked at Peter" (Luke 22:61)—but this time with the knowing smile of affectionate approval. As if to say, "Yes, Simon, I do know all things; I know that you love Me." The erring disciple and his Master had been reunited, bound together with the ties of love that were never again to be broken!

But Simon was to continue to prove his love. "Feed My lambs ... tend My sheep . . . feed My sheep." Preach My Gospel to young and old. The first requirement of true discipleship is faith, love, and devotion to the Savior; but where faith, love, and devotion are found, there the second requirement is sure to follow, namely, willing service to the Savior and His Church. "Feed My lambs"—the little ones at home, in school, in Sunday School. "Tend . . . feed My sheep"—at home, in church, in Bible class, and through the Church's far-flung ministry. "Care for the church of God," says Paul (Acts 20:28).

Are we proving our love to the Savior by a life of willing, consecrated service? Are we helping by our prayers, our efforts, and our contributions to feed the lambs and sheep whom Christ has purchased with His blood? His question to us today is still the same as His question to Simon Peter: "Do you love Me?" Let our answer, then, be "Lord, You know everything; You know that I love You." And then let us resolve to step out into the world with renewed determination to prove our love for Christ by a life of sacrificial service. Let us feed the lambs and sheep. Let us love not in word only, but also in deed and in truth.

Prayer
Jesus, Thou art mine forever,
Dearer far than earth to me;
Neither life nor death shall sever
Those sweet ties which bind to Thee.

All were drear to me and lonely
If Thy presence gladdened not;
While I sing to Thee, Thee only,
Mine's an ever blissful lot.

Thou alone art all my Treasure,
Who hast died that I may live;
Thou conferrest noblest pleasure,
Who dost all my sins forgive.

Lamb of God, I do implore Thee,
Guard, support me, lest I fall.
Let me evermore adore Thee;
Be my everlasting All. Amen.
(TLH 357:1–3, 6)

JESUS, PETER, AND JOHN

John 21:20–25

IT is most appropriate that the last three characters on the stage, as the curtain falls on St. John's Gospel, are Jesus, Peter, and John himself. There can be no doubt that these three (plus John the Baptist in the earlier chapters) have played the leading roles in St. John's narrative.

The Savior had just given Peter a glimpse of things to come. He had predicted that Peter would die the death of a martyr—a fact Peter was never able to forget for the rest of his life (2 Peter 1:14). But Peter, still the impetuous and inquisitive Peter of old, wants to know more about the future. Turning around, he points to John and asks the Savior, "What about this man?" In other words, "What will his destiny be?"

It is this incident that the evangelist now describes:

Jesus and the Beloved Apostle

Peter turned and saw the disciple whom Jesus loved following them, the one who had been reclining at table close to Him and had said, "Lord, who is it that is going to betray you?" When Peter saw him, he said to Jesus, "Lord, what about this man?" Jesus said to him, "If it is My will that he remain until I come, what is that to you? You follow Me!" So the saying spread abroad among the brothers that this disciple was not to die; yet Jesus did not say to him that he was not to die, but, "If it is My will that he remain until I come, what is that to you?"

This is the disciple who is bearing witness about these things, and who has written these things, and we know that his testimony is true.

Now there are also many other things that Jesus did. Were every one of them to be written, I suppose that the world itself could not contain the books that would be written.

Our Lord does not reveal the future to us to satisfy our curiosity. In His merciful wisdom, He often withholds from us the things it is better for us not to know. And so, when Peter, full of curiosity, tried to prevail upon the Savior to grant him a glimpse into the future life of John, the Savior rebukes him gently but firmly, If I want John to remain here until I return again, what business is that of yours?

Peter had just been given his final command—"Follow Me." He had not been given the command to pry into the future. Let us remember, when the future looms ominous and forbidding before us, our Savior's command is clear and single: Follow Me! Don't ask questions; just follow Him. He will take care of the future.

The Savior's words were misunderstood by some of the disciples. The rumor soon spread that John would never die. And so John finds it necessary to deny this rumor in the closing verses of his Gospel. He reminds his readers that Jesus did not promise that John would never die, but that He had merely said, "If it is My will that he remain until I come, what is that to you?" He had not said that John would remain alive until His second coming! We ask, How did this rumor get started? We answer, In the same way all false doctrine starts. Someone said that Jesus had said something that He hadn't. Let us always be sure that we have the Word of God for every doctrine on which we build our faith. Let us never be content with a hearsay religion but only build our faith on what our Savior says in the pages of His blessed Word!

John concludes his Gospel with a confident assurance of the trustworthiness of everything he has written. "This is the disciple who is bearing witness about these things, and who has written these things, and we know that his testimony is true." Already in the midst of the Passion account, at the very foot of the cross, John was eager to vouch for the truthfulness and accuracy of everything he had written. "He who saw it has borne witness," he says, "his testimony is true, and he knows that he is telling the truth—that you also may believe" (John 19:35).

John wrote only what he saw and heard (John 1:15; 19:35; 21:24–25; 1 John 1:1–3; 3 John 12). But by no means did he write all that he saw and heard. "Now there are also many other things that Jesus did"—so many, indeed, that, if they were written, "the world itself could not contain" them.

But these things that are written—incomplete though they may be—are written for a purpose: "That you may believe that Jesus is the Christ, the Son of God, and that by believing you may have life in His name" (John 20:31).

Prayer
Lord, give us such a faith as this;
And then, whate'er may come,
We'll taste e'en now the hallowed bliss
Of an eternal home. Amen. (TLH 396:6)